수능기출 베스트셀러
리 얼 오 리 지 널

수능 내신 1등급 대비 전국연합 학력평가

20일 완성 영어 독해

빈칸 순서 삽입

완성

수능 모의고사 전문 출판
입시플라이

수능 내신 영어 1등급

결론은 '빈순삽'

수능과 내신에서 영어 1등급을 위한 핵심은 [빈칸 추론·글의 순서·문장 삽입] 유형입니다. **이 세 가지 유형은 8문항으로 전체 45문항 중 18% 밖에 안 되지만, [빈칸 추론·글의 순서·문장 삽입] 유형의 정답 여부로 1등급, 2등급, 3등급이 결정**됩니다.

해마다 수능에서 **영어 등급을 결정하는 대표적 '오답률 1위'는 역시 [빈칸 추론]이며, 그 뒤로 [글의 순서, 문장 삽입]**으로 이어지기 때문에 **수능과 내신 '영어 1등급을 목표'한다면 반드시 이 세 가지 유형을 정복**해야 합니다.

[빈칸·순서·삽입] 문항 수 & 오답률

※ 7개년 영어 영역 고1~고3 학평·수능·모평 '오답률' 분석

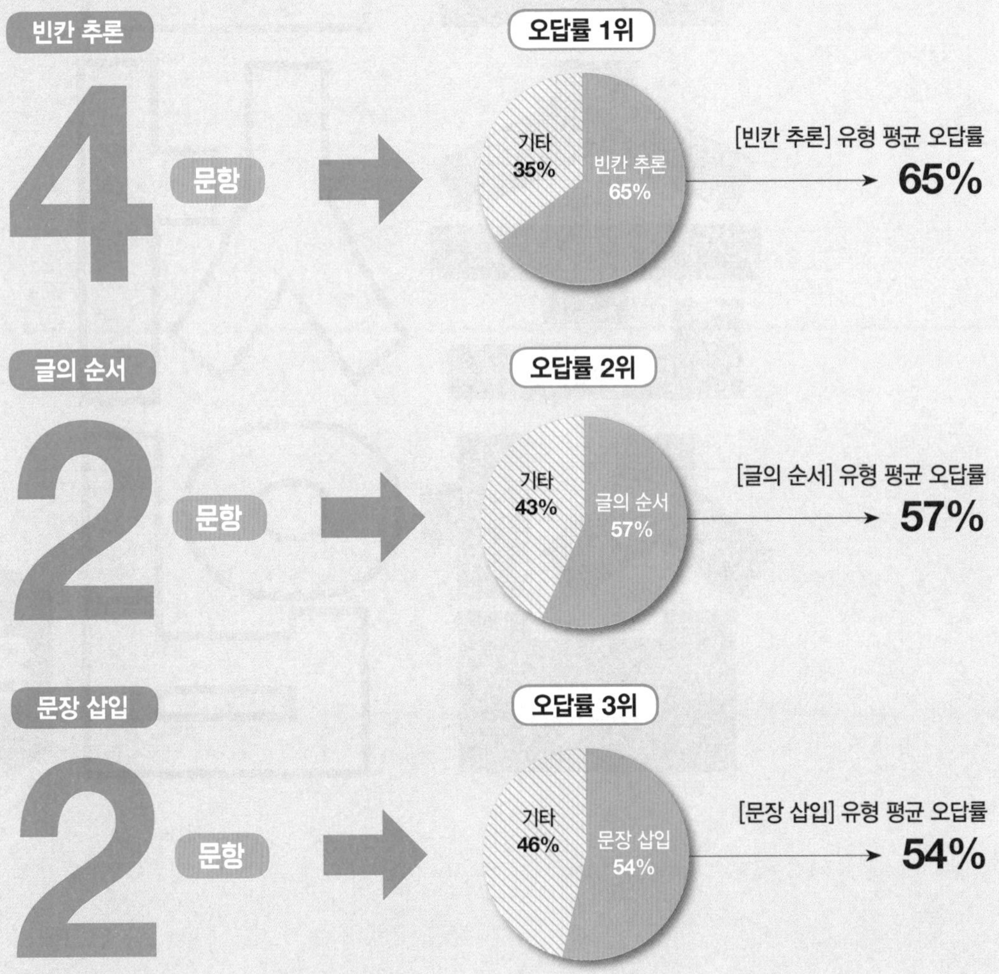

※ 오답률 **60%** 이상의 고난도 문제 중 **70%**는 [빈칸 · 순서 · 삽입] 유형이며, 최근에는 ***[빈칸 추론] 문제뿐 아니라 [글의 순서]와 [문장 삽입] 문제들도 어렵게 출제***된 경우가 많았습니다.

※ 오답률 집계는 기관에 따라 오차가 있을 수 있습니다.

하루 12문제 20분 20일
영어 '1등급' 완성

[빈칸 추론•글의 순서•문장 삽입] 유형의 문제가 모두 어려운 것은 아닙니다. **하루 12문제씩, 20분 학습에는 평이한 문제부터 고난도 2점, 고난도 3점 문항까지 적절히 난이도를 분산 배치해 학습 부담은 낮추고, 효과는 최대한 올릴 수 있도록 '20일 완성'으로 구성**했습니다.
[빈칸 추론•글의 순서•문장 삽입] 유형의 문제를 대비하는 **가장 좋은 방법은 최근 수능에 출제되었던 기출 문제와 학력평가 문제들을 토대로 '다양한 지문의 문제를 풀어보는 것'**입니다.

12문제 + 20분 + 20일 = 영어 1등급

하루 12문제 학습

12 questions →

하루 12문제로 영어 1등급 도전!

- 고2 7개년 학력평가 **[빈칸•순서•삽입] 240문항**
- 수능•모의평가 고3 학력평가 **[우수 문항]** 추가
- 1등급 대비 **[고난도 2점, 3점] 문항** 분산 배치

하루 20분 학습

20 minutes →

가볍게~ 하루 20분 유형별 학습!

- **20분** 학습으로 유형별 **[고난도 문제]까지 정복**
- 고난도 문항 해설에 **문제 해결 [꿀~팁]** 수록
- 지문의 이해를 돕는 해설 **직독직해, 구문 풀이**

20일 완성 프로젝트

20 day →

20일 학습으로 영어 1등급 완성!

- 하루 **6쪽, 20일** 구성으로 **부담 없는 학습 분량**
- **[빈칸 10일, 순서 5일, 삽입 5일]** 유형별 **PLAN**
- 일반 유형별 기출 문제집의 **약 2배 문항 수록**

※ 영어 독해 [빈칸•순서•삽입] 세 가지 유형의 문제는 *수능과 학력평가 뿐만 아니라 학교시험 내신에서도 비슷한 유형으로 출제되기 때문에 수능, 내신 모두 영어 1등급'을 위한 필수 유형*입니다.

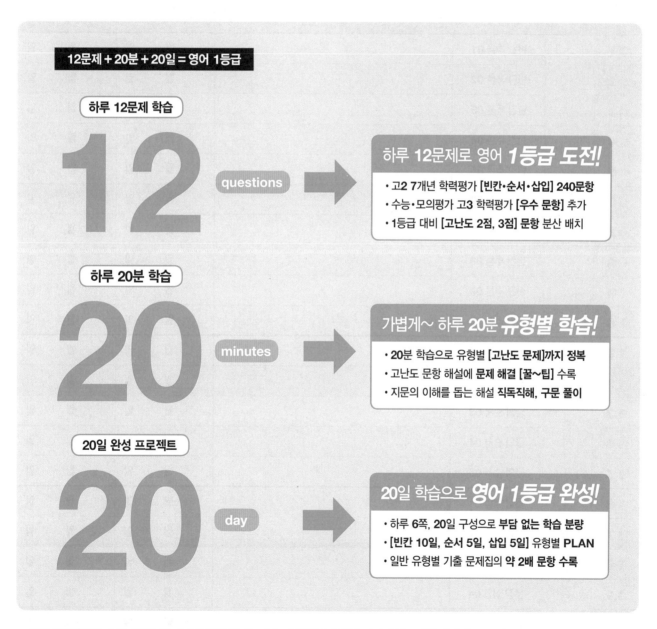

영어 독해 '빈칸·순서·삽입'

20 Day_ planner

완성

- 날짜별로 정해진 **학습 분량에 맞춰 공부하고 학습 결과를 기록**합니다.
- **planner**를 이용해 학습 일정을 계획하고 **자신의 성적을 체크하면서 20일 완성으로 목표**를 세우세요.
- 학습 분량은 하루 **12**문제로 하시되 **자신의 학습 패턴과 상황에 따라 10일 완성으로 학습**하셔도 좋습니다.

Day	구분	영어 독해 유형	틀린 문제 & 복습해야 할 문제	학습 날짜	복습 날짜
01	빈칸 추론	빈칸 추론 01		월 일	월 일
02		빈칸 추론 02		월 일	월 일
03		빈칸 추론 03		월 일	월 일
04		빈칸 추론 04		월 일	월 일
05		빈칸 추론 05		월 일	월 일
06		빈칸 추론 06		월 일	월 일
07		빈칸 추론 07		월 일	월 일
08		빈칸 추론 08		월 일	월 일
09		빈칸 추론 09		월 일	월 일
10		빈칸 추론 10		월 일	월 일
11	글의 순서	글의 순서 01		월 일	월 일
12		글의 순서 02		월 일	월 일
13		글의 순서 03		월 일	월 일
14		글의 순서 04		월 일	월 일
15		글의 순서 05		월 일	월 일
16	문장 삽입	문장 삽입 01		월 일	월 일
17		문장 삽입 02		월 일	월 일
18		문장 삽입 03		월 일	월 일
19		문장 삽입 04		월 일	월 일
20		문장 삽입 05		월 일	월 일

영어 독해 '빈칸·순서·삽입'

Contents

차례

빈칸 추론

영어 독해에서 가장 문항수가 많고, 배점이 높아 문항의 난이도 또한 기본으로 높은 게 특징이며, 오답률 1위에 해당할 만큼 까다로운 문제가 많이 출제되고 있습니다. 최근 수능 유형은 주어진 지문이 어려워 해석이 쉽지 않은 경우도 있지만, 선택지에 매력적인 오답이 있어 헷갈리는 1~2문제 때문에 등급이 달라지는 사례가 많았습니다.

▶ 빈칸 추론 유형

[31~34] 다음 빈칸에 들어갈 말로 가장 적절한 것을 고르시오.

영어 영역 **31~34**번에 해당하는 **빈칸 추론은 주어진 제시문을 읽고 그 내용을 이해한 후 빈칸이 포함된 문장과 절 이외의 나머지 부분을 통해 질문에 알맞은 적절한 내용을 빈칸에 완성하는 문제**입니다.
중요한 것은 지문의 내용만 묻는 게 아니고 **핵심 어구와 절을 완성하는 유형도 있어** 빈칸 추론 **기출문제 중** 고난도 2점, 고난도 3점 문항들을 집중적으로 풀어보고, 지문을 분석하는 논리적 훈련을 통해 고난도 문항에 대한 확실한 대비를 해야 합니다.

꿀팁! 지문 속 표현들을 통해 핵심 내용을 파악 후 선지를 빈칸에 넣고 전후 흐름이 연결되는지, 빈칸에 들어갈 내용과 잘 통하는지 확인한다.

▶ 빈칸 추론 교재 구성

하루 12문항 _ 20분 학습 _ 10일 완성 = 총 120문항

빈칸 추론은 **제시문부터 선지까지 모두 영어로 읽고 답을 해야 하는 부담이 있는 유형**입니다. 특히 소재가 정치, 과학, 예술, 철학 등 다양하게 출제되고 있어 **"빈칸이 [전반부, 중반부, 후반부]에 있을 때로 기출 문제를 구분"**하여 **학습의 효율성**을 높였습니다.

Day 01~02

빈칸이 '전반부'에 있을 때
글의 나머지 내용을 종합해야하는 경우가 많으니 끝까지 쭉 읽고 내용을 파악한다.

Day 03~05

빈칸이 '중반부'에 있을 때
글의 흐름이 하나가 아니고 반전이 있거나 주제를 반박하는 함정이 있으니 주의한다.

Day 06~10

빈칸이 '후반부'에 있을 때
글의 전체 내용을 종합하여 주제문에 자주 등장하는 핵심어 위주로 결론을 완성한다.

2020 하루 20분 20일 완성

PART I
빈칸 추론

Day 01~Day 10

[해설편 p.002]

DAY 01

※ 점수 표기가 없는 문항은 모두 2점입니다.

빈칸이 전반부에 있을 때 **빈칸 추론 01**

● 날짜 : 월 일 ● 시작 시각 : 시 분 초 ● 목표 시간 : 20분

01

고2 • 2019년 11월 31번

다음 빈칸에 들어갈 말로 가장 적절한 것을 고르시오.

Once we own something, we're far more likely to ______________ it. In a study conducted at Duke University, students who won basketball tickets in an extremely onerous lottery (one that they had to wait in line to enter for more than a day) said they wouldn't sell their tickets for less than, on average, $2,400. But students who had waited and hadn't won said they would only pay, on average, $170 per ticket. Once a student owned the tickets, he or she saw them as being worth much more in the market than they were. In another example, during the housing market crash of 2008, a real estate website conducted a survey to see how homeowners felt the crash affected the price of their homes. 92% of respondents, aware of nearby foreclosures, asserted these had hurt the price of homes in their neighborhood. However, when asked about the price of their *own* home, 62% believed it had increased.

* onerous: 성가신 ** foreclosure: 압류

① overvalue ② exchange
③ disregard ④ conceal
⑤ share

02

고2 • 2018년 11월 31번

다음 빈칸에 들어갈 말로 가장 적절한 것을 고르시오. [3점]

A good many scientists and artists have noticed the ____________ of creativity. At the Sixteenth Nobel Conference, held in 1980, scientists, musicians, and philosophers all agreed, to quote Freeman Dyson, that "the analogies between science and art are very good as long as you are talking about the creation and the performance. The creation is certainly very analogous. The aesthetic pleasure of the craftsmanship of performance is also very strong in science." A few years later, at another multidisciplinary conference, physicist Murray Gell-Mann found that "everybody agrees on where ideas come from. We had a seminar here, about ten years ago, including several painters, a poet, a couple of writers, and the physicists. Everybody agrees on how it works. All of these people, whether they are doing artistic work or scientific work, are trying to solve a problem."

① formality ② objectivity
③ complexity ④ universality
⑤ uncertainty

03

고2 • 2019년 9월 32번

다음 빈칸에 들어갈 말로 가장 적절한 것을 고르시오.

Much of the spread of fake news occurs through ______________________. A 2016 study from Columbia University in New York City and Inria, a French technology institute, found that 59 percent of the news from links shared on social media wasn't read first. People see an intriguing headline or photo in their news feed or on another website and then click the Share button to repost the item to their social media friends — without ever clicking through to the full article. Then they may be sharing fake news. To stop the spread of fake news, read stories before you share them. Respect your social media friends enough to know what information you are sending their way. You may discover, on close inspection, that an article you were about to share is obviously fraudulent, that it doesn't really say what the headline promises, or that you actually disagree with it.

* fraudulent: 속이는

① political campaigns
② irrational censorship
③ irresponsible sharing
④ overheated marketing
⑤ statistics manipulation

04

고2 • 2022년 9월 34번

다음 빈칸에 들어갈 말로 가장 적절한 것을 고르시오.

Psychologist Christopher Bryan finds that when we ______________________________, people evaluate choices differently. His team was able to cut cheating in half: instead of "Please don't cheat," they changed the appeal to "Please don't be a cheater." When you're urged not to cheat, you can do it and still see an ethical person in the mirror. But when you're told not to be a cheater, the act casts a shadow; immorality is tied to your identity, making the behavior much less attractive. Cheating is an isolated action that gets evaluated with the logic of consequence: Can I get away with it? Being a cheater evokes a sense of self, triggering the logic of appropriateness: What kind of person am I, and who do I want to be? In light of this evidence, Bryan suggests that we should embrace nouns more thoughtfully. "Don't Drink and Drive" could be rephrased as: "Don't Be a Drunk Driver." The same thinking can be applied to originality. When a child draws a picture, instead of calling the artwork creative, we can say "You are creative."

① ignore what experts say
② keep a close eye on the situation
③ shift our emphasis from behavior to character
④ focus on appealing to emotion rather than reason
⑤ place more importance on the individual instead of the group

05

고2 • 2017년 11월 32번

다음 빈칸에 들어갈 말로 가장 적절한 것을 고르시오. [3점]

Hearing is basically ______________________________. Sound is simply vibrating air which the ear picks up and converts to electrical signals, which are then interpreted by the brain. The sense of hearing is not the only sense that can do this; touch can do this too. If you are standing by the road and a large truck goes by, do you hear or feel the vibration? The answer is both. With very low frequency vibration the ear starts becoming inefficient and the rest of the body's sense of touch starts to take over. For some reason we tend to make a distinction between hearing a sound and feeling a vibration, but in reality they are the same thing. Deafness does not mean that you can't hear, only that there is something wrong with the ears. Even someone who is totally deaf can still hear/feel sounds.

① a specialized form of touch
② an instinct rather than a learnt skill
③ a sense resistant to frequency changes
④ an excellent way to build better understanding
⑤ an experience different from feeling vibrations

06

고2 • 2018년 3월 33번

다음 빈칸에 들어갈 말로 가장 적절한 것을 고르시오. [3점]

The desire for fame has its roots in the ______________________________. No one would want to be famous who hadn't also, somewhere in the past, been made to feel extremely insignificant. We sense the need for a great deal of admiring attention when we have been painfully exposed to earlier deprivation. Perhaps one's parents were hard to impress. They never noticed one much, they were so busy with other things, focusing on other famous people, unable to have or express kind feelings, or just working too hard. There were no bedtime stories and one's school reports weren't the subject of praise and admiration. That's why one dreams that one day the world will pay attention. When we're famous, our parents will have to admire us too.

① spread of media
② experience of neglect
③ freedom from authority
④ curiosity about the unknown
⑤ misunderstanding of popularity

07 1등급 대비 고난도 2점 문제

고2·2023년 3월 31번

다음 빈칸에 들어갈 말로 가장 적절한 것을 고르시오.

Free play is nature's means of teaching children that they are not ____________. In play, away from adults, children really do have control and can practice asserting it. In free play, children learn to make their own decisions, solve their own problems, create and follow rules, and get along with others as equals rather than as obedient or rebellious subordinates. In active outdoor play, children deliberately dose themselves with moderate amounts of fear and they thereby learn how to control not only their bodies, but also their fear. In social play children learn how to negotiate with others, how to please others, and how to manage and overcome the anger that can arise from conflicts. None of these lessons can be taught through verbal means; they can be learned only through experience, which free play provides.

* rebellious: 반항적인

① noisy
② sociable
③ complicated
④ helpless
⑤ selective

08 1등급 대비 고난도 2점 문제

고2·2021년 9월 32번

다음 빈칸에 들어갈 말로 가장 적절한 것을 고르시오.

Philosophical activity is based on the ________________________. The philosopher's thirst for knowledge is shown through attempts to find better answers to questions even if those answers are never found. At the same time, a philosopher also knows that being too sure can hinder the discovery of other and better possibilities. In a philosophical dialogue, the participants are aware that there are things they do not know or understand. The goal of the dialogue is to arrive at a conception that one did not know or understand beforehand. In traditional schools, where philosophy is not present, students often work with factual questions, they learn specific content listed in the curriculum, and they are not required to solve philosophical problems. However, we know that awareness of what one does not know can be a good way to acquire knowledge. Knowledge and understanding are developed through thinking and talking. Putting things into words makes things clearer. Therefore, students must not be afraid of saying something wrong or talking without first being sure that they are right.

① recognition of ignorance
② emphasis on self-assurance
③ conformity to established values
④ achievements of ancient thinkers
⑤ comprehension of natural phenomena

09 1등급 대비 고난도 3점 문제

고2 • 2020년 3월 34번

다음 빈칸에 들어갈 말로 가장 적절한 것을 고르시오. [3점]

The growing field of genetics is showing us what many scientists have suspected for years — ______________________________. This information helps us better understand that genes are under our control and not something we must obey. Consider identical twins; both individuals are given the same genes. In mid-life, one twin develops cancer, and the other lives a long healthy life without cancer. A specific gene instructed one twin to develop cancer, but in the other the same gene did not initiate the disease. One possibility is that the healthy twin had a diet that turned off the cancer gene — the same gene that instructed the other person to get sick. For many years, scientists have recognized other environmental factors, such as chemical toxins (tobacco for example), can contribute to cancer through their actions on genes. The notion that food has a specific influence on gene expression is relatively new.

① identical twins have the same genetic makeup
② our preference for food is influenced by genes
③ balanced diet is essential for our mental health
④ genetic engineering can cure some fatal diseases
⑤ foods can immediately influence the genetic blueprint

10 1등급 대비 고난도 3점 문제

고2 • 2021년 11월 34번

다음 빈칸에 들어갈 말로 가장 적절한 것을 고르시오. [3점]

One vivid example of how ______________________________ is given by Dan Ariely in his book *Predictably Irrational*. He tells the story of a day care center in Israel that decided to fine parents who arrived late to pick up their children, in the hope that this would discourage them from doing so. In fact, the exact opposite happened. Before the imposition of fines, parents felt guilty about arriving late, and guilt was effective in ensuring that only a few did so. Once a fine was introduced, it seems that in the minds of the parents the entire scenario was changed from a social contract to a market one. Essentially, they were paying for the center to look after their children after hours. Some parents thought it worth the price, and the rate of late arrivals increased. Significantly, once the center abandoned the fines and went back to the previous arrangement, late arrivals remained at the high level they had reached during the period of the fines.

① people can put aside their interests for the common good
② changing an existing agreement can cause a sense of guilt
③ imposing a fine can compensate for broken social contracts
④ social bonds can be insufficient to change people's behavior
⑤ a market mindset can transform and undermine an institution

11 1등급 대비 고난도 3점 문제

고2•2021년 3월 33번

다음 빈칸에 들어갈 말로 가장 적절한 것을 고르시오. [3점]

Psychological research has shown that people naturally ________________________, often without thinking about it. Imagine you're cooking up a special dinner with a friend. You're a great cook, but your friend is the wine expert, an amateur sommelier. A neighbor drops by and starts telling you both about the terrific new wines being sold at the liquor store just down the street. There are many new wines, so there's a lot to remember. How hard are you going to try to remember what the neighbor has to say about which wines to buy? Why bother when the information would be better retained by the wine expert sitting next to you? If your friend wasn't around, you might try harder. After all, it would be good to know what a good wine would be for the evening's festivities. But your friend, the wine expert, is likely to remember the information without even trying.

① divide up cognitive labor
② try to avoid disagreements
③ seek people with similar tastes
④ like to share old wisdom
⑤ balance work and leisure

12 1등급 대비 고난도 3점 문제

고2•2018년 11월 34번

다음 빈칸에 들어갈 말로 가장 적절한 것을 고르시오. [3점]

Scientific knowledge cannot ________________________ because science represents natural objects as members of a specific class, rather than as individual entities. The science-based approach claims that aesthetically relevant properties are only those properties that all members of a natural kind share with each other. But this is not true. When we experience nature, we do not experience it as species, but as individual objects. And as separated into individual objects, nature can have aesthetic properties that are not entailed by its scientific description. Natural science can explain, for instance, the formation of the waterfall, but it has nothing to say about our experience of the majestic Victoria Falls when viewed at sunset, its reds and oranges countless and captivating; geology can explain the formation of the Ngorongoro Crater in Tanzania, but not its painful and breathtaking beauty at sunrise, the fog slowly lifting above the crater and a lone hippopotamus dark and heavy in the lake.

* entity: 독립체

① devalue the true beauty of mother nature
② rely on the perspectives of artistic professionals
③ explain the evolutionary process of every species
④ give up its trust in the usefulness of classification
⑤ account for correct aesthetic appreciation of nature

학습 Check!

▶ 몰라서 틀린 문항 × 표기 ▶ 헷갈렸거나 찍은 문항 △ 표기 ▶ ×, △ 문항은 다시 풀고 ✔ 표기를 하세요.

종료 시각	시 분 초	문항 번호	01	02	03	04	05	06	07	08	09	10	11	12
소요 시간	분 초	채점 결과												
초과 시간	분 초	틀린 문항 복습												

DAY 02 ※ 점수 표기가 없는 문항은 모두 2점입니다.

빈칸이 전반부에 있을 때 **빈칸 추론 02**

● 날짜 : 월 일 ● 시작 시각 : 시 분 초 ● 목표 시간 : 20분

01

고2 • 2021년 9월 31번

다음 빈칸에 들어갈 말로 가장 적절한 것을 고르시오.

_____________ works as a general mechanism for the mind, in many ways and across many different areas of life. For example, Brian Wansink, author of *Mindless Eating*, showed that it can also affect our waistlines. We decide how much to eat not simply as a function of how much food we actually consume, but by a comparison to its alternatives. Say we have to choose between three burgers on a menu, at 8, 10, and 12 ounces. We are likely to pick the 10-ounce burger and be perfectly satisfied at the end of the meal. But if our options are instead 10, 12, and 14 ounces, we are likely again to choose the middle one, and again feel equally happy and satisfied with the 12-ounce burger at the end of the meal, even though we ate more, which we did not need in order to get our daily nourishment or in order to feel full.

① Originality ② Relativity
③ Visualization ④ Imitation
⑤ Forgetfulness

02

고2 • 2021년 3월 31번

다음 빈칸에 들어갈 말로 가장 적절한 것을 고르시오. [3점]

Even the most respectable of all musical institutions, the symphony orchestra, carries inside its DNA the legacy of the _____________. The various instruments in the orchestra can be traced back to these primitive origins — their earliest forms were made either from the animal (horn, hide, gut, bone) or the weapons employed in bringing the animal under control (stick, bow). Are we wrong to hear this history in the music itself, in the formidable aggression and awe-inspiring assertiveness of those monumental symphonies that remain the core repertoire of the world's leading orchestras? Listening to Beethoven, Brahms, Mahler, Bruckner, Berlioz, Tchaikovsky, Shostakovich, and other great composers, I can easily summon up images of bands of men starting to chase animals, using sound as a source and symbol of dominance, an expression of the will to predatory power.

* legacy: 유산 ** formidable: 강력한

① hunt ② law
③ charity ④ remedy
⑤ dance

03

고2 • 2020년 3월 33번

다음 빈칸에 들어갈 말로 가장 적절한 것을 고르시오. [3점]

Translating academic language into everyday language can be an essential tool for you as a writer to ______________________________. For, as writing theorists often note, writing is generally not a process in which we start with a fully formed idea in our heads that we then simply transcribe in an unchanged state onto the page. On the contrary, writing is more often a means of discovery in which we use the writing process to figure out what our idea is. This is why writers are often surprised to find that what they end up with on the page is quite different from what they thought it would be when they started. What we are trying to say here is that everyday language is often crucial for this discovery process. Translating your ideas into more common, simpler terms can help you figure out what your ideas really are, as opposed to what you initially imagined they were.

* transcribe: 옮겨 쓰다

① finish writing quickly
② reduce sentence errors
③ appeal to various readers
④ come up with creative ideas
⑤ clarify your ideas to yourself

04

고2 • 2022년 9월 33번

다음 빈칸에 들어갈 말로 가장 적절한 것을 고르시오.

As well as making sense of events through narratives, historians in the ancient world established the tradition of history as a(n) ______________________________. The history writing of Livy or Tacitus, for instance, was in part designed to examine the behavior of heroes and villains, meditating on the strengths and weaknesses in the characters of emperors and generals, providing exemplars for the virtuous to imitate or avoid. This continues to be one of the functions of history. French chronicler Jean Froissart said he had written his accounts of chivalrous knights fighting in the Hundred Years' War "so that brave men should be inspired thereby to follow such examples." Today, historical studies of Lincoln, Churchill, Gandhi, or Martin Luther King, Jr. perform the same function.

* chivalrous: 기사도적인

① source of moral lessons and reflections
② record of the rise and fall of empires
③ war against violence and oppression
④ means of mediating conflict
⑤ integral part of innovation

05

고2 • 2020년 9월 33번

다음 빈칸에 들어갈 말로 가장 적절한 것을 고르시오.

A recent study shows that dogs appear to ______________________________. Scientists placed 28 dogs in front of a computer monitor blocked by an opaque screen, then played a recording of the dog's human guardian or a stranger saying the dog's name five times through speakers in the monitor. Finally, the screen was removed to reveal either the face of the dog's human companion or a stranger's face. The dogs' reactions were videotaped. Naturally, the dogs were attentive to the sound of their name, and they typically stared about six seconds at the face after the screen was removed. But they spent significantly more time gazing at a strange face after they had heard the familiar voice of their guardian. That they paused for an extra second or two suggests that they realized something was wrong. The conclusion drawn is that dogs form a picture in their mind, and that they can think about it and make predictions based on that picture. And, like us, they are puzzled when what they see or hear doesn't match what they were expecting.

* opaque: 불투명한

① form mental images of people's faces
② sense people's moods from their voices
③ detect possible danger and prepare for it
④ imitate their guardians' habitual behaviors
⑤ selectively obey commands from strangers

06

고2 • 2021년 11월 33번

다음 빈칸에 들어갈 말로 가장 적절한 것을 고르시오. [3점]

When it comes to climates in the interior areas of continents, mountains ______________________________. A great example of this can be seen along the West Coast of the United States. Air moving from the Pacific Ocean toward the land usually has a great deal of moisture in it. When this humid air moves across the land, it encounters the Coast Range Mountains. As the air moves up and over the mountains, it begins to cool, which causes precipitation on the windward side of the mountains. Once the air moves down the opposite side of the mountains (called the leeward side) it has lost a great deal of moisture. The air continues to move and then hits the even higher Sierra Nevada mountain range. This second uplift causes most of the remaining moisture to fall out of the air, so by the time it reaches the leeward side of the Sierras, the air is extremely dry. The result is that much of the state of Nevada is a desert.

① increase annual rainfall in dry regions
② prevent drastic changes in air temperature
③ play a huge role in stopping the flow of moisture
④ change wind speed as air ascends and descends them
⑤ equalize the amount of moisture of surrounding land areas

07 1등급 대비 고난도 2점 문제

고2 • 2018년 3월 31번

다음 빈칸에 들어갈 말로 가장 적절한 것을 고르시오.

Most importantly, money needs to be __________ in a predictable way. Precious metals have been desirable as money across the millennia not only because they have intrinsic beauty but also because they exist in fixed quantities. Gold and silver enter society at the rate at which they are discovered and mined; additional precious metals cannot be produced, at least not cheaply. Commodities like rice and tobacco can be grown, but that still takes time and resources. A dictator like Zimbabwe's Robert Mugabe could not order the government to produce 100 trillion tons of rice. He was able to produce and distribute trillions of new Zimbabwe dollars, which is why they eventually became more valuable as toilet paper than currency.

* intrinsic: 내재적인

① invested
② scarce
③ transferred
④ divisible
⑤ deposited

08 1등급 대비 고난도 3점 문제

고2 • 2020년 11월 33번

다음 빈칸에 들어갈 말로 가장 적절한 것을 고르시오. [3점]

We are now ______________________________, instead of the other way around. Perhaps the clearest way to see this is to look at changes in the biomass — the total worldwide weight — of mammals. A long time ago, all of us humans together probably weighed only about two-thirds as much as all the bison in North America, and less than one-eighth as much as all the elephants in Africa. But in the Industrial Era our population exploded and we killed bison and elephants at industrial scale and in terrible numbers. The balance shifted greatly as a result. At present, we humans weigh more than 350 times as much as all bison and elephants put together. We weigh over ten times more than all the earth's wild mammals combined. And if we add in all the mammals we've domesticated — cattle, sheep, pigs, horses, and so on — the comparison becomes truly ridiculous: we and our tamed animals now represent 97 percent of the earth's mammalian biomass. This comparison illustrates a fundamental point: instead of being limited by the environment, we learned to shape it to our own ends.

* bison: 들소

① imposing ourselves on nature
② limiting our ecological impact
③ yielding our land to mammals
④ encouraging biological diversity
⑤ doing useful work for the environment

09 1등급 대비 고난도 3점 문제

고2 • 2019년 3월 32번

다음 빈칸에 들어갈 말로 가장 적절한 것을 고르시오. [3점]

Sometimes a person is acclaimed as "the greatest" because ______________________. For example, violinist Jan Kubelik was acclaimed as "the greatest" during his first tour of the United States, but when impresario Sol Hurok brought him back to the United States in 1923, several people thought that he had slipped a little. However, Sol Elman, the father of violinist Mischa Elman, thought differently. He said, "My dear friends, Kubelik played the Paganini concerto tonight as splendidly as ever he did. Today you have a different standard. You have Elman, Heifetz, and the rest. All of you have developed and grown in artistry, technique, and, above all, in knowledge and appreciation. The point is: you know more; not that Kubelik plays less well."

* acclaim: 칭송하다 ** impresario: 기획자, 단장

① there are moments of inspiration
② there is little basis for comparison
③ he or she longs to be such a person
④ other people recognize his or her efforts
⑤ he or she was born with great artistic talent

10 1등급 대비 고난도 3점 문제

고2 • 2022년 6월 33번

다음 빈칸에 들어갈 말로 가장 적절한 것을 고르시오. [3점]

What is unusual about journalism as a profession is ______________________. In theory, practitioners in the classic professions, like medicine or the clergy, contain the means of production in their heads and hands, and therefore do not have to work for a company or an employer. They can draw their income directly from their clients or patients. Because the professionals hold knowledge, moreover, their clients are dependent on them. Journalists hold knowledge, but it is not theoretical in nature; one might argue that the public depends on journalists in the same way that patients depend on doctors, but in practice a journalist can serve the public usually only by working for a news organization, which can fire her or him at will. Journalists' income depends not on the public, but on the employing news organization, which often derives the large majority of its revenue from advertisers.

① its lack of independence
② the constant search for truth
③ the disregard of public opinion
④ its balance of income and faith
⑤ its overconfidence in its social influence

11 1등급 대비 고난도 3점 문제

(고2 • 2023년 9월 33번)

다음 빈칸에 들어갈 말로 가장 적절한 것을 고르시오. [3점]

As always happens with natural selection, bats and their prey have ______________________ for millions of years. It's believed that hearing in moths arose specifically in response to the threat of being eaten by bats. (Not all insects can hear.) Over millions of years, moths have evolved the ability to detect sounds at ever higher frequencies, and, as they have, the frequencies of bats' vocalizations have risen, too. Some moth species have also evolved scales on their wings and a fur-like coat on their bodies; both act as "acoustic camouflage," by absorbing sound waves in the frequencies emitted by bats, thereby preventing those sound waves from bouncing back. The B-2 bomber and other "stealth" aircraft have fuselages made of materials that do something similar with radar beams.

* frequency: 주파수 ** camouflage: 위장
*** fuselage: (비행기의) 기체

① been in a fierce war over scarce food sources
② been engaged in a life-or-death sensory arms race
③ invented weapons that are not part of their bodies
④ evolved to cope with other noise-producing wildlife
⑤ adapted to flying in night skies absent of any lights

12 1등급 대비 고난도 3점 문제

(고2 • 2018년 11월 33번)

다음 빈칸에 들어갈 말로 가장 적절한 것을 고르시오. [3점]

A vast academic literature provides empirical support for the thesis that ______________________. Large data sets have been constructed, measuring firm environmental behavior and financial performance across a wide number of industries and over many years. While the results are not unequivocal, there is evidence suggestive of a positive correlation between environmental performance and financial performance. In our own work, we find that, on average, a 10% decrease in a company's toxic emissions as reported in the US Environmental Protection Agency's Toxic Release Inventory — a database of toxic emissions from US manufacturing facilities — results in an average 3% increase in a firm's financial performance as measured by return on assets. Another study suggests that a 10% reduction in emissions could result in a $34 million increase in market value.

* unequivocal: 명료한

① it pays to be green
② toxins destroy markets
③ green products are on the rise
④ environmental problems persist
⑤ our faith in statistics is unfounded

학습 Check!

▶ 몰라서 틀린 문항 × 표기 ▶ 헷갈렸거나 찍은 문항 △ 표기 ▶ ×, △ 문항은 다시 풀고 ✔ 표기를 하세요.

종료 시각	시	분	초
소요 시간		분	초
초과 시간		분	초

문항 번호	01	02	03	04	05	06	07	08	09	10	11	12
채점 결과												
틀린 문항 복습												

[해설편 p.015]

DAY 03

※ 점수 표기가 없는 문항은 모두 2점입니다.

빈칸이 중반부에 있을 때 **빈칸 추론 03**

● 날짜 : 월 일 ● 시작 시각 : 시 분 초 ● 목표 시간 : 20분

01

고2 · 2021년 11월 31번

다음 빈칸에 들어갈 말로 가장 적절한 것을 고르시오.

The elements any particular animal needs are relatively predictable. They are predictable based on the past: what an animal's ancestors needed is likely to be what that animal also needs. ______________________, therefore, can be hardwired. Consider sodium (Na). The bodies of terrestrial vertebrates, including those of mammals, tend to have a concentration of sodium nearly fifty times that of the primary producers on land, plants. This is, in part, because vertebrates evolved in the sea and so evolved cells dependent upon the ingredients that were common in the sea, including sodium. To remedy the difference between their needs for sodium and that available in plants, herbivores can eat fifty times more plant material than they otherwise need (and eliminate the excess). Or they can seek out other sources of sodium. The salt taste receptor rewards animals for doing the latter, seeking out salt in order to satisfy their great need.

*terrestrial: 육생의 **vertebrate: 척추동물
***herbivore: 초식 동물

① Taste preferences
② Hunting strategies
③ Migration patterns
④ Protective instincts
⑤ Periodic starvations

02

고2 · 2022년 9월 31번

다음 빈칸에 들어갈 말로 가장 적절한 것을 고르시오. [3점]

It is not the peasant's goal to produce the highest possible time-averaged crop yield, averaged over many years. If your time-averaged yield is marvelously high as a result of the combination of nine great years and one year of crop failure, you will still starve to death in that one year of crop failure before you can look back to congratulate yourself on your great time-averaged yield. Instead, the peasant's aim is to make sure to produce a yield above the starvation level in every single year, even though the time-averaged yield may not be highest. That's why ____________________ may make sense. If you have just one big field, no matter how good it is on the average, you will starve when the inevitable occasional year arrives in which your one field has a low yield. But if you have many different fields, varying independently of each other, then in any given year some of your fields will produce well even when your other fields are producing poorly.

① land leveling
② weed trimming
③ field scattering
④ organic farming
⑤ soil fertilization

03

고2 • 2020년 6월 32번

다음 빈칸에 들어갈 말로 가장 적절한 것을 고르시오.

We are often faced with high-level decisions, where we are unable to predict the results of those decisions. In such situations, most people end up quitting the option altogether, because the stakes are high and results are very unpredictable. But there is a solution for this. You should use the process of ____________________. In many situations, it's wise to dip your toe in the water rather than dive in headfirst. Recently, I was about to enroll in an expensive coaching program. But I was not fully convinced of how the outcome would be. Therefore, I used this process by enrolling in a low-cost mini course with the same instructor. This helped me understand his methodology, style, and content; and I was able to test it with a lower investment, and less time and effort before committing fully to the expensive program.

* stakes: (계획·행동 등의 성공 여부에) 걸려 있는 것

① trying out what other people do
② erasing the least preferred options
③ testing the option on a smaller scale
④ sharing your plans with professionals
⑤ collecting as many examples as possible

04

고2 • 2023년 3월 34번

다음 빈칸에 들어갈 말로 가장 적절한 것을 고르시오. [3점]

It seems natural to describe certain environmental conditions as 'extreme', 'harsh', 'benign' or 'stressful'. It may seem obvious when conditions are 'extreme': the midday heat of a desert, the cold of an Antarctic winter, the salinity of the Great Salt Lake. But this only means that these conditions are extreme *for us*, given our particular physiological characteristics and tolerances. To a cactus there is nothing extreme about the desert conditions in which cacti have evolved; nor are the icy lands of Antarctica an extreme environment for penguins. It is lazy and dangerous for the ecologist to assume that ____________________. Rather, the ecologist should try to gain a worm's-eye or plant's-eye view of the environment: to see the world as others see it. Emotive words like harsh and benign, even relativities such as hot and cold, should be used by ecologists only with care.

* benign: 온화한 ** salinity: 염도

① complex organisms are superior to simple ones
② technologies help us survive extreme environments
③ ecological diversity is supported by extreme environments
④ all other organisms sense the environment in the way we do
⑤ species adapt to environmental changes in predictable ways

05

고2 • 2022년 11월 34번

다음 빈칸에 들어갈 말로 가장 적절한 것을 고르시오. [3점]

Observational studies of humans cannot be properly controlled. Humans live different lifestyles and in different environments. Thus, they are insufficiently homogeneous to be suitable experimental subjects. These *confounding factors* undermine our ability to draw sound causal conclusions from human epidemiological surveys. Confounding factors are variables (known or unknown) that make it difficult for epidemiologists to ________________. For example, Taubes argued that since many people who drink also smoke, researchers have difficulty determining the link between alcohol consumption and cancer. Similarly, researchers in the famous Framingham study identified a significant correlation between coffee drinking and coronary heart disease. However, most of this correlation disappeared once researchers corrected for the fact that many coffee drinkers also smoke. If the confounding factors are known, it is often possible to correct for them. However, if they are unknown, they will undermine the reliability of the causal conclusions we draw from epidemiological surveys.

* homogeneous: 동질적인 ** epidemiological: 역학의

① distort the interpretation of the medical research results
② isolate the effects of the specific variable being studied
③ conceal the purpose of their research from subjects
④ conduct observational studies in an ethical way
⑤ refrain from intervening in their experiments

06

고2 • 2019년 9월 34번

다음 빈칸에 들어갈 말로 가장 적절한 것을 고르시오. [3점]

If you want to use the inclined plane to help you move an object (and who wouldn't?), then you have to move the object over a longer distance to get to the desired height than if you had started from directly below and moved upward. This is probably already clear to you from a lifetime of stair climbing. Consider all the stairs you climb compared to the actual height you reach from where you started. This height is always less than the distance you climbed in stairs. In other words, ________________ to reach the intended height. Now, if we were to pass on the stairs altogether and simply climb straight up to your destination (from directly below it), it would be a shorter climb for sure, but the needed force to do so would be greater. Therefore, we have stairs in our homes rather than ladders.

* inclined plane: (경)사면

① more distance in stairs is traded for less force
② a ladder should be positioned at a steep angle
③ the distance needs to be measured precisely
④ an object's weight has to be reduced
⑤ slopes are often preferred to stairs

07

고3 • 2024학년도 수능 32번

다음 빈칸에 들어갈 말로 가장 적절한 것을 고르시오.

A musical score within any film can add an additional layer to the film text, which goes beyond simply imitating the action viewed. In films that tell of futuristic worlds, composers, much like sound designers, have added freedom to create a world that is unknown and new to the viewer. However, unlike sound designers, composers often shy away from creating unique pieces that reflect these new worlds and often present musical scores that possess familiar structures and cadences. While it is possible that this may interfere with creativity and a sense of space and time, it in fact ______________________________. Through recognizable scores, visions of the future or a galaxy far, far away can be placed within a recognizable context. Such familiarity allows the viewer to be placed in a comfortable space so that the film may then lead the viewer to what is an unfamiliar, but acceptable vision of a world different from their own.

* score: 악보 ** cadence: (율동적인) 박자

① frees the plot of its familiarity
② aids in viewer access to the film
③ adds to an exotic musical experience
④ orients audiences to the film's theme
⑤ inspires viewers to think more deeply

08 1등급 대비 고난도 2점 문제

고2 • 2022년 6월 31번

다음 빈칸에 들어갈 말로 가장 적절한 것을 고르시오.

Followers can be defined by their position as subordinates or by their behavior of going along with leaders' wishes. But followers also have power to lead. Followers empower leaders as well as vice versa. This has led some leadership analysts like Ronald Heifetz to avoid using the word *followers* and refer to the others in a power relationship as "citizens" or "constituents." Heifetz is correct that too simple a view of followers can produce misunderstanding. In modern life, most people wind up being both leaders and followers, and the categories can become quite ____________. Our behavior as followers changes as our objectives change. If I trust your judgment in music more than my own, I may follow your lead on which concert we attend (even though you may be formally my subordinate in position). But if I am an expert on fishing, you may follow my lead on where we fish, regardless of our formal positions or the fact that I followed your lead on concerts yesterday.

* vice versa: 반대로, 거꾸로

① rigid
② unfair
③ fluid
④ stable
⑤ apparent

09 1등급 대비 고난도 3점 문제

고2 • 2020년 9월 32번

다음 빈칸에 들어갈 말로 가장 적절한 것을 고르시오. [3점]

When we are emotionally charged, we often use anger to hide our more primary and deeper emotions, such as sadness and fear, which doesn't allow for true resolution to occur. Separating yourself from an emotionally upsetting situation gives you the space you need to better understand what you are truly feeling so you can more clearly articulate your emotions in a logical and less emotional way. A time-out also helps ______________________. When confronted with situations that don't allow us to deal with our emotions or that cause us to suppress them, we may transfer those feelings to other people or situations at a later point. For instance, if you had a bad day at work, you may suppress your feelings at the office, only to find that you release them by getting into a fight with your kids or spouse when you get home later that evening. Clearly, your anger didn't originate at home, but you released it there. When you take the appropriate time to digest and analyze your feelings, you can mitigate hurting or upsetting other people who have nothing to do with the situation.

* mitigate: 완화하다

① restrain your curiosity
② mask your true emotions
③ spare innocent bystanders
④ provoke emotional behavior
⑤ establish unhealthy relationships

10 1등급 대비 고난도 3점 문제

고2 • 2019년 6월 33번

다음 빈칸에 들어갈 말로 가장 적절한 것을 고르시오. [3점]

At the pharmaceutical giant Merck, CEO Kenneth Frazier decided to motivate his executives to take a more active role in leading innovation and change. He asked them to do something radical: generate ideas that would put Merck out of business. For the next two hours, the executives worked in groups, pretending to be one of Merck's top competitors. Energy soared as they developed ideas for drugs that would crush theirs and key markets they had missed. Then, their challenge was to reverse their roles and figure out how to defend against these threats. This "kill the company" exercise is powerful because ______________________. When deliberating about innovation opportunities, the leaders weren't inclined to take risks. When they considered how their competitors could put them out of business, they realized that it was a risk not to innovate. The urgency of innovation was apparent.

* crush: 짓밟다 ** deliberate: 심사숙고하다

① the unknown is more helpful than the negative
② it highlights the progress they've already made
③ it is not irrational but is consumer-based practice
④ it reframes a gain-framed activity in terms of losses
⑤ they discuss how well it fits their profit-sharing plans

11 1등급 대비 고난도 3점 문제

고2•2020년 11월 34번

다음 빈칸에 들어갈 말로 가장 적절한 것을 고르시오. [3점]

In the modern world, we look for certainty in uncertain places. We search for order in chaos, the right answer in ambiguity, and conviction in complexity. "We spend far more time and effort on trying to control the world," best-selling writer Yuval Noah Harari says, "than on trying to understand it." We look for the easy-to-follow formula. Over time, we ______________________. Our approach reminds me of the classic story of the drunk man searching for his keys under a street lamp at night. He knows he lost his keys somewhere on the dark side of the street but looks for them underneath the lamp, because that's where the light is. Our yearning for certainty leads us to pursue seemingly safe solutions — by looking for our keys under street lamps. Instead of taking the risky walk into the dark, we stay within our current state, however inferior it may be.

① weigh the pros and cons of our actions
② develop the patience to bear ambiguity
③ enjoy adventure rather than settle down
④ gain insight from solving complex problems
⑤ lose our ability to interact with the unknown

12 1등급 대비 고난도 3점 문제

고2•2023년 6월 32번

다음 빈칸에 들어갈 말로 가장 적절한 것을 고르시오. [3점]

It's hard to pay more for the speedy but highly skilled person, simply because there's less effort being observed. Two researchers once did a study in which they asked people how much they would pay for data recovery. They found that people would pay a little more for a greater quantity of rescued data, but what they were most sensitive to was the number of hours the technician worked. When the data recovery took only a few minutes, willingness to pay was low, but when it took more than a week to recover the same amount of data, people were willing to pay much more. Think about it: They were willing to pay more for the slower service with the same outcome. Fundamentally, when we ______________________, we're paying for incompetence. Although it is actually irrational, we *feel* more rational, and more comfortable, paying for incompetence.

① prefer money to time
② ignore the hours put in
③ value effort over outcome
④ can't stand any malfunction
⑤ are biased toward the quality

학습 Check!

▶ 몰라서 틀린 문항 × 표기 ▶ 헷갈렸거나 찍은 문항 △ 표기 ▶ ×, △ 문항은 다시 풀고 ✔ 표기를 하세요.

종료 시각	시 분 초	문항 번호	01	02	03	04	05	06	07	08	09	10	11	12
소요 시간	분 초	채점 결과												
초과 시간	분 초	틀린 문항 복습												

[해설편 p.022]

DAY 04 ※ 점수 표기가 없는 문항은 모두 2점입니다. 빈칸이 중반부에 있을 때 빈칸 추론 04

● 날짜 : 월 일 ● 시작 시각 : 시 분 초 ● 목표 시간 : 20분

01

고2 • 2020년 6월 31번

다음 빈칸에 들어갈 말로 가장 적절한 것을 고르시오. [3점]

When is the right time for the predator to consume the fruit? The plant uses the color of the fruit to signal to predators that it is ripe, which means that the seed's hull has hardened — and therefore the sugar content is at its height. Incredibly, the plant has chosen to manufacture fructose, instead of glucose, as the sugar in the fruit. Glucose raises insulin levels in primates and humans, which initially raises levels of leptin, a hunger-blocking hormone — but fructose does not. As a result, the predator never receives the normal message that it is ____________. That makes for a win-win for predator and prey. The animal obtains more calories, and because it keeps eating more and more fruit and therefore more seeds, the plant has a better chance of distributing more of its babies.

*hull: 겉껍질 **primate: 영장류

① full
② strong
③ tired
④ dangerous
⑤ hungry

02

고2 • 2018년 9월 32번

다음 빈칸에 들어갈 말로 가장 적절한 것을 고르시오. [3점]

Verbal and nonverbal signs are not only relevant but also significant to intercultural communication. The breakdown of them helps to identify aspects of conversations. Here is an excellent example. Newly hired Indian and Pakistani assistants in a staff cafeteria at Heathrow Airport were often perceived as rude or uncooperative by their supervisors and the airport staff, while the Indian and Pakistani women complained of discrimination. Observation revealed that ____________ ____________ were the primary cause. When the staff ordered meat, the cafeteria assistant was supposed to ask them whether they would like to have some gravy. Instead of saying "gravy?" with a rising intonation, the Asian assistants would say "gravy" with a falling intonation, which is their normal way of asking a question. However, this may appear rude to native speakers of English: "gravy" with falling intonation came across as a statement, suggesting "This is gravy. Take it or leave it."

*gravy: 육즙·밀가루·우유로 만든 소스

① frequent pauses
② moral standards
③ first impressions
④ food preferences
⑤ intonation patterns

03

고2 • 2022년 11월 32번

다음 빈칸에 들어갈 말로 가장 적절한 것을 고르시오.

The connectedness of the global economic market makes it vulnerable to potential "infection." A financial failure can make its way from borrowers to banks to insurers, spreading like a flu. However, there are unexpected characteristics when it comes to such infection in the market. Infection can occur even without any contact. A bank might become insolvent even without having any of its investments fail. ______________________________ to financial markets, just as cascading failures due to bad investments. If we all woke up tomorrow and believed that Bank X would be insolvent, then it would become insolvent. In fact, it would be enough for us to fear that others believed that Bank X was going to fail, or just to fear our collective fear! We might all even know that Bank X was well-managed with healthy investments, but if we expected others to pull their money out, then we would fear being the last to pull our money out. Financial distress can be self-fulfilling and is a particularly troublesome aspect of financial markets.

* insolvent: 지급 불능의, 파산한 ** cascading: 연속된

① Fear and uncertainty can be damaging
② Unaffordable personal loans may pose a risk
③ Ignorance about legal restrictions may matter
④ Accurate knowledge of investors can be poisonous
⑤ Strong connections between banks can create a scare

04

고2 • 2019년 6월 32번

다음 빈칸에 들어갈 말로 가장 적절한 것을 고르시오. [3점]

As entrepreneur Derek Sivers put it, "The first follower is what transforms a lone nut into a leader." If you were sitting with seven other people and six group members picked the wrong answer, but the remaining one chose the correct answer, conformity dropped dramatically. "The presence of a supporting partner depleted the majority of much of its pressure," Asch wrote. Merely knowing that ______________________________ makes it substantially easier to reject the crowd. Emotional strength can be found even in small numbers. In the words of Margaret Mead, "Never doubt that a small group of thoughtful citizens can change the world; indeed, it's the only thing that ever has." To feel that you're not alone, you don't need a whole crowd to join you. Research by Sigal Barsade and Hakan Ozcelik shows that in business and government organizations, just having one friend is enough to significantly decrease loneliness.

* conformity: 순응 ** deplete: 고갈시키다

① you're not the only resister
② the leader cannot be defeated
③ conforming to the rule is good
④ men are supposed to live alone
⑤ competition discourages cooperation

05

고2 • 2023년 9월 32번

다음 빈칸에 들어갈 말로 가장 적절한 것을 고르시오. [3점]

A typical soap opera creates an abstract world, in which a highly complex web of relationships connects fictional characters that exist first only in the minds of the program's creators and are then recreated in the minds of the viewer. If you were to think about how much human psychology, law, and even everyday physics the viewer must know in order to follow and speculate about the plot, you would discover it is considerable — at least as much as the knowledge required to follow and speculate about a piece of modern mathematics, and in most cases, much more. Yet viewers follow soap operas with ease. How are they able to cope with such abstraction? Because, of course, the abstraction ______________________. The characters in a soap opera and the relationships between them are very much like the real people and relationships we experience every day. The abstraction of a soap opera is only a step removed from the real world. The mental "training" required to follow a soap opera is provided by our everyday lives.

* soap opera: 드라마, 연속극

① is separated from the dramatic contents
② is a reflection of our unrealistic desires
③ demonstrates our poor taste in TV shows
④ is built on an extremely familiar framework
⑤ indicates that unnecessary details are hidden

06

고2 • 2021년 6월 33번

다음 빈칸에 들어갈 말로 가장 적절한 것을 고르시오. [3점]

When self-handicapping, you're engaging in behaviour that you know will harm your chances of succeeding: you know that you won't do as well on the test if you go out the night before, but you do it anyway. Why would anyone intentionally harm their chances of success? Well, here's a possible answer. Say that you do study hard. You go to bed at a decent time and get eight hours of sleep. Then you take the maths test, but don't do well: you only get a C. What can you conclude about yourself? Probably that you're just not good at maths, which is a pretty hard blow to your self-esteem. But if you self-handicap, you'll never be in this position because ______________________. You were bound to get a C, you can tell yourself, because you went out till 1 a.m. That C doesn't mean that you're bad at maths; it just means that you like to party. Self-handicapping seems like a paradox, because people are deliberately harming their chances of success.

① getting some rest from studying is necessary
② failure serves as the foundation for success
③ you're creating a reason for your failure
④ studying is not about winning or losing
⑤ you have already achieved a lot

07

고3 • 2022학년도 6월 32번

다음 빈칸에 들어갈 말로 가장 적절한 것을 고르시오.

Some of the most insightful work on information seeking emphasizes "strategic self-ignorance," understood as "the use of ignorance as an excuse to engage excessively in pleasurable activities that may be harmful to one's future self." The idea here is that if people are present-biased, they might avoid information that would ______________ — perhaps because it would produce guilt or shame, perhaps because it would suggest an aggregate trade-off that would counsel against engaging in such activities. St. Augustine famously said, "God give me chastity — tomorrow." Present-biased agents think: "Please let me know the risks — tomorrow." Whenever people are thinking about engaging in an activity with short-term benefits but long-term costs, they might prefer to delay receipt of important information. The same point might hold about information that could make people sad or mad: "Please tell me what I need to know — tomorrow."

* aggregate: 합계의 ** chastity: 정결

① highlight the value of preferred activities
② make current activities less attractive
③ cut their attachment to past activities
④ enable them to enjoy more activities
⑤ potentially become known to others

08 1등급 대비 고난도 2점 문제

고2 • 2022년 3월 31번

다음 빈칸에 들어갈 말로 가장 적절한 것을 고르시오.

Around the boss, you will always find people coming across as friends, good subordinates, or even great sympathizers. But some do not truly belong. One day, an incident will blow their cover, and then you will know where they truly belong. When it is all cosy and safe, they will be there, loitering the corridors and fawning at the slightest opportunity. But as soon as difficulties arrive, they are the first to be found missing. And difficult times are the true test of ______________. Dr. Martin Luther King said, "The ultimate test of a man is not where he stands in moments of comfort and convenience, but where he stands at times of challenge and controversy." And so be careful of friends who are always eager to take from you but reluctant to give back even in their little ways. If they lack the commitment to sail with you through difficult weather, then they are more likely to abandon your ship when it stops.

* loiter: 서성거리다 ** fawn: 알랑거리다

① leadership ② loyalty
③ creativity ④ intelligence
⑤ independence

09 1등급 대비 고난도 3점 문제

고2 · 2018년 6월 31번

다음 빈칸에 들어갈 말로 가장 적절한 것을 고르시오. [3점]

Do you advise your kids to keep away from strangers? That's a tall order for adults. After all, you expand your network of friends and create potential business partners by meeting strangers. Throughout this process, however, analyzing people to understand their personalities is not all about potential economic or social benefit. There is your safety to think about, as well as the safety of your loved ones. For that reason, Mary Ellen O'Toole, who is a retired FBI profiler, emphasizes the need to ____________________ in order to understand them. It is not safe, for instance, to assume that a stranger is a good neighbor, just because they're polite. Seeing them follow a routine of going out every morning well-dressed doesn't mean that's the whole story. In fact, O'Toole says that when you are dealing with a criminal, even your feelings may fail you. That's because criminals have perfected the art of manipulation and deceit.

* tall order: 무리한 요구

① narrow down your network in social media
② go beyond a person's superficial qualities
③ focus on intelligence rather than wealth
④ trust your first impressions of others
⑤ take advantage of criminals

10 1등급 대비 고난도 3점 문제

고2 · 2017년 6월 32번

다음 빈칸에 들어갈 말로 가장 적절한 것을 고르시오. [3점]

Honeybees have evolved what we call "swarm intelligence," with up to 50,000 workers in a single colony coming together to make democratic decisions. When a hive gets too crowded in springtime, colonies send scouts to look for a new home. If any scouts disagree on where the colony should build its next hive, they argue their case the civilized way: through a dance-off. Each scout performs a "waggle dance" for other scouts in an attempt to convince them of their spot's merit. The more enthusiastic the dance is, the happier the scout is with his spot. The remainder of the colony ____________________, flying to the spot they prefer and joining in the dance until one potential hive overcomes all other dances of the neighborhood. It would be great if Congress settled their disagreements the same way.

* colony: (개미, 벌 등의) 집단, 군집

① votes with their bodies
② invades other bees' hives
③ searches for more flowers
④ shows more concern for mates
⑤ improves their communication skills

11 1등급 대비 고난도 3점 문제

고2•2017년 9월 33번

다음 빈칸에 들어갈 말로 가장 적절한 것을 고르시오. [3점]

One of the most curious paintings of the Renaissance is a careful depiction of a weedy patch of ground by Albrecht Dürer. Dürer extracts design and harmony from an apparently random collection of weeds and grasses that we would normally not think twice to look at. By taking such an ordinary thing, he is able to convey his artistry in a pure form. In a similar way, scientists often ________________ when trying to understand the essence of a problem. Studying relatively simple systems avoids unnecessary complications, and can allow deeper insights to be obtained. This is particularly true when we are trying to understand something as problematic as our ability to learn. Human reactions are so complex that they can be difficult to interpret objectively. It sometimes helps to step back and consider how more modest creatures, like bacteria or weeds, deal with the challenges they face.

① depend on personal experience
② choose to study humble subjects
③ work in close cooperation with one another
④ look for solutions to problems from the past
⑤ test a hypothesis through lots of experiments

12 1등급 대비 고난도 3점 문제

고2•2022년 6월 34번

다음 빈칸에 들어갈 말로 가장 적절한 것을 고르시오. [3점]

In most of the world, capitalism and free markets are accepted today as constituting the best system for allocating economic resources and encouraging economic output. Nations have tried other systems, such as socialism and communism, but in many cases they have either switched wholesale to or adopted aspects of free markets. Despite the widespread acceptance of the free-market system, ________________. Government involvement takes many forms, ranging from the enactment and enforcement of laws and regulations to direct participation in the economy through entities like the U.S.'s mortgage agencies. Perhaps the most important form of government involvement, however, comes in the attempts of central banks and national treasuries to control and affect the ups and downs of economic cycles.

* enactment: (법률의) 제정 ** entity: 실체

① markets are rarely left entirely free
② governments are reluctant to intervene
③ supply and demand are not always balanced
④ economic inequality continues to get worse
⑤ competition does not guarantee the maximum profit

DAY 04

학습 Check!

▶ 몰라서 틀린 문항 × 표기 ▶ 헷갈렸거나 찍은 문항 △ 표기 ▶ ×, △ 문항은 다시 풀고 ✔ 표기를 하세요.

종료 시각	시 분 초	문항 번호	01	02	03	04	05	06	07	08	09	10	11	12
소요 시간	분 초	채점 결과												
초과 시간	분 초	틀린 문항 복습												

DAY 05 ※ 점수 표기가 없는 문항은 모두 2점입니다.

빈칸이 중반부에 있을 때 빈칸 추론 05

● 날짜 : 월 일 ● 시작 시각 : 시 분 초 ● 목표 시간 : 20분

01

고2•2017년 6월 31번

다음 빈칸에 들어갈 말로 가장 적절한 것을 고르시오. [3점]

There are countless examples of scientific inventions that have been generated by accident. However, often this accident has required a person with above-average knowledge in the field to interpret it. One of the better-known examples of the cooperation between ______________________________ is the invention of penicillin. In 1928, Scottish biologist Alexander Fleming went on a vacation. As a slightly careless man, Fleming left some bacterial cultures on his desk. When he returned, he noticed mold in one of his cultures, with a bacteria-free zone around it. The mold was from the *penicillium notatum* species, which had killed the bacteria on the Petri dish. This was a lucky coincidence. For a person who does not have expert knowledge, the bacteria-free zone would not have had much significance, but Fleming understood the magical effect of the mold. The result was penicillin — a medication that has saved countless people on the planet.

* culture: (세균 등의) 배양균
** mold: 곰팡이

① trial and error
② idea and a critic
③ risk and stability
④ chance and a researcher
⑤ a professional and an amateur

02

고3•2024학년도 6월 32번

다음 빈칸에 들어갈 말로 가장 적절한 것을 고르시오.

In labor-sharing groups, people contribute labor to other people on a regular basis (for seasonal agricultural work such as harvesting) or on an irregular basis (in the event of a crisis such as the need to rebuild a barn damaged by fire). Labor sharing groups are part of what has been called a "moral economy" since no one keeps formal records on how much any family puts in or takes out. Instead, accounting is ______________________. The group has a sense of moral community based on years of trust and sharing. In a certain community of North America, labor sharing is a major economic factor of social cohesion. When a family needs a new barn or faces repair work that requires group labor, a barn-raising party is called. Many families show up to help. Adult men provide manual labor, and adult women provide food for the event. Later, when another family needs help, they call on the same people.

* cohesion: 응집성

① legally established
② regularly reported
③ socially regulated
④ manually calculated
⑤ carefully documented

03

고2 • 2018년 11월 32번

다음 빈칸에 들어갈 말로 가장 적절한 것을 고르시오.

For several years much research in psychology was based on the assumption that human beings are driven by base motivations such as aggression, egoistic self-interest, and the pursuit of simple pleasures. Since many psychologists began with that assumption, they inadvertently designed research studies that supported their own presuppositions. Consequently, the view of humanity that prevailed in psychology was that of a species barely keeping its aggressive tendencies in check and managing to live in social groups more out of motivated self-interest than out of a genuine affinity for others or a true sense of community. Both Sigmund Freud and the early behaviorists led by John B. Watson believed that humans were motivated primarily by ____________________. From that perspective, social interaction is possible only by exerting control over those baser emotions and, therefore, it is always vulnerable to eruptions of violence, greed, and selfishness. The fact that humans actually live together in social groups has traditionally been seen as a tenuous arrangement that is always just one step away from violence.

* inadvertently: 무심코 ** affinity: 친밀감
*** tenuous: 미약한

① ethical ideas
② selfish drives
③ rational thoughts
④ extrinsic rewards
⑤ social punishments

04

고2 • 2022년 11월 33번

다음 빈칸에 들어갈 말로 가장 적절한 것을 고르시오.

Negative numbers are a lot more abstract than positive numbers — you can't see negative 4 cookies and you certainly can't eat them — but you can think about them, and you *have to*, in all aspects of daily life, from debts to contending with freezing temperatures and parking garages. Still, many of us haven't quite made peace with negative numbers. People have invented all sorts of funny little mental strategies to ______________________________________. On mutual fund statements, losses (negative numbers) are printed in red or stuck in parentheses with no negative sign to be found. The history books tell us that Julius Caesar was born in 100 B.C., not −100. The underground levels in a parking garage often have designations like B1 and B2. Temperatures are one of the few exceptions: folks do say, especially here in Ithaca, New York, that it's −5 degrees outside, though even then, many prefer to say 5 below zero. There's something about that negative sign that just looks so unpleasant.

* parentheses: 괄호

① sidestep the dreaded negative sign
② resolve stock market uncertainties
③ compensate for complicated calculating processes
④ unify the systems of expressing numbers below zero
⑤ face the truth that subtraction can create negative numbers

DAY 05

05

고2 • 2020년 6월 34번

다음 빈칸에 들어갈 말로 가장 적절한 것을 고르시오. [3점]

The availability heuristic refers to a common mistake that our brains make by assuming that the instances or examples that come to mind easily are also the most important or prevalent. It shows that we make our decisions based on the recency of events. We often misjudge the frequency and magnitude of the events that have happened recently because of the limitations of our memories. According to Harvard professor, Max Bazerman, managers conducting performance appraisals often fall victim to the availability heuristic. The recency of events highly influences a supervisor's opinion during performance appraisals. Managers give more weight to performance during the three months prior to the evaluation than to the previous nine months of the evaluation period because ____. The availability heuristic is influenced by the ease of recall or retrievability of information of some event. Ease of recall suggests that if something is more easily recalled in your memory, you think that it will occur with a high probability.

* appraisal: 평가 ** retrievability: 회복력

① there is little reliable data about workers
② the frequent contacts help the relationship
③ they want to evaluate employees objectively
④ the recent instances dominate their memories
⑤ distorted data have no impact on the evaluation

06

고2 • 2016년 11월 32번

다음 빈칸에 들어갈 말로 가장 적절한 것을 고르시오. [3점]

The Neanderthals would have faced a problem when it was daylight: the light quality is much poorer at high latitudes and this would have meant that they couldn't see things in the distance so well. For a hunter, this is a serious problem, because you really don't want to make the mistake of not noticing the mother rhinoceros hiding in a dark corner of the forest edge when trying to spear her calf. Living under low light conditions places a much heavier premium on vision than most researchers imagine. The evolutionary response to low light levels is ____. It is the familiar principle from conventional star-gazing telescopes: under the dim lighting of the night sky, a larger mirror allows you to gather more of the light from whatever you want to look at. By the same token, a larger retina allows you to receive more light to compensate for poor light levels.

① to get big enough to frighten animals
② to move their habitats to lower latitudes
③ to increase the size of the visual processing system
④ to develop auditory sense rather than visual system
⑤ to focus our attention on what we perceive to be the threat

07 1등급 대비 고난도 3점 문제

고2 • 2018년 9월 31번

다음 빈칸에 들어갈 말로 가장 적절한 것을 고르시오. [3점]

Online environments vary widely in how easily you can save whatever happens there, what I call its *recordability* and *preservability*. Even though the design, activities, and membership of social media might change over time, the content of what people posted usually remains intact. Email, video, audio, and text messages can be saved. When perfect preservation is possible, time has been suspended. Whenever you want, you can go back to reexamine those events from the past. In other situations, ______________ slips between our fingers, even challenging our reality testing about whether something existed at all, as when an email that we seem to remember receiving mysteriously disappears from our inbox. The slightest accidental tap of the finger can send an otherwise everlasting document into nothingness.

① scarcity ② creativity
③ acceleration ④ permanency
⑤ mysteriousness

08 1등급 대비 고난도 3점 문제

고2 • 2018년 6월 32번

다음 빈칸에 들어갈 말로 가장 적절한 것을 고르시오. [3점]

"Survivorship bias" is a common logical fallacy. We're prone to listen to the success stories from survivors because the others aren't around to tell the tale. A dramatic example from history is the case of statistician Abraham Wald who, during World War Ⅱ, was hired by the U.S. Air Force to determine how to make their bomber planes safer. The planes that returned tended to have bullet holes along the wings, body, and tail, and commanders wanted to reinforce those areas because they seemed to get hit most often. Wald, however, saw that the important thing was that these bullet holes had not destroyed the planes, and what needed more protection were ____________________________. Those were the parts where, if a plane was struck by a bullet, it would never be seen again. His calculations based on that logic are still in use today, and they have saved many pilots.

* fallacy: 오류

① the areas that were not hit
② high technologies to make airplanes
③ military plans for bombing the targets
④ the data that analyzed broken parts
⑤ the commanders of the army

DAY 05

09 1등급 대비 고난도 3점 문제

고2•2019년 6월 31번

다음 빈칸에 들어갈 말로 가장 적절한 것을 고르시오. [3점]

Psychologists Leon Festinger, Stanley Schachter, and sociologist Kurt Back began to wonder how friendships form. Why do some strangers build lasting friendships, while others struggle to get past basic platitudes? Some experts explained that friendship formation could be traced to infancy, where children acquired the values, beliefs, and attitudes that would bind or separate them later in life. But Festinger, Schachter, and Back pursued a different theory. The researchers believed that ______________ was the key to friendship formation; that "friendships are likely to develop on the basis of brief and passive contacts made going to and from home or walking about the neighborhood." In their view, it wasn't so much that people with similar attitudes became friends, but rather that people who passed each other during the day tended to become friends and so came to adopt similar attitudes over time.

* platitude: 상투적인 말

① shared value
② physical space
③ conscious effort
④ similar character
⑤ psychological support

10 1등급 대비 고난도 3점 문제

고2•2021년 6월 32번

다음 빈칸에 들어갈 말로 가장 적절한 것을 고르시오. [3점]

While leaders often face enormous pressures to make decisions quickly, premature decisions are the leading cause of decision failure. This is primarily because leaders respond to the superficial issue of a decision rather than taking the time to explore the underlying issues. Bob Carlson is a good example of a leader ______________ in the face of diverse issues. In the economic downturn of early 2001, Reell Precision Manufacturing faced a 30 percent drop in revenues. Some members of the senior leadership team favored layoffs and some favored salary reductions. While it would have been easy to push for a decision or call for a vote in order to ease the tension of the economic pressures, as co-CEO, Bob Carlson helped the team work together and examine all of the issues. The team finally agreed on salary reductions, knowing that, to the best of their ability, they had thoroughly examined the implications of both possible decisions.

* revenue: 총수입 ** implication: 영향

① justifying layoffs
② exercising patience
③ increasing employment
④ sticking to his opinions
⑤ training unskilled members

11 1등급 대비 고난도 3점 문제

고2 • 2017년 11월 33번

다음 빈칸에 들어갈 말로 가장 적절한 것을 고르시오. [3점]

Veblen goods are named after Thorstein Veblen, a US economist who formulated the theory of “conspicuous consumption”. They are strange because demand for them increases as their price rises. According to Veblen, these goods must signal high status. A willingness to pay higher prices is due to a desire to advertise wealth rather than to acquire better quality. A true Veblen good, therefore, should not be noticeably higher quality than the lower-priced equivalents. If the price falls so much that __________________________________, the rich will stop buying it. There is much evidence of this behavior in the markets for luxury cars, champagne, watches, and certain clothing labels. A reduction in prices might see a temporary increase in sales for the seller, but then sales will begin to fall.

* conspicuous: 과시적인

① the government starts to get involved in the industry
② manufacturers finally decide not to supply the market
③ the law of supply and demand does not work anymore
④ there is no quality competition remaining in the market
⑤ it is no longer high enough to exclude the less well off

12 1등급 대비 고난도 3점 문제

고2 • 2019년 3월 33번

다음 빈칸에 들어갈 말로 가장 적절한 것을 고르시오. [3점]

Theseus was a great hero to the people of Athens. When he returned home after a war, the ship that had carried him and his men was so treasured that the townspeople preserved it for years and years, replacing its old, rotten planks with new pieces of wood. The question Plutarch asks philosophers is this: is the repaired ship still the same ship that Theseus had sailed? Removing one plank and replacing it might not make a difference, but can that still be true once all the planks have been replaced? Some philosophers argue that the ship must be ____________________________. But if this is true, then as the ship got pushed around during its journey and lost small pieces, it would already have stopped being the ship of Theseus.

* plank: 널빤지

① the reminder of victory
② the sum of all its parts
③ fit for the intended use
④ the property of the country
⑤ around for a long period of time

학습 Check!

▶ 몰라서 틀린 문항 × 표기 ▶ 헷갈렸거나 찍은 문항 △ 표기 ▶ ×, △ 문항은 다시 풀고 ✔ 표기를 하세요.

종료 시각	시 분 초
소요 시간	분 초
초과 시간	분 초

문항 번호	01	02	03	04	05	06	07	08	09	10	11	12
채점 결과												
틀린 문항 복습												

[해설편 p.036]

● 날짜 :　　월　　일 ● 시작 시각 :　　시　　분　　초　　● 목표 시간 : 20분

01

고2 • 2020년 9월 31번

다음 빈칸에 들어갈 말로 가장 적절한 것을 고르시오.

Firms in almost every industry tend to be clustered. Suppose you threw darts at random on a map of the United States. You'd find the holes left by the darts to be more or less evenly distributed across the map. But the real map of any given industry looks nothing like that; it looks more as if someone had thrown all the darts in the same place. This is probably in part because of reputation; buyers may be suspicious of a software firm in the middle of the cornfields. It would also be hard to recruit workers if every time you needed a new employee you had to persuade someone to move across the country, rather than just poach one from your neighbor. There are also regulatory reasons: zoning laws often try to concentrate dirty industries in one place and restaurants and bars in another. Finally, people in the same industry often have similar preferences (computer engineers like coffee, financiers show off with expensive bottles of wine). ________________ makes it easier to provide the amenities they like.

* poach: (인력을) 빼내다

① Automation　② Concentration
③ Transportation　④ Globalization
⑤ Liberalization

02

고3 • 2017학년도 수능 31번

다음 빈칸에 들어갈 말로 가장 적절한 것을 고르시오. [3점]

The creativity that children possess needs to be cultivated throughout their development. Research suggests that overstructuring the child's environment may actually limit creative and academic development. This is a central problem with much of science instruction. The exercises or activities are devised to eliminate different options and to focus on predetermined results. The answers are structured to fit the course assessments, and the wonder of science is lost along with cognitive intrigue. We define cognitive intrigue as the wonder that stimulates and intrinsically motivates an individual to voluntarily engage in an activity. The loss of cognitive intrigue may be initiated by the sole use of play items with predetermined conclusions and reinforced by rote instruction in school. This is exemplified by toys, games, and lessons that are a(n) ____________ in and of themselves and require little of the individual other than to master the planned objective.

* rote: 기계적인 암기

① end　② input
③ puzzle　④ interest
⑤ alternative

03

고2 • 2017년 9월 32번

다음 빈칸에 들어갈 말로 가장 적절한 것을 고르시오. [3점]

In many regions of Central America, native people can but do not grow green vegetables packed with vital nutrients such as vitamin A. Generally speaking, the people do not have a tradition of raising these crops. They often have limited education in general and almost no exposure to health and nutrition advice, and they grow what feeds the most people. They often have plenty of tortillas and beans, so they have sufficient protein, and they eat until full. Yet the lack of micronutrients leads to their children developing blindness, iron deficiency, and other growth disorders. In these situations, families have to be educated about nutrition, encouraged to diversify their diets, plant more green vegetables, and sometimes receive nutritional assistance to ______________________.

* micronutrient: 미량 영양소

① eliminate obesity
② improve digestion
③ correct imbalances
④ consume more protein
⑤ preserve their tradition

04

고2 • 2020년 3월 32번

다음 빈칸에 들어갈 말로 가장 적절한 것을 고르시오.

Nothing happens immediately, so in the beginning we can't see any results from our practice. This is like the example of the man who tries to make fire by rubbing two sticks of wood together. He says to himself, "They say there's fire here," and he begins rubbing energetically. He rubs on and on, but he's very impatient. He wants to have that fire, but the fire doesn't come. So he gets discouraged and stops to rest for a while. Then he starts again, but the going is slow, so he rests again. By then the heat has disappeared; he didn't keep at it long enough. He rubs and rubs until he gets tired and then he stops altogether. Not only is he tired, but he becomes more and more discouraged until he gives up completely, "There's no fire here." Actually, he was doing the work, but there wasn't enough heat to start a fire. The fire was there all the time, but ______________________.

① he didn't carry on to the end
② someone told him not to give up
③ the sticks were not strong enough
④ he started without planning in advance
⑤ the weather was not suitable to start a fire

05

고2 • 2022년 3월 33번

다음 빈칸에 들어갈 말로 가장 적절한 것을 고르시오. [3점]

According to many philosophers, there is a purely logical reason why science will never be able to explain everything. For in order to explain something, whatever it is, we need to invoke something else. But what explains the second thing? To illustrate, recall that Newton explained a diverse range of phenomena using his law of gravity. But what explains the law of gravity itself? If someone asks *why* all bodies exert a gravitational attraction on each other, what should we tell them? Newton had no answer to this question. In Newtonian science the law of gravity was a fundamental principle: it explained other things, but could not itself be explained. The moral generalizes. However much the science of the future can explain, the explanations it gives will have to make use of certain fundamental laws and principles. Since nothing can explain itself, it follows that at least some of these laws and principles ____________________.

* invoke: 언급하다

① govern human's relationship with nature
② are based on objective observations
③ will themselves remain unexplained
④ will be compared with other theories
⑤ are difficult to use to explain phenomena

06

고2 • 2023년 6월 33번

다음 빈칸에 들어갈 말로 가장 적절한 것을 고르시오. [3점]

In adolescence many of us had the experience of falling under the sway of a great book or writer. We became entranced by the novel ideas in the book, and because we were so open to influence, these early encounters with exciting ideas sank deeply into our minds and became part of our own thought processes, affecting us decades after we absorbed them. Such influences enriched our mental landscape, and in fact our intelligence depends on the ability to absorb the lessons and ideas of those who are older and wiser. Just as the body tightens with age, however, so does the mind. And just as our sense of weakness and vulnerability motivated the desire to learn, so does our creeping sense of superiority slowly close us off to new ideas and influences. Some may advocate that we all become more skeptical in the modern world, but in fact a far greater danger comes from ____________________ that burdens us as individuals as we get older, and seems to be burdening our culture in general.

* entrance: 매료시키다

① the high dependence on others
② the obsession with our inferiority
③ the increasing closing of the mind
④ the misconception about our psychology
⑤ the self-destructive pattern of behavior

07

고2 • 2017년 6월 34번

다음 빈칸에 들어갈 말로 가장 적절한 것을 고르시오. [3점]

We are extremely responsive to what we perceive people around us to be doing. This unconscious function has helped us make quick and good life-saving decisions throughout history. A study has shown how powerful this factor is. One practical experiment was an experiment conducted where a hotel wished their guests to reuse the towels in their rooms. They decided to put out a few signs. The first sign cited environmental reasons and the second sign said the hotel would donate a portion of end-of-year laundry savings. The third sign showed the majority of guests reused their towels at least once during their stay. To their surprise, guests responded most positively to the third sign. If you want to influence people to act a certain way, there are few more powerful methods than to give the impression that ____________________.

① others are doing the action you desire them to do
② humans support the policy meeting their personal needs
③ people are encouraged to reuse their towels in most hotels
④ you are expected to have positive influence in the world
⑤ hotels are not providing guests with valuable services

08

고3 • 2021학년도 6월 34번

다음 빈칸에 들어갈 말로 가장 적절한 것을 고르시오. [3점]

A large part of what we see is what we expect to see. This explains why we "see" faces and figures in a flickering campfire, or in moving clouds. This is why Leonardo da Vinci advised artists to discover their motifs by staring at patches on a blank wall. A fire provides a constant flickering change in visual information that never integrates into anything solid and thereby allows the brain to engage in a play of hypotheses. On the other hand, the wall does not present us with very much in the way of visual clues, and so the brain begins to make more and more hypotheses and desperately searches for confirmation. A crack in the wall looks a little like the profile of a nose and suddenly a whole face appears, or a leaping horse, or a dancing figure. In cases like these the brain's visual strategies are ____________________.

* flicker: 흔들리다

① ignoring distracting information unrelated to visual clues
② projecting images from within the mind out onto the world
③ categorizing objects into groups either real or imagined
④ strengthening connections between objects in the real world
⑤ removing the broken or missing parts of an original image

DAY 06

09 1등급 대비 고난도 2점 문제

고2·2019년 3월 31번

다음 빈칸에 들어갈 말로 가장 적절한 것을 고르시오.

Would you expect the physical expression of pride to be biologically based or culturally specific? The psychologist Jessica Tracy has found that young children can recognize when a person feels pride. Moreover, she found that isolated populations with minimal Western contact also accurately identify the physical signs. These signs include a smiling face, raised arms, an expanded chest, and a pushed-out torso. Tracy and David Matsumoto examined pride responses among people competing in judo matches in the 2004 Olympic and Paralympic Games. Sighted and blind athletes from 37 nations competed. After victory, the behaviors displayed by sighted and blind athletes were very similar. These findings suggest that pride responses are ____________.

① innate ② creative
③ unidentifiable ④ contradictory
⑤ offensive

10 1등급 대비 고난도 3점 문제

고2·2020년 3월 31번

다음 빈칸에 들어갈 말로 가장 적절한 것을 고르시오. [3점]

When he was dying, the contemporary Buddhist teacher Dainin Katagiri wrote a remarkable book called *Returning to Silence*. Life, he wrote, "is a dangerous situation." It is the weakness of life that makes it precious; his words are filled with the very fact of his own life passing away. "The china bowl is beautiful because sooner or later it will break.... The life of the bowl is always existing in a dangerous situation." Such is our struggle: this unstable beauty. This inevitable wound. We forget — how easily we forget — that love and loss are intimate companions, that we love the real flower so much more than the plastic one and love the cast of twilight across a mountainside lasting only a moment. It is this very ____________ that opens our hearts.

① fragility ② stability
③ harmony ④ satisfaction
⑤ diversity

11 1등급 대비 고난도 3점 문제

고2·2021년 6월 34번

다음 빈칸에 들어갈 말로 가장 적절한 것을 고르시오. [3점]

Early in the term, our art professor projected an image of a monk, his back to the viewer, standing on the shore, looking off into a blue sea and an enormous sky. The professor asked the class, "What do you see?" The darkened auditorium was silent. We looked and looked and thought and thought as hard as possible to unearth the hidden meaning, but came up with nothing — we must have missed it. With dramatic exasperation she answered her own question, "It's a painting of a monk! His back is to us! He is standing near the shore! There's a blue sea and enormous sky!" Hmm... why didn't we see it? So as not to bias us, she'd posed the question without revealing the artist or title of the work. In fact, it was Caspar David Friedrich's *The Monk by the Sea*. To better understand your world, ______________________________ rather than guess at what you think you are supposed to see.

* exasperation: 격분

① consciously acknowledge what you actually see
② accept different opinions with a broad mind
③ reflect on what you've already learned
④ personally experience even a small thing
⑤ analyze the answers from various perspectives

12 1등급 대비 고난도 3점 문제

고2·2019년 11월 34번

다음 빈칸에 들어갈 말로 가장 적절한 것을 고르시오. [3점]

Attitude has been conceptualized into four main components: affective (feelings of liking or disliking), cognitive (beliefs and evaluation of those beliefs), behavioral intention (a statement of how one would behave in a certain situation), and behavior. Public attitudes toward a wildlife species and its management are generated based on the interaction of those components. In forming our attitudes toward wolves, people strive to keep their affective components of attitude consistent with their cognitive component. For example, I could dislike wolves; I believe they have killed people (cognitive belief), and having people killed is of course bad (evaluation of belief). The behavioral intention that could result from this is to support a wolf control program and actual behavior may be a history of shooting wolves. In this example, ______________________________, producing a negative overall attitude toward wolves.

① attitude drives the various forms of belief
② all aspects of attitude are consistent with each other
③ cognitive components of attitude outweigh affective ones
④ the components of attitude are not simultaneously evaluated
⑤ our biased attitudes get in the way of preserving biodiversity

DAY 06

학습 Check!

▶ 몰라서 틀린 문항 × 표기 ▶ 헷갈렸거나 찍은 문항 △ 표기 ▶ ×, △ 문항은 다시 풀고 ✔ 표기를 하세요.

종료 시각	시 분 초
소요 시간	분 초
초과 시간	분 초

문항 번호	01	02	03	04	05	06	07	08	09	10	11	12
채점 결과												
틀린 문항 복습												

[해설편 p.043]

DAY 07 ※ 점수 표기가 없는 문항은 모두 2점입니다.
빈칸이 후반부에 있을 때 빈칸 추론 07

● 날짜 : 월 일 ● 시작 시각 : 시 분 초 ● 목표 시간 : 20분

01

고2•2017년 11월 31번

다음 빈칸에 들어갈 말로 가장 적절한 것을 고르시오. [3점]

What is the true nature of the brain? The brain is a slow-changing machine, and that's a good thing. If your brain could completely change overnight, you would be unstable. Let's just say that your norm is to wake up, read the paper with coffee and a bagel, walk your dog, and watch the news. This is your habitual routine. Then one night, you get a phone call at 3 a.m. and have to run outside in your underwear to check on your neighbors. What if your brain latched on to this new routine and you continued to run outside at 3 a.m. every night in your underwear? Nobody would want that, so it's a good thing our brains require more repetition than that! Let's accept and be thankful for the ____________ our slow-changing brains provide us.

* latch on to: ~을 자기 것으로 하다

① stability
② maturity
③ curiosity
④ variability
⑤ productivity

02

고2•2022년 6월 32번

다음 빈칸에 들어갈 말로 가장 적절한 것을 고르시오.

Color is an interpretation of wavelengths, one that only exists internally. And it gets stranger, because the wavelengths we're talking about involve only what we call "visible light", a spectrum of wavelengths that runs from red to violet. But visible light constitutes only a tiny fraction of the electromagnetic spectrum — less than one ten-trillionth of it. All the rest of the spectrum — including radio waves, microwaves, X-rays, gamma rays, cell phone conversations, wi-fi, and so on — all of this is flowing through us right now, and we're completely unaware of it. This is because we don't have any specialized biological receptors to pick up on these signals from other parts of the spectrum. The slice of reality that we can see is ____________________.

* electromagnetic: 전자기의 ** receptor: 수용체

① hindered by other wavelengths
② derived from our imagination
③ perceived through all senses
④ filtered by our stereotypes
⑤ limited by our biology

03

고2 • 2018년 9월 33번

다음 빈칸에 들어갈 말로 가장 적절한 것을 고르시오. [3점]

Science can only tell us how the world appears to us, not how it is independent of our observation of it, and therefore *right now* will always elude science. When you look into space, you are looking into an ancient past. Some of the stars are already long dead yet we still see them because of their traveling light. Let's say that we are on one of those stars situated roughly sixty million light-years away. If we had a really awesome telescope pointed at the earth, we would see the dinosaurs walking around. The end of the universe is probably so old that if we had that telescope, we might be able to see the beginning. Besides faraway things, even the immediate objects around us are ______________________ because there is still a time lag for the reflection of light to reach our eyes. Every sensation our body feels has to wait for the information to be carried to the brain.

* elude: 교묘하게 벗어나다[피하다]

① results of the big bang
② derived from exploration
③ all afterimages of the past
④ mixes of light, colors, and shading
⑤ signs directly encoded in our genes

04

고3 • 2018학년도 수능 31번

다음 빈칸에 들어갈 말로 가장 적절한 것을 고르시오. [3점]

Apocalypse Now, a film produced and directed by Francis Ford Coppola, gained widespread popularity, and for good reason. The film is an adaptation of Joseph Conrad's novel *Heart of Darkness*, which is set in the African Congo at the end of the 19th century. Unlike the original novel, *Apocalypse Now* is set in Vietnam and Cambodia during the Vietnam War. The setting, time period, dialogue and other incidental details are changed but the fundamental narrative and themes of *Apocalypse Now* are the same as those of *Heart of Darkness*. Both describe a physical journey, reflecting the central character's mental and spiritual journey, down a river to confront the deranged Kurtz character, who represents the worst aspects of civilisation. By giving *Apocalypse Now* a setting that was contemporary at the time of its release, audiences were able to experience and identify with its themes more easily than they would have if the film had been ______________________.

* deranged: 제정신이 아닌

① a literal adaptation of the novel
② a source of inspiration for the novel
③ a faithful depiction of the Vietnam War
④ a vivid dramatisation of a psychological journey
⑤ a critical interpretation of contemporary civilisation

05

고2 • 2017년 3월 32번

다음 빈칸에 들어갈 말로 가장 적절한 것을 고르시오. [3점]

In 1944 the German rocket-bomb attacks on London suddenly escalated. Over two thousand V-1 flying bombs fell on the city, killing more than five thousand people and wounding many more. Somehow, however, the Germans consistently missed their targets. Bombs that were intended for Tower Bridge, or Piccadilly, would fall well short of the city, landing in the less populated suburbs. This was because, in fixing their targets, the Germans relied on secret agents they had planted in England. They did not know that these agents had been discovered, and that in their place, English-controlled agents were giving them subtly deceptive information. The bombs would hit farther and farther from their targets every time they fell. By the end of the attack they were landing on cows in the country. By ______________________________, the English army gained a strong advantage.

① being honest with the public
② giving the enemy a chance to retreat
③ feeding the enemy wrong information
④ focusing on one goal consistently
⑤ exploring the unknown places

06

고2 • 2022년 3월 34번

다음 빈칸에 들어갈 말로 가장 적절한 것을 고르시오. [3점]

In one example of the important role of laughter in social contexts, Devereux and Ginsburg examined frequency of laughter in matched pairs of strangers or friends who watched a humorous video together compared to those who watched it alone. The time individuals spent laughing was nearly twice as frequent in pairs as when alone. Frequency of laughing was only slightly shorter for friends than strangers. According to Devereux and Ginsburg, laughing with strangers served to create a social bond that made each person in the pair feel comfortable. This explanation is supported by the fact that in their stranger condition, when one person laughed, the other was likely to laugh as well. Interestingly, the three social conditions (alone, paired with a stranger, or paired with a friend) did not differ in their ratings of funniness of the video or of feelings of happiness or anxiousness. This finding implies that their frequency of laughter was not because we find things funnier when we are with others but instead we ______________________________.

① have similar tastes in comedy and humor
② are using laughter to connect with others
③ are reluctant to reveal our innermost feelings
④ focus on the content rather than the situation
⑤ feel more comfortable around others than alone

07

고2 • 2021년 9월 33번

다음 빈칸에 들어갈 말로 가장 적절한 것을 고르시오. [3점]

The most powerful emotional experiences are those that bring joy, inspiration, and the kind of love that makes suffering bearable. These emotional experiences are the result of choices and behaviors that result in our feeling happy. When we look at happiness through a spiritual filter, we realize that it does not mean the absence of pain or heartache. Sitting with a sick or injured child, every parent gets to know the profound joy that bubbles over when a son or daughter begins to heal. This is a simple example of how we can be flooded with happiness that becomes more intense as we contrast it with previous suffering. Experiences such as this go into the chemical archives of the limbic system. Each time you experience true happiness, the stored emotions are activated as you are flooded with even deeper joy than you remembered. Your spiritual genes are, in a sense, ______________________.

* limbic system: 변연계(인체의 기본적인 감정·욕구 등을 관장하는 신경계)

① your biological treasure map to joy
② your hidden key to lasting friendships
③ a mirror showing your unique personality
④ a facilitator for communication with others
⑤ a barrier to looking back to your joyful childhood

08

고3 • 2018학년도 6월 32번

다음 빈칸에 들어갈 말로 가장 적절한 것을 고르시오. [3점]

Politics cannot be suppressed, whichever policy process is employed and however sensitive and respectful of differences it might be. In other words, there is no end to politics. It is wrong to think that proper institutions, knowledge, methods of consultation, or participatory mechanisms can make disagreement go away. Theories of all sorts promote the view that there are ways by which disagreement can be processed or managed so as to make it disappear. The assumption behind those theories is that disagreement is wrong and consensus is the desirable state of things. In fact, consensus rarely comes without some forms of subtle coercion and the absence of fear in expressing a disagreement is a source of genuine freedom. Debates cause disagreements to evolve, often for the better, but a positively evolving debate does not have to equal a reduction in disagreement. The suppression of disagreement should never be made into a goal in political deliberation. A defense is required against any suggestion that ______________________.

* consensus: 합의 ** coercion: 강압

① political development results from the freedom of speech
② political disagreement is not the normal state of things
③ politics should not restrict any form of difference
④ freedom could be achieved only through tolerance
⑤ suppression could never be a desirable tool in politics

09 1등급 대비 고난도 2점 문제

고2・2020년 11월 31번

다음 빈칸에 들어갈 말로 가장 적절한 것을 고르시오.

Over 4.5 billion years ago, the Earth's primordial atmosphere was probably largely water vapour, carbon dioxide, sulfur dioxide and nitrogen. The appearance and subsequent evolution of exceedingly primitive living organisms (bacteria-like microbes and simple single-celled plants) began to change the atmosphere, liberating oxygen and breaking down carbon dioxide and sulfur dioxide. This made it possible for higher organisms to develop. When the earliest known plant cells with nuclei evolved about 2 billion years ago, the atmosphere seems to have had only about 1 percent of its present content of oxygen. With the emergence of the first land plants, about 500 million years ago, oxygen reached about one-third of its present concentration. It had risen to almost its present level by about 370 million years ago, when animals first spread on to land. Today's atmosphere is thus not just a requirement to sustain life as we know it — it is also ____________________.

* primordial: 원시의 ** sulfur dioxide: 이산화황

① a barrier to evolution
② a consequence of life
③ a record of primitive culture
④ a sign of the constancy of nature
⑤ a reason for cooperation among species

10 1등급 대비 고난도 3점 문제

고2・2017년 9월 31번

다음 빈칸에 들어갈 말로 가장 적절한 것을 고르시오. [3점]

We are the CEOs of our own lives. We work hard to urge ourselves to get up and go to work and do what we must do day after day. We also try to encourage the people working for and with us, those who are doing business with us, and even those who regulate us. We do this in our personal lives, too: From a very young age, kids try to persuade their parents to do things for them ("Dad, I'm too scared to do this!") with varying degrees of success. As adults, we try to encourage our significant others to do things for us ("Sweetie, I had such a stressful day today, can you please put the kids to bed and do the dishes?"). We attempt to get our kids to clean up their rooms. We try to induce our neighbors to help out with a neighborhood party. Whatever our official job descriptions, we are all part-time __________.

① judges ② motivators
③ inventors ④ analysts
⑤ observers

11 1등급 대비 고난도 3점 문제

고2•2023년 6월 34번

다음 빈칸에 들어갈 말로 가장 적절한 것을 고르시오. [3점]

Many people look for safety and security in popular thinking. They figure that if a lot of people are doing something, then it must be right. It must be a good idea. If most people accept it, then it probably represents fairness, equality, compassion, and sensitivity, right? Not necessarily. Popular thinking said the earth was the center of the universe, yet Copernicus studied the stars and planets and proved mathematically that the earth and the other planets in our solar system revolved around the sun. Popular thinking said surgery didn't require clean instruments, yet Joseph Lister studied the high death rates in hospitals and introduced antiseptic practices that immediately saved lives. Popular thinking said that women shouldn't have the right to vote, yet people like Emmeline Pankhurst and Susan B. Anthony fought for and won that right. We must always remember ________________________. People may say that there's safety in numbers, but that's not always true.

* antiseptic: 멸균의

① majority rule should be founded on fairness
② the crowd is generally going in the right direction
③ the roles of leaders and followers can change at any time
④ people behave in a different fashion to others around them
⑤ there is a huge difference between acceptance and intelligence

12 1등급 대비 고난도 3점 문제

고2•2019년 9월 33번

다음 빈칸에 들어갈 말로 가장 적절한 것을 고르시오. [3점]

New technology tends to come from new ventures — startups. From the Founding Fathers in politics to the Royal Society in science to Fairchild Semiconductor's "traitorous eight" in business, small groups of people bound together by a sense of mission have changed the world for the better. The easiest explanation for this is negative: it's hard to develop new things in big organizations, and it's even harder to do it by yourself. Bureaucratic hierarchies move slowly, and entrenched interests shy away from risk. In the most dysfunctional organizations, signaling that work is being done becomes a better strategy for career advancement than actually doing work. At the other extreme, a lone genius might create a classic work of art or literature, but he could never create an entire industry. Startups operate on the principle that you need to work with other people to get stuff done, but you also need to ________________________.

* entrenched: 굳어진

① stay small enough so that you actually can
② give yourself challenges as often as possible
③ outperform rival businesses in other countries
④ employ the efficient system of big enterprises
⑤ control the organization with consistent policies

DAY 07

학습 Check!

▶ 몰라서 틀린 문항 × 표기 ▶ 헷갈렸거나 찍은 문항 △ 표기 ▶ ×, △ 문항은 다시 풀고 ✔ 표기를 하세요.

종료 시각	시 분 초
소요 시간	분 초
초과 시간	분 초

문항 번호	01	02	03	04	05	06	07	08	09	10	11	12
채점 결과												
틀린 문항 복습												

DAY 08

※ 점수 표기가 없는 문항은 모두 2점입니다.

빈칸이 후반부에 있을 때 **빈칸 추론 08**

● 날짜 : 월 일 ● 시작 시각 : 시 분 초 ● 목표 시간 : 20분

01

고2 • 2017년 3월 31번

다음 빈칸에 들어갈 말로 가장 적절한 것을 고르시오. [3점]

When Charles Darwin developed his theory of natural selection, he created a picture of the evolutionary process in which organismic adaptation was ultimately caused by competition for survival and reproduction. This biological "struggle for existence" bears considerable resemblance to the human struggle between businessmen who are striving for economic success in competitive markets. Long before Darwin published his work, social scientist Adam Smith had already considered that in business life, competition is the driving force behind economic efficiency and adaptation. It is indeed very striking how ______________ the ideas are on which the founders of modern theory in evolutionary biology and economics based their main thoughts.

* organismic: 유기체의

① similar ② confusing
③ unrealistic ④ conventional
⑤ complex

02

고3 • 2024학년도 수능 31번

다음 빈칸에 들어갈 말로 가장 적절한 것을 고르시오.

Over the last decade the attention given to how children learn to read has foregrounded the nature of *textuality*, and of the different, interrelated ways in which readers of all ages make texts mean. 'Reading' now applies to a greater number of representational forms than at any time in the past: pictures, maps, screens, design graphics and photographs are all regarded as text. In addition to the innovations made possible in picture books by new printing processes, design features also predominate in other kinds, such as books of poetry and information texts. Thus, reading becomes a more complicated kind of interpretation than it was when children's attention was focused on the printed text, with sketches or pictures as an adjunct. Children now learn from a picture book that words and illustrations complement and enhance each other. Reading is not simply ______________________________. Even in the easiest texts, what a sentence 'says' is often not what it means.

* adjunct: 부속물

① knowledge acquisition
② word recognition
③ imaginative play
④ subjective interpretation
⑤ image mapping

03

고2 • 2023년 3월 32번

다음 빈칸에 들어갈 말로 가장 적절한 것을 고르시오.

Many early dot-com investors focused almost entirely on revenue growth instead of net income. Many early dot-com companies earned most of their revenue from selling advertising space on their Web sites. To boost reported revenue, some sites began exchanging ad space. Company A would put an ad for its Web site on company B's Web site, and company B would put an ad for its Web site on company A's Web site. No money ever changed hands, but each company recorded revenue (for the value of the space that it gave up on its site) and expense (for the value of its ad that it placed on the other company's site). This practice did little to boost net income and ____________________ — but it did boost *reported* revenue. This practice was quickly put to an end because accountants felt that it did not meet the criteria of the revenue recognition principle.

* revenue: 수익 ** net income: 순이익

① simplified the Web design process
② resulted in no additional cash inflow
③ decreased the salaries of the employees
④ intensified competition among companies
⑤ triggered conflicts on the content of Web ads

04

고2 • 2021년 3월 34번

다음 빈칸에 들어갈 말로 가장 적절한 것을 고르시오. [3점]

Even companies that sell physical products to make profit are forced by their boards and investors to reconsider their underlying motives and to collect as much data as possible from consumers. Supermarkets no longer make all their money selling their produce and manufactured goods. They give you loyalty cards with which they track your purchasing behaviors precisely. Then supermarkets sell this purchasing behavior to marketing analytics companies. The marketing analytics companies perform machine learning procedures, slicing the data in new ways, and resell behavioral data back to product manufacturers as marketing insights. When data and machine learning become currencies of value in a capitalist system, then every company's natural tendency is to maximize its ability to conduct surveillance on its own customers because ____________________.

* surveillance: 관찰, 감시

① its success relies on the number of its innovative products
② more customers come through word-of-mouth marketing
③ it has come to realize the importance of offline stores
④ the customers are themselves the new value-creation devices
⑤ questions are raised on the effectiveness of the capitalist system

05

고2 • 2020년 9월 34번

다음 빈칸에 들어갈 말로 가장 적절한 것을 고르시오. [3점]

In the current landscape, social enterprises tend to rely either on grant capital (e.g., grants, donations, or project funding) or commercial financing products (e.g., bank loans). Ironically, many social enterprises at the same time report of significant drawbacks related to each of these two forms of financing. Many social enterprises are for instance reluctant to make use of traditional commercial finance products, fearing that they might not be able to pay back the loans. In addition, a significant number of social enterprise leaders report that relying too much on grant funding can be a risky strategy since individual grants are time limited and are not reliable in the long term. Grant funding can also lower the incentive for leaders and employees to professionalize the business aspects, thus leading to unhealthy business behavior. In other words, there seems to be a substantial need among social enterprises for ____________________________________.

* grant: (정부나 단체에서 주는) 보조금

① alternatives to the traditional forms of financing
② guidelines for promoting employee welfare
③ measures to protect employees' privacy
④ departments for better customer service
⑤ incentives to significantly increase productivity

06

고2 • 2018년 3월 32번

다음 빈칸에 들어갈 말로 가장 적절한 것을 고르시오. [3점]

In one experiment, children were told they could have one marshmallow treat if they chose to eat it immediately, but two treats if they waited. Most of the children, who ranged in age from 4 to 8, chose to wait, but the strategies they used differed significantly. The 4-year-olds often chose to look at the marshmallows while waiting, a strategy that was not terribly effective. In contrast, 6- and 8-year-olds used language to help overcome temptation, although in different ways. The 6-year-olds spoke and sang to themselves, reminding themselves they would get more treats if they waited. The 8-year-olds focused on aspects of the marshmallows unrelated to taste, such as appearance, which helped them to wait. In short, children used "self-talk" to ____________________________________.

① change their habit
② get more things done
③ regulate their behavior
④ build their self-esteem
⑤ improve their speaking skills

07

고3 • 2021학년도 수능 33번

다음 빈칸에 들어갈 말로 가장 적절한 것을 고르시오. [3점]

Thanks to newly developed neuroimaging technology, we now have access to the specific brain changes that occur during learning. Even though all of our brains contain the same basic structures, our neural networks are as unique as our fingerprints. The latest developmental neuroscience research has shown that the brain is much more malleable throughout life than previously assumed; it develops in response to its own processes, to its immediate and distant "environments," and to its past and current situations. The brain seeks to create meaning through establishing or refining existing neural networks. When we learn a new fact or skill, our neurons communicate to form networks of connected information. Using this knowledge or skill results in structural changes to allow similar future impulses to travel more quickly and efficiently than others. High-activity synaptic connections are stabilized and strengthened, while connections with relatively low use are weakened and eventually pruned. In this way, our brains are ________________________.

* malleable: 순응성이 있는 ** prune: 잘라 내다

① sculpted by our own history of experiences
② designed to maintain their initial structures
③ geared toward strengthening recent memories
④ twinned with the development of other organs
⑤ portrayed as the seat of logical and creative thinking

08 1등급 대비 고난도 2점 문제

고2 • 2022년 9월 32번

다음 빈칸에 들어갈 말로 가장 적절한 것을 고르시오.

There are several reasons why support may not be effective. One possible reason is that receiving help could be a blow to self-esteem. A recent study by Christopher Burke and Jessica Goren at Lehigh University examined this possibility. According to the threat to self-esteem model, help can be perceived as supportive and loving, or it can be seen as threatening if that help is interpreted as implying incompetence. According to Burke and Goren, support is especially likely to be seen as threatening if it is in an area that is self-relevant or self-defining — that is, in an area where your own success and achievement are especially important. Receiving help with a self-relevant task can ________________________, and this can undermine the potential positive effects of the help. For example, if your self-concept rests, in part, on your great cooking ability, it may be a blow to your ego when a friend helps you prepare a meal for guests because it suggests that you're not the master chef you thought you were.

① make you feel bad about yourself
② improve your ability to deal with challenges
③ be seen as a way of asking for another favor
④ trick you into thinking that you were successful
⑤ discourage the person trying to model your behavior

09 1등급 대비 고난도 2점 문제

고3 • 2021학년도 9월 32번

다음 빈칸에 들어갈 말로 가장 적절한 것을 고르시오.

Genetic engineering followed by cloning to distribute many identical animals or plants is sometimes seen as a threat to the diversity of nature. However, humans have been replacing diverse natural habitats with artificial monoculture for millennia. Most natural habitats in the advanced nations have already been replaced with some form of artificial environment based on mass production or repetition. The real threat to biodiversity is surely the need to convert ever more of our planet into production zones to feed the ever-increasing human population. The cloning and transgenic alteration of domestic animals makes little difference to the overall situation. Conversely, the renewed interest in genetics has led to a growing awareness that there are many wild plants and animals with interesting or useful genetic properties that could be used for a variety of as-yet-unknown purposes. This has led in turn to a realization that ______________________________ because they may harbor tomorrow's drugs against cancer, malaria, or obesity.

* monoculture: 단일 경작

① ecological systems are genetically programmed
② we should avoid destroying natural ecosystems
③ we need to stop creating genetically modified organisms
④ artificial organisms can survive in natural environments
⑤ living things adapt themselves to their physical environments

10 1등급 대비 고난도 3점 문제

고2 • 2019년 9월 31번

다음 빈칸에 들어갈 말로 가장 적절한 것을 고르시오. [3점]

Children develop the capacity for solitude in the presence of an attentive other. Consider the silences that fall when you take a young boy on a quiet walk in nature. The child comes to feel increasingly aware of what it is to be alone in nature, supported by being "with" someone who is introducing him to this experience. Gradually, the child takes walks alone. Or imagine a mother giving her two-year-old daughter a bath, allowing the girl's reverie with her bath toys as she makes up stories and learns to be alone with her thoughts, all the while knowing her mother is present and available to her. Gradually, the bath, taken alone, is a time when the child is comfortable with her imagination. ______________ enables solitude.

* reverie: 공상

① Hardship
② Attachment
③ Creativity
④ Compliment
⑤ Responsibility

11 1등급 대비 고난도 3점 문제

고2 • 2023년 9월 34번

다음 빈칸에 들어갈 말로 가장 적절한 것을 고르시오. [3점]

Much of human thought is designed to screen out information and to sort the rest into a manageable condition. The inflow of data from our senses could create an overwhelming chaos, especially given the enormous amount of information available in culture and society. Out of all the sensory impressions and possible information, it is vital to find a small amount that is most relevant to our individual needs and to organize that into a usable stock of knowledge. Expectancies accomplish some of this work, helping to screen out information that is irrelevant to what is expected, and focusing our attention on clear contradictions. The processes of learning and memory ______________________________. People notice only a part of the world around them. Then, only a fraction of what they notice gets processed and stored into memory. And only part of what gets committed to memory can be retrieved.

* retrieve: 생각해 내다

① tend to favor learners with great social skills
② are marked by a steady elimination of information
③ require an external aid to support our memory capacity
④ are determined by the accuracy of incoming information
⑤ are facilitated by embracing chaotic situations as they are

12 1등급 대비 고난도 3점 문제

고2 • 2021년 11월 32번

다음 빈칸에 들어갈 말로 가장 적절한 것을 고르시오. [3점]

We might think that our gut instinct is just an inner feeling — a secret interior voice — but in fact it is shaped by a perception of something visible around us, such as a facial expression or a visual inconsistency so fleeting that often we're not even aware we've noticed it. Psychologists now think of this moment as a 'visual matching game'. So a stressed, rushed or tired person is more likely to resort to this visual matching. When they see a situation in front of them, they quickly match it to a sea of past experiences stored in a mental knowledge bank and then, based on a match, they assign meaning to the information in front of them. The brain then sends a signal to the gut, which has many hundreds of nerve cells. So the visceral feeling we get in the pit of our stomach and the butterflies we feel are a(n) ______________________________.

* gut: 직감, 창자 ** visceral: 본능적인

① result of our cognitive processing system
② instance of discarding negative memories
③ mechanism of overcoming our internal conflicts
④ visual representation of our emotional vulnerability
⑤ concrete signal of miscommunication within the brain

학습 Check!

▶ 몰라서 틀린 문항 × 표기 ▶ 헷갈렸거나 찍은 문항 △ 표기 ▶ ×, △ 문항은 다시 풀고 ✔ 표기를 하세요.

종료 시각	시 분 초	문항 번호	01	02	03	04	05	06	07	08	09	10	11	12
소요 시간	분 초	채점 결과												
초과 시간	분 초	틀린 문항 복습												

DAY 09

※ 점수 표기가 없는 문항은 모두 2점입니다.

빈칸이 후반부에 있을 때

빈칸 추론 09

● 날짜 : 월 일 ● 시작 시각 : 시 분 초 ● 목표 시간 : 20분

01

고3 • 2019학년도 수능 31번

다음 빈칸에 들어갈 말로 가장 적절한 것을 고르시오.

Finkenauer and Rimé investigated the memory of the unexpected death of Belgium's King Baudouin in 1993 in a large sample of Belgian citizens. The data revealed that the news of the king's death had been widely socially shared. By talking about the event, people gradually constructed a social narrative and a collective memory of the emotional event. At the same time, they consolidated their own memory of the personal circumstances in which the event took place, an effect known as "flashbulb memory." The more an event is socially shared, the more it will be fixed in people's minds. Social sharing may in this way help to counteract some natural tendency people may have. Naturally, people should be driven to "forget" undesirable events. Thus, someone who just heard a piece of bad news often tends initially to deny what happened. The ______________ social sharing of the bad news contributes to realism.

* consolidate: 공고히 하다

① biased
② illegal
③ repetitive
④ temporary
⑤ rational

02

고2 • 2022년 11월 31번

다음 빈칸에 들어갈 말로 가장 적절한 것을 고르시오.

No learning is possible without an error signal. Organisms only learn when events violate their expectations. In other words, surprise is one of the fundamental drivers of learning. Imagine hearing a series of identical notes, AAAAA. Each note draws out a response in the auditory areas of your brain — but as the notes repeat, those responses progressively decrease. This is called "adaptation," a deceptively simple phenomenon that shows that your brain is learning to anticipate the next event. Suddenly, the note changes: AAAAA#. Your primary auditory cortex immediately shows a strong surprise reaction: not only does the adaptation fade away, but additional neurons begin to vigorously fire in response to the unexpected sound. And it is not just repetition that leads to adaptation: what matters is whether the notes are ____________. For instance, if you hear an alternating set of notes, such as ABABA, your brain gets used to this alternation, and the activity in your auditory areas again decreases. This time, however, it is an unexpected repetition, such as ABABB, that triggers a surprise response.

① audible
② predictable
③ objective
④ countable
⑤ recorded

03

고2 • 2023년 3월 33번

다음 빈칸에 들어갈 말로 가장 적절한 것을 고르시오. [3점]

Scholars of myth have long argued that myth gives structure and meaning to human life; that meaning is amplified when a myth evolves into a world. A virtual world's ability to fulfill needs grows when lots and lots of people believe in the world. Conversely, a virtual world cannot be long sustained by a mere handful of adherents. Consider the difference between a global sport and a game I invent with my nine friends and play regularly. My game might be a great game, one that is completely immersive, one that consumes all of my group's time and attention. If its reach is limited to the ten of us, though, then it's ultimately just a weird hobby, and it has limited social function. For a virtual world to provide lasting, wide-ranging value, its participants must ____________________________________. When that threshold is reached, psychological value can turn into wide-ranging social value.

* adherent: 추종자 ** threshold: 기준점

① be a large enough group to be considered a society
② have historical evidence to make it worth believing
③ apply their individual values to all of their affairs
④ follow a strict order to enhance their self-esteem
⑤ get approval in light of the religious value system

04

고2 • 2020년 11월 32번

다음 빈칸에 들어갈 말로 가장 적절한 것을 고르시오.

One of the primary ways by which music is able to take on significance in our inner world is by the way it interacts with memory. Memories associated with important emotions tend to be more deeply embedded in our memory than other events. Emotional memories are more likely to be vividly remembered and are more likely to be recalled with the passing of time than neutral memories. Since music can be extremely emotionally evocative, key life events can be emotionally heightened by the presence of music, ensuring that memories of the event become deeply encoded. Retrieval of those memories is then enhanced by contextual effects, in which a recreation of a similar context to that in which the memories were encoded can facilitate their retrieval. Thus, ____ can activate intensely vivid memories of the event.

* evocative: 불러일으키는 ** retrieval: 회복

① analyzing memories of the event thoroughly
② increasing storage space for recalling the event
③ re-hearing the same music associated with the event
④ reconstructing the event in the absence of background music
⑤ enhancing musical competence to deliver emotional messages

05

고2 • 2022년 3월 32번

다음 빈칸에 들어갈 말로 가장 적절한 것을 고르시오.

When you're driving a car, your memory of how to operate the vehicle comes from one set of brain cells; the memory of how to navigate the streets to get to your destination springs from another set of neurons; the memory of driving rules and following street signs originates from another family of brain cells; and the thoughts and feelings you have about the driving experience itself, including any close calls with other cars, come from yet another group of cells. You do not have conscious awareness of all these separate mental plays and cognitive neural firings, yet they somehow work together in beautiful harmony to synthesize your overall experience. In fact, we don't even know the real difference between how we remember and how we think. But, we do know they are strongly intertwined. That is why truly improving memory can never simply be about using memory tricks, although they can be helpful in strengthening certain components of memory. Here's the bottom line: To improve and preserve memory at the cognitive level, you have to ______________________.

* close call: 위기일발 ** intertwine: 뒤얽히게 하다

① keep your body and mind healthy
② calm your mind in stressful times
③ concentrate on one thing at a time
④ work on all functions of your brain
⑤ share what you learn with other people

06

고2 • 2019년 11월 33번

다음 빈칸에 들어갈 말로 가장 적절한 것을 고르시오. [3점]

Thomas Edison was indeed a creative genius, but it was not until he discovered some of the principles of marketing that he found increased success. One of his first inventions was, although much needed, a failure. In 1869, he created and patented an electronic vote recorder, which recorded and totalled the votes in the Massachusetts state legislature faster than the chamber's old manual system. To Edison's astonishment, it failed. Edison had not taken into account legislators' habits. They didn't like to vote quickly and efficiently. They liked to lobby their fellow legislators as voting took place. Edison had a great idea, but he completely misunderstood the needs of his customers. He learned from his failure the relationship between invention and marketing. Edison learned that marketing and invention must be integrated. "Anything that won't sell, I don't want to invent," he said. "Its sale is proof of utility, and utility is success." He realized he needed to ______________________ and tailor his thinking accordingly.

① consider the likelihood of mass production
② simplify the design of his inventions
③ work with other inventors regularly
④ have knowledge of law in advance
⑤ put the customers' needs first

07

고2 • 2019년 3월 34번

다음 빈칸에 들어갈 말로 가장 적절한 것을 고르시오. [3점]

Credit arrangements of one kind or another have existed in all known human cultures. The problem in previous eras was not that no one had the idea or knew how to use it. It was that people seldom wanted to extend much credit because they didn't trust that the future would be better than the present. They generally believed that times past had been better than their own times and that the future would be worse. To put that in economic terms, they believed that the total amount of wealth was limited. People therefore considered it a bad bet to assume that they would be producing more wealth ten years down the line. Business looked like a zero-sum game. Of course, the profits of one particular bakery might rise, but only at the expense of the bakery next door. The king of England might enrich himself, but only by robbing the king of France. You could cut the pie in many different ways, but ______________________.

* credit arrangement: 신용 거래

① it never got any bigger
② its value changed in time
③ it made everybody wealthier
④ there always was another pie
⑤ everyone could get an even share of it

08 1등급 대비 고난도 2점 문제

고2 • 2021년 3월 32번

다음 빈칸에 들어갈 말로 가장 적절한 것을 고르시오.

Our brains have evolved to remember unexpected events because basic survival depends on the ability to perceive causes and predict effects. If the brain predicts one event and experiences another, the unusualness will be especially interesting and will be encoded accordingly. Neurologist and classroom teacher Judith Willis has claimed that surprise in the classroom is one of the most effective ways of teaching with brain stimulation in mind. If students are exposed to new experiences via demonstrations or through the unexpected enthusiasm of their teachers or peers, they will be much more likely to connect with the information that follows. Willis has written that encouraging active discovery in the classroom allows students to interact with new information, moving it beyond working memory to be processed in the frontal lobe, which is devoted to advanced cognitive functioning. ______________ sets us up for learning by directing attention, providing stimulation to developing perceptual systems, and feeding curious and exploratory behavior.

* frontal lobe: (대뇌의) 전두엽

① Awareness of social responsibility
② Memorization of historical facts
③ Competition with rivals
④ Preference for novelty
⑤ Fear of failure

DAY 09

09 1등급 대비 고난도 3점 문제

고2•2023년 9월 31번

다음 빈칸에 들어갈 말로 가장 적절한 것을 고르시오. [3점]

Rebels may think they're rebels, but clever marketers influence them just like the rest of us. Saying, "Everyone is doing it" may turn some people off from an idea. These people will look for alternatives, which (if cleverly planned) can be exactly what a marketer or persuader wants you to believe. If I want you to consider an idea, and know you strongly reject popular opinion in favor of maintaining your independence and uniqueness, I would present the majority option first, which you would reject in favor of my actual preference. We are often tricked when we try to maintain a position of defiance. People use this ____________ to make us "independently" choose an option which suits their purposes. Some brands have taken full effect of our defiance towards the mainstream and positioned themselves as rebels; which has created even stronger brand loyalty.

* defiance: 반항

① reversal
② imitation
③ repetition
④ conformity
⑤ collaboration

10 1등급 대비 고난도 3점 문제

고2•2017년 6월 33번

다음 빈칸에 들어갈 말로 가장 적절한 것을 고르시오. [3점]

Confident leaders are not afraid to ask the basic questions: the questions to which you may feel embarrassed about not already knowing the answers. When you don't know something, admit it as quickly as possible and immediately take action — ask a question. If you have forgotten who the governor is or how many hydrogen atoms are in a molecule of water, quietly ask a friend but one way or the other, quit hiding, and take action. Paradoxically, when you ask basic questions, you will more than likely be perceived by others to be smarter. And more importantly, you'll end up knowing far more over your lifetime. This approach will cause you to be more successful than you would have been had you employed the common practice of ________________________________. To make good leaders, effective teachers encourage, invite, and even force their students to ask those fundamental questions.

① showing caring attitudes to others
② admitting you are less than perfect
③ wanting to feel triumph over reality
④ arguing against any opposing opinion
⑤ pretending to know more than you do

11 1등급 대비 고난도 3점 문제

고2 • 2020년 6월 33번

다음 빈칸에 들어갈 말로 가장 적절한 것을 고르시오. [3점]

Sociologists have proven that people bring their own views and values to the culture they encounter; books, TV programs, movies, and music may affect everyone, but they affect different people in different ways. In a study, Neil Vidmar and Milton Rokeach showed episodes of the sitcom *All in the Family* to viewers with a range of different views on race. The show centers on a character named Archie Bunker, an intolerant bigot who often gets into fights with his more progressive family members. Vidmar and Rokeach found that viewers who didn't share Archie Bunker's views thought the show was very funny in the way it made fun of Archie's absurd racism — in fact, this was the producers' intention. On the other hand, though, viewers who were themselves bigots thought Archie Bunker was the hero of the show and that the producers meant to make fun of his foolish family! This demonstrates why it's a mistake to assume that a certain cultural product ____________________.

* bigot: 고집쟁이

① can provide many valuable views
② reflects the idea of the sociologists
③ forms prejudices to certain characters
④ will have the same effect on everyone
⑤ might resolve social conflicts among people

12 1등급 대비 고난도 3점 문제

고3 • 2018학년도 수능 34번

다음 빈칸에 들어갈 말로 가장 적절한 것을 고르시오. [3점]

Over the past 60 years, as mechanical processes have replicated behaviors and talents we thought were unique to humans, we've had to change our minds about what sets us apart. As we invent more species of AI, we will be forced to surrender more of what is supposedly unique about humans. Each step of surrender — we are not the only mind that can play chess, fly a plane, make music, or invent a mathematical law — will be painful and sad. We'll spend the next three decades — indeed, perhaps the next century — in a permanent identity crisis, continually asking ourselves what humans are good for. If we aren't unique toolmakers, or artists, or moral ethicists, then what, if anything, makes us special? In the grandest irony of all, the greatest benefit of an everyday, utilitarian AI will not be increased productivity or an economics of abundance or a new way of doing science — although all those will happen. The greatest benefit of the arrival of artificial intelligence is that ____________________.

* replicate: 복제하다

① AIs will help define humanity
② humans could also be like AIs
③ humans will be liberated from hard labor
④ AIs could lead us in resolving moral dilemmas
⑤ AIs could compensate for a decline in human intelligence

DAY 09

학습 Check!

▶ 몰라서 틀린 문항 × 표기 ▶ 헷갈렸거나 찍은 문항 △ 표기 ▶ ×, △ 문항은 다시 풀고 ✔ 표기를 하세요.

종료 시각	시 분 초
소요 시간	분 초
초과 시간	분 초

문항 번호	01	02	03	04	05	06	07	08	09	10	11	12
채점 결과												
틀린 문항 복습												

DAY 10 빈칸 추론 10

※ 점수 표기가 없는 문항은 모두 2점입니다.

빈칸이 후반부에 있을 때

● 날짜 : 월 일 ● 시작 시각 : 시 분 초 ● 목표 시간 : 20분

01

고3 • 2020학년도 9월 31번

다음 빈칸에 들어갈 말로 가장 적절한 것을 고르시오.

When you begin to tell a story again that you have retold many times, what you retrieve from memory is the index to the story itself. That index can be embellished in a variety of ways. Over time, even the embellishments become standardized. An old man's story that he has told hundreds of times shows little variation, and any variation that does exist becomes part of the story itself, regardless of its origin. People add details to their stories that may or may not have occurred. They are recalling indexes and reconstructing details. If at some point they add a nice detail, not really certain of its validity, telling the story with that same detail a few more times will ensure its permanent place in the story index. In other words, the stories we tell time and again are ____________ to the memory we have of the events that the story relates.

* retrieve: 회수하다 ** embellish: 윤색하다

① identical
② beneficial
③ alien
④ prior
⑤ neutral

02

고2 • 2021년 6월 31번

다음 빈칸에 들어갈 말로 가장 적절한 것을 고르시오.

The tendency for one purchase to lead to another one has a name: the Diderot Effect. The Diderot Effect states that obtaining a new possession often creates a spiral of consumption that leads to additional purchases. You can spot this pattern everywhere. You buy a dress and have to get new shoes and earrings to match. You buy a toy for your child and soon find yourself purchasing all of the accessories that go with it. It's a chain reaction of purchases. Many human behaviors follow this cycle. You often decide what to do next based on what you have just finished doing. Going to the bathroom leads to washing and drying your hands, which reminds you that you need to put the dirty towels in the laundry, so you add laundry detergent to the shopping list, and so on. No behavior happens in ____________. Each action becomes a cue that triggers the next behavior.

① isolation
② comfort
③ observation
④ fairness
⑤ harmony

03

고3 • 2020학년도 9월 33번

다음 빈칸에 들어갈 말로 가장 적절한 것을 고르시오. [3점]

If one looks at the Oxford definition, one gets the sense that post-truth is not so much a claim that truth *does not exist* as that *facts are subordinate to our political point of view*. The Oxford definition focuses on "*what*" post-truth is: the idea that feelings sometimes matter more than facts. But just as important is the next question, which is *why* this ever occurs. Someone does not argue against an obvious or easily confirmable fact for no reason; he or she does so when it is to his or her advantage. When a person's beliefs are threatened by an "inconvenient fact," sometimes it is preferable to challenge the fact. This can happen at either a conscious or unconscious level (since sometimes the person we are seeking to convince is ourselves), but the point is that this sort of post-truth relationship to facts occurs only when we are seeking to assert something ________________________.

* subordinate: 종속하는

① to hold back our mixed feelings
② that balances our views on politics
③ that leads us to give way to others in need
④ to carry the constant value of absolute truth
⑤ that is more important to us than the truth itself

04

고2 • 2018년 6월 33번

다음 빈칸에 들어갈 말로 가장 적절한 것을 고르시오. [3점]

In the early 2000s, British psychologist Richard Wiseman performed a series of experiments with people who viewed themselves as either 'lucky'(they were successful and happy, and events in their lives seemed to favor them) or 'unlucky'(life just seemed to go wrong for them). What he found was that the 'lucky' people were good at spotting opportunities. In one experiment he told both groups to count the number of pictures in a newspaper. The 'unlucky' diligently ground their way through the task; the 'lucky' usually noticed that the second page contained an announcement that said: "Stop counting — there are 43 photographs in this newspaper." On a later page, the 'unlucky' were also too busy counting images to spot a note reading: "Stop counting, tell the experimenter you have seen this, and win $250." Wiseman's conclusion was that, when faced with a challenge, 'unlucky' people were less flexible. They focused on a specific goal, and failed to notice that ________________________.

① instructions should be followed at all costs
② their mission was impossible to complete
③ other options were passing them by
④ counting was such a demanding task
⑤ efforts would pay off in the long run

05

고2 • 2018년 9월 34번

다음 빈칸에 들어갈 말로 가장 적절한 것을 고르시오. [3점]

For many centuries European science, and knowledge in general, was recorded in Latin — a language that no one spoke any longer and that had to be learned in schools. Very few individuals, probably less than one percent, had the means to study Latin enough to read books in that language and therefore to participate in the intellectual discourse of the times. Moreover, few people had access to books, which were handwritten, scarce, and expensive. The great explosion of scientific creativity in Europe was certainly helped by the sudden spread of information brought about by Gutenberg's use of movable type in printing and by the legitimation of everyday languages, which rapidly replaced Latin as the medium of discourse. In sixteenth-century Europe it became much easier to make a creative contribution not necessarily because more creative individuals were born then than in previous centuries or because social supports became more favorable, but because ____________________________________.

① the number of rich people increased
② information became more widely accessible
③ people were able to learn Latin more easily
④ education provided equal opportunities for all
⑤ new methods of scientific research were introduced

06

고2 • 2017년 9월 34번

다음 빈칸에 들어갈 말로 가장 적절한 것을 고르시오. [3점]

This true story is about a government-owned shoe factory in Poland in the days when the country had a much more socialist economy. Every month, the Polish government gave the factory materials, and the manager was told to produce a fixed number of shoes. Because there was no profit motive involved, the manager's basic goal was to meet the quota in the easiest possible way — by producing only small shoes. This production strategy created a problem for people who had big feet, and so the government revised the system. Now the factory received the same amount of materials, but instead of producing a fixed number of shoes, the factory was expected to produce a fixed number of tons of shoes. In other words, the factory's output would now be weighed rather than counted. And again, the factory's manager responded in the most efficient way, by producing nothing but huge shoes. In either situation, the government's strategy did not provide any motivation to ____________________________________.

① improve the working environment for employees
② simplify the production process to reduce costs
③ increase the number of factories to make more profit
④ produce shoes in various sizes that met people's needs
⑤ adopt new technology to compete against foreign shoes

07

고3 • 2019학년도 9월 34번

다음 빈칸에 들어갈 말로 가장 적절한 것을 고르시오. [3점]

Modern psychological theory states that the process of understanding is a matter of construction, not reproduction, which means that the process of understanding takes the form of the interpretation of data coming from the outside and generated by our mind. For example, the perception of a moving object as a car is based on an interpretation of incoming data within the framework of our knowledge of the world. While the interpretation of simple objects is usually an uncontrolled process, the interpretation of more complex phenomena, such as interpersonal situations, usually requires active attention and thought. Psychological studies indicate that it is knowledge possessed by the individual that determines which stimuli become the focus of that individual's attention, what significance he or she assigns to these stimuli, and how they are combined into a larger whole. This subjective world, interpreted in a particular way, is for us the "objective" world; we cannot know any world other than ______________________________.

① the reality placed upon us through social conventions
② the one we know as a result of our own interpretations
③ the world of images not filtered by our perceptual frame
④ the external world independent of our own interpretations
⑤ the physical universe our own interpretations fail to explain

08 1등급 대비 고난도 2점 문제

고2 • 2019년 11월 32번

다음 빈칸에 들어갈 말로 가장 적절한 것을 고르시오.

Are the different types of mobile device, smartphones and tablets, substitutes or complements? Let's explore this question by considering the case of Madeleine and Alexandra, two users of these devices. Madeleine uses her tablet to take notes in class. These notes are synced to her smartphone wirelessly, via a cloud computing service, allowing Madeleine to review her notes on her phone during the bus trip home. Alexandra uses both her phone and tablet to surf the Internet, write emails and check social media. Both of these devices allow Alexandra to access online services when she is away from her desktop computer. For Madeleine, smartphones and tablets are *complements*. She gets greater functionality out of her two devices when they are used together. For Alexandra, they are *substitutes*. Both smartphones and tablets fulfil more or less the same function in Alexandra's life. This case illustrates the role that an ______________________________ plays in determining the nature of the relationship between two goods or services.

① interaction with other people
② individual consumer's behavior
③ obvious change in social status
④ innovative technological advancement
⑤ objective assessment of current conditions

09 1등급 대비 고난도 3점 문제

고2 · 2019년 6월 34번

다음 빈칸에 들어갈 말로 가장 적절한 것을 고르시오. [3점]

The whole history of mathematics is one long sequence of taking the best ideas of the moment and finding new extensions, variations, and applications. Our lives today are totally different from the lives of people three hundred years ago, mostly owing to scientific and technological innovations that required the insights of calculus. Isaac Newton and Gottfried von Leibniz independently discovered calculus in the last half of the seventeenth century. But a study of the history reveals that mathematicians had thought of all the essential elements of calculus before Newton or Leibniz came along. Newton himself acknowledged this flowing reality when he wrote, "If I have seen farther than others it is because I have stood on the shoulders of giants." Newton and Leibniz came up with their brilliant insight at essentially the same time because ______________________________. All creative people, even ones who are considered geniuses, start as nongeniuses and take baby steps from there.

* calculus: 미적분학

① calculus was considered to be the study of geniuses
② it was not a huge leap from what was already known
③ it was impossible to make a list of the uses of calculus
④ they pioneered a breakthrough in mathematic calculations
⑤ other mathematicians didn't accept the discovery as it was

10 1등급 대비 고난도 3점 문제

고2 · 2018년 3월 34번

다음 빈칸에 들어갈 말로 가장 적절한 것을 고르시오. [3점]

When the late Theodore Roosevelt came back from Africa, just after he left the White House in 1909, he made his first public appearance at Madison Square Garden. Before he would agree to make the appearance, he carefully arranged for nearly one thousand *paid applauders* to be scattered throughout the audience to applaud his entrance on the platform. For more than 15 minutes, these paid hand-clappers made the place ring with their enthusiasm. The rest of the audience took up the suggestion and joined in for another quarter hour. The newspaper men present were literally swept off their feet by the tremendous applause given the American hero, and his name was emblazoned across the headlines of the newspapers in letters two inches high. Roosevelt ______________________________.

* emblazon: 선명히 새기다

① understood and made intelligent use of personal promotion
② made public policies that were beneficial to his people
③ knew when was the right time for him to leave office
④ saw the well-being of his supporters as the top priority
⑤ didn't appear before the public in an arranged setting

[해설편 p.068]

11 1등급 대비 고난도 3점 문제

고2 • 2021년 9월 34번

다음 빈칸에 들어갈 말로 가장 적절한 것을 고르시오. [3점]

Deep-fried foods are tastier than bland foods, and children and adults develop a taste for such foods. Fatty foods cause the brain to release oxytocin, a powerful hormone with a calming, antistress, and relaxing influence, said to be the opposite of adrenaline, into the blood stream; hence the term “comfort foods.” We may even be genetically programmed to eat too much. For thousands of years, food was very scarce. Food, along with salt, carbs, and fat, was hard to get, and the more you got, the better. All of these things are necessary nutrients in the human diet, and when their availability was limited, you could never get too much. People also had to hunt down animals or gather plants for their food, and that took a lot of calories. It’s different these days. We have food at every turn — lots of those fast-food places and grocery stores with carry-out food. But that ingrained “caveman mentality” says that we can’t ever get too much to eat. So craving for “unhealthy” food may ______________________.

① actually be our body’s attempt to stay healthy
② ultimately lead to harm to the ecosystem
③ dramatically reduce our overall appetite
④ simply be the result of a modern lifestyle
⑤ partly strengthen our preference for fresh food

12 1등급 대비 고난도 3점 문제

고2 • 2016년 11월 33번

다음 빈칸에 들어갈 말로 가장 적절한 것을 고르시오. [3점]

It’s possible to lie with numbers, even those that are accurate, because numbers rarely speak for themselves. They need to be interpreted by writers. And writers almost always have purposes that shape the interpretations. For example, you might want to announce the good news that unemployment in the United States stands at just a little over 5 percent. That means 95 percent of Americans have jobs, an employment rate much higher than that of most other industrial nations. But let’s spin the figure another way. In a country as populous as the United States, unemployment at 5 percent means that millions of Americans don’t earn a daily wage. Indeed, one out of every twenty adults who wants work can’t find it. Suddenly that’s a sobering number. And, as you can see, the same statistic can ______________________.

* sobering: 정신이 번쩍 들게 하는

① be influenced by the data collection strategy
② be cited as a cause for celebration or shame
③ be obtained from different experimental data
④ cause various social problems in many cases
⑤ trigger minimum wage protests across the U.S.

학습 Check!

▶ 몰라서 틀린 문항 × 표기 ▶ 헷갈렸거나 찍은 문항 △ 표기 ▶ ×, △ 문항은 다시 풀고 ✔ 표기를 하세요.

종료 시각	시 분 초
소요 시간	분 초
초과 시간	분 초

문항 번호	01	02	03	04	05	06	07	08	09	10	11	12
채점 결과												
틀린 문항 복습												

글의 순서

최근 수능에서는 **글의 순서가 빈칸 추론 못지않게 어렵고 까다롭게 출제된** 경우가 많았습니다. 실제 **수능과 내신 1~2등급을 받는 수험생들도 글의 순서 문제를 어려워하는 경향**이 있습니다. 영어 영역에서 1등급을 목표한다면 반드시 글의 순서 2문항도 확실한 대비를 해야 합니다.

▶ 글의 순서 유형

[36~37] 주어진 글 다음에 이어질 글의 순서로 가장 적절한 것을 고르시오.

영어 영역 **36~37**번에 해당하는 글의 순서는 **주어진 한 문단의 글과 이어지는 나머지 (A), (B), (C) 세 문단의 연결고리를 찾아 논리적으로 순서를 정하는 문제**입니다.
글의 순서는 해석을 기본으로 하기 때문에 **어법과 구문에 대한 실력이 있어야하며, A글과 B글이 연결되는 근거를 찾아서 단락들을 연결하는 것이므로 연결고리가 되는 대명사나 연결사, 지시어가 가리키는 것을 잘 파악**해야 합니다. 특히 연결고리의 단서가 주어지지 않는 고난도 문제에 대한 대응력도 키워야합니다.

꿀팁! 수능에 자주 출제되는 연결사를 익히고, 순서를 연결 한 후 전체 글을 다시 읽으며 흐름이 처음부터 끝까지 잘 이어지는지 확인한다.

▶ 글의 순서 교재 구성

하루 12문항 _ 20분 학습 _ 5일 완성 = 총 60문항

글의 순서는 주어진 글부터 (A), (B), (C) 문단이 순차적으로 자연스럽게 연결고리를 찾을 수 있는 문항의 경우 정답률이 높습니다. 하지만 **주어진 글 뒤에 어떤 단락이 와야 하는지 명확하지 않은 경우가 있는데 기출문제를 통해서 단락을 연결하는 연습과 전체적인 흐름을 확인하는 훈련**을 할 수 있도록 했습니다.

소재를 파악하자

주어진 글을 어떻게 연결할지 고민하지 말고, 일단 **글을 읽고 정확히 어떤 내용에 관한 글인지를 소재를 파악**한다.

단서가 핵심이다

this, that, it 등 지시어가 가리키는 것과 **문장 간의 연결 고리가 되는 대명사, 연결사 및 부사구를 단서로 활용**한다.

결정 NO, 임시 OK

예를 들어 **주어진 글과 (B), (C)가 순서라고 생각이 들어도 바로 결정하지 말고, 임시적으로 연결만 해 놓은 다음 글의 전체적인 흐름을 다시 한 번 확인한 후 결정하는 습관**을 길러야한다.

2020 하루 20분 20일 완성

PART Ⅱ 글의 순서

Day 11~Day 15

[해설편 p.070]

DAY 11 글의 순서 01

※ 점수 표기가 없는 문항은 모두 2점입니다.

● 날짜 : 월 일 ● 시작 시각 : 시 분 초 ● 목표 시간 : 20분

01

고2・2023년 6월 36번

주어진 글 다음에 이어질 글의 순서로 가장 적절한 것을 고르시오.

> When evaluating a policy, people tend to concentrate on how the policy will fix some particular problem while ignoring or downplaying other effects it may have. Economists often refer to this situation as *The Law of Unintended Consequences*.

(A) But an unintended consequence is that the jobs of some autoworkers will be lost to foreign competition. Why? The tariff that protects steelworkers raises the price of the steel that domestic automobile makers need to build their cars.

(B) For instance, suppose that you impose a tariff on imported steel in order to protect the jobs of domestic steelworkers. If you impose a high enough tariff, their jobs will indeed be protected from competition by foreign steel companies.

(C) As a result, domestic automobile manufacturers have to raise the prices of their cars, making them relatively less attractive than foreign cars. Raising prices tends to reduce domestic car sales, so some domestic autoworkers lose their jobs.

① (A) – (C) – (B) ② (B) – (A) – (C)
③ (B) – (C) – (A) ④ (C) – (A) – (B)
⑤ (C) – (B) – (A)

02

고2・2022년 9월 36번

주어진 글 다음에 이어질 글의 순서로 가장 적절한 것을 고르시오.

> If DNA were the only thing that mattered, there would be no particular reason to build meaningful social programs to pour good experiences into children and protect them from bad experiences.

(A) This number came as a surprise to biologists: given the complexity of the brain and the body, it had been assumed that hundreds of thousands of genes would be required.

(B) So how does the massively complicated brain, with its eighty-six billion neurons, get built from such a small recipe book? The answer relies on a clever strategy implemented by the genome: build incompletely and let world experience refine.

(C) But brains require the right kind of environment if they are to correctly develop. When the first draft of the Human Genome Project came to completion at the turn of the millennium, one of the great surprises was that humans have only about twenty thousand genes.

① (A) – (C) – (B) ② (B) – (A) – (C)
③ (B) – (C) – (A) ④ (C) – (A) – (B)
⑤ (C) – (B) – (A)

03

고2•2019년 3월 36번

주어진 글 다음에 이어질 글의 순서로 가장 적절한 것을 고르시오.

One of the first things I did in each classroom in South Milwaukee was to draw a diagram of the students' desks, labelled with their names, as an aid to recognizing them.

(A) One said, "Where's your name?" and was not satisfied until I included a sketch of the chair by the bookcase where I was sitting, labelled with my name. It had not occurred to me that I needed to be included: after all, I knew where I was sitting, and knew my name.

(B) At lunch in the first grade classroom the first day I was present, a group of students came over, saw the diagram, and began finding their names on my picture.

(C) But to her, my presence in the classroom was the newest, most noteworthy thing that had occurred that day, and it was logical to include me. Her point of view was different from mine, and resulted in a different diagram of the classroom.

① (A) – (C) – (B)
② (B) – (A) – (C)
③ (B) – (C) – (A)
④ (C) – (A) – (B)
⑤ (C) – (B) – (A)

04

고2•2018년 11월 36번

주어진 글 다음에 이어질 글의 순서로 가장 적절한 것을 고르시오.

During the late 1800s, printing became cheaper and faster, leading to an explosion in the number of newspapers and magazines and the increased use of images in these publications.

(A) This "yellow journalism" sometimes took the form of gossip about public figures, as well as about socialites who considered themselves private figures, and even about those who were not part of high society but had found themselves involved in a scandal, crime, or tragedy that journalists thought would sell papers.

(B) Photographs, as well as woodcuts and engravings of them, appeared in newspapers and magazines. The increased number of newspapers and magazines created greater competition — driving some papers to print more salacious articles to attract readers.

(C) Gossip was of course nothing new, but the rise of mass media in the form of widely distributed newspapers and magazines meant that gossip moved from limited (often oral only) distribution to wide, printed dissemination.

* engraving: 판화 ** salacious: 외설스러운
*** dissemination: 보급

① (A) – (C) – (B)
② (B) – (A) – (C)
③ (B) – (C) – (A)
④ (C) – (A) – (B)
⑤ (C) – (B) – (A)

05

고2 • 2018년 3월 36번

주어진 글 다음에 이어질 글의 순서로 가장 적절한 것을 고르시오.

Studies show that no one is "born" to be an entrepreneur and that everyone has the potential to become one.

(A) These traits are developed over time and evolve from an individual's social context. For example, people with parents who were self-employed are more likely to become entrepreneurs.

(B) Whether someone does or doesn't is a function of environment, life experiences, and personal choices. However, there are personality traits and characteristics commonly associated with entrepreneurs.

(C) After witnessing a father's or mother's independence in the workplace, an individual is more likely to find independence appealing. Similarly, people who personally know an entrepreneur are more than twice as likely to be involved in starting a new firm as those with no entrepreneur acquaintances or role models.

* entrepreneur: 기업가

① (A) – (C) – (B)
② (B) – (A) – (C)
③ (B) – (C) – (A)
④ (C) – (A) – (B)
⑤ (C) – (B) – (A)

06

고2 • 2021년 3월 36번

주어진 글 다음에 이어질 글의 순서로 가장 적절한 것을 고르시오. [3점]

Once we recognize the false-cause issue, we see it everywhere. For example, a recent long-term study of University of Toronto medical students concluded that medical school class presidents lived an average of 2.4 years less than other medical school graduates.

(A) Perhaps this extra stress, and the corresponding lack of social and relaxation time — rather than being class president per se — contributes to lower life expectancy. If so, the real lesson of the study is that we should all relax a little and not let our work take over our lives.

(B) Probably not. Just because being class president is correlated with shorter life expectancy does not mean that it *causes* shorter life expectancy. In fact, it seems likely that the sort of person who becomes medical school class president is, on average, extremely hard-working, serious, and ambitious.

(C) At first glance, this seemed to imply that being a medical school class president is bad for you. Does this mean that you should avoid being medical school class president at all costs?

* per se: 그 자체로

① (A) – (C) – (B)
② (B) – (A) – (C)
③ (B) – (C) – (A)
④ (C) – (A) – (B)
⑤ (C) – (B) – (A)

07

고2 • 2022년 6월 37번

주어진 글 다음에 이어질 글의 순서로 가장 적절한 것을 고르시오. [3점]

One interesting feature of network markets is that "history matters." A famous example is the QWERTY keyboard used with your computer.

(A) Replacing the QWERTY keyboard with a more efficient design would have been both expensive and difficult to coordinate. Thus, the placement of the letters stays with the obsolete QWERTY on today's English-language keyboards.

(B) You might wonder why this particular configuration of keys, with its awkward placement of the letters, became the standard. The QWERTY keyboard in the 19th century was developed in the era of manual typewriters with physical keys.

(C) The keyboard was designed to keep frequently used keys (like E and O) physically separated in order to prevent them from jamming. By the time the technology for electronic typing evolved, millions of people had already learned to type on millions of QWERTY typewriters.

* obsolete: 구식의 ** configuration: 배열

① (A) – (C) – (B)
② (B) – (A) – (C)
③ (B) – (C) – (A)
④ (C) – (A) – (B)
⑤ (C) – (B) – (A)

08

고2 • 2020년 11월 37번

주어진 글 다음에 이어질 글의 순서로 가장 적절한 것을 고르시오. [3점]

When we think of culture, we first think of human cultures, of *our* culture. We think of computers, airplanes, fashions, teams, and pop stars. For most of human cultural history, none of those things existed.

(A) Sadly, this remains true as the final tribal peoples get overwhelmed by those who value money above humanity. We are living in their end times and, to varying extents, we're all contributing to those endings. Ultimately our values may even prove self-defeating.

(B) They held extensive knowledge, knew deep secrets of their lands and creatures. And they experienced rich and rewarding lives; we know so because when their ways were threatened, they fought to hold on to them, to the death.

(C) For hundreds of thousands of years, no human culture had a tool with moving parts. Well into the twentieth century, various human foraging cultures retained tools of stone, wood, and bone. We might pity human hunter-gatherers for their stuck simplicity, but we would be making a mistake.

* forage: 수렵 채집하다

① (A) – (C) – (B)
② (B) – (A) – (C)
③ (B) – (C) – (A)
④ (C) – (A) – (B)
⑤ (C) – (B) – (A)

09

고3 • 2022학년도 수능 36번

주어진 글 다음에 이어질 글의 순서로 가장 적절한 것을 고르시오.

According to the market response model, it is increasing prices that drive providers to search for new sources, innovators to substitute, consumers to conserve, and alternatives to emerge.

(A) Many examples of such "green taxes" exist. Facing landfill costs, labor expenses, and related costs in the provision of garbage disposal, for example, some cities have required households to dispose of all waste in special trash bags, purchased by consumers themselves, and often costing a dollar or more each.

(B) Taxing certain goods or services, and so increasing prices, should result in either decreased use of these resources or creative innovation of new sources or options. The money raised through the tax can be used directly by the government either to supply services or to search for alternatives.

(C) The results have been greatly increased recycling and more careful attention by consumers to packaging and waste. By internalizing the costs of trash to consumers, there has been an observed decrease in the flow of garbage from households.

① (A) – (C) – (B)
② (B) – (A) – (C)
③ (B) – (C) – (A)
④ (C) – (A) – (B)
⑤ (C) – (B) – (A)

10 1등급 대비 고난도 2점 문제

고2 • 2023년 9월 36번

주어진 글 다음에 이어질 글의 순서로 가장 적절한 것을 고르시오.

If you drive down a busy street, you will find many competing businesses, often right next to one another. For example, in most places a consumer in search of a quick meal has many choices, and more fast-food restaurants appear all the time.

(A) Yes, costs rise, but consumers also gain information to help make purchasing decisions. Consumers also benefit from added variety, and we all get a product that's pretty close to our vision of a perfect good — and no other market structure delivers that outcome.

(B) However, this misconception doesn't account for why firms advertise. In markets where competitors sell slightly differentiated products, advertising enables firms to inform their customers about new products and services.

(C) These competing firms advertise heavily. The temptation is to see advertising as driving up the price of a product without any benefit to the consumer.

① (A) – (C) – (B)
② (B) – (A) – (C)
③ (B) – (C) – (A)
④ (C) – (A) – (B)
⑤ (C) – (B) – (A)

[해설편 p.075]

11 1등급 대비 고난도 2점 문제

고2•2016년 11월 36번

주어진 글 다음에 이어질 글의 순서로 가장 적절한 것을 고르시오.

> Twins provide a unique opportunity to study genes. Some pairs of twins are identical: they share the exact same genes in their DNA.

(A) In the same way, scientists can estimate the role genes play in any other trait by comparing the similarity of identical twins to the similarity of fraternal twins. If there is a difference, then the magnitude of the difference gives a clue as to how much genes are involved.

(B) Other pairs are fraternal, sharing only half of their genes on average. Differences in genetic similarity turn out to be a powerful natural experiment, allowing us to estimate how much genes influence a given trait.

(C) For example, identical twins almost always have the same eye color, but fraternal twins often do not. This suggests that genes play a role in eye color, and in fact geneticists have identified several specific genes that are involved.

① (A) − (C) − (B) ② (B) − (A) − (C)
③ (B) − (C) − (A) ④ (C) − (A) − (B)
⑤ (C) − (B) − (A)

12 1등급 대비 고난도 3점 문제

고2•2019년 11월 37번

주어진 글 다음에 이어질 글의 순서로 가장 적절한 것을 고르시오. [3점]

> Like the physiological discoveries of the late nineteenth century, today's biological breakthrough has fundamentally altered our understanding of how the human organism works and will change medical practice fundamentally and thoroughly.

(A) Remember the scientific method, which you probably first learned about back in elementary school? It has a long and difficult process of observation, hypothesis, experiment, testing, modifying, retesting, and retesting again and again and again.

(B) That's how science works, and the breakthrough understanding of the relationship between our genes and chronic disease happened in just that way, building on the work of scientists from decades — even centuries — ago. In fact, it is still happening; the story continues to unfold as the research presses on.

(C) The word "breakthrough," however, seems to imply in many people's minds an amazing, unprecedented revelation that, in an instant, makes everything clear. Science doesn't actually work that way.

① (A) − (C) − (B) ② (B) − (A) − (C)
③ (B) − (C) − (A) ④ (C) − (A) − (B)
⑤ (C) − (B) − (A)

학습 Check!

▶ 몰라서 틀린 문항 × 표기 ▶ 헷갈렸거나 찍은 문항 △ 표기 ▶ ×, △ 문항은 다시 풀고 ✔ 표기를 하세요.

종료 시각	시 분 초
소요 시간	분 초
초과 시간	분 초

문항 번호	01	02	03	04	05	06	07	08	09	10	11	12
채점 결과												
틀린 문항 복습												

[해설편 p.077]

DAY 12 ※ 점수 표기가 없는 문항은 모두 2점입니다.

글의 순서 02

● 날짜 : 월 일 ● 시작 시각 : 시 분 초 ● 목표 시간 : 20분

01

고2 • 2023년 3월 36번

주어진 글 다음에 이어질 글의 순서로 가장 적절한 것을 고르시오.

> Like positive habits, bad habits exist on a continuum of easy-to-change and hard-to-change.

(A) But this kind of language (and the approaches it spawns) frames these challenges in a way that isn't helpful or effective. I specifically hope we will stop using this phrase: "break a habit." This language misguides people. The word "break" sets the wrong expectation for how you get rid of a bad habit.

(B) This word implies that if you input a lot of force in one moment, the habit will be gone. However, that rarely works, because you usually cannot get rid of an unwanted habit by applying force one time.

(C) When you get toward the "hard" end of the spectrum, note the language you hear — *breaking* bad habits and *battling* addiction. It's as if an unwanted behavior is a nefarious villain to be aggressively defeated.

* spawn: 낳다 ** nefarious: 사악한

① (A) – (C) – (B)
② (B) – (A) – (C)
③ (B) – (C) – (A)
④ (C) – (A) – (B)
⑤ (C) – (B) – (A)

02

고2 • 2021년 11월 36번

주어진 글 다음에 이어질 글의 순서로 가장 적절한 것을 고르시오.

> Regarding food production, under the British government, there was a different conception of responsibility from that of French government. In France, the responsibility for producing good food lay with the producers.

(A) It would be unfair to interfere with the shopkeeper's right to make money. In the 1840s, a patent was granted for a machine designed for making fake coffee beans out of chicory, using the same technology that went into manufacturing bullets.

(B) The state would police their activities and, if they should fail, would punish them for neglecting the interests of its citizens. By contrast, the British government — except in extreme cases — placed most of the responsibility with the individual consumers.

(C) This machine was clearly designed for the purposes of swindling, and yet the government allowed it. A machine for forging money would never have been licensed, so why this? As one consumer complained, the British system of government was weighted against the consumer in favour of the swindler.

* swindle: 사기 치다 ** forge: 위조하다

① (A) – (C) – (B)
② (B) – (A) – (C)
③ (B) – (C) – (A)
④ (C) – (A) – (B)
⑤ (C) – (B) – (A)

03

고2 • 2020년 6월 36번

주어진 글 다음에 이어질 글의 순서로 가장 적절한 것을 고르시오.

The invention of the mechanical clock was influenced by monks who lived in monasteries that were the examples of order and routine.

(A) Time was determined by watching the length of the weighted rope. The discovery of the pendulum in the seventeenth century led to the widespread use of clocks and enormous public clocks. Eventually, keeping time turned into serving time.

(B) They had to keep accurate time so that monastery bells could be rung at regular intervals to announce the seven hours of the day reserved for prayer. Early clocks were nothing more than a weight tied to a rope wrapped around a revolving drum.

(C) People started to follow the mechanical time of clocks rather than their natural body time. They ate at meal time, rather than when they were hungry, and went to bed when it was time, rather than when they were sleepy. Even periodicals and fashions became "yearly." The world had become orderly.

* monastery: 수도원 ** pendulum: 흔들리는 추

① (A) – (C) – (B)
② (B) – (A) – (C)
③ (B) – (C) – (A)
④ (C) – (A) – (B)
⑤ (C) – (B) – (A)

04

고2 • 2019년 9월 37번

주어진 글 다음에 이어질 글의 순서로 가장 적절한 것을 고르시오.

Testing strategies relating to direct assessment of content knowledge still have their value in an inquiry-driven classroom.

(A) For these reasons, we need a measure of a student's content understanding. To do this right, we need to make sure our assessment is getting us accurate measures of whether our students understand the content they use in an inquiry.

(B) However, it also could be that they did not understand the content that they were trying to build patterns with. Sometimes students will understand the processes of inquiry well, and be capable of skillfully applying social studies disciplinary strategies, yet fail to do so because they misinterpret the content.

(C) Let's pretend for a moment that we wanted to ignore content and only assess a student's skill with investigations. The problem is that the skills and the content are interconnected. When a student fails at pattern analysis, it could be because they do not understand how to do the pattern analysis properly.

* inquiry-driven classroom: 탐구 주도형 교실

① (A) – (C) – (B)
② (B) – (A) – (C)
③ (B) – (C) – (A)
④ (C) – (A) – (B)
⑤ (C) – (B) – (A)

05

고2 · 2017년 9월 37번

주어진 글 다음에 이어질 글의 순서로 가장 적절한 것을 고르시오.

Both taxi and bus drivers use a part of their brain called the hippocampus to navigate routes that can sometimes be very complicated. Who would you guess has the larger hippocampus: the taxi driver or bus driver?

(A) In contrast, most bus drivers follow the same route every day and therefore do not stimulate their hippocampus as much. Over time, the taxi driver's role triggers a growth of neurons and synapses in the hippocampus, resulting in its increased size.

(B) Brain changes like this are the basis for seeing improvement in mental performance. So if you put away your satellite navigation system and regularly use your memory instead, you may end up with a larger hippocampus and perhaps a better memory, too.

(C) The answer is the taxi driver. This is because taxi drivers need to take new routes quite often. To do this, they use their hippocampus intensively to memorize all kinds of routes and figure out the quickest way to reach their destinations.

* hippocampus: (뇌의) 해마

① (A) – (C) – (B)
② (B) – (A) – (C)
③ (B) – (C) – (A)
④ (C) – (A) – (B)
⑤ (C) – (B) – (A)

06

고2 · 2018년 9월 35번

주어진 글 다음에 이어질 글의 순서로 가장 적절한 것을 고르시오.

Calling your pants "blue jeans" almost seems redundant because practically all denim is blue. While jeans are probably the most versatile pants in your wardrobe, blue actually isn't a particularly neutral color.

(A) The natural indigo dye used in the first jeans, on the other hand, would stick only to the outside of the threads. When the indigo-dyed denim is washed, tiny amounts of that dye get washed away, and the thread comes with them.

(B) Ever wonder why it's the most commonly used hue? Blue was the chosen color for denim because of the chemical properties of blue dye. Most dyes will permeate fabric in hot temperatures, making the color stick.

(C) The more denim was washed, the softer it would get, eventually achieving that worn-in, made-just-for-me feeling you probably get with your favorite jeans. That softness made jeans the trousers of choice for laborers.

* hue: 색상 ** permeate: 스며[배어]들다

① (A) – (C) – (B)
② (B) – (A) – (C)
③ (B) – (C) – (A)
④ (C) – (A) – (B)
⑤ (C) – (B) – (A)

07

고2 • 2023년 9월 37번

주어진 글 다음에 이어질 글의 순서로 가장 적절한 것을 고르시오. [3점]

Architects might say a machine can never design an innovative or impressive building because a computer cannot be "creative." Yet consider the Elbphilharmonie, a new concert hall in Hamburg, which contains a remarkably beautiful auditorium composed of ten thousand interlocking acoustic panels.

(A) Are these systems behaving "creatively"? No, they are using lots of processing power to blindly generate varied possible designs, working in a very different way from a human being.

(B) It is the sort of space that makes one instinctively think that only a human being — and a human with a remarkably refined creative sensibility, at that — could design something so aesthetically impressive. Yet the auditorium was, in fact, designed algorithmically, using a technique known as "parametric design."

(C) The architects gave the system a set of criteria, and it generated a set of possible designs for the architects to choose from. Similar software has been used to design lightweight bicycle frames and sturdier chairs, among much else.

* aesthetically: 미적으로 ** sturdy: 튼튼한, 견고한

① (A) – (C) – (B)
② (B) – (A) – (C)
③ (B) – (C) – (A)
④ (C) – (A) – (B)
⑤ (C) – (B) – (A)

08

고2 • 2018년 11월 37번

주어진 글 다음에 이어질 글의 순서로 가장 적절한 것을 고르시오. [3점]

Some fad diets might have you running a caloric deficit, and while this might encourage weight loss, it has no effect on improving body composition, and it could actually result in a loss of muscle mass.

(A) Timing is also important. By eating the right combinations of these key macronutrients at strategic intervals throughout the day, we can help our bodies heal and grow even faster.

(B) Your body also needs the right balance of key macronutrients to heal and grow stronger. These macronutrients, which include protein, carbohydrates, and healthy fats, can help your body maximize its ability to repair, rebuild, and grow stronger.

(C) Calorie restriction can also cause your metabolism to slow down, and significantly reduce energy levels. Controlling caloric intake to deliver the proper amount of calories so that the body has the energy it needs to function and heal is the only proper approach.

* fad: (일시적인) 유행 ** macronutrient: 다량 영양소

① (A) – (C) – (B)
② (B) – (A) – (C)
③ (B) – (C) – (A)
④ (C) – (A) – (B)
⑤ (C) – (B) – (A)

09

고2·2017년 6월 36번

주어진 글 다음에 이어질 글의 순서로 가장 적절한 것을 고르시오. [3점]

Most habits are probably good when they are first formed. That is, for many of the habits that you do not create intentionally, there must have been some value to performing that particular behavior.

(A) Overeating is one such habit. You may know conceptually that eating too much is a problem. But when you actually overeat, there are few really negative consequences in the moment.

(B) That value is what causes you to repeat the behavior often enough to create the habit. Some habits become bad, because a behavior that has rewarding elements to it at one time also has negative consequences that may not have been obvious when the habit began.

(C) So you do it again and again. Eventually, though, you'll start to gain weight. By the time you really notice this, your habit of eating too much is deeply rooted.

① (A) – (C) – (B) ② (B) – (A) – (C)
③ (B) – (C) – (A) ④ (C) – (A) – (B)
⑤ (C) – (B) – (A)

10 1등급 대비 고난도 2점 문제

고2·2022년 11월 36번

주어진 글 다음에 이어질 글의 순서로 가장 적절한 것을 고르시오.

The right to be forgotten is a right distinct from but related to a right to privacy. The right to privacy is, among other things, the right for information traditionally regarded as protected or personal not to be revealed.

(A) One motivation for such a right is to allow individuals to move on with their lives and not be defined by a specific event or period in their lives. For example, it has long been recognized in some countries, such as the UK and France, that even past criminal convictions should eventually be "spent" and not continue to affect a person's life.

(B) The right to be forgotten, in contrast, can be applied to information that has been in the public domain. The right to be forgotten broadly includes the right of an individual not to be forever defined by information from a specific point in time.

(C) Despite the reason for supporting the right to be forgotten, the right to be forgotten can sometimes come into conflict with other rights. For example, formal exceptions are sometimes made for security or public health reasons.

① (A) – (C) – (B) ② (B) – (A) – (C)
③ (B) – (C) – (A) ④ (C) – (A) – (B)
⑤ (C) – (B) – (A)

11 1등급 대비 고난도 3점 문제

고2 • 2022년 9월 37번

주어진 글 다음에 이어질 글의 순서로 가장 적절한 것을 고르시오. [3점]

> One benefit of reasons and arguments is that they can foster humility. If two people disagree without arguing, all they do is yell at each other. No progress is made.

(A) That is one way to achieve humility — on one side at least. Another possibility is that neither argument is refuted. Both have a degree of reason on their side. Even if neither person involved is convinced by the other's argument, both can still come to appreciate the opposing view.

(B) Both still think that they are right. In contrast, if both sides give arguments that articulate reasons for their positions, then new possibilities open up. One of the arguments gets refuted — that is, it is shown to fail. In that case, the person who depended on the refuted argument learns that he needs to change his view.

(C) They also realize that, even if they have some truth, they do not have the whole truth. They can gain humility when they recognize and appreciate the reasons against their own view.

* humility: 겸손 ** articulate: 분명히 말하다

① (A) – (C) – (B)
② (B) – (A) – (C)
③ (B) – (C) – (A)
④ (C) – (A) – (B)
⑤ (C) – (B) – (A)

12 1등급 대비 고난도 3점 문제

고2 • 2017년 11월 37번

주어진 글 다음에 이어질 글의 순서로 가장 적절한 것을 고르시오. [3점]

> The online world is an artificial universe — entirely human-made and designed. The design of the underlying system shapes how we appear and what we see of other people.

(A) They determine whether we see each other's faces or instead know each other only by name. They can reveal the size and makeup of an audience, or provide the impression that one is writing intimately to only a few, even if millions are in fact reading.

(B) Architects, however, do not control how the residents of those buildings present themselves or see each other — but the designers of virtual spaces do, and they have far greater influence on the social experience of their users.

(C) It determines the structure of conversations and who has access to what information. Architects of physical cities determine the paths people will take and the sights they will see. They affect people's mood by creating cathedrals that inspire awe and schools that encourage playfulness.

* cathedral: 대성당

① (A) – (C) – (B)
② (B) – (A) – (C)
③ (B) – (C) – (A)
④ (C) – (A) – (B)
⑤ (C) – (B) – (A)

학습 Check!

▶ 몰라서 틀린 문항 × 표기 ▶ 헷갈렸거나 찍은 문항 △ 표기 ▶ ×, △ 문항은 다시 풀고 ✔ 표기를 하세요.

종료 시각	시 분 초
소요 시간	분 초
초과 시간	분 초

문항 번호	01	02	03	04	05	06	07	08	09	10	11	12
채점 결과												
틀린 문항 복습												

[해설편 p.084]

DAY 13 글의 순서 03

※ 점수 표기가 없는 문항은 모두 2점입니다.

● 날짜 : 월 일 ● 시작 시각 : 시 분 초 ● 목표 시간 : 20분

01

고2 • 2023년 6월 37번

주어진 글 다음에 이어질 글의 순서로 가장 적절한 것을 고르시오.

> Species that are found in only one area are called endemic species and are especially vulnerable to extinction.

(A) But warmer air from global climate change caused these clouds to rise, depriving the forests of moisture, and the habitat for the golden toad and many other species dried up. The golden toad appears to be one of the first victims of climate change caused largely by global warming.

(B) They exist on islands and in other unique small areas, especially in tropical rain forests where most species are highly specialized. One example is the brilliantly colored golden toad once found only in a small area of lush rain forests in Costa Rica's mountainous region.

(C) Despite living in the country's well-protected Monteverde Cloud Forest Reserve, by 1989, the golden toad had apparently become extinct. Much of the moisture that supported its rain forest habitat came in the form of moisture-laden clouds blowing in from the Caribbean Sea.

* lush: 무성한, 우거진

① (A) − (C) − (B)
② (B) − (A) − (C)
③ (B) − (C) − (A)
④ (C) − (A) − (B)
⑤ (C) − (B) − (A)

02

고2 • 2021년 3월 37번

주어진 글 다음에 이어질 글의 순서로 가장 적절한 것을 고르시오.

> We commonly argue about the fairness of taxation — whether this or that tax will fall more heavily on the rich or the poor.

(A) Taxes on tobacco, alcohol, and casinos are called "sin taxes" because they seek to discourage activities considered harmful or undesirable. Such taxes express society's disapproval of these activities by raising the cost of engaging in them. Proposals to tax sugary sodas (to combat obesity) or carbon emissions (to address climate change) likewise seek to change norms and shape behavior.

(B) But the expressive dimension of taxation goes beyond debates about fairness, to the moral judgements societies make about which activities are worthy of honor and recognition, and which ones should be discouraged. Sometimes, these judgements are explicit.

(C) Not all taxes have this aim. We do not tax income to express disapproval of paid employment or to discourage people from engaging in it. Nor is a general sales tax intended as a deterrent to buying things. These are simply ways of raising revenue.

* deterrent: 억제책

① (A) − (C) − (B)
② (B) − (A) − (C)
③ (B) − (C) − (A)
④ (C) − (A) − (B)
⑤ (C) − (B) − (A)

03

고2・2020년 9월 37번

주어진 글 다음에 이어질 글의 순서로 가장 적절한 것을 고르시오.

When an important change takes place in your life, observe your response. If you resist accepting the change it is because you are afraid; afraid of losing something.

(A) To learn to let go, to not cling and allow the flow of the river, is to live without resistances; being the creators of constructive changes that bring about improvements and widen our horizons.

(B) In life, all these things come and go and then others appear, which will also go. It is like a river in constant movement. If we try to stop the flow, we create a dam; the water stagnates and causes a pressure which accumulates inside us.

(C) Perhaps you might lose your position, property, possession, or money. The change might mean that you lose privileges or prestige. Perhaps with the change you lose the closeness of a person or a place.

* stagnate: (물이) 고이다

① (A) – (C) – (B)
② (B) – (A) – (C)
③ (B) – (C) – (A)
④ (C) – (A) – (B)
⑤ (C) – (B) – (A)

04

고2・2019년 11월 36번

주어진 글 다음에 이어질 글의 순서로 가장 적절한 것을 고르시오.

The lotus plant (a white water lily) grows in the dirty, muddy bottom of lakes and ponds, yet despite this, its leaves are always clean.

(A) As a result of this investigation, a German company produced a house paint. On the market in Europe and Asia, the product even came with a guarantee that it would stay clean for five years without detergents or sandblasting.

(B) That is because whenever the smallest particle of dust lands on the plant, it immediately waves the leaf, directing the dust particles to one particular spot. Raindrops falling on the leaves are sent to that same place, to thus wash the dirt away.

(C) This property of the lotus led researchers to design a new house paint. Researchers began working on how to develop paints that wash clean in the rain, in much the same way as lotus leaves do.

① (A) – (C) – (B)
② (B) – (A) – (C)
③ (B) – (C) – (A)
④ (C) – (A) – (B)
⑤ (C) – (B) – (A)

05

고2 • 2018년 6월 35번

주어진 글 다음에 이어질 글의 순서로 가장 적절한 것을 고르시오.

> Your story is what makes you special. But the tricky part is showing how special you are without talking about yourself. Effective personal branding isn't about talking about yourself all the time.

(A) By doing so, you promote their victories and their ideas, and you become an influencer. You are seen as someone who is not only helpful, but is also a valuable resource. That helps your brand more than if you just talk about yourself over and over.

(B) Although everyone would like to think that friends and family are eagerly waiting by their computers hoping to hear some news about what you're doing, they're not.

(C) Actually, they're hoping you're sitting by your computer, waiting for news about them. The best way to build your personal brand is to talk more about other people, events, and ideas than you talk about yourself.

＊tricky: 교묘한, 까다로운

① (A) – (C) – (B)
② (B) – (A) – (C)
③ (B) – (C) – (A)
④ (C) – (A) – (B)
⑤ (C) – (B) – (A)

06

고2 • 2017년 3월 36번

주어진 글 다음에 이어질 글의 순서로 가장 적절한 것을 고르시오. [3점]

> James Francis was born in England and emigrated to the United States at age 18. One of his first contributions to water engineering was the invention of the sprinkler system now widely used in buildings for fire protection.

(A) Once the system was activated by opening the valve, water would flow out everywhere. If the building did not burn down, it would certainly be completely flooded.

(B) Francis's design involved a series of perforated pipes running throughout the building. It had two defects: it had to be turned on manually, and it had only *one* valve.

(C) Only some years later, when other engineers perfected the kind of sprinkler heads in use nowadays, did the concept become popular. They turned on automatically and were activated only where actually needed.

＊perforate: 구멍을 내다

① (A) – (C) – (B)
② (B) – (A) – (C)
③ (B) – (C) – (A)
④ (C) – (A) – (B)
⑤ (C) – (B) – (A)

DAY 13

07

고2 • 2021년 11월 37번

주어진 글 다음에 이어질 글의 순서로 가장 적절한 것을 고르시오. [3점]

Because we are told that the planet is doomed, we do not register the growing number of scientific studies demonstrating the resilience of other species. For instance, climate-driven disturbances are affecting the world's coastal marine ecosystems more frequently and with greater intensity.

(A) Similarly, kelp forests hammered by intense El Niño water-temperature increases recovered within five years. By studying these "bright spots," situations where ecosystems persist even in the face of major climatic impacts, we can learn what management strategies help to minimize destructive forces and nurture resilience.

(B) In a region in Western Australia, for instance, up to 90 percent of live coral was lost when ocean water temperatures rose, causing what scientists call coral bleaching. Yet in some sections of the reef surface, 44 percent of the corals recovered within twelve years.

(C) This is a global problem that demands urgent action. Yet, as detailed in a 2017 paper in *BioScience*, there are also instances where marine ecosystems show remarkable resilience to acute climatic events.

* doomed: 운이 다한 ** resilience: 회복력
*** kelp: 켈프(해초의 일종)

① (A) – (C) – (B)
② (B) – (A) – (C)
③ (B) – (C) – (A)
④ (C) – (A) – (B)
⑤ (C) – (B) – (A)

08

고2 • 2019년 3월 37번

주어진 글 다음에 이어질 글의 순서로 가장 적절한 것을 고르시오. [3점]

A little boy sees and hears birds with delight. Then the "good father" comes along and feels he should "share" the experience and help his son "develop."

(A) But most of the members of the human race have lost the capacity to be painters, poets, or musicians, and are not left the option of seeing and hearing directly even if they can afford to; they must get it secondhand.

(B) He says: "That's a jay, and this is a sparrow." The moment the little boy is concerned with which is a jay and which is a sparrow, he can no longer see the birds or hear them sing. He has to see and hear them the way the father wants him to.

(C) Father has good reasons on his side, since few people can go through life listening to the birds sing, and the sooner the boy starts his "education" the better. Maybe he will be an ornithologist when he grows up. A few people, however, can still see and hear in the old way.

* ornithologist: 조류학자

① (A) – (C) – (B)
② (B) – (A) – (C)
③ (B) – (C) – (A)
④ (C) – (A) – (B)
⑤ (C) – (B) – (A)

09

고3 • 2024학년도 9월 36번

주어진 글 다음에 이어질 글의 순서로 가장 적절한 것을 고르시오.

The intuitive ability to classify and generalize is undoubtedly a useful feature of life and research, but it carries a high cost, such as in our tendency to stereotype generalizations about people and situations.

(A) Intuitively and quickly, we mentally sort things into groups based on what we perceive the differences between them to be, and that is the basis for stereotyping. Only afterwards do we examine (or not examine) more evidence of how things are differentiated, and the degree and significance of the variations.

(B) Our brain performs these tasks efficiently and automatically, usually without our awareness. The real danger of stereotypes is not their inaccuracy, but their lack of flexibility and their tendency to be preserved, even when we have enough time to stop and consider.

(C) For most people, the word stereotype arouses negative connotations: it implies a negative bias. But, in fact, stereotypes do not differ in principle from all other generalizations; generalizations about groups of people are not necessarily always negative.

* intuitive: 직관적인 ** connotation: 함축

① (A) – (C) – (B)
② (B) – (A) – (C)
③ (B) – (C) – (A)
④ (C) – (A) – (B)
⑤ (C) – (B) – (A)

10 1등급 대비 고난도 2점 문제

고2 • 2022년 3월 37번

주어진 글 다음에 이어질 글의 순서로 가장 적절한 것을 고르시오.

There is no doubt that the length of some literary works is overwhelming. Reading or translating a work in class, hour after hour, week after week, can be such a boring experience that many students never want to open a foreign language book again.

(A) Moreover, there are some literary features that cannot be adequately illustrated by a short excerpt: the development of plot or character, for instance, with the gradual involvement of the reader that this implies; or the unfolding of a complex theme through the juxtaposition of contrasting views.

(B) Extracts provide one type of solution. The advantages are obvious: reading a series of passages from different works produces more variety in the classroom, so that the teacher has a greater chance of avoiding monotony, while still giving learners a taste at least of an author's special flavour.

(C) On the other hand, a student who is only exposed to 'bite-sized chunks' will never have the satisfaction of knowing the overall pattern of a book, which is after all the satisfaction most of us seek when we read something in our own language.

* excerpt: 발췌 ** juxtaposition: 병치

① (A) – (C) – (B)
② (B) – (A) – (C)
③ (B) – (C) – (A)
④ (C) – (A) – (B)
⑤ (C) – (B) – (A)

11 1등급 대비 고난도 3점 문제

고2·2018년 3월 37번

주어진 글 다음에 이어질 글의 순서로 가장 적절한 것을 고르시오. [3점]

According to the consulting firm McKinsey, knowledge workers spend up to 60 percent of their time looking for information, responding to emails, and collaborating with others.

(A) Think of it as the robot-assisted human, given superpowers through the aid of technology. Our jobs become enriched by relying on robots to do the tedious while we work on increasingly more sophisticated tasks.

(B) The solution is to enable people to work smarter, not just by saying it, but by putting smart tools and improved processes in place so that people can perform at enhanced levels.

(C) By using social technologies, those workers can become up to 25 percent more productive. The need for productivity gains through working harder and longer has a limit and a human toll.

* tedious: 지루한, 싫증 나는

① (A) – (C) – (B)
② (B) – (A) – (C)
③ (B) – (C) – (A)
④ (C) – (A) – (B)
⑤ (C) – (B) – (A)

12 1등급 대비 고난도 3점 문제

고2·2022년 11월 37번

주어진 글 다음에 이어질 글의 순서로 가장 적절한 것을 고르시오. [3점]

To an economist who succeeds in figuring out a person's preference structure — understanding whether the satisfaction gained from consuming one good is greater than that of another — explaining behavior in terms of changes in underlying likes and dislikes is usually highly problematic.

(A) When income rises, for example, people want more children (or, as you will see later, more satisfaction derived from children), even if their inherent desire for children stays the same.

(B) To argue, for instance, that the baby boom and then the baby bust resulted from an increase and then a decrease in the public's inherent taste for children, rather than a change in relative prices against a background of stable preferences, places a social scientist in an unsound position.

(C) In economics, such an argument about birth rates would be equivalent to saying that a rise and fall in mortality could be attributed to an increase in the inherent desire change for death. For an economist, changes in income and prices, rather than changes in tastes, affect birth rates.

① (A) – (C) – (B)
② (B) – (A) – (C)
③ (B) – (C) – (A)
④ (C) – (A) – (B)
⑤ (C) – (B) – (A)

학습 Check!

▶ 몰라서 틀린 문항 × 표기 ▶ 헷갈렸거나 찍은 문항 △ 표기 ▶ ×, △ 문항은 다시 풀고 ✔ 표기를 하세요.

종료 시각	시 분 초
소요 시간	분 초
초과 시간	분 초

문항 번호	01	02	03	04	05	06	07	08	09	10	11	12
채점 결과												
틀린 문항 복습												

[해설편 p.090]

DAY 14 글의 순서 04

※ 점수 표기가 없는 문항은 모두 2점입니다.

● 날짜 : 월 일 ● 시작 시각 : 시 분 초 ● 목표 시간 : 20분

01

고2 • 2022년 3월 36번

주어진 글 다음에 이어질 글의 순서로 가장 적절한 것을 고르시오.

The ancient Greeks used to describe two very different ways of thinking — *logos* and *mythos*. *Logos* roughly referred to the world of the logical, the empirical, the scientific.

(A) But lots of scholars then and now — including many anthropologists, sociologists and philosophers today — see a more complicated picture, where *mythos* and *logos* are intertwined and interdependent. Science itself, according to this view, relies on stories.

(B) *Mythos* referred to the world of dreams, storytelling and symbols. Like many rationalists today, some philosophers of Greece prized *logos* and looked down at *mythos*. Logic and reason, they concluded, make us modern; storytelling and mythmaking are primitive.

(C) The frames and metaphors we use to understand the world shape the scientific discoveries we make; they even shape what we see. When our frames and metaphors change, the world itself is transformed. The Copernican Revolution involved more than just scientific calculation; it involved a new story about the place of Earth in the universe.

* empirical: 경험적인

① (A) – (C) – (B)
② (B) – (A) – (C)
③ (B) – (C) – (A)
④ (C) – (A) – (B)
⑤ (C) – (B) – (A)

02

고2 • 2020년 11월 36번

주어진 글 다음에 이어질 글의 순서로 가장 적절한 것을 고르시오.

Mark Granovetter examined the extent to which information about jobs flowed through weak versus strong ties among a group of people.

(A) This means that they might have information that is most relevant to us, but it also means that it is information to which we may already be exposed. In contrast, our weaker relationships are often with people who are more distant both geographically and demographically.

(B) Their information is more novel. Even though we talk to these people less frequently, we have so many weak ties that they end up being a sizable source of information, especially of information to which we don't otherwise have access.

(C) He found that only a sixth of jobs that came via the network were from strong ties, with the rest coming via medium or weak ties; and with more than a quarter coming via weak ties. Strong ties can be more homophilistic. Our closest friends are often those who are most like us.

* demographically: 인구통계학적으로
** homophilistic: 동족친화적인

① (A) – (C) – (B)
② (B) – (A) – (C)
③ (B) – (C) – (A)
④ (C) – (A) – (B)
⑤ (C) – (B) – (A)

03

고2·2020년 9월 36번

주어진 글 다음에 이어질 글의 순서로 가장 적절한 것을 고르시오.

When a change in the environment occurs, there is a relative increase or decrease in the rate at which the neurons fire, which is how intensity is coded. Furthermore, relativity operates to calibrate our sensations.

(A) Although both hands are now in the same water, one feels that it is colder and the other feels warmer because of the relative change from prior experience. This process, called *adaptation*, is one of the organizing principles operating throughout the central nervous system.

(B) For example, if you place one hand in hot water and the other in iced water for some time before immersing them both into lukewarm water, you will experience conflicting sensations of temperature because of the relative change in the receptors registering hot and cold.

(C) It explains why you can't see well inside a dark room if you have come in from a sunny day. Your eyes have to become accustomed to the new level of luminance. Adaptation explains why apples taste sour after eating sweet chocolate and why traffic seems louder in the city if you normally live in the country.

* calibrate: 조정하다 ** luminance: (빛의) 밝기

① (A) – (C) – (B)
② (B) – (A) – (C)
③ (B) – (C) – (A)
④ (C) – (A) – (B)
⑤ (C) – (B) – (A)

04

고2·2017년 11월 36번

주어진 글 다음에 이어질 글의 순서로 가장 적절한 것을 고르시오.

A researcher in adult education at the University of Toronto, Allen Tough wrote a paper called "The Iceberg of Informal Adult Learning." Tough formulated a reverse 20/80 rule for adult learning.

(A) Tough researched the reasons why people chose to learn on their own rather than attend a class. "People seem to want to be in control," he wrote. "They want to set their own pace and use their own style of learning; they want to keep it flexible."

(B) Twenty percent of an adult learner's efforts were formal, organized by an institution. Eighty percent was informal, organized by the learner. He used the metaphor of an iceberg to describe the large portion of learning, informal learning, that remains invisible.

(C) People also seem to consider informal learning experiential and social. Lifelong learning organized around one's interests might be seen as a new form of recreation.

① (A) – (C) – (B)
② (B) – (A) – (C)
③ (B) – (C) – (A)
④ (C) – (A) – (B)
⑤ (C) – (B) – (A)

05

고2 • 2018년 6월 36번

주어진 글 다음에 이어질 글의 순서로 가장 적절한 것을 고르시오.

Many years ago I visited the chief investment officer of a large financial firm, who had just invested some tens of millions of dollars in the stock of the ABC Motor Company.

(A) Instead, he had listened to his intuition; he liked the cars, he liked the company, and he liked the idea of owning its stock. From what we know about the accuracy of stock picking, it is reasonable to believe that he did not know what he was doing.

(B) His response made it very clear that he trusted his gut feeling and was satisfied with himself and with his decision. I found it remarkable that he had apparently not considered the one question that an economist would call relevant: Is the ABC stock currently underpriced?

(C) When I asked how he had made that decision, he replied that he had recently attended an automobile show and had been impressed. He said, "Boy, they do know how to make a car!"

* gut feeling: 직감

① (A) – (C) – (B)
② (B) – (A) – (C)
③ (B) – (C) – (A)
④ (C) – (A) – (B)
⑤ (C) – (B) – (A)

06

고2 • 2023년 3월 37번

주어진 글 다음에 이어질 글의 순서로 가장 적절한 것을 고르시오. [3점]

A common but incorrect assumption is that we are creatures of reason when, in fact, we are creatures of both reason and emotion. We cannot get by on reason alone since any reason always eventually leads to a feeling. Should I get a wholegrain cereal or a chocolate cereal?

(A) These deep-seated values, feelings, and emotions we have are rarely a result of reasoning, but can certainly be influenced by reasoning. We have values, feelings, and emotions before we begin to reason and long before we begin to reason effectively.

(B) I can list all the reasons I want, but the reasons have to be based on something. For example, if my goal is to eat healthy, I can choose the wholegrain cereal, but what is my reason for wanting to be healthy?

(C) I can list more and more reasons such as wanting to live longer, spending more quality time with loved ones, etc., but what are the reasons for those reasons? You should be able to see by now that reasons are ultimately based on non-reason such as values, feelings, or emotions.

① (A) – (C) – (B)
② (B) – (A) – (C)
③ (B) – (C) – (A)
④ (C) – (A) – (B)
⑤ (C) – (B) – (A)

07

고2・2021년 9월 36번

주어진 글 다음에 이어질 글의 순서로 가장 적절한 것을 고르시오. [3점]

When trying to sustain an independent ethos, cultures face a problem of critical mass. No single individual, acting on his or her own, can produce an ethos.

(A) They manage this feat through a combination of trade, to support their way of life, and geographic isolation. The Inuit occupy remote territory, removed from major population centers of Canada. If cross-cultural contact were to become sufficiently close, the Inuit ethos would disappear.

(B) Rather, an ethos results from the interdependent acts of many individuals. This cluster of produced meaning may require some degree of insulation from larger and wealthier outside forces. The Canadian Inuit maintain their own ethos, even though they number no more than twenty-four thousand.

(C) Distinct cultural groups of similar size do not, in the long run, persist in downtown Toronto, Canada, where they come in contact with many outside influences and pursue essentially Western paths for their lives.

* ethos: 민족(사회) 정신 ** insulation: 단절

① (A) – (C) – (B)
② (B) – (A) – (C)
③ (B) – (C) – (A)
④ (C) – (A) – (B)
⑤ (C) – (B) – (A)

08

고2・2019년 6월 37번

주어진 글 다음에 이어질 글의 순서로 가장 적절한 것을 고르시오. [3점]

Brain research provides a framework for understanding how the brain processes and internalizes athletic skills.

(A) This internalization transfers the swing from a consciously controlled left-brain function to a more intuitive or automatic right-brain function. This description, despite being an oversimplification of the actual processes involved, serves as a model for the interaction between conscious and unconscious actions in the brain, as it learns to perfect an athletic skill.

(B) In practicing a complex movement such as a golf swing, we experiment with different grips, positions and swing movements, analyzing each in terms of the results it yields. This is a conscious, left-brain process.

(C) Once we identify those elements of the swing that produce the desired results, we rehearse them over and over again in an attempt to record them permanently in "muscle memory." In this way, we internalize the swing as a kinesthetic feeling that we trust to recreate the desired swing on demand.

* kinesthetic: 운동 감각의

① (A) – (C) – (B)
② (B) – (A) – (C)
③ (B) – (C) – (A)
④ (C) – (A) – (B)
⑤ (C) – (B) – (A)

09

고3·2023학년도 6월 36번

주어진 글 다음에 이어질 글의 순서로 가장 적절한 것을 고르시오.

The fossil record provides evidence of evolution. The story the fossils tell is one of change. Creatures existed in the past that are no longer with us. Sequential changes are found in many fossils showing the change of certain features over time from a common ancestor, as in the case of the horse.

(A) If multicelled organisms were indeed found to have evolved before single-celled organisms, then the theory of evolution would be rejected. A good scientific theory always allows for the possibility of rejection. The fact that we have not found such a case in countless examinations of the fossil record strengthens the case for evolutionary theory.

(B) The fossil record supports this prediction — multicelled organisms are found in layers of earth millions of years after the first appearance of single-celled organisms. Note that the possibility always remains that the opposite could be found.

(C) Apart from demonstrating that evolution did occur, the fossil record also provides tests of the predictions made from evolutionary theory. For example, the theory predicts that single-celled organisms evolved before multicelled organisms.

① (A) – (C) – (B)　② (B) – (A) – (C)
③ (B) – (C) – (A)　④ (C) – (A) – (B)
⑤ (C) – (B) – (A)

10 1등급 대비 고난도 2점 문제

고2·2021년 6월 36번

주어진 글 다음에 이어질 글의 순서로 가장 적절한 것을 고르시오.

Consider the story of two men quarreling in a library. One wants the window open and the other wants it closed. They argue back and forth about how much to leave it open: a crack, halfway, or three-quarters of the way.

(A) The librarian could not have invented the solution she did if she had focused only on the two men's stated positions of wanting the window open or closed. Instead, she looked to their underlying interests of fresh air and no draft.

(B) After thinking a minute, she opens wide a window in the next room, bringing in fresh air without a draft. This story is typical of many negotiations. Since the parties' problem appears to be a conflict of positions, they naturally tend to talk about positions — and often reach an impasse.

(C) No solution satisfies them both. Enter the librarian. She asks one why he wants the window open: "To get some fresh air." She asks the other why he wants it closed: "To avoid a draft."

* draft: 외풍 ** impasse: 막다름

① (A) – (C) – (B)　② (B) – (A) – (C)
③ (B) – (C) – (A)　④ (C) – (A) – (B)
⑤ (C) – (B) – (A)

11 1등급 대비 고난도 3점 문제

고2・2016년 11월 37번

주어진 글 다음에 이어질 글의 순서로 가장 적절한 것을 고르시오. [3점]

> For years business leaders and politicians have portrayed environmental protection and jobs as mutually exclusive.

(A) Pollution control, protection of natural areas and endangered species, and limits on use of nonrenewable resources, they claim, will choke the economy and throw people out of work. Ecological economists dispute this claim, however.

(B) Recycling, for instance, makes more new jobs than extracting raw materials. This doesn't necessarily mean that recycled goods are more expensive than those from raw resources. We're simply substituting labor in the recycling center for energy and huge machines used to extract new materials in remote places.

(C) Their studies show that only 0.1 percent of all large-scale layoffs in the United States in recent years were due to government regulations. Environmental protection, they argue, not only is necessary for a healthy economic system, but it actually creates jobs and stimulates business.

① (A) – (C) – (B)　② (B) – (A) – (C)　③ (B) – (C) – (A)　④ (C) – (A) – (B)　⑤ (C) – (B) – (A)

12 1등급 대비 고난도 3점 문제

고2・2020년 3월 37번

주어진 글 다음에 이어질 글의 순서로 가장 적절한 것을 고르시오. [3점]

> Regardless of whether the people existing after agriculture were happier, healthier, or neither, it is undeniable that there were more of them. Agriculture both supports and requires more people to grow the crops that sustain them.

(A) And a larger population doesn't just mean increasing the size of everything, like buying a bigger box of cereal for a larger family. It brings qualitative changes in the way people live.

(B) Estimates vary, of course, but evidence points to an increase in the human population from 1-5 million people worldwide to a few hundred million once agriculture had become established.

(C) For example, more people means more kinds of diseases, particularly when those people are sedentary. Those groups of people can also store food for long periods, which creates a society with haves and have-nots.

＊sedentary: 한 곳에 정착해 있는

① (A) – (C) – (B)　② (B) – (A) – (C)　③ (B) – (C) – (A)　④ (C) – (A) – (B)　⑤ (C) – (B) – (A)

DAY 14

학습 Check!

▶ 몰라서 틀린 문항 × 표기 ▶ 헷갈렸거나 찍은 문항 △ 표기 ▶ ×, △ 문항은 다시 풀고 ✔ 표기를 하세요.

종료 시각	시 분 초
소요 시간	분 초
초과 시간	분 초

문항 번호	01	02	03	04	05	06	07	08	09	10	11	12
채점 결과												
틀린 문항 복습												

DAY 15 글의 순서 05

※ 점수 표기가 없는 문항은 모두 2점입니다.

● 날짜 : 월 일 ● 시작 시각 : 시 분 초 ● 목표 시간 : 20분

01

고2 • 2022년 6월 36번

주어진 글 다음에 이어질 글의 순서로 가장 적절한 것을 고르시오.

Touch receptors are spread over all parts of the body, but they are not spread evenly. Most of the touch receptors are found in your fingertips, tongue, and lips.

(A) But if the fingers are spread far apart, you can feel them individually. Yet if the person does the same thing on the back of your hand (with your eyes closed, so that you don't see how many fingers are being used), you probably will be able to tell easily, even when the fingers are close together.

(B) You can test this for yourself. Have someone poke you in the back with one, two, or three fingers and try to guess how many fingers the person used. If the fingers are close together, you will probably think it was only one.

(C) On the tip of each of your fingers, for example, there are about five thousand separate touch receptors. In other parts of the body there are far fewer. In the skin of your back, the touch receptors may be as much as 2 inches apart.

① (A) – (C) – (B) ② (B) – (A) – (C)
③ (B) – (C) – (A) ④ (C) – (A) – (B)
⑤ (C) – (B) – (A)

02

고2 • 2021년 6월 37번

주어진 글 다음에 이어질 글의 순서로 가장 적절한 것을 고르시오.

In one survey, 61 percent of Americans said that they supported the government spending more on 'assistance to the poor'.

(A) Therefore, the framing of a question can heavily influence the answer in many ways, which matters if your aim is to obtain a 'true measure' of what people think. And next time you hear a politician say 'surveys prove that the majority of the people agree with me', be very wary.

(B) But when the same population was asked whether they supported spending more government money on 'welfare', only 21 percent were in favour. In other words, if you ask people about individual welfare programmes — such as giving financial help to people who have long-term illnesses and paying for school meals for families with low income — people are broadly in favour of them.

(C) But if you ask about 'welfare' — which refers to those exact same programmes that you've just listed — they're against it. The word 'welfare' has negative connotations, perhaps because of the way many politicians and newspapers portray it.

* wary: 조심성 있는 ** connotation: 함축

① (A) – (C) – (B) ② (B) – (A) – (C)
③ (B) – (C) – (A) ④ (C) – (A) – (B)
⑤ (C) – (B) – (A)

03

고2 • 2019년 6월 36번

주어진 글 다음에 이어질 글의 순서로 가장 적절한 것을 고르시오.

> Without money, people could only barter. Many of us barter to a small extent, when we return favors.

(A) There is no need to find someone who wants what you have to trade; you simply pay for your goods with money. The seller can then take the money and buy from someone else. Money is transferable and deferrable — the seller can hold on to it and buy when the time is right.

(B) What would happen if you wanted a loaf of bread and all you had to trade was your new car? Barter depends on the double coincidence of wants, where not only does the other person happen to have what I want, but I also have what he wants. Money solves all these problems.

(C) A man might offer to mend his neighbor's broken door in return for a few hours of babysitting, for instance. Yet it is hard to imagine these personal exchanges working on a larger scale.

* barter: 물물 교환(하다)

① (A) – (C) – (B)
② (B) – (A) – (C)
③ (B) – (C) – (A)
④ (C) – (A) – (B)
⑤ (C) – (B) – (A)

04

고2 • 2017년 6월 35번

주어진 글 다음에 이어질 글의 순서로 가장 적절한 것을 고르시오.

> Suppose that the price of frozen yogurt falls. The law of demand says that you will buy more frozen yogurt. At the same time, you will probably buy less ice cream.

(A) Yet, in this case, you will likely buy more ice cream as well, since ice cream and topping are often used together. When a fall in the price of one good raises the demand for another good, the two goods are called complements.

(B) They are often pairs of goods that are used in place of each other, like hot dogs and hamburgers. Now suppose that the price of chocolate topping falls. According to the law of demand, you will buy more chocolate topping.

(C) This is because ice cream and frozen yogurt are both cold and sweet desserts, satisfying similar desires. When a fall in the price of one good reduces the demand for another good, the two goods are called substitutes.

① (A) – (C) – (B)
② (B) – (A) – (C)
③ (B) – (C) – (A)
④ (C) – (A) – (B)
⑤ (C) – (B) – (A)

05

고2 • 2018년 9월 36번

주어진 글 다음에 이어질 글의 순서로 가장 적절한 것을 고르시오.

> Your concepts are a primary tool for your brain to guess the meaning of incoming sensory inputs.

(A) When Westerners hear Indonesian gamelan music for the first time, which is based on seven pitches per octave with varied tunings, it's more likely to sound like noise. A brain that's been wired by listening to twelve-tone scales doesn't have a concept for that music.

(B) All people of Western culture with normal hearing have a concept for this ubiquitous scale, even if they can't explicitly describe it. Not all music uses this scale, however.

(C) For example, concepts give meaning to changes in sound pressure so you hear them as words or music instead of random noise. In Western culture, most music is based on an octave divided into twelve equally spaced pitches: the equal-tempered scale codified by Johann Sebastian Bach in the 17th century.

① (A) – (C) – (B)
② (B) – (A) – (C)
③ (B) – (C) – (A)
④ (C) – (A) – (B)
⑤ (C) – (B) – (A)

06

고2 • 2021년 9월 37번

주어진 글 다음에 이어질 글의 순서로 가장 적절한 것을 고르시오. [3점]

> Heat is lost at the surface, so the more surface area you have relative to volume, the harder you must work to stay warm. That means that little creatures have to produce heat more rapidly than large creatures.

(A) Despite the vast differences in heart rates, nearly all mammals have about 800 million heartbeats in them if they live an average life. The exception is humans. We pass 800 million heartbeats after twenty-five years, and just keep on going for another fifty years and 1.6 billion heartbeats or so.

(B) They must therefore lead completely different lifestyles. An elephant's heart beats just thirty times a minute, a human's sixty, a cow's between fifty and eighty, but a mouse's beats six hundred times a minute — ten times a second. Every day, just to survive, the mouse must eat about 50 percent of its own body weight.

(C) We humans, by contrast, need to consume only about 2 percent of our body weight to supply our energy requirements. One area where animals are curiously uniform is with the number of heartbeats they have in a lifetime.

① (A) – (C) – (B)
② (B) – (A) – (C)
③ (B) – (C) – (A)
④ (C) – (A) – (B)
⑤ (C) – (B) – (A)

07

고2 • 2020년 3월 36번

주어진 글 다음에 이어질 글의 순서로 가장 적절한 것을 고르시오. [3점]

> Habits create the foundation for mastery. In chess, it is only after the basic movements of the pieces have become automatic that a player can focus on the next level of the game. Each chunk of information that is memorized opens up the mental space for more effortful thinking.

(A) You fall into mindless repetition. It becomes easier to let mistakes slide. When you can do it "good enough" automatically, you stop thinking about how to do it better.

(B) However, the benefits of habits come at a cost. At first, each repetition develops fluency, speed, and skill. But then, as a habit becomes automatic, you become less sensitive to feedback.

(C) This is true for anything you attempt. When you know the simple movements so well that you can perform them without thinking, you are free to pay attention to more advanced details. In this way, habits are the backbone of any pursuit of excellence.

① (A) – (C) – (B) ② (B) – (A) – (C)
③ (B) – (C) – (A) ④ (C) – (A) – (B)
⑤ (C) – (B) – (A)

08

고2 • 2017년 9월 36번

주어진 글 다음에 이어질 글의 순서로 가장 적절한 것을 고르시오. [3점]

> Crossing the street in Los Angeles is a tricky business, but luckily, at the press of a button, we can stop traffic. Or can we?

(A) Clever technicians create the illusion of control by installing fake temperature dials. This reduces energy bills — and complaints. Such tricks are called "placebo buttons" and they are being pushed in all sorts of contexts.

(B) The button's real purpose is to make us believe we have an influence on the traffic lights, and thus we're better able to endure the wait for the signal to change with more patience.

(C) The same goes for "door-open" and "door-close" buttons in elevators: Many are not even connected to the electrical panel. Such tricks are also designed in offices: For some people it will always be too hot, for others, too cold.

① (A) – (C) – (B) ② (B) – (A) – (C)
③ (B) – (C) – (A) ④ (C) – (A) – (B)
⑤ (C) – (B) – (A)

09

고2 • 2019년 9월 36번

주어진 글 다음에 이어질 글의 순서로 가장 적절한 것을 고르시오. [3점]

You know that forks don't fly off to the Moon and that neither apples nor anything else on Earth cause the Sun to crash down on us.

(A) The Earth has more mass than tables, trees, or apples, so almost everything in the world is pulled towards the Earth. That's why apples fall from trees. Now, you might know that the Sun is much bigger than Earth and has much more mass.

(B) The reason these things don't happen is that the strength of gravity's pull depends on two things. The first is the mass of the object. The apple is very small, and doesn't have much mass, so its pull on the Sun is absolutely tiny, certainly much smaller than the pull of all the planets.

(C) So why don't apples fly off towards the Sun? The reason is that the pull of gravity also depends on the distance to the object doing the pulling. Although the Sun has much more mass than the Earth, we are much closer to the Earth, so we feel its gravity more.

① (A) – (C) – (B)
② (B) – (A) – (C)
③ (B) – (C) – (A)
④ (C) – (A) – (B)
⑤ (C) – (B) – (A)

10

고3 • 2021학년도 6월 36번

주어진 글 다음에 이어질 글의 순서로 가장 적절한 것을 고르시오.

Studies of people struggling with major health problems show that the majority of respondents report they derived benefits from their adversity. Stressful events sometimes force people to develop new skills, reevaluate priorities, learn new insights, and acquire new strengths.

(A) High levels of adversity predicted poor mental health, as expected, but people who had faced intermediate levels of adversity were healthier than those who experienced little adversity, suggesting that moderate amounts of stress can foster resilience. A follow-up study found a similar link between the amount of lifetime adversity and subjects' responses to laboratory stressors.

(B) Intermediate levels of adversity were predictive of the greatest resilience. Thus, having to deal with a moderate amount of stress may build resilience in the face of future stress.

(C) In other words, the adaptation process initiated by stress can lead to personal changes for the better. One study that measured participants' exposure to thirty-seven major negative events found a curvilinear relationship between lifetime adversity and mental health.

* resilience: 회복력

① (A) – (C) – (B)
② (B) – (A) – (C)
③ (B) – (C) – (A)
④ (C) – (A) – (B)
⑤ (C) – (B) – (A)

11 1등급 대비 고난도 2점 문제

고2·2017년 3월 37번

주어진 글 다음에 이어질 글의 순서로 가장 적절한 것을 고르시오.

> The difference between selling and marketing is very simple. Selling focuses mainly on the firm's desire to sell products for revenue.

(A) When a product or service is marketed in the proper manner, very little selling is necessary because the consumer need already exists and the product or service is merely being produced to satisfy the need.

(B) Salespeople and other forms of promotion are used to create demand for a firm's current products. Clearly, the needs of the seller are very strong.

(C) Marketing, however, focuses on the needs of the consumer, ultimately benefiting the seller as well. When a product or service is truly marketed, the needs of the consumer are considered from the very beginning of the new product development process, and the product-service mix is designed to meet the unsatisfied needs of the consuming public.

* revenue: 수익

① (A) – (C) – (B)
② (B) – (A) – (C)
③ (B) – (C) – (A)
④ (C) – (A) – (B)
⑤ (C) – (B) – (A)

12 1등급 대비 고난도 3점 문제

고2·2020년 6월 37번

주어진 글 다음에 이어질 글의 순서로 가장 적절한 것을 고르시오. [3점]

> Since we know we can't completely eliminate our biases, we need to try to limit the harmful impacts they can have on the objectivity and rationality of our decisions and judgments.

(A) If it did, we can move on and make an objective and informed decision. If it didn't, we can try the same strategy again or implement a new one until we are ready to make a rational judgment.

(B) Then we can choose an appropriate de-biasing strategy to combat it. After we have implemented a strategy, we should check in again to see if it worked in the way we had hoped.

(C) It is important that we are aware when one of our cognitive biases is activated and make a conscious choice to overcome that bias. We need to be aware of the impact the bias has on our decision making process and our life.

① (A) – (C) – (B)
② (B) – (A) – (C)
③ (B) – (C) – (A)
④ (C) – (A) – (B)
⑤ (C) – (B) – (A)

DAY 15

학습 Check!

▶ 몰라서 틀린 문항 × 표기 ▶ 헷갈렸거나 찍은 문항 △ 표기 ▶ ×, △ 문항은 다시 풀고 ✔ 표기를 하세요.

종료 시각	시 분 초
소요 시간	분 초
초과 시간	분 초

문항 번호	01	02	03	04	05	06	07	08	09	10	11	12
채점 결과												
틀린 문항 복습												

문장 삽입

수능 영어 **문장 삽입에서 무엇보다 중요한 것은 연결사를 정확히 알고 이해를 하는 것**입니다. 단순히 **뜻만 알고 있는 것이 아니고, 연결사 앞 문장과 뒤에 나오는 문장이 어떤 관계에 있는지를 추론**할 수 있어야합니다.
영어 영역 1등급을 위한 '오답 3대장' 중 마지막 관문인 '문장 삽입'을 반드시 정복해 목표를 이루시기를 바랍니다.

▶ 문장 삽입 유형

[38~39] 글의 흐름으로 보아 주어진 문장이 들어가기에 가장 적절한 곳을 고르시오.

영어 영역 **38~39**번에 해당하는 **문장 삽입은 연결어 등의 단서를 이용해 주어진 한 문장을 끼워 넣어 논리적인 흐름에 맞게 만드는 문제**입니다.
글을 쭉 읽으며 문장 사이의 대비가 자연스럽지 않거나 연결이 어색한 문장들 사이에 주어진 문장을 그 사이에 넣어 흐름이 매끄러운지 확인하는 훈련을 해야 하며, 충분한 연습이 가능하도록 기출문제를 수록했습니다.

꿀팁! 갑자기 흐름이 끊겨서 어색한 곳을 찾아내 주어진 문장을 알맞은 위치에 넣고, 전 후 흐름이 자연스럽게 이어졌는지 확인한다.

▶ 문장 삽입 교재 구성

하루 12문항 _ 20분 학습 _ 5일 완성 = 총 60문항

문장 삽입은 **앞 문장에는 등장하지 않았던 어구가 갑자기 나오거나 문맥상 원인이 주어지지 않았는데 결과가 갑자기 등장한다면, 또는 글의 흐름이 아무 연결어 없이 완전히 전환되거나 화재가 넘어가는 부분이 정답**일 수 있습니다. **일관성을 유지하는 주제를 파악하여 '주어진 문장의 위치를 찾는 연습'이 영어 '1등급으로 향하는 실력'**이 됩니다.

단서에 유의하자

한정사(such, both…), 대명사, 지시어, 정관사, 대동사, 연결어, 시간 흐름 등의 단서에 유의해서 해석한다.

흐름을 파악하자

글의 전반부가 부정이고 후반으로 갈수록 긍정이라면 삽입 문장은 역접이 시작하는 부분일 가능성이 높다.

논리의 비약을 찾자

주어진 문장에서 논리적 흐름이 이상한 곳과 글에서 내용상의 단절되는 부분을 찾으면 쉽게 답을 찾을 수 있다.

2020 하루 20분 20일 완성

PART Ⅲ
문장 삽입

Day 16~Day 20

[해설편 p.104]

DAY 16 문장 삽입 01

※ 점수 표기가 없는 문항은 모두 2점입니다.

● 날짜 : 월 일 ● 시작 시각 : 시 분 초

● 목표 시간 : 20분

01

고2•2023년 9월 38번

글의 흐름으로 보아, 주어진 문장이 들어가기에 가장 적절한 곳을 고르시오.

> You don't sit back and speculate about the meaning of life when you are stressed.

The brain is a high-energy consumer of glucose, which is its fuel. Although the brain accounts for merely 3 percent of a person's body weight, it consumes 20 percent of the available fuel. (①) Your brain can't store fuel, however, so it has to "pay as it goes." (②) Since your brain is incredibly adaptive, it economizes its fuel resources. (③) Thus, during a period of high stress, it shifts away from the analysis of the nuances of a situation to a singular and fixed focus on the stressful situation at hand. (④) Instead, you devote all your energy to trying to figure out what action to take. (⑤) Sometimes, however, this shift from the higher-thinking parts of the brain to the automatic and reflexive parts of the brain can lead you to do something too quickly, without thinking.

* glucose: 포도당

02

고2•2022년 3월 38번

글의 흐름으로 보아, 주어진 문장이 들어가기에 가장 적절한 곳을 고르시오.

> For instance, the revolutionary ideas that earned Einstein his Nobel Prize — concerning the special theory of relativity and the photoelectric effect — appeared as papers in the *Annalen der Physik*.

In the early stages of modern science, scientists communicated their creative ideas largely by publishing books. (①) This modus operandi is illustrated not only by Newton's *Principia*, but also by Copernicus' *On the Revolutions of the Heavenly Spheres*, Kepler's *The Harmonies of the World*, and Galileo's *Dialogues Concerning the Two New Sciences*. (②) With the advent of scientific periodicals, such as the *Transactions of the Royal Society of London*, books gradually yielded ground to the technical journal article as the chief form of scientific communication. (③) Of course, books were not abandoned altogether, as Darwin's *Origin of Species* shows. (④) Even so, it eventually became possible for scientists to establish a reputation for their creative contributions without publishing a single book-length treatment of their ideas. (⑤) His status as one of the greatest scientists of all time does not depend on the publication of a single book.

* photoelectric effect: 광전 효과
** modus operandi: 작업 방식[절차]

03

고2 • 2019년 11월 38번

글의 흐름으로 보아, 주어진 문장이 들어가기에 가장 적절한 곳을 고르시오.

> In describing the service, a recent newspaper article warned consumers that sharing the yacht means "there is no guarantee you will always be able to use it when you want."

Car-sharing is now a familiar concept, but creative companies are making it possible for their clients to share ownership and access to just about everything, such as villas, handbags and even diamond necklaces. (①) According to a Portuguese saying, "You should never have a yacht; you should have a friend with a yacht." (②) By joining a yacht sharing service, members can live the Portuguese dream by sharing a yacht with up to seven other people. (③) This apparent limitation is precisely what helps consumers make it a treat. (④) Limiting your access to everything from sandwiches to luxury cars helps to reset your cheerometer. (⑤) That is, knowing you can't have access to something all the time may help you appreciate it more when you do.

04

고2 • 2017년 6월 37번

글의 흐름으로 보아, 주어진 문장이 들어가기에 가장 적절한 곳을 고르시오.

> This instinctive exchange gradually helped the sick twin to recover and regain his health.

The world can be a different and better place if, while you are here, you give of yourself. This concept became clear to Azim one day when he was watching television at an airport terminal while waiting for a flight. A priest was sharing a story about newborn twins, one of whom was ill. (①) The twins were in separate incubators, as per hospital rules. (②) A nurse on the floor repeatedly suggested that the twins be kept together in one incubator. (③) The doctors finally agreed to try this. (④) When the twins were brought into contact with each other, the healthy twin immediately put his arms around his sick brother. (⑤) The babies' family and the doctors witnessed the intangible force of love and the incredible power of giving.

* intangible: 만질 수 없는

05

고2・2020년 3월 39번

글의 흐름으로 보아, 주어진 문장이 들어가기에 가장 적절한 곳을 고르시오. [3점]

> In some cases, their brains had ceased to function altogether.

Of all the medical achievements of the 1960s, the most widely known was the first heart transplant, performed by the South African surgeon Christiaan Barnard in 1967. (①) The patient's death 18 days later did not weaken the spirits of those who welcomed a new era of medicine. (②) The ability to perform heart transplants was linked to the development of respirators, which had been introduced to hospitals in the 1950s. (③) Respirators could save many lives, but not all those whose hearts kept beating ever recovered any other significant functions. (④) The realization that such patients could be a source of organs for transplantation led to the setting up of the Harvard Brain Death Committee, and to its recommendation that the absence of all "discernible central nervous system activity" should be "a new criterion for death". (⑤) The recommendation has since been adopted, with some modifications, almost everywhere.

* respirator: 인공호흡기 ** discernible: 식별 가능한
*** criterion: 기준

06

고2・2023년 3월 39번

글의 흐름으로 보아, 주어진 문장이 들어가기에 가장 적절한 곳을 고르시오. [3점]

> For others, whose creativity is more focused on methods and technique, creativity may lead to solutions that drastically reduce the work necessary to solve a problem.

Creativity can have an effect on productivity. Creativity leads some individuals to recognize problems that others do not see, but which may be very difficult. (①) Charles Darwin's approach to the speciation problem is a good example of this; he chose a very difficult and tangled problem, speciation, which led him into a long period of data collection and deliberation. (②) This choice of problem did not allow for a quick attack or a simple experiment. (③) In such cases creativity may actually decrease productivity (as measured by publication counts) because effort is focused on difficult problems. (④) We can see an example in the development of the polymerase chain reaction (PCR) which enables us to amplify small pieces of DNA in a short time. (⑤) This type of creativity might reduce the number of steps or substitute steps that are less likely to fail, thus increasing productivity.

* speciation: 종(種) 분화
** polymerase chain reaction: 중합 효소 연쇄 반응

07

고2 • 2022년 11월 39번

글의 흐름으로 보아, 주어진 문장이 들어가기에 가장 적절한 곳을 고르시오. [3점]

> However, the rigidity of rock means that land rises and falls with the tides by a much smaller amount than water, which is why we notice only the ocean tides.

The difference in the Moon's gravitational pull on different parts of our planet effectively creates a "stretching force." (①) It makes our planet slightly stretched out along the line of sight to the Moon and slightly compressed along a line perpendicular to that. (②) The tidal stretching caused by the Moon's gravity affects our entire planet, including both land and water, inside and out. (③) The stretching also explains why there are generally *two* high tides (and two low tides) in the ocean each day. (④) Because Earth is stretched much like a rubber band, the oceans bulge out both on the side facing toward the Moon and on the side facing away from the Moon. (⑤) As Earth rotates, we are carried through both of these tidal bulges each day, so we have high tide when we are in each of the two bulges and low tide at the midpoints in between.

* rigidity: 단단함 ** perpendicular: 직각을 이루는
*** bulge: 팽창하다

08 1등급 대비 고난도 2점 문제

고2 • 2023년 6월 39번

글의 흐름으로 보아, 주어진 문장이 들어가기에 가장 적절한 곳을 고르시오.

> These healthful, non-nutritive compounds in plants provide color and function to the plant and add to the health of the human body.

Why do people in the Mediterranean live longer and have a lower incidence of disease? Some people say it's because of what they eat. Their diet is full of fresh fruits, fish, vegetables, whole grains, and nuts. Individuals in these cultures drink red wine and use great amounts of olive oil. Why is that food pattern healthy? (①) One reason is that they are eating a palette of colors. (②) More and more research is surfacing that shows us the benefits of the thousands of colorful "phytochemicals" (*phyto* = plant) that exist in foods. (③) Each color connects to a particular compound that serves a specific function in the body. (④) For example, if you don't eat purple foods, you are probably missing out on anthocyanins, important brain protection compounds. (⑤) Similarly, if you avoid green-colored foods, you may be lacking chlorophyll, a plant antioxidant that guards your cells from damage.

* antioxidant: 산화 방지제

DAY 16

09 1등급 대비 고난도 2점 문제

고2·2018년 11월 38번

글의 흐름으로 보아, 주어진 문장이 들어가기에 가장 적절한 곳을 고르시오.

> However, living off big game in the era before refrigeration meant humans had to endure alternating periods of feast and famine.

The problem of amino acid deficiency is not unique to the modern world by any means. (①) Preindustrial humanity probably dealt with protein and amino acid insufficiency on a regular basis. (②) Sure, large hunted animals such as mammoths provided protein and amino acids aplenty. (③) Droughts, forest fires, superstorms, and ice ages led to long stretches of difficult conditions, and starvation was a constant threat. (④) The human inability to synthesize such basic things as amino acids certainly worsened those crises and made surviving on whatever was available that much harder. (⑤) During a famine, it's not the lack of calories that is the ultimate cause of death; it's the lack of proteins and the essential amino acids they provide.

* synthesize: 합성하다

10 1등급 대비 고난도 2점 문제

고2·2017년 3월 38번

글의 흐름으로 보아, 주어진 문장이 들어가기에 가장 적절한 곳을 고르시오.

> On the other hand, if you are saving for auto repairs and pay down your debt a little slower, you will feel proud that you planned for the auto repair.

If you apply all your extra money to paying off debt without saving for the things that are guaranteed to happen, you will feel like you've failed when something does happen. You will end up going further into debt. (①) Let's use an example of an unexpected auto repair bill of $500. (②) If you don't save for this, you'll end up with another debt to pay off. (③) You'll feel frustrated that you have been working so hard to pay things off and yet you just added more debt to your list. (④) You will have cash to pay for it, and you are still paying down your debt uninterrupted and on schedule. (⑤) Instead of frustration and disappointment from the unexpected auto repair, you feel proud and excited.

11 1등급 대비 고난도 3점 문제

고2 • 2021년 9월 39번

글의 흐름으로 보아, 주어진 문장이 들어가기에 가장 적절한 곳을 고르시오. [3점]

> There isn't really a way for us to pick up smaller pieces of debris such as bits of paint and metal.

The United Nations asks that all companies remove their satellites from orbit within 25 years after the end of their mission. This is tricky to enforce, though, because satellites can (and often do) fail. (①) To tackle this problem, several companies around the world have come up with novel solutions. (②) These include removing dead satellites from orbit and dragging them back into the atmosphere, where they will burn up. (③) Ways we could do this include using a harpoon to grab a satellite, catching it in a huge net, using magnets to grab it, or even firing lasers to heat up the satellite, increasing its atmospheric drag so that it falls out of orbit. (④) However, these methods are only useful for large satellites orbiting Earth. (⑤) We just have to wait for them to naturally re-enter Earth's atmosphere.

* harpoon: 작살

12 1등급 대비 고난도 3점 문제

고2 • 2020년 11월 39번

글의 흐름으로 보아, 주어진 문장이 들어가기에 가장 적절한 곳을 고르시오. [3점]

> However, according to Christakis and Fowler, we cannot transmit ideas and behaviours much beyond our friends' friends' friends (in other words, across just three degrees of separation).

In the late twentieth century, researchers sought to measure how fast and how far news, rumours or innovations moved. (①) More recent research has shown that ideas — even emotional states and conditions — can be transmitted through a social network. (②) The evidence of this kind of contagion is clear: 'Students with studious roommates become more studious. Diners sitting next to heavy eaters eat more food.' (③) This is because the transmission and reception of an idea or behaviour requires a stronger connection than the relaying of a letter or the communication that a certain employment opportunity exists. (④) Merely knowing people is not the same as being able to influence them to study more or over-eat. (⑤) Imitation is indeed the sincerest form of flattery, even when it is unconscious.

* flattery: 아첨

DAY 16

학습 Check!

▶ 몰라서 틀린 문항 × 표기 ▶ 헷갈렸거나 찍은 문항 △ 표기 ▶ ×, △ 문항은 다시 풀고 ✔ 표기를 하세요.

종료 시각	시 분 초	문항 번호	01	02	03	04	05	06	07	08	09	10	11	12
소요 시간	분 초	채점 결과												
초과 시간	분 초	틀린 문항 복습												

[해설편 p.110]

DAY 17 문장 삽입 02

※ 점수 표기가 없는 문항은 모두 2점입니다.

● 날짜 :　　월　　일 ● 시작 시각 :　　시　　분　　초　　● 목표 시간 : 20분

01

고2 • 2022년 6월 39번

글의 흐름으로 보아, 주어진 문장이 들어가기에 가장 적절한 곳을 고르시오.

> But by the 1970s, psychologists realized there was no such thing as a general "creativity quotient."

The holy grail of the first wave of creativity research was a personality test to measure general creativity ability, in the same way that IQ measured general intelligence. (①) A person's creativity score should tell us his or her creative potential in any field of endeavor, just like an IQ score is not limited to physics, math, or literature. (②) Creative people aren't creative in a general, universal way; they're creative in a specific sphere of activity, a particular domain. (③) We don't expect a creative scientist to also be a gifted painter. (④) A creative violinist may not be a creative conductor, and a creative conductor may not be very good at composing new works. (⑤) Psychologists now know that creativity is domain specific.

* quotient: 지수　** holy grail: 궁극적 목표

02

고2 • 2016년 11월 39번

글의 흐름으로 보아, 주어진 문장이 들어가기에 가장 적절한 곳을 고르시오.

> When you were first learning to read, you may have studied specific facts about the sounds of letters.

There are different kinds of knowledge. Some is domain-specific knowledge that relates to a particular task or subject. For example, knowing that the shortstop plays between second and third base is specific to the domain of baseball. (①) Some knowledge, on the other hand, is general — it applies to many different situations. (②) For example, general knowledge about how to read or write or use a computer is useful both in and out of school. (③) Of course, there is no absolute line between general and domain-specific knowledge. (④) At that time, knowledge about letter sounds was specific to the domain of reading. (⑤) But now you can use both knowledge about sounds and the ability to read in more general ways.

03

고2 • 2018년 6월 38번

글의 흐름으로 보아, 주어진 문장이 들어가기에 가장 적절한 곳을 고르시오.

> Recently, however, some researchers found that how people are praised is very important.

A child bounces up to you holding her school work; perhaps she's your daughter, cousin, or neighbour. (①) She proudly shows you a big red A at the bottom of her test paper. (②) How do you praise her? (③) For decades, people have been told that praise is vital for happy and healthy children and that the most important job in raising a child is nurturing her self-esteem. (④) They discovered that if you say "What a very clever girl you are!" to the child showing you an A, you may cause her more harm than good. (⑤) For your children to succeed and be happy, you need to convince them that success comes from effort, not from some talent that they're born with or without.

04

고2 • 2019년 3월 38번

글의 흐름으로 보아, 주어진 문장이 들어가기에 가장 적절한 곳을 고르시오.

> Granted, it's not quite the same thing, and the computer is not going to tell you when something doesn't "sound right."

It can be helpful to read your own essay aloud to hear how it sounds, and it can sometimes be even more beneficial to hear someone else read it. (①) Either reading will help you to hear things that you otherwise might not notice when editing silently. (②) If you feel uncomfortable having someone read to you, however, or if you simply don't have someone you can ask to do it, you can have your computer read your essay to you. (③) The computer also won't stumble over things that are awkward — it will just plow right on through. (④) But hearing the computer read your writing is a very different experience from reading it yourself. (⑤) If you have never tried it, you might find that you notice areas for revision, editing, and proofreading that you didn't notice before.

* stumble: 말을 더듬다

DAY 17

05

고2 • 2019년 11월 39번

글의 흐름으로 보아, 주어진 문장이 들어가기에 가장 적절한 곳을 고르시오. [3점]

> Houses in the historic district of Key West, Florida, for example, whether new or remodeled, must be built of wood in a traditional style, and there are only a few permissible colors of paint, white being preferred.

In the US, regional styles of speech have always been associated with regional styles of building: the Midwestern farmhouse, the Southern plantation mansion, and the Cape Cod cottage all have their equivalent in spoken dialect. (①) These buildings may be old and genuine, or they may be recent reproductions, the equivalent of an assumed rather than a native accent. (②) As James Kunstler says, "half-baked versions of Scarlett O'Hara's Tara now stand replicated in countless suburban subdivisions around the United States." (③) In some cities and towns, especially where tourism is an important part of the economy, zoning codes may make a sort of artificial authenticity compulsory. (④) From the street these houses may look like the simple sea captains' mansions they imitate. (⑤) Inside, however, where zoning does not reach, they often contain modern lighting and state-of-the-art kitchens and bathrooms.

06

고2 • 2023년 9월 39번

글의 흐름으로 보아, 주어진 문장이 들어가기에 가장 적절한 곳을 고르시오. [3점]

> It is, however, noteworthy that although engagement drives job performance, job performance also drives engagement.

Much research has been carried out on the causes of engagement, an issue that is important from both a theoretical and practical standpoint: identifying the drivers of work engagement may enable us to manipulate or influence it. (①) The causes of engagement fall into two major camps: situational and personal. (②) The most influential situational causes are job resources, feedback and leadership, the latter, of course, being responsible for job resources and feedback. (③) Indeed, leaders influence engagement by giving their employees honest and constructive feedback on their performance, and by providing them with the necessary resources that enable them to perform their job well. (④) In other words, when employees are able to do their jobs well — to the point that they match or exceed their own expectations and ambitions — they will engage more, be proud of their achievements, and find work more meaningful. (⑤) This is especially evident when people are employed in jobs that align with their values.

* align with: ~과 일치하다

07

고2 • 2021년 11월 39번

글의 흐름으로 보아, 주어진 문장이 들어가기에 가장 적절한 곳을 고르시오. [3점]

> In full light, seedlings reduce the amount of energy they allocate to stem elongation.

Scientists who have observed plants growing in the dark have found that they are vastly different in appearance, form, and function from those grown in the light. (①) This is true even when the plants in the different light conditions are genetically identical and are grown under identical conditions of temperature, water, and nutrient level. (②) Seedlings grown in the dark limit the amount of energy going to organs that do not function at full capacity in the dark, like cotyledons and roots, and instead initiate elongation of the seedling stem to propel the plant out of darkness. (③) The energy is directed to expanding their leaves and developing extensive root systems. (④) This is a good example of phenotypic plasticity. (⑤) The seedling adapts to distinct environmental conditions by modifying its form and the underlying metabolic and biochemical processes.

* elongation: 연장 ** cotyledon: 떡잎
*** phenotypic plasticity: 표현형 적응성

08

고3 • 2023학년도 6월 38번

글의 흐름으로 보아, 주어진 문장이 들어가기에 가장 적절한 곳을 고르시오.

> Also, it has become difficult for companies to develop new pesticides, even those that can have major beneficial effects and few negative effects.

Simply maintaining yields at current levels often requires new cultivars and management methods, since pests and diseases continue to evolve, and aspects of the chemical, physical, and social environment can change over several decades. (①) In the 1960s, many people considered pesticides to be mainly beneficial to mankind. (②) Developing new, broadly effective, and persistent pesticides often was considered to be the best way to control pests on crop plants. (③) Since that time, it has become apparent that broadly effective pesticides can have harmful effects on beneficial insects, which can negate their effects in controlling pests, and that persistent pesticides can damage non-target organisms in the ecosystem, such as birds and people. (④) Very high costs are involved in following all of the procedures needed to gain government approval for new pesticides. (⑤) Consequently, more consideration is being given to other ways to manage pests, such as incorporating greater resistance to pests into cultivars by breeding and using other biological control methods.

* pesticide: 살충제 ** cultivar: 품종
*** breed: 개량하다

09 1등급 대비 고난도 2점 문제

고2•2023년 3월 38번

글의 흐름으로 보아, 주어진 문장이 들어가기에 가장 적절한 곳을 고르시오.

> In the electric organ the muscle cells are connected in larger chunks, which makes the total current intensity larger than in ordinary muscles.

Electric communication is mainly known in fish. The electric signals are produced in special electric organs. When the signal is discharged the electric organ will be negatively loaded compared to the head and an electric field is created around the fish. (①) A weak electric current is created also in ordinary muscle cells when they contract. (②) The fish varies the signals by changing the form of the electric field or the frequency of discharging. (③) The system is only working over small distances, about one to two meters. (④) This is an advantage since the species using the signal system often live in large groups with several other species. (⑤) If many fish send out signals at the same time, the short range decreases the risk of interference.

10 1등급 대비 고난도 2점 문제

고2•2017년 9월 39번

글의 흐름으로 보아, 주어진 문장이 들어가기에 가장 적절한 곳을 고르시오.

> However, concerns have been raised that cookies, which can track what people do online, may be violating privacy by helping companies or government agencies accumulate personal information.

Favorite websites sometimes greet users like old friends. Online bookstores welcome their customers by name and suggest new books they might like to read. (①) Real estate sites tell their visitors about new properties that have come on the market. (②) These tricks are made possible by cookies, small files that an Internet server stores inside individuals' web browsers so it can remember them. (③) Therefore, cookies can greatly benefit individuals. (④) For example, cookies save users the chore of having to enter names and addresses into e-commerce websites every time they make a purchase. (⑤) Security is another concern: Cookies make shared computers far less secure and offer hackers many ways to break into systems.

11 1등급 대비 고난도 2점 문제

고2·2018년 9월 38번

글의 흐름으로 보아, 주어진 문장이 들어가기에 가장 적절한 곳을 고르시오.

> This allows the solids to carry the waves more easily and efficiently, resulting in a louder sound.

Tap your finger on the surface of a wooden table or desk, and observe the loudness of the sound you hear. Then, place your ear flat on top of the table or desk. (①) With your finger about one foot away from your ear, tap the table top and observe the loudness of the sound you hear again. (②) The volume of the sound you hear with your ear on the desk is much louder than with it off the desk. (③) Sound waves are capable of traveling through many solid materials as well as through air. (④) Solids, like wood for example, transfer the sound waves much better than air typically does because the molecules in a solid substance are much closer and more tightly packed together than they are in air. (⑤) The density of the air itself also plays a determining factor in the loudness of sound waves passing through it.

* molecule: 분자

12 1등급 대비 고난도 3점 문제

고2·2018년 3월 39번

글의 흐름으로 보아, 주어진 문장이 들어가기에 가장 적절한 곳을 고르시오. [3점]

> A clay pot is an example of a material artifact, which, although transformed by human activity, is not all that far removed from its natural state.

By acting on either natural or artificial resources, through techniques, we alter them in various ways. (①) Thus we create *artifacts*, which form an important aspect of technologies. (②) A plastic cup, a contact lens, and a computer chip, on the other hand, are examples of artifacts that are far removed from the original states of the natural resources needed to create them. (③) Artifacts can serve as resources in other technological processes. (④) This is one of the important interaction effects within the technological system. (⑤) In other words, each new technology increases the stock of available tools and resources that can be employed by other technologies to produce new artifacts.

* artifact: 가공품

DAY 17

학습 Check!

▶ 몰라서 틀린 문항 × 표기 ▶ 헷갈렸거나 찍은 문항 △ 표기 ▶ ×, △ 문항은 다시 풀고 ✔ 표기를 하세요.

종료 시각	시 분 초
소요 시간	분 초
초과 시간	분 초

문항 번호	01	02	03	04	05	06	07	08	09	10	11	12
채점 결과												
틀린 문항 복습												

DAY 18 문장 삽입 03

※ 점수 표기가 없는 문항은 모두 2점입니다.

● 날짜 : 월 일 ● 시작 시각 : 시 분 초 ● 목표 시간 : 20분

01

고2 • 2021년 6월 39번

글의 흐름으로 보아, 주어진 문장이 들어가기에 가장 적절한 곳을 고르시오.

While other competitors were in awe of this incredible volume, Henry Ford dared to ask, "Can we do even better?"

Ransom Olds, the father of the Oldsmobile, could not produce his "horseless carriages" fast enough. In 1901 he had an idea to speed up the manufacturing process — instead of building one car at a time, he created the assembly line. (①) The acceleration in production was unheard-of — from an output of 425 automobiles in 1901 to an impressive 2,500 cars the following year. (②) He was, in fact, able to improve upon Olds's clever idea by introducing conveyor belts to the assembly line. (③) As a result, Ford's production went through the roof. (④) Instead of taking a day and a half to manufacture a Model T, as in the past, he was now able to spit them out at a rate of one car every ninety minutes. (⑤) The moral of the story is that good progress is often the herald of great progress.

* in awe of: ~에 깊은 감명을 받은 ** herald: 선구자

02

고2 • 2020년 3월 38번

글의 흐름으로 보아, 주어진 문장이 들어가기에 가장 적절한 곳을 고르시오.

Yet today if you program that same position into an ordinary chess program, it will immediately suggest the exact moves that Fischer made.

The boundary between uniquely human creativity and machine capabilities continues to change. (①) Returning to the game of chess, back in 1956, thirteen-year-old child prodigy Bobby Fischer made a pair of remarkably creative moves against grandmaster Donald Byrne. (②) First he sacrificed his knight, seemingly for no gain, and then exposed his queen to capture. (③) On the surface, these moves seemed insane, but several moves later, Fischer used these moves to win the game. (④) His creativity was praised at the time as the mark of genius. (⑤) It's not because the computer has memorized the Fischer-Byrne game, but rather because it searches far enough ahead to see that these moves really do pay off.

* prodigy: 신동, 영재

03

고2 • 2017년 6월 38번

글의 흐름으로 보아, 주어진 문장이 들어가기에 가장 적절한 곳을 고르시오.

> If this goes on for any length of time the reactions in our cells cannot continue and we die.

It is vitally important that wherever we go and whatever we do the body temperature is maintained at the temperature at which our enzymes work best. It is not the temperature at the surface of the body which matters. (①) It is the temperature deep inside the body which must be kept stable. (②) At only a few degrees above or below normal body temperature our enzymes cannot function properly. (③) All sorts of things can affect internal body temperature, including heat generated in the muscles during exercise, fevers caused by disease, and the external temperature. (④) We can control our temperature in lots of ways: we can change our clothing, the way we behave and how active we are. (⑤) But we also have an internal control mechanism: when we get too hot we start to sweat.

* enzyme: 효소

04

고2 • 2017년 11월 38번

글의 흐름으로 보아, 주어진 문장이 들어가기에 가장 적절한 곳을 고르시오.

> But it was more than just a centre for physical improvement.

In 1996, as construction workers cleared a site in downtown Athens for the foundations of a new Museum of Modern Art, they found traces of a large structure sitting on the bedrock. (①) A building had occupied this same spot some two-and-a-half thousand years earlier, when it was part of a wooded sanctuary outside the original city walls, on the banks of the River Ilissos. (②) The excavation uncovered the remains of a gymnasium, a wrestling arena, changing rooms and baths. (③) This had been a place for athletics and exercise, where the young men of Athens had trained to become soldiers and citizens. (④) The archaeologists soon realised that they had found one of the most significant sites in all of western European intellectual culture, a site referred to continually by history's greatest philosophers: the Lyceum of Aristotle. (⑤) It was the world's first university.

* sanctuary: 신전

05

고2 • 2019년 3월 39번

글의 흐름으로 보아, 주어진 문장이 들어가기에 가장 적절한 곳을 고르시오. [3점]

> Rather, it is the air moving through a small hole into a closed container, as a result of air being blown out of the container by a fan on the inside.

Hubert Cecil Booth is often credited with inventing the first powered mobile vacuum cleaner. (①) In fact, he only claimed to be the first to coin the term "vacuum cleaner" for devices of this nature, which may explain why he is so credited. (②) As we all know, the term "vacuum" is an inappropriate name, because there exists no vacuum in a vacuum cleaner. (③) But I suppose a "rapid air movement in a closed container to create suction" cleaner would not sound as scientific or be as handy a name. (④) Anyway, we are stuck with it historically, and it is hard to find any references to "vacuum" prior to Booth. (⑤) Interestingly, Booth himself did not use the term "vacuum" when he filed a provisional specification describing in general terms his intended invention.

* provisional specification: 임시 제품 설명서

06

고2 • 2022년 6월 38번

글의 흐름으로 보아, 주어진 문장이 들어가기에 가장 적절한 곳을 고르시오. [3점]

> This temperature is of the surface of the star, the part of the star which is emitting the light that can be seen.

One way of measuring temperature occurs if an object is hot enough to visibly glow, such as a metal poker that has been left in a fire. (①) The color of a glowing object is related to its temperature: as the temperature rises, the object is first red and then orange, and finally it gets white, the "hottest" color. (②) The relation between temperature and the color of a glowing object is useful to astronomers. (③) The color of stars is related to their temperature, and since people cannot as yet travel the great distances to the stars and measure their temperature in a more precise way, astronomers rely on their color. (④) The interior of the star is at a much higher temperature, though it is concealed. (⑤) But the information obtained from the color of the star is still useful.

07

고2 • 2022년 9월 38번

글의 흐름으로 보아, 주어진 문장이 들어가기에 가장 적절한 곳을 고르시오. [3점]

> However, the capacity to produce skin pigments is inherited.

Adaptation involves changes in a population, with characteristics that are passed from one generation to the next. This is different from acclimation — an individual organism's changes in response to an altered environment. (①) For example, if you spend the summer outside, you may acclimate to the sunlight: your skin will increase its concentration of dark pigments that protect you from the sun. (②) This is a temporary change, and you won't pass the temporary change on to future generations. (③) For populations living in intensely sunny environments, individuals with a good ability to produce skin pigments are more likely to thrive, or to survive, than people with a poor ability to produce pigments, and that trait becomes increasingly common in subsequent generations. (④) If you look around, you can find countless examples of adaptation. (⑤) The distinctive long neck of a giraffe, for example, developed as individuals that happened to have longer necks had an advantage in feeding on the leaves of tall trees.

* pigment: 색소

08

고3 • 2022학년도 6월 38번

글의 흐름으로 보아, 주어진 문장이 들어가기에 가장 적절한 곳을 고르시오.

> A problem, however, is that supervisors often work in locations apart from their employees and therefore are not able to observe their subordinates' performance.

In most organizations, the employee's immediate supervisor evaluates the employee's performance. (①) This is because the supervisor is responsible for the employee's performance, providing supervision, handing out assignments, and developing the employee. (②) Should supervisors rate employees on performance dimensions they cannot observe? (③) To eliminate this dilemma, more and more organizations are implementing assessments referred to as *360-degree evaluations*. (④) Employees are rated not only by their supervisors but by coworkers, clients or citizens, professionals in other agencies with whom they work, and subordinates. (⑤) The reason for this approach is that often coworkers and clients or citizens have a greater opportunity to observe an employee's performance and are in a better position to evaluate many performance dimensions.

* subordinate: 부하 직원

09 1등급 대비 고난도 2점 문제

고2 • 2022년 11월 38번

글의 흐름으로 보아, 주어진 문장이 들어가기에 가장 적절한 곳을 고르시오.

> It does this by making your taste buds perceive these flavors as bad and even disgusting.

In the natural world, if an animal consumes a plant with enough antinutrients to make it feel unwell, it won't eat that plant again. Intuitively, animals also know to stay away from these plants. Years of evolution and information being passed down created this innate intelligence. (①) This "intuition," though, is not just seen in animals. (②) Have you ever wondered why most children hate vegetables? (③) Dr. Steven Gundry justifies this as part of our genetic programming, our inner intelligence. (④) Since many vegetables are full of antinutrients, your body tries to keep you away from them while you are still fragile and in development. (⑤) As you grow and your body becomes stronger enough to tolerate these antinutrients, suddenly they no longer taste as bad as before.

* taste bud: 미뢰(味蕾)

10 1등급 대비 고난도 2점 문제

고2 • 2016년 11월 38번

글의 흐름으로 보아, 주어진 문장이 들어가기에 가장 적절한 곳을 고르시오.

> It is possible to obtain more natural-looking portraits when the camera shoots from the same level as the child's eyeline instead of being tilted.

The birth of a child in a family is often the reason why people begin to take up or rediscover photography. (①) In many ways, photographing a child is little different from photographing any other person. (②) What makes it different, however, is the relative height between a young child and an adult. (③) Using the camera at your own head height works well for photographing adults, but for children the camera will be tilted downward. (④) You are looking down on the child, literally and metaphorically, and the resulting picture can make the child look smaller and less significant than most parents would like. (⑤) For an eight year old, this might mean sitting down when shooting; and for a crawling baby, the best approach may be to lie on the floor.

11 1등급 대비 고난도 3점 문제

고2•2018년 9월 37번

글의 흐름으로 보아, 주어진 문장이 들어가기에 가장 적절한 곳을 고르시오. [3점]

> However, when a bill was introduced in Congress to outlaw such rules, the credit card lobby turned its attention to language.

Framing matters in many domains. (①) When credit cards started to become popular forms of payment in the 1970s, some retail merchants wanted to charge different prices to their cash and credit card customers. (②) To prevent this, credit card companies adopted rules that forbade their retailers from charging different prices to cash and credit customers. (③) Its preference was that if a company charged different prices to cash and credit customers, the credit price should be considered the "normal" (default) price and the cash price a discount — rather than the alternative of making the cash price the usual price and charging a surcharge to credit card customers. (④) The credit card companies had a good intuitive understanding of what psychologists would come to call "framing." (⑤) The idea is that choices depend, in part, on the way in which problems are stated.

12 1등급 대비 고난도 3점 문제

고2•2020년 6월 39번

글의 흐름으로 보아, 주어진 문장이 들어가기에 가장 적절한 곳을 고르시오. [3점]

> We have a continual desire to communicate our feelings and yet at the same time the need to conceal them for proper social functioning.

For hundreds of thousands of years our hunter-gatherer ancestors could survive only by constantly communicating with one another through nonverbal cues. Developed over so much time, before the invention of language, that is how the human face became so expressive, and gestures so elaborate. (①) With these counterforces battling inside us, we cannot completely control what we communicate. (②) Our real feelings continually leak out in the form of gestures, tones of voice, facial expressions, and posture. (③) We are not trained, however, to pay attention to people's nonverbal cues. (④) By sheer habit, we fixate on the words people say, while also thinking about what we'll say next. (⑤) What this means is that we are using only a small percentage of the potential social skills we all possess.

* counterforce: 반대 세력 ** sheer: 순전한

DAY 18

학습 Check!

▶ 몰라서 틀린 문항 × 표기 ▶ 헷갈렸거나 찍은 문항 △ 표기 ▶ ×, △ 문항은 다시 풀고 ✔ 표기를 하세요.

종료 시각	시 분 초
소요 시간	분 초
초과 시간	분 초

문항 번호	01	02	03	04	05	06	07	08	09	10	11	12
채점 결과												
틀린 문항 복습												

DAY 19 문장 삽입 04

※ 점수 표기가 없는 문항은 모두 2점입니다.

● 날짜 : 월 일 ● 시작 시각 : 시 분 초 ● 목표 시간 : 20분

01

고2 • 2023년 6월 38번

글의 흐름으로 보아, 주어진 문장이 들어가기에 가장 적절한 곳을 고르시오.

> Rather, we have to create a situation that doesn't actually occur in the real world.

The fundamental nature of the experimental method is manipulation and control. Scientists manipulate a variable of interest, and see if there's a difference. At the same time, they attempt to control for the potential effects of all other variables. The importance of controlled experiments in identifying the underlying causes of events cannot be overstated. (①) In the real-uncontrolled-world, variables are often correlated. (②) For example, people who take vitamin supplements may have different eating and exercise habits than people who don't take vitamins. (③) As a result, if we want to study the health effects of vitamins, we can't merely observe the real world, since any of these factors (the vitamins, diet, or exercise) may affect health. (④) That's just what scientific experiments do. (⑤) They try to separate the naturally occurring relationship in the world by manipulating one specific variable at a time, while holding everything else constant.

02

고2 • 2020년 11월 38번

글의 흐름으로 보아, 주어진 문장이 들어가기에 가장 적절한 곳을 고르시오.

> But the flowing takes time, and if your speed of impact is too great, the water won't be able to flow away fast enough, and so it pushes back at you.

Liquids are destructive. Foams feel soft because they are easily compressed; if you jump on to a foam mattress, you'll feel it give beneath you. (①) Liquids don't do this; instead they flow. (②) You see this in a river, or when you turn on a tap, or if you use a spoon to stir your coffee. (③) When you jump off a diving board and hit a body of water, the water has to flow away from you. (④) It's that force that stings your skin as you belly-flop into a pool, and makes falling into water from a great height like landing on concrete. (⑤) The incompressibility of water is also why waves can have such deadly power, and in the case of tsunamis, why they can destroy buildings and cities, tossing cars around easily.

* compress: 압축하다 ** give: (힘을 받아) 휘다

03

고2 • 2019년 9월 38번

글의 흐름으로 보아, 주어진 문장이 들어가기에 가장 적절한 곳을 고르시오.

> In much the same way, an array of technological, political, economic, cultural, and linguistic factors can exist and create a similar kind of pull or drag or friction.

Open international online access is understood using the metaphor "flat earth." It represents a world where information moves across the globe as easily as a hockey puck seems to slide across an ice rink's flat surface. (①) This framework, however, can be misleading — especially if we extend the metaphor. (②) As anyone who has crossed an ice rink can confirm, just because the surface of the rink appears flat and open does not necessarily mean that surface is smooth or even. (③) Rather, such surfaces tend to be covered by a wide array of dips and cracks and bumps that create a certain degree of pull or drag or friction on any object moving across it. (④) They affect how smoothly or directly information can move from point to point in global cyberspace. (⑤) Thus, while the earth might appear to be increasingly flat from the perspective of international online communication, it is far from frictionless.

04

고2 • 2017년 9월 38번

글의 흐름으로 보아, 주어진 문장이 들어가기에 가장 적절한 곳을 고르시오.

> Yet, although the robot is sophisticated, it lacks all motivation to act.

Emotion plays an essential role in all our pursuits — including our pursuit of happiness. (①) It is nearly impossible for us to imagine a life without emotion. (②) Think of an emotionless robot that, other than the capacity for emotions, has exactly the same physical and cognitive characteristics as humans. (③) The robot thinks and behaves in the same way that humans do. (④) It can discuss deep philosophical issues and follow complex logic; it can dig tunnels and build skyscrapers. (⑤) This is because even the most basic desires are dependent on emotions — the one thing this robot lacks.

05

고2 • 2021년 3월 38번

글의 흐름으로 보아, 주어진 문장이 들어가기에 가장 적절한 곳을 고르시오. [3점]

> However, some types of beliefs cannot be tested for truth because we cannot get external evidence in our lifetimes (such as a belief that the Earth will stop spinning on its axis by the year 9999 or that there is life on a planet 100-million light-years away).

Most beliefs — but not all — are open to tests of verification. This means that beliefs can be tested to see if they are correct or false. (①) Beliefs can be verified or falsified with objective criteria external to the person. (②) There are people who believe the Earth is flat and not a sphere. (③) Because we have objective evidence that the Earth is in fact a sphere, the flat Earth belief can be shown to be false. (④) Also, the belief that it will rain tomorrow can be tested for truth by waiting until tomorrow and seeing whether it rains or not. (⑤) Also, meta-physical beliefs (such as the existence and nature of a god) present considerable challenges in generating evidence that everyone is willing to use as a truth criterion.

* verification: 검증, 확인 ** falsify: 거짓임을 입증하다

06

고2 • 2022년 3월 39번

글의 흐름으로 보아, 주어진 문장이 들어가기에 가장 적절한 곳을 고르시오. [3점]

> Although sport clubs and leagues may have a fixed supply schedule, it is possible to increase the number of consumers who watch.

A supply schedule refers to the ability of a business to change their production rates to meet the demand of consumers. Some businesses are able to increase their production level quickly in order to meet increased demand. However, sporting clubs have a fixed, or inflexible(inelastic) production capacity. (①) They have what is known as a fixed supply schedule. (②) It is worth noting that this is not the case for sales of clothing, equipment, memberships and memorabilia. (③) But clubs and teams can only play a certain number of times during their season. (④) If fans and members are unable to get into a venue, that revenue is lost forever. (⑤) For example, the supply of a sport product can be increased by providing more seats, changing the venue, extending the playing season or even through new television, radio or Internet distribution.

* memorabilia: 기념품 ** venue: 경기장

07

고2 • 2019년 6월 39번

글의 흐름으로 보아, 주어진 문장이 들어가기에 가장 적절한 곳을 고르시오. [3점]

> The most profitable information likely comes through network connections that provide "inside" information.

You're probably already starting to see the tremendous value of network analysis for businesspeople. (①) In the business world, information is money: a tip about anything from a cheap supplier to a competitor's marketing campaign to an under-the-table merger discussion can inform strategic decisions that might yield millions of dollars in profits. (②) You might catch it on TV or in the newspaper, but that's information everyone knows. (③) And it isn't just information that travels through network connections — it's influence as well. (④) If you have a connection at another company, you can possibly ask your connection to push that company to do business with yours, to avoid a competitor, or to hold off on the launch of a product. (⑤) So clearly, any businessperson wants to increase their personal network.

* merger: 합병

08

고3 • 2021학년도 9월 38번

글의 흐름으로 보아, 주어진 문장이 들어가기에 가장 적절한 곳을 고르시오.

> As long as you do not run out of copies before completing this process, you will know that you have a sufficient number to go around.

We sometimes solve number problems almost without realizing it. (①) For example, suppose you are conducting a meeting and you want to ensure that everyone there has a copy of the agenda. (②) You can deal with this by labelling each copy of the handout in turn with the initials of each of those present. (③) You have then solved this problem without resorting to arithmetic and without explicit counting. (④) There are numbers at work for us here all the same and they allow precise comparison of one collection with another, even though the members that make up the collections could have entirely different characters, as is the case here, where one set is a collection of people, while the other consists of pieces of paper. (⑤) What numbers allow us to do is to compare the relative size of one set with another.

* arithmetic: 산수

09 1등급 대비 고난도 2점 문제

고2•2021년 9월 38번

글의 흐름으로 보아, 주어진 문장이 들어가기에 가장 적절한 곳을 고르시오.

> It is possible to argue, for example, that, today, the influence of books is vastly overshadowed by that of television.

Interest in ideology in children's literature arises from a belief that children's literary texts are culturally formative, and of massive importance educationally, intellectually, and socially. (①) Perhaps more than any other texts, they reflect society as it wishes to be, as it wishes to be seen, and as it unconsciously reveals itself to be, at least to writers. (②) Clearly, literature is not the only socialising agent in the life of children, even among the media. (③) There is, however, a considerable degree of interaction between the two media. (④) Many so-called children's literary classics are televised, and the resultant new book editions strongly suggest that viewing can encourage subsequent reading. (⑤) Similarly, some television series for children are published in book form.

* resultant: 그 결과로 생긴

10 1등급 대비 고난도 2점 문제

고2•2017년 11월 39번

글의 흐름으로 보아, 주어진 문장이 들어가기에 가장 적절한 곳을 고르시오.

> However, some say that a freer flow of capital has raised the risk of financial instability.

The liberalization of capital markets, where funds for investment can be borrowed, has been an important contributor to the pace of globalization. Since the 1970s there has been a trend towards a freer flow of capital across borders. (①) Current economic theory suggests that this should aid development. (②) Developing countries have limited domestic savings with which to invest in growth, and liberalization allows them to tap into a global pool of funds. (③) A global capital market also allows investors greater scope to manage and spread their risks. (④) The East Asian crisis of the late 1990s came in the wake of this kind of liberalization. (⑤) Without a strong financial system and a sound regulatory environment, capital market globalization can sow the seeds of instability in economies rather than growth.

11 1등급 대비 고난도 3점 문제

고2 • 2021년 11월 38번

글의 흐름으로 보아, 주어진 문장이 들어가기에 가장 적절한 곳을 고르시오. [3점]

> But this is a short-lived effect, and in the long run, people find such sounds too bright.

Brightness of sounds means much energy in higher frequencies, which can be calculated from the sounds easily. A violin has many more overtones compared to a flute and sounds brighter. (①) An oboe is brighter than a classical guitar, and a crash cymbal brighter than a double bass. (②) This is obvious, and indeed people like brightness. (③) One reason is that it makes sound subjectively louder, which is part of the loudness war in modern electronic music, and in the classical music of the 19th century. (④) All sound engineers know that if they play back a track to a musician that just has recorded this track and add some higher frequencies, the musician will immediately like the track much better. (⑤) So it is wise not to play back such a track with too much brightness, as it normally takes quite some time to convince the musician that less brightness serves his music better in the end.

12 1등급 대비 고난도 3점 문제

고2 • 2020년 9월 38번

글의 흐름으로 보아, 주어진 문장이 들어가기에 가장 적절한 곳을 고르시오. [3점]

> In terms of the overall value of an automobile, you can't drive without tires, but you can drive without cup holders and a portable technology dock.

Some resources, decisions, or activities are *important* (highly valuable on average) while others are *pivotal* (small changes make a big difference). Consider how two components of a car relate to a consumer's purchase decision: tires and interior design. Which adds more value on average? The tires. (①) They are essential to the car's ability to move, and they impact both safety and performance. (②) Yet tires generally do not influence purchase decisions because safety standards guarantee that all tires will be very safe and reliable. (③) Differences in interior features — optimal sound system, portable technology docks, number and location of cup holders — likely have far more effect on the consumer's buying decision. (④) Interior features, however, clearly have a greater impact on the purchase decision. (⑤) In our language, the tires are important, but the interior design is pivotal.

DAY 19

학습 Check!

▶ 몰라서 틀린 문항 × 표기 ▶ 헷갈렸거나 찍은 문항 △ 표기 ▶ ×, △ 문항은 다시 풀고 ✔ 표기를 하세요.

종료 시각	시 분 초	문항 번호	01	02	03	04	05	06	07	08	09	10	11	12
소요 시간	분 초	채점 결과												
초과 시간	분 초	틀린 문항 복습												

[해설편 p.129]

DAY 20 문장 삽입 05

※ 점수 표기가 없는 문항은 모두 2점입니다.

● 날짜 : 월 일 ● 시작 시각 : 시 분 초 ● 목표 시간 : 20분

01

고2•2022년 9월 39번

글의 흐름으로 보아, 주어진 문장이 들어가기에 가장 적절한 곳을 고르시오.

> This inequality produces the necessary conditions for the operation of a huge, global-scale engine that takes on heat in the tropics and gives it off in the polar regions.

On any day of the year, the tropics and the hemisphere that is experiencing its warm season receive much more solar radiation than do the polar regions and the colder hemisphere. (①) Averaged over the course of the year, the tropics and latitudes up to about 40° receive more total heat than they lose by radiation. (②) Latitudes above 40° receive less total heat than they lose by radiation. (③) Its working fluid is the atmosphere, especially the moisture it contains. (④) Air is heated over the warm earth of the tropics, expands, rises, and flows away both northward and southward at high altitudes, cooling as it goes. (⑤) It descends and flows toward the equator again from more northerly and southerly latitudes.

* latitude: 위도

02

고2•2020년 6월 38번

글의 흐름으로 보아, 주어진 문장이 들어가기에 가장 적절한 곳을 고르시오.

> A computer cannot make independent decisions, however, or formulate steps for solving problems, unless programmed to do so by humans.

It is important to remember that computers can only carry out instructions that humans give them. Computers can process data accurately at far greater speeds than people can, yet they are limited in many respects — most importantly, they lack common sense. (①) However, combining the strengths of these machines with human strengths creates synergy. (②) Synergy occurs when combined resources produce output that exceeds the sum of the outputs of the same resources employed separately. (③) A computer works quickly and accurately; humans work relatively slowly and make mistakes. (④) Even with sophisticated artificial intelligence, which enables the computer to learn and then implement what it learns, the initial programming must be done by humans. (⑤) Thus, a human-computer combination allows the results of human thought to be translated into efficient processing of large amounts of data.

03

고2 • 2018년 3월 38번

글의 흐름으로 보아, 주어진 문장이 들어가기에 가장 적절한 곳을 고르시오.

> However, this solution does not work in all situations because we also become increasingly sensitive to glare.

Two major kinds of age-related structural changes occur in the eye. One is a decrease in the amount of light that passes through the eye, resulting in the need for more light to do tasks such as reading. (①) As you might suspect, this change is one reason why older adults do not see as well in the dark, which may account in part for their reluctance to go places at night. (②) One possible logical response to the need for more light would be to increase illumination levels in general. (③) In addition, our ability to adjust to changes in illumination, called adaptation, declines. (④) Going from outside into a darkened movie theater involves dark adaptation; going back outside involves light adaptation. (⑤) Research indicates that the time it takes for both types of adaptation increases with age.

* illumination: 조도, 조명

04

고2 • 2017년 3월 39번

글의 흐름으로 보아, 주어진 문장이 들어가기에 가장 적절한 곳을 고르시오.

> Only after everyone had finished lunch would the hostess inform her guests that what they had just eaten was neither tuna salad nor chicken salad but rather rattlesnake salad.

A dramatic example of how culture can influence our biological processes was provided by anthropologist Clyde Kluckhohn, who spent much of his career in the American Southwest studying the Navajo culture. (①) Kluckhohn tells of a non-Navajo woman he knew in Arizona who took a somewhat perverse pleasure in causing a cultural response to food. (②) At luncheon parties she often served sandwiches filled with a light meat that resembled tuna or chicken but had a distinctive taste. (③) Invariably, someone would vomit upon learning what they had eaten. (④) Here, then, is an excellent example of how the biological process of digestion was influenced by a cultural idea. (⑤) Not only was the process influenced, it was reversed: the culturally based *idea* that rattlesnake meat is a disgusting thing to eat triggered a violent reversal of the normal digestive process.

* perverse: 심술궂은

05

고2 • 2018년 11월 39번

글의 흐름으로 보아, 주어진 문장이 들어가기에 가장 적절한 곳을 고르시오. [3점]

> Even though there may be a logically easy set of procedures to follow, it's still an emotional battle to change your habits and introduce new, uncomfortable behaviors that you are not used to.

Charisma is eminently learnable and teachable, and in many ways, it follows one of Newton's famed laws of motion: *For every action, there is an equal and opposite reaction*. (①) That is to say that all of charisma and human interaction is a set of signals and cues that lead to other signals and cues, and there is a science to deciphering which signals and cues work the most in your favor. (②) In other words, charisma can often be simplified as a checklist of what to do at what time. (③) However, it will require brief forays out of your comfort zone. (④) I like to say that it's just a matter of using muscles that have long been dormant. (⑤) It will take some time to warm them up, but it's only through practice and action that you will achieve your desired goal.

* decipher: 판독하다 ** foray: 시도
*** dormant: 활동을 중단한

06

고2 • 2021년 6월 38번

글의 흐름으로 보아, 주어진 문장이 들어가기에 가장 적절한 곳을 고르시오. [3점]

> However, transfer of one kind of risk often means inheriting another kind.

Risk often arises from uncertainty about how to approach a problem or situation. (①) One way to avoid such risk is to contract with a party who is experienced and knows how to do it. (②) For example, to minimize the financial risk associated with the capital cost of tooling and equipment for production of a large, complex system, a manufacturer might subcontract the production of the system's major components to suppliers familiar with those components. (③) This relieves the manufacturer of the financial risk associated with the tooling and equipment to produce these components. (④) For example, subcontracting work for the components puts the manufacturer in the position of relying on outsiders, which increases the risks associated with quality control, scheduling, and the performance of the end-item system. (⑤) But these risks often can be reduced through careful management of the suppliers.

* subcontract: 하청을 주다(일감을 다른 사람에게 맡기다)

07

고2 • 2019년 9월 39번

글의 흐름으로 보아, 주어진 문장이 들어가기에 가장 적절한 곳을 고르시오. [3점]

> Attitudes and values, however, are subjective to begin with, and therefore they are easily altered to fit our ever-changing circumstances and goals.

In physics, the principle of relativity requires that all equations describing the laws of physics have the same form regardless of inertial frames of reference. The formulas should appear identical to any two observers and to the same observer in a different time and space. (①) Thus, the same task can be viewed as boring one moment and engaging the next. (②) Divorce, unemployment, and cancer can seem devastating to one person but be perceived as an opportunity for growth by another person, depending on whether or not the person is married, employed, and healthy. (③) It is not only beliefs, attitudes, and values that are subjective. (④) Our brains comfortably change our perceptions of the physical world to suit our needs. (⑤) We will never see the same event and stimuli in exactly the same way at different times.

* inertial frame of reference: 관성좌표계

08

고3 • 2020학년도 수능 38번

글의 흐름으로 보아, 주어진 문장이 들어가기에 가장 적절한 곳을 고르시오.

> Thus, individuals of many resident species, confronted with the fitness benefits of control over a productive breeding site, may be forced to balance costs in the form of lower nonbreeding survivorship by remaining in the specific habitat where highest breeding success occurs.

Resident-bird habitat selection is seemingly a straightforward process in which a young dispersing individual moves until it finds a place where it can compete successfully to satisfy its needs. (①) Initially, these needs include only food and shelter. (②) However, eventually, the young must locate, identify, and settle in a habitat that satisfies not only survivorship but reproductive needs as well. (③) In some cases, the habitat that provides the best opportunity for survival may not be the same habitat as the one that provides for highest reproductive capacity because of requirements specific to the reproductive period. (④) Migrants, however, are free to choose the optimal habitat for survival during the nonbreeding season and for reproduction during the breeding season. (⑤) Thus, habitat selection during these different periods can be quite different for migrants as opposed to residents, even among closely related species.

* disperse: 흩어지다 ** optimal: 최적의

09 1등급 대비 고난도 2점 문제

고2 • 2019년 6월 38번

글의 흐름으로 보아, 주어진 문장이 들어가기에 가장 적절한 곳을 고르시오.

> The illusion of relative movement works the other way, too.

You are in a train, standing at a station next to another train. Suddenly you seem to start moving. But then you realize that you aren't actually moving at all. (①) It is the second train that is moving in the opposite direction. (②) You think the other train has moved, only to discover that it is your own train that is moving. (③) It can be hard to tell the difference between apparent movement and real movement. (④) It's easy if your train starts with a jolt, of course, but not if your train moves very smoothly. (⑤) When your train overtakes a slightly slower train, you can sometimes fool yourself into thinking your train is still and the other train is moving slowly backwards.

* apparent: 외견상의 ** jolt: 덜컥하고 움직임

10 1등급 대비 고난도 2점 문제

고2 • 2021년 3월 39번

글의 흐름으로 보아, 주어진 문장이 들어가기에 가장 적절한 곳을 고르시오.

> But the necessary and useful instinct to generalize can distort our world view.

Everyone automatically categorizes and generalizes all the time. Unconsciously. It is not a question of being prejudiced or enlightened. Categories are absolutely necessary for us to function. (①) They give structure to our thoughts. (②) Imagine if we saw every item and every scenario as truly unique — we would not even have a language to describe the world around us. (③) It can make us mistakenly group together things, or people, or countries that are actually very different. (④) It can make us assume everything or everyone in one category is similar. (⑤) And, maybe, most unfortunate of all, it can make us jump to conclusions about a whole category based on a few, or even just one, unusual example.

11 1등급 대비 고난도 3점 문제

고2・2018년 6월 37번

글의 흐름으로 보아, 주어진 문장이 들어가기에 가장 적절한 곳을 고르시오. [3점]

> Thinking of an internal cause for a person's behaviour is easy — the strict teacher is a stubborn person, the devoted parents just love their kids.

You may be wondering why people prefer to prioritize internal disposition over external situations when seeking causes to explain behaviour. One answer is simplicity. (①) In contrast, situational explanations can be complex. (②) Perhaps the teacher appears stubborn because she's seen the consequences of not trying hard in generations of students and wants to develop self-discipline in them. (③) Perhaps the parents who're boasting of the achievements of their children are anxious about their failures, and conscious of the cost of their school fees. (④) These situational factors require knowledge, insight, and time to think through. (⑤) Whereas, jumping to a dispositional attribution is far easier.

* disposition: 성질, 기질

12 1등급 대비 고난도 3점 문제

고2・2020년 9월 39번

글의 흐름으로 보아, 주어진 문장이 들어가기에 가장 적절한 곳을 고르시오. [3점]

> When an overall silence appears on beats 4 and 13, it is not because each musician is thinking, "On beats 4 and 13, I will rest."

In the West, an individual composer writes the music long before it is performed. The patterns and melodies we hear are pre-planned and intended. (①) Some African tribal music, however, results from collaboration by the players on the spur of the moment. (②) The patterns heard, whether they are the silences when all players rest on a beat or the accented beats when all play together, are not planned but serendipitous. (③) Rather, it occurs randomly as the patterns of all the players converge upon a simultaneous rest. (④) The musicians are probably as surprised as their listeners to hear the silences at beats 4 and 13. (⑤) Surely that surprise is one of the joys tribal musicians experience in making their music.

* serendipitous: 우연히 얻은 ** converge: 한데 모아지다

DAY 20

학습 Check!

▶ 몰라서 틀린 문항 × 표기 ▶ 헷갈렸거나 찍은 문항 △ 표기 ▶ ×, △ 문항은 다시 풀고 ✔ 표기를 하세요.

종료 시각	시 분 초
소요 시간	분 초
초과 시간	분 초

문항 번호	01	02	03	04	05	06	07	08	09	10	11	12
채점 결과												
틀린 문항 복습												

MEMO

SPEED 정답 체크 영어 독해 | 빈칸 순서 삽입 완성

PART Ⅰ • 빈칸 추론 [Day 01~Day 10]

Day 01 빈칸 추론 01

01 ① 02 ④ 03 ③ 04 ③ 05 ① 06 ② 07 ④ 08 ① 09 ⑤ 10 ⑤
11 ① 12 ⑤

Day 02 빈칸 추론 02

01 ② 02 ① 03 ⑤ 04 ① 05 ① 06 ③ 07 ② 08 ① 09 ② 10 ①
11 ② 12 ①

Day 03 빈칸 추론 03

01 ① 02 ③ 03 ③ 04 ④ 05 ② 06 ① 07 ② 08 ③ 09 ③ 10 ④
11 ⑤ 12 ③

Day 04 빈칸 추론 04

01 ① 02 ⑤ 03 ① 04 ① 05 ④ 06 ③ 07 ② 08 ② 09 ② 10 ①
11 ② 12 ①

Day 05 빈칸 추론 05

01 ④ 02 ③ 03 ② 04 ① 05 ④ 06 ③ 07 ④ 08 ① 09 ② 10 ②
11 ⑤ 12 ②

Day 06 빈칸 추론 06

01 ② 02 ① 03 ③ 04 ① 05 ③ 06 ③ 07 ① 08 ② 09 ① 10 ①
11 ① 12 ②

Day 07 빈칸 추론 07

01 ① 02 ⑤ 03 ③ 04 ① 05 ③ 06 ② 07 ① 08 ② 09 ② 10 ②
11 ⑤ 12 ①

Day 08 빈칸 추론 08

01 ① 02 ② 03 ② 04 ④ 05 ① 06 ③ 07 ① 08 ① 09 ② 10 ②
11 ② 12 ①

Day 09 빈칸 추론 09

01 ③ 02 ② 03 ① 04 ③ 05 ④ 06 ⑤ 07 ① 08 ④ 09 ① 10 ⑤
11 ④ 12 ①

Day 10 빈칸 추론 10

01 ① 02 ① 03 ⑤ 04 ③ 05 ② 06 ④ 07 ② 08 ② 09 ② 10 ①
11 ① 12 ②

PART Ⅱ • 글의 순서 [Day 11~Day 15]

Day 11 글의 순서 01

01 ② 02 ④ 03 ② 04 ② 05 ② 06 ⑤ 07 ③ 08 ⑤ 09 ② 10 ⑤
11 ③ 12 ④

Day 12 글의 순서 02

01 ④ 02 ② 03 ② 04 ⑤ 05 ④ 06 ② 07 ③ 08 ⑤ 09 ② 10 ②
11 ② 12 ⑤

Day 13 글의 순서 03

01 ③ 02 ② 03 ⑤ 04 ③ 05 ③ 06 ② 07 ⑤ 08 ③ 09 ④ 10 ③
11 ⑤ 12 ③

Day 14 글의 순서 04

01 ② 02 ④ 03 ② 04 ② 05 ⑤ 06 ③ 07 ② 08 ③ 09 ⑤ 10 ⑤
11 ① 12 ②

Day 15 글의 순서 05

01 ⑤ 02 ③ 03 ⑤ 04 ⑤ 05 ⑤ 06 ③ 07 ⑤ 08 ③ 09 ② 10 ④
11 ③ 12 ⑤

PART Ⅲ • 문장 삽입 [Day 16~Day 20]

Day 16 문장 삽입 01

01 ④ 02 ⑤ 03 ③ 04 ⑤ 05 ④ 06 ④ 07 ③ 08 ③ 09 ③ 10 ④
11 ⑤ 12 ③

Day 17 문장 삽입 02

01 ② 02 ④ 03 ④ 04 ③ 05 ④ 06 ④ 07 ③ 08 ④ 09 ② 10 ⑤
11 ⑤ 12 ②

Day 18 문장 삽입 03

01 ② 02 ⑤ 03 ③ 04 ④ 05 ③ 06 ④ 07 ③ 08 ② 09 ⑤ 10 ⑤
11 ③ 12 ①

Day 19 문장 삽입 04

01 ④ 02 ④ 03 ④ 04 ⑤ 05 ⑤ 06 ⑤ 07 ③ 08 ③ 09 ③ 10 ④
11 ⑤ 12 ④

Day 20 문장 삽입 05

01 ③ 02 ④ 03 ③ 04 ③ 05 ④ 06 ④ 07 ① 08 ④ 09 ② 10 ③
11 ① 12 ③

※ 절취선을 따라 잘라서 쓰실 수 있습니다.

수능 내신 1등급 대비 전국연합 학력평가

20일 완성 영어 독해

수능기출 베스트셀러
리 얼 오 리 지 널

빈칸 순서 삽입

The Real series ipsifly provide questions in previous real test and you can practice as real college scholastic ability test.

20 Days completed

2020

하루 20분

20일 완성

완성
해설편

- 고2 최근 7개년 전국연합학력평가 기출 [빈칸·순서·삽입] 총 240문항 수록
- 하루 12문제를 20분씩 학습하는 [20일 완성] 영어 1등급 PLAN
- 평이한 2점, 3점 문항과 [고난도 2점, 3점] 문항을 매회 체계적으로 배치
- 지문의 이해를 돕는 [직독직해, 구문풀이] 해설 및 고난도 문제 해결 꿀팁

수능 모의고사 전문 출판
입시플라이

SPEED 정답 체크 영어 독해 | 빈칸 순서 삽입 완성

PART Ⅰ • 빈칸 추론 [Day 01~Day 10]

Day 01 빈칸 추론 01

01 ① 02 ④ 03 ③ 04 ③ 05 ① 06 ② 07 ④ 08 ① 09 ⑤ 10 ⑤ 11 ① 12 ⑤

Day 02 빈칸 추론 02

01 ② 02 ① 03 ⑤ 04 ① 05 ① 06 ③ 07 ② 08 ① 09 ② 10 ① 11 ② 12 ①

Day 03 빈칸 추론 03

01 ① 02 ③ 03 ③ 04 ④ 05 ② 06 ① 07 ② 08 ③ 09 ③ 10 ④ 11 ⑤ 12 ③

Day 04 빈칸 추론 04

01 ① 02 ⑤ 03 ① 04 ① 05 ④ 06 ③ 07 ② 08 ② 09 ② 10 ① 11 ② 12 ①

Day 05 빈칸 추론 05

01 ④ 02 ③ 03 ② 04 ① 05 ④ 06 ③ 07 ④ 08 ① 09 ② 10 ② 11 ⑤ 12 ②

Day 06 빈칸 추론 06

01 ② 02 ① 03 ③ 04 ① 05 ③ 06 ③ 07 ① 08 ② 09 ① 10 ① 11 ① 12 ②

Day 07 빈칸 추론 07

01 ① 02 ⑤ 03 ③ 04 ① 05 ③ 06 ② 07 ① 08 ② 09 ② 10 ② 11 ⑤ 12 ①

Day 08 빈칸 추론 08

01 ① 02 ② 03 ② 04 ④ 05 ① 06 ③ 07 ① 08 ① 09 ② 10 ② 11 ② 12 ①

Day 09 빈칸 추론 09

01 ③ 02 ② 03 ① 04 ③ 05 ④ 06 ⑤ 07 ① 08 ④ 09 ① 10 ⑤ 11 ④ 12 ①

Day 10 빈칸 추론 10

01 ① 02 ① 03 ⑤ 04 ③ 05 ② 06 ④ 07 ② 08 ② 09 ② 10 ① 11 ① 12 ②

PART Ⅱ • 글의 순서 [Day 11~Day 15]

Day 11 글의 순서 01

01 ② 02 ④ 03 ② 04 ② 05 ② 06 ⑤ 07 ③ 08 ⑤ 09 ② 10 ⑤ 11 ③ 12 ④

Day 12 글의 순서 02

01 ④ 02 ② 03 ② 04 ⑤ 05 ④ 06 ② 07 ③ 08 ⑤ 09 ② 10 ② 11 ② 12 ⑤

Day 13 글의 순서 03

01 ③ 02 ② 03 ⑤ 04 ③ 05 ③ 06 ② 07 ⑤ 08 ③ 09 ④ 10 ③ 11 ⑤ 12 ③

Day 14 글의 순서 04

01 ② 02 ④ 03 ② 04 ② 05 ⑤ 06 ③ 07 ② 08 ③ 09 ⑤ 10 ⑤ 11 ① 12 ②

Day 15 글의 순서 05

01 ⑤ 02 ③ 03 ⑤ 04 ⑤ 05 ⑤ 06 ③ 07 ⑤ 08 ③ 09 ② 10 ④ 11 ③ 12 ⑤

PART Ⅲ • 문장 삽입 [Day 16~Day 20]

Day 16 문장 삽입 01

01 ④ 02 ⑤ 03 ③ 04 ⑤ 05 ④ 06 ④ 07 ③ 08 ③ 09 ③ 10 ④ 11 ⑤ 12 ③

Day 17 문장 삽입 02

01 ② 02 ④ 03 ④ 04 ③ 05 ④ 06 ④ 07 ③ 08 ④ 09 ② 10 ⑤ 11 ⑤ 12 ②

Day 18 문장 삽입 03

01 ② 02 ⑤ 03 ③ 04 ④ 05 ③ 06 ④ 07 ③ 08 ② 09 ⑤ 10 ⑤ 11 ③ 12 ①

Day 19 문장 삽입 04

01 ④ 02 ④ 03 ④ 04 ⑤ 05 ⑤ 06 ⑤ 07 ③ 08 ③ 09 ③ 10 ④ 11 ⑤ 12 ④

Day 20 문장 삽입 05

01 ③ 02 ④ 03 ③ 04 ③ 05 ④ 06 ④ 07 ① 08 ④ 09 ② 10 ③ 11 ① 12 ③

20일 완성 영어독해

빈칸 순서 삽입 완성

해설편

Contents

PART Ⅰ 빈칸 추론

PART Ⅱ 글의 순서

PART Ⅲ 문장 삽입

REAL ORIGINAL

수록된 정답률은 실제와 차이가 있을 수 있습니다. 문제 난도를 파악하는데 참고용으로 활용하시기 바랍니다.

DAY 01 빈칸 추론 01

01 ①	02 ④	03 ③	04 ③	05 ①
06 ②	07 ④	08 ①	09 ⑤	10 ⑤
11 ①	12 ⑤			

01 자기 소유의 물건의 가치를 과대평가하는 경향

정답률 71% | 정답 ①

다음 빈칸에 들어갈 말로 가장 적절한 것을 고르시오.

✓ overvalue – 과대평가할
② exchange – 교환할
③ disregard – 무시할
④ conceal – 숨길
⑤ share – 공유할

Once we own something, / we're far more likely to overvalue it.
일단 우리가 어떤 것을 소유하면, / 우리는 그것을 과대평가할 가능성이 훨씬 더 높다.

In a study conducted at Duke University, / students who won basketball tickets / in an extremely onerous lottery / (one that they had to wait in line to enter for more than a day) / said they wouldn't sell their tickets / for less than, on average, $2,400.
Duke 대학교에서 실시된 한 연구에서, / 농구 티켓을 얻은 학생들은 / 극도로 성가신 추첨에서 / (그들이 참여하기 위해 하루 이상 줄을 서서 기다려야 하는 것) / 자신의 티켓을 팔지 않을 것이라고 말했다. / 평균적으로 2,400달러 아래로는

But students who had waited and hadn't won / said they would only pay, on average, $170 per ticket.
그러나 기다렸지만 티켓을 얻지 못한 학생들은 / 단지 평균적으로 티켓당 170달러를 지불할 것이라고 말했다.

Once a student owned the tickets, / he or she saw them / as being worth much more in the market / than they were.
일단 학생이 티켓을 소유하면 / 그 또는 그녀는 그것을 여겼다. / 시장에서 훨씬 더 많은 가치가 있다고 / 실제로 그러한 것보다

In another example, / during the housing market crash of 2008, / a real estate website conducted a survey / to see / how homeowners felt the crash affected the price of their homes.
또 다른 사례에서 / 2008년의 주택시장 붕괴 동안에 / 부동산 웹 사이트가 설문조사를 실시했다. / 알아보기 위해 / 주택 소유자들이 느끼기에 그 붕괴가 자신들의 주택의 가격에 어떻게 영향을 미쳤는지를

92% of respondents, aware of nearby foreclosures, asserted / these had hurt the price of homes in their neighborhood.
인근의 압류를 인식하고 있는 응답자 중 92%가 단언했다. / 이것이 자신의 지역에 있는 주택의 가격을 손상시켰다고

However, when asked about the price of their *own* home, / 62% believed it had increased.
하지만 그들 *소유의* 주택 가격에 대해 질문을 받았을 때, / 62%는 그것이 상승했다고 믿었다.

일단 우리가 어떤 것을 소유하면, 우리는 그것을 과대평가할 가능성이 훨씬 더 높다. Duke 대학에서 실시된 한 연구에서, 극도로 성가신 추첨(참여하기 위해 하루 이상 줄을 서서 기다려야 하는 것)에서 농구 티켓을 얻은 학생들은 평균적으로 2,400달러 아래로는 자신의 티켓을 팔지 않을 것이라고 말했다. 그러나 기다렸지만 티켓을 얻지 못한 학생들은 단지 평균적으로 티켓당 170달러를 지불할 것이라고 말했다. 일단 학생이 티켓을 소유하면 그 또는 그녀는 실제로 그러한 것보다 그것이 시장에서 훨씬 더 많은 가치가 있다고 여겼다. 또 다른 사례에서 2008년의 주택시장 붕괴 동안에 부동산 웹 사이트가 주택 소유자들이 느끼기에 그 붕괴가 자신들의 주택의 가격에 어떻게 영향을 미쳤는지를 알아보기 위해 설문조사를 실시했다. 인근의 압류를 인식하고 있는 응답자 중 92%가 이것이 자신의 지역에 있는 주택의 가격을 손상시켰다고 단언했다. 하지만 그들 *소유의* 주택 가격에 대해 질문을 받았을 때, 62%는 그것이 상승했다고 믿었다.

Why? 왜 정답일까?

첫 문장인 주제문을 완성하는 빈칸 문제로, 빈칸 이후의 두 예시를 적절히 일반화하여 빈칸에 들어갈 말을 추론해야 한다. 예시의 결론 문장에서 각각 티켓을 소유한 학생은 실제보다 티켓의 가치를 높게 보았고, 자기 소유의 주택가에 대해 질문을 받은 사람들은 가격이 상승했다고 믿었다는 내용이 나온다. 이를 일반화하면, 사람들은 자신이 소유하게 된 것의 가치를 실제보다 크게 추산하는 경향이 있다는 결론을 도출할 수 있다. 따라서 빈칸에 들어갈 말로 가장 적절한 것은 ① '과대평가할'이다.

- extremely ad 극도로
- wait in line 줄을 서서 기다리다
- real estate 부동산
- overvalue ⓥ 과대평가하다
- lottery ⓝ 추첨, 도박, 복권
- crash ⓝ 붕괴, 도산
- assert ⓥ 단언하다, 확고히 하다
- disregard ⓥ 무시하다

구문 풀이

2행 In a study conducted at Duke University, / students [who won basketball tickets in an extremely onerous lottery] / (one [that they had to wait in line to enter for more than a day]) / said (that) they wouldn't sell their tickets for less than, on average, $2,400.

(conducted: 과거분사 / students: 주어(선행사) / who: 주격 관계대명사 / one: =a lottery / that: 목적격 관계대명사 / to enter: 부사적 용법(~하기 위해) / said: 동사 / (that): 생략(접속사))

02 과학과 예술 분야에서 창의성의 보편성

정답률 40% | 정답 ④

다음 빈칸에 들어갈 말로 가장 적절한 것을 고르시오. [3점]

① formality – 형식성
② objectivity – 객관성
③ complexity – 복잡성
✓ universality – 보편성
⑤ uncertainty – 불확실성

A good many scientists and artists / have noticed the universality of creativity.
상당한 수의 과학자들과 예술가들이 / 창의성의 보편성에 대해 주목해 왔다.

At the Sixteenth Nobel Conference, / held in 1980, / scientists, musicians, and philosophers all agreed, / to quote Freeman Dyson, / that "the analogies between science and art are very good / as long as you are talking / about the creation and the performance.
제16차 노벨 회의에서 / 1980년에 열린 / 과학자들, 음악가들 그리고 철학자들은 모두 동의했다. / Freeman Dyson의 말을 인용하여 / "과학과 예술 사이의 유사성은 매우 높습니다. / 여러분이 이야기하고 있는 한 / 창조와 행위에 관해

The creation is certainly very analogous.
창조는 분명 매우 유사합니다.

The aesthetic pleasure / of the craftsmanship of performance / is also very strong in science."
미적 쾌감은 / 행위의 솜씨에서 나오는 / 과학에서도 매우 큽니다."라는 것에

A few years later, / at another multidisciplinary conference, / physicist Murray Gell-Mann found / that "everybody agrees on / where ideas come from.
몇 년 후, / 또 다른 여러 학문 분야에 걸친 회의에서 / 물리학자인 Murray Gell-Mann은 알아냈다. / "모두가 동의합니다. / 아이디어가 어디에서 오는지에 대해

We had a seminar here, / about ten years ago, / including several painters, a poet, a couple of writers, and the physicists.
우리는 이곳에서 세미나를 했습니다. / 약 10년 전 / 몇 명의 화가, 시인 한 명, 두 세 명의 작가 그리고 물리학자들을 포함하여

Everybody agrees on / how it works.
모두는 동의합니다. / 그것이 어떻게 진행되는지에 대해

All of these people, / whether they are doing artistic work or scientific work, / are trying to solve a problem."
이 사람들 모두는 / 자신들이 예술적인 일이든 과학적인 일을 하고 있든 / 문제를 해결하려고 노력하고 있습니다."라는 것을

상당한 수의 과학자들과 예술가들이 창의성의 보편성에 대해 주목해 왔다. 1980년에 열린 제16차 노벨 회의에서 과학자들, 음악가들 그리고 철학자들은 Freeman Dyson의 말을 인용하여 "여러분이 창조와 행위에 관해 이야기하고 있는 한 과학과 예술 사이의 유사성은 매우 높습니다. 창조는 분명 매우 유사합니다. 행위의 솜씨에서 나오는 미적 쾌감은 과학에서도 매우 큽니다."라는 것에 모두 동의했다. 몇 년 후, 또 다른 여러 학문 분야에 걸친 회의에서 물리학자인 Murray Gell-Mann은 "모두가 아이디어가 어디에서 오는지에 대해 동의합니다. 우리는 화가 여러 명, 시인 한 명, 작가 두서넛 명 그리고 물리학자들을 포함하여 약 10년 전 이곳에서 세미나를 했습니다. 모두는 그것이 어떻게 진행되는지에 대해 동의합니다. 이 사람들 모두는 자신들이 예술적인 일을 하고 있든 과학적인 일을 하고 있든 문제를 해결하려고 노력하고 있습니다."라는 것을 알아냈다.

Why? 왜 정답일까?

과학과 예술이라는 서로 다른 분야에서도 창조의 행위는 서로 유사하며(~ **the analogies between science and art are very good as long as you are talking about the creation and the performance. The creation is certainly very analogous.**), 과학자들과 예술가들 모두 아이디어가 어디서 나오고 창조가 어떻게 진행되는가에 대해 의견을 같이한다는 내용의 글이다. 따라서 주제를 요약해 나타내는 빈칸에 들어갈 말로 가장 적절한 것은 ④ '보편성'이다.

- a good many 상당한 수의
- analogy ⓝ 유사성, 유추
- craftsmanship ⓝ (훌륭한) 솜씨
- quote ⓥ 인용하다
- aesthetic ⓐ 미적인
- multidisciplinary ⓐ 여러 학문 분야에 걸친

구문 풀이

2행 At the Sixteenth Nobel Conference, (which was) held in 1980, / scientists, musicians, and philosophers all agreed, to quote Freeman Dyson, {that "the analogies between science and art are very good / as long as you are talking about the creation and the performance}.

선행사 / 생략 / 주어 / 동사 / 주어 / 동사 / ~하는 한 / { }: 목적어

03 가짜 뉴스의 확산을 막는 방법

정답률 67% | 정답 ③

다음 빈칸에 들어갈 말로 가장 적절한 것을 고르시오.

① political campaigns – 정치 운동
② irrational censorship – 불합리한 검열
③ irresponsible sharing – 무책임한 공유
④ overheated marketing – 과열된 마케팅
⑤ statistics manipulation – 통계 수치 조작

Much of the spread of fake news / occurs through irresponsible sharing.
많은 가짜 뉴스 확산은 / 무책임한 공유를 통해 일어난다.

A 2016 study from Columbia University in New York City / and Inria, a French technology institute, / found / that 59 percent of the news from links / shared on social media / wasn't read first.
2016년 뉴욕에 위치한 Columbia University와 / 프랑스의 기술원인 Inria의 연구는 / 밝혀냈다. / 링크로부터의 뉴스 중 59퍼센트가 / 소셜 미디어에서 공유된 / 먼저 읽히지 않았음을

People see an intriguing headline or photo / in their news feed or on another website / and then click the Share button / to repost the item to their social media friends / — without ever clicking through to the full article.
사람들은 흥미로운 제목이나 사진을 보고, / 자신의 뉴스 피드나 다른 웹 사이트에 있는 / '공유하기' 버튼을 클릭한다. / 자신의 소셜 미디어 친구들을 대상으로 다시 게시하기 위해 / 클릭해서 기사 전체를 살펴보지도 않은 채

Then they may be sharing fake news.
그러면 그들은 가짜 뉴스를 공유하고 있는지도 모른다.

To stop the spread of fake news, / read stories before you share them.
가짜 뉴스의 확산을 막기 위해, / 기사를 공유하기 전에 그것을 읽어보아라.

Respect your social media friends / enough to know what information you are sending their way.
여러분의 소셜 미디어 친구들을 존중하라. / 여러분이 그들에게 어떤 정보를 보내고 있는지 알 만큼 충분히

You may discover, on close inspection, / that an article you were about to share / is obviously fraudulent, / that it doesn't really say what the headline promises, / or that you actually disagree with it.
자세히 들여다보면, 여러분은 발견할지도 모른다. / 여러분이 공유하려는 기사가 / 분명 속이는 것이라거나, / 그것이 제목이 약속하는 것을 정말로 이야기하지 않는다거나, / 또는 여러분이 실제로 그것에 동의하지 않는다는 것을

많은 가짜 뉴스 확산은 무책임한 공유를 통해 일어난다. 2016년 뉴욕에 위치한 Columbia University와 프랑스의 기술원인 Inria의 연구는 소셜 미디어에서 공유된 링크로부터의 뉴스 중 59퍼센트가 먼저 읽히지 않았음을 밝혀냈다. 사람들은 자신의 뉴스 피드나 다른 웹 사이트에 있는 흥미로운 제목이나 사진을 보고, 클릭해서 기사 전체를 살펴보지도 않은 채, 자신의 소셜 미디어 친구들을 대상으로 다시 게시하기 위해 '공유하기' 버튼을 클릭한다. 그러면 그들은 가짜 뉴스를 공유하고 있는지도 모른다. 가짜 뉴스의 확산을 막기 위해, 기사를 공유하기 전에 그것을 읽어보아라. 여러분이 그들에게 어떤 정보를 보내고 있는지 알 만큼 충분히 여러분의 소셜 미디어 친구들을 존중하라. 자세히 들여다보면, 여러분은 공유하려는 기사가 분명 속이는 것이라거나, 제목이 약속하는 것을 정말로 이야기하지 않는다거나, 또는 여러분이 실제로 그것에 동의하지 않는다는 것을 발견할지도 모른다.

Why? 왜 정답일까?

'**People see an intriguing headline or photo in their news feed or on another website and then click the Share button to repost the item to their social media friends—without ever clicking through to the full article. Then they may be sharing fake news.**'에서 뉴스를 공유하기 전에 그것을 제대로 읽어보지 않음으로 인해 가짜 뉴스가 확산되고 있다고 지적한 후, 이를 막기 위해서는 뉴스를 공유하기 앞서 전체 내용을 확인할 필요가 있음을 주장한 글이다. 따라서 빈칸에 들어갈 말로 가장 적절한 것은 ③ '무책임한 공유'이다.

- spread ⓝ 확산
- inspection ⓝ 검토, 조사
- irrational ⓐ 불합리한, 비이성적인
- overheated ⓐ 과열된
- intriguing ⓐ 흥미로운
- be about to ~하려고 하다
- censorship ⓝ 검열
- manipulation ⓝ 조작

구문 풀이

6행 People see an intriguing headline or photo in their news feed or on another website and then click the Share button to repost the item to their social media friends — without ever clicking through to the full article.

동사1 / 동사2 / ~하기 위해 / 「without + 동명사 : ~하지 않은 채」

04 어떤 행동을 막을 수 있는 효과적인 기법

정답률 57% | 정답 ③

다음 빈칸에 들어갈 말로 가장 적절한 것을 고르시오.

① ignore what experts say
전문가들의 말을 무시할
② keep a close eye on the situation
상황을 면밀히 관찰할
③ shift our emphasis from behavior to character
행동에서 품성으로 강조점을 옮길
④ focus on appealing to emotion rather than reason
이성보다 감정에 호소하는 데 초점을 둘
⑤ place more importance on the individual instead of the group
집단 대신 개인에 더 중점을 둘

Psychologist Christopher Bryan finds / that when we shift our emphasis from behavior to character, / people evaluate choices differently.
심리학자인 Christopher Bryan은 밝힌다. / 우리가 행동에서 품성으로 강조점을 옮길 때, / 사람들은 선택을 다르게 평가한다는 것을

His team was able to cut cheating in half: / instead of "Please don't cheat," / they changed the appeal / to "Please don't be a cheater."
그의 팀은 속이는 행위를 반으로 줄일 수 있었는데, / '속이지 마세요'라는 문구 대신에, / 그들은 호소를 전환했다. / '속이는 사람이 되지 마세요'라는 문구로

When you're urged not to cheat, / you can do it / and still see an ethical person in the mirror.
당신이 속이지 말라고 강요받을 때, / 당신은 그렇게 하고도 / 여전히 거울 속에서 도덕적인 사람을 마주할 수 있다.

But when you're told not to be a cheater, / the act casts a shadow; / immorality is tied to your identity, / making the behavior much less attractive.
하지만 당신이 속이는 사람이 되지 말라고 들을 때는 / 그 행동이 그림자를 드리우는데, / 비도덕성이 당신의 정체성과 결부되어 / 그 행동을 훨씬 덜 매력적으로 만든다.

Cheating is an isolated action / that gets evaluated with the logic of consequence: / Can I get away with it?
속이는 행동은 독립적인 행위이다. / 결과의 논리에 따라 평가되는 / 내가 들키지 않을 수 있을까?

Being a cheater evokes a sense of self, / triggering the logic of appropriateness: / What kind of person am I, / and who do I want to be?
속이는 사람이 되는 것은 자의식을 환기시키며 / 적절함에 대한 논리를 촉발한다. / 나는 어떤 종류의 사람인가, / 그리고 나는 어떤 사람이 되고 싶은가?

In light of this evidence, / Bryan suggests / that we should embrace nouns more thoughtfully.
이러한 증거에 비추어 볼 때, / Bryan은 제안한다. / 우리가 명사를 더욱 사려 깊게 받아들여야 한다고

"Don't Drink and Drive" could be rephrased as: / "Don't Be a Drunk Driver."
'음주운전 하지 마세요'는 ~라고 바꿔 말할 수 있다. / '음주 운전자가 되지 마세요'

The same thinking can be applied to originality.
같은 논리가 독창성에도 적용될 수 있다.

When a child draws a picture, / instead of calling the artwork creative, / we can say "You are creative."
아이가 그림을 그릴 때, / 작품이 창의적이라고 말하는 대신에 / 우리는 '너는 창의적이구나'라고 말해줄 수 있다.

심리학자인 Christopher Bryan은 우리가 행동에서 품성으로 강조점을 옮길 때, 사람들은 선택을 다르게 평가한다는 것을 밝힌다. 그의 팀은 속이는 행위를 반으로 줄일 수 있었는데, '속이지 마세요'라는 문구 대신에, 그들은 '속이는 사람이 되지 마세요'라는 문구로 호소를 전환했다. 당신이 속이지 말라고 강요받을 때, 당신은 속이고 나서도 여전히 거울 속에서 도덕적인 사람을 마주할 수 있다. 하지만 당신이 속이는 사람이 되지 말라고 들을 때는 그 행동이 그림자를 드리우는데, 비도덕성이 당신의 정체성과 결부되어 그 행동을 훨씬 덜 매력적으로 만든다. 속이는 행동은 결과의 논리에 따라 평가되는 독립적인 행위이다. 내가 들키지 않을 수 있을까? 속이는 사람이 되는 것은 자의식을 환기시키며 적절함에 대한 논리를 촉발한다. 나는 어떤 종류의 사람인가, 그리고 나는 어떤 사람이 되고 싶은가? 이러한 증거에 비추어 볼 때, Bryan은 우리가 명사를 더욱 사려 깊게 받아들여야 한다고 제안한다. '음주운전 하지 마세요'는 '음주 운전자가 되지 마세요'로 바꿔 말할 수 있다. 같은 논리가 독창성에도 적용될 수 있다. 아이가 그림을 그릴 때, 작품이 창의적이라고 말하는 대신에 우리는 '너는 창의적이구나'라고 말해줄 수 있다.

[문제편 p.010]

Why? 왜 정답일까?

빈칸 뒤의 예시에 따르면, 어떤 행동을 막고 싶을 때 단지 그 행동을 하지 말라는 메시지보다는, 그 행동과 정체성을 연결시킨 메시지를 이용할 때 더 효과적일 수 있다고 한다. 즉, 단지 '~하지 말라'는 메시지보다는 '~하는 사람이 되지 말라'는 식으로 자의식이나 품성을 건드릴 수 있는 진술이 행동 방지 효과를 더 크게 나타낸다는 것이다. 따라서 빈칸에 들어갈 말로 가장 적절한 것은 ③ '행동에서 품성으로 강조점을 옮길'이다.

- **cut in half** 절반으로 줄이다
- **urge** ⓥ 촉구하다
- **cast a shadow** 그림자를 드리우다
- **be tied to** ~와 결부되다
- **get away with** ~에서 벗어나다
- **appropriateness** ⓝ 적절성
- **emphasis** ⓝ 강조, 역점
- **cheat** ⓥ 속이다
- **ethical** ⓐ 도덕적인, 윤리적인
- **immorality** ⓝ 부도덕함
- **isolated** ⓐ 고립된, 동떨어진
- **evoke** ⓥ (감정 등을) 불러일으키다
- **in light of** ~에 비추어볼 때
- **place importance on** ~에 중점을 두다

구문 풀이

7행 But when you're told not to be a cheater, the act casts a shadow; immorality is tied to your identity, making the behavior much less attractive.
(be told not＋to부정사 : ~하지 말라고 듣다 / 분사구문)

05 촉각과 청각의 유사성

정답률 48% | 정답 ①

다음 빈칸에 들어갈 말로 가장 적절한 것을 고르시오. [3점]

✔ a specialized form of touch
촉각의 분화된 한 형태
② an instinct rather than a learnt skill
학습된 능력이기보다는 본능
③ a sense resistant to frequency changes
진동수 변화에 내성이 있는 감각
④ an excellent way to build better understanding
더 나은 이해를 쌓아나가는 탁월한 방법
⑤ an experience different from feeling vibrations
진동을 느끼는 것과는 다른 경험

Hearing is basically a specialized form of touch.
청각은 기본적으로 촉각의 분화된 한 형태이다.
Sound is simply vibrating air / which the ear picks up / and converts to electrical signals, / which are then interpreted by the brain.
소리는 공기 진동이고, / 단순히 귀가 포착하여 / 전기 신호로 전환하는 / 그 전기 신호들은 이후 뇌에 의해 해석된다.
The sense of hearing is not the only sense / that can do this; / touch can do this too.
청각이라는 감각이 유일한 감각은 아니다. / 이렇게 할 수 있는 / 촉각도 이렇게 할 수 있다.
If you are standing by the road / and a large truck goes by, / do you hear or feel the vibration?
만약 여러분이 길가에 서 있는데 / 큰 트럭이 지나가면 / 여러분은 그 진동을 듣는 것인가 아니면 느끼는 것인가?
The answer is both.
답은 둘 다이다.
With very low frequency vibration / the ear starts becoming inefficient / and the rest of the body's sense of touch / starts to take over.
매우 낮은 주파수 진동에 / 귀가 비효율적으로 되기 시작하고 / 나머지 신체의 촉각이 / 더 중요해지기 시작한다.
For some reason / we tend to make a distinction / between hearing a sound and feeling a vibration, / but in reality they are the same thing.
어떤 이유에서인지 / 우리는 구분하는 경향이 있지만, / 소리를 듣는 것과 진동을 느끼는 것을 / 실제로 그것들은 똑같은 것이다.
Deafness does not mean that you can't hear, / only that there is something wrong with the ears.
귀먹음이란 여러분이 들을 수 없다는 것이 아니라, / 귀가 뭔가 잘못되었다는 것을 의미할 뿐이다.
Even someone who is totally deaf / can still hear/feel sounds.
심지어 완전히 귀가 먹은 사람도 / 여전히 소리를 듣거나 느낄 수 있다.

청각은 기본적으로 촉각의 분화된 한 형태이다. 소리는 단순히 귀가 포착하여 전기 신호로 전환하는 공기 진동이고, 그 전기 신호들은 이후 뇌에 의해 해석된다. 청각이라는 감각이 이렇게 할 수 있는 유일한 감각은 아니다. 촉각도 이렇게 할 수 있다. 만약 여러분이 길가에 서 있는데 큰 트럭이 지나가면 여러분은 그 진동을 듣는 것인가 아니면 느끼는 것인가? 답은 둘 다이다. 매우 낮은 주파수 진동에 귀가 비효율적으로 되기 시작하고 나머지 신체의 촉각이 더 중요해지기 시작한다. 어떤 이유에서인지 우리는 소리를 듣는 것과 진동을 느끼는 것을 구분하는 경향이 있지만, 실제로 그것들은 똑같은 것이다. 귀먹음이란 여러분이 들을 수 없다는 것이 아니라, 귀가 뭔가 잘못되었다는 것을 의미할 뿐이다. 심지어 완전히 귀가 먹은 사람도 여전히 소리를 듣거나 느낄 수 있다.

Why? 왜 정답일까?

빈칸 뒤의 세 문장에서 청각은 공기의 진동을 감지하는 것인데 이는 청각뿐만 아니라 촉각 또한 담당할 수 있는 기능임을 설명한 데 이어, '**For some reason we tend to make a distinction between hearing a sound and feeling a vibration, but in reality they are the same thing.**'에서는 촉각과 청각이 본질적으로 같다고 여겨질 수 있다는 내용을 말하고 있다. 따라서 빈칸에 들어갈 말로 가장 적절한 것은 두 감각이 유사하다는 뜻의 ① '촉각의 분화된 한 형태'이다.

- **basically** ad 본질적으로, 기본적으로
- **convert to** ~로 변환하다, 바꾸다
- **interpret** ⓥ 해석하다, 이해하다
- **make a distinction** (~을) 구별하다
- **vibrate** ⓥ 진동하다, 떨리다
- **electrical** ⓐ 전기의
- **frequency** ⓝ 진동수
- **in reality** 사실은, 실제로는

구문 풀이

2행 Sound is simply vibrating air [which the ear picks up and converts to electrical signals], which are then interpreted by the brain.
(목적격 관계대명사 / 동사1 / 동사2(~로 바꾸다) / 선행사 / 계속적 용법)

06 명성에 대한 욕망의 근원

정답률 42% | 정답 ②

다음 빈칸에 들어갈 말로 가장 적절한 것을 고르시오. [3점]

① spread of media – 대중 매체의 보급
✔ experience of neglect – 무시 당한 경험
③ freedom from authority – 권위로부터의 자유
④ curiosity about the unknown – 미지의 것에 대한 호기심
⑤ misunderstanding of popularity – 인기에 대한 오해

The desire for fame has its roots / in the experience of neglect.
명성에 대한 욕망은 그 뿌리를 두고 있다. / 무시당한 경험에
No one would want to be famous / who hadn't also, somewhere in the past, / been made to feel extremely insignificant.
어느 누구도 유명해지고 싶지 않을 것이다. / 과거 어느 시점에 또한 겪어보지 못했던 사람은 / 자신이 대단히 하찮은 사람이라는 느낌을
We sense the need for a great deal of admiring attention / when we have been painfully exposed to earlier deprivation.
우리는 (우리를) 대단하다고 보는 많은 관심의 필요를 느낀다. / 우리가 더 일찍이 고통스럽게 박탈감을 겪게 되었을 때
Perhaps one's parents were hard to impress.
어쩌면 어떤 이의 부모는 감명시키기가 어려웠을 것이다.
They never noticed one much, / they were so busy with other things, / focusing on other famous people, / unable to have or express kind feelings, / or just working too hard.
그들은 결코 그에게 많은 주의를 기울이지 못했고, / 그들은 다른 일로 너무 바빴다. / 다른 유명한 사람들에게 집중하거나, / 다정한 감정을 갖거나 이를 표현할 수 없었거나, / 그저 너무 열심히 일하며
There were no bedtime stories / and one's school reports weren't the subject of praise and admiration.
잠들기 전에 (부모가 읽어준) 이야기가 없었고, / 그의 성적 통지표는 칭찬과 감탄의 대상이 아니었다.
That's why one dreams / that one day the world will pay attention.
그러한 이유로 그는 꿈꾼다. / 언젠가 세상이 관심을 가져 주기를
When we're famous, / our parents will have to admire us too.
우리가 유명하면, / 우리의 부모 역시 우리를 대단하게 볼 수밖에 없을 것이다.

명성에 대한 욕망은 무시 당한 경험에 그 뿌리를 두고 있다. 과거 어느 시점에 자신이 대단히 하찮은 사람이라는 느낌을 또한 겪어보지 못했던 사람은 어느 누구도 유명해지고 싶지 않을 것이다. 우리는 더 일찍이 고통스럽게 박탈감을 겪게 되었을 때 우리를 대단하다고 보는 많은 관심의 필요를 느낀다. 어쩌면 어떤 이의 부모는 감명시키기가 어려웠을 것이다. 그들(부모)은 결코 그에게 많은 주의를 기울이지 못했고, 다른 유명한 사람들에게 집중하거나, 다정한 감정을 갖거나 이를 표현할 수 없었거나, 그저 너무 열심히 일하며 다른 일로 너무 바빴다. 잠들기 전에 이야기를 읽어준 적이 없었고, 그의 성적 통지표는 칭찬과 감탄의 대상이 아니었다. 그러한 이유로 그는 언젠가 세상이 관심을 가져 주기를 꿈꾼다. 우리가 유명하면, 우리의 부모 역시 우리를 대단하게 볼 수밖에 없을 것이다.

Why? 왜 정답일까?

빈칸 뒤의 두 문장에서 자신이 대단히 하찮은 사람이라고 여겨지는 경험을 했거나 (~ **made to feel extremely insignificant.**) 고통스러운 박탈감을 겪었던 사람 (~ **painfully exposed to earlier deprivation.**)이 명성에 대한 욕망을 갖게 된다고 이야기하므로, 빈칸에 들어갈 말로 가장 적절한 것은 ② '무시 당한 경험'이다.

- fame ⓝ 명성
- insignificant ⓐ 하찮은, 중요하지 않은
- attention ⓝ 주목
- deprivation ⓝ 결핍
- school report 성적 통지표
- extremely ad 극도로, 극히
- admire ⓥ 대단하게 여기다, 감탄하다
- expose ⓥ 겪게 하다, 노출하다
- impress ⓥ 감명을 주다

구문 풀이

2행 No one would want to be famous [who hadn't also, (somewhere in the past), been made to feel extremely insignificant].
선행사 / 주격 관계대명사 과거완료 / 과거완료 / 「be made＋to부정사 : ~하게 만들어지다」

★★★ 1등급 대비 고난도 2점 문제

07 자유 놀이의 기능 — 정답률 29% | 정답 ④

다음 빈칸에 들어갈 말로 가장 적절한 것을 고르시오.

① noisy – 시끄럽지
② sociable – 사교적이지
③ complicated – 복잡하지
④ helpless – 무력하지
⑤ selective – 선택적이지

Free play is nature's means of teaching children / that they are not helpless.
자유 놀이는 아이들에게 가르치는 자연적 수단이다. / 자신이 무력하지 않다는 것을
In play, away from adults, / children really do have control / and can practice asserting it.
어른과 떨어져 놀면서, / 아이들은 통제력을 정말로 가지고 / 그것을 발휘하는 것을 연습할 수 있다.
In free play, / children learn / to make their own decisions, / solve their own problems, / create and follow rules, / and get along with others as equals / rather than as obedient or rebellious subordinates.
자유 놀이를 통해, / 아이들은 배운다. / 스스로 결정을 내리고, / 자신들만의 문제를 해결하고, / 규칙을 만들고 지키며, / 동등한 사람 자격으로 다른 사람과 어울리는 것을 / 복종적이거나 반항적인 아랫사람이라기보다는
In active outdoor play, / children deliberately dose themselves with moderate amounts of fear / and they thereby learn / how to control not only their bodies, but also their fear.
활동적인 야외 놀이를 통해, / 아이들은 의도적으로 자기 자신에게 적절한 수준의 두려움을 주고, / 그렇게 하여 그들은 배운다. / 자기 신체뿐만 아니라 두려움 또한 통제하는 법을
In social play / children learn / how to negotiate with others, / how to please others, / and how to manage and overcome the anger / that can arise from conflicts.
사회적인 놀이를 통해 / 아이들은 배운다. / 어떻게 다른 사람과 협상하고, / 다른 사람을 기쁘게 하며, / 분노를 다스리고 극복할 수 있는지를 / 갈등으로부터 생길 수 있는
None of these lessons / can be taught through verbal means; / they can be learned only through experience, / which free play provides.
이러한 교훈 중 어느 것도 / 언어적 수단을 통해서는 배울 수 없다. / 그것들은 오로지 경험을 통해서만 배울 수 있는데, / 그것은 자유 놀이가 제공하는 것이다.

자유 놀이는 아이들에게 자신이 무력하지 않다는 것을 가르치는 자연적 수단이다. 어른과 떨어져 놀면서, 아이들은 통제력을 정말로 가지고 그것을 발휘하는 것을 연습할 수 있다. 자유 놀이를 통해, 아이들은 스스로 결정을 내리고, 자신들만의 문제를 해결하고, 규칙을 만들고 지키며, 복종적이거나 반항적인 아랫사람보다는 동등한 사람 자격으로 다른 사람과 어울리는 것을 배운다. 활동적인 야외 놀이를 통해, 아이들은 의도적으로 자기 자신에게 적절한 수준의 두려움을 주고, 그렇게 하여 자기 신체뿐만 아니라 두려움 또한 통제하는 법을 배운다. 사회적인 놀이를 통해 아이들은 어떻게 다른 사람과 협상하고, 다른 사람을 기쁘게 하며, 갈등으로부터 생길 수 있는 분노를 다스리고 극복할 수 있는지를 배운다. 이러한 교훈 중 어느 것도 언어적 수단을 통해서는 배울 수 없다. 그것들은 오로지 경험을 통해서만 배울 수 있는데, 그것은 자유 놀이가 제공하는 것이다.

Why? 왜 정답일까?

두 번째 문장에서 자유 놀이를 통해 아이들은 통제력을 갖고 발휘하는 연습(~ **do have control and can practice asserting it.**)을 해볼 수 있다는 핵심 내용이 나온다. 이어서 글 전체에 걸쳐 아이들은 놀이 속에서 스스로 결정하고 문제를 해결하며, 타인과 동등한 인격체로 어울리고 협상하는 법을 익히는 한편, 자신의 감정을 통제하는 법도 익혀나간다는 보충 설명이 제시된다. 이때 빈칸 바로 앞에는 **not**이 있으므로, 빈칸에는 '통제력이 없는' 상태에 관한 말이 들어가야 '**not＋빈칸**'이 주제를 나타낼 수 있다. 따라서 빈칸에 들어갈 말로 가장 적절한 것은 ④ '무력하지'이다.

- assert ⓥ (권리 등을) 행사하다, 주장하다
- rebellious ⓐ 반항적인
- deliberately ad 의도적으로
- moderate ⓐ 적당한
- obedient ⓐ 복종하는
- subordinate ⓝ 하급자, 부하
- dose ⓥ (약을) 투여하다, 먹이다
- thereby ad 그렇게 함으로써

- negotiate ⓥ 협상하다
- arise from ~에서 발생하다
- verbal ⓐ 언어적인
- helpless ⓐ 무력한
- overcome ⓥ 극복하다
- conflict ⓝ 갈등
- sociable ⓐ 사교적인
- selective ⓐ 선택적인

구문 풀이

11행 In social play children learn how to negotiate with others, how to please others, and how to manage and overcome the anger [that can arise from conflicts].
명사구1 / 명사구2 / 명사구3(~하는 방법) / [ ]: anger 수식

★★ 문제 해결 꿀~팁 ★★

▶ 많이 틀린 이유는?
글에 **get along with others**, **social play** 등의 표현이 나와 ②가 답으로 적절해 보일 수 있다. 하지만 아이들의 놀이의 의미를 설명하는 두 번째 문장을 보면, 놀이를 통해 아이들은 스스로 '통제력'을 지니고 있음을 알고, 그것을 행사하는 방법을 익히게 된다고 한다. 이는 아이들이 '무력한 존재가 아니라' 놀이 속 경험을 통해 행동이나 감정의 조절, 사회적 규칙 등을 배워갈 수 있는 힘을 지닌 존재라는 뜻이다.
▶ 문제 해결 방법은?
빈칸 앞에 **not**이 있으므로, '**not＋빈칸**'이 함께 주제를 나타내려면 빈칸에는 주제와 반대되는 말이 들어가야 한다. 즉 **do have control**과 의미상 반대되는 표현이 빈칸에 적합하다.

★★★ 1등급 대비 고난도 2점 문제

08 철학적 대화에서 이루어지는 무지의 인식 — 정답률 36% | 정답 ①

다음 빈칸에 들어갈 말로 가장 적절한 것을 고르시오.

① recognition of ignorance – 무지의 인식
② emphasis on self-assurance – 자기 확신에 대한 강조
③ conformity to established values – 확립된 가치관에 대한 순응
④ achievements of ancient thinkers – 고대 사상가들의 업적
⑤ comprehension of natural phenomena – 자연 현상에 대한 이해

Philosophical activity is based on the recognition of ignorance.
철학적 활동은 무지의 인식에 기초를 둔다.
The philosopher's thirst for knowledge / is shown through attempts / to find better answers to questions / even if those answers are never found.
지식에 대한 철학자의 갈망은 / 시도를 통해 나타나게 된다. / 질문에 대한 더 나은 답을 찾으려는 / 그 답이 결코 발견되지 않는다 하더라도
At the same time, / a philosopher also knows / that being too sure / can hinder the discovery of other and better possibilities.
동시에, / 철학자는 또한 알고 있다. / 지나치게 확신하는 것이 / 다른 가능성들과 더 나은 가능성들의 발견을 방해할 수 있다는 것을
In a philosophical dialogue, / the participants are aware / that there are things / they do not know or understand.
철학적 대화에서 / 참여자들은 인식한다. / 일들이 있다는 것을 / 자신이 알지 못하거나 이해하지 못하는
The goal of the dialogue is / to arrive at a conception / that one did not know or understand beforehand.
그 대화의 목표는 / 생각에 도달하는 것이다. / 아무도 전부터 알지 못했거나 이해하지 못했다는
In traditional schools, / where philosophy is not present, / students often work with factual questions, / they learn specific content listed in the curriculum, / and they are not required to solve philosophical problems.
전통적 학교에서, / 철학이 존재하지 않는 / 학생들은 흔히 사실적 질문에 대해 공부하고, / 그들은 교육과정에 실린 특정한 내용을 배우며, / 그들은 철학적인 문제를 해결하도록 요구받지 않는다.
However, / we know / that awareness of what one does not know / can be a good way to acquire knowledge.
하지만 / 우리는 안다. / 누구도 알지 못하는 것에 대한 인식이 / 지식을 습득하는 좋은 방법이 될 수 있다는 것을
Knowledge and understanding are developed / through thinking and talking.
지식과 이해는 발달한다. / 사색과 토론을 통해
Putting things into words makes things clearer.
생각을 말로 표현하는 것은 생각을 더 분명하게 만든다.
Therefore, / students must not be afraid of / saying something wrong / or talking without first being sure that they are right.
따라서 / 학생들은 두려워해서는 안 된다. / 틀린 것을 말하거나 / 처음에 그들이 옳다는 것을 확신하지 못하는 상태로 이야기하는 것을

철학적 활동은 무지의 인식에 기초를 둔다. 지식에 대한 철학자의 갈망은 그 답이 결코 발견되지 않는다 하더라도 질문에 대한 더 나은 답을 찾으려는 시도를 통해 나타나게 된다. 동시에, 철학자는 또한 지나치게 확신하는 것이 다른

[문제편 p.012]

가능성들과 더 나은 가능성들의 발견을 방해할 수 있다는 것을 알고 있다. 철학적 대화에서 참여자들은 자신이 알지 못하거나 이해하지 못하는 것이 있다는 것을 인식한다. 그 대화의 목표는 아무도 전부터 알지 못했거나 이해하지 못했다는 생각에 도달하는 것이다. 철학이 존재하지 않는 전통적 학교에서, 학생들은 흔히 사실적 질문에 대해 공부하고, 교육과정에 실린 특정한 내용을 배우며, 철학적인 문제를 해결하도록 요구받지 않는다. 하지만 우리는 누구도 알지 못하는 것에 대한 인식이 지식을 습득하는 좋은 방법이 될 수 있다는 것을 안다. 지식과 이해는 사색과 토론을 통해 발달한다. 생각을 말로 표현하는 것은 생각을 더 분명하게 만든다. 따라서 학생들은 틀린 것을 말하거나 처음에 그들이 옳다는 것을 확신하지 못하는 상태로 이야기하는 것을 두려워해서는 안 된다.

Why? 왜 정답일까?

'In a philosophical dialogue, the participants are aware that there are things they do not know or understand.'에서 철학적 대화를 하다 보면 사람들은 자신이 모르고 있거나 이해하지 못하고 있는 것이 있음을 알게 된다고 언급한 후, 'However, we know that awareness of what one does not know can be a good way to acquire knowledge.'에서는 이러한 무지에 대한 인식이 우리가 지식을 습득하는 좋은 방법이 될 수 있다고 설명한다. 따라서 빈칸에 들어갈 말로 가장 적절한 것은 ① '무지의 인식'이다.

- philosophical ⓐ 철학적인
- discovery ⓝ 발견
- specific ⓐ 특정한
- acquire ⓥ 습득하다
- ignorance ⓝ 무지
- self-assurance ⓝ 자기 확신
- phenomenon ⓝ 현상
- hinder ⓥ 방해하다
- factual ⓐ 사실적인
- awareness ⓝ 인식
- put into words 말로 옮기다
- emphasis ⓝ 강조
- conformity ⓝ 순응

구문 풀이

10행 In traditional schools, where philosophy is not present, students often work with factual questions, they learn specific content listed in the curriculum, and they are not required to solve philosophical problems.
(선행사: traditional schools / 관계부사: where / 주어1: students / 동사1: work / 주어2: they / 동사2: learn / 주어3: they / 동사3: are not required)

★★ 문제 해결 꿀~팁 ★★

▶ 많이 틀린 이유는?
'In a philosophical dialogue, ~'와 'The goal of the dialogue ~'에서 철학적 대화를 통해 인간은 스스로 알지 못하거나 모르고 있다는 사실을 인지하게 된다고 했다. 따라서 철학적 대화나 활동을 통해 인간이 자기 확신에 이른다는 내용인, self-assurance를 포함한 ②는 답으로 적절하지 않다.
▶ 문제 해결 방법은?
주제를 제시하는 However가 포함된 문장의 'awareness of what one does not know'를 재진술한 표현이 바로 ①의 'recognition of ignorance'임을 파악하면 쉽게 답을 고를 수 있다.

★★★ 1등급 대비 고난도 3점 문제

09 유전자 발현에 영향을 주는 음식 — 정답률 37% | 정답 ⑤

다음 빈칸에 들어갈 말로 가장 적절한 것을 고르시오. [3점]

① identical twins have the same genetic makeup
일란성 쌍둥이는 똑같은 유전자 구성을 지니고 있다
② our preference for food is influenced by genes
우리의 음식 선호는 유전자에 영향을 받는다
③ balanced diet is essential for our mental health
균형잡힌 식사가 우리의 정신 건강에 필수적이다
④ genetic engineering can cure some fatal diseases
유전공학은 몇몇 치명적인 질병을 고칠 수 있다
✔ foods can immediately influence the genetic blueprint
식품이 유전자 청사진에 직접 영향을 줄 수 있다

The growing field of genetics is showing us / what many scientists have suspected for years / — foods can immediately influence the genetic blueprint.
성장하고 있는 유전학 분야는 우리에게 보여주고 있다. / 많은 과학자가 여러 해 동안 의구심을 가져왔던 것을 / 즉 식품이 유전자 청사진에 직접 영향을 줄 수 있다는 것
This information helps us better understand / that genes are under our control / and not something we must obey.
이 정보는 우리가 더 잘 이해하도록 도와준다. / 유전자가 우리의 통제 하에 있는 것이지 / 우리가 복종해야 하는 것이 아니라는 것을
Consider identical twins; / both individuals are given the same genes.
일란성 쌍둥이를 생각해보자. / 두 사람은 모두 똑같은 유전자를 부여받는다.
In mid-life, one twin develops cancer, / and the other lives a long healthy life without cancer.
중년에, 쌍둥이 중 한 명은 암에 걸리고, / 다른 한 명은 암 없이 건강하게 오래 산다.
A specific gene instructed one twin to develop cancer, / but in the other the same gene did not initiate the disease.
특정 유전자가 쌍둥이 중 한 명에게 암에 걸리도록 명령했지만, / 나머지 한 명에서는 똑같은 유전자가 그 질병을 발생시키지 않았다.
One possibility is / that the healthy twin had a diet / that turned off the cancer gene / — the same gene that instructed the other person to get sick.
한 가지 가능성은 / 쌍둥이 중 건강한 사람이 식사를 했다는 것이다. / 암 유전자를 차단하는 / 즉 나머지 한 명이 병에 걸리도록 명령했던 바로 그 유전자를
For many years, scientists have recognized / other environmental factors, / such as chemical toxins (tobacco for example), / can contribute to cancer through their actions on genes.
여러 해 동안 과학자들은 인정해 왔다. / 다른 환경적 요인들이 / 화학적 독소(예를 들어 담배)와 같은 / 유전자에 작용하여 암의 원인이 될 수 있다는 것을
The notion / that food has a specific influence on gene expression / is relatively new.
생각은 / 음식이 유전자 발현에 특정한 영향을 미친다는 / 비교적 새로운 것이다.

성장하고 있는 유전학 분야는 많은 과학자가 여러 해 동안 의구심을 가져왔던 것, 즉 식품이 유전자 청사진에 직접 영향을 줄 수 있다는 것을 우리에게 보여주고 있다. 이 정보는 유전자가 우리의 통제 하에 있는 것이지 우리가 복종해야 하는 것이 아니라는 것을 더 잘 이해하도록 도와준다. 일란성 쌍둥이를 생각해보자. 두 사람은 모두 똑같은 유전자를 부여받는다. 중년에, 쌍둥이 중 한 명은 암에 걸리고, 다른 한 명은 암 없이 건강하게 오래 산다. 특정 유전자가 쌍둥이 중 한 명에게 암에 걸리도록 명령했지만, 나머지 한 명에서는 똑같은 유전자가 그 질병을 발생시키지 않았다. 한 가지 가능성은 쌍둥이 중 건강한 사람이 암 유전자, 즉 나머지 한 명이 병에 걸리도록 명령했던 바로 그 유전자를 차단하는 식사를 했다는 것이다. 여러 해 동안 과학자들은 화학적 독소(예를 들어 담배)와 같은 다른 환경적 요인들이 유전자에 작용하여 암의 원인이 될 수 있다는 것을 인정해 왔다. 음식이 유전자 발현에 특정한 영향을 미친다는 생각은 비교적 새로운 것이다.

Why? 왜 정답일까?

유전자가 완전히 서로 같지만 둘 중 한 사람만 암에 걸린 일란성 쌍둥이를 생각해 볼 때, 음식이 유전자 발현에 특정한 영향을 끼친다는 사실(The notion that food has a specific influence on gene expression ~)을 알 수 있음을 소개한 글이다. 따라서 빈칸에 들어갈 말로 가장 적절한 것은 ⑤ '식품이 유전자 청사진에 직접 영향을 줄 수 있다'이다.

- genetics ⓝ 유전학
- under control 통제 하에 있는, 통제되는
- identical twin 일란성 쌍둥이
- initiate ⓥ 시작되게 하다
- contribute to ~의 원인이 되다
- makeup ⓝ 구성
- immediately ad 직접적으로, 즉각
- suspect ⓥ 의심하다
- obey ⓥ 복종하다
- instruct ⓥ 명령하다, 지시하다
- environmental ⓐ 환경적인
- relatively ad 비교적
- preference ⓝ 선호
- blueprint ⓝ 청사진, 설계도

구문 풀이

10행 One possibility is that the healthy twin had a diet [that turned off the cancer gene] — the same gene [that instructed the other person to get sick].
(접속사(~것): that / 선행사: a diet → 주격 관·대 / 동격(=the cancer gene) / 주격 관·대 「instruct+목적어+to부정사: ~이 …하도록 지시하다」)

★★ 문제 해결 꿀~팁 ★★

▶ 많이 틀린 이유는?
우리가 먹는 음식이 유전자 발현에 영향을 미칠 수 있다는 내용으로 ④에서 언급하는 genetic engineering(유전공학)이나 fatal diseases(치명적인 질병)에 대한 언급은 없다. 또한 ②는 유전자가 음식 선호에 영향을 준다는 내용으로 이 글의 내용과 반대되는 내용이다.
▶ 문제 해결 방법은?
글의 주제가 처음과 마지막에서 두 번 언급되고 있고 이를 예를 들어 설명한 내용이 가운데에 배치된 글이다. 빈칸이 주제를 나타내고 있으므로 예시를 잘 파악하고 주제가 다시 언급되는 부분에 주목하여 읽는다.

★★★ 1등급 대비 고난도 3점 문제

10 시장 사고방식에 의한 관습의 변질 정답률 20% | 정답 ⑤

다음 빈칸에 들어갈 말로 가장 적절한 것을 고르시오. [3점]

① people can put aside their interests for the common good
사람들이 공익을 위해 그들의 이익을 제쳐둘 수 있는지
② changing an existing agreement can cause a sense of guilt
기존의 합의를 바꾸는 것은 죄책감을 유발할 수 있는지
③ imposing a fine can compensate for broken social contracts
벌금 부과가 사회 계약 위반을 보상할 수 있는지
④ social bonds can be insufficient to change people's behavior
사회적 유대감이 사람들의 행동을 바꾸기에 불충분할 수 있는지
⑤ a market mindset can transform and undermine an institution
시장 사고방식이 관습을 변질시키고 훼손시킬 수 있는지

One vivid example / of how a market mindset can transform and undermine an institution / is given by Dan Ariely in his book *Predictably Irrational*.
한 생생한 예가 / 어떻게 시장 사고방식이 관습을 변질시키고 훼손시킬 수 있는지에 대한 / Dan Ariely의 저서 *Predictably Irrational*에서 주어진다.

He tells the story of a day care center in Israel / that decided to fine parents / who arrived late to pick up their children, / in the hope that this would discourage them from doing so.
그는 이스라엘의 한 어린이집에 관한 이야기를 들려준다. / 부모들에게 벌금을 부과하기로 결정했던 / 아이를 데리러 늦게 도착한 / 이것이 그들이 그렇게 행동하는 것을 막을 수 있기를 바라면서

In fact, the exact opposite happened.
실제로는 정반대의 일이 일어났다.

Before the imposition of fines, / parents felt guilty about arriving late, / and guilt was effective / in ensuring that only a few did so.
벌금 부과 전에 / 부모들은 늦게 도착한 것에 대해 죄책감을 느꼈고 / 죄책감은 효과적이었다. / 몇 안 되는 사람들만이 그렇게 하도록 하는 데

Once a fine was introduced, / it seems / that in the minds of the parents / the entire scenario was changed / from a social contract to a market one.
일단 벌금이 도입되자 / ~처럼 보인다. / 부모들의 마음속에서 / 전체 시나리오가 바뀌었던 / 사회 계약에서 시장 계약으로

Essentially, / they were paying for the center / to look after their children after hours.
근본적으로 / 그들은 어린이집에 비용을 지불하고 있었다. / 방과 후에 아이를 봐주도록

Some parents thought it worth the price, / and the rate of late arrivals increased.
일부 부모들은 그것이 값어치를 한다고 생각했고 / 늦은 도착의 비율이 증가했다.

Significantly, / once the center abandoned the fines / and went back to the previous arrangement, / late arrivals remained at the high level / they had reached during the period of the fines.
중요하게는, / 어린이집이 벌금을 포기하고 / 이전 방식으로 돌아갔을 때, / 늦은 도착은 그 높은 수준으로 유지되었다. / 그들이 벌금 기간 중 달했던

어떻게 시장 사고방식이 관습을 변질시키고 훼손시킬 수 있는지에 대한 한 생생한 예가 Dan Ariely의 저서 *Predictably Irrational*에서 주어진다. 그는 아이를 데리러 늦게 도착한 부모들에게 벌금을 부과하기로 결정했던 이스라엘의 한 어린이집에 관한 이야기를 들려주는데, 이는 벌금이 그들의 그런 행동을 막을 수 있기를 바라서였다. 실제로는 정반대의 일이 일어났다. 벌금 부과 전에 부모들은 늦게 도착한 것에 대해 죄책감을 느꼈고, 죄책감은 늦는 사람이 얼마 없도록 하는 데 효과적이었다. 일단 벌금이 도입되자 부모들의 마음속에서 전체 시나리오가 사회 계약에서 시장 계약으로 바뀌었던 것으로 보인다. 근본적으로 그들은 방과 후에 아이를 돌봐주는 데 대해 어린이집에 비용을 지불하고 있었다. 일부 부모들은 그것이 값어치를 한다고 생각했고 늦은 도착의 비율이 증가했다. 중요하게는, 어린이집이 벌금을 포기하고 이전 방식으로 돌아갔을 때, 늦은 도착은 벌금 기간 중 달했던 그 높은 수준으로 유지되었다.

Why? 왜 정답일까?

예시에 따르면 어린이집이 아이를 늦게 데리러 온 부모들에 벌금을 물리기 시작하자 부모들이 점차 어린이집에 지불하는 '비용'을 의식하게 되면서 오히려 더 많이 늦게 왔다고 한다. 이어서 마지막 문장에서는 이후 결국 어린이집이 벌금을 없앴음에도 이 늦는 비율이 줄어들지 않았다고 한다. 즉 이 예시는 사회 계약으로 인식되던 관계가 '시장 계약'으로 변화했을 때 기존의 관습이 어떻게 무너지는지를 보여준다고 정리할 수 있다. 따라서 빈칸에 들어갈 말로 가장 적절한 것은 ⑤ '시장 사고방식이 관습을 변질시키고 훼손시킬 수 있는지'이다.

- vivid ⓐ 생생한
- irrational ⓐ 불합리한
- discourage A from B A를 B하지 못하게 하다
- imposition ⓝ 부과
- guilty ⓐ 죄책감이 드는
- contract ⓝ 계약
- abandon ⓥ (하다가) 포기하다
- put aside ~을 무시하다, 제쳐두다
- compensate for ~을 보상하다
- insufficient ⓐ 불충분한
- undermine ⓥ 훼손하다, 약화시키다
- institution ⓝ 제도, 관습

구문 풀이

14행 Some parents thought it worth the price, and the rate of late arrivals increased.
(thought: 5형식 동사 / it: 목적어 / worth the price: 목적격 보어(worth+명사 : ~할 가치가 있는))

★★ 문제 해결 꿀~팁 ★★

▶ 많이 틀린 이유는?
글에 따르면 부모들과 어린이집은 본래 '사회 계약' 관계에 있었지만, 어린이집이 지각하는 부모들에게 벌금을 물리기 시작하며 '돈'이 매개가 되는 '시장 계약'으로 관계가 변화했다고 한다. 오답 중 ③은 벌금이 사회 계약을 복구시키는 수단이 될 수 있다는 의미이므로 답으로 적절하지 않다. 또한, 이 글이 사회적 유대 관계가 행동을 바꾼다는 내용도 아니므로 ④도 답으로 부적절하다.
▶ 문제 해결 방법은?
⑤의 **an institution**은 본문의 **a social contract**과 문맥적 의미가 같다. 즉 부모들에게 벌금을 물리기 이전에 '부모가 어린이집에 제때 와 아이를 데려가기로 하는' 암묵적 합의가 있었던 상황을 요약하는 말이다.

★★★ 1등급 대비 고난도 3점 문제

11 인간의 무의식적인 인지 과업 분담 정답률 37% | 정답 ①

다음 빈칸에 들어갈 말로 가장 적절한 것을 고르시오. [3점]

① divide up cognitive labor – 인지 노동을 나누는데
② try to avoid disagreements – 의견 불일치를 피하려고 노력하는데
③ seek people with similar tastes – 비슷한 취향을 가진 사람을 찾는데
④ like to share old wisdom – 옛 지혜를 공유하기 좋아하는데
⑤ balance work and leisure – 일과 여가의 균형을 맞추는데

Psychological research has shown / that people naturally divide up cognitive labor, / often without thinking about it.
심리학 연구는 보여준다. / 사람들은 자연스럽게 인지 노동을 나누는데, / 흔히 그것에 대해서 별 생각 없이 그렇게 한다고

Imagine you're cooking up a special dinner with a friend.
여러분이 친구와 함께 특별한 저녁식사를 요리하고 있다고 상상해 보라.

You're a great cook, / but your friend is the wine expert, an amateur sommelier.
여러분은 요리를 잘하지만, / 친구는 아마추어 소믈리에라고 할 수 있는 와인 전문가이다.

A neighbor drops by / and starts telling you both / about the terrific new wines / being sold at the liquor store just down the street.
이웃이 들르더니 / 여러분 두 사람에게 말하기 시작한다. / 기막히게 좋은 새로운 와인에 대해 / 거리를 따라가면 바로 있는 주류 가게에서 파는

There are many new wines, / so there's a lot to remember.
많은 새로운 와인이 있어서 / 기억해야 할 것이 많다.

How hard are you going to try / to remember what the neighbor has to say about which wines to buy?
여러분은 얼마나 열심히 노력할까? / 어떤 와인을 사야 하는지에 관해 이웃이 할 말을 기억하기 위해

Why bother / when the information would be better retained / by the wine expert sitting next to you?
무엇 하러 그러겠는가? / 그 정보가 더 잘 기억될 텐데 / 여러분 옆에 앉아 있는 와인 전문가에 의해

If your friend wasn't around, / you might try harder.
여러분의 친구가 곁에 없다면 / 여러분은 더 열심히 애쓸지도 모른다.

After all, / it would be good to know / what a good wine would be for the evening's festivities.
어쨌든 / 아는 것은 좋은 일일 것이다. / 뭐가 저녁 만찬을 위해 좋은 와인일지

But / your friend, the wine expert, / is likely to remember the information without even trying.
하지만, / 와인 전문가인 여러분의 친구는 / 애쓰지도 않고 그 정보를 기억하기가 쉽다.

심리학 연구에 따르면, 사람들은 자연스럽게 인지 노동을 나누는데, 흔히 그것에 대해서 별 생각 없이 그렇게 한다. 여러분이 친구와 함께 특별한 저녁식사를 요리하고 있다고 상상해 보라. 여러분은 요리를 잘하지만, 친구는 아마추어 소믈리에라고 할 수 있는 와인 전문가이다. 이웃이 들르더니 여러분 두 사람에게 거리를 따라가면 바로 있는 주류 가게에서 파는 기막히게 좋은 새로운 와인에 대해 말하기 시작한다. 많은 새로운 와인이 있어서 기억해야 할 것이 많다. 어떤 와인을 사야 하는지에 관해 이웃이 할 말을 기억하기 위해 여러분은 얼마나 열심히 노력할까? 여러분 옆에 앉아 있는 와인 전문가가 그 정보를 더 잘 기억하고 있는데 무엇 하러 그러겠는가? 여러분의 친구가 곁에 없다면 더 열심히 애쓸지도 모른다. 어쨌든 뭐가 저녁 만찬을 위해 좋은 와인일지 아는 것은 좋은 일일 것이다. 하지만, 와인 전문가인 여러분의 친구는 애쓰지도 않고 그 정보를 기억하기가 쉽다.

[문제편 p.013]

Why? 왜 정답일까?

첫 문장에서 주제를 제시하고 두 번째 문장부터 주제를 뒷받침하는 예를 소개한다. 예시에 따르면 와인 전문가인 친구와 함께 새로 들어온 와인에 관한 이야기를 들을 때, 친구가 그 정보를 큰 노력 없이 더 잘 기억할 것이기 때문에 우리는 무의식적으로 별 노력을 들이지 않게 된다고 한다. 이에 근거할 때, 우리는 무의식적으로 함께 있는 사람과 인지적인 노력을 '분담해서' 효율적으로 정보를 처리하려는 경향이 있다는 내용을 추론할 수 있다. 따라서 빈칸에 들어갈 말로 가장 적절한 것은 ① '인지 노동을 나누는데'이다.

- **expert** ⓝ 전문가
- **terrific** ⓐ 아주 멋진
- **retain** ⓥ 보유하다
- **cognitive** ⓐ 인지적인
- **leisure** ⓝ 여가
- **sommelier** ⓝ 소믈리에(와인 담당 웨이터)
- **liquor** ⓝ (독한) 술
- **festivity** ⓝ 축제 기분
- **disagreement** ⓝ 불일치

구문 풀이

9행 How hard are you going to try to remember what the neighbor has to say about which wines to buy?

(what: 관계대명사(~것) / which wines to buy: 「which+명+to부정사 : 어떤 ~을 …할지」)

★★ 문제 해결 꿀~팁 ★★

▶ 많이 틀린 이유는?

어떤 정보를 더 잘 기억할 사람이 옆에 있다면 우리는 무의식적으로 그 정보를 기억하려는 노력을 덜 들일 것이라는 내용의 글이다. 의견 불일치를 피하거나 서로 비슷한 취향을 가진 사람을 찾는다는 내용은 언급되지 않으므로 ②, ③은 모두 답으로 부적절하다.

▶ 문제 해결 방법은?

빈칸 뒤의 예시를 읽고 그 전체적인 내용을 근거로 도출할 수 있는 논리적 결론을 추론해내는 문제이다. 와인에 대한 정보를 별로 애쓰지도 않고 쉽게 기억해낼 친구가 있다면, 이웃이 와인에 대한 정보를 이야기해줄 때 그 정보를 처리하기 위한 인지적 노력을 덜 기울일 것이라는 내용을 통해, 인간은 무의식 속에서도 '인지적 부담'을 나눌 수 있는지 살펴보고 행동한다는 내용이 빈칸에 들어가야 한다.

★★★ 1등급 대비 고난도 3점 문제

12 자연에 대한 심미적 감상을 설명할 수 없는 과학 　정답률 36% | 정답 ⑤

다음 빈칸에 들어갈 말로 가장 적절한 것을 고르시오. [3점]

① devalue the true beauty of mother nature
대자연의 진정한 아름다움을 평가절하할
② rely on the perspectives of artistic professionals
전문 예술가들의 관점에 의지할
③ explain the evolutionary process of every species
모든 종의 진화 과정을 설명할
④ give up its trust in the usefulness of classification
분류의 유용성에 대한 믿음을 포기할
⑤ account for correct aesthetic appreciation of nature
자연에 대한 정확한 심미적 감상을 설명할

Scientific knowledge cannot account for / correct aesthetic appreciation of nature / because science represents natural objects / as members of a specific class, / rather than as individual entities.
과학적 지식은 설명할 수 없다. / 자연에 대한 정확한 심미적 감상을 / 과학은 자연물을 나타내기 때문에 / 특정한 부류에 속하는 요소로 / 개별적인 독립체라기보다는

The science-based approach claims / that aesthetically relevant properties are only those properties / that all members of a natural kind / share with each other.
과학에 기초한 접근법은 주장한다. / 심미적으로 관련된 특성들은 특성들일 뿐이라고 / 한 자연종의 모든 요소들이 / 서로 공유하는

But this is not true.
하지만 이것은 사실이 아니다.

When we experience nature, / we do not experience it as species, / but as individual objects.
우리가 자연을 경험할 때 / 우리는 그것을 종으로서 경험하는 것이 아니라 / 개별적인 대상으로서 경험한다.

And as separated into individual objects, / nature can have aesthetic properties / that are not entailed by its scientific description.
그리고 개별적인 대상으로 분리될 때, / 자연은 심미적 특성들을 가질 수 있다. / 그것의 과학적인 설명에 의해 수반되지 않는

Natural science can explain, for instance, / the formation of the waterfall, / but it has nothing to say / about our experience of the majestic Victoria Falls / when viewed at sunset, / its reds and oranges countless and captivating; / geology can explain the formation of the Ngorongoro Crater in Tanzania, / but not its painful and breathtaking beauty at sunrise, / the fog slowly lifting above the crater / and a lone hippopotamus dark and heavy in the lake.

예를 들어, 자연 과학은 설명할 수 있지만, / 폭포의 형성을 / 할 말이 없다. / 장엄한 빅토리아 폭포에 대한 우리의 경험, / 일몰에 본 / 즉 무수히 많고 매혹적인 그것의 붉은색과 주황색에 대해서는 / 즉 지질학은 탄자니아에 있는 Ngorongoro 분화구의 형성을 설명할 수 있지만, / 일출의 가슴 아프고 숨 막히는 아름다움, / 그 분화구 위로 천천히 떠오르는 안개 / 그리고 호수 안에 있는 어둡고 육중한 한 마리의 하마를 설명할 수는 없다.

과학은 자연물을 개별적인 독립체라기보다는 특정한 부류에 속하는 요소로 나타내기 때문에 과학적 지식은 자연에 대한 정확한 심미적 감상을 설명할 수 없다. 과학에 기초한 접근법은 심미적으로 관련된 특성들은 한 자연종의 모든 요소들이 서로 공유하는 특성들일 뿐이라고 주장한다. 하지만 이것은 사실이 아니다. 우리가 자연을 경험할 때 우리는 그것을 종으로서 경험하는 것이 아니라 개별적인 대상으로서 경험한다. 그리고 개별적인 대상으로 분리될 때, 자연은 과학적인 설명에 의해 수반되지 않는 심미적 특성들을 가질 수 있다. 예를 들어, 자연 과학은 폭포의 형성을 설명할 수 있지만, 일몰에 본 장엄한 빅토리아 폭포에 대한 우리의 경험, 무수히 많고 매혹적인 붉은색과 주황색에 대해서는 할 말이 없다. 지질학은 탄자니아에 있는 Ngorongoro 분화구의 형성을 설명할 수 있지만, 일출 때의 가슴 아프고 숨 막히는 아름다움, 그 분화구 위로 천천히 떠오르는 안개 그리고 호수 안에 있는 어둡고 육중한 한 마리의 하마를 설명할 수는 없다.

Why? 왜 정답일까?

과학은 자연을 개별적인 대상보다는 특정 종이나 부류의 개념으로 설명하는 데 반해 우리는 자연을 개별적인 대상으로서 경험하므로 각 대상의 심미적 특성을 과학적으로 모두 설명하기는 어렵다(**When we experience nature, we do not experience it as species, but as individual objects. And as separated into individual objects, nature can have aesthetic properties that are not entailed by its scientific description.**)는 내용을 주제로 다룬 글이다. 빈칸 앞에 **not**이 있으므로 빈칸에는 주제와 반대되는 내용을 넣어 주제문을 완성해야 한다. 따라서 빈칸에 들어갈 말로 가장 적절한 것은 ⑤ '자연에 대한 정확한 심미적 감상을 설명할'이다.

- **represent** ⓥ 나타내다, 대표하다
- **relevant** ⓐ 관련된, 적절한
- **separate** ⓥ 분리하다
- **formation** ⓝ 형성
- **captivating** ⓐ 매혹적인, 마음을 사로잡는
- **devalue** ⓥ 평가절하하다, 가치를 낮춰보다
- **account for** 설명하다
- **aesthetically** ad 미적으로
- **property** ⓝ 특성, 성질
- **entail** ⓥ 수반하다
- **majestic** ⓐ 장엄한, 위풍당당한
- **breathtaking** ⓐ 숨이 막히는
- **classification** ⓝ 분류, 유형, 범주
- **appreciation** ⓝ 감상, 감탄

구문 풀이

11행 Natural science can explain, for instance, the formation of the waterfall, but it has nothing to say about our experience of the majestic Victoria Falls when viewed at sunset, its reds and oranges (being) countless and captivating; / geology can explain [the formation of the Ngorongoro Crater in Tanzania], but not [{its painful and breathtaking beauty at sunrise}, {the fog slowly lifting above the crater} and {a lone hippopotamus (being) dark and heavy in the lake}].

(Natural science: 주어1 / can explain: 동사1 / it: 주어2 / has: 동사2 / when viewed at sunset: 분사구문(~할 때) / its reds and oranges: 의미상 주어 / (being): 생략(분사구문) / 「[A], but not+[B] : A이지만 B는 아닌」 / the fog: 의미상 주어 / lifting: 분사구문(현재분사) / a lone hippopotamus: 의미상 주어 / (being): 생략(분사구문))

★★ 문제 해결 꿀~팁 ★★

▶ 많이 틀린 이유는?

과학이 자연의 심미적 특징을 기술하지 못하는 이유를 설명하는 추상적인 글로, 구문 또한 까다로워 난이도가 높다. 부정어인 **cannot** 뒤에 빈칸이 나오므로 답은 주제와 반대되는 내용이어야 한다. 최다 오답인 ③은 모든 종의 진화 과정을 설명한다는 의미로 이 글에서는 자연에서의 진화에 대한 언급 자체가 없었으므로 답으로 적절하지 않다.

▶ 문제 해결 방법은?

예문 앞에 핵심 표현이 있다. '**~ nature can have aesthetic properties that are not entailed by its scientific description.**'를 근거로 보고, **cannot** 뒤에 각 선택지를 대입해 읽으며 근거 문장과 빈칸 문장의 의미가 서로 같게 만들어 주는 말을 답으로 찾도록 한다.

DAY 02 빈칸 추론 02

01 ②	02 ①	03 ⑤	04 ①	05 ①
06 ③	07 ②	08 ①	09 ②	10 ①
11 ②	12 ①			

01　상대적 비교에 따라 결정되는 음식 양　　정답률 54% | 정답 ②

다음 빈칸에 들어갈 말로 가장 적절한 것을 고르시오.

① Originality – 독창성　　✔ Relativity – 상대성
③ Visualization – 시각화　　④ Imitation – 모방
⑤ Forgetfulness – 건망증

Relativity works as a general mechanism for the mind, / in many ways and across many different areas of life.
상대성은 정신을 위한 일반적인 메커니즘으로 작용한다. / 여러 면에서 그리고 삶의 많은 다른 영역에 걸쳐

For example, / Brian Wansink, author of *Mindless Eating*, / showed / that it can also affect our waistlines.
예를 들어, / *Mindless Eating*의 저자 Brian Wansink는 / 보여주었다. / 이것이 우리의 허리 둘레에도 영향을 미칠 수 있다는 것을

We decide how much to eat / not simply as a function of how much food we actually consume, / but by a comparison to its alternatives.
우리는 우리가 먹을 양을 결정한다. / 단순히 우리가 실제로 먹는 음식 양의 함수로서가 아니라 / 그것의 대안과의 비교를 통해서

Say we have to choose / between three burgers on a menu, / at 8, 10, and 12 ounces.
우리가 선택해야 한다고 하자. / 메뉴에 있는 버거 세 개 사이에서 / 8온스, 10온스, 12온스의

We are likely to pick the 10-ounce burger / and be perfectly satisfied at the end of the meal.
우리는 10온스 버거를 고르고 / 식사가 끝날 때쯤이면 완벽하게 만족할 수 있을 것이다.

But if our options are instead 10, 12, and 14 ounces, / we are likely again to choose the middle one, / and again feel equally happy and satisfied / with the 12-ounce burger / at the end of the meal, / even though we ate more, / which we did not need / in order to get our daily nourishment / or in order to feel full.
하지만 만약 대신에 우리의 선택권이 10온스, 12온스, 14온스라면, / 우리는 다시 중간의 것을 선택할 것이고, / 똑같이 행복감과 만족감을 다시 느낄 수 있을 것이다. / 12온스의 햄버거에 / 식사가 끝날 때 / 비록 우리가 더 많이 먹었더라도, / 우리가 필요하지 않았던 / 매일 영양분을 섭취하기 위해 / 혹은 포만감을 느끼기 위해

상대성은 여러 면에서 그리고 삶의 많은 다른 영역에 걸쳐 정신을 위한 일반적인 메커니즘으로 작용한다. 예를 들어, *Mindless Eating*의 저자 Brian Wansink는 이것이 우리의 허리 둘레에도 영향을 미칠 수 있다는 것을 보여주었다. 우리는 단순히 우리가 실제로 먹는 음식 양의 함수로서가 아니라 대안과의 비교를 통해서 우리가 먹을 양을 결정한다. 우리가 메뉴에 있는 8온스, 10온스, 12온스의 버거 세 개 중 하나를 선택해야 한다고 하자. 우리는 10온스 버거를 고르고 식사가 끝날 때쯤이면 완벽하게 만족할 수 있을 것이다. 하지만 만약 대신에 우리의 선택권이 10온스, 12온스, 14온스라면, 우리는 다시 중간의 것을 선택할 것이고, 비록 우리가 더 많이 먹었더라도, 식사가 끝날 때 매일 영양분을 섭취하거나 포만감을 느끼기 위해 필요하지 않았던 12온스의 햄버거에 똑같이 행복감과 만족감을 다시 느낄 수 있을 것이다.

Why? 왜 정답일까?

예시 앞의 'We decide how much to eat not simply as a function of how much food we actually consume, but by a comparison to its alternatives.'에서 우리는 대안 간의 비교를 통해 얼마나 먹을지를 결정하게 된다고 하므로, 빈칸에 들어갈 말로 가장 적절한 것은 '비교'를 다른 말로 재진술한 ② '상대성'이다.

- function ⓝ (수학) 함수
- consume ⓥ 먹다, 마시다
- alternative ⓝ 대안
- nourishment ⓝ 영양분
- originality ⓝ 독창성
- relativity ⓝ 상대성
- forgetfulness ⓝ 건망증, 잘 잊어버림

구문 풀이

5행 We decide how much to eat not simply as a function (of how much food we actually consume), but by a comparison (to its alternatives).
(not simply[only] + A + but (also) + B : A뿐 아니라 B도)

02　사냥의 역사를 지니고 있는 음악　　정답률 57% | 정답 ①

다음 빈칸에 들어갈 말로 가장 적절한 것을 고르시오.

✔ hunt – 사냥　　② law – 법
③ charity – 자선 (행위)　　④ remedy – 치료법
⑤ dance – 춤

Even the most respectable of all musical institutions, / the symphony orchestra, / carries inside its DNA the legacy of the hunt.
심지어 모든 음악 단체 중 가장 훌륭한 단체인 / 교향악단도 / 자신의 DNA 안에 사냥의 유산을 지니고 있다.

The various instruments in the orchestra / can be traced back to these primitive origins / — their earliest forms were made / either from the animal (horn, hide, gut, bone) / or the weapons employed in bringing the animal under control (stick, bow).
교향악단에 있는 다양한 악기들은 / 다음의 원시적인 기원으로 거슬러 올라갈 수 있는데, / 그것들의 초기 형태는 만들어졌다. / 동물(뿔, 가죽, 내장, 뼈) / 또는 동물을 진압하기 위해 사용된 무기(막대, 활)로

Are we wrong to hear this history in the music itself, / in the formidable aggression and awe-inspiring assertiveness of those monumental symphonies / that remain the core repertoire of the world's leading orchestras?
음악 그 자체에서 이러한 역사를 듣는다면 우리가 틀린 것인가? / 기념비적인 교향곡들의 강력한 공격성과 경외감을 자아내는 당당함에서 / 세계의 주요한 교향악단의 핵심 레퍼토리로 남아 있는

Listening to Beethoven, Brahms, Mahler, Bruckner, Berlioz, Tchaikovsky, Shostakovich, and other great composers, / I can easily summon up images of bands of men / starting to chase animals, / using sound as a source and symbol of dominance, / an expression of the will to predatory power.
베토벤, 브람스, 말러, 브루크너, 베를리오즈, 차이코프스키, 쇼스타코비치 및 다른 위대한 작곡가들의 음악을 들으며, / 나는 사람들 무리의 이미지를 쉽게 떠올릴 수 있다. / 동물을 쫓기 시작하는 / 소리를 지배의 원천이자 상징으로 사용하면서 / 공격적인 힘에 대한 의지의 표현으로

심지어 모든 음악 단체 중 가장 훌륭한 단체인 교향악단도 자신의 DNA 안에 사냥의 유산을 지니고 있다. 교향악단에 있는 다양한 악기들은 다음의 원시적인 기원으로 거슬러 올라갈 수 있는데, 그것들의 초기 형태는 동물(뿔, 가죽, 내장, 뼈) 또는 동물을 진압하기 위해 사용된 무기(막대, 활)로 만들어졌다. 음악 그 자체에서, 세계의 주요한 교향악단의 핵심 레퍼토리로 남아 있는 기념비적인 교향곡들의 강력한 공격성과 경외감을 자아내는 당당함에서 이러한 역사를 듣는다면 우리가 틀린 것인가? 베토벤, 브람스, 말러, 브루크너, 베를리오즈, 차이코프스키, 쇼스타코비치 및 다른 위대한 작곡가들의 음악을 들으며, 나는 소리를 지배의 원천이자 상징으로, 공격적인 힘에 대한 의지의 표현으로 사용하면서 동물을 쫓기 시작하는 사람들 무리의 이미지를 쉽게 떠올릴 수 있다.

Why? 왜 정답일까?

두 번째 문장에서 초기 악기는 동물의 신체 부위로 만들어지거나 동물을 진압하기 위한 무기(either from the animal ~ or the weapons employed in bringing the animal under control)에서 기원했다고 설명한다. 마지막 문장에서는 유명한 음악가의 음악을 들으면 과거 조상들이 소리로 공격의 의지를 표명하면서 동물들을 사냥하던 모습을 상상할 수 있다고 언급한다. 따라서 빈칸에 들어갈 말로 가장 적절한 것은 ① '사냥'이다.

- respectable ⓐ 훌륭한, 존경할 만한
- institution ⓝ 기관, 제도
- trace back to ~으로 거슬러 올라가다
- primitive ⓐ 원시적인
- hide ⓝ (동물의) 가죽
- aggression ⓝ 공격성
- awe-inspiring ⓐ 경외감을 불러일으키는
- assertiveness ⓝ 적극성, 자기 주장
- monumental ⓐ 기념비적인, 엄청난
- summon up (생각 등을) 불러일으키다
- predatory ⓐ 포식하는, 생물을 잡아먹는

구문 풀이

11행 Listening to Beethoven, Brahms, Mahler, Bruckner, Berlioz, (분사구문(~하면서))
Tchaikovsky, Shostakovich, and other great composers, I can easily (동사구)
summon up images of bands of men starting to chase animals, (목적어) (꾸밈 받는 명사) (현재분사)
using sound as a source and symbol of dominance, an expression (분사구문(~하면서)) (전치사(~로서))
of the will to predatory power.

03　생각을 일상 언어로 풀어보기　　정답률 47% | 정답 ⑤

다음 빈칸에 들어갈 말로 가장 적절한 것을 고르시오. [3점]

① finish writing quickly – 글쓰기를 빨리 끝낼
② reduce sentence errors – 문장의 오류를 줄일
③ appeal to various readers – 다양한 독자의 흥미를 끌

④ come up with creative ideas – 창의적인 생각을 떠올릴
✔ clarify your ideas to yourself – 자신의 생각을 스스로에게 명료하게 할

Translating academic language into everyday language / can be an essential tool for you as a writer / to clarify your ideas to yourself.
학문적인 언어를 일상 언어로 바꿔 보는 것은 / 작가인 여러분에게 필수적인 도구가 될 수 있다. / 자신의 생각을 스스로에게 명료하게 할 수 있는
For, as writing theorists often note, / writing is generally not a process / in which we start with a fully formed idea in our heads / that we then simply transcribe / in an unchanged state onto the page.
왜냐하면, 글쓰기 이론가들이 흔히 지적하듯이, / 글쓰기는 일반적으로 과정이 아니기 때문이다. / 머릿속에 완전하게 만들어진 한 가지 생각으로 시작하는 / 우리가 단순히 옮겨 쓰는 / 본래 그대로의 상태로 페이지 위에
On the contrary, / writing is more often a means of discovery / in which we use the writing process / to figure out what our idea is.
도리어 / 글쓰기는 발견의 수단인 경우가 더 흔하다. / 우리가 글쓰기 과정을 사용하는 / 우리의 생각이 무엇인지를 알아내기 위해
This is why writers are often surprised to find / that what they end up with on the page / is quite different / from what they thought it would be when they started.
이것이 글을 쓰는 사람들이 발견하고는 자주 놀라는 이유이다. / 결국 그들이 페이지 위에 적는 내용이 / 상당히 다르다는 것을 / 그들이 처음에 시작할 때 그렇게 되리라고 생각했던 것과
What we are trying to say here is / that everyday language is often crucial for this discovery process.
우리가 여기서 하고자 하는 말은 / 일상 언어가 이런 발견 과정에 흔히 매우 중요하다는 것이다.
Translating your ideas into more common, simpler terms / can help you figure out what your ideas really are, / as opposed to what you initially imagined they were.
여러분의 생각을 더 평범하고 더 간단한 말로 바꿔 보는 것은 / 실제 여러분의 생각이 무엇인지 알아내도록 도와줄 수 있을 것이다. / 여러분이 처음에 그럴 것이라고 상상했던 것이 아니라

학문적인 언어를 일상 언어로 바꿔 보는 것은 여러분이 작가로서 자신의 생각을 스스로에게 명료하게 할 수 있는 필수적인 도구가 될 수 있다. 왜냐하면, 글쓰기 이론가들이 흔히 지적하듯이, 글쓰기는 일반적으로 머릿속에 완전하게 만들어진 한 가지 생각으로 시작하여, 그 생각을 본래 그대로의 상태로 페이지 위에 단순히 옮겨 쓰는 과정이 아니기 때문이다. 도리어 글쓰기는 글쓰기 과정을 사용하여 우리의 생각이 무엇인지를 알아내는 발견의 수단인 경우가 더 흔하다. 이래서 글을 쓰는 사람들은 결국 페이지 위에 적히는 내용이 처음에 시작할 때 그렇게 되리라고 생각했던 것과 상당히 다르다는 것을 발견하고는 자주 놀란다. 우리가 여기서 하고자 하는 말은 일상 언어가 이런 발견 과정에 흔히 매우 중요하다는 것이다. 여러분의 생각을 더 평범하고 더 간단한 말로 바꿔 보는 것은 여러분이 처음에 그럴 것이라고 상상했던 것이 아니라 실제 여러분의 생각이 무엇인지 알아내도록 도와줄 수 있을 것이다.

Why? 왜 정답일까?

'Translating your ideas into more common, simpler terms can help you figure out what your ideas really are, as opposed to what you initially imagined they were.'에서 머릿속 생각을 쉬운 말로 풀어보면 그 생각의 내용이 실제로 어떤지 깨닫는 데 도움이 될 것이라고 하므로, 빈칸에 들어갈 말로 가장 적절한 것은 ⑤ '자신의 생각을 스스로에게 명료하게 할'이다.

- translate A into B A를 B로 번역하다
- theorist ⓝ 이론가
- unchanged ⓐ 변하지 않은
- end up with 결국 ~하게 되다
- as opposed to ~이 아니라
- come up with ~을 떠올리다
- essential ⓐ 필수적인
- generally ad 일반적으로
- discovery ⓝ 발견
- crucial ⓐ 중요한
- initially ad 처음에
- clarify ⓥ 명확하게 하다

구문 풀이

3행 For, as writing theorists often note, writing is generally not a process [in which we start with a fully formed idea in our heads {that we then simply transcribe in an unchanged state onto the page}]. (a process: 선행사, in which: 「전치사+관·대」, a fully formed idea: 선행사, in our heads: 전명구, that: 목적격 관·대) { }: a fully formed idea 수식

04 도덕적 성찰을 돕기 위한 역사 연구

정답률 47% | 정답 ①

다음 빈칸에 들어갈 말로 가장 적절한 것을 고르시오.

✔ source of moral lessons and reflections – 도덕적 교훈과 성찰의 근원
② record of the rise and fall of empires – 제국의 흥망성쇠에 관한 기록
③ war against violence and oppression – 폭력과 억압에 대항하는 전쟁
④ means of mediating conflict – 갈등 중재의 수단
⑤ integral part of innovation – 혁신의 필수 요소

As well as making sense of events through narratives, / historians in the ancient world established the tradition of history / as a source of moral lessons and reflections.
이야기를 통해서 사건을 이해했을 뿐 아니라 / 고대 사회의 역사가들은 역사의 전통을 확립했다. / 도덕적 교훈과 성찰의 근원으로서
The history writing of Livy or Tacitus, / for instance, / was in part designed / to examine the behavior of heroes and villains, / meditating on the strengths and weaknesses / in the characters of emperors and generals, / providing exemplars for the virtuous to imitate or avoid.
Livy나 Tacitus의 역사적인 기술은 / 예를 들면, / 부분적으로는 만들어져, / 영웅과 악당의 행동을 살펴보도록 / 장점과 단점을 숙고해 / 황제와 장군들의 성격에서의 / 도덕적인 사람들이 모방하거나 피해야 할 표본을 제공한다.
This continues to be one of the functions of history.
이것이 계속되어 역사의 기능 중 하나가 된다.
French chronicler Jean Froissart said / he had written his accounts of chivalrous knights / fighting in the Hundred Years' War / "so that brave men should be inspired thereby / to follow such examples."
프랑스의 연대기 학자인 Jean Froissart는 말했다. / 그가 기사도적인 기사들의 이야기를 썼다고 / 백년전쟁에서 싸운 / '용맹스러운 자들이 영감을 받아 이러한 본보기를 따르도록'
Today, / historical studies of Lincoln, Churchill, Gandhi, or Martin Luther King, Jr. / perform the same function.
오늘날 / Lincoln, Churchill, Gandhi 또는 Martin Luther King, Jr.에 대한 역사적 연구는 / 같은 기능을 수행한다.

고대 사회의 역사가들은 이야기를 통해서 사건을 이해했을 뿐 아니라 도덕적 교훈과 성찰의 근원으로서 역사의 전통을 확립했다. 예를 들면, Livy나 Tacitus의 역사적인 기술은 부분적으로는 황제와 장군들의 성격적 장점과 단점을 숙고해 영웅과 악당의 행동을 살펴보도록 만들어져, 도덕적인 사람들이 모방하거나 피해야 할 표본을 제공한다. 이것이 계속되어 역사의 기능 중 하나가 된다. 프랑스의 연대기 학자인 Jean Froissart는 백년전쟁에서 싸운 기사도적인 기사들의 이야기로 '용맹스러운 자들이 영감을 받아 이러한 본보기를 따르도록' 썼다고 말했다. 오늘날 Lincoln, Churchill, Gandhi 또는 Martin Luther King, Jr.에 대한 역사적 연구는 같은 기능을 수행한다.

Why? 왜 정답일까?

빈칸 뒤의 예시에서 역사적 인물의 장단점을 연구해 사람들이 보고 따를 만한 도덕적 인간의 표본을 만들어낸다(~ providing exemplars for the virtuous to imitate or avoid.)고 하므로, 빈칸에 들어갈 말로 가장 적절한 것은 ① '도덕적 교훈과 성찰의 근원'이다.

- villain ⓝ 악당
- emperor ⓝ 황제
- virtuous ⓐ 도덕적인
- account ⓝ 설명
- empire ⓝ 제국
- meditate on ~에 관해 곰곰이 생각해보다
- exemplar ⓝ 본보기
- chronicler ⓝ 연대기 작가, 기록가
- rise and fall 흥망성쇠
- oppression ⓝ 억압

구문 풀이

9행 French chronicler Jean Froissart said he had written his accounts of chivalrous knights fighting in the Hundred Years' War "so that brave men should be inspired thereby to follow such examples." (had written: 과거완료, so that: 접속사(~하도록), be inspired + to부정사: ~하도록 영감을 받다)

05 사람들의 얼굴을 머릿속에 그릴 수 있는 개들

정답률 59% | 정답 ①

다음 빈칸에 들어갈 말로 가장 적절한 것을 고르시오.

✔ form mental images of people's faces
사람들의 얼굴에 대한 심상을 형성하는
② sense people's moods from their voices
사람들의 목소리로부터 그들의 기분을 파악하는
③ detect possible danger and prepare for it
가능한 위험을 감지하고 그것에 대비하는
④ imitate their guardians' habitual behaviors
그들의 보호자의 습관적 행동을 따라 하는
⑤ selectively obey commands from strangers
낯선 사람들의 명령에 선택적으로 복종하는

A recent study shows / that dogs appear to form mental images of people's faces.
최근의 한 연구는 보여준다. / 개들이 사람들의 얼굴에 대한 심상을 형성하는 것처럼 보인다는 것을

Scientists placed 28 dogs / in front of a computer monitor / blocked by an opaque screen, / then played a recording / of the dog's human guardian or a stranger / saying the dog's name five times / through speakers in the monitor.
과학자들은 28마리의 개들을 놓고, / 컴퓨터 모니터 앞에 / 불투명한 스크린으로 가려진 / 그리고 나서 녹음을 틀어주었다. / 개의 보호자나 낯선 사람이 / 개의 이름을 5번 부르는 / 모니터의 스피커를 통해
Finally, / the screen was removed / to reveal / either the face of the dog's human companion / or a stranger's face.
마지막으로 / 스크린을 제거했다. / 드러내기 위해 / 개의 인간 동반자의 얼굴이나 / 낯선 사람의 얼굴을
The dogs' reactions were videotaped.
개들의 반응이 비디오로 녹화되었다.
Naturally, / the dogs were attentive to the sound of their name, / and they typically stared about six seconds at the face / after the screen was removed.
당연히, / 개들은 자신의 이름을 부르는 소리에 주의를 기울였고, / 그들은 일반적으로 약 6초 동안 얼굴을 응시했다. / 스크린이 제거된 후
But they spent significantly more time / gazing at a strange face / after they had heard the familiar voice of their guardian.
그러나 그들은 훨씬 더 많은 시간을 보냈다. / 낯선 사람의 얼굴을 응시하는 것에 / 그들이 보호자의 친숙한 목소리를 들은 후
That they paused for an extra second or two / suggests / that they realized something was wrong.
그들이 1～2초 동안 더 멈췄다는 것은 / 보여준다. / 그들이 뭔가 잘못된 것을 파악했음을
The conclusion drawn is / that dogs form a picture in their mind, / and that they can think about it / and make predictions / based on that picture.
도출된 결론은 ~이다. / 개들이 머릿속에 그림을 형성하고 / 그들이 그것에 대해서 생각할 수 있고 / 예측할 수 있다는 것 / 그 그림을 바탕으로
And, like us, / they are puzzled / when what they see or hear doesn't match / what they were expecting.
그리고 우리와 마찬가지로, / 개들은 당황한다. / 그들이 보거나 듣는 것이 일치하지 않을 때 / 그들이 기대했던 것과

최근의 한 연구는 개들이 사람들의 얼굴에 대한 심상을 형성하는 것처럼 보인다는 것을 보여준다. 과학자들은 28마리의 개들을 불투명한 스크린으로 가려진 컴퓨터 모니터 앞에 놓고, 그러고 나서 모니터의 스피커를 통해 개의 보호자나 낯선 사람이 개의 이름을 5번 부르는 녹음을 틀어주었다. 마지막으로 스크린을 제거해 개의 인간 동반자의 얼굴이나 낯선 사람의 얼굴을 드러냈다. 개들의 반응이 비디오로 녹화되었다. 당연히, 개들은 자신의 이름을 부르는 소리에 주의를 기울였고, 스크린이 제거된 후 그들은 일반적으로 약 6초 동안 얼굴을 응시했다. 그러나 그들은 보호자의 친숙한 목소리를 들은 후 낯선 사람의 얼굴을 응시하는 데 훨씬 더 많은 시간을 보냈다. 그들이 1～2초 동안 더 멈췄다는 것은 그들이 뭔가 잘못된 것을 파악했음을 보여준다. 도출된 결론은 개들이 머릿속에 그림을 형성하고 그것에 대해서 생각할 수 있고 그 그림을 바탕으로 예측할 수 있다는 것이다. 그리고 우리와 마찬가지로, 개들은 그들이 보거나 듣는 것이 기대했던 것과 일치하지 않을 때 당황한다.

Why? 왜 정답일까?

연구의 결론을 제시하는 '**The conclusion drawn is that dogs form a picture in their mind, and that they can think about it and make predictions based on that picture.**'에서 개들은 목소리 녹음을 듣고 목소리 주인의 얼굴에 대한 머릿속 이미지를 만들어냈으며 그 이미지를 바탕으로 예측도 할 수 있었던 것으로 보인다고 언급하므로, 빈칸에 들어갈 말로 가장 적절한 것은 ① '사람들의 얼굴에 대한 심상을 형성하는'이다.

- **companion** ⓝ 동반자
- **typically** ad 일반적으로, 전형적으로
- **significantly** ad 상당히, 현저히
- **make a prediction** 예측하다
- **detect** ⓥ 감지하다
- **selectively** ad 선택적으로
- **attentive** ⓐ 주의를 기울이는
- **stare** ⓥ 응시하다
- **gaze at** ⓥ ~을 응시하다
- **puzzled** ⓐ 당황한
- **habitual** ⓐ 습관적인

구문 풀이

16행 The conclusion drawn is that dogs form a picture in their mind, and that they can think about it and make predictions based on that picture.
(The conclusion: 주어 / drawn: 과거분사 / is: 동사 / that: 접속사1 / dogs: 주어 / form: 동사 / that: 접속사2 / they: 주어 / can think: 동사1 / make: 동사2 / based on: 분사구문(~을 바탕으로))

06 내륙 지역의 기후를 건조하게 만드는 산

정답률 52% | 정답 ③

다음 빈칸에 들어갈 말로 가장 적절한 것을 고르시오. [3점]

① increase annual rainfall in dry regions
건조한 지역에서 연간 강우량을 늘리다
② prevent drastic changes in air temperature
급격한 기온 변화를 방지하다
✔ play a huge role in stopping the flow of moisture
수분의 흐름을 막는 데 큰 역할을 한다
④ change wind speed as air ascends and descends them
공기가 오르내림에 따라 풍속을 바꾸다
⑤ equalize the amount of moisture of surrounding land areas
주변 토지의 습도를 균등하게 하다

When it comes to climates / in the interior areas of continents, / mountains play a huge role / in stopping the flow of moisture.
기후에 있어서 / 대륙의 내륙 지역의 / 산은 큰 역할을 한다. / 수분의 흐름을 막는 데
A great example of this / can be seen along the West Coast of the United States.
이것의 좋은 예를 / 미국의 서해안을 따라 확인할 수 있다.
Air moving from the Pacific Ocean toward the land / usually has a great deal of moisture in it.
태평양에서 육지로 이동하는 공기는 / 보통 많은 수분을 함유한다.
When this humid air moves across the land, / it encounters the Coast Range Mountains.
이 습한 공기가 육지를 가로질러 이동할 때, / 그것은 코스트산맥 산들과 마주친다.
As the air moves up and over the mountains, / it begins to cool, / which causes precipitation on the windward side of the mountains.
공기가 상승하여 산맥 위로 이동하면서 / 그것은 식기 시작하고, / 이는 산의 풍상측(風上側)에 강수를 발생시킨다.
Once the air moves down the opposite side of the mountains / (called the leeward side) / it has lost a great deal of moisture.
공기가 산의 반대편으로 내려갈 때쯤이면 / (풍하측(風下側)이라고 불리는) / 그것은 많은 수분을 잃어버린다.
The air continues to move / and then hits the even higher Sierra Nevada mountain range.
공기는 계속 움직이며 / 그러고 나서 훨씬 더 높은 시에라네바다 산맥과 부딪친다.
This second uplift causes most of the remaining moisture / to fall out of the air, / so by the time it reaches the leeward side of the Sierras, / the air is extremely dry.
이 두 번째 상승은 남아 있는 수분 대부분이 ~하게 하며 / 공기로부터 빠져나오게 / 그래서 그것이 시에라 산맥의 풍하측에 도달할 때쯤이면 / 공기는 극도로 건조하다.
The result is / that much of the state of Nevada is a desert.
그 결과는 ~이다. / 네바다주 대부분이 사막이라는 것

대륙의 내륙 지역의 기후에 있어서 산은 수분의 흐름을 막는 데 큰 역할을 한다. 이것의 좋은 예를 미국의 서해안을 따라 확인할 수 있다. 태평양에서 육지로 이동하는 공기는 보통 많은 수분을 함유한다. 이 습한 공기가 육지를 가로질러 이동할 때, 그것은 코스트산맥 산들과 마주친다. 공기는 상승하여 산맥 위로 이동하면서 시기 시작하고, 이는 산의 풍상측(風上側)에 강수를 발생시킨다. 공기가 (풍하측(風下側)이라고 불리는) 산의 반대편으로 내려갈 때쯤이면 그것은 많은 수분을 잃어버린다. 공기는 계속 움직이며 그러고 나서 훨씬 더 높은 시에라네바다 산맥과 부딪친다. 이 두 번째 상승은 남아 있는 수분 대부분을 공기로부터 빠져나오게 하며, 그래서 공기는 시에라 산맥의 풍하측에 도달할 때쯤이면 극도로 건조하다. 그 결과 네바다주 대부분이 사막이 된다.

Why? 왜 정답일까?

태평양에서 육지로 이동하는 공기는 본래 많은 수분을 포함하고 있지만 산 위로 상승해 온도가 떨어져 비로 내리는 과정 속에서 그 수분을 거의 잃고 건조해진다(**~ most of the remaining moisture to fall out of the air, so ~ the air is extremely dry.**)고 한다. 따라서 빈칸에 들어갈 말로 가장 적절한 것은 ③ '수분의 흐름을 막는 데 큰 역할을 한다'이다.

- **continent** ⓝ 대륙
- **precipitation** ⓝ 강수
- **leeward** ⓐ 바람이 가려지는 쪽의
- **uplift** ⓝ 상승
- **extremely** ad 매우, 극도로
- **ascend** ⓥ 올라가다
- **encounter** ⓥ 마주치다, 접하다
- **windward** ⓐ 바람이 불어오는 쪽의
- **a great deal of** 많은 양의
- **fall out of** ~에서 빠져나오다
- **drastic** ⓐ 급격한, 과감한
- **equalize** ⓥ 균등하게 하다

구문 풀이

14행 This second uplift causes most of the remaining moisture to fall out of the air, so by the time it reaches the leeward side of the Sierras, the air is extremely dry.
(causes ~ to fall: 「cause + 목적어 + to부정사 : ~이 …하게 야기하다」 / by the time: 접속사(~할 무렵))

★★★ **1등급 대비 고난도 2점 문제**

07 화폐의 희소성

정답률 17% | 정답 ②

다음 빈칸에 들어갈 말로 가장 적절한 것을 고르시오.

① invested – 투자될
✔ scarce – 희소성이 있을

③ transferred – 이동될 ④ divisible – 나뉠 수 있을
⑤ deposited – 예치될

Most importantly, / money needs to be scarce in a predictable way.
가장 중요하게도, / 돈은 예측 가능한 방식으로 희소성이 있을 필요가 있다.
Precious metals have been desirable as money / across the millennia / not only because they have intrinsic beauty / but also because they exist in fixed quantities.
귀금속은 돈으로서 바람직했다. / 수 천 년에 걸쳐 / 내재적인 아름다움을 지니고 있을 뿐만 아니라 / 고정된 양으로 존재하기 때문에
Gold and silver enter society at the rate / at which they are discovered and mined; / additional precious metals cannot be produced, / at least not cheaply.
금과 은은 속도만큼 사회에 유입되는데, / 그것들이 발견되고 채굴되는 / 추가적인 귀금속은 생산될 수가 없다. / 적어도 싸게는
Commodities like rice and tobacco can be grown, / but that still takes time and resources.
쌀과 담배와 같은 상품들은 재배할 수 있지만, / 여전히 시간과 자원이 든다.
A dictator like Zimbabwe's Robert Mugabe / could not order the government / to produce 100 trillion tons of rice.
Zimbabwe의 Robert Mugabe와 같은 독재자도 / 정부에 명령할 수 없었다. / 100조 톤의 쌀을 생산하라고
He was able to produce and distribute trillions of new Zimbabwe dollars, / which is why / they eventually became more valuable / as toilet paper than currency.
그는 수조의 새로운 Zimbabwe 달러를 만들어 유통시킬 수 있었는데, / 이것은 이유이다. / 결국 그것이 더 가치가 있게 되었던 / 통화(通貨)보다 휴지로서

가장 중요하게도, 돈은 예측 가능한 방식으로 희소성이 있을 필요가 있다. 귀금속은 내재적인 아름다움을 지니고 있을 뿐만 아니라 고정된 양으로 존재하기 때문에 수 천 년에 걸쳐 돈으로서 바람직했다. 금과 은은 발견되고 채굴되는 만큼 사회에 유입되는데, 추가적인 귀금속은 적어도 싸게는 생산될 수가 없다. 쌀과 담배와 같은 상품들은 재배할 수 있지만, 여전히 시간과 자원이 든다. Zimbabwe의 Robert Mugabe와 같은 독재자도 정부에 100조 톤의 쌀을 생산하라고 명령할 수 없었다. 그는 수조의 새로운 Zimbabwe 달러를 만들어 유통시킬 수 있었는데, 이것은 결국 그것이 통화(通貨)보다 휴지로서 더 가치가 있게 되었던 이유이다.

Why? 왜 정답일까?

빈칸 뒤에서 귀금속은 고정된 양으로 존재하기 때문에(~ **they exist in fixed quantities.**) 돈으로서 기능하기 바람직했다는 내용에 이어 추가적인 귀금속은 싸게 생산될 수 없다고 덧붙이고 있다. 이는 귀금속이 수요에 따라 무한정 늘어나지 못하고 늘 욕구에 비해 '희소한' 상태를 유지했기에 돈으로서의 가치를 지녔다는 뜻으로 이해할 수 있다. 따라서 빈칸에 들어갈 말로 가장 적절한 것은 ② '희소성이 있을'이다.

- **predictable** ⓐ 예측 가능한
- **desirable** ⓐ 바람직한
- **intrinsic** ⓐ 내재적인, 본질적인, 고유한
- **quantity** ⓝ 양
- **dictator** ⓝ 독재자
- **distribute** ⓥ 유통시키다, 배포하다
- **precious** ⓐ 귀중한, 소중한
- **millennium** ⓝ 1천 년
- **fixed** ⓐ 고정된
- **commodity** ⓝ 상품
- **trillion** ⓐ 1조의
- **currency** ⓝ 통화

구문 풀이

11행 **He was able to produce and distribute trillions of new Zimbabwe dollars, which is (the reason) why they eventually became more valuable as toilet paper than currency.**
「be able to + 동사원형1 and 동사원형2 : ~하고 …할 수 있다」 / 계속적 용법(앞 문장 받음) / 생략된 선행사 / 관계부사 / 2형식 동사 / 보어

★★ 문제 해결 꿀~팁 ★★

▶ 많이 틀린 이유는?
지문의 다른 부분에 빈칸과 대응될 말이 없어 까다로운 문제였다. 귀금속은 애초에 양도 정해져 있고 추가로 만들어질 수도 없기에 '희소성'을 지니고 있고, 이로 인해 화폐로 쓰이기 적합했다는 내용상의 흐름을 이해하도록 한다. 오답으로 많이 꼽힌 ①, ③의 경우 지문의 내용보다는 상식을 근거로 할 때 답으로 고르기 쉬운 선택지였다.
▶ 문제 해결 방법은?
'**not only ~ but also** …'가 들어간 문장은 많은 경우 주제를 제시하며, 특히 **but also** 이하에는 핵심 소재가 나온다. 여기서도 **but also** 뒤에 나온 '**exist in fixed quantities**'가 정답에 대한 결정적인 힌트를 제공하고 있다.

★★★ 1등급 대비 고난도 3점 문제

08 환경에 대한 인간의 영향력 정답률 45% | 정답 ①

다음 빈칸에 들어갈 말로 가장 적절한 것을 고르시오. [3점]
① imposing ourselves on nature – 우리 자신을 자연에게 강요하고 있으며
② limiting our ecological impact – 우리의 생물학적 영향력을 제한하고 있으며
③ yielding our land to mammals – 우리의 땅을 포유류에게 내주고 있으며
④ encouraging biological diversity – 생물학적 다양성을 장려하고 있으며
⑤ doing useful work for the environment – 환경에 유용한 일을 하고 있으며

We are now imposing ourselves on nature, / instead of the other way around.
우리는 지금 우리 자신을 자연에게 강요하고 있다. / 그 반대의 경우는 대신
Perhaps the clearest way to see this / is to look at changes / in the biomass — the total worldwide weight — of mammals.
아마도 이것을 알 수 있는 가장 분명한 방법은 / 변화를 보는 것이다. / 전 세계 포유류 무게의 총합, 즉 생물량의
A long time ago, / all of us humans together / probably weighed only about two-thirds as much / as all the bison in North America, / and less than one-eighth as much / as all the elephants in Africa.
오래전에 / 우리 인간은 모두 합쳐도 / 아마 대략 3분의 2 정도의 무게였고, / 북미에 있는 모든 들소 무게의 / 8분의 1 무게보다 적었다. / 아프리카의 모든 코끼리의
But in the Industrial Era / our population exploded / and we killed bison and elephants / at industrial scale and in terrible numbers.
하지만 산업 시대에 / 우리의 인구는 폭발적으로 증가했고 / 우리는 들소와 코끼리를 죽였다. / 엄청난 규모와 끔찍한 숫자로
The balance shifted greatly as a result.
그 결과 균형이 엄청나게 바뀌었다.
At present, / we humans weigh more than 350 times as much / as all bison and elephants put together.
현재는 / 우리 인간이 350배가 넘는 무게가 나간다. / 모든 들소와 코끼리를 합친 무게의
We weigh over ten times more / than all the earth's wild mammals combined.
우리는 10배 이상 무게가 나간다. / 지구상의 모든 야생 포유류를 합친 것보다
And if we add in all the mammals we've domesticated / — cattle, sheep, pigs, horses, and so on — / the comparison becomes truly ridiculous: / we and our tamed animals / now represent 97 percent of the earth's mammalian biomass.
그리고 만약 우리가 사육해 온 모든 포유류를 포함한다면 / 소, 양, 돼지, 말 등 / 그 비교는 정말로 터무니없어지는데, / 우리와 우리가 길들인 동물은 / 현재 지구 포유류 생물량의 97%에 해당한다.
This comparison illustrates a fundamental point: / instead of being limited by the environment, / we learned to shape it to our own ends.
이러한 비교는 기본적인 핵심을 보여주고 있는데, / 환경에 의해 제약을 받는 것이 아니라, / 우리는 우리 자신의 목적에 맞게 그것을 만들도록 배웠다.

우리는 지금 우리 자신을 자연에게 강요하고 있으며, 그 반대의 경우는 아니다. 아마도 이것을 알 수 있는 가장 분명한 방법은 전 세계 포유류 무게의 총합, 즉 생물량의 변화를 보는 것이다. 오래전에 우리 인간은 모두 합쳐도 아마 북미에 있는 모든 들소 무게의 대략 3분의 2 정도의 무게였고, 아프리카의 모든 코끼리의 8분의 1 무게보다 적었다. 하지만 산업 시대에 우리의 인구는 폭발적으로 증가했고 우리는 엄청난 규모와 끔찍한 숫자의 들소와 코끼리를 죽였다. 그 결과 균형이 엄청나게 바뀌었다. 현재는 우리 인간이 모든 들소와 코끼리를 합친 무게의 350배가 넘는 무게가 나간다. 우리는 지구상의 모든 야생 포유류를 합친 것보다 10배 이상 무게가 나간다. 그리고 만약 우리가 사육해 온 소, 양, 돼지, 말 등 모든 포유류를 포함한다면 그 비교는 정말로 터무니없어지는데, 우리와 우리가 길들인 동물은 현재 지구 포유류 생물량의 97%에 해당한다. 이러한 비교는 기본적인 핵심을 보여주고 있는데, 우리는 환경에 의해 제약을 받는 것이 아니라, 우리 자신의 목적에 맞게 그것을 만들도록 배웠다.

Why? 왜 정답일까?

마지막 문장에서 생물량을 비교해보면 우리 인간은 환경에 제약을 받는 대신 오히려 우리 자신의 목적에 맞게 환경을 만들어나가는 법을 배웠다(~ **instead of being limited by the environment, we learned to shape it to our own ends.**)는 점을 알 수 있다고 했다. 따라서 빈칸에 들어갈 말로 가장 적절한 것은 인간이 환경에 영향을 받는 대상이라기보다는 영향력을 직접 행사하는 주체라는 뜻의 ① '우리 자신을 자연에게 강요하고 있으며'이다.

- **the other way around** 반대로, 거꾸로
- **mammal** ⓝ 포유류
- **at industrial scale** 대규모로
- **domesticate** ⓥ 가축화하다, 길들이다
- **tame** ⓥ 길들이다
- **illustrate** ⓥ (예를 들어) 보여주다
- **biomass** ⓝ (특정 지역 내의) 생물량
- **explode** ⓥ 폭발적으로 증가하다
- **shift** ⓥ 변화하다, 바뀌다
- **ridiculous** ⓐ 터무니없는, 우스꽝스러운
- **represent** ⓥ 나타내다
- **fundamental** ⓐ 기본적인

- to one's end ~의 목적을 위해서
- impose ⓥ 강요하다, 부과하다
- yield ⓥ (~에게) 양도하다

구문 풀이

13행 We weigh over ten times more than all the earth's wild mammals combined.
「배수사+비교급+than : ~보다 … 배 더 ~한/하게」
과거분사

★★ 문제 해결 꿀~팁 ★★

▶ 많이 틀린 이유는?
본래 인간은 북미 모든 들소 무게의 약 2/3, 아프리카 모든 코끼리 무게의 1/8 미만 정도를 차지했으나, 산업화 이후 인구는 폭발적으로 늘고 들소와 코끼리는 죽어 나가면서 비중이 완전히 역전되었다는 것이 글의 주된 내용이다. ②, ③은 모두 인간이 자연에서 차지하는 비중이 '늘었다'는 내용과 정반대되는 선택지이다.
▶ 문제 해결 방법은?
마지막 문장 이전까지 부연과 예시가 주를 이루다가 마지막 문장에서 결론을 제시하고 있다. 앞은 숫자 위주로 비교적 가볍게 읽고 마지막 문장의 의미를 정확히 파악한 뒤, 오답 선택지를 소거하며 풀도록 한다.

★★★ 1등급 대비 고난도 3점 문제

09 비교군에 좌우되는 연주 평가 정답률 30% | 정답 ②

다음 빈칸에 들어갈 말로 가장 적절한 것을 고르시오. [3점]

① there are moments of inspiration
영감이 떠오르는 순간들이 있기
② there is little basis for comparison
비교할 만한 근거가 거의 없기
③ he or she longs to be such a person
그가 그러한 사람이 되기를 간절히 바라기
④ other people recognize his or her efforts
다른 사람들이 그의 노력을 알아보기
⑤ he or she was born with great artistic talent
그가 위대한 예술적 재능을 갖고 태어났기

Sometimes / a person is acclaimed as "the greatest" / because there is little basis for comparison.
때때로 / 누군가는 '가장 위대하다'고 칭송받는다. / 비교할 만한 근거가 거의 없기 때문에
For example, / violinist Jan Kubelik was acclaimed as "the greatest" / during his first tour of the United States, / but when impresario Sol Hurok brought him back / to the United States in 1923, / several people thought / that he had slipped a little.
예를 들어, / 바이올리니스트 Jan Kubelik는 '가장 위대하다'고 칭송받았지만, / 그의 첫 번째 미국 순회공연 기간 동안 / 기획자 Sol Hurok이 그를 다시 데려왔을 때, / 1923년에 미국으로 / 몇몇 사람들은 생각했다. / 그가 실력이 약간 떨어졌다고
However, / Sol Elman, / the father of violinist Mischa Elman, / thought differently.
그러나 / Sol Elman은 / 바이올리니스트 Mischa Elman의 아버지인 / 다르게 생각했다.
He said, / "My dear friends, / Kubelik played the Paganini concerto tonight / as splendidly as ever he did.
그는 말했다. / "친애하는 친구들이여, / Kubelik는 오늘 밤 Paganini 협주곡을 연주했습니다. / 그가 늘 했던 것만큼 훌륭하게
Today you have a different standard.
오늘 여러분은 다른 기준을 가지고 있습니다.
You have Elman, Heifetz, and the rest.
여러분에게는 Elman, Heifetz, 그리고 그 밖의 연주자가 있습니다.
All of you have developed and grown / in artistry, technique, / and, above all, / in knowledge and appreciation.
여러분 모두 발전하고 성장했습니다. / 예술성, 기법, / 그리고 무엇보다 / 지식과 감식력에서
The point is: / you know more; / not that Kubelik plays less well."
요점은 / 여러분이 더 많이 알고 있는 것이지, / Kubelik가 연주 실력이 더 떨어진 것이 아닙니다."라고

때때로 누군가는 비교할 만한 근거가 거의 없기 때문에 '가장 위대하다'고 칭송받는다. 예를 들어, 바이올리니스트 Jan Kubelik는 그의 첫 번째 미국 순회공연 동안 '가장 위대하다'고 칭송받았지만, 1923년에 기획자 Sol Hurok이 그를 미국으로 다시 데려왔을 때, 몇몇 사람들은 그가 실력이 약간 떨어졌다고 생각했다. 그러나 바이올리니스트 Mischa Elman의 아버지인 Sol Elman은 다르게 생각했다. "친애하는 친구들이여, 오늘 밤 Kubelik는 그가 늘 했던 것만큼 훌륭하게 Paganini 협주곡을 연주했습니다. 오늘날 여러분은 다른 기준을 가지고 있습니다. 여러분에게는 Elman, Heifetz, 그리고 그 밖의 연주자가 있습니다. 여러분 모두 예술성, 기법, 그리고 무엇보다 지식과 감식력에서 발전하고 성장했습니다. 요점은 여러분이 더 많이 알고 있는 것이지, Kubelik가 연주 실력이 더 떨어진 것이 아닙니다."라고 그는 말했다.

Why? 왜 정답일까?

첫 미국 순회공연에서 연주 실력을 극찬 받았던 Jan Kubelik은 후에 다시 미국에서 공연했을 때에는 일부 사람들에 의해 실력이 떨어졌다고 평가되었는데, 이는 Sol Elman에 따르면 사람들의 비교 기준이 달라졌기 때문이었다(Today you have a different standard.). 새로운 비교 대상이 생기면서 같은 실력에 비해 보다 낮게 평가하게 된 것이라는 내용의 마지막 문장(The point is: you know more; ~)을 근거로 할 때, Jan Kubelik이 최고라고 칭송받았던 이유는 당시에 비교 대상이 없었기 때문이었을 것임을 유추할 수 있으므로, 빈칸에 들어갈 말로 가장 적절한 것은 ② '비교할 만한 근거가 거의 없기'이다.

- slip ⓥ 떨어지다, 미끄러지다
- splendidly ad 훌륭하게, 멋지게, 근사하게
- standard ⓝ 수준, 기준
- artistry ⓝ 예술적 기교
- appreciation ⓝ 평가, 감식, 감상
- inspiration ⓝ 영감
- basis ⓝ 근거

구문 풀이

3행 For example, violinist Jan Kubelik was acclaimed as "the greatest" during his first tour of the United States, but (when impresario Sol Hurok brought him back to the United States in 1923), several people thought {that he had slipped a little}.
주어1 / 동사1(~로 칭송받다) / ( ) : 부사절 / 주어2 / 동사2 / 접속사(~것)

★★ 문제 해결 꿀~팁 ★★

▶ 많이 틀린 이유는?
첫 문장인 주제문을 완성하는 빈칸 문제로, 글의 다른 부분에 빈칸의 재진술로 볼 수 있는 표현이 없어 까다롭다. 본문이 비교 기준에 따라 실력에 대한 평가가 달라진다는 내용을 다루고 있는 것으로 볼 때, 노력을 언급하는 ④는 주제와 관계가 없다.
▶ 문제 해결 방법은?
일화 형식의 글이므로 결론이 중요하다. 마지막 세 문장의 'You have Elman, Heifetz, and the rest.', '~ you know more; ~' 등이 의미하는 바에 주목하며 답을 찾도록 한다.

★★★ 1등급 대비 고난도 3점 문제

10 일반 전문직과 저널리즘의 차이점 정답률 32% | 정답 ①

다음 빈칸에 들어갈 말로 가장 적절한 것을 고르시오. [3점]

① its lack of independence – 그것의 독립성의 부족
② the constant search for truth – 지속적인 진리 추구
③ the disregard of public opinion – 여론의 무시
④ its balance of income and faith – 수입과 신념의 균형
⑤ its overconfidence in its social influence – 사회적 영향에 대한 과신

What is unusual about journalism as a profession / is its lack of independence.
직업으로서의 저널리즘에서 특이한 점은 / 그것의 독립성의 부족이다.
In theory, / practitioners in the classic professions, / like medicine or the clergy, / contain the means of production in their heads and hands, / and therefore do not have to work / for a company or an employer.
이론적으로, / 고전적 전문직에 종사하는 사람들은 / 의학이나 성직자처럼 / 머리와 손 안에 생산 수단을 지니고 있으므로, / 일할 필요가 없다. / 회사나 고용주를 위해
They can draw their income / directly from their clients or patients.
그들은 수입을 끌어낼 수 있다. / 고객이나 환자로부터 직접
Because the professionals hold knowledge, moreover, / their clients are dependent on them.
게다가, 전문직 종사자들은 지식을 보유하고 있기 때문에, / 그들의 고객은 이들에게 의존한다.
Journalists hold knowledge, / but it is not theoretical in nature; / one might argue / that the public depends on journalists / in the same way that patients depend on doctors, / but in practice a journalist can serve the public / usually only by working for a news organization, / which can fire her or him at will.
언론인들은 지식을 보유하고 있지만, / 그것은 본질적으로 이론적이지 않다. / 어떤 사람들은 주장할지도 모르지만, / 대중이 언론인들에게 의존한다고 / 환자들이 의사들에게 의존하는 것과 같은 방식으로 / 실제로 언론인은 대중들에게 봉사할 수 있으며, / 일반적으로 뉴스 기관을 위해 일해야만 / 그 기관은 그 사람을 마음대로 해고할 수 있다.
Journalists' income depends not on the public, / but on the employing news organization, / which often derives the large majority of its revenue from advertisers.
언론인들의 수입은 대중에 의존하지 않고 / 고용한 뉴스 기관에 의존하는데, / 이는 종종 광고주들로부터 수익의 대부분을 얻는다.

[문제편 p.019]

직업으로서의 저널리즘에서 특이한 점은 그것의 독립성의 부족이다. 이론적으로, 의학이나 성직자처럼 고전적인 전문직에 종사하는 사람들은 머리와 손 안에 생산 수단을 지니고 있으므로, 회사나 고용주를 위해 일할 필요가 없다. 그들은 고객이나 환자로부터 직접 수입을 끌어낼 수 있다. 게다가, 전문직 종사자들은 지식을 보유하고 있기 때문에, 고객은 이들에게 의존한다. 언론인들은 지식을 보유하고 있지만, 그것은 본질적으로 이론적이지 않다. 어떤 사람들은 환자들이 의사들에게 의존하는 것과 같은 방식으로 대중이 언론인들에게 의존한다고 주장할지도 모르지만, 실제로 언론인은 일반적으로 뉴스 기관을 위해 일해야만 대중들에게 봉사할 수 있으며, 그 기관은 그 사람을 마음대로 해고할 수 있다. 언론인들의 수입은 대중이 아닌, 고용한 뉴스 기관에 의존하는데, 이 기관들은 종종 광고주들로부터 수익의 대부분을 얻는다.

Why? 왜 정답일까?

마지막 두 문장(~ but in practice a journalist can serve the public usually only by working for a news organization, which can fire her or him at will. Journalists' income depends not on the public, but on the employing news organization, ~)에서, 언론인은 고전적인 전문직과는 달리 지식을 보유하고 있어도 독립적이지 못한 채 자신을 고용한 뉴스 기관을 위해 일해야 한다고 설명한다. 따라서 빈칸에 들어갈 말로 가장 적절한 것은 ① '그것의 독립성의 부족'이다.

- practitioner ⓝ 전문직 종사자, 현역
- means of production 생산 수단
- theoretical ⓐ 이론적인
- at will 마음대로
- disregard ⓝ 무시
- overconfidence ⓝ 과신
- clergy ⓝ 성직자
- draw A from B A를 B로부터 끌어내다
- in nature 본질적으로
- derive A from B A를 B로부터 얻다
- faith ⓝ 믿음

구문 풀이

1행 {What is unusual about journalism as a profession} is its lack of independence.
{ }: 주어(명사절) / as: 전치사(~로서) / is: 동사(단수)

★★ 문제 해결 꿀~팁 ★★

▶ 많이 틀린 이유는?
저널리스트를 설명하는 글 중후반부에 the public이 많이 등장하므로, 얼핏 보면 public이 포함된 ③이 정답처럼 보인다. 하지만 저널리스트들이 '대중의 의견을 무시'한다는 내용은 글 어디에도 없다.

▶ 문제 해결 방법은?
전문직과 저널리스트를 구별하는 부분을 잘 봐야 한다. 전문직은 자기 분야에 대한 전문성과 지식을 인정받기 때문에, 회사를 위해서 일할 필요가 없으며 의뢰인도 이들의 지식을 신뢰한다는 내용이 글 중반까지 나온다. 하지만 'Journalists hold knowledge, ~' 이후로는 저널리스트들의 상황이 '다르다'는 내용이 주를 이룬다. 이들은 회사에 '종속되어' 일하므로 '업무 독립성에 제약이 있다'는 것이다.

★★★ 1등급 대비 고난도 3점 문제

11 진화적 군비 경쟁 — 정답률 32% | 정답 ②

다음 빈칸에 들어갈 말로 가장 적절한 것을 고르시오. [3점]

① been in a fierce war over scarce food sources
희소한 식량 자원을 두고 맹렬한 전쟁을 치러
✔② been engaged in a life-or-death sensory arms race
수백만 년 동안 생사를 가르는 감각 군비 경쟁에 참여해
③ invented weapons that are not part of their bodies
그들의 신체 일부가 아닌 무기를 발명해
④ evolved to cope with other noise-producing wildlife
소음을 만들어내는 다른 야생 생물에 대처하도록 진화해
⑤ adapted to flying in night skies absent of any lights
아무 빛도 없는 밤하늘을 나는 데 적응해

As always happens with natural selection, / bats and their prey / have been engaged in a life-or-death sensory arms race / for millions of years.
자연 선택에서 항상 그렇듯이, / 박쥐와 그 먹잇감은 / 생사를 가르는 감각 군비 경쟁에 참여해 왔다. / 수백만 년 동안

It's believed / that hearing in moths arose / specifically in response to the threat of being eaten by bats.
여겨진다. / 나방의 청력은 생겨났다고 / 특히 박쥐에게 잡아먹히는 위협에 대한 반응으로

(Not all insects can hear.)
(모든 곤충이 들을 수 있는 것은 아니다.)

Over millions of years, / moths have evolved the ability / to detect sounds at ever higher frequencies, / and, as they have, / the frequencies of bats' vocalizations have risen, too.
수백만 년 동안, / 나방은 능력을 발달시켰고, / 계속 더 높아진 주파수의 소리를 감지하는 / 그것들이 그렇게 하면서 / 박쥐의 발성 주파수도 높아졌다.

Some moth species have also evolved / scales on their wings / and a fur-like coat on their bodies; / both act as "acoustic camouflage," / by absorbing sound waves in the frequencies / emitted by bats, / thereby preventing those sound waves from bouncing back.
또한 일부 나방 종은 진화시켰다. / 날개의 비늘과 / 몸에 모피와 같은 외피를 / 둘 다 '음향 위장'의 역할을 한다. / 주파수의 음파를 흡수함으로써 / 박쥐에 의해 방출되는 / 그렇게 하여 음파가 박쥐에게로 되돌아가는 것을 방지함으로써

The B-2 bomber and other "stealth" aircraft / have fuselages / made of materials / that do something similar with radar beams.
B-2 폭격기와 그 밖의 '스텔스' 항공기는 / 재료로 만들어진 기체를 가지고 있다. / 레이더 전파에 유사하게 반응하는

자연 선택에서 항상 그렇듯이, 박쥐와 그 먹잇감은 수백만 년 동안 생사를 가르는 감각 군비 경쟁에 참여해 왔다. 나방의 청력은 특히 박쥐에게 잡아먹히는 위협에 대한 반응으로 생겨났다고 여겨진다. (모든 곤충이 들을 수 있는 것은 아니다.) 수백만 년 동안, 나방은 계속 더 높아진 주파수의 소리를 감지하는 능력을 발달시켰고, 그것들이 그렇게 하면서 박쥐의 발성 주파수도 높아졌다. 또한 일부 나방 종은 날개의 비늘과 몸에 모피와 같은 외피를 진화시켰다. 둘 다 '음향 위장'의 역할을 해서, 박쥐에 의해 방출되는 주파수의 음파를 흡수하여 음파가 박쥐에게로 되돌아가는 것을 방지한다. B-2 폭격기와 그 밖의 '스텔스' 항공기는 레이더 전파에 유사하게 반응하는 재료로 만들어진 기체를 가지고 있다.

Why? 왜 정답일까?

박쥐의 먹잇감인 나방은 잡아먹히지 않기 위해 박쥐가 내는 고주파음을 듣도록 진화해왔고, 그에 따라 박쥐는 더 높은 주파수를 낼 수 있도록 같이 진화해왔다는 내용이다. 이렇듯 두 종이 더 잡아먹고 덜 잡아먹히기 위해 경쟁적으로 진화하는 과정을 '군비 경쟁'으로 볼 수 있으므로, 빈칸에 들어갈 말로 가장 적절한 것은 ② '수백만 년 동안 생사를 가르는 감각 군비 경쟁에 참여해'이다.

- natural selection 자연 선택
- moth ⓝ 나방
- detect ⓥ 감지하다
- vocalization ⓝ 발성
- acoustic ⓐ 청각적인
- absorb ⓥ 흡수하다
- bounce back 반향하다, 되돌아가다
- stealth ⓐ 스텔스기의, 숨어서 하는
- fierce ⓐ 맹렬한
- wildlife ⓝ 야생 생물
- prey ⓝ 먹이 동물
- threat ⓝ 위협
- frequency ⓝ 주파수
- scale ⓝ 비늘
- camouflage ⓝ 위장
- emit ⓥ 방출하다
- bomber ⓝ 폭격기
- fuselage ⓝ (비행기의) 기체
- arms race 군비 경쟁
- absent of ~이 없는

구문 풀이

3행 It's believed that hearing in moths arose specifically in response to the threat of being eaten by bats.
=Hearing in moths is believed to have arisen ~ / being eaten: 동명사의 수동태(being p.p.)

★★ 문제 해결 꿀~팁 ★★

▶ 많이 틀린 이유는?
예시의 지엽적 내용에만 집중하면 '소음을 만들어낸다'는 표현이 들어간 ④를 고르기 쉽다. 하지만 빈칸 뒤에 예시가 나오면 이를 적절히 일반화해야 정답을 도출할 수 있다.

▶ 문제 해결 방법은?
박쥐가 더 높은 주파수의 소리를 내고, 나방이 소리를 더 잘 듣게 계속 진화하는 이유는 각자 더 '생존'에 유리해지기 위함이다. 이 진화가 '경쟁적으로' 일어난다는 점도 포인트이다.

★★★ 1등급 대비 고난도 3점 문제

12 친환경적인 행위의 경제적 이득 — 정답률 25% | 정답 ①

다음 빈칸에 들어갈 말로 가장 적절한 것을 고르시오. [3점]

✔① it pays to be green – 친환경적인 것이 이득이 된다
② toxins destroy markets – 독소가 시장을 파괴한다
③ green products are on the rise – 친환경적인 제품들이 상승세에 있다
④ environmental problems persist – 환경 문제들이 지속된다
⑤ our faith in statistics is unfounded – 통계 수치에 대한 우리의 믿음은 근거가 없다

A vast academic literature / provides empirical support for the thesis / that it pays to be green.

방대한 학술 문헌은 / 논지에 대한 경험적인 증거를 제공한다. / 친환경적인 것이 이득이 된다는

Large data sets have been constructed, / measuring firm environmental behavior and financial performance / across a wide number of industries / and over many years.

많은 양의 데이터 집합이 구축되어 왔다. / 기업 환경 행위와 재무 성과를 측정하면서 / 광범위한 산업들을 대상으로 / 여러 해 동안

While the results are not unequivocal, / there is evidence / suggestive of a positive correlation / between environmental performance and financial performance.

그 결과들이 명료하지는 않지만, / 증거가 있다. / 양의 상관관계를 시사하는 / 환경 행위와 재무 성과 사이의

In our own work, / we find that, / on average, a 10% decrease in a company's toxic emissions / as reported in the US Environmental Protection Agency's Toxic Release Inventory / — a database of toxic emissions from US manufacturing facilities — / results in an average 3% increase / in a firm's financial performance / as measured by return on assets.

우리 자신의 연구에서, / 우리는 알아냈다. / 평균적으로 한 회사의 유해 물질 배출에서의 10퍼센트 감소가 / 미국 환경 보호국의 유해 물질 배출 목록에서 보고한 바와 같이, / — 미국 제조 시설들에서 나오는 유해 물질 배출에 대한 데이터베이스 — / 평균 3퍼센트의 증가를 가져온다는 것을 / 기업의 재무 성과에서 / 자산 수익률을 측정했을 때

Another study suggests / that a 10% reduction in emissions / could result in a $34 million increase / in market value.

또 다른 연구는 시사한다. / 배출물의 10퍼센트 감소가 / 3천4백만 달러의 증가를 가져올 수도 있다는 것을 / 시장 가치에서

방대한 학술 문헌은 친환경적인 것이 이득이 된다는 논지에 대한 경험적인 증거를 제공한다. 대규모 데이터 집합이 많은 수의 산업들을 대상으로 여러 해 동안 기업 환경 행위와 재무 성과를 측정하면서 구축되어 왔다. 그 결과들이 명료하지는 않지만, 환경 행위와 재무 성과 사이의 양의 상관관계를 시사하는 증거가 있다. 우리 자신의 연구에서, 우리는 미국 환경 보호국의 유해 물질 배출 목록 — 미국 제조 시설들에서 나오는 유해 물질 배출에 대한 데이터베이스 — 에서 보고한 바와 같이, 평균적으로 한 회사의 유해 물질 배출에서의 10퍼센트 감소가 자산 수익률로 측정된 기업의 재무 성과에서 평균 3퍼센트의 증가를 가져온다는 것을 알아냈다. 또 다른 연구는 배출물의 10퍼센트 감소가 시장 가치에서 3천4백만 달러의 증가를 가져올 수도 있다는 것을 시사한다.

Why? 왜 정답일까?

'While the results are not unequivocal, there is evidence suggestive of a positive correlation between environmental performance and financial performance.'의 주절에서 환경 행위와 재무 성과 사이에는 양의 상관관계가 나타난다는, 즉 친환경적인 행위를 할 때 경제적인 이득이 따를 수 있다는 증거가 있음을 언급하므로, 이 내용을 재진술하는 빈칸에 들어갈 말로 가장 적절한 것은 ① '친환경적인 것이 이득이 된다'이다.

- empirical ⓐ 경험적인
- suggestive of ~을 시사하는, 암시하는
- on the rise 상승세에 있는, 떠오르는
- unfounded ⓐ 근거 없는
- thesis ⓝ 논지, 학위 논문
- correlation ⓝ 상관관계
- persist ⓥ 지속되다, 계속되다

구문 풀이

9행 In our own work, we find {that, on average, a 10% decrease (주어) in a company's toxic emissions (as reported in the US Environmental Protection Agency's Toxic Release Inventory — a database of toxic emissions from US manufacturing facilities) — results (동사(~을 야기하다)) in an average 3% increase (목적어) in a firm's financial performance (as measured by return on assets)}. ( ): 분사구문, 동격, { }: find의 목적어

★★ 문제 해결 꿀~팁 ★★

▶ 많이 틀린 이유는?

친환경적 행위의 경제적 효과라는 낯선 주제를 다룬 글로, ②는 예시에 지엽적으로 나오는 유해 물질을 언급하여 답으로 적절치 않다. ③ 또한 이 글이 기업의 환경 행위를 다룰 뿐 친환경 제품에 대한 내용을 다루지 않으므로 부적절한 선택지이다.

▶ 문제 해결 방법은?

예시 앞의 문장은 보통 주제를 말한다. 이 지문 또한 'In our own work ~' 이하로 예가 제시되기에 앞서 '~ there is evidence suggestive of a positive correlation between environmental performance and financial performance.'라는 핵심 표현이 나오고 있다.

[문제편 p.020]

DAY 03 빈칸 추론 03

01 ①	02 ③	03 ③	04 ④	05 ②
06 ①	07 ②	08 ③	09 ③	10 ④
11 ⑤	12 ③			

01 맛 선호도의 발달

정답률 54% | 정답 ①

다음 빈칸에 들어갈 말로 가장 적절한 것을 고르시오.

① Taste preferences – 맛 선호도
② Hunting strategies – 사냥 전략
③ Migration patterns – 이주 패턴
④ Protective instincts – 보호 본능
⑤ Periodic starvations – 주기적 굶주림

The elements any particular animal needs / are relatively predictable.

어떤 특정한 동물이 필요로 하는 요소들은 / 상대적으로 예측 가능하다.

They are predictable based on the past: / what an animal's ancestors needed / is likely to be what that animal also needs.

그것들은 과거에 기반하여 예측 가능한데, / 즉 어떤 동물의 조상들이 필요로 했던 것은 / 그 동물이 현재에도 필요로 하는 것일 가능성이 있다.

Taste preferences, therefore, can be hardwired.

그러므로 맛 선호도는 타고나는 것일 수 있다.

Consider sodium (Na).

나트륨(Na)을 생각해 보라.

The bodies of terrestrial vertebrates, / including those of mammals, / tend to have a concentration of sodium / nearly fifty times that of the primary producers on land, / plants.

육생 척추동물의 몸은 / 포유동물의 몸을 포함하여 / 나트륨 농도를 지니고 있는 경향이 있다. / 육지의 주된 생산자의 농도의 50배인 / 즉, 식물

This is, in part, because vertebrates evolved in the sea / and so evolved cells / dependent upon the ingredients / that were common in the sea, / including sodium.

이는 부분적으로는 척추동물이 바다에서 진화했고 / 따라서 세포를 진화시켰기 때문이다. / 성분들에 의존한 / 바다에서 흔했던 / 나트륨을 포함하여

To remedy the difference / between their needs for sodium and that available in plants, / herbivores can eat fifty times more plant material / than they otherwise need / (and eliminate the excess).

격차를 해결하기 위해 / 나트륨에 대한 욕구와 식물에서 얻을 수 있는 나트륨 사이의 / 초식 동물은 50배 더 많은 식물을 섭취할 수 있다. / 그들이 그렇지 않은 경우 필요로 하는 것보다 / (그리고 초과분을 배설한다)

Or they can seek out other sources of sodium.

또는 나트륨의 다른 공급원을 찾아다닐 수 있다.

The salt taste receptor rewards animals for doing the latter, / seeking out salt / in order to satisfy their great need.

짠맛 수용기는 후자의 행위에 대해 동물에게 보상을 한다. / 즉 소금을 찾아다니는 것 / 그들의 엄청난 욕구를 충족시키기 위해

어떤 특정한 동물이 필요로 하는 요소들은 상대적으로 예측 가능하다. 그것들은 과거에 기반하여 예측 가능한데, 즉 어떤 동물의 조상들이 필요로 했던 것은 그 동물이 현재에도 필요로 하는 것일 가능성이 있다. 그러므로 맛 선호도는 타고나는 것일 수 있다. 나트륨(Na)을 생각해 보라. 포유동물의 몸을 포함하여 육생 척추동물의 몸은 육지의 주된 생산자인 식물보다 나트륨 농도가 거의 50배인 경향이 있다. 이는 부분적으로는 척추동물이 바다에서 진화했고, 따라서 나트륨을 포함하여 바다에서 흔했던 성분들에 의존한 세포를 진화시켰기 때문이다. 나트륨에 대한 욕구와 식물에서 얻을 수 있는 나트륨 사이의 격차를 해결하기 위해 초식 동물은 그렇지 않은 경우 필요로 하는 것보다 50배 더 많은 식물을 섭취할 수 있다(그리고 초과분을 배설한다). 또는 나트륨의 다른 공급원을 찾아다닐 수 있다. 짠맛 수용기는 후자의 행위, 즉 엄청난 욕구를 충족시키기 위해 소금을 찾아다니는 것에 대해 동물에게 보상을 한다.

Why? 왜 정답일까?

예시에 따르면 본래 바다에서 진화한 육생 동물들은 식물에 비해 체내 나트륨 비율이 훨씬 높아서, 필요한 만큼 나트륨을 먹으려면 식물을 아주 많이 먹어야 하거나 다른 나트륨 공급원을 찾아야 하는 상황이라고 한다. 그리고 마지막 문장에서는 이들의 짠맛 수용기가 나트륨을 더 찾아나서는 행위에 '보상'을 해준다고 한다. 이는 짠맛에 대한 선호로 이어지게 될 것이므로, 빈칸에 들어갈 말로 가장 적절한 것은 ① '맛 선호도'이다.

- predictable ⓐ 예측 가능한
- concentration ⓝ 농도
- remedy ⓥ 해결하다, 바로잡다
- hardwired ⓐ 타고난, 내장된
- dependent upon ~에 의존하는
- eliminate ⓥ 배설하다, 제거하다

[문제편 p.020]

- receptor ⓝ (신체의) 수용기, 감각기
- periodic ⓐ 주기적인
- reward ⓥ 보상하다

구문 풀이

12행 To remedy the difference between their needs for sodium and that available in plants, herbivores can eat fifty times more plant material than they otherwise need (and eliminate the excess).
부사적 용법(~하기 위해) / 「between + A + and + B : A와 B 사이에」 / 「배수표현 + 비교급 + than : ~보다 …배 더 한」

02 농지 분산의 이점

정답률 57% | 정답 ③

다음 빈칸에 들어갈 말로 가장 적절한 것을 고르시오. [3점]

① land leveling – 땅 평평하게 고르기
② weed trimming – 잡초 손질
③ field scattering – 농지 흩어놓기 ✔
④ organic farming – 유기농법
⑤ soil fertilization – 토지 비옥하게 만들기

It is not the peasant's goal / to produce the highest possible time-averaged crop yield, / averaged over many years.
농부의 목표가 아니다. / 최고로 가능한 시간 평균적인 농작물 생산량을 만드는 것은 / 여러 해에 걸쳐서 평균을 내는

If your time-averaged yield is marvelously high / as a result of the combination of nine great years and one year of crop failure, / you will still starve to death in that one year of crop failure / before you can look back / to congratulate yourself on your great time-averaged yield.
당신의 시간 평균적인 생산량이 엄청나게 높더라도, / 좋았던 9년과 농사에 실패한 1년을 합친 결과로 / 당신은 농사에 실패한 바로 그 한 해에 굶어 죽을 것이다. / 당신이 돌아보기도 전에 / 훌륭한 시간 평균적인 생산량에 있어서 스스로를 축하하려고

Instead, / the peasant's aim is / to make sure to produce a yield above the starvation level in every single year, / even though the time-averaged yield may not be highest.
대신에, / 농부의 목표는 ~이다. / 굶어 죽지 않을 수준 이상의 생산량을 매년 확실히 만들어내는 것이다. / 시간 평균적인 생산량이 가장 높지 않을지라도

That's why field scattering may make sense.
그것이 바로 농지 흩어놓기가 합리적인 이유이다.

If you have just one big field, / no matter how good it is on the average, / you will starve / when the inevitable occasional year arrives / in which your one field has a low yield.
만일 당신이 그냥 하나의 큰 농지를 가지고 있다면, / 그것이 평균적으로 아무리 좋다고 할지라도, / 당신은 굶주리게 될 것이다. / 그 가끔 오는 불가피한 때가 오면 / 당신의 유일한 농지가 낮은 생산량을 내는

But if you have many different fields, / varying independently of each other, / then in any given year / some of your fields will produce well / even when your other fields are producing poorly.
그러나 만일 당신이 농지들을 가지고 있다면, / 서로 상관없는 다른 / 어느 해에 / 당신의 농지 중 일부는 잘 생산할 것이다. / 당신의 다른 농지들이 빈약하게 생산하고 있을 때조차도

여러 해에 걸쳐서 평균을 내는, 최고로 가능한 시간 평균적인 농작물 생산량을 만드는 것은 농부의 목표가 아니다. 당신의 시간 평균적인 생산량이 (농사 결과가) 좋았던 9년과 농사에 실패한 1년을 합친 결과로 엄청나게 높더라도, 당신은 훌륭한 시간 평균적인 생산량에 있어서 스스로를 축하하려고 돌아보기도 전에 농사에 실패한 바로 그 한 해에 굶어 죽을 것이다. 대신에, 농부의 목표는 시간 평균적인 생산량이 가장 높지 않을지라도, 굶어 죽지 않을 수준 이상의 생산량을 매년 확실히 만들어내는 것이다. 그것이 바로 농지 흩어놓기가 합리적인 이유이다. 만일 당신이 그냥 하나의 큰 농지를 가지고 있다면, 그것이 평균적으로 아무리 좋다고 할지라도, 당신은 유일한 농지가 낮은 생산량을 내는 그 가끔 오는 불가피한 때가 오면 굶주리게 될 것이다. 그러나 만일 당신이 서로 상관없는 다른 농지들을 가지고 있다면, 어느 해에 당신의 다른 농지들이 빈약하게 생산하고 있을 때조차도 당신의 농지 중 일부는 잘 생산할 것이다.

Why? 왜 정답일까?

빈칸 뒤에서 큰 농지를 하나 가지고 있을 때와 여러 개의 분산된 농지를 갖고 있을 때를 대조하며, 전자의 경우 그 농지 수확이 낮으면 꼼짝없이 위기를 맞지만 후자의 경우 어느 한 땅이 안 좋아도 다른 땅이 벌충해줄 수 있어 좋다(**But if you have many different fields, varying independently of each other, then in any given year some of your fields will produce well** ~)고 설명하고 있다. 따라서 빈칸에 들어갈 말로 가장 적절한 것은 ③ '농지 흩어놓기'이다.

- peasant ⓝ 농부, 소작농
- marvelously ad 놀랍도록
- make sure to 확실히 ~하다
- occasional ⓐ 이따금의
- leveling (땅을) 고름, 평평하게 함
- fertilization ⓝ (땅을) 비옥하게 하기
- yield ⓝ 수확량, 산출량
- starve to death 굶어 죽다
- inevitable ⓐ 불가피한
- independently of ~와 상관없이
- scatter ⓥ 흩어놓다

구문 풀이

3행 If your time-averaged yield is marvelously high as a result of the combination of nine great years and one year of crop failure, you will still starve to death in that one year of crop failure before you can look back to congratulate yourself on your great time-averaged yield.
접속사(조건) / 현재시제 / ~의 결과로 / 미래시제 / 부사적 용법(목적)

03 어떤 것을 선택하기 전에 먼저 작게 시도해보기

정답률 67% | 정답 ③

다음 빈칸에 들어갈 말로 가장 적절한 것을 고르시오.

① trying out what other people do – 다른 사람들이 하는 것을 시험 삼아 해보는
② erasing the least preferred options – 가장 선호하지 않는 선택권을 지우는
③ testing the option on a smaller scale – 선택을 좀 더 작은 규모로 시험해보는 ✔
④ sharing your plans with professionals – 전문가와 계획을 상의하는
⑤ collecting as many examples as possible – 가능한 한 많은 사례를 모으는

We are often faced with high-level decisions, / where we are unable to predict the results of those decisions.
우리는 종종 높은 수준의 결정에 직면하는데, / 거기에서 우리는 그 결정의 결과를 예측할 수 없다.

In such situations, / most people end up quitting the option altogether, / because the stakes are high / and results are very unpredictable.
그런 경우에, / 대부분의 사람들은 결국 선택권을 전적으로 포기하는데, / 왜냐하면 위험성이 높고 / 결과가 매우 예측 불가능하기 때문이다.

But there is a solution for this.
그러나 여기에는 해결책이 있다.

You should use the process / of testing the option on a smaller scale.
당신은 과정을 활용해야 한다. / 선택을 좀 더 작은 규모로 시험해보는

In many situations, it's wise / to dip your toe in the water / rather than dive in headfirst.
많은 경우에, 현명하다. / 발끝을 담그는 것이 / 물속에 머리부터 뛰어들기보다는

Recently, I was about to enroll / in an expensive coaching program.
최근에, 나는 등록을 하려고 했었다. / 비싼 코칭 프로그램에

But I was not fully convinced / of how the outcome would be.
그러나 나는 완전히 확신하지 못했다. / 그 결과가 어떠할지

Therefore, I used this process / by enrolling in a low-cost mini course with the same instructor.
그러므로 나는 이러한 과정을 활용했다. / 똑같은 강사의 저렴한 미니 코스에 등록함으로써

This helped me understand his methodology, style, and content; / and I was able to test it / with a lower investment, and less time and effort / before committing fully to the expensive program.
이것은 내가 그의 방법론, 스타일, 그리고 교육 내용을 이해하도록 도왔고, / 나는 그것을 시험해 볼 수 있었다. / 더 적은 투자, 그리고 더 적은 시간과 노력으로 / 비싼 프로그램에 완전히 전념하기 전에

우리는 종종 높은 수준의 결정에 직면하는데, 거기에서 우리는 그 결정의 결과를 예측할 수 없다. 그런 경우에, 대부분의 사람들은 결국 선택권을 전적으로 포기하는데, 왜냐하면 위험성이 높고 결과가 매우 예측 불가능하기 때문이다. 그러나 여기에는 해결책이 있다. 당신은 선택을 좀 더 작은 규모로 시험해보는 과정을 활용해야 한다. 많은 경우에, 물속에 머리부터 뛰어들기보다는 발끝을 담그는 것이 현명하다. 최근에, 나는 비싼 코칭 프로그램에 등록을 하려고 했었다. 그러나 나는 그 결과가 어떠할지 완전히 확신하지 못했다. 그러므로 나는 똑같은 강사의 저렴한 미니 코스에 등록함으로써 이러한 과정을 활용했다. 이것은 내가 그의 방법론, 스타일, 그리고 교육 내용을 이해하도록 도왔고, 비싼 프로그램에 완전히 전념하기 전에 나는 그것을 더 적은 투자, 그리고 더 적은 시간과 노력으로 시험해 볼 수 있었다.

Why? 왜 정답일까?

빈칸 뒤의 '**In many situations, it's wise to dip your toe in the water rather than dive in headfirst.**'에서 물속에 머리부터 다 뛰어들기보다는 발끝을 담가보는게 현명하다는 비유적인 표현을 통해 어떤 것을 선택하기 앞서 작게 시도해보라는 조언을 제시하고 있다. 이어서 마지막 두 문장 또한 필자가 비싼 코칭 프로그램을 듣기로 결정하기 전에 먼저 미니 코스부터 들어 보아서 비교적 저렴한 비용과 노력으로 의사 결정에 참고할 만한 정보를 얻었다고 언급하고 있다. 따라서 빈칸에 들어갈 말로 가장 적절한 것은 ③ '선택을 좀 더 작은 규모로 시험해보는'이다.

- predict ⓥ 예측하다
- altogether ad 전적으로, 완전히
- enroll in ~에 등록하다
- outcome ⓝ 결과
- content ⓝ 내용
- end up 결국 ~하게 되다
- dip ⓥ 담그다, 적시다
- convinced ⓐ 확신하는
- methodology ⓝ 방법론
- investment ⓝ 투자

구문 풀이

1행 We are often faced with high-level decisions, where we are unable to predict the results of those decisions.
선행사(추상적 공간) 관계부사 ~할 수 없다

04 생태 환경에 대한 감정적 묘사에 신중하기

정답률 44% | 정답 ④

다음 빈칸에 들어갈 말로 가장 적절한 것을 고르시오. [3점]

① complex organisms are superior to simple ones
다세포 생물이 단세포보다 우월하다
② technologies help us survive extreme environments
기술은 우리가 극심한 환경에서 생존하도록 돕는다
③ ecological diversity is supported by extreme environments
생태적 다양성이 극심한 환경들에 의해 뒷받침된다
④ all other organisms sense the environment in the way we do
모든 다른 유기체가 우리가 느끼는 방식으로 환경을 느낀다
⑤ species adapt to environmental changes in predictable ways
생물 종들은 예측 가능한 방식으로 환경 변화에 적응한다

It seems natural / to describe certain environmental conditions / as 'extreme', 'harsh', 'benign' or 'stressful'.
당연해 보인다. / 특정한 환경 조건을 묘사하는 것은 / '극심한', '혹독한', '온화한' 또는 '스트레스를 주는'이라고
It may seem obvious / when conditions are 'extreme': / the midday heat of a desert, / the cold of an Antarctic winter, / the salinity of the Great Salt Lake.
그것이 명백해 보일지도 모른다. / 상태가 '극심한' 경우에는 / 사막 한낮의 열기, / 남극 겨울의 추위, / 그레이트 솔트호의 염도와 같이
But this only means / that these conditions are extreme *for us*, / given our particular physiological characteristics and tolerances.
하지만 이것은 의미할 뿐이다. / 이러한 조건이 *우리에게* 극심하다는 것을 / 우리의 특정한 생리적 특징과 내성을 고려할 때
To a cactus / there is nothing extreme about the desert conditions / in which cacti have evolved; / nor are the icy lands of Antarctica / an extreme environment for penguins.
선인장에게 / 사막의 환경 조건은 전혀 극심한 것이 아니며, / 선인장들이 진화해 온 / 남극의 얼음에 뒤덮인 땅도 아니다 / 펭귄에게 극심한 환경이
It is lazy and dangerous / for the ecologist to assume / that all other organisms sense the environment / in the way we do.
나태하고 위험하다. / 생태학자가 추정하는 것은 / 모든 다른 유기체가 환경을 느낀다고 / 우리가 느끼는 방식으로
Rather, / the ecologist should try to gain a worm's-eye or plant's-eye view of the environment: / to see the world as others see it.
오히려 / 생태학자는 환경에 대한 벌레의 관점이나 식물의 관점을 취하려고 노력해야 한다. / 다른 유기체가 세계를 보는 방식으로 세계를 바라보기 위해
Emotive words like harsh and benign, / even relativities such as hot and cold, / should be used by ecologists / only with care.
혹독한, 그리고 온화한 같은 감정적 단어들, / 심지어 덥고 추운 것과 같은 상대적인 단어들은 / 생태학자들에 의해 사용되어야 한다. / 오로지 신중하게

특정한 환경 조건을 '극심한', '혹독한', '온화한' 또는 '스트레스를 주는'이라고 묘사하는 것은 당연해 보인다. 사막 한낮의 열기, 남극 겨울의 추위, 그레이트 솔트호의 염도와 같이 상태가 '극심한' 경우에는 그것이 명백해 보일지도 모른다. 하지만 이것은 우리의 특정한 생리적 특징과 내성을 고려할 때 이러한 조건이 *우리에게* 극심하다는 것을 의미할 뿐이다. 선인장에게 선인장들이 진화해 온 사막의 환경 조건은 전혀 극심한 것이 아니며, 펭귄에게 남극의 얼음에 뒤덮인 땅은 극심한 환경이 아니다. 생태학자가 모든 다른 유기체가 우리가 느끼는 방식으로 환경을 느낀다고 추정하는 것은 나태하고 위험하다. 오히려 생태학자는 다른 유기체가 세계를 보는 방식으로 세계를 바라보기 위해 환경에 대한 벌레의 관점이나 식물의 관점을 취하려고 노력해야 한다. 혹독한, 그리고 온화한 같은 감정적 단어들, 심지어 덥고 추운 것과 같은 상대적인 단어들은 생태학자들에 의해 오로지 신중하게 사용되어야 한다.

Why? 왜 정답일까?

Rather로 시작하는 문장에서, 생태학자는 우리 자신의 시각으로 어떤 환경을 바라보기보다, 그 환경에 적응해 사는 다른 생물의 관점을 두루 취할 의무가 있다(~ **the ecologist should try to gain a worm's-eye or plant's-eye view of the environment: to see the world as others see it.**)고 한다. 즉 '모두가 우리와 같게 느낄 것이라고' 나태하게 가정하지 말아야 한다는 것이 글의 주제이다. 따라서 빈칸에 들어갈 말로 가장 적절한 것은 ④ '모든 다른 유기체가 우리가 느끼는 방식으로 환경을 느낀다'이다.

- extreme ⓐ 극심한, 극도의
- harsh ⓐ 혹독한
- benign ⓐ 온화한
- obvious ⓐ 명백한
- Antarctic ⓐ 남극의
- salinity ⓝ 염도
- physiological ⓐ 생리적인
- characteristic ⓝ 특성
- tolerance ⓝ 내성, 저항력, 인내
- cactus (*pl.* cacti) ⓝ 선인장
- lazy ⓐ 나태한, 게으른
- ecologist ⓝ 생태학자
- emotive ⓐ 감정적인, 감정을 나타내는
- relativity ⓝ 상대성
- complex organism 다세포 생물

구문 풀이

11행 It is lazy and dangerous for the ecologist to assume that all other organisms sense the environment in the way we do.
가주어 의미상 주어 진주어 대동사(= sense)

05 인간에 대한 연구를 어렵게 하는 교란 변수

정답률 34% | 정답 ②

다음 빈칸에 들어갈 말로 가장 적절한 것을 고르시오. [3점]

① distort the interpretation of the medical research results
의학 연구 결과의 해석을 왜곡하기
② isolate the effects of the specific variable being studied
연구되고 있는 특정한 변수의 영향을 분리하기
③ conceal the purpose of their research from subjects
자신의 연구 목적을 실험 참가자로부터 숨기기
④ conduct observational studies in an ethical way
관찰 연구를 윤리적 방식으로 수행하기
⑤ refrain from intervening in their experiments
자신의 실험에 개입하기를 자제하기

Observational studies of humans / cannot be properly controlled.
인간에 대한 관찰 연구는 / 적절하게 통제될 수 없다.
Humans live different lifestyles and in different environments.
인간은 다양한 생활 방식으로 다양한 환경에서 산다.
Thus, / they are insufficiently homogeneous / to be suitable experimental subjects.
따라서 / 그들은 충분히 동질적이지 않다. / 적절한 실험 대상이 되기에
These *confounding factors* undermine our ability / to draw sound causal conclusions / from human epidemiological surveys.
이러한 *교란 변수*는 우리의 능력을 약화시킨다. / 타당한 인과적 결론을 도출하는 / 인간 역학 조사로부터
Confounding factors are variables (known or unknown) / that make it difficult / for epidemiologists / to isolate the effects of the specific variable being studied.
교란 변수는 (알려지거나 알려지지 않은) 변수이다. / 어렵게 하는 / 역학자가 / 연구되고 있는 특정한 변수의 영향을 분리하기
For example, / Taubes argued / that since many people who drink also smoke, / researchers have difficulty determining the link / between alcohol consumption and cancer.
예를 들어, / Taubes는 주장했다. / 술을 마시는 많은 사람들이 흡연도 하기 때문에 / 연구자들이 연관성을 파악하는 데 어려움을 겪는다고 / 알코올 섭취와 암 사이의
Similarly, / researchers in the famous Framingham study / identified a significant correlation / between coffee drinking and coronary heart disease.
마찬가지로 / 유명한 Framingham 연구의 연구자들은 / 상당한 상관관계를 확인했다. / 커피를 마시는 것과 관상 동맥성 심장 질환 사이에
However, / most of this correlation disappeared / once researchers corrected for the fact / that many coffee drinkers also smoke.
그러나 / 이러한 상관관계의 대부분은 사라졌다. / 연구자들이 사실에 대해 수정하자 / 커피를 마시는 많은 사람들이 흡연도 한다는
If the confounding factors are known, / it is often possible / to correct for them.
교란 변수들이 알려져 있다면 / 종종 가능하다. / 그것들을 수정하는 것이
However, if they are unknown, / they will undermine the reliability of the causal conclusions / we draw from epidemiological surveys.
그러나 그것들이 알려져 있지 않다면, / 그것들은 인과적 결론의 신뢰성을 손상시킬 것이다. / 우리가 역학 조사로부터 도출하는

인간에 대한 관찰 연구는 적절하게 통제될 수 없다. 인간은 다양한 생활 방식으로 다양한 환경에서 산다. 따라서 그들은 적절한 실험 대상이 되기에 충분히 동질적이지 않다. 이러한 *교란 변수*는 인간 역학 조사로부터 타당한 인과적 결론을 도출하는 우리의 능력을 약화시킨다. 교란 변수는 역학자가 연구되고 있는 특정한 변수의 영향을 분리하기 어렵게 하는 (알려지거나 알려지지 않은) 변수이다. 예를 들어, Taubes는 술을 마시는 많은 사람들이 흡연도 하기 때문에 연구자들이 알코올 섭취와 암 사이의 연관성을 파악하는 데 어려움을 겪는다고 주장했다. 마찬가지로 유명한 Framingham 연구의 연구자들은 커피를 마시는 것과 관상 동맥성 심장 질환 사이에 상당한 상관관계를 확인했다. 그러나 연구자들이 커피를 마시는 많은 사람들이 흡연도 한다는 사실에 대해 수정하자 이러한 상관관계의 대부분은 사라졌다. 교란 변수들이 알려져 있다면 그것들을 수정하는 것이 종종 가능하다. 그러나 그것들이 알려져 있지 않다면, 그것들은 우리가 역학 조사로부터 도출하는 인과적 결론의 신뢰성을 손상시킬 것이다.

DAY 03

[문제편 p.022]

Why? 왜 정답일까?

첫 문장과 마지막 두 문장의 내용을 종합하면, 교란 변수가 알려진 경우에는 이를 수정할 수 있지만 알려지지 않은 경우 수정되기 어렵기 때문에, 인간을 대상으로 한 연구는 적절히 통제되기 어렵다는 것이 글의 결론이다. 여기서 '통제되기 어렵다'는 말은 결국 실험 결과에 영향을 미치는 다른 변수, 즉 교란 변수를 연구 대상인 변수로부터 '분리해내' 수정하기가 어렵다는 의미로 이해할 수 있다. 따라서 빈칸에 들어갈 말로 가장 적절한 것은 ② '연구되고 있는 특정한 변수의 영향을 분리하기'이다.

- observational ⓐ 관찰의
- homogeneous ⓐ 동질적인
- confounding factor 교란 변수
- draw a conclusion 결론을 내리다
- epidemiologist ⓝ 전염병학자, 역학자
- coronary ⓐ 관상 동맥의
- distort ⓥ 왜곡하다
- conceal ⓥ 숨기다, 가리다
- intervene ⓥ 간섭하다
- insufficiently ad 불충분하게
- suitable ⓐ 적절한
- undermine ⓥ 약화시키다
- epidemiological ⓐ 역학의
- correlation ⓝ 상관관계
- reliability ⓝ 신뢰도
- isolate ⓥ 분리하다
- refrain from ~을 자제하다, 삼가다

구문 풀이

7행 Confounding factors are variables (known or unknown) [that make it difficult for epidemiologists to isolate the effects of the specific variable being studied].
가목적어 / 목적격 보어 / 의미상 주어 / 진목적어 / 분사구(진행수동)

06 같은 높이의 경사면과 직선 비교

정답률 56% | 정답 ①

다음 빈칸에 들어갈 말로 가장 적절한 것을 고르시오. [3점]

① more distance in stairs is traded for less force
계단을 이용했을 때의 더 먼 거리는 더 작은 힘과 교환된다
② a ladder should be positioned at a steep angle
사다리는 가파른 각도로 놓여야 한다
③ the distance needs to be measured precisely
거리는 정확하게 측정되어야 한다
④ an object's weight has to be reduced
물체의 무게를 줄여야 한다
⑤ slopes are often preferred to stairs
경사면이 계단보다 종종 선호된다

If you want to use the inclined plane / to help you move an object / (and who wouldn't?), / then you have to move the object over a longer distance / to get to the desired height / than if you had started from directly below and moved upward.
여러분이 경사면을 이용하기를 원한다면, / 물체를 이동시키는 데 도움이 되도록 / (그리고 누가 안 그러겠는가?) / 여러분은 그 물체를 더 긴 거리로 이동시켜야 한다. / 원하는 높이에 도달하게 하기 위해서는 / 바로 아래에서 시작하여 위로 이동시켰을 때보다
This is probably already clear to you / from a lifetime of stair climbing.
이것은 아마도 이미 여러분에게 명백할 것이다. / 평생 계단을 올랐던 것으로 인해
Consider all the stairs you climb / compared to the actual height / you reach from where you started.
여러분이 오르는 모든 계단을 고려해 보라. / 실제 높이와 비교하여 / 여러분이 출발한 곳으로부터 도달하는
This height is always less / than the distance you climbed in stairs.
이 높이는 항상 짧다. / 계단으로 오른 거리보다
In other words, more distance in stairs / is traded for less force / to reach the intended height.
다시 말해, 계단을 이용했을 때의 더 먼 거리는 / 더 작은 힘과 교환된다. / 의도한 높이에 도달하기 위해서
Now, if we were to pass on the stairs altogether / and simply climb straight up to your destination / (from directly below it), / it would be a shorter climb for sure, / but the needed force to do so would be greater.
이제 우리가 계단을 완전히 지나쳐 / 단순히 여러분의 목적지까지 곧바로 올라가려고 한다면, / (바로 아래로부터) / 확실히 더 짧은 거리를 오르는 것이지만, / 그렇게 하는 데 필요한 힘은 더 커질 것이다.
Therefore, we have stairs in our homes rather than ladders.
그러므로 우리는 집에 사다리가 아닌 계단을 가지고 있는 것이다.

여러분이 물체를 이동시키는 데 도움이 되도록 경사면을 이용하기를 원한다면(그리고 누가 안 그러겠는가?), 여러분은 그 물체를 원하는 높이에 도달하게 하기 위해서는 바로 아래에서 시작하여 위로 이동시켰을 때보다 더 긴 거리로 이동시켜야 한다. 이것은 아마도 평생 계단을 올랐던 것으로 인해 이미 여러분에게 명백할 것이다. 여러분이 출발한 곳으로부터 도달하는 실제 높이와 비교하여 여러분이 오르는 모든 계단을 고려해 보라. 이 높이는 항상 계단으로 오른 거리보다 짧다. 다시 말해, 의도한 높이에 도달하기 위해서 계단을 이용했을 때의 더 먼 거리는 더 작은 힘과 교환된다. 이제 우리가 계단을 완전히 지나쳐 (바로 아래로부터) 단순히 여러분의 목적지까지 곧바로 올라가려고 한다면, 확실히 더 짧은 거리를 오르는 것이지만, 그렇게 하는 데 필요한 힘은 더 커질 것이다. 그러므로 우리는 집에 사다리가 아닌 계단을 가지고 있는 것이다.

Why? 왜 정답일까?

'If you want to use the inclined plane to help you move an object ~, then you have to move the object over a longer distance to get to the desired height ~'에 따르면 경사면을 이용하여 물체를 더 높은 위치로 이동시킬 경우 바로 아래에서 직선으로 올릴 때보다 더 먼 거리로 이동시키게 된다. 한편 빈칸 뒤의 문장에서는 직선으로 올라올 때 거리는 더 짧지만 힘이 더 많이 든다고 설명한다. 즉 같은 높이에 도달하는 경사면과 직선을 비교하면 경사면이 거리는 더 길지만 힘은 직선에 비해 덜 든다는 것이 글의 주된 내용이므로, 빈칸에 들어갈 말로 가장 적절한 것은 ① '계단을 이용했을 때의 더 먼 거리는 더 작은 힘과 교환된다'이다.

- desired ⓐ 원하는
- altogether ad 완전히
- ladder ⓝ 사다리
- precisely ad 정확히
- height ⓝ 높이
- destination ⓝ 목적지
- steep ⓐ 가파른
- slope ⓝ 경사면

구문 풀이

11행 Now, if we were to pass on the stairs altogether and simply climb straight up to your destination (from directly below it), it would be a shorter climb for sure, but the needed force to do so would be greater.
「if + 주어 + were to + 동사원형 ~, 주어 + would + 동사원형 : 가정법 미래(만에 하나 ~한다면 …할 것이다)」

07 영화 속에서 음악의 역할

정답률 42% | 정답 ②

다음 빈칸에 들어갈 말로 가장 적절한 것을 고르시오.

① frees the plot of its familiarity – 줄거리에서 친숙함을 없애다
② aids in viewer access to the film – 관객이 영화에 접근하는 데 도움이 된다
③ adds to an exotic musical experience – 이국적인 음악 경험을 더해준다
④ orients audiences to the film's theme – 관객이 영화의 주제 쪽으로 향하게 한다
⑤ inspires viewers to think more deeply – 관객이 더 깊이 생각하도록 자극을 준다

A musical score within any film / can add an additional layer to the film text, / which goes beyond simply imitating the action viewed.
어떤 영화 속에서든 악보는 / 영화 텍스트에 추가적인 층을 추가할 수 있는데, / 이것은 보이는 연기를 단순히 흉내 내기를 넘어선다.
In films / that tell of futuristic worlds, / composers, much like sound designers, / have added freedom to create a world / that is unknown and new to the viewer.
미래 세계에 관해 말하는 영화에서, / 작곡가는 꼭 사운드 디자이너처럼 / 자유를 추가해서 세계를 창조해 왔다. / 관객에게 알려지지 않은 새로운
However, / unlike sound designers, / composers often shy away from creating unique pieces / that reflect these new worlds / and often present musical scores / that possess familiar structures and cadences.
그러나 / 사운드 디자이너와 달리, / 작곡가는 흔히 독특한 곡을 만들어 내기를 피하고, / 이러한 새로운 세계를 반영하는 / 흔히 악보를 제시한다. / 익숙한 구조와 박자를 가진
While it is possible / that this may interfere with creativity and a sense of space and time, / it in fact aids in viewer access to the film.
가능성이 있지만, / 이것이 창의성과 시공간 감각을 저해할 / 사실 그것은 관객이 영화에 접근하는 데 도움이 된다.
Through recognizable scores, / visions of the future or a galaxy far, far away / can be placed within a recognizable context.
쉽게 파악되는 악보를 통해 / 미래나 멀고 먼 은하계에 대한 비전이 / 쉽게 파악되는 맥락 안에 놓일 수 있다.
Such familiarity allows the viewer / to be placed in a comfortable space / so that the film may then lead the viewer / to what is an unfamiliar, but acceptable vision of a world / different from their own.
그러한 친숙함은 관객이 ~하게 하고 / 편안한 공간에 놓일 수 있게 / 그러면 영화는 관객을 안내할 수 있을 것이다. / 세계에 관한 낯설지만 받아들일 수 있는 비전으로 / 자신들의 세계와는 다른

어떤 영화 속에서든 악보는 영화 텍스트에 추가적인 층을 추가할 수 있는데, 이것은 보이는 연기를 단순히 흉내 내기를 넘어선다. 미래 세계에 관해 말하는 영화에서, 작곡가는 꼭 사운드 디자이너처럼, 자유를 추가해서 관객에게 알려지지 않은 새로운 세계를 창조해 왔다. 그러나 사운드 디자이너와 달리, 작곡가는 흔히 이러한 새로운 세계를 반영하는 독특한 곡을 만들어 내기를 피하고, 흔히 익숙한 구조와 박자를 가진 악보를 제시한다. 이는 창의성과 시공간 감각을 저해할 가능성이 있지만, 사실 그것은 관객이 영화에 접근하는 데 도움이 된다. 미래나 멀고 먼 은하계에 대한 비전이 쉽게 파악되는 악보를 통해 쉽게 파악되는 맥락 안에 놓일 수 있다. 그러한 친숙함을 통해 관객은 편안한 공간

에 놓이게 되고, 그러면 영화는 관객을 자신들의 세계와는 다른 세계에 관한 낯설지만 받아들일 수 있는 비전으로 안내할 수 있을 것이다.

Why? 왜 정답일까?

빈칸 뒤에서 친숙한 악보가 영화 속 낯선 세계나 비전을 쉽게 이해하는 데 도움을 주고 관객에게 편안함을 준다(**Through recognizable scores, visions ~ can be placed within a recognizable context.**)는 내용이 전개되는 것으로 보아, 빈칸에 들어갈 말로 가장 적절한 것은 ② '관객이 영화에 접근하는 데 도움이 된다'이다.

- score ⓝ 악보
- go beyond ~을 넘어서다
- composer ⓝ 작곡가
- unknown ⓐ 미지의
- shy away from ~을 피하다
- structure ⓝ 구조
- cadence ⓝ (율동적인) 박자
- interfere with ~을 방해하다
- galaxy ⓝ 은하계
- free A of B A에서 B를 없애다
- exotic ⓐ 이국적인
- layer ⓝ 층
- futuristic ⓐ 미래의
- add A to B A를 B에 더하다
- unlike prep ~와는 달리
- unique ⓐ 독특한
- familiar ⓐ 친숙한
- reflect ⓥ 반영하다
- recognizable ⓐ 쉽게 파악되는
- acceptable ⓐ 받아들일 수 있는
- aid ⓥ 돕다

구문 풀이

14행 Such familiarity allows the viewer to be placed in a comfortable space so that the film may then lead the viewer to {what is an unfamiliar, but acceptable vision of a world different from their own}.
(「allow+목적어+to부정사 : ~이 …하게 하다」 / so that: 접속사(~하도록) / what: 관계대명사(~것) / different from their own: 형용사구)

★★★ 1등급 대비 고난도 2점 문제

08 리더 및 추종자 역할의 유동성 — 정답률 45% | 정답 ③

다음 빈칸에 들어갈 말로 가장 적절한 것을 고르시오.

① rigid – 엄격할
② unfair – 불공평할
③ fluid – 유동적일 ✔
④ stable – 안정적일
⑤ apparent – 분명할

Followers can be defined by their position as subordinates / or by their behavior of going along with leaders' wishes.
추종자는 부하라는 직책에 의해 정의될 수 있다. / 또는 리더의 바람에 따르는 행동에 의해
But followers also have power to lead.
그러나 추종자도 이끌 힘이 있다.
Followers empower leaders as well as vice versa.
추종자는 리더에게 힘을 주기도 하고, 그 반대도 마찬가지이다.
This has led some leadership analysts like Ronald Heifetz / to avoid using the word *followers* / and refer to the others in a power relationship / as "citizens" or "constituents."
이로 인해 Ronald Heifetz와 같은 일부 리더십 분석가들은 / *추종자*라는 단어를 사용하는 것을 피하고 / 권력 관계에 있는 다른 사람들을 지칭하게 되었다. / '시민' 또는 '구성원'으로
Heifetz is correct / that too simple a view of followers / can produce misunderstanding.
Heifetz의 말은 옳다. / 추종자에 대한 너무 단순한 관점이 / 오해를 불러일으킬 수 있다는
In modern life, / most people wind up being both leaders and followers, / and the categories can become quite fluid.
현대의 삶에서, / 대부분의 사람들은 결국 리더와 추종자 둘 다가 되고, / 그 범주는 꽤 유동적일 수 있다.
Our behavior as followers changes / as our objectives change.
추종자로서의 우리의 행동도 바뀐다. / 우리의 목표가 변함에 따라
If I trust your judgment in music more than my own, / I may follow your lead / on which concert we attend / (even though you may be formally my subordinate in position).
만약 내가 음악에 대한 나의 판단보다 당신의 판단을 더 신뢰한다면, / 나는 당신의 주도를 따를 수 있다. / 우리가 어떤 콘서트에 참석할지에 대해서는 / (당신이 비록 공식적으로 지위상 나의 부하일지라도)
But if I am an expert on fishing, / you may follow my lead on where we fish, / regardless of our formal positions / or the fact that I followed your lead on concerts yesterday.
하지만 내가 낚시 전문가라면, / 당신은 낚시할 장소에 대해서는 나를 따를 수 있다. / 공식적인 지위와는 관계없이 / 혹은 내가 어제 콘서트에 대해 당신을 따랐다는 사실과

추종자는 부하라는 직책이나 리더의 바람에 따르는 행동에 의해 정의될 수 있다. 그러나 추종자도 이끌 힘이 있다. 추종자는 리더에게 힘을 주기도 하고, 그 반대도 마찬가지이다. 이로 인해 Ronald Heifetz와 같은 일부 리더십 분석가들은 *추종자*라는 단어를 사용하는 것을 피하고, 권력 관계에 있는 다른 사람들을 '시민' 또는 '구성원'으로 지칭하게 되었다. 추종자에 대한 너무 단순한 관점이 오해를 불러일으킬 수 있다는 Heifetz의 말은 옳다. 현대의 삶에서, 대부분의 사람들은 결국 리더와 추종자 둘 다가 되고, 그 범주는 꽤 유동적일 수 있다. 우리의 목표가 변함에 따라 추종자로서의 우리의 행동도 바뀐다. 만약 내가 음악에 대한 나의 판단보다 당신의 판단을 더 신뢰한다면, (당신이 비록 공식적으로 지위상 나의 부하일지라도) 우리가 어떤 콘서트에 참석할지에 대해서는 당신의 주도를 따를 수 있다. 하지만 내가 낚시 전문가라면, 우리의 공식적인 지위나 내가 어제 콘서트에 대해 당신을 따랐다는 사실과는 관계없이, 낚시할 장소에 대해서는 당신이 나를 따를 수 있다.

Why? 왜 정답일까?

'**Our behavior as followers changes as our objectives change.**'에서 목표가 변함에 따라 추종자로서의 행동이 바뀐다고 언급한 후, 상황에 따라 리더와 추종자의 역할이 달라지는 경우를 예로 들고 있다. 따라서 빈칸에 들어갈 말로 가장 적절한 것은 리더와 추종자의 범주가 '변할 수 있다'는 의미의 ③ '유동적일'이다.

- subordinate ⓝ 부하, 추종자
- analyst ⓝ 분석가
- constituent ⓝ 구성원, 구성 요소
- formally ad 공식적으로
- rigid ⓐ 엄격한
- empower ⓥ 권한을 주다
- refer to A as B A를 B라고 지칭하다
- objective ⓝ 목표
- regardless of ~에 관계없이
- fluid ⓐ 유동적인

구문 풀이

6행 Heifetz is correct {that too simple a view of followers can produce misunderstanding}.
(too simple a view of followers: 주어(too+형+a(n)+명 : 너무 ~한 …) / can produce: 동사구)

★★ 문제 해결 꿀~팁 ★★

▶ 많이 틀린 이유는?
④가 나타내듯이 추종자와 리더의 분류가 '안정적'이라면, 빈칸 뒤와 마찬가지로 '목적에 따라 추종자로서의 행동이 바뀌는' 상황이 발생하기 어렵다. 리더의 역할, 추종자의 역할이 안정적인 분류 체계에 따라 굳어질 것이기 때문이다.
▶ 문제 해결 방법은?
빈칸 바로 뒤가 빈칸을 뒷받침하는 내용이다. 즉 '목적이 변하면 행동도 변한다'는 내용을 요약할 수 있는 말을 찾아 빈칸에 넣는다.

★★★ 1등급 대비 고난도 3점 문제

09 격앙된 감정을 다스리는 데 도움이 되는 타임아웃 — 정답률 27% | 정답 ③

다음 빈칸에 들어갈 말로 가장 적절한 것을 고르시오. [3점]

① restrain your curiosity – 호기심을 억누르는
② mask your true emotions – 진실된 감정을 가리는
③ spare innocent bystanders – 무고한 구경꾼들을 구하는 ✔
④ provoke emotional behavior – 감정적 행동을 촉발시키는
⑤ establish unhealthy relationships – 건강하지 않은 관계를 만드는

When we are emotionally charged, / we often use anger / to hide our more primary and deeper emotions, / such as sadness and fear, / which doesn't allow / for true resolution to occur.
우리가 감정적으로 격앙되어 있을 때, / 우리는 자주 분노를 사용하는데, / 우리의 더 원초적이고 더 깊은 감정을 숨기기 위해 / 슬픔과 공포와 같은 / 그것은 허용하지 않는다. / 진정한 해결책이 생기는 것을
Separating yourself / from an emotionally upsetting situation / gives you the space you need / to better understand what you are truly feeling / so you can more clearly articulate your emotions / in a logical and less emotional way.
자신을 분리하는 것은 / 감정적으로 화가 나는 상황으로부터 / 당신에게 필요한 공간을 제공하기에 / 당신이 진정으로 느끼고 있는 것을 더 잘 이해하기 위해 / 당신은 감정을 더 명확하게 표현할 수 있다. / 논리적이고 덜 감정적인 방법으로
A time-out also helps spare innocent bystanders.
타임아웃은 또한 무고한 구경꾼들을 구하는 데 도움이 된다.
When confronted with situations / that don't allow us to deal with our emotions / or that cause us to suppress them, / we may transfer those feelings / to other people or situations / at a later point.
우리가 상황들에 직면했을 때, / 우리가 우리의 감정을 다스리도록 허용되지 않는 / 혹은 우리가 그 감정들을 억누르게 만드는 / 우리는 그러한 감정을 전이할 수도 있다. / 다른 사람들이나 상황에 / 나중에
For instance, / if you had a bad day at work, / you may suppress your feelings at the office, / only to find / that you release them / by getting into a fight with your kids or spouse / when you get home / later that evening.

[문제편 p.024]

예를 들어, / 만약 당신이 직장에서 기분이 나쁜 하루를 보냈다면, / 당신은 사무실에서 당신의 감정을 억누를 수 있지만, / 결과적으로 발견하게 된다. / 당신이 그것들을 표출하는 것을 / 당신의 아이들이나 배우자와 다툼으로써 / 당신이 집에 도착했을 때 / 그 후 저녁에

Clearly, / your anger didn't originate at home, / but you released it there.

분명히, / 당신의 분노는 집에서 비롯된 것이 아니었지만, / 당신은 거기서 그것을 표출했다.

When you take the appropriate time / to digest and analyze your feelings, / you can mitigate hurting or upsetting other people / who have nothing to do with the situation.

당신이 적절한 시간을 가질 때, / 당신의 감정을 소화하고 분석하는 데 / 당신은 다른 사람들을 상처주거나 화나게 하는 것을 완화시킬 수 있다. / 그 상황과 무관한

우리가 감정적으로 격앙되어 있을 때, 우리는 자주 슬픔과 공포와 같은 우리의 더 원초적이고 더 깊은 감정을 숨기기 위해 분노를 사용하는데, 그것은 진정한 해결책이 생기는 것을 허용하지 않는다. 감정적으로 화가 나는 상황으로부터 자신을 분리하는 것은 당신이 진정으로 느끼고 있는 것을 더 잘 이해하는 데 필요한 공간을 제공하기에 당신은 논리적이고 덜 감정적인 방법으로 감정을 더 명확하게 표현할 수 있다. 타임아웃은 또한 무고한 구경꾼들을 구하는 데 도움이 된다. 우리가 우리의 감정을 다스리도록 허용되지 않는 상황 혹은 그 감정을 억누르게 만드는 상황에 직면했을 때, 우리는 그러한 감정을 나중에 다른 사람들이나 상황에 전이할 수도 있다. 예를 들어, 만약 당신이 직장에서 기분이 나쁜 하루를 보냈다면, 당신은 사무실에서 당신의 감정을 억누를 수 있지만, 결과적으로 그 후 저녁에 당신이 집에 도착했을 때 당신의 아이들이나 배우자와 다툼으로써 그것들을 표출하는 것을 발견하게 된다. 분명히, 당신의 분노는 집에서 비롯된 것이 아니었지만, 당신은 거기서 그것을 표출했다. 당신의 감정을 소화하고 분석하는 데 적절한 시간을 가질 때, 당신은 그 상황과 무관한 다른 사람들을 상처 주거나 화나게 하는 것을 완화시킬 수 있다.

Why? 왜 정답일까?

마지막 문장인 '**When you take the appropriate time to digest and analyze your feelings, you can mitigate hurting or upsetting other people who have nothing to do with the situation.**'에서 감정을 소화하고 분석할 시간을 갖고 나면 무관한 사람들에게 상처를 주고 화나게 할 일이 적어진다고 서술하고 있다. 따라서 빈칸에 들어갈 말로 가장 적절한 것은 ③ '무고한 구경꾼들을 구하는'이다.

- primary ⓐ 원초적인, 기본적인
- articulate ⓥ 명확하게 표현하다
- suppress ⓥ 억누르다
- spouse ⓝ 배우자
- appropriate ⓐ 적절한
- analyze ⓥ 분석하다
- restrain ⓥ 억누르다, 제한하다
- provoke ⓥ 촉발시키다, 자극하다
- resolution ⓝ 해결책, 결심
- confront ⓥ 직면하게 하다
- transfer ⓥ 전이하다, 옮기다
- originate ⓥ 비롯되다, 기원하다
- digest ⓥ 소화하다
- have nothing to do with ~와 무관하다
- innocent ⓐ 무고한, 순진한

구문 풀이

4행 Separating yourself from an emotionally upsetting situation gives you the space [you need to better understand what you are truly feeling] so (that) you can more clearly articulate your emotions in a logical and less emotional way.

(동명사구 주어 「separate+A+from+B : A를 B로부터 분리시키다」 / 동사(단수) / 간·목 / 직·목 / ~하기 위해 / 관계대명사(~것) / (~해서) …하다)

★★ 문제 해결 꿀~팁 ★★

▶ 많이 틀린 이유는?

글에서 감정을 '식히기' 위한 시간을 가질 것을 조언하고 있지만, 이는 감정을 '숨기라'는 의미는 아니므로 ②는 답으로 부적절하다. 또한 감정을 식히는 시간을 갖는데 '감정적인 행위가 촉발되지는' 않을 것이므로 ④도 답으로 부적합하다.

▶ 문제 해결 방법은?

빈칸 문장에 also가 있는 것으로 보아, 앞에 이어 새로이 추가되는 내용이 중요함을 알 수 있다. 즉 빈칸 앞보다는 뒤를 중점적으로 읽고 핵심을 요약하여 빈칸에 들어갈 말을 찾아야 한다.

★★★ 1등급 대비 고난도 3점 문제

10 혁신에 대한 동기 부여 　　정답률 37% | 정답 ④

다음 빈칸에 들어갈 말로 가장 적절한 것을 고르시오. [3점]

① the unknown is more helpful than the negative
미지의 것이 부정적인 것보다 더 도움이 되기
② it highlights the progress they've already made
그들이 이미 이룬 진전을 강조하기
③ it is not irrational but is consumer-based practice
불합리하지 않지만 소비자 중심의 관행이기
④ it reframes a gain-framed activity in terms of losses
손실의 관점에서 수익 (창출로) 구조화된 활동을 재구조화하기
⑤ they discuss how well it fits their profit-sharing plans
그것이 그들의 수익 공유 계획에 얼마나 적합한지 그들이 논의하기

At the pharmaceutical giant Merck, / CEO Kenneth Frazier decided to motivate his executives / to take a more active role / in leading innovation and change.

거대 제약회사 Merck에서 / CEO인 Kenneth Frazier는 그의 간부들에게 동기를 부여하기로 결심하였다. / 보다 적극적인 역할을 취하도록 / 혁신과 변화를 이끄는 데

He asked them to do something radical: / generate ideas / that would put Merck out of business.

그는 그들이 급진적인 무엇인가를 하도록 요청하였는데, / 아이디어들을 만들어내라는 것이었다. / Merck를 폐업시킬

For the next two hours, / the executives worked in groups, / pretending to be one of Merck's top competitors.

다음 두 시간 동안 / 회사 간부들은 그룹으로 작업을 하였다. / Merck의 주요 경쟁사 가운데 하나인 체하면서

Energy soared as they developed ideas / for drugs that would crush theirs / and key markets they had missed.

그들이 아이디어를 발전시키는 동안 에너지가 치솟았다. / 그들의 회사를 짓밟을 만한 약과 / 그들이 놓쳤던 주요 시장에 대한

Then, their challenge was / to reverse their roles / and figure out how to defend against these threats.

그러고 나서, 그들의 과제는 / 그들의 역할을 반대로 하여 / 이러한 위협을 어떻게 방어할 수 있는지를 알아내는 것이었다.

This "kill the company" exercise is powerful / because it reframes a gain-framed activity / in terms of losses.

이러한 "회사 무너뜨리기" 활동은 강력하다. / 수익 (창출로) 구조화된 활동을 재구조화하기 때문에 / 손실의 관점에서

When deliberating about innovation opportunities, / the leaders weren't inclined to take risks.

혁신 기회에 대해 심사숙고할 때, / 리더들은 위험을 무릅쓰지 않는 경향이 있었다.

When they considered / how their competitors could put them out of business, / they realized that it was a risk not to innovate.

그들이 고려했을 때, / 그들의 경쟁자들이 그들을 어떻게 폐업시킬 수 있을지를 / 그들은 혁신하지 않는 것이 위험한 것이라는 것을 깨달았다.

The urgency of innovation was apparent.

혁신의 다급함이 명확해졌다.

거대 제약회사 Merck에서 CEO인 Kenneth Frazier는 그의 간부들이 혁신과 변화를 이끄는 데 보다 적극적인 역할을 취하도록 동기를 부여하기로 결심하였다. 그는 그들이 급진적인 무엇인가를 하도록 요청하였는데, Merck를 폐업시킬 아이디어들을 만들어내라는 것이었다. 다음 두 시간 동안 회사 간부들은 Merck의 주요 경쟁사 가운데 하나인 체하면서 그룹으로 작업을 하였다. 그들이 그들의 회사를 짓밟을 만한 약과 그들이 놓쳤던 주요 시장에 대한 아이디어를 발전시키는 동안 에너지가 치솟았다. 그러고 나서, 그들의 과제는 그들의 역할을 반대로 하여 이러한 위협을 어떻게 방어할 수 있는지를 알아내는 것이었다. 이러한 "회사 무너뜨리기" 활동은 손실의 관점에서 수익 (창출로) 구조화된 활동을 재구조화하기 때문에 강력하다. 혁신 기회에 대해 심사숙고할 때, 리더들은 위험을 무릅쓰지 않는 경향이 있었다. 그들이 그들의 경쟁자들이 그들을 어떻게 폐업시킬 수 있을지를 고려했을 때, 그들은 혁신하지 않는 것이 위험한 것이라는 것을 깨달았다. 혁신의 다급함이 명확해졌다.

Why? 왜 정답일까?

간부들에게 혁신의 동기를 부여하기 위해 경쟁사의 입장에서 회사를 망하게 할 아이디어를 먼저 떠올려 보게 했던 Merck 사의 이야기를 다룬 글이다. '**Then, their challenge was to reverse their roles and figure out how to defend against these threats.**'에서 뒤이어 간부들은 다시 입장을 바꾸어 회사가 그런 아이디어들로 망하지 않기 위해서는 어떻게 해야 하는가를 알아내야 했다는 이야기가 나오는데, 이는 곧 회사가 손실을 보거나 큰 위기에 처하는 상황을 먼저 생각해본 뒤 그에 맞추어서 혁신의 기회를 재고할 기회를 갖게 된 것으로 이해할 수 있다. 따라서 빈칸에 들어갈 말로 가장 적절한 것은 ④ '손실의 관점에서 수익 (창출로) 구조화된 활동을 재구조화하기'이다.

- pharmaceutical ⓐ 제약의, 약학의
- executive ⓝ 임원, 간부
- radical ⓐ 급진적인
- put out of business ~을 문 닫게 하다
- soar ⓥ 치솟다, 급등하다
- defend ⓥ 방어하다, 막다
- urgency ⓝ 다급함
- irrational ⓐ 비이성적인
- motivate ⓥ 동기를 부여하다
- innovation ⓝ 혁신
- generate ⓥ 만들어내다, 창출하다
- pretend ⓥ ~인 척하다
- reverse ⓥ 뒤집다
- be inclined to ~하는 경향이 있다
- apparent ⓐ 명백한
- reframe ⓥ 다시 구성하다

구문 풀이

7행 Energy soared / as they developed ideas for drugs [that would crush theirs] and key markets [they had missed].
(주어 / 자동사 / ~하면서, ~함에 따라 / 전치사 / 목적어1 / 목적어2)

★★ 문제 해결 꿀~팁 ★★

▶ 많이 틀린 이유는?
오답률이 선택지 별로 고르게 포진한 것으로 볼 때, 매력적인 오답이 두드러지지는 않았지만 정답 선택지의 표현이 어려워 틀린 수험생이 많았다는 점을 유추할 수 있다.
▶ 문제 해결 방법은?
경쟁사 입장에서 회사에 손실을 끼칠 방법을 먼저 생각하게 한 후 이를 방어할 아이디어를 다시 찾게 함으로써 혁신의 필요성을 일깨웠다는 것이 글의 주제이다. ④의 a gain-framed activity가 '혁신'을, 'reframes ~ in terms of losses'가 실험의 과정을 묘사한다.

★★★ 1등급 대비 고난도 3점 문제

11 확실성을 추구하는 인간 정답률 43% | 정답 ⑤

다음 빈칸에 들어갈 말로 가장 적절한 것을 고르시오. [3점]

① weigh the pros and cons of our actions
우리 행동의 장단점을 따져 본다
② develop the patience to bear ambiguity
모호함을 참을 수 있는 인내심을 기른다
③ enjoy adventure rather than settle down
안주하기보다 모험을 즐긴다
④ gain insight from solving complex problems
복잡한 문제를 해결하여 통찰력을 얻는다
⑤ lose our ability to interact with the unknown
미지의 것과 상호 작용하는 우리의 능력을 잃어버린다

In the modern world, / we look for certainty in uncertain places.
현대 세계에서 / 우리는 불확실한 곳에서 확실성을 찾는다.
We search for order in chaos, / the right answer in ambiguity, / and conviction in complexity.
우리는 혼란 속에서 질서를 찾는다. / 애매모호함에서 정답을, / 복잡함에서 확신을
"We spend far more time and effort / on trying to control the world," / best-selling writer Yuval Noah Harari says, / "than on trying to understand it."
"우리는 훨씬 더 많은 시간과 노력을 쏟는다. / 세상을 통제하려고 하는 것에" / 베스트셀러 작가인 Yuval Noah Harari가 말하기를, / "세상을 이해하려고 하는 것보다"
We look for the easy-to-follow formula.
우리는 쉽게 따라할 수 있는 공식을 찾는다.
Over time, / we lose our ability to interact with the unknown.
시간이 지나면서 / 우리는 미지의 것과 상호 작용하는 우리의 능력을 잃어버린다.
Our approach reminds me / of the classic story of the drunk man / searching for his keys under a street lamp at night.
우리의 접근법은 나에게 떠올리게 한다. / 술 취한 남자에 대한 전형적인 이야기를 / 밤에 가로등 아래에서 자신의 열쇠를 찾는
He knows / he lost his keys somewhere on the dark side of the street / but looks for them underneath the lamp, / because that's where the light is.
그는 알지만 / 자신이 열쇠를 어두운 길가 어딘가에서 잃어버렸다는 것을 / 가로등 밑에서 그것을 찾는데, / 왜냐하면 그곳이 빛이 있는 곳이기 때문이다.
Our yearning for certainty / leads us to pursue seemingly safe solutions / — by looking for our keys under street lamps.
확실성에 대한 우리의 열망은 / 우리가 겉으로 보기에 안전한 해결책을 추구하도록 이끈다. / 가로등 아래에서 우리의 열쇠를 찾음으로써
Instead of taking the risky walk into the dark, / we stay within our current state, / however inferior it may be.
어둠 속으로 위험한 걸음을 내딛는 대신, / 우리는 우리의 현재 상태 안에 머문다. / 그것이 아무리 열등할지 몰라도

현대 세계에서 우리는 불확실한 곳에서 확실성을 찾는다. 우리는 혼란 속에서 질서를, 애매모호함에서 정답을, 복잡함에서 확신을 찾는다. 베스트셀러 작가인 Yuval Noah Harari가 말하기를, "우리는 세상을 이해하려고 하는 것보다 세상을 통제하려고 하는 것에 훨씬 더 많은 시간과 노력을 쏟는다." 우리는 쉽게 따라할 수 있는 공식을 찾는다. 시간이 지나면서 우리는 미지의 것과 상호 작용하는 우리의 능력을 잃어버린다. 우리의 접근법은 내게 밤에 가로등 아래에서 자신의 열쇠를 찾는 술 취한 남자에 대한 전형적인 이야기를 떠올리게 한다. 그는 자신이 열쇠를 어두운 길가 어딘가에서 잃어버렸다는 것을 알지만 가로등 밑에서 그것을 찾는데, 왜냐하면 그곳에 빛이 있기 때문이다. 확실성에 대한 우리의 열망은 우리가 가로등 아래에서 열쇠를 찾음으로써 겉으로 보기에 안전한 해결책을 추구하도록 이끈다. 어둠 속으로 위험한 걸음을 내딛는 대신, 우리는 우리의 현재 상태가 아무리 열등할지 몰라도 그 안에 머문다.

Why? 왜 정답일까?

마지막 두 문장에서 우리는 확실성을 추구하기 때문에 겉보기에 안전해 보이는 선택지를 취하려 하며, 미지의 어둠 속을 탐색하는 대신 부족하고 열등한 현재 상태일지라도 그대로 유지하려는 경향이 있다(**Our yearning for certainty leads us to pursue seemingly safe solutions ~. Instead of taking the risky walk into the dark, we stay within our current state, however inferior it may be.**)고 언급한다. 따라서 빈칸에 들어갈 말로 가장 적절한 것은 새롭고 불확실한 것을 점점 덜 알아보려 한다는 의미의 ⑤ '미지의 것과 상호 작용하는 우리의 능력을 잃어버린다'이다.

- certainty ⓝ 확실성
- ambiguity ⓝ 애매모호함
- complexity ⓝ 복잡성
- formula ⓝ 공식, 제조법
- pursue ⓥ 추구하다
- inferior ⓐ 열등한
- patience ⓝ 인내심
- insight ⓝ 통찰력
- uncertain ⓐ 불확실한
- conviction ⓝ 확신
- easy-to-follow ⓐ 따르기 쉬운
- yearning ⓝ 갈망, 열망
- seemingly ad 겉보기에
- pros and cons 장단점
- bear ⓥ 참다, (아이를) 낳다
- unknown ⓐ 미지의, 알려지지 않은

구문 풀이

3행 "We spend far more time and effort on trying to control the world," (best-selling writer Yuval Noah Harari says), "than on trying to understand it."
「spend + 시간/노력 + on + 동명사 : ~하는 데 시간/노력을 들이다」 / ( ) : 삽입절 / 병렬구조(than 앞의 on trying과 연결됨)

★★ 문제 해결 꿀~팁 ★★

▶ 많이 틀린 이유는?
빈칸이 있는 문장 바로 앞의 'We look for ~'에서 우리는 쉽게 따라할 수 있는 것을 좇는 경향이 있다고 하므로, '어려운 문제를 풀며 영감을 얻는다'는 의미의 ④는 맥락상 상충한다.
▶ 문제 해결 방법은?
어두운 길가에서 열쇠를 잃어버렸음에도 빛이 있는 가로등 밑에서 열쇠를 찾아 헤매는 남자의 예는 '새롭고 위험할지라도 시도해봐야 하지만 안전한 현재 상태만 고수하고 있는' 우리의 모습을 비유한 것이다. 빈칸 문장은 이 상태가 지속되면 결국 우리가 '미지의 것을 살펴보는 능력 자체를 잃게 된다는' 전망을 제시하는 것이다.

★★★ 1등급 대비 고난도 3점 문제

12 능력보다도 시간이나 노력에 돈을 치르려는 경향 정답률 39% | 정답 ③

다음 빈칸에 들어갈 말로 가장 적절한 것을 고르시오. [3점]

① prefer money to time – 시간보다 돈을 선호할
② ignore the hours put in – 들인 시간을 무시할
③ value effort over outcome – 결과보다 노력을 중시할
④ can't stand any malfunction – 어떤 불량도 참지 못할
⑤ are biased toward the quality – 질 쪽으로 편향될

It's hard to pay more / for the speedy but highly skilled person, / simply because there's less effort being observed.
더 많은 돈을 지불하기는 어려운데, / 빠르지만 고도로 숙련된 사람에게 / 그 이유는 단순히 관찰되고 있는 노력이 적기 때문이다.
Two researchers once did a study / in which they asked people / how much they would pay for data recovery.
두 명의 연구원이 연구를 한 적이 있다. / 그들이 사람들에게 묻는 / 그들이 데이터 복구에 얼마를 지불할 것인지를
They found / that people would pay a little more / for a greater quantity of rescued data, / but what they were most sensitive to / was the number of hours / the technician worked.
그들은 발견했다. / 사람들이 조금 더 많은 돈을 지불할 것이었지만 / 더 많은 양의 복구된 데이터에 / 사람들이 가장 민감하게 여기는 것은 / 시간이었다는 것을 / 기술자가 일한
When the data recovery took only a few minutes, / willingness to pay was low, / but when it took more than a week / to recover the same amount of data, / people were willing to pay much more.
데이터 복구에 몇 분밖에 걸리지 않았을 때, / 지불 의사는 낮았지만, / 일주일 이상이 걸렸을 때, / 같은 양의 데이터를 복구하는 데 / 사람들은 훨씬 더 많은 비용을 지불할 의사가 있었다.
Think about it: / They were willing to pay more / for the slower service / with the same outcome.
생각해 보라. / 그들은 더 많은 비용을 기꺼이 지불하고자 했다. / 더 느린 서비스에 / 같은 결과를 내는
Fundamentally, / when we value effort over outcome, / we're paying for incompetence.
근본적으로, / 우리가 결과보다 노력을 중시할 때, / 우리는 무능함에 비용을 지불하는 것이다.

DAY 03

[문제편 p.026]

Although it is actually irrational, / we *feel* more rational, / and more comfortable, / paying for incompetence.
비록 그것이 실제로는 비합리적이지만, / 우리는 더 합리적이라고 *느낀다*. / 그리고 더 편하다 / 무능함에 지불하면서

빠르지만 고도로 숙련된 사람에게 더 많은 돈을 지불하기는 어려운데, 그 이유는 단순히 관찰되고 있는 노력이 적기 때문이다. 두 명의 연구원이 사람들에게 데이터 복구에 얼마를 지불할 것인지를 묻는 연구를 한 적이 있다. 그들은 사람들이 복구된 데이터가 더 많으면 조금 더 많은 돈을 지불할 것이었지만, 사람들이 가장 민감하게 여기는 것은 기술자가 일한 시간이었다는 것을 발견했다. 데이터 복구에 몇 분밖에 걸리지 않았을 때 지불 의사는 낮았지만, 같은 양의 데이터를 복구하는 데 일주일 이상이 걸렸을 때, 사람들은 훨씬 더 많은 비용을 지불할 의사가 있었다. 생각해 보라. 그들은 같은 결과에 대해 더 느린 서비스에 더 많은 비용을 기꺼이 지불하고자 했다. 근본적으로, 우리가 결과보다 노력을 중시할 때, 우리는 무능함에 비용을 지불하는 것이다. 비록 그것이 실제로는 비합리적이지만, 우리는 무능함에 지불하면서 더 합리적이고 더 편하다고 *느낀다*.

Why? 왜 정답일까?

유능해도 보이는 노력이 적으면 우리는 비용을 덜 치르고 싶어 한다(**It's hard to pay more for the speedy but highly skilled person, simply because there's less effort being observed.**)는 내용이다. 예시로 언급된 실험에 관해 주제와 같은 결론이 내려져야 하므로, 빈칸에 들어갈 말로 가장 적절한 것은 ③ '결과보다 노력을 중시할'이다.

- rescue ⓥ 복구하다, 구조하다
- fundamentally ad 근본적으로
- incompetence ⓝ 무능
- malfunction ⓝ 불량

구문 풀이

1행 It's hard to pay more for the speedy but highly skilled person, simply because there's less effort being observed.
(It's: 가주어, to pay ~: 진주어, being observed: 진행 수동(~되고 있는))

★★ 문제 해결 꿀~팁 ★★

▶ 많이 틀린 이유는?
①에 '시간'과 '돈'이라는 핵심어가 다 포함되어 있지만, 이 글은 '시간보다 돈이 선호된다'는 내용이 아니다. 똑같은 일에 더 오랜 시간이 소요되었을 때 오히려 돈을 더 기꺼이 내려는 경향을 소개하는 것이 글의 중심 내용이다.

▶ 문제 해결 방법은?
빈칸 문제에서는 핵심어의 반복보다는 주제의 '적절한 재진술'을 찾는 것이 중요하다. 실제로 정답인 ③은 '일에 들인 시간'을 effort로, '복구된 데이터 양'을 outcome으로 재진술하였다.

DAY 04 빈칸 추론 04

01 ①	02 ⑤	03 ①	04 ①	05 ④
06 ③	07 ②	08 ②	09 ②	10 ①
11 ②	12 ①			

01 과일이 당분으로 과당을 선택한 이유

정답률 48% | 정답 ①

다음 빈칸에 들어갈 말로 가장 적절한 것을 고르시오. [3점]

✔ full – 배가 부르다
② strong – 튼튼하다
③ tired – 피곤하다
④ dangerous – 위험하다
⑤ hungry – 배가 고프다

When is the right time / for the predator to consume the fruit?
적절한 시기는 언제인가? / 포식자가 과일을 섭취하기에

The plant uses the color of the fruit / to signal to predators that it is ripe, / which means that the seed's hull has hardened / — and therefore the sugar content is at its height.
식물은 과일의 색깔을 이용하며, / 포식자에게 과일이 익었음을 알려주기 위해 / 이는 씨의 껍질이 딱딱해졌음을, / 그리하여 당도가 최고에 이르렀음을 의미한다.

Incredibly, the plant has chosen / to manufacture fructose, instead of glucose, / as the sugar in the fruit.
놀랍게도, 식물은 선택해왔다. / 포도당 대신 과당을 만들기로 / 과일의 당분으로서

Glucose raises insulin levels in primates and humans, / which initially raises levels of leptin, a hunger-blocking hormone / — but fructose does not.
포도당은 영장류와 인간의 인슐린 수치를 높여서, / 처음에는 배고픔을 막는 호르몬인 렙틴의 수치를 높이지만, / 과당은 그렇지 않다.

As a result, / the predator never receives the normal message / that it is full.
그 결과 / 포식자는 결코 일반적인 메시지를 받지 못한다. / 배가 부르다는

That makes for a win-win for predator and prey.
그것이 포식자와 먹이에게 상호 이익이 된다.

The animal obtains more calories, / and because it keeps eating more and more fruit / and therefore more seeds, / the plant has a better chance of distributing more of its babies.
동물은 더 많은 열량을 얻고, / 그것이 계속해서 더 많은 과일을 먹기 때문에, / 따라서 더 많은 씨를 / 식물은 더 많은 후손을 퍼뜨릴 더 높은 가능성을 얻는다.

포식자가 과일을 섭취하기에 적절한 시기는 언제인가? 식물은 포식자에게 과일이 익었음을 알려주기 위해 과일의 색깔을 이용하며, 이는 씨의 껍질이 딱딱해졌음을, 그리하여 당도가 최고에 이르렀음을 의미한다. 놀랍게도, 식물은 과일의 당분으로서 포도당 대신 과당을 만들기로 선택해왔다. 포도당은 영장류와 인간의 인슐린 수치를 높여서, 처음에는 배고픔을 막는 호르몬인 렙틴의 수치를 높이지만, 과당은 그렇지 않다. 그 결과 포식자는 결코 배가 부르다는 일반적인 메시지를 받지 못한다. 그것이 포식자와 먹이에게 상호 이익이 된다. 동물은 더 많은 열량을 얻고, 그것이 계속해서 더 많은 과일을, 따라서 더 많은 씨를 먹기 때문에 식물은 더 많은 후손을 퍼뜨릴 더 높은 가능성을 얻는다.

Why? 왜 정답일까?

'Glucose raises insulin levels in primates and humans, which initially raises levels of leptin, a hunger–blocking hormone – but fructose does not.'에서 포도당과는 달리 과당은 배고픔을 막는 호르몬 분비 증가를 유도하지 않는다고 설명하는 것으로 보아, 빈칸에는 동물이 이로 인해 '배부름'을 느끼지 못한다는 의미를 완성하는 ① '배가 부르다'가 들어가야 적절하다. 마지막 두 문장은 이로 인해 동물이 계속해서 과일을 먹고 결과적으로 과일의 씨도 더 많이 먹게 되므로 과일이 번식할 가능성을 높여준다는 결론을 제시하고 있다.

- predator ⓝ 포식자
- ripe ⓐ (과일 등이) 다 익은
- harden ⓥ 딱딱해지다
- content ⓝ 함량
- at one's height 최고조에 이른
- incredibly ad 놀랍게도, 믿기 힘들게도
- manufacture ⓥ 생산하다
- fructose ⓝ 과당
- glucose ⓝ 포도당
- initially ad 처음에는
- distribute ⓥ 퍼뜨리다, 분포시키다

구문 풀이

2행 The plant uses the color of the fruit to signal to predators that it is ripe, which means that the seed's hull has hardened — and therefore the sugar content is at its height.
(to signal의 목적어(선행사) / 목적(~하기 위해) / 계속적 용법 / 접속사(~것) / 주어1 / 동사1(현재완료) / 주어2 / 동사2)

02 억양 패턴 등 비언어적 신호의 차이로 생기는 오해

정답률 53% | 정답 ⑤

다음 빈칸에 들어갈 말로 가장 적절한 것을 고르시오. [3점]

① frequent pauses – 잦은 휴지(休止)
② moral standards – 도덕적 기준
③ first impressions – 첫인상
④ food preferences – 음식에 대한 선호
✔ intonation patterns – 억양 패턴

Verbal and nonverbal signs / are not only relevant but also significant / to intercultural communication.
언어적, 비언어적 신호들은 / 관련되어 있을 뿐만 아니라 중요하다. / 문화 간 의사소통에서
The breakdown of them / helps to identify aspects of conversations.
그것들을 분석하는 것은 / 대화의 양상을 파악하는 데 도움이 된다.
Here is an excellent example.
여기 아주 훌륭한 예가 있다.
Newly hired Indian and Pakistani assistants / in a staff cafeteria at Heathrow Airport / were often perceived as rude or uncooperative / by their supervisors and the airport staff, / while the Indian and Pakistani women complained of discrimination.
새로 고용된 인도, 파키스탄 직원들은 / Heathrow 공항 직원 식당에 / 종종 무례하고 비협조적이라고 여겨졌던 / 관리자들과 공항 직원들로부터 / 반면, 인도와 파키스탄 여성들은 차별에 대해 불평했다.
Observation revealed / that intonation patterns were the primary cause.
관찰은 밝혀주었다. / 억양 패턴이 주요 이유임을
When the staff ordered meat, / the cafeteria assistant was supposed to ask them / whether they would like to have some gravy.
공항 직원이 고기를 주문했을 때, / 그 식당 직원은 그들에게 물어봐야 했다. / 그레이비 소스가 조금 필요한지 아닌지
Instead of saying "gravy?" with a rising intonation, / the Asian assistants would say "gravy" with a falling intonation, / which is their normal way of asking a question.
상승조의 억양으로 "그레이비요?"라고 말하는 대신에, / 아시아계 직원들은 하강조로 "그레이비"라고 말하곤 했는데, / 그것은 그들의 일반적인 질문 방식이다.
However, this may appear rude to native speakers of English: / "gravy" with falling intonation came across as a statement, / suggesting "This is gravy. Take it or leave it."
그러나 이것은 영어를 모국어로 쓰는 사람들에게는 무례하게 비춰질지도 모르는데, / 하강조의 "그레이비"는 말이라는 인상을 주었다. / "이것이 그레이비 소스예요. 가져가든지 말든지."를 암시하는

언어적, 비언어적 신호들은 문화 간 의사소통과 관련되어 있을 뿐만 아니라 문화 간 의사소통에서 중요하다. 그것들을 분석하는 것은 대화의 양상을 파악하는 데 도움이 된다. 여기 아주 훌륭한 예가 있다. Heathrow 공항 직원 식당에 새로 고용된 인도, 파키스탄 직원들은 관리자들과 공항 직원들로부터 종종 무례하고 비협조적이라고 여겨졌던 반면, 인도와 파키스탄 여성들은 차별에 대해 불평했다. 관찰을 통해 억양 패턴이 주요 이유임이 밝혀졌다. 공항 직원이 고기를 주문했을 때, 그 식당 직원은 그레이비 소스가 조금 필요한지 아닌지 물어봐야 했다. 상승조의 억양으로 "그레이비요?"라고 말하는 대신에, 아시아계 직원들은 하강조로 "그레이비"라고 말하곤 했는데, 그것은 그들의 일반적인 질문 방식이다. 그러나 이것은 영어를 모국어로 쓰는 사람들에게는 무례하게 비춰질지도 모르는데, 하강조의 "그레이비"는 "이것이 그레이비 소스예요. 가져가든지 말든지."를 암시하는 말이라는 인상을 주었다.

Why? 왜 정답일까?

빈칸 뒤의 'Instead of saying "gravy?" with a rising intonation, the Asian assistants would say "gravy" with a falling intonation ~'에서 하강조의 억양에 대한 이해와 사용의 차이로 인해 의사소통상 오해가 발생하게 되었다는 예시를 제시하므로, 빈칸에 들어갈 말로 가장 적절한 것은 ⑤ '억양 패턴'이다.

- nonverbal ⓐ 비언어적인
- intercultural ⓐ 문화 간의
- uncooperative ⓐ 비협조적인
- intonation ⓝ 억양
- significant ⓐ 중요한, 유의미한
- breakdown ⓝ (자료 등의) 분석, 분해
- discrimination ⓝ 차별
- come across as ~라는 인상을 주다

구문 풀이

13행 Instead of saying "gravy?" with a rising intonation, / the Asian assistants would say "gravy" with a falling intonation, / which is their normal way of asking a question.
(~ 대신에 / 동명사 / ~하곤 했다 / 선행사 / 계속적 용법)

03 두려움과 불확실성이 금융 시장에 미치는 영향

정답률 53% | 정답 ①

다음 빈칸에 들어갈 말로 가장 적절한 것을 고르시오.

✔ Fear and uncertainty can be damaging
두려움과 불확실성은 해가 될 수 있다
② Unaffordable personal loans may pose a risk
감당 못할 개인 부채는 위험을 끼칠 수도 있다
③ Ignorance about legal restrictions may matter
법적 제재에 대한 무지가 문제가 될 수 있다
④ Accurate knowledge of investors can be poisonous
투자자에 대한 정확한 정보가 유해할 수 있다
⑤ Strong connections between banks can create a scare
은행 간의 강한 유대가 두려움을 낳을 수 있다

The connectedness of the global economic market / makes it vulnerable to potential "infection."
전 세계 경제 시장의 연결성은 / 시장이 잠재적 '감염'에 취약하게 만든다.
A financial failure can make its way / from borrowers to banks to insurers, / spreading like a flu.
금융상의 실패는 나아갈 수 있다. / 채무자에서부터 은행, 보증인까지 / 독감처럼 퍼지면서
However, / there are unexpected characteristics / when it comes to such infection in the market.
그러나 / 예상치 못한 특징들이 있다. / 시장 내 그러한 감염에 관한
Infection can occur / even without any contact.
감염은 일어날 수 있다. / 심지어 아무런 접촉 없이도
A bank might become insolvent / even without having any of its investments fail.
은행은 지급 불능이 될 수 있다. / 어떠한 투자에 실패하지 않고도
Fear and uncertainty / can be damaging to financial markets, / just as cascading failures due to bad investments.
두려움과 불확실성은 / 금융 시장에 해가 될 수 있다. / 어떤 나쁜 투자들 때문에 일어나는 연속된 실패처럼
If we all woke up tomorrow / and believed that Bank X would be insolvent, / then it would become insolvent.
만약 우리 모두가 내일 일어나서 / X은행이 지급 불능이 될 것이라고 믿는다면, / 그러면 그것은 지급 불능이 될 것이다.
In fact, / it would be enough for us to fear / that others believed that Bank X was going to fail, / or just to fear our collective fear!
사실 / 우리가 두려워하는 것으로 충분할 것이다. / 다른 사람들이 X은행이 망할 거라고 믿고 있다는 것을 / 혹은 단지 우리의 집단적인 두려움을 겁내는 것으로
We might all even know / that Bank X was well-managed with healthy investments, / but if we expected others to pull their money out, / then we would fear being the last / to pull our money out.
우리 모두 심지어 알 것이다 / X은행이 건전한 투자로 잘 운영된다는 것을 / 하지만 만약 우리가 다른 사람들이 자기 돈을 인출해 갈 것이라고 예상한다면, / 우리는 마지막 사람이 되기를 겁낼 것이다. / 자기 돈을 인출하는
Financial distress can be self-fulfilling / and is a particularly troublesome aspect of financial markets.
재정적인 고통은 자기 충족적일 수 있으며, / 금융 시장에서 각별히 골치 아픈 측면이다.

전 세계 경제 시장의 연결성은 시장이 잠재적 '감염'에 취약하게 만든다. 금융상의 실패는 독감처럼 퍼지면서 채무자에서부터 은행, 보증인까지 나아갈 수 있다. 그러나 시장 내 그러한 감염에 관한 예상치 못한 특징들이 있다. 감염은 심지어 아무런 접촉 없이도 일어날 수 있다. 은행은 어떠한 투자에 실패하지 않고도 지급 불능이 될 수 있다. 어떤 나쁜 투자들 때문에 일어나는 연속된 실패처럼, 두려움과 불확실성은 금융 시장에 해가 될 수 있다. 만약 우리 모두가 내일 일어나서 X은행이 지급 불능이 될 것이라고 믿는다면, 그것은 지급 불능이 될 것이다. 사실 우리가 다른 사람들이 X은행이 망할 거라고 믿고 있다는 것을 두려워하거나, 단지 우리의 집단적인 두려움을 겁내는 것으로 충분할 것이다. 우리 모두 심지어 X은행이 건전한 투자로 잘 운영된다는 것을 알지라도 만약 우리가 다른 사람들이 (거기서) 자기 돈을 인출해 갈 것이라고 예상한다면, 우리는 자기 돈을 인출하는 마지막 사람이 되기를 겁낼 것이다(남들보다 돈을 먼저 인출하려 할 것이다). 재정적인 고통은 자기 충족적일 수 있으며, 금융 시장에서 각별히 골치 아픈 측면이다.

Why? 왜 정답일까?

빈칸 뒤 예시에 따르면 X은행이 실제로 잘 운영되고 있음에도 불구하고, 사람들이 X은행이 망할까봐 '두려워하는' 마음만으로 X은행에 위기가 닥칠 수 있다고 한다. 즉 재정적

[문제편 p.027]
고통이 닥칠지도 모른다는 두려움과 불확실성 자체가 금융 시장에 생각지 못한 위기를 가져올 수 있다는 것이므로, 빈칸에 들어갈 말로 가장 적절한 것은 ① '두려움과 불확실성은 해가 될 수 있다'이다.

- infection ⓝ 감염
- insolvent ⓐ 지급 불능의, 파산한
- cascading ⓐ 연속된
- well-managed ⓐ 잘 경영되는
- self-fulfilling ⓐ 자기 충족적인
- uncertainty ⓝ 불확실성
- unaffordable ⓐ 감당할 수 없는
- insurer ⓝ 보증인, 보험업자
- investment ⓝ 투자
- collective ⓐ 집단적인
- distress ⓝ 고통
- troublesome ⓐ 골치 아픈
- damaging ⓐ 해로운
- restriction ⓝ 제재, 제한

구문 풀이

1행 The connectedness of the global economic market makes it vulnerable to potential "infection."
대명사(= the global economic market)

04 단 한 명의 친구 또는 지지자가 미치는 영향

정답률 45% | 정답 ①

다음 빈칸에 들어갈 말로 가장 적절한 것을 고르시오. [3점]

① you're not the only resister – 당신이 유일한 저항가가 아니라는
② the leader cannot be defeated – 리더는 패배할 수 없다는
③ conforming to the rule is good – 규칙에 순응하는 것이 좋다는
④ men are supposed to live alone – 사람들은 혼자 살아가게 되어 있다는
⑤ competition discourages cooperation – 경쟁은 협력을 단념시킨다는

As entrepreneur Derek Sivers put it, / "The first follower is / what transforms a lone nut into a leader."
기업가 Derek Sivers가 말했듯이, / "첫 추종자가 / 외로운 괴짜를 지도자로 바꾸는 것이다."
If you were sitting with seven other people / and six group members picked the wrong answer, / but the remaining one chose the correct answer, / conformity dropped dramatically.
만약 당신이 7명의 다른 사람들과 앉아 있고 / 여섯 명이 틀린 답을 고르지만 / 나머지 한 사람이 옳은 답을 선택한다면 / 순응은 급격하게 떨어진다.
"The presence of a supporting partner / depleted the majority of much of its pressure," / Asch wrote.
"한 명의 지지자의 존재가 / 다수에게서 그것(행동을 같이 해야 한다는 것)의 많은 압박감을 고갈시켰다."라고 / Asch가 썼다.
Merely knowing that you're not the only resister / makes it substantially easier / to reject the crowd.
당신이 유일한 저항가가 아니라는 것을 단지 아는 것은 / 상당히 더 쉽게 만든다. / 군중에게 반대하는 것을
Emotional strength can be found / even in small numbers.
정서적인 힘이 발견될 수 있다. / 심지어 소수에게서도
In the words of Margaret Mead, / "Never doubt / that a small group of thoughtful citizens / can change the world; / indeed, it's the only thing that ever has."
Margaret Mead의 말에 따르면, / "결코 의심하지 마라. / 소수의 사려 깊은 시민이 / 세상을 바꿀 수 있다는 것을 / 사실상 그것이 지금껏 세상을 바꾼 유일한 것이다."
To feel that you're not alone, / you don't need a whole crowd to join you.
당신이 혼자가 아니라는 것을 느끼기 위해, / 당신과 함께할 전체 군중이 필요한 것은 아니다.
Research by Sigal Barsade and Hakan Ozcelik shows / that in business and government organizations, / just having one friend is enough / to significantly decrease loneliness.
Sigal Barsade와 Hakan Ozcelik에 의한 연구는 보여준다. / 사업과 정부 조직에서 / 단지 한 명의 친구를 갖는 것만으로도 충분하다는 것을 / 외로움을 상당히 줄이기에

기업가 Derek Sivers가 말했듯이, "첫 추종자가 외로운 괴짜를 지도자로 바꾸는 것이다." 만약 당신이 7명의 다른 사람들과 앉아 있고 여섯 명이 틀린 답을 고르지만 나머지 한 사람이 옳은 답을 선택한다면 순응은 급격하게 떨어진다. "한 명의 지지자의 존재가 다수에게서 그것(행동을 같이 해야 한다는 것)의 많은 압박감을 고갈시켰다."라고 Asch가 썼다. 당신이 유일한 저항가가 아니라는 것을 단지 아는 것은 군중에게 반대하는 것을 상당히 더 쉽게 만든다. 정서적인 힘이 심지어 소수에게서도 발견될 수 있다. Margaret Mead의 말에 따르면, "소수의 사려 깊은 시민이 세상을 바꿀 수 있다는 것을 결코 의심하지 마라. 사실상 그것이 지금껏 세상을 바꾼 유일한 것이다." 당신이 혼자가 아니라는 것을 느끼기 위해, 당신과 함께할 전체 군중이 필요한 것은 아니다. Sigal Barsade와 Hakan Ozcelik에 의한 연구는 사업과 정부 조직에서 단지 한 명의 친구를 갖는 것만으로도 외로움을 상당히 줄이기에 충분하다는 것을 보여준다.

Why? 왜 정답일까?

빈칸 앞의 인용구인 'The presence of a supporting partner depleted the majority of much of its pressure ~'에서 지지하는 사람이 한 명만 있어도 다수에 순응해야 한다는 압박이 줄어든다고 한 데 이어, 마지막 두 문장 또한 친구가 한 명만 있어도 외로움을 줄이기에는 충분하다는(~ just having one friend is enough to significantly decrease loneliness.) 내용을 언급하고 있다. 따라서 빈칸에 들어갈 말로 가장 적절한 것은 ① '당신이 유일한 저항가가 아니라는'이다.

- entrepreneur ⓝ 기업가
- lone ⓐ 혼자인
- dramatically ad 극적으로
- merely ad 단지
- emotional ⓐ 정서의
- significantly ad 상당히
- resister ⓝ 저항가
- discourage ⓥ 낙담시키다, 단념시키다
- transform ⓥ 변형하다
- nut ⓝ 괴짜, 미친 사람
- presence ⓝ 존재
- substantially ad 상당히
- thoughtful ⓐ 사려 깊은
- loneliness ⓝ 외로움, 고독
- defeat ⓥ 패배시키다, 이기다

구문 풀이

7행 Merely knowing {that you're not the only resister} makes it substantially easier to reject the crowd.
동명사구 주어 / { }: 명사절 / 5형식 동사(단수) / 가목적어 / 목적격 보어 / 진목적어

05 드라마 속 추상적인 세계

정답률 47% | 정답 ④

다음 빈칸에 들어갈 말로 가장 적절한 것을 고르시오. [3점]

① is separated from the dramatic contents
극적인 내용과 분리되어 있기
② is a reflection of our unrealistic desires
비현실적인 욕망의 반영이기
③ demonstrates our poor taste in TV shows
TV 쇼에 대한 우리의 형편없는 취향을 보여주기
④ is built on an extremely familiar framework
매우 친숙한 틀 위에서 만들어졌기
⑤ indicates that unnecessary details are hidden
불필요한 세부사항이 숨겨져 있다는 의미이기

A typical soap opera creates an abstract world, / in which a highly complex web of relationships connects fictional characters / that exist first only in the minds of the program's creators / and are then recreated in the minds of the viewer.
전형적인 드라마는 추상적인 세계를 만들어내는데, / 그 세계에서는 매우 복잡한 관계망이 허구의 캐릭터들을 연결한다. / 프로그램 제작자들의 마음속에만 먼저 존재하다가 / 이후에 시청자의 마음속에 재현되는
If you were to think about / how much human psychology, law, and even everyday physics the viewer must know / in order to follow and speculate about the plot, / you would discover it is considerable / — at least as much as the knowledge / required to follow and speculate about a piece of modern mathematics, / and in most cases, much more.
만약 여러분이 생각해보면 / 시청자가 얼마나 많은 인간 심리학, 법, 그리고 심지어 일상에서의 물리학을 알아야 하는지 / 줄거리를 따라가고 그것에 대해 추측하려면 / 여러분은 그 양이 상당하다는 것을 알게 된다. / 적어도 지식만큼, / 현대 수학의 한 부분을 따라가고 거기에 대해 추측하는 데 필요한 / 나아가 대부분의 경우 훨씬 더 많다는 것을 알게 된다.
Yet viewers follow soap operas with ease.
하지만 시청자들은 드라마를 쉽게 따라간다.
How are they able to cope with such abstraction?
그들은 어떻게 그런 추상에 대처할 수 있을까?
Because, of course, / the abstraction is built on an extremely familiar framework.
왜냐면 당연하게도, / 그 추상은 매우 친숙한 틀 위에서 만들어졌기 때문이다.
The characters in a soap opera / and the relationships between them / are very much like the real people and relationships / we experience every day.
드라마 속 인물들과 / 그들 사이의 관계는 / 실제 사람들 및 관계와 매우 흡사하다. / 우리가 매일 경험하는
The abstraction of a soap opera / is only a step / removed from the real world.
드라마의 추상은 / 불과 한 걸음이다. / 현실 세계에서 떨어져 있는
The mental "training" required to follow a soap opera / is provided by our everyday lives.
드라마를 따라가는 데 필요한 정신적 '훈련'은 / 우리의 일상생활에 의해 제공된다.

전형적인 드라마는 추상적인 세계를 만들어내는데, 그 세계에서는 매우 복잡한 관계망이 프로그램 제작자들의 마음속에만 먼저 존재하다가 이후에 시청자의 마음속에 재현되는 허구의 캐릭터들을 연결한다. 만약 줄거리를 따라가고 그것에 대해 추측하려면 시청자가 얼마나 많은 인간 심리학, 법, 그리고 심지어 일상에서의 물리학을 알아야 하는지 생각해보면, 여러분은 그 양이 상당하다는 것을 알게 된다. 적어도 현대 수학의 한 부분을 따라가고 거기에 대해 추측하는 데 필요한 지식만큼, 나아가 대부분의 경우 훨씬 더 많다는 것을 알게 된다. 하지만 시청자들은 드라마를 쉽게 따라간다. 그들은 어떻게 그런 추상에

대처할 수 있을까? 왜냐면 당연하게도, 그 추상은 매우 친숙한 틀 위에서 만들어졌기 때문이다. 드라마 속 인물들과 그들 사이의 관계는 우리가 매일 경험하는 실제 사람들 및 관계와 매우 흡사하다. 드라마의 추상은 현실 세계에서 불과 한 걸음 떨어져 있다. 드라마를 따라가는 데 필요한 정신적 '훈련'은 우리의 일상생활에 의해 제공된다.

Why? 왜 정답일까?

빈칸 뒤 내용의 핵심은 드라마 속의 추상이 우리 일상과 가깝다는 것이다(The mental "training" required to follow a soap opera is provided by our everyday lives.). 따라서 빈칸에 들어갈 말로 가장 적절한 것은 ④ '매우 친숙한 틀 위에서 만들어졌기'이다.

- soap opera 드라마, 연속극
- complex ⓐ 복잡한
- fictional ⓐ 허구의
- psychology ⓝ 심리
- speculate ⓥ 추측하다
- cope with ~에 대처하다
- reflection ⓝ 반영
- framework ⓝ 틀, 뼈대
- abstract ⓐ 추상적인
- web ⓝ 망
- recreate ⓥ 되살리다
- physics ⓝ 물리학
- considerable ⓐ 상당한
- abstraction ⓝ 추상
- demonstrate ⓥ 입증하다, 보여주다

구문 풀이

5행 If you were to think about {how much human psychology, law, and even everyday physics the viewer must know in order to follow and speculate about the plot}, you would discover it is considerable — at least as much as the knowledge required to follow and speculate about a piece of modern mathematics, and in most cases, much more.

(가정법 미래 종속절(if+주어+were to+동사원형 ~) / { }: 명사절 / 가정법 미래 주절(주어+조동사 과거형+동사원형 ~) / 과거분사)

06 자기불구화 전략

정답률 60% | 정답 ③

다음 빈칸에 들어갈 말로 가장 적절한 것을 고르시오. [3점]

① getting some rest from studying is necessary – 공부하다가 약간 쉬는 것은 필요하기
② failure serves as the foundation for success – 실패는 성공의 기초 역할을 하기
✔ you're creating a reason for your failure – 실패에 대한 이유를 만들기
④ studying is not about winning or losing – 공부는 이기고 지는 것의 문제가 아니기
⑤ you have already achieved a lot – 당신은 이미 많은 것을 성취했기

When self-handicapping, / you're engaging in behaviour / that you know will harm your chances of succeeding: / you know / that you won't do as well on the test / if you go out the night before, / but you do it anyway.
자기불구화를 할 때, / 당신은 행동에 관여하고 있는 것인데, / 당신이 알기로 당신의 성공 가능성을 해칠 / 당신은 알고 있지만, / 당신이 시험을 그만큼 잘 치지 못할 것임을 / 당신이 전날 밤 놀러 나가면 / 당신은 어찌되었든 그렇게 한다.

Why would anyone intentionally harm their chances of success?
어떤 사람이 왜 의도적으로 자신의 성공 가능성을 해치겠는가?

Well, here's a possible answer.
여기에 가능한 답이 있다.

Say that you do study hard.
당신이 공부를 정말로 열심히 한다고 해 보자.

You go to bed at a decent time / and get eight hours of sleep.
당신은 적당한 시간에 잠자리에 들고 / 8시간 동안 잠을 잔다.

Then you take the maths test, / but don't do well: / you only get a C.
그러고 나서 당신은 수학 시험에 응시하지만, / 잘 치지 못해서 / 당신은 겨우 C를 받는다.

What can you conclude about yourself?
당신은 당신 자신에 대해 어떤 결론을 내릴 수 있는가?

Probably that you're just not good at maths, / which is a pretty hard blow to your self-esteem.
아마도 당신은 그저 수학을 잘 못한다는 것일 텐데, / 이것은 당신의 자존감에 꽤 큰 타격이다.

But if you self-handicap, / you'll never be in this position / because you're creating a reason for your failure.
하지만 만약 당신이 자기불구화를 한다면, / 당신은 결코 이런 상황에 처하지 않을 것이다. / 당신이 실패에 대한 이유를 만들기 때문에

You were bound to get a C, / you can tell yourself, / because you went out till 1 a.m.
당신이 C를 받을 수밖에 없었다고 / 당신은 스스로에게 말할 수 있는 것이다. / 당신이 새벽 1시까지 밖에 있었기 때문에

That C doesn't mean that you're bad at maths; / it just means that you like to party.
그 C는 당신이 수학을 못한다는 것을 뜻하지는 않으며, / 그것은 단지 당신이 파티하는 것을 좋아한다는 것을 의미한다.

Self-handicapping seems like a paradox, / because people are deliberately harming their chances of success.
자기불구화 현상은 역설처럼 보이는데, / 사람들이 의도적으로 자신의 성공 가능성을 해치고 있는 것이기 때문이다.

자기불구화를 할 때, 당신은 당신이 알기로 당신의 성공 가능성을 해칠 행동에 관여하고 있는 것인데, 당신은 (시험) 전날 밤 놀러 나가면 시험을 그만큼 잘 치지 못할 것임을 알고 있지만, 어찌되었든 그렇게 한다. 어떤 사람이 왜 의도적으로 성공 가능성을 해치겠는가? 여기에 가능한 답이 있다. 당신이 공부를 정말로 열심히 한다고 해 보자. 당신은 적당한 시간에 잠자리에 들고 8시간 동안 잠을 잔다. 그러고 나서 당신은 수학 시험에 응시하지만, 잘 치지 못해서 겨우 C를 받는다. 당신은 당신 자신에 대해 어떤 결론을 내릴 수 있는가? 아마도 당신은 그저 수학을 잘 못한다는 결론일 텐데, 이것은 당신의 자존감에 꽤 큰 타격이다. 하지만 만약 당신이 자기불구화를 한다면, 당신은 실패에 대한 이유를 만들기 때문에 결코 이런 상황에 처하지 않을 것이다. 당신은 새벽 1시까지 밖에 있었기 때문에 C를 받을 수밖에 없었다고 스스로에게 말할 수 있는 것이다. 그 C는 당신이 수학을 못한다는 것을 뜻하지는 않으며, 단지 당신이 파티하는 것을 좋아한다는 것을 의미한다. 자기불구화 현상은 역설처럼 보이는데, 사람들이 의도적으로 자신의 성공 가능성을 해치고 있는 것이기 때문이다.

Why? 왜 정답일까?

빈칸 앞에서 수학 시험 공부를 열심히 하고 나서 시험을 쳤지만 결과가 좋지 않았을 때에는 능력을 탓할 수 밖에 없을 것이라고 설명하고 있다. 한편 빈칸이 포함된 문장부터는 우리가 자기불구화 전략을 택하는 경우, 즉 시험 전날 늦게까지 나가 놀아서 C를 받을 수밖에 없는 상황을 만드는 경우에는 우리가 능력이 아닌 다른 이유를 탓할 수 있다는 내용이 이어지고 있다. 이로 인해 마지막 문장에서는 자기불구화 전략을 채택하는 경우 사람들은 의도적으로 자신이 성공할 가능성을 망치고 있는 것(~ people are deliberately harming their chances of success.)이라는 결론을 내린다. 따라서 빈칸에 들어갈 말로 가장 적절한 것은 사람들이 스스로 '실패의 핑계를 만들기 위해' 자기불구화 전략을 채택한다는 의미를 완성하는 ③ '실패에 대한 이유를 만들기'이다.

- engage in ~에 관여하다
- intentionally ad 의도적으로
- deliberately ad 의도적으로, 고의로
- foundation ⓝ 기반, 기초
- harm ⓥ 해를 입히다
- paradox ⓝ 역설
- serve as ~의 역할을 하다

구문 풀이

1행 When self-handicapping, you're engaging in behaviour [that (you know) will harm your chances of succeeding]: you know that you won't do as well on the test if you go out the night before, but you do it anyway.

(접속사 / 분사구문 / 선행사 / ( ): 삽입절 / [ ]: 주격 관계대명사절 / 동사(미래) / 조건 접속사 / 동사(현재))

07 전략적 자기 무지

정답률 47% | 정답 ②

다음 빈칸에 들어갈 말로 가장 적절한 것을 고르시오.

① highlight the value of preferred activities – 선호되는 활동의 가치를 강조할
✔ make current activities less attractive – 현재의 활동을 덜 매력적으로 만들
③ cut their attachment to past activities – 과거 활동에 대한 자신들의 애착을 끊을
④ enable them to enjoy more activities – 자신들로 하여금 더 많은 활동을 즐기게 해줄
⑤ potentially become known to others – 다른 사람들에게 잠재적으로 알려지게 될

Some of the most insightful work on information seeking / emphasizes "strategic self-ignorance," / understood as "the use of ignorance as an excuse / to engage excessively in pleasurable activities / that may be harmful to one's future self."
정보 탐색에 관한 가장 통찰력 있는 연구 중 일부는 / '전략적 자기 무지'를 강조하는데, / 이는 '무지를 핑계로 이용하는 것'으로 이해된다. / '즐거운 활동을 과도하게 할 / 자신의 미래 자아에 해로울 수도 있는'

The idea here is / that if people are present-biased, / they might avoid information / that would make current activities less attractive / — perhaps because it would produce guilt or shame, / perhaps because it would suggest an aggregate trade-off / that would counsel against engaging in such activities.
여기서의 생각은 / 만약 사람들이 현재에 편향되어 있다면, / 정보를 피할 수도 있다는 것인데, / 현재의 활동을 덜 매력적으로 만들 / 아마도 그것이 죄책감이나 수치심을 유발할 것이고, / 총체적 절충을 제안할 것이기 때문일 것이다. / 그러한 활동을 하지 말라고 충고할

St. Augustine famously said, / "God give me chastity — tomorrow."
성 아우구스티누스는 유명한 말을 했다. / "하나님 제게 정결을 내일 주시옵소서."라는

[문제편 p.029]

Present-biased agents think: / "Please let me know the risks — tomorrow."
현재에 편향되어 있는 행위자들은 생각한다. / "제가 위험을 내일 알게 해주세요."라고

Whenever people are thinking about engaging in an activity / with short-term benefits but long-term costs, / they might prefer to delay receipt of important information.
사람들이 활동을 하려고 생각하고 있을 때마다, / 단기적인 혜택은 있지만 장기적인 대가가 있는 / 그들은 중요한 정보의 수신을 미루는 것을 선호할 수도 있다.

The same point might hold about information / that could make people sad or mad: / "Please tell me what I need to know — tomorrow."
정보에 관해서도 똑같은 점이 있을 수 있다. / 사람들을 슬프게 하거나 화나게 할 수 있는 / "제가 알아야 할 것을 내일 말해 주세요."

정보 탐색에 관한 가장 통찰력 있는 연구 중 일부는 '전략적 자기 무지'를 강조하는데, 이는 '자신의 미래 자아에 해로울 수도 있는 즐거운 활동을 과도하게 할 핑계로 무지를 이용하는 것'으로 이해된다. 여기서의 생각은 만약 사람들이 현재에 편향되어 있다면, 현재의 활동을 덜 매력적으로 만들 정보를 피할 수도 있다는 것인데, 아마도 그것이 죄책감이나 수치심을 유발할 것이고, 그러한 활동을 하지 말라고 충고할 총체적 절충을 제안할 것이기 때문일 것이다. 성 아우구스티누스는 "하나님 제게 정결을 내일 주시옵소서."라는 유명한 말을 했다. 현재에 편향되어 있는 행위자들은 "제가 위험을 내일 알게 해주세요."라고 생각한다. 사람들이 단기적인 혜택은 있지만 장기적인 대가가 있는 활동을 하려고 생각하고 있을 때마다, 그들은 중요한 정보의 수신을 미루는 것을 선호할 수도 있다. 사람들을 슬프게 하거나 화나게 할 수 있는 정보에 관해서도 똑같은 점이 있을 수 있다. "제가 알아야 할 것을 내일 말해 주세요."

Why? 왜 정답일까?

'**Whenever people are thinking about engaging in an activity with short-term benefits but long-term costs, they might prefer to delay receipt of important information.**'에서 단기적으로는 이득이 되지만 장기적으로는 대가가 따르는 행동을 할 때 사람들은 '중요한' 정보 입수를 미룰 수도 있다고 언급하고 있다. 여기서 중요한 정보란 '~ **perhaps because it would produce guilt or shame, because it would suggest an aggregate trade-off that would counsel against engaging in such activities.**'에 따르면 그러한 행동을 하려는 것에 대해 수치심이나 죄책감이 들게 하여 활동에 참여하지 못하게 만들 수 있는 정보를 가리킨다. 따라서 빈칸에 들어갈 말로 가장 적절한 것은 ② '현재의 활동을 덜 매력적으로 만들'이다.

- **insightful** ⓐ 통찰력 있는
- **strategic** ⓐ 전략적인
- **excessively** ad 과도하게
- **harmful** ⓐ 해로운
- **delay** ⓥ 미루다
- **attachment** ⓝ 애착
- **emphasize** ⓥ 강조하다
- **ignorance** ⓝ 무지
- **pleasurable** ⓐ 즐거운
- **guilt** ⓝ 죄책감
- **highlight** ⓥ 강조하다

구문 풀이

1행 Some of the most insightful work on information seeking (주어) emphasizes (동사(단수)) "strategic self-ignorance," (목적어(선행사)) (which is) (생략) understood as "the use of ignorance as (전치사(~로서)) an excuse to engage (형용사적 용법) excessively in pleasurable activities (선행사) [that (주격 관계대명사) may be harmful to one's future self]."

★★★ 1등급 대비 고난도 2점 문제

08 충성심의 시험대가 되는 어려운 시기 — 정답률 36% | 정답 ②

다음 빈칸에 들어갈 말로 가장 적절한 것을 고르시오.

① leadership – 지도력
✔ loyalty – 충성심
③ creativity – 창의력
④ intelligence – 지성
⑤ independence – 독립성

Around the boss, / you will always find people / coming across as friends, good subordinates, or even great sympathizers.
우두머리 주변에서, / 여러분은 항상 사람들을 발견할 수 있다. / 친구나 좋은 부하, 심지어는 대단한 동조자라는 인상을 주는

But some do not truly belong.
그러나 일부는 진정으로 속해 있는 것은 아니다.

One day, / an incident will blow their cover, / and then you will know where they truly belong.
언젠가는, / 어떤 사건이 그들의 껍데기를 날려 버릴 것이고, / 여러분은 그들이 진정으로 속한 곳을 알게 될 것이다.

When it is all cosy and safe, / they will be there, / loitering the corridors and fawning at the slightest opportunity.
모든 것이 편안하고 안전할 때, / 그들은 그곳에 있을 것이다. / 복도를 서성거리고 아주 작은 기회에도 알랑거리면서

But as soon as difficulties arrive, / they are the first to be found missing.
하지만 어려움이 닥치자마자, / 그들은 가장 먼저 보이지 않을 것이다.

And difficult times are the true test of loyalty.
그래서 어려운 시기는 충성심의 진정한 시험대이다.

Dr. Martin Luther King said, / "The ultimate test of a man / is not where he stands in moments of comfort and convenience, / but where he stands at times of challenge and controversy."
Dr. Martin Luther King은 말했다. / "어떤 사람을 판단하는 궁극적인 시험대는 / 그 사람이 편안함과 안락함의 순간에 있는 곳이 아니라, / 도전과 논쟁의 시기에 있는 곳이다."라고

And so be careful of friends / who are always eager to take from you / but reluctant to give back even in their little ways.
그러므로 친구를 조심하라. / 항상 여러분에게서 뭔가 얻어가려고 열망하면서 / 사소하게라도 돌려주기를 꺼리는

If they lack the commitment / to sail with you through difficult weather, / then they are more likely to abandon your ship / when it stops.
만약 그들에게 헌신이 부족하다면, / 여러분과 함께 악천후를 뚫고 항해하려는 / 그렇다면 그들은 여러분의 배를 버릴 가능성이 더 크다. / 그것이 멈출 때

우두머리 주변에서, 여러분은 항상 친구나 좋은 부하, 심지어는 대단한 동조자라는 인상을 주는 사람들을 발견할 수 있다. 그러나 일부는 진정으로 속해 있는 것은 아니다. 언젠가는, 어떤 사건이 그들의 껍데기를 날려 버릴 것이고, 여러분은 그들이 진정으로 속한 곳을 알게 될 것이다. 모든 것이 편안하고 안전할 때, 그들은 복도를 서성거리고 아주 작은 기회에도 알랑거리면서 그곳에 있을 것이다. 하지만 어려움이 닥치자마자, 그들은 가장 먼저 보이지 않을 것이다. 그래서 어려운 시기는 충성심의 진정한 시험대이다. Dr. Martin Luther King은 "어떤 사람을 판단하는 궁극적인 시험대는 그 사람이 편안함과 안락함의 순간에 있는 곳이 아니라, 도전과 논쟁의 시기에 있는 곳이다."라고 말했다. 그러므로 항상 여러분에게서 뭔가 얻어가려고 열망하면서 사소하게라도 돌려주기를 꺼리는 친구를 조심하라. 만약 그들에게 여러분과 함께 악천후를 뚫고 항해하려는 헌신이 부족하다면, 여러분의 배가 멈출 때 그것을 버릴 가능성이 더 크다.

Why? 왜 정답일까?

마지막 문장에서 어려운 시기를 악천후에 빗대어, '헌신(**commitment**)'이 부족한 친구라면 이러한 악천후의 시기에 우리 곁을 떠나고 말 것이라는 내용을 제시하고 있다. 따라서 빈칸에 들어갈 말로 가장 적절한 것은 '헌신'과 같은 의미인 ② '충성심'이다.

- **subordinate** ⓝ 부하
- **incident** ⓝ 사건, 일
- **corridor** ⓝ 복도
- **controversy** ⓝ 논란
- **reluctant** ⓐ (~하기를) 꺼리는
- **abandon** ⓥ 버리다
- **sympathizer** ⓝ 동조자
- **blow** ⓥ 날리다, 불다
- **ultimate** ⓐ 궁극적인
- **be eager to** ~하려고 열망하는
- **commitment** ⓝ 헌신

구문 풀이

7행 But as soon as (접속사(~하자마자)) difficulties arrive, they are the first to be found missing. 「be found + 형용사 : ~한 것으로 발견되다」

★★ 문제 해결 꿀~팁 ★★

▶ 많이 틀린 이유는?
첫 문장에 the boss가 언급되므로 얼핏 보면 '리더십'에 관한 글처럼 보여 ①을 고르기 쉽다. 하지만 글에서 팀이나 무리를 이끄는 상황, 리더의 자질 등에 관해서는 전혀 언급되지 않는다.
▶ 문제 해결 방법은?
시기가 좋을 때와 어려울 때를 나눠, 좋을 때 곁에 있고 어려울 때 떠나는 사람을 경계해야 한다고 언급하는 글이다. 즉 '어려운' 시기는 곁에 있는 이들의 '진실성, 충실함'을 시험할 계기 역할을 한다는 것이다.

★★★ 1등급 대비 고난도 3점 문제

09 타인을 보이는 대로 판단해서는 안 되는 이유 — 정답률 40% | 정답 ②

다음 빈칸에 들어갈 말로 가장 적절한 것을 고르시오. [3점]

① narrow down your network in social media – 소셜 미디어에서 네트워크를 좁힐
✔ go beyond a person's superficial qualities – 그들의 피상적인 특성을 넘어설
③ focus on intelligence rather than wealth – 부보다는 지능에 집중할

④ trust your first impressions of others – 타인의 첫인상을 믿을
⑤ take advantage of criminals – 범죄자들을 이용할

Do you advise your kids to keep away from strangers?
당신은 당신의 아이들에게 낯선 사람을 멀리 하라고 조언하는가?
That's a tall order for adults.
그것은 어른들에게는 무리한 요구이다.
After all, you expand your network of friends / and create potential business partners / by meeting strangers.
결국, 당신은 친구 관계를 확장하고 / 잠재적인 사업 파트너를 만든다. / 낯선 사람들을 만남으로써
Throughout this process, however, / analyzing people to understand their personalities / is not all about potential economic or social benefit.
그러나 이 과정에서, / 사람들의 성격을 이해하기 위해 그들을 분석하는 것은 / 잠재적인 경제적 또는 사회적 이익에 관한 것만은 아니다.
There is your safety to think about, / as well as the safety of your loved ones.
당신의 안전도 생각해봐야 한다. / 당신이 사랑하는 사람들의 안전뿐 아니라.
For that reason, / Mary Ellen O'Toole, who is a retired FBI profiler, / emphasizes the need to go beyond a person's superficial qualities / in order to understand them.
그런 이유로, / 은퇴한 FBI 프로파일러인 Mary Ellen O'Toole은 / 사람들의 피상적인 특성을 넘어설 필요성을 강조한다. / 그들을 이해하기 위해
It is not safe, for instance, / to assume that a stranger is a good neighbor, / just because they're polite.
예를 들어, 안전하지 않다. / 낯선 이들이 좋은 이웃이라고 가정하는 것은 / 단지 그들이 공손하다는 이유로
Seeing them follow a routine / of going out every morning well-dressed / doesn't mean that's the whole story.
그들이 관행을 따르는 것을 보는 것이 / 매일 아침 잘 차려 입고 외출하는 / 이야기의 전부인 것은 아니다(전부인 것은 아니다).
In fact, O'Toole says / that when you are dealing with a criminal, / even your feelings may fail you.
사실, O'Toole은 말한다. / 당신이 범죄자를 다룰 때, / 심지어 당신의 느낌도 당신을 틀리게 할 수 있다고
That's because criminals have perfected the art of manipulation and deceit.
그것은 범죄자들이 조작과 사기의 기술에 통달했기 때문이다.

당신은 당신의 아이들에게 낯선 사람을 멀리 하라고 조언하는가? 그것은 어른들에게는 무리한 요구이다. 결국, 당신은 낯선 사람들을 만남으로써 친구 관계를 확장하고 잠재적인 사업 파트너를 만든다. 그러나 이 과정에서, 사람들의 성격을 이해하기 위해 그들을 분석하는 것은 잠재적인 경제적 또는 사회적 이익에 관한 것만은 아니다. 당신이 사랑하는 사람들의 안전뿐 아니라, 당신의 안전도 생각해봐야 한다. 그런 이유로, 은퇴한 FBI 프로파일러인 Mary Ellen O'Toole은 사람들을 이해하기 위해 그들의 피상적인 특성을 넘어설 필요성을 강조한다. 예를 들어, 단지 낯선 이들이 공손하다는 이유로 좋은 이웃이라고 가정하는 것은 안전하지 않다. 매일 아침 잘 차려 입고 외출하는 관행을 따르는 그들을 보는 것이 이야기의 전부인 것은 아니다(매일 아침 그들이 관행처럼 잘 차려입고 외출하는 모습을 본다고 그들의 사정 전부를 알 수는 없다). 사실, O'Toole은 당신이 범죄자를 다룰 때, 심지어 당신의 느낌도 당신을 틀리게 할 수 있다고 말한다. 그것은 범죄자들이 조작과 사기의 기술에 통달했기 때문이다.

Why? 왜 정답일까?

빈칸 뒤의 예시에서 보이는 모습이 공손하다고 하여 어떤 이웃이 좋은 이웃이라고 가정하는 것은 안전하지 않다는 이야기를 통해, 타인을 '보이는 대로 판단하지 않을' 필요성에 대해 언급하고 있다. 따라서 빈칸에 들어갈 말로 가장 적절한 것은 ② '그들의 피상적인 특성을 넘어설'이다.

- keep away from ~을 멀리하다
- analyze ⓥ 분석하다
- retired ⓐ 은퇴한, 퇴직한
- well-dressed 잘 차려입은, 복장이 훌륭한
- manipulation ⓝ 조작, 교묘한 처리
- superficial ⓐ 피상적인, 얄팍한
- potential ⓐ 가능성이 있는
- personality ⓝ 성격
- emphasize ⓥ (중요성을) 강조하다
- criminal ⓝ 범죄자 ⓐ 형사상의, 범죄의
- deceit ⓝ 사기, 기만, 속임수
- take advantage of ~을 이용하다

구문 풀이

13행 Seeing them follow a routine of going out every morning well-dressed doesn't mean {that's the whole story}. { }: 목적어
(Seeing: 동명사구 주어, doesn't: 원형부정사 / 동사(단수))

★★ 문제 해결 꿀~팁 ★★

▶ 많이 틀린 이유는?
빈칸이 주제 부분에 있고 답의 근거는 예시에 주로 나오므로, 예시를 읽고 이해한 뒤 이 내용을 일반화하여 최종적으로 답을 골라야 하는 문제이다. 'Seeing ~ doesn't mean the whole story.'에서 '보기에' 공손하고 옷을 잘 차려입는다고 하여 모든 것을 판단할 수는 없다는 일반적인 내용을 추론하여, '피상적인' 특성을 넘어서야 한다는 말을 답으로 고르도록 한다. 오답 중 ①은 'social media'라는 단어가 주제와 무관하며, ④는 주로 보이는 데 의존하기 마련인 '첫인상을 믿으라'는 뜻이므로 주제와 반대되는 내용에 가깝다.
▶ 문제 해결 방법은?
빈칸이 글 중간 부분에 있다면 힌트는 주로 뒤에 있다. 따라서 이 글 또한 후반부를 중점적으로 읽도록 한다.

★★★ 1등급 대비 고난도 3점 문제

10 꿀벌의 집단 지성 — 정답률 42% | 정답 ①

다음 빈칸에 들어갈 말로 가장 적절한 것을 고르시오. [3점]

① votes with their bodies – 몸으로 투표한다
② invades other bees' hives – 다른 벌들의 집에 쳐들어간다
③ searches for more flowers – 더 많은 꽃을 찾아 나선다
④ shows more concern for mates – 짝에 대한 걱정을 더 많이 보인다
⑤ improves their communication skills – 의사소통 기술을 향상시킨다

Honeybees have evolved / what we call "swarm intelligence," / with up to 50,000 workers in a single colony coming together / to make democratic decisions.
꿀벌은 발전시켜 왔다. / 우리가 "집단 지성"이라고 부르는 것을 / 한 군집 내 최대 5만 마리의 일벌이 함께 모여서 / 민주적인 결정을 내리기 위해
When a hive gets too crowded in springtime, / colonies send scouts to look for a new home.
봄철에 벌집이 너무 붐빌 때 / 군집들은 새로운 집을 찾기 위해 정찰병을 보낸다.
If any scouts disagree / on where the colony should build its next hive, / they argue their case the civilized way: / through a dance-off.
어느 정찰병이라도 동의하지 않으면, / 어디에 다음 벌집을 지을지에 대해 / 그들은 문명화된 방법으로 문제를 논의한다. / 즉 춤을 통해
Each scout performs a "waggle dance" for other scouts / in an attempt to convince them of their spot's merit.
각 정찰병은 다른 정찰병들을 위해 "waggle dance(8자 춤)"를 춘다. / 그들에게 자신이 찾은 장소의 장점을 납득시키기 위해
The more enthusiastic the dance is, / the happier the scout is with his spot.
춤이 더 열정적일수록 / 그 정찰병은 그 장소를 더 마음에 들어 하는 것이다.
The remainder of the colony votes with their bodies, / flying to the spot they prefer / and joining in the dance / until one potential hive overcomes all other dances of the neighborhood.
군집의 나머지 벌들은 몸으로 투표한다. / 그들이 선호하는 장소로 날아가서 / 춤에 합류하여 / 벌집이 될 가능성이 있는 한 장소가 주변의 모든 다른 춤들을 이길 때까지
It would be great / if Congress settled their disagreements the same way.
멋질 것이다. / 의회가 의견 불일치를 똑같은 방법으로 해결한다면

꿀벌은 한 군집 내 최대 5만 마리의 일벌이 함께 민주적인 결정을 내리기 위해 모여서 소위 "집단 지성"을 발전시켜 왔다. 봄철에 벌집이 너무 붐빌 때 군집들은 새로운 집을 찾기 위해 정찰병을 보낸다. 어느 정찰병이라도 어디에 다음 벌집을 지을지에 대해 동의하지 않으면, 그들은 문명화된 방법으로, 즉 춤을 통해 문제를 논의한다. 각 정찰병은 다른 정찰병들에게 자신이 찾은 장소의 장점을 납득시키기 위해 "waggle dance(8자 춤)"를 춘다. 춤이 더 열정적일수록 그 정찰병은 그 장소를 더 마음에 들어 하는 것이다. 군집의 나머지 벌들은 그들이 선호하는 장소로 날아가서 벌집이 될 가능성이 있는 한 장소가 주변의 모든 다른 춤들을 이길 때까지 춤에 합류하여 몸으로 투표한다. 의회가 의견 불일치를 똑같은 방법으로 해결한다면 멋질 것이다.

Why? 왜 정답일까?

'If any scouts disagree on where the colony should build its next hive, they argue their case the civilized way: through a dance-off.'에서 벌은 마음에 드는 벌집 장소를 결정함에 있어 '춤'이라는 수단을 이용한다고 이야기하는데, 이는 결국 춤이 벌들에게 있어 의사를 표현하는 중대한 수단임을 말하는 것이다. 따라서 빈칸에 들어갈 말로 가장 적절한 것은 '춤'을 간접적으로 풀어 쓴 ① '몸으로 투표한다'이다.

- evolve ⓥ 발전시키다, 진화하다
- up to ~까지
- democratic ⓐ 민주적인
- scout ⓝ 정찰병
- enthusiastic ⓐ 열정적인
- potential ⓐ ~일 가능성이 있는
- swarm ⓝ 떼
- colony ⓝ 군집
- hive ⓝ 벌집
- convince ⓥ 납득시키다, 설득하다
- remainder ⓝ 나머지
- overcome ⓥ 이기다, 극복하다

DAY 04

[문제편 p.031]

- congress ⓝ 의회
- settle ⓥ (혼란이나 갈등을) 해결하다

구문 풀이

1행 Honeybees have evolved what we call "swarm intelligence," with up to 50,000 workers in a single colony coming together to make democratic decisions.
동사(현재완료) / 관계대명사(~것) / 목적격 보어 / 「with + 명사 + 분사 : ~하면서」 / 부사적 용법(~하기 위해)

★★ 문제 해결 꿀~팁 ★★

▶ 많이 틀린 이유는?

'꿀벌이 춤으로 의사를 표현한다'는 주제를 파악했어도 정답 선택지에 '춤'이라는 단어가 직접 등장하지 않기에 한 번 더 생각을 요하는 문제였다. 최다 오답인 ②는 다른 선택지와는 달리 본문에 비교적 많이 나온 '벌집'이라는 단어를 포함하고 있지만 이 글은 '벌집 장소 결정'보다는 그 결정 방법인 '춤'에 더 무게중심을 두고 있다. 더구나 다른 벌집을 '침입'한다는 이야기는 글의 다른 부분에 나온 바 없다.

▶ 문제 해결 방법은?

주제를 잡는 데 어려움이 있었다면 글에서 가장 많이 반복된 단어가 무엇인지 먼저 파악해 본다('dance', 'hive'). 그리고 그 핵심 소재가 서로 어떤 연관성이 있는지 (dance → hive 장소 결정)에 중점을 두어 독해한다.

★★★ 1등급 대비 고난도 3점 문제

11 과학에서 보잘것없는 대상을 연구하는 이유

정답률 35% | 정답 ②

다음 빈칸에 들어갈 말로 가장 적절한 것을 고르시오. [3점]

① depend on personal experience
개인적인 경험에 의존한다
✔② choose to study humble subjects
보잘것없는 대상을 연구하기로 한다
③ work in close cooperation with one another
서로 긴밀하게 협력하여 일한다
④ look for solutions to problems from the past
과거로부터 문제에 대한 해결을 찾는다
⑤ test a hypothesis through lots of experiments
많은 실험을 통해 가설을 시험한다

One of the most curious paintings of the Renaissance / is a careful depiction of a weedy patch of ground / by Albrecht Dürer.
르네상스 시대의 가장 흥미를 돋우는 그림 중 하나는 / 잡초가 무성한 땅의 정교한 묘사이다. / Albrecht Dürer에 의한

Dürer extracts design and harmony / from an apparently random collection of weeds and grasses / that we would normally not think twice to look at.
Dürer는 디자인과 조화를 끌어낸다. / 겉보기에는 잡초나 풀이 아무렇게나 모여 있는 것으로부터 / 우리가 평소에는 다시 쳐다볼 생각조차 하지 않을

By taking such an ordinary thing, / he is able to convey his artistry in a pure form.
그런 평범한 사물을 취하여 / 그는 자신의 예술적 재능을 순수한 형태로 전달할 수 있다.

In a similar way, / scientists often choose to study humble subjects / when trying to understand the essence of a problem.
마찬가지로, / 과학자들은 흔히 보잘것없는 대상을 연구하기로 한다. / 문제의 본질을 이해하려 노력할 때

Studying relatively simple systems / avoids unnecessary complications, / and can allow deeper insights to be obtained.
비교적 단순한 체계를 연구하는 것은 / 불필요한 문제를 피하고 / 보다 깊은 통찰력을 얻게 할 수 있다.

This is particularly true / when we are trying to understand something as problematic / as our ability to learn.
이는 특히 그렇다. / 우리가 문제가 많은 것을 이해하려고 애쓰고 있을 때 / 우리의 학습 능력만큼이나

Human reactions are so complex / that they can be difficult to interpret objectively.
인간의 반응은 너무 복잡해서 / 객관적으로 해석하기가 어려울 수 있다.

It sometimes helps to step back / and consider / how more modest creatures, / like bacteria or weeds, / deal with the challenges they face.
때로는 한 발 뒤로 물러서 / 생각해 보는 것이 도움이 된다. / 어떻게 좀 더 보잘것없는 생물들이 / 박테리아나 잡초와 같은 / 그들이 직면하는 어려움에 대처하는지

르네상스 시대의 가장 흥미를 돋우는 그림 중 하나는 잡초가 무성한 땅을 정교하게 그린, Albrecht Dürer의 그림이다. Dürer는 우리가 평소에는 다시 쳐다볼 생각조차 하지 않을, 겉보기에는 아무렇게나 모여 있는 잡초나 풀로부터 디자인과 조화를 끌어낸다. 그런 평범한 사물을 취하여 그는 자신의 예술적 재능을 순수한 형태로 전달할 수 있다. 마찬가지로, 과학자들은 문제의 본질을 이해하려 노력할 때 흔히 보잘것없는 대상을 연구하기로 한다. 비교적 단순한 체계를 연구하는 것은 불필요한 문제를 피하고 보다 깊은 통찰력을 얻게 할 수 있다. 이는 우리가 우리의 학습 능력만큼이나 문제가 많은 것을 이해하려고 애쓰고 있을 때 특히 그렇다. 인간의 반응은 너무 복잡해서 객관적으로 해석하기가 어려울 수 있다. 때로는 한 발 뒤로 물러서서 박테리아나 잡초와 같은 좀 더 보잘것없는 생물들이 직면하는 어려움에 어떻게 대처하는지 생각해 보는 것이 도움이 된다.

Why? 왜 정답일까?

'Studying relatively simple systems avoids unnecessary complications, and can allow deeper insights to be obtained.'와 **'It sometimes helps to step back and consider how more modest creatures, like bacteria or weeds, deal with the challenges they face.'**에서 비교적 단순한 체계를 연구하면 도리어 불필요한 문제를 피하고 깊은 통찰력을 얻을 수 있어서, 박테리아나 잡초처럼 언뜻 보아 별 의미가 없어 보이는 대상들이 어려움에 어떻게 대처하는지 생각해 보면 보다 복잡한 대상을 연구할 때 도움을 받을 수 있다고 이야기 한다. 따라서 빈칸에 들어갈 말로 가장 적절한 것은 ② '보잘것없는 대상을 연구하기로 한다'이다.

- weedy ⓐ 잡초가 무성한
- apparently ad 겉보기에
- convey ⓥ 전달하다
- essence ⓝ 본질
- complication ⓝ (복잡함이 야기하는) 문제
- problematic ⓐ 문제가 많은
- modest ⓐ 보잘것없는, 대단하지는 않은
- extract ⓥ 추출하다, 끌어내다
- ordinary ⓐ 평범한, 보통의
- artistry ⓝ 예술가적 재능, 예술적 기교
- relatively ad 비교적, 상대적으로
- insight ⓝ 통찰력
- interpret ⓥ 해석하다

구문 풀이

11행 This is particularly true / when we are trying to understand something as problematic as our ability to learn.
접속사(~할 때) / ~하려고 애쓰다(현재진행) / 원급 비교 / 형용사적 용법

★★ 문제 해결 꿀~팁 ★★

▶ 많이 틀린 이유는?

앞에서 르네상스 예술가의 작업 방식을 예로 든 뒤 과학자의 연구 방법을 주제로 연결시키는데, 이는 얼핏 보아 서로 연관성이 없는 내용이다. 이 점이 지문을 이해하는 데 어려움을 야기한 것으로 보인다. 오답 선택지가 모두 주제와 무관하게 구성된 가운데, ④는 글의 앞부분에 나온 '르네상스'를 일반화한 듯이 '과거'라는 단어를 언급하고 있어 오답률이 높았다.

▶ 문제 해결 방법은?

앞에 나온 예술가는 비유 또는 예시에 해당하므로 빈칸 앞보다는 뒤에 주력하여 답을 찾는다. 특히 마지막 두 문장에서 '과학 연구: 복잡한 체계 < 단순한 체계'라는 요약을 이끌어내도록 한다.

★★★ 1등급 대비 고난도 3점 문제

12 어느 정도의 정부 개입이 필요한 자유 시장 경제

정답률 33% | 정답 ①

다음 빈칸에 들어갈 말로 가장 적절한 것을 고르시오. [3점]

✔① markets are rarely left entirely free
시장이 완전히 자유로운 상태로 맡겨지는 경우는 드물다
② governments are reluctant to intervene
정부는 개입하기를 꺼린다
③ supply and demand are not always balanced
수요와 공급은 항상 균형이 맞는 것은 아니다
④ economic inequality continues to get worse
경제적 불평등은 계속해서 심해지고 있다
⑤ competition does not guarantee the maximum profit
경쟁은 최대 이익을 보장해주지 못한다

In most of the world, / capitalism and free markets are accepted today / as constituting the best system / for allocating economic resources and encouraging economic output.
세계 대부분에서 / 오늘날 자본주의와 자유 시장은 받아들여지고 있다. / 최고의 시스템을 구성하는 것으로 / 경제적 자원을 분배하고 경제적 생산을 장려하기 위한

Nations have tried other systems, / such as socialism and communism, / but in many cases / they have either switched wholesale to / or adopted aspects of free markets.
국가들은 다른 시스템들을 시도했지만, / 사회주의나 공산주의와 같은 / 많은 경우 / 그들은 (자유 시장)으로 완전히 전환하거나 / 자유 시장의 측면들을 받아들였다.

Despite the widespread acceptance of the freemarket system, / markets are rarely left entirely free.
자유 시장 시스템의 광범위한 수용에도 불구하고, / 시장이 완전히 자유로운 상태로 맡겨지는 경우는 드물다.

Government involvement takes many forms, / ranging from the enactment and enforcement of laws and regulations / to direct participation in the economy / through entities like the U.S.'s mortgage agencies.

정부의 개입은 다양한 형태를 취한다. / 법과 규정의 제정과 집행에서부터 / 직접적인 경제 참여에 이르기까지 / 미국의 담보 기관과 같은 실체를 통한

Perhaps the most important form of government involvement, / however, / comes in the attempts of central banks and national treasuries / to control and affect the ups and downs of economic cycles.

아마도 가장 중요한 형태의 정부 개입은 / 그러나 / 중앙은행과 국가 재무기관의 시도로 나타날 것이다. / 경기 주기의 흥망성쇠를 통제하고 영향을 미치려는

오늘날 세계 대부분에서 자본주의와 자유 시장은 경제적 자원을 분배하고 경제적 생산을 장려하기 위한 최고의 시스템을 구성하는 것으로 받아들여지고 있다. 국가들은 사회주의나 공산주의와 같은 다른 시스템들을 시도했지만, 많은 경우 그들은 자유 시장으로 완전히 전환하거나 자유 시장의 측면들을 받아들였다. 자유 시장 시스템의 광범위한 수용에도 불구하고, 시장이 완전히 자유로운 상태로 맡겨지는 경우는 드물다. 정부의 개입은 법과 규정의 제정과 집행에서부터 미국의 담보 기관과 같은 실체를 통한 직접적인 경제 참여에 이르기까지 다양한 형태를 취한다. 그러나 아마도 가장 중요한 형태의 정부 개입은 중앙은행과 국가 재무기관이 경기 주기의 흥망성쇠를 통제하고 영향을 미치려는 시도로 나타날 것이다.

Why? 왜 정답일까?

빈칸 앞에서 오늘날 세계 대부분의 국가가 자유 시장 경제를 받아들였다고 이야기하는데, 빈칸 뒤에서는 자유 시장 경제 체제 안에서도 이루어질 수밖에 없는 정부 개입(Government involvement)에 관해 설명하고 있다. 따라서 빈칸에 들어갈 말로 가장 적절한 것은 ① '시장이 완전히 자유로운 상태로 맡겨지는 경우는 드물다'이다.

- capitalism ⓝ 자본주의
- allocate ⓥ 배분하다, 할당하다
- communism ⓝ 공산주의
- enforcement ⓝ 시행, 집행
- mortgage ⓝ (담보) 대출
- ups and downs 흥망성쇠
- intervene ⓥ 개입하다
- constitute ⓥ 구성하다
- socialism ⓝ 사회주의
- wholesale ad 완전히, 모조리
- regulation ⓝ 규정, 규제
- treasury ⓝ 재무부, 금고
- reluctant ⓐ 꺼리는, 마지못해 하는

구문 풀이

7행 Despite the widespread acceptance of the freemarket system, markets are rarely left entirely free.
(Despite: 전치사(~에도 불구하고) / are rarely left: 5형식 수동태 / entirely free: 보어(형용사구))

★★ 문제 해결 꿀~팁 ★★

▶ 많이 틀린 이유는?

②는 '정부가 개입을 꺼린다'는 의미인데, 빈칸 뒤를 보면 실제 자본주의 체계에서 일어나는 다양한 정부 개입의 형태를 언급하고 있다. 이는 정부가 시장 개입을 자제한다기보다 오히려 단행한다는 뜻이다.

▶ 문제 해결 방법은?

글 중간에 나온 빈칸에 대한 힌트는 빈칸 뒤에 있음을 명심하자. 여기서도 빈칸 뒤를 보면, 정부 개입은 실제로 다양한 형태로 발생하고, 그중에서도 가장 중요한 개입은 중앙 은행이나 국가 재무기관의 조치로 나타난다는 내용이 제시된다. 이를 토대로 볼 때, '정부 개입이 이뤄진다 = 시장을 가만히 내버려두는 경우는 잘 없다'는 내용이 빈칸에 들어가야 한다.

[문제편 p.032]

DAY 05 빈칸 추론 05

01 ④	02 ③	03 ②	04 ①	05 ④
06 ③	07 ④	08 ①	09 ②	10 ②
11 ⑤	12 ②			

01 우연과 전문가가 만나 탄생한 과학적 발명의 예 　정답률 44% | 정답 ④

다음 빈칸에 들어갈 말로 가장 적절한 것을 고르시오. [3점]

① trial and error – 시행착오
② idea and a critic – 생각과 비평가
③ risk and stability – 위험과 안정성
④ chance and a researcher – 우연과 연구자
⑤ a professional and an amateur – 프로와 아마추어

There are countless examples of scientific inventions / that have been generated by accident.
과학적 발명의 예는 셀 수 없이 많다. / 우연히 만들어진

However, / often this accident has required a person / with above-average knowledge in the field / to interpret it.
하지만 / 종종 이러한 우연은 사람을 필요로 해 왔다. / 해당 분야에서 평균 이상의 지식을 가진 / 이를 해석할 수 있는

One of the better-known examples / of the cooperation between chance and a researcher / is the invention of penicillin.
보다 잘 알려진 예 중 하나는 / 우연과 연구자의 협업에 대해 / 페니실린의 발명이다.

In 1928, / Scottish biologist Alexander Fleming went on a vacation.
1928년, / 스코틀랜드의 생물학자인 Alexander Fleming이 휴가를 떠났다.

As a slightly careless man, / Fleming left some bacterial cultures on his desk.
다소 부주의한 사람이었던 / Fleming은 책상 위에 몇몇 박테리아 배양균을 두고 갔다.

When he returned, / he noticed mold in one of his cultures, / with a bacteria-free zone around it.
그는 돌아왔을 때 / 배양균들 중 하나에서 곰팡이를 발견했는데 / 그 주변에는 박테리아가 없었다.

The mold was from the *penicillium notatum* species, / which had killed the bacteria on the Petri dish.
그 곰팡이는 *penicillium notatum* 종에서 나온 것인데, / 이것이 Petri 접시 위의 박테리아를 죽였던 것이다.

This was a lucky coincidence.
이는 운 좋은 우연의 일치였다.

For a person who does not have expert knowledge, / the bacteria-free zone would not have had much significance, / but Fleming understood the magical effect of the mold.
전문적 지식이 없는 사람에게는 / 박테리아가 없는 부분이 그리 중요하지 않았겠지만, / Fleming은 그 곰팡이의 마법 같은 작용을 이해했다.

The result was penicillin / — a medication / that has saved countless people on the planet.
그 결과는 페니실린이었다. / 약물인 / 지구의 수많은 사람들을 구한

우연히 만들어진 과학적 발명의 예는 셀 수 없이 많다. 하지만 종종 이러한 우연은 이를 해석할 수 있는, 해당 분야에서 평균 이상의 지식을 가진 사람을 필요로 해 왔다. 우연과 연구자의 협업에 대해 보다 잘 알려진 예 중 하나는 페니실린의 발명이다. 1928년, 스코틀랜드의 생물학자인 Alexander Fleming이 휴가를 떠났다. 다소 부주의한 사람이었던 Fleming은 책상 위에 몇몇 박테리아 배양균을 두고 갔다. 그는 돌아왔을 때 배양균들 중 하나에서 곰팡이를 발견했는데 그 주변에는 박테리아가 없었다. 그 곰팡이는 '*penicillium notatum*' 종에서 나온 것인데, 이것이 Petri 접시 위의 박테리아를 죽였던 것이다. 이는 운 좋은 우연의 일치였다. 전문적 지식이 없는 사람에게는 박테리아가 없는 부분이 그리 중요하지 않았겠지만, Fleming은 그 곰팡이의 마법 같은 작용을 이해했다. 그 결과는 지구의 수많은 사람들을 구한 약물인 페니실린이었다.

Why? 왜 정답일까?

'**There are countless examples of scientific inventions that have been generated by accident. However, often this accident has required a person with above-average knowledge in the field to interpret it.**'에서 과학적 발명이 만들어질 수 있는 우연은 그 우연의 의미를 헤아릴 수 있는, 해당 분야에서 평균 이상의 지식을 지닌 사람을 필요로 했다고 이야기하므로, 빈칸에 들어갈 말로 가장 적절한 것은 ④ '우연과 연구자'이다.

DAY 05

[문제편 p.032]

- countless ⓐ 셀 수 없이 많은
- accident ⓝ 우연
- interpret ⓥ 해석하다, 이해하다
- slightly ad 다소, 약간
- notice ⓥ 발견하다, 알아채다
- coincidence ⓝ 우연의 일치
- medication ⓝ 약물, 약
- generate ⓥ 만들어 내다, 발생시키다
- above-average 평균 이상의
- cooperation ⓝ 협업, 협력
- careless ⓐ 부주의한
- species ⓝ (생물의) 종
- significance ⓝ 중요성

구문 풀이

11행 The mold **was** from the *penicillium notatum* species, which had killed the bacteria on the Petri dish.

(was: 동사(과거) / species: 선행사 / which: 계속적 용법 / had killed: 동사(대과거) : was보다 먼저 일어남)

02 노동력 공유 체계

정답률 54% | 정답 ③

다음 빈칸에 들어갈 말로 가장 적절한 것을 고르시오.

① legally established – 법적으로 확립된다
② regularly reported – 정기적으로 보고된다
✔ socially regulated – 사회적으로 규제된다
④ manually calculated – 수동으로 계산된다
⑤ carefully documented – 신중하게 문서화된다

In labor-sharing groups, / people contribute labor to other people / on a regular basis / (for seasonal agricultural work such as harvesting) / or on an irregular basis / (in the event of a crisis / such as the need to rebuild a barn damaged by fire).
노동력 공유 집단에서 / 사람들은 다른 사람들에게 노동력을 제공한다. / 정기적으로 / (수확과 같은 계절적인 농사일을 위해) / 혹은 비정기적으로 / (위기 상황 발생 시 / 화재로 손상된 헛간을 다시 지어야 하는 것과 같은)

Labor sharing groups / are part of what has been called a "moral economy" / since no one keeps formal records / on how much any family puts in or takes out.
노동력 공유 집단은 / '도덕적 경제'라고 불린 것의 일부다. / 아무도 공식적인 기록을 남기지 않으므로 / 어떤 가족이 얼마나 많이 투입하고 얼마나 많이 가져갔는지에 대해

Instead, accounting is socially regulated.
대신에, 정산은 사회적으로 규제된다.

The group has a sense of moral community / based on years of trust and sharing.
그 집단은 도덕적 공동체 의식을 지닌다. / 다년간의 신뢰와 나눔을 바탕으로 하는

In a certain community of North America, / labor sharing is a major economic factor of social cohesion.
북미의 특정 지역 사회에서는 / 노동력 공유가 사회적 응집성의 주요 경제적 요소이다.

When a family needs a new barn / or faces repair work / that requires group labor, / a barn-raising party is called.
한 가족이 새 헛간이 필요하거나, / 수리 작업에 직면할 때, / 단체 노동력을 필요로 하는 / 헛간 조성 모임이 소집된다.

Many families show up to help.
여러 가족이 도우러 온다.

Adult men provide manual labor, / and adult women provide food for the event.
성인 남성은 육체노동을 제공하고, / 성인 여성은 행사를 위한 음식을 제공한다.

Later, / when another family needs help, / they call on the same people.
나중에, / 다른 가족이 도움이 필요할 때 / 그들은 똑같은 사람에게 부탁한다.

동력 공유 집단에서 사람들은 정기적으로(수확과 같은 계절적인 농사일을 위해) 혹은 비정기적으로(화재로 손상된 헛간을 다시 지어야 하는 것과 같은 위기 상황 발생 시) 다른 사람들에게 노동력을 제공한다. 아무도 어떤 가족이 얼마나 많이 투입하고 얼마나 많이 가져갔는지에 대해 공식적인 기록을 남기지 않으므로, 노동력 공유 집단은 '도덕적 경제'라고 불린 것의 일부다. 대신에, 정산은 사회적으로 규제된다. 그 집단은 다년간의 신뢰와 나눔을 바탕으로 하는 도덕적 공동체 의식을 지닌다. 북미의 특정 지역 사회에서는 노동력 공유가 사회적 응집성의 주요 경제적 요소이다. 한 가족이 새 헛간이 필요하거나, 단체 노동력을 필요로 하는 수리 작업에 직면할 때, 헛간 조성 모임이 소집된다. 여러 가족이 도우러 온다. 성인 남성은 육체노동을 제공하고, 성인 여성은 행사를 위한 음식을 제공한다. 나중에, 다른 가족이 도움이 필요할 때 그들은 똑같은 사람들에게 부탁한다.

Why? 왜 정답일까?

빈칸 뒤에서 북미 어느 지역의 예를 통해, 노동력 공유 집단은 다년간의 신뢰와 나눔을 바탕으로 한 도덕적 공동체여서 한 집에서 일이 필요하면 부르고, 대가로 음식을 나눠 먹고, 다음 번에 다른 집에서 일손을 필요로 하면 또 똑같은 이들이 동원되는 식이라고 한다. 결국 정산이 공동체 안에서 '사회적으로' 이뤄졌다는 결론이 적합하므로, 빈칸에 들어갈 말로 가장 적절한 것은 ③ '사회적으로 규제된다'이다.

- labor ⓝ 노동력
- on a regular basis 정기적으로
- agricultural ⓐ 농업의
- irregular ⓐ 비정기적인
- barn ⓝ 헛간
- put in ~을 투입하다
- trust ⓝ 신뢰
- factor ⓝ 요인
- manual ⓐ 손으로 하는, 육체 노동의
- regulate ⓥ 규제하다
- contribute ⓥ 기여하다, 기증하다
- seasonal ⓐ 계절적인
- harvesting ⓝ 수확
- rebuild ⓥ 다시 짓다
- formal ⓐ 공식적인
- accounting ⓝ 정산, 회계
- community ⓝ 공동체, 지역사회
- cohesion ⓝ 응집성
- call on ~에게 부탁하다, 시키다
- document ⓥ 문서화하다

구문 풀이

5행 Labor sharing groups are part of {what has been called a "moral economy"} since no one keeps formal records on [how much any family puts in or takes out].

(has been called: 현재완료 수동태 / a "moral economy": 보어 / since: 접속사(~ 때문에) / on: 전치사 / how much: 의문부사(얼마나))

03 인간에 대한 심리학의 가정

정답률 38% | 정답 ②

다음 빈칸에 들어갈 말로 가장 적절한 것을 고르시오.

① ethical ideas – 윤리적인 생각들
✔ selfish drives – 이기적인 욕구들
③ rational thoughts – 합리적인 사고들
④ extrinsic rewards – 외적인 보상들
⑤ social punishments – 사회적인 처벌들

For several years / much research in psychology / was based on the assumption / that human beings are driven by base motivations / such as aggression, egoistic self-interest, and the pursuit of simple pleasures.
수년 동안 / 심리학에서 많은 연구는 / 가정에 바탕을 두었다. / 인간이 저급한 동기들에 의해 움직인다는 / 공격성, 이기적인 사욕 그리고 단순한 즐거움의 추구와 같은

Since many psychologists began with that assumption, / they inadvertently designed research studies / that supported their own presuppositions.
많은 심리학자가 그 가정에서 출발했기 때문에 / 그들은 조사 연구를 무심코 설계했다. / 자신들의 가정을 뒷받침하는

Consequently, / the view of humanity / that prevailed in psychology / was that of a species / barely keeping its aggressive tendencies in check / and managing to live in social groups / more out of motivated self-interest / than out of a genuine affinity for others / or a true sense of community.
그 결과 / 인류에 대한 관점은 / 심리학에서 우세한 / 종이라는 관점이었다. / 그것의 공격적 성향을 가까스로 억제하고, / 사회 집단 속에서 간신히 살아가고 있는 / 동기화된 사욕에 의해 / 타인에 대한 진실한 친밀감 / 혹은 진정한 공동체 의식보다는

Both Sigmund Freud / and the early behaviorists led by John B. Watson / believed that humans were motivated / primarily by selfish drives.
Sigmund Freud와 / John B. Watson이 이끈 초기 행동주의자들 모두는 / 인간들이 동기 부여되었다고 믿었다. / 주로 이기적인 욕구들에 의해서

From that perspective, / social interaction is possible / only by exerting control over those baser emotions / and, therefore, / it is always vulnerable / to eruptions of violence, greed, and selfishness.
그러한 관점에서 / 사회적 상호 작용은 가능하고, / 그러한 더 저급한 감정들에 통제를 가함으로써만 / 그러므로 / 그것은 항상 취약하다. / 폭력, 탐욕 그리고 이기심의 분출에

The fact / that humans actually live together in social groups / has traditionally been seen / as a tenuous arrangement / that is always just one step away from violence.
사실은 / 인간들이 실제로 사회 집단 안에서 함께 산다는 / 전통적으로 여겨져 왔다. / 미약한 합의라고 / 폭력으로부터 언제나 단지 한 걸음 떨어져 있는

수년 동안 심리학에서 많은 연구는 인간이 공격성, 이기적인 사욕 그리고 단순한 즐거움의 추구와 같은 저급한 동기들에 의해 움직인다는 가정에 바탕을 두었다. 많은 심리학자가 그 가정에서 출발했기 때문에 그들은 무심코 자신들의 가정을 뒷받침하는 조사 연구를 설계했다. 그 결과 심리학에서 우세했던 인류에 대한 관점은 그것이 공격적 성향을 가까스로 억제하고, 타인에 대한 진실한 친밀감 혹은 진정한 공동체 의식보다는 동기화된 사욕에 의해 사회 집단 속에서 간신히 살아가고 있는 종이라는 관점이었다. Sigmund Freud와 John B. Watson이 이끈 초기 행동주의자들 모두는 인간들이 주로 이기적인 욕구들에 의해서 동기 부여된다고 믿었다. 그러한 관점에서 사회적 상호 작용은 그러한 더 저급한 감정들에 통제를 가함으로써만 가능하고, 그러므로 그것은 폭력, 탐욕 그리고 이기심의 분출에 항상 취약하다. 인간들이 실제로 사회 집단 안에서 함께 산다는 사실은 폭력으로부터 언제나 단지 한 걸음 떨어져 있는 미약한 합의라고 전통적으로 여겨져 왔다.

Why? 왜 정답일까?

첫 문장인 'For several years much research in psychology was based on the assumption that human beings are driven by base motivations such as aggression, egoistic self-interest, and the pursuit of simple pleasures.'에서 심리학에서는 한동안 인간이 공격성, 사리사욕, 단순한 쾌락 추구와 같은 동기에 기반하여 행동한다는 가정 하에 연구를 진행해 왔다는 주제를 제시하므로, 빈칸에 들어갈 말로 가장 적절한 것은 ② '이기적인 욕구들'이다.

- assumption ⓝ 가정, 추정
- aggression ⓝ 공격, 침략
- presupposition ⓝ 예상, 추정
- barely ad 간신히, 가까스로
- genuine ⓐ 진정한, 진짜의
- exert ⓥ 행사하다, 가하다
- eruption ⓝ 분출, 폭발
- drive ⓝ 충동, 욕구, 추진력
- motivation ⓝ 동기 부여
- egoistic ⓐ 이기주의의, 제멋대로의
- prevail ⓥ 우세하다, 만연하다, 팽배하다
- keep in check ~을 억누르다, 억제하다
- behaviorist ⓝ 행동주의 심리학자
- vulnerable ⓐ 취약한, 연약한
- greed ⓝ 탐욕, 식탐

구문 풀이

7행 Consequently, the view of humanity [that prevailed in psychology] was that of a species [barely keeping its aggressive tendencies in check and managing to live in social groups more {out of motivated self-interest} than {out of a genuine affinity for others or a true sense of community}].

(주어(선행사) / 주격 관계대명사 / 동사 / =the view / 현재분사1 / 현재분사2 / { }: 전명구 병렬)

---

04 음수 기호 사용을 꺼리는 경향

정답률 37% | 정답 ①

다음 빈칸에 들어갈 말로 가장 적절한 것을 고르시오.

✔ sidestep the dreaded negative sign
그 두려운 음수의 기호를 피하기
② resolve stock market uncertainties
주식 시장의 불확실성을 해결하기
③ compensate for complicated calculating processes
복잡한 계산 과정을 보완하기
④ unify the systems of expressing numbers below zero
영 이하의 수를 표현하는 체계를 통합하기
⑤ face the truth that subtraction can create negative numbers
뺄셈으로 음수가 생길 수 있다는 진리를 직시하기

Negative numbers are a lot more abstract than positive numbers / — you can't see negative 4 cookies / and you certainly can't eat them — / but you can think about them, / and you *have to*, / in all aspects of daily life, / from debts to contending with freezing temperatures and parking garages.
음수는 양수에 비해 훨씬 더 추상적이다 / 여러분이 -4개의 쿠키를 볼 수 없고 / 여러분이 분명 이를 먹지 못한다는 점에서 / 그러나 여러분은 음수에 관해 생각할 수 있으며, / 여러분은 생각*해야만 한다*. / 일상의 모든 측면에서 / 빚부터 시작해서 몹시 추운 기온과 주차장에서 씨름하는 것에 이르기까지

Still, / many of us haven't quite made peace with negative numbers.
그럼에도 불구하고, / 우리들 중 많은 사람들은 음수와 잘 지내지 못했다.

People have invented all sorts of funny little mental strategies / to sidestep the dreaded negative sign.
사람들은 온갖 우스꽝스럽고 사소한 정신적 전략들을 만들어 냈다. / 그 두려운 음수의 기호를 피하기 위해

On mutual fund statements, / losses (negative numbers) are printed in red / or stuck in parentheses / with no negative sign to be found.
뮤추얼 펀드 설명서에서 / 손실(음수)은 빨갛게 인쇄되거나 / 괄호 안에 갇혀 있다. / 음수 기호를 찾아볼 수 없는 채로

The history books tell us / that Julius Caesar was born in 100 B.C., / not -100.
역사책은 우리에게 알려준다. / Julius Caesar는 기원전 100년에 태어났다고 / -100년이 아닌

The underground levels in a parking garage / often have designations / like B1 and B2.
주차장의 지하층은 / 종종 명칭을 가지고 있다. / B1과 B2와 같은

Temperatures are one of the few exceptions: / folks do say, / especially here in Ithaca, New York, / that it's -5 degrees outside, / though even then, / many prefer to say 5 below zero.
기온은 몇 안 되는 예외 중 하나인데, / 사람들은 정말로 말한다 / 특히 이곳 New York의 Ithaca에서 / 바깥의 기온이 -5도라고 / 하지만 심지어 이때도 / 많은 이들이 영하 5도라고 말하길 선호한다.

There's something about that negative sign / that just looks so unpleasant.
그 음수의 기호에 관해서는 무언가가 있다. / 정말 불쾌하게만 보이는

음수는 여러분이 −4개의 쿠키를 볼 수 없고 분명 이를 먹지 못한다는 점에서 양수에 비해 훨씬 더 추상적이지만, 여러분은 음수에 관해 생각할 수 있으며, 빚부터 시작해서 몹시 추운 기온과 주차장에서 씨름하는 것에 이르기까지 일상의 모든 측면에서 생각*해야만 한다*. 그럼에도 불구하고, 우리들 중 많은 사람들은 음수와 잘 지내지 못했다. 사람들은 그 두려운 음수의 기호를 피하기 위해 온갖 우스꽝스럽고 사소한 정신적 전략들을 만들어 냈다. 뮤추얼 펀드(계약형 투자 신탁) 설명서에서 손실(음수)은 빨갛게 인쇄되거나 음수 기호를 찾아볼 수 없는 채로 괄호 안에 갇혀 있다. 역사책에서 우리에게 알려주기로 Julius Caesar는 −100년이 아닌 기원전 100년에 태어났다고 한다. 주차장의 지하층은 종종 B1과 B2와 같은 명칭을 가지고 있다. 기온은 몇 안 되는 예외 중 하나인데, 특히 이곳 New York의 Ithaca에서 사람들은 바깥의 기온이 −5도라고 하지만 심지어 이때도 많은 이들이 영하 5도라고 말하길 선호한다. 그 음수의 기호에 관해서는 정말 불쾌하게만 보이는 무언가가 있다.

Why? 왜 정답일까?

빈칸 뒤에서 음수를 괄호 처리하거나, −100년 대신 '기원전' 100년이라는 호칭을 쓰거나, 지하 1층, 2층을 'B1, B2'와 같이 표시함으로써 음수 기호 사용을 최대한 피하는 경우를 예로 들고 있다. 따라서 이러한 예시를 아우르는 빈칸에 들어갈 말로 가장 적절한 것은 ① '그 두려운 음수의 기호를 피하기'이다. 마지막 문장에서 음수 기호가 '불쾌하다(unpleasant)'고 언급한 것을 통해서도 결론에 대한 힌트를 얻을 수 있다.

- negative ⓐ (수가) 음수인
- positive ⓐ (수가) 양수인
- freezing ⓐ 몹시 추운
- all sorts of 온갖
- parentheses ⓝ 괄호
- designation ⓝ 명칭, 직함
- unpleasant ⓐ 불쾌한
- dread ⓥ 두려워하다, 겁내다
- subtraction ⓝ 빼기, 뺄셈
- abstract ⓐ 추상적인
- contend with ~와 씨름하다
- make peace with ~와 잘 지내다
- statement ⓝ 설명(서)
- underground ⓐ 지하의
- folks ⓝ 사람들
- sidestep ⓥ 회피하다
- resolve ⓥ 해결하다

구문 풀이

1행 Negative numbers are a lot more abstract than positive numbers — (you can't see negative 4 cookies and you certainly can't eat them) — but you can think about them, and you *have to*, in all aspects of daily life, from debts to contending with freezing temperatures and parking garages.

(비교급 수식(훨씬) / 대동사(= have to think about them) / ( ): 삽입절 / 대명사(= negative numbers))

05 가용성 휴리스틱

정답률 54% | 정답 ④

다음 빈칸에 들어갈 말로 가장 적절한 것을 고르시오. [3점]

① there is little reliable data about workers
직원들에 대한 신뢰성 있는 데이터가 거의 없기
② the frequent contacts help the relationship
잦은 접촉이 관계에 도움이 되기
③ they want to evaluate employees objectively
그들은 직원들을 객관적으로 평가하고 싶어 하기
✔ the recent instances dominate their memories
최근의 사례들이 그들의 기억을 지배하기
⑤ distorted data have no impact on the evaluation
왜곡된 데이터는 평가에 전혀 영향을 미치지 않기

The availability heuristic refers to a common mistake / that our brains make / by assuming / that the instances or examples / that come to mind easily / are also the most important or prevalent.
가용성 휴리스틱은 일반적인 오류를 가리킨다. / 우리의 뇌가 저지르는 / 가정함으로써 / 사례들이나 예시들이 / 머릿속에 쉽게 떠오르는 / 역시 가장 중요하거나 널리 퍼져 있다고

It shows that we make our decisions / based on the recency of events.
그것은 우리가 의사 결정을 한다는 것을 보여준다. / 사건들의 최신성에 기반하여

We often misjudge the frequency and magnitude of the events / that have happened recently / because of the limitations of our memories.
우리는 종종 사건들의 빈도와 규모를 잘못 판단한다. / 최근에 발생한 / 우리 기억의 한계 때문에

According to Harvard professor, Max Bazerman, / managers conducting performance appraisals / often fall victim to the availability heuristic.
Harvard 대학교의 교수인 Max Bazerman에 따르면, / 직무 수행 평가를 수행하는 관리자들은 / 종종 이 가용성 휴리스틱의 희생양이 된다.

The recency of events / highly influences a supervisor's opinion / during performance appraisals.
사건의 최신성은 / 관리자의 의견에 크게 영향을 미친다. / 직무 수행 평가 기간 중

Managers give more weight to performance / during the three months prior to the evaluation / than to the previous nine months of the evaluation period / because the recent instances dominate their memories.
관리자들은 수행에 더 무게를 둔다. / 평가 직전 3개월 동안의 / 평가 기간 앞의 9개월보다 / 최근의 사례들이 그들의 기억을 지배하기 때문에

The availability heuristic is influenced / by the ease of recall or retrievability / of information of some event.

가용성 휴리스틱은 영향을 받는다. / 회상의 용이함 또는 복구 가능성에 의해서 / 어떤 사건에 대한 정보의
Ease of recall suggests / that if something is more easily recalled in your memory, / you think that it will occur with a high probability.
회상의 용이함은 시사한다. / 만약 어떤 것이 당신의 기억 속에서 더 쉽게 회상된다면, / 당신은 그것이 높은 가능성으로 일어날 것이라고 생각한다는 것을

가용성 휴리스틱은 우리의 뇌가 머릿속에 쉽게 떠오르는 사례들이 역시 가장 중요하거나 널리 퍼져 있다고 가정함으로써 저지르는 일반적인 오류를 가리킨다. 그것은 우리가 사건들의 최신성에 기반하여 의사 결정을 한다는 것을 보여준다. 우리 기억의 한계 때문에 우리는 종종 최근에 발생한 사건들의 빈도와 규모를 잘못 판단한다. Harvard 대학교의 교수인 Max Bazerman에 따르면, 직무 수행 평가를 수행하는 관리자들은 종종 이 가용성 휴리스틱의 희생양이 된다. 사건의 최신성은 직무 수행 평가 기간 중 관리자의 의견에 크게 영향을 미친다. 최근의 사례들이 그들의 기억을 지배하기 때문에 관리자들은 평가 기간 앞의 9개월 보다 평가 직전 3개월 동안의 수행에 더 무게를 둔다. 가용성 휴리스틱은 어떤 사건에 대한 정보의 회상 또는 복구 가능성의 용이함에 의해서 영향을 받는다. 회상의 용이함은 만약 어떤 것이 기억 속에서 더 쉽게 회상된다면 당신은 그것이 높은 가능성으로 일어날 것이라고 생각한다는 것을 시사한다.

Why? 왜 정답일까?

가용성 휴리스틱의 특성을 설명하는 '**It shows that we make our decisions based on the recency of events.**'에서 우리의 의사 결정은 사건의 최신성에 영향을 받을 수 있다는 내용을 제시하고 있다. 이를 근거로 볼 때, 직무 수행을 평가하고 있는 관리자들은 평가 시점 기준으로 최근에 일어난 사건들에 영향을 받아 의견을 형성하게 될 것임을 유추할 수 있다. 따라서 빈칸에 들어갈 말로 가장 적절한 것은 ④ '최근의 사례들이 그들의 기억을 지배하기'이다.

- **availability** ⓝ 가용성, 이용 가능성
- **come to mind** 떠오르다
- **recency** ⓝ 최신성
- **magnitude** ⓝ 규모
- **fall victim to** ~의 희생양이 되다
- **evaluation** ⓝ 평가
- **reliable** ⓐ 신뢰할 만한
- **objectively** ad 객관적으로
- **heuristic** ⓐ (교수법·교육이) 체험적인
- **prevalent** ⓐ 널리 퍼진, 만연한
- **misjudge** ⓥ 잘못 판단하다
- **limitation** ⓝ 한계
- **supervisor** ⓝ 관리자, 상사
- **probability** ⓝ 가능성
- **frequent** ⓐ 잦은
- **distorted** ⓐ 왜곡된

구문 풀이

1행 The availability heuristic refers to a common mistake [that our brains make by assuming that the instances or examples {that come to mind easily} are also the most important or prevalent].
(목적격 관·대 / ~함으로써 / 접속사(~것) / 선행사 / 주어 / 동사(복수) / 보어(최상급 형용사))

06 어두운 환경에서 살면서 망막 크기가 커진 인간 　정답률 55% | 정답 ③

다음 빈칸에 들어갈 말로 가장 적절한 것을 고르시오. [3점]

① to get big enough to frighten animals
동물들에게 겁을 주기 위해 덩치가 커지는 것
② to move their habitats to lower latitudes
저위도로 서식지를 옮기는 것
✔ to increase the size of the visual processing system
시각 처리 기관의 크기를 증가시키는 것
④ to develop auditory sense rather than visual system
시각 체계보다는 청각을 발달시키는 것
⑤ to focus our attention on what we perceive to be the threat
위험이 될 수 있다고 여기는 요소에 주의를 집중시키는 것

The Neanderthals would have faced a problem / when it was daylight: / the light quality is much poorer at high latitudes / and this would have meant / that they couldn't see things in the distance so well.
네안데르탈인들은 한 가지 문제에 직면했을 것인데, / 대낮이었을 때 / 고위도에서는 빛의 질이 훨씬 나쁘고 / 이는 곧 뜻했을 것이다. / 그들이 멀리 있는 사물을 그다지 잘 볼 수 없었다는 것을
For a hunter, this is a serious problem, / because you really don't want to make the mistake / of not noticing the mother rhinoceros / hiding in a dark corner of the forest edge / when trying to spear her calf.
사냥꾼에게 이는 심각한 문제였는데, / 왜냐하면 여러분은 실수를 하기를 진정 원치 않기 때문이다. / 어미 코뿔소를 알아채지 못하는 / 숲가 어두운 구석에 숨어 있는 / 그녀의 새끼를 창으로 찌르려고 할 때
Living under low light conditions / places a much heavier premium on vision / than most researchers imagine.
조도가 낮은 환경에서 사는 것은 / 시력에 훨씬 더 중요한 가치를 부여한다. / 대부분의 연구자들이 상상하는 것 이상으로
The evolutionary response to low light levels / is to increase the size of the visual processing system.
어두운 빛 밝기에 대한 진화적인 반응은 / 시각 처리 기관의 크기를 증가시키는 것이다.
It is the familiar principle / from conventional star-gazing telescopes: / under the dim lighting of the night sky, / a larger mirror allows you to gather more of the light / from whatever you want to look at.
이는 비슷한 원리이다. / 별을 관측하는 일반적인 망원경과 / 밤하늘의 흐릿한 빛 아래에서 / 더 큰 거울은 더 많은 빛을 모으게 해준다. / 무엇이든 당신이 보고 싶은 것으로부터
By the same token, / a larger retina allows you to receive more light / to compensate for poor light levels.
같은 이유로, / 더 큰 망막은 더 많은 빛을 받아들이게 해 준다. / 빈약한 빛의 수준을 보완하고자

네안데르탈인들은 대낮에 한 가지 문제에 직면했을 것인데, 고위도에서는 빛의 질이 훨씬 나쁘고 이는 곧 그들이 멀리 있는 사물을 그다지 잘 볼 수 없었다는 것을 뜻했을 것이다. 사냥꾼에게 이는 심각한 문제였는데, 왜냐하면 새끼를 창으로 찌르려고 할 때 어미 코뿔소가 숲가 어두운 구석에 숨어 있다는 것을 알아채지 못하는 실수를 하기를 진정 원치 않기 때문이다. 조도가 낮은 환경에서 사는 것은 대부분의 연구자들이 상상하는 것 이상으로 시력에 훨씬 더 중요한 가치를 부여한다. 어두운 빛 밝기에 대한 진화적인 반응은 시각 처리 기관의 크기를 증가시키는 것이다. 이는 별을 관측하는 일반적인 망원경과 비슷한 원리인, 밤하늘의 흐릿한 빛 아래에서 더 큰 거울은 무엇이든 당신이 보고 싶은 것으로부터 더 많은 빛을 모으게 해준다. 같은 이유로, 더 큰 망막은 빈약한 빛의 수준을 보완하고자 더 많은 빛을 받아들이게 해 준다.

Why? 왜 정답일까?

첫 두 문장에서 수렵 사회의 조상 인류였던 네안데르탈인은 어두운 환경에서 살아 멀리서는 사물을 잘 볼 수 없었고, 이 때문에 사냥꾼으로서는 심각한 문제를 안고 있었다고 말하는데, 마지막 두 문장에서는 이에 따라 인류는 진화하면서 더 많은 빛을 받아들이도록 망막이 커지게 되었다(**By the same token, a larger retina allows you to receive more light to compensate for poor light levels.**)고 설명한다. 따라서 빈칸에 들어갈 말로 가장 적절한 것은 ③ '시각 처리 기관의 크기를 증가시키는 것'이다.

- **latitude** ⓝ 위도
- **rhinocero** ⓝ 코뿔소
- **place a premium on** ~에 중요성을 부여하다
- **evolutionary** ⓐ 진화적인
- **telescope** ⓝ 망원경
- **retina** ⓝ 망막
- **in the distance** 멀리 있는, 멀리서
- **calf** ⓝ (동물의) 새끼
- **conventional** ⓐ 일반적인, 전통적인
- **by the same token** 같은 이유로
- **compensate for** ~을 보완하다

구문 풀이

1행 The Neanderthals would have faced a problem when it was daylight: [the light quality is much poorer at high latitudes and this would have meant that they couldn't see things in the distance so well]. [ ] : a problem의 내용 설명
(「would have + 과거분사 : ~했을 것이다」 / 비교급 강조(훨씬) / 비교급 / 지시대명사(and 앞 내용) / ~했을 것이다)

★★★ **1등급 대비 고난도 3점 문제**

07 온라인에 저장된 정보의 양면적인 특성 　정답률 37% | 정답 ④

다음 빈칸에 들어갈 말로 가장 적절한 것을 고르시오. [3점]

① scarcity – 희소성
② creativity – 창의력
③ acceleration – 가속화
✔ permanency – 영속성
⑤ mysteriousness – 신비성

Online environments vary widely / in how easily you can save whatever happens there, / what I call its *recordability* and *preservability*.
온라인 환경은 아주 다양하다. / 거기에서 일어나는 일이 무엇이든지 간에 얼마나 쉽게 저장할 수 있는지에 있어서 / 즉 내가 그것의 *기록 가능성*과 *저장 가능성*이라고 부르는 것
Even though the design, activities, and membership of social media / might change over time, / the content of what people posted usually remains intact.
비록 소셜 미디어의 디자인, 활동, 멤버십이 / 시간이 지남에 따라 바뀔지도 모르겠지만, / 사람들이 게시했던 내용은 보통 훼손되지 않고 남아 있다.
Email, video, audio, and text messages can be saved.
이메일, 동영상, 음성, 텍스트 메시지는 저장될 수 있다.
When perfect preservation is possible, / time has been suspended.
완벽한 보존이 가능할 때, / 시간은 멈춰 있다.
Whenever you want, / you can go back to reexamine those events from the past.
당신은 원할 때마다 / 그러한 과거의 사건들을 다시 돌아보기 위해 되돌아 갈 수 있다.
In other situations, permanency slips between our fingers, / even challenging our reality testing / about whether something existed at all, / as when an email / that we seem to remember receiving mysteriously / disappears from our inbox.

또 다른 상황에서, 영속성은 우리 손가락 사이로 빠져나간다. / 실재 검증에 심지어 이의를 제기하면서, / 어떤 것이 어떤 식으로든 존재했었는지에 대한 / 이메일이 / 우리가 받았다고 기억하는 듯한 / 우리의 받은 편지함에서 불가사의하게 사라질 때처럼

The slightest accidental tap of the finger / can send an otherwise everlasting document into nothingness.

손가락으로 우연하게 살짝 톡 친 것이 / 그렇게 하지 않았으면 영원히 존재했을 문서를 무(無)의 상태로 보내 버릴 수 있다.

온라인 환경은 거기에서 일어나는 일이 무엇이든지 간에 얼마나 쉽게 저장할 수 있는지, 즉 내가 그것의 *기록 가능성*과 *저장 가능성*이라고 부르는 것에 있어서 아주 다양하다. 비록 소셜 미디어의 디자인, 활동, 멤버십이 시간이 지남에 따라 바뀔지도 모르겠지만, 사람들이 게시했던 내용은 보통 훼손되지 않고 남아 있다. 이메일, 동영상, 음성, 텍스트 메시지는 저장될 수 있다. 완벽한 보존이 가능할 때, 시간은 멈춰 있다. 당신은 원할 때마다 그러한 과거의 사건들을 다시 돌아보기 위해 되돌아 갈 수 있다. 또 다른 상황에서, 우리가 받았다고 기억하는 듯한 이메일이 우리의 받은 편지함에서 불가사의하게 사라질 때처럼, 어떤 것이 어떤 식으로든 존재했었는지에 대한 실재 검증에 심지어 이의를 제기하면서, 영속성은 우리 손가락 사이로 빠져나간다. 손가락으로 우연하게 살짝 톡 친 것이 그렇게 하지 않았으면 영원히 존재했을 문서를 무(無)의 상태로 보내 버릴 수 있다.

Why? 왜 정답일까?

In other situations 앞뒤로 온라인에 저장된 정보에 관한 서로 다른 내용이 대조된다. 이 앞에서는 정보가 온라인에서 비교적 한결같은 상태로 보존될 수 있다는 내용을 다루지만, 뒤에서는 손가락으로 우연히 살짝 잘못 건드리기만 해도 문서가 무의 상태로 돌아가 버릴 수도 있다(**The slightest accidental tap of the finger can send an otherwise everlasting document into nothingness.**)는 내용을 다루고 있다. 빈칸은 **In other situations** 뒤에 있으므로, 빈칸을 포함한 문장은 정보의 '영속성'이 순식간에 우리 손을 빠져나갈 수도 있다는 의미를 나타내야 한다. 따라서 빈칸에 들어갈 말로 가장 적절한 것은 ④ '영속성'이다.

- **recordability** ⓝ 기록 가능성
- **preservability** ⓝ 저장 가능성, 보존 가능성
- **intact** ⓐ 손상되지 않은, 온전한
- **preservation** ⓝ 보존
- **suspend** ⓥ (공식적으로) 멈추다, 유예하다
- **reexamine** ⓥ 다시 검토하다
- **inbox** ⓝ 받은 편지함, 수신함
- **accidental** ⓐ 우연한, 돌발적인
- **otherwise** ad 그렇지 않으면
- **everlasting** ⓐ 영원한, 변치 않는
- **nothingness** ⓝ 무, 공허, 존재하지 않음

구문 풀이

1행 Online environments vary widely in {how easily you can save whatever happens there}, {what I call its *recordability* and *preservability*}.

vary: 자동사(다르다) / how: 의문부사 / { }: 서로 동격 / whatever: 복합관계대명사(무엇이 ~하든 간에) / what: 관계대명사

★★ 문제 해결 꿀~팁 ★★

▶ 많이 틀린 이유는?

온라인에 저장된 정보의 특성을 설명하는 추상적인 글이다. ①의 '희소성'은 본문의 다른 부분에서 언급된 바 없으며, ⑤는 빈칸 뒤의 'mysteriously'를 품사만 바꾼 것이다.

▶ 문제 해결 방법은?

In other situations를 기점으로 글의 흐름이 반전되며, 빈칸은 이 뒤에 있으므로 답의 근거 또한 후반부에서 찾는 것이 정석이다. 하지만 빈칸 뒤의 '**slips between our fingers**'가 '~이 빠져나간다'라는 뜻으로서 부정적인 의미를 내포하므로, 빈칸에는 **In other situations** 뒤가 아닌 앞을 요약하는 표현이 들어가야 적절하다.

★★★ 1등급 대비 고난도 3점 문제

08 생존 편향의 개념과 사례 — 정답률 40% | 정답 ①

다음 빈칸에 들어갈 말로 가장 적절한 것을 고르시오. [3점]

✔ the areas that were not hit – (총알을) 맞지 않은 부분
② high technologies to make airplanes – 비행기를 만드는 고도의 기술
③ military plans for bombing the targets – 목표물을 폭격하기 위한 군사 계획
④ the data that analyzed broken parts – 부서진 부품을 분석한 데이터
⑤ the commanders of the army – 군대의 지휘관들

"Survivorship bias" is a common logical fallacy.

'생존 편향'은 흔한 논리적 오류이다.

We're prone to listen to the success stories from survivors / because the others aren't around to tell the tale.

우리는 생존자들의 성공담을 듣는 경향이 있는데, / 왜냐하면 이야기를 해 줄 다른 이들은 주변에 없기 때문이다.

A dramatic example from history / is the case of statistician Abraham Wald / who, during World War Ⅱ, was hired by the U.S. Air Force / to determine how to make their bomber planes safer.

역사상 극적인 예는 / 통계학자 Abraham Wald의 경우이다. / 2차 세계대전 동안 미국 공군에 의해 고용된 / 폭격기를 더 안전하게 만들 방법을 정하기 위해

The planes that returned / tended to have bullet holes along the wings, body, and tail, / and commanders wanted to reinforce those areas / because they seemed to get hit most often.

살아 돌아온 비행기는 / 날개, 본체, 그리고 꼬리 부분을 따라 총알 자국이 있는 경향이 있었고, / 지휘관들은 이 부분들을 강화하기를 원했다. / 그 부분들이 가장 총알을 자주 맞는 것처럼 보였기 때문에

Wald, however, saw / that the important thing was / that these bullet holes had not destroyed the planes, / and what needed more protection / were the areas that were not hit.

그러나 Wald는 알게 되었다. / 중요한 것은 / 이 총알 구멍들이 비행기를 파괴한 것이 아니며, / 보호가 더 필요한 쪽은 / (총알을) 맞지 않은 부분이라는 것을

Those were the parts / where, if a plane was struck by a bullet, / it would never be seen again.

그 부분들은 부분들이었다. / 만약 비행기가 총알을 맞았다면 / 다시는 그것을 볼 수 없게 했었을

His calculations based on that logic / are still in use today, / and they have saved many pilots.

그 논리에 기초한 그의 계산은 / 오늘날에도 여전히 사용되며, / 그것은 많은 조종사들의 목숨을 구했다.

'생존 편향'은 흔한 논리적 오류이다. 우리는 생존자들의 성공담을 듣는 경향이 있는데, 왜냐하면 이야기를 해 줄 다른 이들은 주변에 없기 때문이다. 역사상 극적인 예는 2차 세계대전 동안 폭격기를 더 안전하게 만들 방법을 정하기 위해 미국 공군에 의해 고용된 통계학자 Abraham Wald의 경우이다. 살아 돌아온 비행기는 날개, 본체, 그리고 꼬리 부분을 따라 총알 자국이 있는 경향이 있었고, 그 부분들이 가장 총알을 자주 맞는 것처럼 보였기 때문에 지휘관들은 이 부분들을 강화하기를 원했다. 그러나 Wald는 중요한 것은 이 총알 구멍들이 비행기를 파괴한 것이 아니며, 보호가 더 필요한 쪽은 (총알을) 맞지 않은 부분이라는 것을 알게 되었다. 그 부분들은 만약 비행기가 총알을 맞았다면 다시는 그것(비행기)을 볼 수 없게 했었을 부분들이었다. 그 논리에 기초한 그의 계산은 오늘날에도 여전히 사용되며, 그것은 많은 조종사들의 목숨을 구했다.

Why? 왜 정답일까?

2차 세계대전에서 폭격기를 만들 당시, 미국 공군에서는 총알을 자주 맞는 부분을 강화하기를 원했지만, 통계학자인 **Abraham Wald**는 혹시라도 총알을 맞았다면 큰 타격을 입었을(~ **if a plane was struck by a bullet, it would never be seen again.**) '다른' 부분들에 초점을 두기를 주장했고, 이것이 오늘날까지도 많은 조종사들의 목숨을 살리는 결과로 이어졌다는 내용을 다룬 글이다. 따라서 빈칸에 들어갈 말로 가장 적절한 것은 ① '(총알을) 맞지 않은 부분'이다.

- **survivorship** ⓝ 생존
- **bias** ⓝ 편견, 편향
- **logical** ⓐ 논리적인
- **fallacy** ⓝ 오류
- **be prone to** ~하기 쉽다
- **statistician** ⓝ 통계학자
- **determine** ⓥ 결정하다
- **commander** ⓝ 지휘관, 사령관
- **reinforce** ⓥ 강화하다, 보강하다
- **protection** ⓝ 보호
- **calculation** ⓝ 계산
- **in use** 사용 중인, 쓰이고 있는
- **military** ⓐ 군사적인, 무력의

구문 풀이

3행 A dramatic example from history is the case of statistician Abraham Wald [who, (during World War Ⅱ), was hired by the U.S. Air Force / to determine how to make their bomber planes safer].

Abraham Wald: 선행사 / who: 주격 관계대명사 / was hired: 동사 / to determine: ~하기 위해 / how to make: 「의문사+to부정사(~하는 방법)」

★★ 문제 해결 꿀~팁 ★★

▶ 많이 틀린 이유는?

앞에서 제시된 '생존 편향'이라는 개념과 예시의 연결이 쉽지 않아 읽기 어려운 지문이다. 이런 경우에는 예시 자체에 집중하여 답을 찾는다. 빈칸 바로 뒤의 문장에서, '총알을 맞았다면 비행기를 볼 수 없게 되었을 만큼 타격을 입었을 다른 부분'이란 것은 결국 '여태까지는 총알을 비껴갔(기에 비행기가 살아남을 수 있었)던 부분'을 뜻한다. 최다 오답인 ④는 '(이미 총알을 맞아) 부서진 부분', 즉 **Wald**가 아닌 사령관들이 주목했던 부분으로서 핵심과는 반대되는 내용이다.

▶ 문제 해결 방법은?

근거 문장에 내포된 가정법에 주의를 기울여 답을 찾도록 한다.

★★★ 1등급 대비 고난도 3점 문제

09 우정이 싹트게 하는 요인 정답률 34% | 정답 ②

다음 빈칸에 들어갈 말로 가장 적절한 것을 고르시오. [3점]

① shared value – 공유된 가치
② physical space – 물리적 공간
③ conscious effort – 의식적 노력
④ similar character – 비슷한 성격
⑤ psychological support – 심리적 지지

Psychologists Leon Festinger, Stanley Schachter, and sociologist Kurt Back / began to wonder / how friendships form.
심리학자 Leon Festinger, Stanley Schachter, 그리고 사회학자 Kurt Back은 / 궁금해 하기 시작했다. / 우정이 어떻게 형성되는지

Why do some strangers build lasting friendships, / while others struggle to get past basic platitudes?
왜 몇몇 타인들은 지속적인 우정을 쌓을까? / 다른 이들은 기본적인 상투적인 말을 넘어서는 데 어려움을 겪는 반면

Some experts explained / that friendship formation could be traced to infancy, / where children acquired the values, beliefs, and attitudes / that would bind or separate them later in life.
몇몇 전문가들은 설명했는데, / 우정 형성이 유아기로 거슬러 올라갈 수 있다고 / 그 시기에 아이들은 가치, 신념, 그리고 태도를 습득했다. / 훗날 삶에서 그들을 결합시키거나 분리시킬 수도 있는

But Festinger, Schachter, and Back / pursued a different theory.
그러나 Festinger, Schachter, 그리고 Back은 / 다른 이론을 추구하였다.

The researchers believed / that physical space was the key to friendship formation; / that "friendships are likely to develop / on the basis of brief and passive contacts / made going to and from home / or walking about the neighborhood."
그 연구자들은 믿었다. / 물리적 공간이 우정 형성의 핵심이라고, / 즉 "우정은 발달하는 것 같다. / 짧고 수동적인 접촉에 근거하여 / 집을 오가거나 / 동네 주변을 걸어 다니면서 이루어지는"이라고

In their view, / it wasn't so much that people with similar attitudes became friends, / but rather that people who passed each other during the day / tended to become friends / and so came to adopt similar attitudes over time.
그들의 관점에서는 / 유사한 태도를 지닌 사람들이 친구가 된다기보다는 / 그날 동안 서로를 지나쳐 가는 사람들이 / 친구가 되는 경향이 있고 / 그래서 시간이 지남에 따라 유사한 태도를 받아들이게 되었다.

심리학자 Leon Festinger, Stanley Schachter, 그리고 사회학자 Kurt Back은 우정이 어떻게 형성되는지 궁금해 하기 시작했다. 왜 몇몇 타인들은 지속적인 우정을 쌓는 반면, 다른 이들은 기본적인 상투적인 말을 넘어서는 데 어려움을 겪을까? 몇몇 전문가들은 우정 형성이 유아기로 거슬러 올라갈 수 있다고 설명했는데, 그 시기에 아이들은 훗날 삶에서 그들을 결합시키거나 분리시킬 수도 있는 가치, 신념, 그리고 태도를 습득했다. 그러나 Festinger, Schachter, 그리고 Back은 다른 이론을 추구하였다. 그 연구자들은 물리적 공간이 우정 형성의 핵심이라고, 즉 "우정은 집을 오가거나 동네 주변을 걸어 다니면서 이루어지는 짧고 수동적인 접촉에 근거하여 발달하는 것 같다."라고 믿었다. 그들의 관점에서는 유사한 태도를 지닌 사람들이 친구가 된다기보다는 그날 동안 서로를 지나쳐 가는 사람들이 친구가 되는 경향이 있고 그래서 시간이 지남에 따라 유사한 태도를 받아들이게 되었다.

Why? 왜 정답일까?

빈칸 뒤의 인용구 '**friendships are likely to develop on the basis of brief and passive contacts made going to and from home or walking about the neighborhood.**'에서 우정은 집을 오가거나 동네 주변을 걸어 다니며 우연히 만나거나 접촉한 사람들 사이에서 발달하는 듯하다는 연구자들의 믿음을 제시하고 있으므로, 빈칸에 들어갈 말로 가장 적절한 것은 ② '물리적 공간'이다.

- psychologist ⓝ 심리학자
- wonder ⓥ 궁금하다, 궁금해 하다
- struggle ⓥ 투쟁하다, 노력하다
- infancy ⓝ 유아기
- attitude ⓝ 태도
- separate ⓥ 분리시키다
- passive ⓐ 수동적인
- similar ⓐ 유사한
- sociologist ⓝ 사회학자
- lasting ⓐ 지속적인
- be traced to ~로 거슬러 올라가다
- acquire ⓥ 습득하다
- bind ⓥ 묶다, 결속하다
- pursue ⓥ 추구하다
- on the basis of ~을 기반으로

구문 풀이

13행 In their view, it wasn't so much {that people with similar attitudes became friends}, but rather {that people [who passed each other during the day] tended to become friends and so came to adopt similar attitudes over time}.
「not so much+A+but+B : A라기보다 B인」, 주어, 동사, 주어, 동사1, 동사2

★★ 문제 해결 꿀~팁 ★★

▶ 많이 틀린 이유는?
빈칸이 글 중간에 나오므로 뒤에 주로 힌트가 있다. 최다 오답인 ④는 서로 스쳐가는 사람들이 친구가 되고 나중에야 비슷한 태도를 받아들이는 것이라는 내용의 마지막 문장을 근거로 할 때 답으로 부적절하다.
▶ 문제 해결 방법은?
'**~ on the basis of brief and passive contacts made going to and from home or walking about the neighborhood.**'와 '**people who passed each other during the day**'가 서로 같은 내용임에 유의한다. 즉 주변에서 오며 가며 자주 보고 스치는 사람끼리 친구가 된다는 것이 글의 주제이다.

★★★ 1등급 대비 고난도 3점 문제

10 섣부른 결정으로 인한 실패를 피하는 방법 정답률 26% | 정답 ②

다음 빈칸에 들어갈 말로 가장 적절한 것을 고르시오. [3점]

① justifying layoffs – 해고를 정당화하는
② exercising patience – 인내심을 발휘하는
③ increasing employment – 고용을 늘리는
④ sticking to his opinions – 자기 의견을 고수하는
⑤ training unskilled members – 미숙한 구성원들을 훈련시키는

While leaders often face enormous pressures / to make decisions quickly, / premature decisions / are the leading cause of decision failure.
리더들은 종종 큰 압박에 직면하지만, / 빨리 결정들을 내려야 하는 / 섣부른 결정들은 / 결정 실패의 주된 원인이다.

This is primarily / because leaders respond / to the superficial issue of a decision / rather than taking the time / to explore the underlying issues.
이것은 주로 / 리더들이 반응하기 때문이다. / 결정의 피상적인 문제에 / 시간을 보내기보다는 / 근원적인 문제들을 탐색하는 데

Bob Carlson is a good example of a leader / exercising patience in the face of diverse issues.
Bob Carlson은 리더의 좋은 예이다. / 다양한 문제들에 직면했을 때 인내심을 발휘하는

In the economic downturn of early 2001, / Reell Precision Manufacturing / faced a 30 percent drop in revenues.
2001년 초의 경기 침체기에, / Reell Precision Manufacturing은 / 총수입의 30퍼센트 하락에 직면했다.

Some members of the senior leadership team favored layoffs / and some favored salary reductions.
몇몇의 고위 지도자 팀의 구성원들은 해고에 찬성했고 / 몇몇은 임금 삭감에 찬성했다.

While it would have been easy / to push for a decision or call for a vote / in order to ease the tension of the economic pressures, / as co-CEO, / Bob Carlson helped the team work together / and examine all of the issues.
쉬웠을 테지만, / 결정을 밀어붙이거나 투표를 요청하는 것이 / 경제적 압박의 긴장 상태를 완화하기 위해서 / 공동 최고 경영자로서, / Bob Carlson은 그 팀이 함께 노력하도록 도왔다. / 그리고 모든 문제들을 검토하도록

The team finally agreed on salary reductions, / knowing that, / to the best of their ability, / they had thoroughly examined the implications of both possible decisions.
그 팀은 마침내 임금 삭감에 동의했다. / 아는 상태로 / 자신들의 최선의 능력으로 / 자신들이 두 가지 가능한 결정 모두의 영향을 철저하게 검토했다는 것을

리더들이 종종 빨리 결정들을 내려야 하는 큰 압박에 직면하지만, 섣부른 결정들은 결정 실패의 주된 원인이다. 이것은 주로 리더들이 근원적인 문제들을 탐색하는 데 시간을 보내기보다는 결정의 피상적인 문제에 반응하기 때문이다. Bob Carlson은 다양한 문제들에 직면했을 때 인내심을 발휘하는 리더의 좋은 예이다. 2001년 초의 경기 침체기에, Reell Precision Manufacturing은 총수입의 30퍼센트 하락에 직면했다. 몇몇의 고위 지도자 팀의 구성원들은 해고에 찬성했고 몇몇은 임금 삭감에 찬성했다. 경제적 압박의 긴장 상태를 완화하기 위해서 결정을 밀어붙이거나 투표를 요청하는 것이 쉬웠을 테지만, 공동 최고 경영자로서, Bob Carlson은 그 팀이 함께 노력하고 모든 문제들을 검토하도록 도왔다. 그 팀은 마침내 자신들이 최선의 능력으로 두 가지 가능한 결정 모두의 영향을 철저하게 검토했다는 것을 아는 상태로 임금 삭감에 동의했다.

Why? 왜 정답일까?

빈칸 뒤에 제시된 예에 따르면 경기 침체기를 맞아 해고 또는 임금 삭감이라는 두 가지 안 중 하나를 선택해야 하는 상황에서, 회사의 공동 경영자였던 **Bob Carlson**은 팀원들 모두가 함께 노력하고 모든 문제를 검토하도록 도와주었다(**~ as co-CEO, Bob Carlson helped the team work together and examine all of the issues.**) 고 한다. 이는 리더가 섣불리 결정하지 않고 팀원들의 논의와 검토 과정을 '인내심 있게

기다리는' 행위로 볼 수 있으므로, 빈칸에 들어갈 말로 가장 적절한 것은 ② '인내심을 발휘하는'이다.

- enormous ⓐ 거대한
- primarily ad 주로
- underlying ⓐ 근본적인
- layoff ⓝ 해고
- examine ⓥ 검토하다
- justify ⓥ 정당화하다
- premature ⓐ 너무 이른, 시기상조의
- superficial ⓐ 피상적인
- in the face of ~에 직면하여
- reduction ⓝ 삭감, 감소
- thoroughly ad 철저하게
- stick to ~을 고수하다

구문 풀이

16행 The team finally agreed on salary reductions, knowing (분사구문) that, (to the best of their ability), they had thoroughly examined the implications of both possible decisions.
접속사(~것) ( ): 삽입구 they: 주어 had thoroughly examined: 동사(과거완료)

★★ 문제 해결 꿀~팁 ★★

▶ 많이 틀린 이유는?
리더들이 섣부른 결정을 내리는 이유를 진단하고 이를 해결할 방법을 제시하는 글이다. '해고'는 예시의 일부로 언급될 뿐 글의 핵심 소재가 아니므로 ①은 답으로 부적절하다. ④는 리더가 '자기 의견만 고수한다'라는 의미인데, 이는 글의 주제와 정반대된다.
▶ 문제 해결 방법은?
글에 'patience(인내심)'이라는 단어가 직접 등장하지는 않지만, 예시에서 리더가 팀원들로 하여금 모든 해결책을 꼼꼼히 검토해볼 수 있도록 도와주었다는 내용을 통해, 섣불리 혼자 결정하지 않고 '시간을 들여 기다리는 것'이 필요하다는 결론을 내릴 수 있다.

★★★ 1등급 대비 고난도 3점 문제

11 배블런재의 특성 정답률 42% | 정답 ⑤

다음 빈칸에 들어갈 말로 가장 적절한 것을 고르시오. [3점]

① the government starts to get involved in the industry
정부가 업계에 관여하기 시작한다
② manufacturers finally decide not to supply the market
제조업자들이 결국 시장에 공급하지 않기로 결정한다
③ the law of supply and demand does not work anymore
공급과 수요의 법칙은 더 이상 작용하지 않는다
④ there is no quality competition remaining in the market
시장에 남아있는 품질 경쟁 상품이 없다
✔ it is no longer high enough to exclude the less well off
덜 부유한 사람들을 배제할 정도로 가격이 더 이상 높지 않다

Veblen goods are named after Thorstein Veblen, / a US economist / who formulated the theory of "conspicuous consumption".
베블런재는 Thorstein Veblen의 이름을 따서 명명되었다. / 미국의 경제학자인 / '과시적 소비' 이론을 만들어낸
They are strange / because demand for them increases / as their price rises.
베블런재들은 기이하다. / 그것들에 대한 수요가 증가하기 때문에 / 그 가격이 상승함에 따라
According to Veblen, / these goods must signal high status.
Veblen에 따르면 / 이러한 재화들은 높은 지위를 나타내야 한다.
A willingness to pay higher prices / is due to a desire to advertise wealth / rather than to acquire better quality.
기꺼이 더 높은 가격을 지불하고자 하는 마음은 / 부유함을 드러내고자 하는 욕망에 기인한다. / 더 나은 품질을 얻기보다는
A true Veblen good, therefore, / should not be noticeably higher quality / than the lower-priced equivalents.
그러므로 진정한 베블런재는 / 눈에 띄게 품질이 더 높지는 않을 것이다. / 더 저렴한 가격의 동등한 물건보다
If the price falls so much / that it is no longer high enough / to exclude the less well off, / the rich will stop buying it.
만약 그 가격이 너무 많이 하락하여 / 가격이 더 이상 높지 않다면, / 덜 부유한 사람들을 배제할 정도로 / 부자들은 그것을 사는 것을 중단할 것이다.
There is much evidence of this behavior / in the markets for luxury cars, champagne, watches, and certain clothing labels.
이러한 행동에 대한 많은 증거가 있다. / 고급 차, 샴페인, 시계 그리고 특정 의류 브랜드 시장에는
A reduction in prices / might see a temporary increase in sales for the seller, / but then sales will begin to fall.
가격 하락은 / 판매자들에게는 일시적인 판매량의 상승을 보일 수 있으나, / 그 이후에는 판매량이 하락하기 시작할 것이다.

베블런재(Veblen goods)는 '과시적 소비' 이론을 만들어낸 미국의 경제학자인 Thorstein Veblen의 이름을 따서 명명되었다. 베블런재들은 그 가격이 상승함에 따라 그것들에 대한 수요가 증가하기 때문에 기이하다. Veblen에 따르면 이러한 재화(베블런재)들은 높은 지위를 나타내야 한다. 기꺼이 더 높은 가격을 지불하고자 하는 마음은 더 나은 품질을 얻기보다는 부유함을 드러내고자 하는 욕망에 기인한다. 그러므로 진정한 베블런재는 더 저렴한 가격의 동등한 물건보다 눈에 띄게 품질이 더 높지는 않을 것이다. 만약 그 가격이 너무 많이 하락하여 덜 부유한 사람들을 배제할 정도로 가격이 더 이상 높지 않다면, 부자들은 그것을 사는 것을 중단할 것이다. 고급 차, 샴페인, 시계 그리고 특정 의류 브랜드 시장에는 이러한 행동에 대한 많은 증거가 있다. 가격 하락은 판매자들에게는 일시적인 판매량의 상승을 보일 수 있으나, 그 이후에는 판매량이 하락하기 시작할 것이다.

Why? 왜 정답일까?

과시적 소비와 관련된 '베블런재'의 특성을 설명한 글로, 베블런재는 일반 재화와는 달리 가격이 높을 때 계속 소비되고 가격이 떨어지면 오히려 소비량이 줄어든다(**A reduction in prices might see a temporary increase in sales for the seller, but then sales will begin to fall.**)는 내용을 다루고 있다. 따라서 가격 하락에 관해 설명하는 빈칸에 들어갈 말로 가장 적절한 것은 ⑤ '덜 부유한 사람들을 배제할 정도로 가격이 더 이상 높지 않다'이다.

- be named after ~의 이름을 따서 명명되다
- formulate ⓥ 만들어내다
- consumption ⓝ 소비
- willingness ⓝ 기꺼이 하는 마음
- noticeably ad 눈에 띄게, 두드러지게
- reduction ⓝ 하락, 감소
- conspicuous ⓐ 과시적인, 과시의
- demand ⓝ 수요
- advertise ⓥ 알리다, 광고하다
- equivalent ⓝ 등가물, ~에 상응하는 것

구문 풀이

5행 A willingness [to pay higher prices] is due to (~ 때문에) a desire [to advertise wealth rather than to acquire better quality].
「A + rather than + B : B라기보다는 A」

★★ 문제 해결 꿀~팁 ★★

▶ 많이 틀린 이유는?
전통적으로 오답이 많은 경제 분야의 지문으로서, 많은 학생들에게 다소 생소할 수 있는 '베블런재' 개념을 다루고 있어 어려운 문제이다.
최다 오답은 ④였는데, 이 지문에서 제품의 '품질'과 관련된 내용은 언급된 바가 없다.
▶ 문제 해결 방법은?
첫 두 문장과 마지막 문장을 중점적으로 읽어 글의 핵심 내용을 파악하는 데 주력해야 한다. 가격이 상승하면 수요가 떨어지는 일반적인 재화나 서비스와는 달리, 가격이 오르면 수요도 오르고 가격이 떨어지면 수요도 떨어지는 양상을 보이는 것이 바로 베블런재임을 이해하도록 한다.

★★★ 1등급 대비 고난도 3점 문제

12 Theseus의 배 정답률 39% | 정답 ②

다음 빈칸에 들어갈 말로 가장 적절한 것을 고르시오. [3점]

① the reminder of victory – 승리를 상기시키는 것
✔ the sum of all its parts – 모든 부분의 총합
③ fit for the intended use – 의도된 용도에 적합한
④ the property of the country – 국가의 재산
⑤ around for a long period of time – 오랜 시간 동안 주위에 있는

Theseus was a great hero / to the people of Athens.
Theseus는 위대한 영웅이었다. / 아테네 사람들에게
When he returned home after a war, / the ship that had carried him and his men / was so treasured / that the townspeople preserved it for years and years, / replacing its old, rotten planks / with new pieces of wood.
그가 전쟁을 마치고 집으로 돌아왔을 때, / 그와 그의 병사들을 태우고 다녔던 배는 / 매우 소중히 여겨져, / 시민들은 그 배를 여러 해 동안 계속 보존했다. / 그 배의 낡고 썩은 널빤지를 교체하면서 / 새로운 나무 조각으로
The question / Plutarch asks philosophers / is this: / is the repaired ship still the same ship / that Theseus had sailed?
질문은 / Plutarch가 철학자들에게 하는 / 이것이다. / 수리된 배는 여전히 바로 그 배인가? / Theseus가 타고 항해했던
Removing one plank and replacing it / might not make a difference, / but can that still be true / once all the planks have been replaced?
널빤지 하나를 제거하여 교체하는 것은 / 차이가 없을 수도 있지만, / 여전히 그러할 수 있을까? / 모든 널빤지가 교체되었을 때도
Some philosophers argue / that the ship must be the sum of all its parts.
일부 철학자들은 주장한다. / 그 배가 모든 부분의 총합이어야 한다고

But if this is true, / then as the ship got pushed around / during its journey / and lost small pieces, / it would already have stopped being the ship of Theseus.
그러나 만일 이것이 사실이라면, / 그 배가 이리저리 밀쳐져 / 항해하는 동안 / 작은 조각들을 잃었을 때, / 그것은 이미 Theseus의 배가 아니게 되었을 것이다.

Theseus는 아테네 사람들에게 위대한 영웅이었다. 그가 전쟁을 마치고 집으로 돌아왔을 때, 그와 그의 병사들을 태우고 다녔던 배는 매우 소중히 여겨져, 시민들은 그 배의 낡고 썩은 널빤지를 새로운 나무 조각으로 교체하면서, 그 배를 여러 해 동안 계속 보존했다. Plutarch가 철학자들에게 하는 질문은 이것이다. 수리된 배는 여전히 Theseus가 타고 항해했던 바로 그 배인가? 널빤지 하나를 제거하여 교체하는 것은 차이가 없을 수도 있지만, 모든 널빤지가 교체되었을 때도 여전히 그러할 수 있을까? 일부 철학자들은 그 배가 모든 부분의 총합이어야 한다고 주장한다. 그러나 만일 이것이 사실이라면, 그 배가 항해하는 동안 이리저리 밀쳐져 작은 조각들을 잃었을 때, 그것은 이미 Theseus의 배가 아니게 되었을 것이다.

Why? 왜 정답일까?

빈칸 뒤의 'But if this is true, then as the ship got pushed around during its journey and lost small pieces, it would already have stopped being the ship of Theseus.'에서 '이것'이 사실이라면 배가 자신의 일부인 조각들을 잃은 경우 그 조각들의 모음이 배의 본질이 바뀌었을 것이라고 말하는데, 이는 배의 일부들이 모여 배라는 본질을 구성한다고 가정할 때 유추될 수 있는 내용이다. 즉 부분이 전체를 구성한다고 믿을 때 부분이 달라지면 전체 또한 달라진다는 결론을 내릴 수 있는 것이므로, 빈칸에 들어갈 말로 가장 적절한 것은 ② '모든 부분의 총합'이다.

- treasure ⓥ 소중히 여기다
- preserve ⓥ 보존하다
- philosopher ⓝ 철학자
- push around 여기저기 밀치다
- sum ⓝ 총합
- property ⓝ 재산
- townspeople ⓝ 도시 주민
- rotten ⓐ 썩은
- make a difference 차이를 낳다
- reminder ⓝ 상기시키는 것
- intended ⓐ 의도된, 계획된
- period ⓝ 기간

구문 풀이

2행 When he returned home after a war, / the ship [that had
~할 때 주어
carried him and his men] was so treasured that the townspeople
「so + 형용사 + that + 주어 + 동사 : 너무 ~해서 …하다」
preserved it for years and years, replacing its old, rotten planks with
분사구문(~하면서)
new pieces of wood.

★★ 문제 해결 꿀~팁 ★★

▶ 많이 틀린 이유는?
부분이 전체의 본질에 어떤 영향을 끼칠 수 있는지 다룬 추상적인 글이다. 선택지별 오답률이 큰 차이가 없는 것으로 보아 지문의 내용이 어려워 정답률이 떨어진 예로 이해할 수 있다.

▶ 문제 해결 방법은?
글의 흐름상 빈칸은 마지막 문장의 결론을 내리게 해주는 전제이므로, 선택지를 하나씩 대입하며 빈칸으로 인해 결론과 같은 내용이 도출되는지를 확인하면 답을 찾을 수 있다.

DAY 06 빈칸 추론 06

01 ②	02 ①	03 ③	04 ①	05 ③
06 ③	07 ①	08 ②	09 ①	10 ①
11 ①	12 ②			

01 산업의 집중화 경향 정답률 43% | 정답 ②

다음 빈칸에 들어갈 말로 가장 적절한 것을 고르시오.

① Automation – 자동화
✓ Concentration – 집중
③ Transportation – 교통
④ Globalization – 세계화
⑤ Liberalization – 자유화

Firms in almost every industry / tend to be clustered.
거의 모든 산업의 회사들은 / 밀집되는 경향이 있다.
Suppose / you threw darts at random / on a map of the United States.
가정해보라. / 당신이 무작위로 다트를 던진다고 / 미국 지도에
You'd find the holes / left by the darts / to be more or less evenly distributed / across the map.
당신은 구멍들을 보게 될 것이다. / 다트에 의해 남겨진 / 다소 고르게 분포된 것을 / 지도 전체에
But the real map of any given industry / looks nothing like that; / it looks / more as if someone had thrown all the darts in the same place.
하지만 어떤 특정 산업의 실제 지도는 / 전혀 그렇게 보이지 않는다. / 그것은 보인다. / 마치 어떤 사람이 던진 것처럼 모든 다트를 같은 지역에
This is probably in part because of reputation; / buyers may be suspicious of a software firm / in the middle of the cornfields.
이것은 아마 부분적으로는 평판 때문일 것이다. / 구매자들은 소프트웨어 회사를 수상쩍게 여길 것이다. / 옥수수밭 한가운데에 있는
It would also be hard / to recruit workers / if every time you needed a new employee / you had to persuade someone / to move across the country, / rather than just poach one from your neighbor.
또한 어려울 것이다. / 직원을 채용하는 것이 / 만약 당신이 새로운 직원을 필요로 할 때마다 / 당신이 누군가를 설득해야 한다면 / 나라를 가로질러 이주하도록 / 근처에서 인력을 빼내기보다는 오히려
There are also regulatory reasons: / zoning laws often try to concentrate / dirty industries in one place / and restaurants and bars in another.
또한 규제상의 이유들도 있다. / 토지 사용 제한법들은 종종 집중시키려 노력한다. / 공해 유발 산업들을 한 지역에, / 그리고 식당들과 술집들을 다른 지역에
Finally, / people in the same industry / often have similar preferences / (computer engineers like coffee, / financiers show off with expensive bottles of wine).
마지막으로, / 같은 산업에 종사하는 사람들은 / 종종 유사한 선호도를 가진다. / 컴퓨터 엔지니어들은 커피를 좋아하고, / 금융업 종사자들은 비싼 와인을 가지고 뽐낸다.
Concentration makes it easier / to provide the amenities they like.
집중이 더 쉽게 해준다. / 그들이 좋아하는 생활 편의시설을 제공하는 것을

거의 모든 산업의 회사들은 밀집되는 경향이 있다. 당신이 미국 지도에 무작위로 다트를 던진다고 가정해보라. 당신은 다트에 의해 남겨진 구멍들이 지도 전체에 다소 고르게 분포된 것을 보게 될 것이다. 하지만 어떤 특정 산업의 실제 지도는 전혀 그렇게 보이지 않고, 마치 어떤 사람이 모든 다트를 같은 지역에 던진 것처럼 보인다. 이것은 아마 부분적으로는 평판 때문일 것이다. 구매자들은 옥수수밭 한가운데 있는 소프트웨어 회사를 수상쩍게 여길 것이다. 당신이 새로운 직원을 필요로 할 때마다 근처에서 인력을 빼내기보다는 오히려 누군가로 하여금 나라를 가로질러 이주하도록 설득해야 한다면 직원을 채용하는 것이 또한 어려울 것이다. 또한 규제상의 이유도 있다. 토지 사용 제한법들은 종종 공해 유발 산업들을 한 지역에, 식당들과 술집들을 다른 지역에 집중시키려 노력한다. 마지막으로, 같은 산업에 종사하는 사람들은 종종 유사한 선호도를 보인다. (컴퓨터 엔지니어들은 커피를 좋아하고 금융업 종사자들은 비싼 와인을 가지고 뽐낸다.) 집중이 그들이 좋아하는 생활 편의시설을 제공하는 것을 더 쉽게 해준다.

Why? 왜 정답일까?

첫 문장인 'Firms in almost every industry tend to be clustered.'에서 어느 산업 부문에서건 회사들은 밀집되는 경향이 있다고 언급하는 것으로 볼 때, 빈칸에 들어갈 말로 가장 적절한 것은 '밀집'을 다른 말로 나타낸 ② '집중'이다.

- cluster ⓥ 밀집하다, 모이다
- distribute ⓥ 분포하다
- suspicious ⓐ 수상쩍어하는, 의심스러운
- evenly ⓐⓓ 고르게
- reputation ⓝ 평판, 명성
- recruit ⓥ 채용하다, 모집하다

- regulatory ⓐ 규제의, 단속력을 지닌
- financier ⓝ 금융업자, 자본가
- automation ⓝ 자동화
- concentrate ⓥ 집중시키다
- amenity ⓝ 편의시설
- liberalization ⓝ 자유화

구문 풀이

4행 But the real map of any given industry looks nothing like that; it looks more as if someone had thrown all the darts in the same place.
「as if＋주어＋had p.p. : 가정법 과거완료(마치 ~했던 것처럼)」

02 아이들이 지닌 인지적 호기심

정답률 35% | 정답 ①

다음 빈칸에 들어갈 말로 가장 적절한 것을 고르시오. [3점]

① end – 목적
② input – 투입
③ puzzle – 퍼즐
④ interest – 흥미
⑤ alternative – 대안

The creativity that children possess / needs to be cultivated throughout their development.
아이들이 지닌 창의성은 / 그들이 성장하는 동안 함양되어야 한다.
Research suggests / that overstructuring the child's environment / may actually limit creative and academic development.
어떤 연구는 시사한다. / 아이의 환경을 과도하게 구조화하는 것이 / 사실은 창의적이고 학문적인 발달을 제한할지도 모른다는 것을
This is a central problem with much of science instruction.
이것은 과학 교육의 많은 부분에서 가장 중요한 문제이다.
The exercises or activities are devised to eliminate different options / and to focus on predetermined results.
연습이나 활동은 다양한 선택권을 없애도록 고안된다. / 그리고 미리 정해진 결과에 집중하도록
The answers are structured to fit the course assessments, / and the wonder of science is lost along with cognitive intrigue.
정답은 수업의 평가에 맞게 구조화되고 / 과학의 경이로움은 인지적인 호기심과 함께 잃게 된다.
We define cognitive intrigue as the wonder / that stimulates and intrinsically motivates an individual / to voluntarily engage in an activity.
우리는 인지적 호기심을 경이로움으로 정의한다. / 한 개인을 자극하고 본질적으로 동기를 부여하는 / 어떤 활동에 자의적으로 참여할 수 있게
The loss of cognitive intrigue may be initiated / by the sole use of play items with predetermined conclusions / and reinforced by rote instruction in school.
인지적인 호기심의 상실은 시작되고 / 미리 정해진 결론을 가지고 놀이 품목을 한 가지 방식으로 사용하면서 / 학교에서 기계적으로 암기하는 교육을 통해 강화될 수 있다.
This is exemplified by toys, games, and lessons / that are an end in and of themselves / and require little of the individual / other than to master the planned objective.
이것은 장난감, 게임, 그리고 수업에서 전형적인 사례를 보여준다. / 그 자체로 목적이 되고 / 개인에게 거의 아무것도 요구하지 않는 / 계획된 목표를 통달하는 것 외에

아이들이 지닌 창의성은 그들이 성장하는 동안 함양되어야 한다. 어떤 연구는 아이의 환경을 과도하게 구조화하는 것이 사실은 창의적이고 학문적인 발달을 제한할지도 모른다는 것을 시사한다. 이것은 과학 교육의 많은 부분에서 가장 중요한 문제이다. 연습이나 활동은 다양한 선택권을 없애고 미리 정해진 결과에 집중하도록 고안된다. 정답은 수업의 평가에 맞게 구조화되고 과학의 경이로움은 인지적인 호기심과 함께 잃게 된다. 우리는 인지적 호기심을 한 개인이 어떤 활동에 자의적으로 참여할 수 있게 자극하고 본질적으로 동기를 부여하는 경이로움으로 정의한다. 인지적인 호기심의 상실은 미리 정해진 결론을 가지고 놀이 품목을 한 가지 방식으로 사용하면서 시작되고 학교에서 기계적으로 암기하는 교육을 통해 강화될 수 있다. 이것은 그 자체로 목적이 되고 계획된 목표를 통달하는 것 외에 개인에게 거의 아무것도 요구하지 않는 장난감, 게임, 그리고 수업에서 전형적인 사례를 보여준다.

Why? 왜 정답일까?

아이의 환경을 지나치게 구조화하는 것이 오히려 아이의 창의력 발달을 제한할 수 있다는 내용을 다룬 글이다. '**The loss of cognitive intrigue may be initiated by the sole use of play items with predetermined conclusions ~**'에서 놀이 품목을 '미리 결정된 단 하나의' 방식으로 사용하게 되면서 아이의 인지적인 호기심이 상실되기 시작할 수 있음을 지적하는데, 이는 놀거나 배우는 방식이 '정해진 결론'을 위해 짜여져 그 자체로 '목적'처럼 기능하고 마는 상황이 일어났음을 뜻한다. 따라서 빈칸에 들어갈 말로 가장 적절한 것은 ① '목적'이다.

- cultivate ⓥ 육성하다, 기르다
- overstructure ⓥ 지나치게 구조화하다
- cognitive ⓐ 인식의, 인지의
- engage in ~에 참여하다
- development ⓝ 발달, 성장, 개발
- instruction ⓝ 교육
- intrigue ⓥ (호기심을) 불러일으키다
- reinforce ⓥ 강화하다, 보강하다

구문 풀이

15행 This is exemplified by toys, games, and lessons [that are an end in and of themselves and require little of the individual other than to master the planned objective].
(주어: This / 동사: is exemplified / 선행사: lessons / 주격 관계대명사: that / 그 자체로: in and of themselves / ~이외에는: other than / 과거분사: planned)

03 중미 토착민의 영양 불균형

정답률 55% | 정답 ③

다음 빈칸에 들어갈 말로 가장 적절한 것을 고르시오. [3점]

① eliminate obesity – 비만을 근절하기
② improve digestion – 소화를 증진하기
③ correct imbalances – 불균형을 바로잡기
④ consume more protein – 단백질을 더 소비하기
⑤ preserve their tradition – 전통을 보존하기

In many regions of Central America, / native people can but do not grow green vegetables / packed with vital nutrients such as vitamin A.
중미의 많은 지역에서 / 토착민들은 녹색 채소를 재배할 수는 있지만, 재배하지 않는다. / 비타민 A와 같은 필수 영양분이 가득한
Generally speaking, / the people do not have a tradition of raising these crops.
일반적으로 말해서, / 이 사람들은 이런 곡물을 재배하는 전통이 없다.
They often have limited education in general / and almost no exposure to health and nutrition advice, / and they grow what feeds the most people.
이들은 흔히 대체로 제한된 교육을 받고, / 건강이나 영양과 관련된 조언에 대한 노출이 거의 없으며, / 그리고 그들은 최대한 많은 사람들이 먹을 수 있는 식량을 재배한다.
They often have plenty of tortillas and beans, / so they have sufficient protein, / and they eat until full.
이들은 흔히 토르티야와 콩을 많이 먹어서 / 충분한 단백질을 섭취하며 / 배가 부를 때까지 먹는다.
Yet the lack of micronutrients / leads to their children / developing blindness, iron deficiency, and other growth disorders.
하지만 미량 영양소의 부족은 / 이들의 자녀에게 초래한다. / 실명, 철분 결핍 및 다른 발육 장애의 발병을
In these situations, / families have to be educated about nutrition, / encouraged to diversify their diets, / plant more green vegetables, / and sometimes receive nutritional assistance / to correct imbalances.
이 상황에서, / 가정들은 영양에 대한 교육을 받아야 한다. / 식단을 다양화하고, / 보다 많은 녹색 채소를 심고, / 영양적 지원을 때때로 받도록 권장 받으면서 / 불균형을 바로잡기 위해

중미의 많은 지역에서 토착민들은 비타민 A와 같은 필수 영양분이 가득한 녹색 채소를 재배할 수는 있지만, 재배하지 않는다. 일반적으로 말해서, 이 사람들은 이런 곡물을 재배하는 전통이 없다. 이들은 흔히 대체로 제한된 교육을 받고, 건강이나 영양과 관련된 조언을 거의 접하지 못하며, 최대한 많은 사람들이 먹을 수 있는 식량을 재배한다. 이들은 흔히 토르티야와 콩을 많이 먹어서 충분한 단백질을 섭취하며 배가 부를 때까지 먹는다. 하지만 미량 영양소의 부족은 이들의 자녀에게 실명, 철분 결핍 및 다른 발육 장애의 발병을 초래한다. 이 상황에서, 가정들은 불균형을 바로잡기 위해 식단을 다양화하고, 보다 많은 녹색 채소를 심고, 영양적 지원을 때때로 받도록 권장 받으면서 영양에 대한 교육을 받아야 한다.

Why? 왜 정답일까?

중미 지역의 토착민들은 녹색 채소를 재배하는 전통을 갖고 있지 않아, '**Yet the lack of micronutrients leads to their children developing blindness, iron deficiency, and other growth disorders.**'에서 언급하듯이 영양 불균형으로 인한 질병에 시달리기도 한다. 따라서 이에 대한 해결책을 다루는 빈칸에 들어갈 말로 가장 적절한 것은 ③ '불균형을 바로잡기'이다.

- region ⓝ 지역
- generally speaking 일반적으로 말해서
- nutrition ⓝ 영양
- feed ⓥ 먹여 살리다, 먹이다
- lack ⓝ 부족, 결여
- disorder ⓝ 장애
- packed with ~이 가득한
- limited ⓐ 제한된
- plenty of 많은
- sufficient ⓐ 충분한
- deficiency ⓝ 결핍
- diversify ⓥ 다양화하다

구문 풀이

12행 In these situations, families have to be educated about nutrition, / encouraged to diversify their diets, plant more green vegetables, and sometimes receive nutritional assistance to correct imbalances.
(조동사 수동태: have to be educated / 수동분사구문: encouraged / 보어1: to diversify / (to 생략) 보어2: plant / (to 생략) 보어3: receive / 부사적 용법(~하기 위해): to correct)

[문제편 p.039]

04 인내심의 중요성

정답률 56% | 정답 ①

다음 빈칸에 들어갈 말로 가장 적절한 것을 고르시오.

✔ he didn't carry on to the end – 그는 끝까지 계속하지 못했다
② someone told him not to give up – 누군가 그에게 그만두지 말라고 했다
③ the sticks were not strong enough – 막대기가 충분히 튼튼하지 않았다
④ he started without planning in advance – 그는 미리 계획하지 않은 채로 시작했다
⑤ the weather was not suitable to start a fire – 불을 피우기에 날씨가 적당하지 않았다

Nothing happens immediately, / so in the beginning / we can't see any results from our practice.
아무것도 즉시 일어나는 것은 없으므로, / 처음에 / 우리는 우리가 하는 일로부터 어떤 결과도 볼 수 없다.
This is like the example of the man / who tries to make fire / by rubbing two sticks of wood together.
이것은 사람의 예와 같다. / 불을 피우려고 하는 / 두 개의 나무 막대기를 서로 문질러서
He says to himself, "They say there's fire here," / and he begins rubbing energetically.
그는 "여기에 불이 있다고들 하잖아."라고 혼잣말을 하고는 / 힘차게 문지르기 시작한다.
He rubs on and on, / but he's very impatient.
그는 계속해서 문지르지만, / 그는 매우 참을성이 없다.
He wants to have that fire, / but the fire doesn't come.
그는 그 불을 갖고 싶어 하지만, / 불은 일어나지 않는다.
So he gets discouraged / and stops to rest for a while.
그래서 그는 풀이 죽어서 / 잠시 쉬려고 멈춘다.
Then he starts again, / but the going is slow, / so he rests again.
그러고 나서 그는 다시 시작하지만, / 진행이 더디므로, / 그는 다시 휴식을 취한다.
By then the heat has disappeared; / he didn't keep at it long enough.
그때쯤에는 열이 사라져 버렸는데, / 그가 충분히 오랫동안 그것을 계속하지 않았기 때문이다.
He rubs and rubs until he gets tired / and then he stops altogether.
그는 결국 지치게 되기까지 문지르고 문지르다가, / 그런 다음에 완전히 멈춘다.
Not only is he tired, / but he becomes more and more discouraged / until he gives up completely, "There's no fire here."
그는 지쳤을 뿐만 아니라, / 점점 더 좌절하여 / "여기에는 불이 없어."라고 하며 완전히 포기한다.
Actually, he was doing the work, / but there wasn't enough heat to start a fire.
사실 그는 작업을 하고 있었지만, / 불을 피울 수 있을 만큼의 충분한 열이 없었다.
The fire was there all the time, / but he didn't carry on to the end.
불은 줄곧 거기에 있었지만, / 그는 끝까지 계속하지 못했다.

아무것도 즉시 일어나는 것은 없으므로, 처음에 우리는 우리가 하는 일로부터 어떤 결과도 볼 수 없다. 이것은 두 개의 나무 막대기를 서로 문질러서 불을 피우려고 하는 사람의 예와 같다. 그는 "여기에 불이 있다고들 하잖아."라고 혼잣말을 하고는 힘차게 문지르기 시작한다. 계속해서 문지르지만, 그는 매우 참을성이 없다. 그는 그 불을 갖고 싶어 하지만, 불은 일어나지 않는다. 그래서 그는 풀이 죽어서 잠시 쉬려고 멈춘다. 그러고 나서 다시 시작하지만, 진행이 더디므로, 그는 다시 휴식을 취한다. 그때쯤에는 열이 사라져 버렸는데, 그가 충분히 오랫동안 그것을 계속하지 않았기 때문이다. 그는 문지르고 또 문지르다가 결국 지치게 되고, 그런 다음에 완전히 멈춘다. 그는 지쳤을 뿐만 아니라, 점점 더 좌절하여 "여기에는 불이 없어."라고 하며 완전히 포기한다. 사실 그는 작업을 하고 있었지만, 불을 피울 수 있을 만큼의 충분한 열이 없었다. 불은 줄곧 거기에 있었지만, 그는 끝까지 계속하지 못했다.

Why? 왜 정답일까?

첫 문장에서 어떤 일도 즉시 일어나지 않으므로 일의 시작 단계에서는 아무런 결실도 볼 수 없다는 내용을 제시한 후 나뭇가지를 비벼 불을 켜려고 시도하는 남자의 예를 든다. 예시에 따르면 남자는 참을성이 없어서(**he's very impatient**), 불을 피울 만큼의 열이 유지되도록 계속해서 비비는 일을 하지 못한다(**he didn't keep at it long enough**)고 한다. 따라서 빈칸에 들어갈 말로 가장 적절한 것은 남자의 인내심 부족을 지적하는 ① '그는 끝까지 계속하지 못했다'이다.

- **immediately** ad 즉시
- **rub** ⓥ 문지르다
- **on and on** 계속해서
- **discouraged** ⓐ 풀이 죽은, 낙담한
- **altogether** ad 완전히
- **in advance** 미리
- **practice** ⓐ 실행
- **energetically** ad 힘차게, 열심히
- **impatient** ⓐ 참을성이 없는
- **rest** ⓥ 쉬다, 휴식을 취하다
- **carry on** ~을 계속하다
- **suitable** ⓐ 적합한

구문 풀이

12행 Not only is he tired, but he becomes more and more discouraged until he gives up completely, "There's no fire here."
(「부정어구+be+주어 : 도치 구문」 / 「not only+A+but (also)+B : A뿐만 아니라 B도」 / until: 시간 접속사(~까지))

05 과학이 모든 것을 설명하지 못하는 이유

정답률 45% | 정답 ③

다음 빈칸에 들어갈 말로 가장 적절한 것을 고르시오. [3점]

① govern human's relationship with nature – 인간이 자연과 맺는 관계를 지배한다
② are based on objective observations – 객관적인 관찰에 기초한다
✔ will themselves remain unexplained – 그 자체로 설명되지 않은 채 남을 것이다
④ will be compared with other theories – 다른 이론들과 비교될 것이다
⑤ are difficult to use to explain phenomena – 현상을 설명하기 위해 사용하기 어렵다

According to many philosophers, / there is a purely logical reason / why science will never be able to explain everything.
많은 철학자에 따르면, / 순전히 논리적인 이유가 있다. / 과학이 결코 모든 것을 설명하지는 못할 것이라는
For in order to explain something, / whatever it is, / we need to invoke something else.
왜냐하면 무언가를 설명하기 위해서는, / 그것이 무엇이든 / 우리는 다른 어떤 것을 언급해야 한다.
But what explains the second thing?
하지만 두 번째 것은 무엇으로 설명하는가?
To illustrate, / recall that Newton explained a diverse range of phenomena / using his law of gravity.
예를 들어, / 뉴턴이 매우 다양한 범위의 현상을 설명했음을 떠올려 보라. / 자신의 중력 법칙을 사용하여
But what explains the law of gravity itself?
하지만 중력 법칙 자체는 무엇이 설명하는가?
If someone asks / *why* all bodies exert a gravitational attraction on each other, / what should we tell them?
만약 누군가가 묻는다면, / *왜* 모든 물체가 서로에게 중력을 행사하는지 / 우리는 그들에게 뭐라고 말해야 하는가?
Newton had no answer to this question.
뉴턴은 이 질문에 답이 없었다.
In Newtonian science / the law of gravity was a fundamental principle: / it explained other things, / but could not itself be explained.
뉴턴의 과학에서 / 중력 법칙은 기본 원리였다. / 그것은 다른 것들을 설명했지만, / 그 자체는 설명될 수 없었다.
The moral generalizes.
이 교훈이 일반화된다.
However much the science of the future can explain, / the explanations it gives / will have to make use of certain fundamental laws and principles.
미래의 과학이 아무리 많이 설명할 수 있다 하더라도, / 그것이 제공하는 설명은 / 어떤 기본 법칙과 원리를 이용해야만 할 것이다.
Since nothing can explain itself, / it follows that / at least some of these laws and principles / will themselves remain unexplained.
어떤 것도 스스로를 설명할 수 없기 때문에, / 결론적으로 ~이다. / 적어도 이러한 법칙과 원리 중 일부는 / 그 자체로 설명되지 않은 채 남을 것

많은 철학자에 따르면, 과학이 결코 모든 것을 설명하지는 못할 것이라는 순전히 논리적인 이유가 있다. 왜냐하면 무언가를 설명하기 위해서는, 우리는 무엇이든 다른 어떤 것을 언급해야 한다. 하지만 두 번째 것은 무엇으로 설명하는가? 예를 들어, 뉴턴이 자신의 중력 법칙을 사용하여 매우 다양한 범위의 현상을 설명했음을 떠올려 보라. 하지만 중력 법칙 자체는 무엇이 설명하는가? 만약 누군가가 *왜* 모든 물체가 서로에게 중력을 행사하는지 묻는다면, 우리는 그들에게 뭐라고 말해야 하는가? 뉴턴은 이 질문에 답이 없었다. 뉴턴의 과학에서 중력 법칙은 기본 원리였다. 즉, 그것이 다른 것들을 설명했지만, 그 자체는 설명될 수 없었다. 이 교훈이 일반화된다. 미래의 과학이 아무리 많이 설명할 수 있다 하더라도, 그것이 제공하는 설명은 어떤 기본 법칙과 원리를 이용해야만 할 것이다. 어떤 것도 스스로를 설명할 수 없기 때문에, 결론적으로 적어도 이러한 법칙과 원리 중 일부는 그 자체로 설명되지 않은 채 남을 것이다.

Why? 왜 정답일까?

첫 두 문장에 따르면 과학은 모든 것을 설명하지 못하는데, 왜냐하면 한 가지를 설명하기 위해 무엇이든 다른 개념을 동원해야만 하기 때문이다. 이어서 마지막 문장에서 어떤 것도 자기 자신을 설명할 수는 없다(**nothing can explain itself**)고 언급하는 것으로 보아, 끝내 설명되지 않고 남는 대상이 존재하기 마련이라는 결론을 내릴 수 있다. 따라서 빈칸에 들어갈 말로 가장 적절한 것은 ③ '그 자체로 설명되지 않은 채 남을 것이다'이다.

- **philosopher** ⓝ 철학자
- **gravity** ⓝ 중력
- **fundamental** ⓐ 기본적인, 근본적인
- **make use of** ~을 이용하다, 활용하다
- **objective** ⓐ 객관적인
- **illustrate** ⓥ (예를 들어) 보여주다
- **attraction** ⓝ 끌어당김
- **generalize** ⓥ 일반화하다
- **govern** ⓥ 지배하다

구문 풀이

3행 For in order to explain something, whatever it is, we need to invoke something else.
(For: ~ 때문이다(앞과 연결) / in order to explain: 부사적 용법(~하기 위해) / whatever: 복합관계대명사(어떤 것이 ~하든 간에))

06 나이가 들수록 닫히는 마음

정답률 43% | 정답 ③

다음 빈칸에 들어갈 말로 가장 적절한 것을 고르시오. [3점]

① the high dependence on others – 타인에 대한 높은 의존
② the obsession with our inferiority – 우리의 열등함에 대한 강박
③ the increasing closing of the mind – 점차적인 마음의 폐쇄
④ the misconception about our psychology – 우리 심리에 대한 오해
⑤ the self-destructive pattern of behavior – 자기 파괴적 행동 패턴

In adolescence / many of us had the experience / of falling under the sway of a great book or writer.
청소년기에 / 우리 중 다수는 경험이 있다. / 위대한 책이나 작가의 영향을 받은
We became entranced / by the novel ideas in the book, / and because we were so open to influence, / these early encounters with exciting ideas / sank deeply into our minds / and became part of our own thought processes, / affecting us decades after we absorbed them.
우리는 매료되었고, / 책 속의 참신한 아이디어에 / 그리고 우리가 영향에 매우 열려 있었기 때문에, / 흥미로운 아이디어와의 이러한 초기 만남은 / 우리의 마음속 깊이 가라앉아 / 우리 사고 과정의 일부가 되었고, / 그것들을 흡수한 지 수십 년이 지난 후에 우리에게 영향을 미쳤다.
Such influences enriched our mental landscape, / and in fact our intelligence depends on the ability / to absorb the lessons and ideas of those / who are older and wiser.
그러한 영향들은 우리의 정신적 풍경을 풍부하게 했고, / 사실 우리의 지성은 능력에 달려 있다. / 사람들의 교훈과 생각을 흡수하는 / 더 나이가 많고 더 현명한
Just as the body tightens with age, / however, / so does the mind.
나이가 들면서 몸이 경직되는 것처럼 / 그러나, / 마음도 그러하다.
And just as our sense of weakness and vulnerability / motivated the desire to learn, / so does our creeping sense of superiority / slowly close us off to new ideas and influences.
그리고 마치 약점과 취약성에 대한 우리의 깨달음이 / 학습 욕구를 자극했듯이, / 슬며시 다가오는 우월감도 / 새로운 생각과 영향력에 대해 서서히 우리를 닫는다.
Some may advocate / that we all become more skeptical in the modern world, / but in fact a far greater danger comes / from the increasing closing of the mind / that burdens us as individuals / as we get older, / and seems to be burdening our culture in general.
어떤 사람들은 주장할지도 모르지만, / 현대 세계에서 우리가 모두 더 회의적이 된다고 / 사실 훨씬 더 큰 위험은 온다. / 점차적인 마음의 폐쇄에서 / 우리에게 개인으로서 부담을 주는 / 우리가 나이 들수록 / 그리고 전반적인 우리 문화에 부담을 주는 듯 보이는

청소년기에 우리 중 다수는 위대한 책이나 작가의 영향을 받은 경험이 있다. 우리는 책 속의 참신한 아이디어에 매료되었고, 영향에 매우 열려 있었기 때문에, 흥미로운 아이디어와의 이러한 초기 만남은 우리의 마음속 깊이 가라앉아 우리 사고 과정의 일부가 되었고, 그것들을 흡수한 지 수십 년이 지난 후에 우리에게 영향을 미쳤다. 그러한 영향들은 우리의 정신적 풍경을 풍부하게 했고, 사실 우리의 지성은 더 나이가 많고 더 현명한 사람들의 교훈과 생각을 흡수하는 능력에 달려 있다. 그러나, 나이가 들면서 몸이 경직되는 것처럼 마음도 그러하다. 그리고 약점과 취약성에 대한 우리의 깨달음이 학습 욕구를 자극했듯이, 슬며시 다가오는 우월감도 새로운 생각과 영향력에 대해 서서히 우리를 닫는다. 어떤 사람들은 현대 세계에서 우리가 모두 더 회의적이 된다고 주장할지도 모르지만, 사실 훨씬 더 큰 위험은 우리가 나이 들수록 우리에게 개인으로서 부담을 주고, 전반적인 우리 문화에 부담을 주는 듯 보이는 점차적인 마음의 폐쇄에서 온다.

Why? 왜 정답일까?

어렸을 때는 위대한 책과 작가의 영향력에 마음이 열려 있지만 나이가 들수록 우리 마음이 닫혀 흡수가 잘 일어나지 않는다(**Just as the body tightens with age, however, so does the mind. And just as our sense of weakness and vulnerability motivated the desire to learn, so does our creeping sense of superiority slowly close us off to new ideas and influences.**)는 내용이다. 따라서 빈칸에 들어갈 말로 가장 적절한 것은 ③ '점차적인 마음의 폐쇄'이다.

- adolescence ⓝ 청소년기, 사춘기
- entrance ⓥ 매료시키다
- encounter ⓝ 만남, 조우
- deeply ad 깊이
- enrich ⓥ 풍부하게 하다
- tighten ⓥ 조여들다, 경직되다
- creeping ⓐ 서서히 진행되는
- close off ~을 닫다
- skeptical ⓐ 회의적인
- obsession ⓝ 강박, 집착
- self-destructive ⓐ 자기 파괴적인
- sway ⓝ 영향, 지배, 장악
- novel ⓐ 새로운, 신기한
- sink into ~로 가라앉다
- thought process 사고 과정
- landscape ⓝ 정경, 풍경
- vulnerability ⓝ 취약함, 상처받기 쉬움
- superiority ⓝ 우월함
- advocate ⓥ 주장하다, 변호하다, 옹호하다
- burden ⓥ 부담을 주다 ⓝ 짐, 부담
- inferiority ⓝ 열등함

구문 풀이

12행 And just as our sense of weakness and vulnerability motivated the desire to learn, so does our creeping sense of superiority slowly close us off to new ideas and influences.
「just as + A + so + B : 마치 A하듯이 B하다(B는 동의 구문 : so + 대동사 + 주어)」

07 다른 사람의 행동에 민감한 인간

정답률 44% | 정답 ①

다음 빈칸에 들어갈 말로 가장 적절한 것을 고르시오. [3점]

① others are doing the action you desire them to do
그 사람들이 했으면 하는 행동을 다른 사람들도 하고 있다
② humans support the policy meeting their personal needs
사람들이 자신의 개인적 필요에 부응하는 정책을 지지한다
③ people are encouraged to reuse their towels in most hotels
대부분의 호텔에서 사람들은 수건을 재사용하도록 권유받는다
④ you are expected to have positive influence in the world
당신이 세상에 긍정적인 영향을 끼치리라 기대된다
⑤ hotels are not providing guests with valuable services
호텔이 값비싼 서비스를 투숙객들에게 제공하고 있지 않다

We are extremely responsive / to what we perceive people around us to be doing.
우리는 굉장히 잘 반응한다. / 우리가 인식하기로 주변 사람들이 하고 있는 것에
This unconscious function / has helped us make quick and good life-saving decisions / throughout history.
이러한 무의식적인 기능은 / 우리가 신속하고 목숨을 구할만한 좋은 판단을 하도록 도와준다. / 역사를 통틀어
A study has shown / how powerful this factor is.
한 연구에서는 보여 주었다. / 이 요소가 얼마나 강력한지
One practical experiment / was an experiment conducted / where a hotel wished their guests / to reuse the towels in their rooms.
한 가지 실질적인 실험은 / 실행된 실험이었다. / 호텔이 투숙객에게 바라는 곳에서 / 그들의 방에서 수건을 재사용하기를
They decided to put out a few signs.
그들은 몇 가지 표지판을 걸어두기로 했다.
The first sign cited environmental reasons / and the second sign said / the hotel would donate a portion of end-of-year laundry savings.
첫 번째 표지판은 환경적인 이유에 대해서 언급했고 / 두 번째는 말했다. / 연말에 절약된 세탁비 일부를 호텔이 기부한다는
The third sign showed / the majority of guests reused their towels / at least once during their stay.
세 번째 표지판은 보여주었다. / 대다수의 투숙객들이 수건을 재사용했다고 / 투숙하는 동안 적어도 한 번은
To their surprise, / guests responded most positively to the third sign.
그들로서는 놀랍게도, / 투숙객들은 세 번째 표지판에 가장 긍정적으로 반응하였다.
If you want to influence people to act a certain way, / there are few more powerful methods / than to give the impression / that others are doing the action / you desire them to do.
만약 사람들에게 어떤 특정한 방식으로 행동하도록 영향을 미치고 싶다면, / 더 강력한 방법은 거의 없다. / 인상을 주는 것보다 / 다른 사람들도 그 행동을 하고 있다는 / 당신이 그 사람들이 하기를 바라는

우리는 우리가 인식하기로 주변 사람들이 하고 있는 것에 굉장히 잘 반응한다. 이러한 무의식적인 기능은 역사를 통틀어 우리가 신속하고 목숨을 구할만한 좋은 판단을 하도록 도와준다. 한 연구에서는 이 요소가 얼마나 강력한지 보여주었다. 한 가지 실질적인 실험은 투숙객이 방에서 수건을 재사용하기를 바라는 호텔에서 실행된 실험이었다. 그들은 몇 가지 표지판을 걸어두기로 했다. 첫 번째 표지판은 환경적인 이유에 대해서 언급했고 두 번째는 연말에 절약된 세탁비 일부를 호텔이 기부한다는 내용이었다. 세 번째 표지판은 대다수의 투숙객들이 투숙하는 동안 적어도 한 번은 수건을 재사용했다는 내용이었다. 놀랍게도, 투숙객들은 세 번째 표지판에 가장 긍정적으로 반응하였다. 만약 사람들에게 어떤 특정한 방식으로 행동하도록 영향을 미치고 싶다면, 그 사람들이 했으면 하는 행동을 다른 사람들도 하고 있다는 인상을 주는 것보다 더 강력한 방법은 거의 없다.

Why? 왜 정답일까?

'**We are extremely responsive to what we perceive people around us to be doing.**'에서 우리는 주변 사람들이 하는 행동에 잘 반응하는 경향이 있다고 말한 데 이어, 뒤에서는 호텔 투숙객을 대상으로 수건을 재사용하도록 유도한 한 실험에서 '다른 사람들도 재사용하고 있다는 인식을 주었을 때' 사람들이 가장 긍정적으로 반응하였다는 내용을 소개한다. 따라서 빈칸에 들어갈 말로 가장 적절한 것은 ① '그 사람들이 했으면 하는 행동을 다른 사람들도 하고 있다'이다.

- extremely ad 매우, 극도로
- unconscious ⓐ 무의식적인
- life-saving 목숨을 구할
- responsive ⓐ 즉각 반응하는, 호응하는
- function ⓝ 기능
- throughout prep ~을 통틀어

DAY 06

[문제편 p.041]

- practical ⓐ 현실적인, 실제적인
- majority ⓝ (대)다수
- influence ⓥ 영향을 미치다
- impression ⓝ 인상
- conduct ⓥ 실행하다, 수행하다
- positively ad 긍정적으로
- method ⓝ 방법

구문 풀이

1행 We are extremely responsive to what we perceive people around us to be doing.
(~에 즉각 반응하다 / 관계대명사(~것) 「perceive + A + to부정사 : A가 ~한다고 인식하다」)

08 우리가 기대하는 것을 보게 하는 우리의 뇌

정답률 44% | 정답 ②

다음 빈칸에 들어갈 말로 가장 적절한 것을 고르시오. [3점]

① ignoring distracting information unrelated to visual clues
시각적 단서와 관련이 없는, 정신을 산만하게 하는 정보를 무시하는 것
② projecting images from within the mind out onto the world
마음속으로부터의 이미지를 세계로 투영하는 것
③ categorizing objects into groups either real or imagined
사물을 실제이거나 상상한 집단으로 (범주화하여) 분류하는 것
④ strengthening connections between objects in the real world
실제 세계의 사물들 간의 관련성을 강화하는 것
⑤ removing the broken or missing parts of an original image
원래의 상(像)에서 부서지거나 유실된 부분을 제거하는 것

A large part of what we see / is what we expect to see.
우리가 보는 것의 많은 부분은 / 우리가 볼 것이라 기대하는 것이다.
This explains why we "see" faces and figures / in a flickering campfire, or in moving clouds.
이것은 왜 우리가 얼굴과 형상을 '보는'지 설명해준다. / 흔들리는 모닥불이나 움직이는 구름 속에서
This is why Leonardo da Vinci advised artists to discover their motifs / by staring at patches on a blank wall.
이것이 레오나르도 다 빈치가 화가들에게 그들의 모티프를 찾으라고 권한 이유다. / 빈 벽의 부분들을 응시함으로써
A fire provides a constant flickering change in visual information / that never integrates into anything solid / and thereby allows the brain to engage in a play of hypotheses.
불은 시각 정보에 있어 지속적으로 흔들리는 변화를 제공하고, / (형태가) 확실한 어떤 것에도 절대 통합되지 않는 / 그렇게 함으로써 뇌가 가설 놀이에 참여할 수 있게 한다.
On the other hand, / the wall does not present us with very much / in the way of visual clues, / and so the brain begins to make more and more hypotheses / and desperately searches for confirmation.
반면에, / 벽은 우리에게 그다지 많이 주지는 않고, / 시각적인 단서의 방식으로 / 그래서 뇌는 점점 더 많은 가설을 세우기 시작하고 / 필사적으로 확인을 모색한다.
A crack in the wall / looks a little like the profile of a nose / and suddenly a whole face appears, / or a leaping horse, or a dancing figure.
벽에 난 금이 / 코의 옆모습과 약간 닮아 / 갑자기 얼굴 전체가 나타나기도 한다. / 또는 도약하는 말, 또는 춤추는 형상이
In cases like these / the brain's visual strategies are / projecting images from within the mind out onto the world.
이와 같은 경우에 / 뇌의 시각적 전략은 / 마음속으로부터의 이미지를 세계로 투영하는 것이다.

우리가 보는 것의 많은 부분은 우리가 볼 것이라 기대하는 것이다. 이것은 왜 우리가 흔들리는 모닥불이나 움직이는 구름 속에서 얼굴과 형상을 '보는'지 설명해준다. 이것이 레오나르도 다 빈치가 화가들에게 빈 벽의 부분들을 응시함으로써 그들의 모티프를 찾으라고 권한 이유다. 불은 (형태가) 확실한 어떤 것에도 절대 통합되지 않는 시각 정보에 있어 지속적으로 흔들리는 변화를 제공하고, 그렇게 함으로써 뇌가 가설 놀이에 참여할 수 있게 한다. 반면에, 벽은 우리에게 시각적인 단서라고 할 만한 것을 그다지 많이 주지는 않고, 그래서 뇌는 점점 더 많은 가설을 세우기 시작하고 필사적으로 확인을 모색한다. 벽에 난 금이 코의 옆모습과 약간 닮아 갑자기 얼굴 전체가 나타나거나, 도약하는 말 또는 춤추는 형상이 나타나기도 한다. 이와 같은 경우에 뇌의 시각적 전략은 마음속으로부터의 이미지를 세계로 투영하는 것이다.

Why? 왜 정답일까?

첫 문장인 'A large part of what we see is what we expect to see.'에서 우리가 보는 것은 결국 우리가 보기를 기대하는 것이라는 주제를 제시한다. 이를 레오나르도 다 빈치가 언급한 빈 벽의 예에 적용하면, 시각적 정보가 많이 없는 빈 벽에서 인간이 갖가지 형상을 목도하는 것은 그들이 마음속으로 기대한 바가 뇌에 의해 투영되어 나타났기 때문임을 추론할 수 있다. 따라서 빈칸에 들어갈 말로 가장 적절한 것은 ② '마음속으로부터의 이미지를 세계로 투영하는 것'이다.

- constant ⓐ 지속적인
- hypothesis ⓝ 가설
- integrate ⓥ 통합되다
- present ⓥ 주다, 제시하다
- desperately ad 필사적으로
- distracting ⓐ 정신을 산만하게 하는
- strengthen ⓥ 강화하다
- confirmation ⓝ 확인
- unrelated to ~와 관계없는

구문 풀이

5행 A fire provides a constant flickering change in visual information [that never integrates into anything solid] and thereby allows the brain to engage in a play of hypotheses.
(동사1 / 선행사(불가산명사) / 주격 관·대 / 동사(단수) / 동사2 「allow + 목적어 + to부정사 : ~이 …하게 해주다」)

★★★ 1등급 대비 고난도 2점 문제

09 자부심과 연관된 신체적 표현의 보편성

정답률 36% | 정답 ①

다음 빈칸에 들어갈 말로 가장 적절한 것을 고르시오.

① innate – 선천적인
② creative – 창의적인
③ unidentifiable – 확인 불가능한
④ contradictory – 모순적인
⑤ offensive – 모욕적인

Would you expect the physical expression of pride / to be biologically based or culturally specific?
여러분은 자부심을 드러내는 신체적 표현이 / 생물학적 기반을 두고 있을 것으로 기대하는가, 아니면 문화적으로 특정할 것으로 기대하는가?
The psychologist Jessica Tracy has found / that young children can recognize / when a person feels pride.
심리학자 Jessica Tracy는 발견했다. / 어린아이들이 알아볼 수 있다는 것을 / 누군가가 자부심을 느끼는 때를
Moreover, / she found / that isolated populations with minimal Western contact / also accurately identify the physical signs.
더욱이, / 그녀는 발견했다. / 서구와의 접촉이 아주 적은 고립된 인구 집단 / 또한 정확하게 그 신체 신호를 알아본다는 것을
These signs include / a smiling face, raised arms, an expanded chest, and a pushed-out torso.
이러한 신호에는 포함된다. / 웃고 있는 얼굴, 들어 올린 두 팔, 펼친 가슴, 그리고 밖으로 내민 상체가
Tracy and David Matsumoto examined pride responses / among people competing in judo matches / in the 2004 Olympic and Paralympic Games.
Tracy와 David Matsumoto는 자부심을 드러내는 반응들을 조사했다. / 유도 경기에서 시합을 치르는 선수들에게서 / 2004년 올림픽 대회와 장애인 올림픽 대회의
Sighted and blind athletes / from 37 nations / competed.
볼 수 있는 선수들과 시각 장애가 있는 선수들이 / 37개 국가 출신의 / 시합을 치렀다.
After victory, / the behaviors / displayed by sighted and blind athletes / were very similar.
승리 후에, / 행동은 / 볼 수 있는 선수들과 시각 장애가 있는 선수들이 보여준 / 매우 비슷했다.
These findings suggest / that pride responses are innate.
이러한 연구 결과는 보여준다. / 자부심을 드러내는 반응이 선천적이라는 것을

여러분은 자부심을 드러내는 신체적 표현이 생물학적 기반을 두고 있을 것으로 기대하는가, 아니면 문화적으로 특정할 것으로 기대하는가? 심리학자 Jessica Tracy는 어린아이들이 누군가가 언제 자부심을 느끼는지를 알아볼 수 있다는 것을 발견했다. 더욱이, 그녀는 서구와의 접촉이 아주 적은 고립된 인구 집단 또한 정확하게 그 신체 신호를 알아본다는 것을 발견했다. 이러한 신호에는 웃고 있는 얼굴, 들어 올린 두 팔, 펼친 가슴, 그리고 밖으로 내민 상체가 포함된다. Tracy와 David Matsumoto는 2004년 올림픽 대회와 장애인 올림픽 대회의 유도 경기에서 시합을 치르는 선수들에게서 자부심을 드러내는 반응들을 조사했다. 37개 국가 출신의 볼 수 있는 선수들과 시각 장애가 있는 선수들이 시합을 치렀다. 승리 후에, 앞을 볼 수 있는 선수들과 시각 장애가 있는 선수들이 보여준 행동은 매우 비슷했다. 이러한 연구 결과는 자부심을 드러내는 반응이 선천적이라는 것을 보여준다.

Why? 왜 정답일까?

첫 문장에서 자부심을 드러내는 신체 표현이 생물학적인 요소 혹은 문화적 요소 중 어느 것에 영향을 받는지 질문한 뒤 예시를 통해 답을 도출하는 글이다. 두 번째와 세 번째 문장에서 아이들 또는 서구 문화권과의 교류가 적은 고립된 인구 집단이 모두 자부심의 신체 신호를 정확히 인지할 수 있었다는 예가 제시된 뒤, 빈칸 앞의 문장에서는 시각 장애가 있(기에 남의 신호를 눈으로 보고 학습할 수 없)는 선수들 또한 비장애인 선수들과 비슷한 자부심의 신체 신호를 보였다는 예가 추가로 제시된다. 이는 자부심으로 인한 신체의 반응이 일종의 문화로서 후천적으로 학습된 것이 아니라 '타고났기에' 어느 정도 보편적임을 보여주는 것이므로, 빈칸에 들어갈 말로 가장 적절한 것은 ① '선천적인'이다.

- pride ⓝ 자랑스러움
- specific ⓐ 특정적인, 구체적인
- biologically ad 생물학적으로
- recognize ⓥ 인식하다, 알아보다

- isolated ⓐ 고립된
- minimal ⓐ 최소의, 아주 적은
- identify ⓥ 알아보다, 확인하다
- pushed-out 밖으로 내밀어진
- compete ⓥ 경쟁하다
- innate ⓐ 타고난, 선천적인
- population ⓝ 인구
- accurately [ad] 정확하게
- expanded ⓐ 펼쳐진, 넓어진, 확대된
- examine ⓥ 조사하다, 검토하다
- sighted ⓐ 앞을 볼 수 있는

구문 풀이

1행 Would you expect the physical expression of pride to be biologically based or culturally specific?
「expect + 목적어 + to부정사 : ~이 …하리라고 기대하다」
biologically based: 보어1 / culturally specific: 보어2

★★ 문제 해결 꿀~팁 ★★

▶ 많이 틀린 이유는?
연구의 결론인 주제문을 완성하는 빈칸 문제로, 예시를 읽고 공통된 결론을 유추해야 한다. 어린 아이들, 문화적으로 고립된 인구 집단, 시각 장애가 있는 선수 집단 모두 나이, 문화, 장애 여부와 상관없이 자부심의 신체 표현을 이해하거나 보여주었다는 내용으로 보아, 자부심의 신체적 반응은 생물학적 기반을 두고 있다고 이해해야 옳다. ③은 자부심의 신체 표현이 어떤 것인지 알아보거나 확인할 수 없다는 뜻이므로 글의 내용과 다르다.
▶ 문제 해결 방법은?
연구 내용에 나오는 어린 아이들, 문화적으로 고립된 인구 집단, 시각 장애가 있는 선수들은 첫 문장의 **biologically based**의 예시이고, 이를 달리 표현한 말이 **innate**임에 유의한다.

★★★ 1등급 대비 고난도 3점 문제

10 연약해서 아름다운 삶 — 정답률 45% | 정답 ①

다음 빈칸에 들어갈 말로 가장 적절한 것을 고르시오. [3점]

✔ fragility – 연약함
② stability – 안정성
③ harmony – 조화
④ satisfaction – 만족감
⑤ diversity – 다양성

When he was dying, / the contemporary Buddhist teacher Dainin Katagiri / wrote a remarkable book called *Returning to Silence*.
그가 죽어가고 있었을 때, / 현대의 불교 스승인 Dainin Katagiri는 / *침묵으로의 회귀*라는 경이로운 책을 집필했다.
Life, he wrote, "is a dangerous situation."
그는 삶이란 "위험한 상황이다."라고 썼다.
It is the weakness of life / that makes it precious; / his words are filled / with the very fact of his own life passing away.
바로 삶의 취약함이며, / 삶을 소중하게 만드는 것은 / 그의 글은 채워져 있다. / 자신의 삶이 끝나가고 있다는 바로 그 사실로
"The china bowl is beautiful / because sooner or later it will break.... / The life of the bowl is always existing in a dangerous situation."
"자기 그릇은 아름답다. / 언젠가 깨질 것이기 때문에… / 그 그릇의 생명은 늘 위험한 상황에 놓여 있다."
Such is our struggle: / this unstable beauty.
그런 것이 우리의 고행이다. / 이 불안정한 아름다움.
This inevitable wound.
이 피할 수 없는 상처.
We forget / — how easily we forget — / that love and loss are intimate companions, / that we love the real flower so much more than the plastic one / and love the cast of twilight across a mountainside / lasting only a moment.
우리는 잊는다 / — 그것도 너무나 쉽게 잊는다. / 사랑과 상실이 친밀한 동반자라는 것을, / 우리가 진짜 꽃을 플라스틱 꽃보다 훨씬 더 사랑하고 / 산 중턱을 가로지르는 황혼의 색조를 사랑한다는 것을 / 한 순간만 지속하는
It is this very fragility / that opens our hearts.
바로 이 연약함이다. / 우리의 마음을 여는 것은

현대의 불교 스승인 Dainin Katagiri는 죽음을 앞두고 *침묵으로의 회귀*라는 경이로운 책을 집필했다. 그는 삶이란 "위험한 상황이다."라고 썼다. 삶을 소중하게 만드는 것은 바로 삶의 취약함이며, 그의 글은 자신의 삶이 끝나가고 있다는 바로 그 사실로 채워져 있다. "자기 그릇은 언젠가 깨질 것이기 때문에 아름답다…. 그 그릇의 생명은 늘 위험한 상황에 놓여 있다." 그런 것이 우리의 고행이다. 이 불안정한 아름다움. 이 피할 수 없는 상처. 우리는 사랑과 상실이 친밀한 동반자라는 것을, 우리가 진짜 꽃을 플라스틱 꽃보다 훨씬 더 사랑하고 산 중턱을 가로지르는 한 순간만 지속하는 황혼의 색조를 사랑한다는 것을 잊는다 — 그것도 너무나 쉽게 잊는다. 우리의 마음을 여는 것은 바로 이 연약함이다.

Why? 왜 정답일까?

'It is the weakness of life that makes it precious; ~'에서 **Dainin Katagiri**는 죽음을 앞두고 쓴 책에서 삶을 소중하게 만드는 것이 삶의 취약함이라고 기술했다는 내용이 나온다. 따라서 빈칸에 들어갈 말로 가장 적절한 것은 **weakness**의 동의어인 ① '연약함'이다.

- contemporary ⓐ 현대의
- pass away (존재하던 것이) 없어지다
- unstable ⓐ 불안정한
- wound ⓝ 상처 ⓥ 상처 입히다
- companion ⓝ 동반자
- stability ⓝ 안정성
- remarkable ⓐ 경이로운, 주목할 만한
- sooner or later 언젠가, 곧, 조만간
- inevitable ⓐ 피할 수 없는
- intimate ⓐ 친밀한
- fragility ⓝ 연약함

구문 풀이

10행 We forget — (how easily we forget) — that love and loss are intimate companions, that we love the real flower so much more than the plastic one and love the cast of twilight across a mountainside lasting only a moment.
forget: 동사 / ( ): 삽입절 / that love…: 접속사1(~것) / that we love…: 접속사2(~것) / so much more: 비교급 강조 / across a mountainside: 전명구 / lasting only a moment: 현재분사구(twilight 꾸밈)

★★ 문제 해결 꿀~팁 ★★

▶ 많이 틀린 이유는?
삶은 언젠가 끝나기 마련인 특유의 연약함 때문에 아름답게 여겨진다는 내용의 글로, ②의 '안정성'은 주제와 반대된다. ③의 '조화', ④의 '만족감'은 글에서 언급되지 않았다.
▶ 문제 해결 방법은?
강조구문인 'It is the weakness of life ~'에서 삶의 연약함을, 도치 구문인 'Such is our struggle: this unstable beauty.'에서 삶의 불안정한 아름다움을 강조하고 있는 것으로 볼 때 ①이 답으로 적절하다.

★★★ 1등급 대비 고난도 3점 문제

11 실제 보이는 것을 인식하기 — 정답률 49% | 정답 ①

다음 빈칸에 들어갈 말로 가장 적절한 것을 고르시오. [3점]

✔ consciously acknowledge what you actually see
여러분이 실제로 보는 것을 의식적으로 인정하라
② accept different opinions with a broad mind
넓은 마음으로 다양한 의견을 받아들이라
③ reflect on what you've already learned
이미 배운 것을 반추해보라
④ personally experience even a small thing
작은 것이라도 직접 경험하라
⑤ analyze the answers from various perspectives
다양한 시각에서 답을 분석하라

Early in the term, / our art professor projected an image of a monk, / his back to the viewer, / standing on the shore, / looking off into a blue sea and an enormous sky.
학기 초, / 우리 미술 교수는 수도승의 이미지를 제시했다. / 보는 이를 등지고 / 바닷가에 서서 / 푸른 바다와 거대한 하늘을 바라보고 있는
The professor asked the class, "What do you see?"
교수는 반 학생들에게 물었다, "무엇이 보이나요?"
The darkened auditorium was silent.
어두컴컴한 강당은 조용했다.
We looked and looked and thought and thought / as hard as possible / to unearth the hidden meaning, / but came up with nothing / — we must have missed it.
우리는 보고 또 보고 생각하고 또 생각했지만, / 가능한 한 열심히 / 그 숨겨진 의미를 파헤치기 위해 / 아무것도 생각해 내지 못했다 / 우리는 그것을 놓쳤음에 틀림없었다.
With dramatic exasperation / she answered her own question, / "It's a painting of a monk! His back is to us! / He is standing near the shore! / There's a blue sea and enormous sky!"
극도로 분노하며 / 그녀는 자신의 질문에 대답했다. / "이것은 수도승의 그림이에요! / 그는 우리를 등지고 있어요! / 그는 해안 근처에 서 있죠! / 푸른 바다와 거대한 하늘이 있네요!"
Hmm... why didn't we see it?
흠… 왜 우리는 그것을 보지 못했을까?
So as not to bias us, / she'd posed the question / without revealing the artist or title of the work.
우리에게 편견을 주지 않기 위해, / 그녀는 질문을 제시했다. / 그 작품의 작가나 제목을 밝히지 않고
In fact, / it was Caspar David Friedrich's *The Monk by the Sea*.
사실, / 그것은 Caspar David Friedrich의 *The Monk by the Sea*였다.

[문제편 p.043]

To better understand your world, / consciously acknowledge what you actually see / rather than guess at / what you think you are supposed to see.
여러분의 세상을 더 잘 이해하려면, / 여러분이 실제로 보는 것을 의식적으로 인정하라. / 추측하기보다는 / 여러분이 생각하기에 봐야 한다고 기대되는 것을

학기 초, 우리 미술 교수는 보는 이를 등지고 바닷가에 서서 푸른 바다와 거대한 하늘을 바라보고 있는 수도승의 이미지를 제시했다. 교수는 반 학생들에게 물었다, "무엇이 보이나요?" 어두컴컴한 강당은 조용했다. 우리는 그 숨겨진 의미를 파헤치기 위해 가능한 한 열심히 보고 또 보고 생각하고 또 생각했지만, 아무것도 생각해 내지 못했다 — 우리는 그것을 놓쳤음에 틀림없었다. 극도로 분노하며 그녀는 자신의 질문에 대답했다. "이것은 수도승의 그림이에요! 그는 우리를 등지고 있어요! 그는 해안 근처에 서 있죠! 푸른 바다와 거대한 하늘이 있네요!" 흠... 왜 우리는 그것을 보지 못했을까? 우리에게 편견을 주지 않기 위해, 그녀는 그 작품의 작가나 제목을 밝히지 않고 질문을 제시했다. 사실, 그것은 Caspar David Friedrich의 *The Monk by the Sea*였다. 여러분의 세상을 더 잘 이해하려면, 여러분이 생각하기에 봐야 한다고 기대되는 것을 추측하기보다는 여러분이 실제로 보는 것을 의식적으로 인정하라.

Why? 왜 정답일까?

제시된 예에 따르면 교수가 바닷가에 등을 보이고 서 있는 수도승의 이미지를 주었을 때, 학생들은 교수가 기대하는 답 또는 그림의 의미를 찾는 데 골몰하다가 그 이미지를 있는 그대로 감상하지 못했다. 이는 애초에 작가와 작품명도 주지 않고 이미지를 최대한 편견 없이 보기를 바랐던 교수의 기대와는 상반된 결과였다. 이 예시를 토대로 빈칸이 포함된 문장은 이미지를 볼 때 이미지 너머의 것을 추론하기보다는 '보이는 것을 보라'는 결론을 도출하고 있다. 따라서 빈칸에 들어갈 말로 가장 적절한 것은 ① '여러분이 실제로 보는 것을 의식적으로 인정하라'이다.

- project ⓥ 제시하다, 투사하다
- auditorium ⓝ 강당
- come up with ~을 떠올리다
- acknowledge ⓥ 인정하다
- analyze ⓥ 분석하다
- enormous ⓐ 거대한
- unearth ⓥ 파헤치다, 밝혀내다
- bias ⓥ 편견을 갖게 하다 ⓝ 편견
- reflect on ~을 반추하다, 되돌아 보다
- perspective ⓝ 시각, 관점

구문 풀이

1행 Early in the term, our art professor(주어) projected(동사) an image of a monk(목적어), his(=the monk's) back to the viewer, standing(현재분사1) on the shore, looking off(현재분사2(a monk 보충 설명)) into a blue sea and an enormousus sky.

★★ 문제 해결 꿀~팁 ★★

▶ 많이 틀린 이유는?
세상을 어떤 기대에 맞추어 바라보려고 하기보다 있는 그대로 이해하는 것이 중요하다는 글로, 일화가 생소하여 내용이 쉽게 와닿지 않을 수 있다. 오답 중 ②와 ⑤는 모두 의견의 '다양성'을 언급하고 있는데, 이는 글에서 언급되지 않은 소재이므로 답으로 적절하지 않다.
▶ 문제 해결 방법은?
교수의 말을 주의 깊게 읽도록 한다. 수도승 그림에 관해 교수가 언급한 내용은 필자가 첫 문장에서 그림 속 수도승을 '보이는 대로' 묘사한 내용과 일치한다.

★★★ 1등급 대비 고난도 3점 문제

12 야생 동물 관리 태도 형성에 영향을 주는 요소 정답률 32% | 정답 ②

다음 빈칸에 들어갈 말로 가장 적절한 것을 고르시오. [3점]

① attitude drives the various forms of belief
태도가 다양한 형태의 믿음을 이끌어내어
✔② all aspects of attitude are consistent with each other
태도의 모든 측면이 서로 일치하여
③ cognitive components of attitude outweigh affective ones
태도의 인지적 요소가 감정적 요소보다 중요하여
④ the components of attitude are not simultaneously evaluated
태도의 요소들이 동시에 평가되지 않아
⑤ our biased attitudes get in the way of preserving biodiversity
우리의 편향된 태도가 생물 다양성 보존을 방해하여

Attitude has been conceptualized into four main components: / affective (feelings of liking or disliking), / cognitive (beliefs and evaluation of those beliefs), / behavioral intention / (a statement of how one would behave / in a certain situation), / and behavior.
태도는 네 가지 주요한 요소로 개념화되어 왔다. / 감정적 요소(좋아하거나 싫어한다는 느낌), / 인지적 요소(신념 및 그러한 신념에 대한 평가), / 행동적 의도 요소 / (누군가 어떻게 행동할 것인가에 대한 진술 / 어떤 상황에서), / 그리고 행동 요소이다.

Public attitudes toward a wildlife species and its management / are generated / based on the interaction of those components.
야생 동물종과 그것의 관리에 대한 대중의 태도는 / 생성된다. / 그러한 요소들의 상호작용에 기초하여
In forming our attitudes toward wolves, / people strive to keep their affective components of attitude / consistent with their cognitive component.
늑대들에 대한 우리의 태도를 형성할 때, / 사람들은 태도의 감정적 요소를 유지하려고 노력한다. / 그들의 인지적 요소에 일치되게
For example, I could dislike wolves; / I believe they have killed people / (cognitive belief), / and having people killed is of course bad / (evaluation of belief).
예를 들어, 나는 늑대를 싫어할 수 있다. / 나는 그것들이 사람들을 죽였다고 믿는다 / (인지적 신념). / 그리고 사람을 죽게 하는 것은 당연히 나쁘다 / (신념에 대한 평가).
The behavioral intention that could result from this / is to support a wolf control program / and actual behavior may be a history of shooting wolves.
이것으로부터 생길 수 있는 행동적 의도는 / 늑대 통제 프로그램을 지지하는 것이고, / 실제 행동은 늑대 사냥의 역사일 것이다.
In this example, / all aspects of attitude are consistent with each other, / producing a negative overall attitude toward wolves.
이 예에서는, / 태도의 모든 측면이 서로 일치하여 / 늑대에 대해 부정적인 전체 태도를 만들어 낸다.

태도는 네 가지 주요한 요소로 개념화되어 왔는데, 바로 감정적 요소(좋아하거나 싫어한다는 느낌), 인지적 요소(신념 및 그러한 신념에 대한 평가), 행동적 의도 요소(누군가 어떤 상황에서 어떻게 행동할 것인가에 대한 진술), 행동 요소이다. 야생 동물종과 그 관리에 대한 대중의 태도는 그러한 요소들의 상호작용에 기초하여 생성된다. 늑대들에 대한 우리의 태도를 형성할 때, 사람들은 태도의 감정적 요소를 그들의 인지적 요소에 일치되게 유지하려고 노력한다. 예를 들어, 나는 늑대를 싫어할 수 있다. 나는 그것들이 사람들을 죽였다고 믿는다(인지적 신념). 그리고 사람을 죽게 하는 것은 당연히 나쁘다(신념에 대한 평가). 이것으로부터 생길 수 있는 행동적 의도는 늑대 통제 프로그램을 지지하는 것이고, 실제 행동은 늑대 사냥의 역사일 것이다. 이 예에서는, 태도의 모든 측면이 서로 일치하여 늑대에 대해 부정적인 전체 태도를 만들어 낸다.

Why? 왜 정답일까?

글의 서두에서 태도에 4가지 주요 요소가 있다고 언급하고, 이 요소들의 상호작용에 의해 대중의 태도가 형성된다고 했다. 또한 For example 앞에서 사람들은 감정적 요소를 인지적 요소에 '일치되게' 유지하려고 노력한다(~, people strive to keep their affective components of attitude consistent with their cognitive component.)고 설명한다. 마지막 문장은 예시의 결론을 다시 한번 정리하는 문장이므로, 빈칸에 들어갈 말로 가장 적절한 것은 예시 앞 문장과 같은 의미를 지닌 ② '태도의 모든 측면이 서로 일치하여'이다.

- conceptualize ⓥ 개념화하다
- affective ⓐ 감정적인
- behavioral ⓐ 행동의
- consistent with ~와 일관되는, 일치하는
- simultaneously ad 동시에
- biodiversity ⓝ 생물 다양성
- component ⓝ 구성 요소
- evaluation ⓝ 평가
- generate ⓥ 생성하다, 만들어 내다
- outweigh ⓥ ~보다 중요하다
- get in the way of ~을 방해하다

구문 풀이

8행 In forming(~함에 있어, ~할 때) our attitudes toward wolves, people strive to keep(동사구(~하기 위해 노력하다)) their affective components of attitude(목적어) consistent with their cognitive component(목적격 보어).

★★ 문제 해결 꿀~팁 ★★

▶ 많이 틀린 이유는?
글에 따르면 태도에는 네 가지 요소가 있고, 우리는 이 요소 각각에 부합하는 방향으로 어떤 대상에 대한 태도를 형성하는 경향이 있다. 글에서 태도의 인지적 요소와 정의적 요소의 영향력을 비교하고 있지는 않으므로 ③은 정답이 아니다. 또한 ①에서 언급하는 '믿음'은 태도의 결과물이 아닌 태도의 구성 요소이다. 따라서 태도가 다양한 믿음을 파생시킨다는 진술은 글의 내용과 다르다.
▶ 문제 해결 방법은?
'주제 – 예시 – 결론(= 주제)' 구조의 글에서 마지막에 빈칸이 나온 문제이므로, 예시 앞 부분을 집중적으로 읽어 답을 도출하도록 한다.

DAY 07 빈칸 추론 07

01 ①	02 ⑤	03 ③	04 ①	05 ③
06 ②	07 ①	08 ②	09 ②	10 ②
11 ⑤	12 ①			

01 천천히 변하는 뇌
정답률 69% | 정답 ①

다음 빈칸에 들어갈 말로 가장 적절한 것을 고르시오. [3점]

✔ stability - 안정감
② maturity - 성숙함
③ curiosity - 호기심
④ variability - 가변성
⑤ productivity - 생산성

What is the true nature of the brain?
뇌의 진정한 본질은 무엇인가?
The brain is a slow-changing machine, / and that's a good thing.
뇌는 천천히 변화하는 기계이며, / 그것은 좋은 것이다.
If your brain could completely change overnight, / you would be unstable.
만약 여러분의 뇌가 하룻밤 사이에 완전히 변할 수 있다면 / 여러분은 불안정해질 것이다.
Let's just say that your norm is to wake up, / read the paper with coffee and a bagel, / walk your dog, / and watch the news.
여러분의 평소 행동 양식이 잠에서 깨서, / 커피와 베이글을 먹으며 신문을 읽고, / 개를 산책시키고, / 뉴스를 보는 것이라고 해 보자.
This is your habitual routine.
이것은 여러분의 습관적인 일상이다.
Then one night, you get a phone call at 3 a.m. / and have to run outside in your underwear / to check on your neighbors.
그런데 어느 날 밤, 여러분이 새벽 3시에 전화를 받고 / 속옷 차림으로 뛰쳐나가야만 한다. / 여러분의 이웃을 확인해 보기 위해
What if your brain latched on to this new routine / and you continued to run outside / at 3 a.m. every night in your underwear?
만약 여러분의 뇌가 이 새로운 일상을 자기 것으로 만들어 / 여러분이 계속해서 밖으로 뛰쳐나가야 한다면 어떻겠는가? / 매일 새벽 3시에 속옷 차림으로
Nobody would want that, / so it's a good thing / our brains require more repetition than that!
누구도 그러길 원치 않을 것이므로 / 좋은 것이다! / 우리의 뇌가 그것보다 더 많은 반복이 필요하다는 것은
Let's accept and be thankful for the stability / our slow-changing brains provide us.
안정감을 받아들이고 고마워하자. / 천천히 변하는 우리 뇌가 우리에게 제공해 주는

뇌의 진정한 본질은 무엇인가? 뇌는 천천히 변화하는 기계이며, 그것은 좋은 것이다. 만약 여러분의 뇌가 하룻밤 사이에 완전히 변할 수 있다면 여러분은 불안정해질 것이다. 여러분의 평소 행동 양식이 잠에서 깨서, 커피와 베이글을 먹으며 신문을 읽고, 개를 산책시키고, 뉴스를 보는 것이라고 해 보자. 이것은 여러분의 습관적인 일상이다. 그런데 어느 날 밤, 여러분이 새벽 3시에 전화를 받고 속옷 차림으로 여러분의 이웃을 확인해 보기 위해 뛰쳐나가야만 한다. 만약 여러분의 뇌가 이 새로운 일상을 자기 것으로 만들어 여러분이 매일 새벽 3시에 속옷 차림으로 계속해서 밖으로 뛰쳐나가야 한다면 어떻겠는가? 누구도 그러길 원치 않을 것이므로 우리의 뇌가 그것보다 더 많은 반복이 필요하다는 것은 좋은 것이다! 천천히 변하는 우리 뇌가 우리에게 제공해 주는 안정감을 받아들이고 고마워하자.

Why? 왜 정답일까?

첫 문장에서 뇌의 본질은 무엇인가 라는 질문을 던진 뒤 이에 대한 답으로서 '뇌는 천천히 변한다'는 내용이 제시되고 있다. 특히 '**If your brain could completely change overnight, you would be unstable.**'에서는 만일 뇌가 지금과는 달리 하루아침에 빠르게 변할 수 있었더라면 불안정했을 것이라는 말을 통해 천천히 변하는 뇌가 인간에게 '안정감'을 줄 수 있다는 내용을 나타내고 있다. 따라서 빈칸에 들어갈 말로 가장 적절한 것은 ① '안정감'이다.

- nature ⓝ 본질, 천성
- completely ad 완전히
- norm ⓝ 행동 양식, 표준, 규범
- routine ⓝ (판에 박힌) 일상
- repetition ⓝ 반복
- slow-changing 천천히 변하는
- overnight ad 하룻밤 사이에, 간밤에
- habitual ⓐ 습관적인
- latch on to ~을 붙들다, ~에 들러붙다
- thankful ⓐ 고마워하는

구문 풀이

2행 If your brain could completely change overnight, / you would be unstable.
「if + 주어 + 과거 동사 + ~, 주어 + 조동사 과거 + 동사원형 : 가정법 과거」

02 생물학적 작용의 한계에서 비롯되는 인식의 한계
정답률 49% | 정답 ⑤

다음 빈칸에 들어갈 말로 가장 적절한 것을 고르시오.

① hindered by other wavelengths - 다른 파장에 의해 방해받는다
② derived from our imagination - 우리의 상상에서 나온다
③ perceived through all senses - 모든 감각을 통해 인식된다
④ filtered by our stereotypes - 우리의 고정관념에 의해 걸러진다
✔ limited by our biology - 우리의 생물학적 작용에 의해 제한된다

Color is an interpretation of wavelengths, / one that only exists internally.
색은 파장에 대한 해석으로, / 내부에서만 존재하는 것이다.
And it gets stranger, / because the wavelengths we're talking about / involve only what we call "visible light", / a spectrum of wavelengths / that runs from red to violet.
그리고 그것은 더 생소하게 느껴진다. / 왜냐하면 우리가 말하고 있는 파장은 / '가시광선'이라고 부르는 것만을 포함하기 때문에, / 파장의 스펙트럼인 / 빨간색에서 보라색까지 이어지는
But visible light constitutes / only a tiny fraction of the electromagnetic spectrum / — less than one ten-trillionth of it.
그러나 가시광선은 구성해서 / 전자기 스펙트럼의 극히 일부만을 / 그중 10조 분의 1도 되지 않는다.
All the rest of the spectrum / — including radio waves, microwaves, Xrays, gamma rays, cell phone conversations, wifi, and so on — / all of this is flowing through us right now, / and we're completely unaware of it.
나머지 모든 스펙트럼이 / 전파, 마이크로파, X선, 감마선, 휴대폰 통화, 와이파이 등 / 이 모든 것이 지금 우리를 통해 흐르고 있으며, / 우리는 그것을 완전히 알지 못한다.
This is because we don't have any specialized biological receptors / to pick up on these signals from other parts of the spectrum.
이것은 우리가 어떤 특별한 생물학적 수용체도 가지고 있지 않기 때문이다. / 스펙트럼의 다른 부분으로부터 이러한 신호를 포착할 수 있는
The slice of reality that we can see / is limited by our biology.
우리가 볼 수 있는 현실의 단면은 / 우리의 생물학적 작용에 의해 제한된다.

색은 파장에 대한 해석으로, 내부에서만 존재하는 것이다. 그리고 이것은 더 생소해지는데, 우리가 말하고 있는 파장은 빨간색에서 보라색까지 이어지는 파장의 스펙트럼인 '가시광선'이라고 부르는 것만을 포함하기 때문이다. 그러나 가시광선은 전자기 스펙트럼의 극히 일부만을 구성해서 그중 10조 분의 1도 되지 않는다. 전파, 마이크로파, X선, 감마선, 휴대폰 통화, 와이파이 등 나머지 모든 스펙트럼이 지금 우리를 통해 흐르고 있으며, 우리는 이 모든 것을 완전히 알지 못한다. 이것은 우리가 스펙트럼의 다른 부분으로부터 이러한 신호를 포착할 수 있는 어떤 특별한 생물학적 수용체도 가지고 있지 않기 때문이다. 우리가 볼 수 있는 현실의 단면은 우리의 생물학적 작용에 의해 제한된다.

Why? 왜 정답일까?

우리 주변에는 온갖 종류의 스펙트럼이 흐르고 있지만 우리는 생물학적 수용체의 한계상 극히 일부만 인식할 수 있다(~ **we don't have any specialized biological receptors to pick up on these signals from other parts of the spectrum.**)는 설명으로 보아, 빈칸에 들어갈 말로 가장 적절한 것은 ⑤ '우리의 생물학적 작용에 의해 제한된다'이다.

- interpretation ⓝ 해석
- internally ad 내부적으로
- constitute ⓥ 구성하다
- rest ⓝ 나머지
- conversation ⓝ 대화
- unaware ⓐ 알지 못하는
- pick up on ~을 알아차리다
- hinder ⓥ 방해하다
- perceive ⓥ 인식하다
- stereotype ⓝ 고정관념
- wavelength ⓝ 파장, 주파수
- visible light 가시광선
- fraction ⓝ 부분, 파편
- radio waves 무선 전파
- completely ad 완전히
- specialized ⓐ 전문화된, 분화된
- signal ⓝ 신호
- derive ⓥ ~에서 나오다
- filter ⓥ 거르다

구문 풀이

2행 And it gets stranger, because the wavelengths we're talking about involve only {what we call "visible light"}, a spectrum of wavelengths [that runs from red to violet].
{ }: 선행사 / 선행사 동격 / 주격 관·대

[문제편 p.045]

03 과거를 다루는 과학

정답률 54% | 정답 ③

다음 빈칸에 들어갈 말로 가장 적절한 것을 고르시오. [3점]

① results of the big bang
빅뱅의 결과
② derived from exploration
탐험에서 유래한 (것)
✔ all afterimages of the past
모두 과거의 잔상
④ mixes of light, colors, and shading
빛과 색깔, 명암의 혼합
⑤ signs directly encoded in our genes
우리의 유전자 속에 직접 부호화되어 있는 신호

Science can only tell us how the world appears to us, / not how it is independent of our observation of it, / and therefore *right now* will always elude science.
과학은 세상이 어떻게 우리에게 보이는지를 말해 줄 수 있을 뿐이고, / 세상이 세상에 대한 우리의 관찰과 어떻게 별개인가가 아니라, / 그러므로 *바로 지금*은 항상 과학을 벗어나게 마련이다.
When you look into space, / you are looking into an ancient past.
당신은 우주를 들여다볼 때 / 먼 옛날의 과거를 들여다보는 것이다.
Some of the stars are already long dead / yet we still see them / because of their traveling light.
몇몇 별들은 이미 오래전에 죽었지만 / 우리는 여전히 그것들을 본다. / 그 별들의 이동하는 빛 때문에
Let's say that we are on one of those stars / situated roughly sixty million light-years away.
별들 중 하나에 우리가 존재한다고 가정해 보자. / 대략 6,000만 광년 떨어진 곳에 위치한
If we had a really awesome telescope pointed at the earth, / we would see the dinosaurs walking around.
만약 우리가 지구를 향해 있는 아주 근사한 망원경을 가지고 있다면, / 공룡이 걸어 다니고 있는 것을 볼 것이다.
The end of the universe is probably so old / that if we had that telescope, / we might be able to see the beginning.
우주의 끝은 아마도 너무 오래되어서 / 만약 우리가 그러한 망원경을 가지고 있다면 / 우주의 시작을 볼 수 있을지도 모른다.
Besides faraway things, / even the immediate objects around us / are all afterimages of the past / because there is still a time lag / for the reflection of light to reach our eyes.
멀리 떨어진 것들 외에도 / 가까이 있는 물체들조차 / 모두 과거의 잔상인데 / 그 이유는 여전히 시간상의 지체가 있기 때문이다. / 빛의 반사가 우리 눈에 도달하는 데
Every sensation our body feels has to wait / for the information to be carried to the brain.
우리 몸이 느끼는 모든 감각은 기다려야 한다. / 그 정보가 뇌에 전달되기까지

과학은 세상이 세상에 대한 우리의 관찰과 어떻게 별개인가가 아니라, 세상이 어떻게 우리에게 보이는지를 말해 줄 수 있을 뿐이고, 그러므로 *바로 지금*은 항상 과학을 벗어나게 마련이다. 당신은 우주를 들여다볼 때 먼 옛날의 과거를 들여다보는 것이다. 몇몇 별들은 이미 오래전에 죽었지만 우리는 그 별들의 이동하는 빛 때문에 여전히 그것들을 본다. 대략 6,000만 광년 떨어진 곳에 위치한 별들 중 하나에 우리가 존재한다고 가정해 보자. 만약 우리가 지구를 향해 있는 아주 근사한 망원경을 가지고 있다면, 공룡이 걸어 다니고 있는 것을 볼 것이다. 우주의 끝은 아마도 너무 오래되어서 만약 우리가 그러한 망원경을 가지고 있다면 우주의 시작을 볼 수 있을지도 모른다. 멀리 떨어진 것들 외에도 가까이 있는 물체들조차 모두 과거의 잔상인데 그 이유는 빛의 반사가 우리 눈에 도달하는 데 여전히 시간상의 지체가 있기 때문이다. 우리 몸이 느끼는 모든 감각은 그 정보가 뇌에 전달되기까지 기다려야 한다.

Why? 왜 정답일까?

'When you look into space, you are looking into an ancient past.'에서 우리가 바라보는 우주는 '먼 과거'임을 말한 데 이어, 빈칸 뒤에서는 우리가 심지어 가까운 물체를 보더라도 정보가 뇌에 도달하는 데 시간이 걸리기 때문에 역시 '과거'의 것을 바라보게 된다(**~ here is still a time lag for the reflection of light to reach our eyes. Every sensation our body feels has to wait for the information to be carried to the brain.**)는 내용을 이야기하므로, 빈칸에 들어갈 말로 가장 적절한 것은 ③ '모두 과거의 잔상'이다.

- **independent of** ~와는 별개인, 독립적인
- **roughly** ad 대략, 약
- **time lag** 시간상의 차이, 시차
- **afterimage** ⓝ 잔상
- **situate** ⓥ 위치하게 하다
- **immediate** ⓐ 가까이 있는, 목전의
- **derived from** ~에서 기인하는, 유래하는
- **encode** ⓥ 부호화하다, 암호화하다

구문 풀이

8행 If we had a really awesome telescope pointed at the earth, / we would see the dinosaurs walking around.
「if+주어+과거 동사+ ~, 주어+조동사 과거형+동사원형 : 가정법 과거(현재 반대)」
walking: 현재분사(see의 목적격 보어)

04 영화 *Apocalypse Now*와 원작과의 비교

정답률 63% | 정답 ①

다음 빈칸에 들어갈 말로 가장 적절한 것을 고르시오. [3점]

✔ a literal adaptation of the novel
소설을 있는 그대로 각색한 것
② a source of inspiration for the novel
소설에 대한 영감의 근원
③ a faithful depiction of the Vietnam War
베트남 전쟁에 대한 충실한 묘사
④ a vivid dramatisation of a psychological journey
심리적 여정의 생생한 극화
⑤ a critical interpretation of contemporary civilisation
현대 문명에 대한 비판적인 해석

Apocalypse Now, a film produced and directed by Francis Ford Coppola, / gained widespread popularity, and for good reason.
Francis Ford Coppola가 제작하고 감독한 영화인 *Apocalypse Now*는 / 폭넓은 인기를 얻었는데, 그럴 만한 이유가 있었다.
The film is an adaptation / of Joseph Conrad's novel *Heart of Darkness*, / which is set in the African Congo at the end of the 19th century.
그 영화는 각색인데, / Joseph Conrad의 소설 *Heart of Darkness*의 / 이 소설은 19세기 말 아프리카의 콩고를 배경으로 한다.
Unlike the original novel, / *Apocalypse Now* is set in Vietnam and Cambodia / during the Vietnam War.
원작 소설과는 달리 / *Apocalypse Now*는 베트남과 캄보디아를 배경으로 한다. / 베트남 전쟁 당시의
The setting, time period, dialogue and other incidental details / are changed / but the fundamental narrative and themes of *Apocalypse Now* / are the same as those of *Heart of Darkness*.
배경, 시기, 대화 및 기타 부수적 세부 사항은 / 바뀌어 있지만, / *Apocalypse Now*의 기본적인 줄거리와 주제는 / *Heart of Darkness*와 같다.
Both describe a physical journey, / reflecting the central character's mental and spiritual journey, / down a river to confront the deranged Kurtz character, / who represents the worst aspects of civilisation.
둘 다 물리적 여정을 묘사하는데, / 이는 주인공의 정신적 여정과 영적 여정을 반영한 것이며, / 제정신이 아닌 Kurtz라는 인물에 맞서려고 강을 따라 내려가는 / Kurtz는 문명의 가장 나쁜 단면을 대표한다.
By giving *Apocalypse Now* / a setting that was contemporary at the time of its release, / audiences were able to experience and identify with its themes more easily / than they would have / if the film had been a literal adaptation of the novel.
*Apocalypse Now*에 제공함으로써, / 영화 개봉 당시와 같은 시대적 배경을 / 더 쉽게 영화의 주제를 접하고 영화와 동질감을 느낄 수 있었다. / 그들이 그러했을 것보다 / 관객들은 영화가 소설을 있는 그대로 각색한 것이었다면

Francis Ford Coppola가 제작하고 감독한 영화인 *Apocalypse Now*는 폭넓은 인기를 얻었는데, 그럴만한 이유가 있었다. 그 영화는 Joseph Conrad의 소설 *Heart of Darkness*를 각색한 것인데, 이 소설은 19세기 말 아프리카의 콩고를 배경으로 한다. 원작 소설과는 달리 *Apocalypse Now*는 베트남 전쟁 당시의 베트남과 캄보디아를 배경으로 한다. 배경, 시기, 대화 및 기타 부수적 세부 사항은 바뀌어 있지만, *Apocalypse Now*의 기본적인 줄거리와 주제는 *Heart of Darkness*와 같다. 둘 다 물리적 여정을 묘사하는데, 이는 제정신이 아닌 Kurtz라는 인물에 맞서려고 강을 따라 내려가는, 주인공의 정신적 여정과 영적 여정을 반영한 것이며, Kurtz는 문명의 가장 나쁜 단면을 대표한다. *Apocalypse Now*에 영화 개봉 당시와 같은 시대적 배경을 제공함으로써, 관객들은 영화가 소설을 있는 그대로 각색한 것이었다면 그러했을 것보다 더 쉽게 영화의 주제를 접하고 영화와 동질감을 느낄 수 있었다.

Why? 왜 정답일까?

글에 따르면 영화 ***Apocalypse Now***는 소설 ***Heart of Darkness***를 각색하여 만든 영화이지만 배경, 시기, 대화, 기타 세부 사항 면에서 변화를 시도했는데, 마지막 문장에 따르면 이는 관객으로 하여금 영화의 주제를 더 쉽게 접하고 영화에 동질감을 느끼게 하기 위한 장치였다. 원작에 '변화를 주어 각색한 것'은 원작을 '그대로 각색한 것'과 비교해야 적절하므로, 빈칸에 들어갈 말로 가장 적절한 것은 ① '소설을 있는 그대로 각색한 것'이다.

- **widespread** ⓐ 널리 퍼진, 만연한
- **unlike** prep ~와는 달리
- **incidental** ⓐ 부수적인
- **contemporary** ⓐ 현대의, 동시대의
- **adaptation** ⓝ 각색, 적응
- **setting** ⓝ (연극 등의) 배경
- **narrative** ⓝ 줄거리, 묘사
- **identify with** ~와 동일시하다

구문 풀이

10행 Both describe a physical journey, [reflecting the central character's mental and spiritual journey, down a river to confront the deranged Kurtz character], {who represents the worst aspects of civilisation}.
[ ]: a physical journey 부연
선행사 / 주격 관계대명사

05 독일군의 포탄 공격에 대한 영국의 교란

정답률 62% | 정답 ③

다음 빈칸에 들어갈 말로 가장 적절한 것을 고르시오. [3점]

① being honest with the public – 대중에게 정직함
② giving the enemy a chance to retreat – 적에게 후퇴할 기회를 제공함
③ feeding the enemy wrong information – 적에게 잘못된 정보를 제공함
④ focusing on one goal consistently – 한 가지 목표에 일관되게 집중함
⑤ exploring the unknown places – 미지의 장소를 탐험함

In 1944 the German rocket-bomb attacks on London / suddenly escalated.
1944년 런던에 대한 독일의 로켓포 공격이 / 갑자기 증가했다.
Over two thousand V-1 flying bombs / fell on the city, / killing more than five thousand people / and wounding many more.
2천 개가 넘는 V-1 비행 폭탄이 / 도시에 떨어져 / 5천 명이 넘는 사람들의 목숨을 앗아 갔고, / 그보다 더 많은 사람들을 부상 입혔다.
Somehow, however, / the Germans consistently missed their targets.
하지만 웬일인지 / 독일군은 시종일관 목표물을 빗맞혔다.
Bombs that were intended for Tower Bridge, or Piccadilly, / would fall well short of the city, / landing in the less populated suburbs.
Tower Bridge나 Piccadilly로 의도된 폭탄은 / 도시에 한참 못 미쳐, / 사람이 더 적게 사는 교외에 떨어지곤 했다.
This was because, in fixing their targets, / the Germans relied on secret agents / they had planted in England.
이는 목표물을 정할 때 / 독일군이 비밀 요원들에게 의지했기 때문이었다. / 그들이 영국에 배치해 두었던
They did not know / that these agents had been discovered, / and that in their place, / English-controlled agents were giving them subtly deceptive information.
그들은 몰랐다. / 이 비밀 요원들이 발각되었고, / 그들 대신에 / 영국의 지휘를 받는 요원들이 자신들에게 교묘하게 거짓 정보를 제공하고 있다는 사실을
The bombs would hit farther and farther from their targets / every time they fell.
폭탄은 목표물에서 점점 더 먼 곳을 맞히곤 했다. / 그것이 떨어질 때마다
By the end of the attack / they were landing on cows in the country.
공격이 끝날 무렵에는, / 폭탄은 시골에 있는 암소 위로 떨어지고 있었다.
By feeding the enemy wrong information, / the English army gained a strong advantage.
적에게 잘못된 정보를 제공함으로써 / 영국군은 큰 이득을 얻었다.

1944년 런던에 대한 독일의 로켓포 공격이 갑자기 증가했다. 2천 개가 넘는 V-1 비행 폭탄이 도시에 떨어져 5천 명이 넘는 사람들의 목숨을 앗아 갔고, 그보다 더 많은 사람들은 부상을 입었다. 하지만 웬일인지 독일군은 시종일관 목표물을 빗맞혔다. Tower Bridge나 Piccadilly로 의도된 폭탄은 도시에 한참 못 미쳐, 사람이 더 적게 사는 교외에 떨어지곤 했다. 이는 독일군이 목표물을 정할 때 그들이 영국에 배치해 두었던 비밀 요원들에게 의지했기 때문이었다. 그들은 이 비밀 요원들이 발각되었고, 그들 대신 영국의 지휘를 받는 요원들이 자신들에게 교묘하게 거짓 정보를 제공하고 있다는 사실을 몰랐다. 폭탄은 떨어질 때마다 목표물에서 점점 더 먼 곳을 맞히곤 했다. 공격이 끝날 무렵에는, 폭탄은 시골에 있는 암소 위로 떨어지고 있었다. 적에게 잘못된 정보를 제공함으로써 영국군은 큰 이득을 얻었다.

Why? 왜 정답일까?

'They did not know that these agents had been discovered, and that in their place, English-controlled agents were giving them subtly deceptive information.'에서 독일군이 영국에 심어두었던 첩자는 발각되었고 영국군 산하의 요원들이 목표물과 관련하여 거짓 정보를 계속해서 흘렸다고 이야기하므로, 빈칸에 들어갈 말로 가장 적절한 것은 ③ '적에게 잘못된 정보를 제공함'이다.

- escalate ⓥ 증가하다
- consistently ad 시종일관, 일관되게
- fall short of ~에 못 미치다
- populate ⓥ 살다, 거주하다
- plant ⓥ 잠입시키다
- in one's place ~을 대신하여
- deceptive ⓐ 거짓된, 기만적인
- wound ⓥ 부상 입히다, 상처 입히다
- intended ⓐ 대상으로 삼은
- land ⓥ 떨어지다, 착륙하다
- rely on ~에 의지하다
- discover ⓥ 발각하다, 발견하다
- subtly ad 미묘하게
- advantage ⓝ 이득, 이점

구문 풀이

2행 Over two thousand V-1 flying bombs(주어) fell(동사(과거)) on the city, / killing(분사구문1) more than five thousand people and(병렬) wounding(분사구문2(그리고 ~하다)) many more.

06 사회적 상황에서의 웃음의 역할

정답률 49% | 정답 ②

다음 빈칸에 들어갈 말로 가장 적절한 것을 고르시오. [3점]

① have similar tastes in comedy and humor
희극과 유머에 대한 비슷한 취향을 갖고 있기
② are using laughter to connect with others
다른 사람과 가까워지기 위해 웃음을 이용하고 있기
③ are reluctant to reveal our innermost feelings
우리의 가장 내밀한 감정을 드러내기를 꺼리기
④ focus on the content rather than the situation
상황보다는 내용에 집중하기
⑤ feel more comfortable around others than alone
혼자보다 다른 사람 곁에 있을 때 더 편안함을 느끼기

In one example of the important role of laughter in social contexts, / Devereux and Ginsburg examined frequency of laughter / in matched pairs of strangers or friends / who watched a humorous video together / compared to those who watched it alone.
사회적 상황에서 웃음의 중요한 역할의 한 예로, / Devereux와 Ginsburg는 웃음의 빈도를 조사했다. / 모르는 사람이나 친구끼리 짝지어진 쌍에서 / 익살스러운 동영상을 함께 본, / 그것을 혼자 본 사람들과 비교하여
The time individuals spent laughing / was nearly twice as frequent in pairs / as when alone.
사람들이 웃은 시간은 / 짝을 이루어 있을 때 거의 두 배 더 잦았다. / 혼자 있을 때보다
Frequency of laughing / was only slightly shorter for friends than strangers.
웃음의 빈도는 / 모르는 사람들보다 친구들의 경우가 약간 더 적었을 뿐이다.
According to Devereux and Ginsburg, / laughing with strangers served to create a social bond / that made each person in the pair feel comfortable.
Devereux와 Ginsburg에 따르면, / 모르는 사람과 함께 웃는 것은 사회적 유대를 형성하는 데 이바지했다. / 쌍을 이루는 각각의 사람을 편안하게 만드는
This explanation is supported by the fact / that in their stranger condition, / when one person laughed, / the other was likely to laugh as well.
이 설명은 사실에 의해 뒷받침된다. / 모르는 사람과 함께 있는 조건에서 / 한 사람이 웃을 때 / 상대방도 웃을 가능성이 있었다는
Interestingly, / the three social conditions / (alone, paired with a stranger, or paired with a friend) / did not differ in their ratings of funniness of the video / or of feelings of happiness or anxiousness.
흥미롭게도, / 세 가지 사회적 조건은 / (혼자인 경우, 모르는 사람과 쌍을 이룬 경우, 친구와 쌍을 이룬 경우) / 동영상의 재미에 대한 그들의 평가에서는 다르지 않았다. / 또는 행복감이나 불안감에 대한
This finding implies / that their frequency of laughter / was not because we find things funnier / when we are with others / but instead we are using laughter to connect with others.
이 발견은 의미한다. / 그들의 웃음의 빈도는 / 우리가 어떤 것이 더 재미있다고 생각하기 때문이 아니라 / 우리가 다른 사람들과 함께 있을 때 / 오히려 우리가 다른 사람과 가까워지기 위해 웃음을 이용하고 있기 때문이었음을

사회적 상황에서 웃음의 중요한 역할의 한 예로, Devereux와 Ginsburg는 익살스러운 동영상을 혼자 본 사람들과 비교하여 그것을 함께 본, 모르는 사람이나 친구끼리 짝지어진 쌍에서 웃음의 빈도를 조사했다. 사람들이 웃은 시간은 혼자 있을 때보다 짝을 이루어 있을 때 거의 두 배 더 잦았다. 웃음의 빈도는 모르는 사람들보다 친구들의 경우가 약간 더 적었을 뿐이다. Devereux와 Ginsburg에 따르면, 모르는 사람과 함께 웃는 것은 쌍을 이루는 각각의 사람을 편안하게 만드는 사회적 유대를 형성하는 데 이바지했다. 이 설명은 모르는 사람과 함께 있는 조건에서 한 사람이 웃을 때 상대방도 웃을 가능성이 있었다는 사실에 의해 뒷받침된다. 흥미롭게도, 세 가지 사회적 조건(혼자인 경우, 모르는 사람과 쌍을 이룬 경우, 친구와 쌍을 이룬 경우)은 동영상의 재미나 행복감 또는 불안감에 대한 그들의 평가에서는 다르지 않았다. 이 발견이 의미하기로, 그들의 웃음 빈도는 우리가 다른 사람들과 함께 있을 때 어떤 것이 더 재미있다고 생각하기 때문이 아니라 오히려 우리가 다른 사람과 가까워지기 위해 웃음을 이용하고 있기 때문이었다.

Why? 왜 정답일까?

글 중반부에서 모르는 사람끼리 함께 웃는 것이 사회적 유대를 형성한다(~ **laughing with strangers served to create a social bond that made each person in the pair feel comfortable.**)는 내용이 나오는 것으로 보아, 빈칸에 들어갈 말로 가장 적절한 것은 ② '다른 사람과 가까워지기 위해 웃음을 이용하고 있기'이다.

- frequency ⓝ 빈도
- bond ⓝ 유대감
- anxiousness ⓝ 불안감
- reveal ⓥ 드러내다
- slightly ad 약간
- rating ⓝ 평가
- connect with ~와 관계를 맺다, 연결하다
- content ⓝ 내용

구문 풀이

5행 The time(주어) [(that)(목적격 관·대) individuals spent laughing] was(동사) nearly twice as frequent in pairs as(「배수사+as+원급+as : ~ 배만큼 …한」) when (they are) alone(부사절 축약(대명사+be 생략)).

DAY 07

[문제편 p.047]

07 기쁨의 경험 정답률 62% | 정답 ①

다음 빈칸에 들어갈 말로 가장 적절한 것을 고르시오. [3점]

① your biological treasure map to joy
기쁨으로 가는 생물학적 보물지도
② your hidden key to lasting friendships
오래 지속되는 우정에 이르는 숨겨진 열쇠
③ a mirror showing your unique personality
독특한 성격을 보여주는 거울
④ a facilitator for communication with others
다른 사람들과의 의사소통에 대한 촉진제
⑤ a barrier to looking back to your joyful childhood
즐거운 어린 시절을 돌아보는 데 있어서의 장애물

The most powerful emotional experiences / are those / that bring joy, inspiration, / and the kind of love / that makes suffering bearable.
가장 강력한 감정적 경험은 / 경험이다. / 기쁨, 영감을 가져다주는 / 그리고 일종의 사랑을 / 고통을 견딜 수 있게 만들어주는

These emotional experiences / are the result of choices and behaviors / that result in our feeling happy.
이러한 감정적 경험은 / 선택과 행동의 결과이다. / 우리가 행복하다고 느끼게 만드는

When we look at happiness through a spiritual filter, / we realize / that it does not mean the absence of pain or heartache.
우리가 정신적 필터를 통해 행복을 바라볼 때, / 우리는 깨닫는다. / 그것이 고통이나 마음의 아픔이 없다는 것을 뜻하는 것이 아님을

Sitting with a sick or injured child, / every parent gets to know the profound joy / that bubbles over / when a son or daughter begins to heal.
아프거나 다친 아이와 함께 앉아 있으면, / 모든 부모는 깊은 기쁨을 알게 된다. / 벅차오르는 / 아들 혹은 딸이 치유되기 시작할 때

This is a simple example / of how we can be flooded with happiness / that becomes more intense / as we contrast it with previous suffering.
이것은 간단한 예이다. / 어떻게 우리가 행복으로 넘쳐날 수 있는지의 / 더욱 강렬해진 / 우리가 그것을 이전의 고통과 대조함에 따라

Experiences such as this / go into the chemical archives of the limbic system.
이와 같은 경험은 / 변연계의 화학적 기록 보관소에 들어간다.

Each time you experience true happiness, / the stored emotions are activated / as you are flooded with even deeper joy / than you remembered.
여러분이 진정한 행복을 경험할 때마다, / 저장된 감정이 활성화된다. / 여러분이 훨씬 더 깊은 기쁨으로 벅차오르면서 / 여러분이 기억했던 것보다

Your spiritual genes are, / in a sense, / <u>your biological treasure map to joy</u>.
당신의 정신적 유전자는 / 어떤 의미에서, / 기쁨으로 가는 생물학적 보물지도이다.

가장 강력한 감정적 경험은 기쁨, 영감, 고통을 견딜 수 있게 만들어주는 일종의 사랑을 가져다주는 경험이다. 이러한 감정적 경험은 우리가 행복하다고 느끼게 만드는 선택과 행동의 결과이다. 우리가 정신적 필터를 통해 행복을 바라볼 때, 우리는 그것이 고통이나 마음의 아픔이 없다는 것을 뜻하는 것이 아님을 깨닫는다. 아프거나 다친 아이와 함께 앉아 있으면, 모든 부모는 아들 혹은 딸이 치유되기 시작할 때 벅차오르는 깊은 기쁨을 알게 된다. 이것은 이전의 고통과 대조함에 따라 어떻게 우리가 더욱 강렬해진 행복으로 넘쳐날 수 있는지의 간단한 예이다. 이와 같은 경험은 변연계의 화학적 기록 보관소에 들어간다. 진정한 행복을 경험할 때마다, 기억했던 것보다 훨씬 더 깊은 기쁨이 벅차오르면서 저장된 감정이 활성화된다. 어떤 의미에서, 당신의 정신적 유전자는 <u>기쁨으로 가는 생물학적 보물지도</u>이다.

Why? 왜 정답일까?

'**Each time you experience true happiness, the stored emotions are activated as you are flooded with even deeper joy than you remembered.**'에서 우리가 행복을 경험할 때마다 우리의 기억 속에 저장되어 있던 기쁨이 한층 증폭되어 활성화된다고 언급하는 것으로 보아, 감정과 관련된 우리의 정신 기제를 설명하는 빈칸에 들어갈 말로 가장 적절한 것은 ① '기쁨으로 가는 생물학적 보물지도'이다.

- inspiration ⓝ 영감
- spiritual ⓐ 정신적인
- profound ⓐ 깊은
- intense ⓐ 강렬한
- archive ⓝ 기록 보관소
- facilitator ⓝ 촉진제
- bearable ⓐ 견딜 수 있는
- absence ⓝ 부재
- be flooded with ~로 넘쳐나다
- contrast A with B A와 B를 대조하다
- lasting ⓐ 지속되는
- look back to ~을 돌아보다

구문 풀이

1행 The most powerful emotional experiences are <u>those</u> [that bring joy, inspiration, and <u>the kind of love</u> [that makes suffering bearable]].
(those: 선행사(=experiences), that: 주격 관·대 / the kind of love: 선행사, that: 주격 관·대)

08 정치 과정에서 다른 의견을 억압하면 안 되는 이유 정답률 42% | 정답 ②

다음 빈칸에 들어갈 말로 가장 적절한 것을 고르시오. [3점]

① political development results from the freedom of speech
정치적 발전은 언론의 자유에서 나온다는
② political disagreement is not the normal state of things
정치적 갈등이 정상적 상태가 아니라는
③ politics should not restrict any form of difference
정치는 그 어떤 형태의 차이도 제한해서는 안 된다는
④ freedom could be achieved only through tolerance
자유는 관용을 통해서만 성취된다는
⑤ suppression could never be a desirable tool in politics
억압은 정치에서 결코 바람직한 도구가 될 수 없다는

Politics cannot be suppressed, / whichever policy process is employed / and however sensitive and respectful of differences it might be.
정치적 견해는 억압될 수 없다. / 어떤 정치 과정이 이용되든, / 그 과정이 얼마나 민감하고 차이를 얼마나 존중하든

In other words, / there is no end to politics.
다시 말해서, / 정치적 견해에는 끝이 없다.

It is wrong to think / that proper institutions, knowledge, methods of consultation, or participatory mechanisms / can make disagreement go away.
생각하는 것은 잘못된 것이다. / 적절한 기관이나 지식, 협의 과정, 또는 참여 기제가 / 의견의 불일치를 없앨 수 있다고

Theories of all sorts promote the view / that there are ways / by which disagreement can be processed or managed / so as to make it disappear.
모든 종류의 이론은 견해를 조장한다. / 방법이 있다는 / 불일치를 처리하고 다룰 수 있는 / 의견 불일치가 사라지게 하기 위하여

The assumption behind those theories is / that disagreement is wrong / and consensus is the desirable state of things.
그런 이론들 뒤에 숨겨진 가정은 / 불일치가 틀린 것이고 / 합의란 만물의 바람직한 상태라는 것이다.

In fact, / consensus rarely comes / without some forms of subtle coercion / and the absence of fear in expressing a disagreement / is a source of genuine freedom.
사실은, / 합의란 좀처럼 이루어지지 않으며, / 어떤 형태로든 미묘한 강요 없이는 / 다른 의견을 표하는 데 두려움이 없는 것은 / 진정한 자유의 원천이다.

Debates cause disagreements to evolve, / often for the better, / but a positively evolving debate / does not have to equal a reduction in disagreement.
논쟁은 갈등이 발전하게 만드는데, / 때때로 보다 나은 쪽으로 / 긍정적으로 발전하는 논쟁이 / 불일치의 감소와 동일시될 필요는 없다.

The suppression of disagreement / should never be made into a goal / in political deliberation.
다른 의견의 억압은 / 결코 목표가 되어서는 안 된다. / 정치적 숙고의

A defense is required against any suggestion / that <u>political disagreement is not the normal state of things</u>.
그 어떤 제안에도 맞서는 항변이 필요하다. / 정치적 갈등이 정상적 상태가 아니라는

어떤 정치 과정이 이용되든, 그 과정이 얼마나 민감하고 차이를 얼마나 존중하든, 정치적 견해는 억압될 수 없다. 다시 말해서, 정치적 견해에는 끝이 없다. 적절한 기관이나 지식, 협의 과정, 또는 참여 기제가 의견의 불일치를 없앨 수 있다고 생각하는 것은 잘못된 것이다. 모든 종류의 이론은 의견 불일치가 사라지게 하기 위하여 불일치를 처리하고 다룰 수 있는 방법이 있다는 견해를 조장한다. 그런 이론들 뒤에 숨겨진 가정은 불일치가 틀린 것이고 합의란 만물의 바람직한 상태라는 것이다. 사실은, 합의란 어떤 형태로든 미묘한 강요 없이는 좀처럼 이루어지지 않으며, 다른 의견을 표하는 데 두려움이 없는 것은 진정한 자유의 원천이다. 논쟁은 갈등이 때때로 보다 나은 쪽으로 발전하게 만드는데, 긍정적으로 발전하는 논쟁이 불일치의 감소와 동일시될 필요는 없다. 다른 의견의 억압은 결코 정치적 숙고의 목표가 되어서는 안 된다. <u>정치적 갈등이 정상적 상태가 아니라는</u> 그 어떤 제안에도 맞서는 항변이 필요하다.

Why? 왜 정답일까?

'**It is wrong to think that proper institutions, knowledge, methods of consultation, or participatory mechanisms can make disagreement go away.**'와 '**The suppression of disagreement should never be made into a goal in political deliberation.**'에서 적절한 방법으로 정치 과정 내 의견의 불일치를 줄이거나 없애겠다고 생각하는 것은 잘못된 것이며 합의를 위해 다른 의견을 억압하는 것은 정치적 숙고 과정의 목표가 될 수 없음을 이야기한다. 이때 빈칸 문장은 '~한 견해에는 항변해야 한다'는 내용이므로, 빈칸 부분에는 '불일치를 나쁘게 보지 말라'는 주제 대신 '불일치를 나쁘게 본다'는 내용이 들어가야 이러한 견해에 항변을 할 수 있어야 한다는 맥락이 성립한다. 따라서 빈칸에 들어갈 말로 가장 적절한 것은 ② '정치적 갈등이 정상적 상태가 아니라는'이다.

- suppress ⓥ 억압하다, 억누르다
- proper ⓐ 적절한
- employ ⓥ 이용하다, 사용하다
- institution ⓝ 기관, 제도

- mechanism ⓝ 기제
- consensus ⓝ 합의, 의견 일치
- coercion ⓝ 강요
- process ⓥ 처리하다
- subtle ⓐ 미묘한, 감지하기 힘든
- deliberation ⓝ 숙고, 숙의

구문 풀이

1행 Politics cannot be suppressed, (whichever policy process is employed) and (however sensitive and respectful of differences it might be). 조동사 수동태 / 복합관계형용사(어떤 ~이든) / 복합관계부사(아무리 ~이든) / ~을 존중하는 / ( ): 부사절

★★★ 1등급 대비 고난도 2점 문제

09 생명체의 출현으로 인한 지구의 대기 변화 정답률 29% | 정답 ②

다음 빈칸에 들어갈 말로 가장 적절한 것을 고르시오.

① a barrier to evolution – 진화에 있어 장벽
② a consequence of life – 생명체의 결과
③ a record of primitive culture – 원시 문화의 기록
④ a sign of the constancy of nature – 자연의 불변성에 대한 신호
⑤ a reason for cooperation among species – 종들 간 협력의 이유

Over 4.5 billion years ago, / the Earth's primordial atmosphere / was probably largely water vapour, carbon dioxide, sulfur dioxide and nitrogen.
45억 년도 더 전에 / 지구의 원시 대기는 / 아마도 대부분 수증기, 이산화탄소, 이산화황과 질소였을 것이다.
The appearance and subsequent evolution of exceedingly primitive living organisms / (bacteria-like microbes and simple single-celled plants) / began to change the atmosphere, / liberating oxygen and breaking down carbon dioxide and sulfur dioxide.
극히 원시적인 생물체의 출현과 연이은 진화는 / (박테리아 같은 미생물과 단순한 단세포 식물) / 대기를 변화시키기 시작했다. / 산소를 유리(遊離)시키고 이산화탄소와 이산화황을 분해하면서
This made it possible / for higher organisms to develop.
이것은 가능하게 했다. / 더 상위 유기체가 발달하는 것을
When the earliest known plant cells with nuclei / evolved about 2 billion years ago, / the atmosphere seems to have had / only about 1 percent of its present content of oxygen.
가장 최초라고 알려진 핵이 있는 식물 세포가 / 약 20억 년 전 진화했을 때, / 대기에 있었던 것 같다. / 현재 산소 함량이 고작 약 1%만이
With the emergence of the first land plants, / about 500 million years ago, / oxygen reached about one-third of its present concentration.
최초의 육지 식물이 출현하면서 / 약 5억 년 전에 / 산소는 현재 농도의 약 3분의 1에 달했다.
It had risen to almost its present level / by about 370 million years ago, / when animals first spread on to land.
그것은 거의 현재 수준으로 증가했고, / 약 3억 7천만 년 전까지 / 그때 동물들이 처음 육지에 퍼졌다.
Today's atmosphere is thus / not just a requirement to sustain life / as we know it — / it is also a consequence of life.
그러므로 오늘날의 대기는 / 생명체를 유지하기 위한 필요조건인 것만이 아니라, / 우리가 알고 있듯이 / 생명체의 결과이기도 하다.

45억 년도 더 전에 지구의 원시 대기는 아마도 대부분 수증기, 이산화탄소, 이산화황과 질소였을 것이다. 극히 원시적인 생물체(박테리아 같은 미생물과 단순한 단세포 식물)의 출현과 연이은 진화는 산소를 유리(遊離)시키고 이산화탄소와 이산화황을 분해하면서 대기를 변화시키기 시작했다. 이것은 더 상위 유기체가 발달하는 것을 가능하게 했다. 가장 최초라고 알려진 핵이 있는 식물 세포가 약 20억 년 전 진화했을 때, 대기에 현재 산소 함량의 고작 약 1%만이 있었던 것 같다. 약 5억 년 전에 최초의 육지 식물이 출현하면서 산소는 현재 농도의 약 3분의 1에 달했다. 그것은 약 3억 7천만 년 전까지 거의 현재 수준으로 증가했고, 그때 동물들이 처음 육지에 퍼졌다. 그러므로 오늘날의 대기는 우리가 알고 있듯이 생명체를 유지하기 위한 필요조건인 것만이 아니라, 생명체의 결과이기도 하다.

Why? 왜 정답일까?

첫 두 문장에서 지구의 원시 대기는 수증기, 이산화탄소, 이산화황, 질소 등으로 이루어져 있었을 것이나 생명체의 탄생 이후 산소가 유리되고 이산화탄소와 이산화황이 분해되는 등 그 변화를 맞이하게 되었다고 한다. 이어서 핵이 있는 최초의 식물 세포, 최초의 육지 식물 등이 출현하며 산소 농도 또한 점점 더 많은 생명체가 살기 적합하도록 높아졌다는 내용이 전개된다. 이러한 흐름으로 보아, 빈칸 문장은 대기가 생명체의 탄생으로 말미암아 '결과적으로' 변화해온 것이라는 결론을 적합하게 제시해야 한다. 따라서 빈칸에 들어갈 말로 가장 적절한 것은 ② '생명체의 결과'이다.

- billion ⓝ 10억
- subsequent ⓐ 연이은, 그다음의
- nitrogen ⓝ 질소
- exceedingly ad 극히, 대단히
- liberate ⓥ (화학) 유리시키다
- emergence ⓝ 출현
- requirement ⓝ 필요조건
- consequence ⓝ 결과
- nucleus ⓝ (생물) 핵, 세포핵 (*pl.* nuclei)
- concentration ⓝ 농도
- sustain ⓥ 유지하다, 지탱하다
- constancy ⓝ 불변성

구문 풀이

15행 It had risen to almost its present level by about 370 million years ago, when animals first spread on to land. 과거완료 / 시간 선행사 / 관계부사(계속적 용법)

★★ 문제 해결 꿀~팁 ★★

▶ 많이 틀린 이유는?
지구의 대기가 생물체 출현에 따라 '변화해' 왔다는 것이 글의 주제이므로, ④의 constancy(불변성, 항구성)는 주제와 정반대되는 단어이다. 또한 글에서 '원시 문화'에 관해 언급하지 않으므로 ③도 답으로 부적절하다.
▶ 문제 해결 방법은?
첫 두 문장에서 초창기 대기는 오늘날과 많이 달랐으나 생물체의 진화에 따라 대기가 변화되기 시작했다는 내용을 파악하면 답이 ②임을 알 수 있다.

★★★ 1등급 대비 고난도 3점 문제

10 타인과 자신을 끊임없이 격려하며 사는 인간 정답률 52% | 정답 ②

다음 빈칸에 들어갈 말로 가장 적절한 것을 고르시오. [3점]

① judges – 재판관
② motivators – 동기부여자
③ inventors – 발명가
④ analysts – 분석가
⑤ observers – 관찰자

We are the CEOs of our own lives.
우리는 우리 삶의 CEO들이다.
We work hard / to urge ourselves / to get up and go to work / and do what we must do day after day.
우리는 열심히 노력한다. / 스스로를 자극하려고 / 일어나 직장에 가고 / 매일 해야 할 일을 하도록
We also try to encourage / the people working for and with us, / those who are doing business with us, / and even those who regulate us.
또한 우리는 격려하기 위해 노력한다. / 우리를 위해 일하고 우리와 함께 일하는 사람들을 / 우리와 거래하고 있는 사람들을, / 그리고 심지어 우리를 통제하는 사람들을
We do this in our personal lives, too:
우리는 사적인 삶에서도 이런 행동을 한다.
From a very young age, / kids try to persuade their parents to do things for them / ("Dad, I'm too scared to do this!") / with varying degrees of success.
아주 어릴 때부터 / 아이들은 부모가 무언가를 해 주도록 설득하려고 노력한다. / ("아빠, 저 너무 무서워서 이거 못 하겠어요!") / 성공의 정도는 각기 다르지만
As adults, / we try to encourage our significant others / to do things for us / ("Sweetie, I had such a stressful day today, / can you please put the kids to bed and do the dishes?").
성인으로서 / 우리는 우리의 배우자를 격려하려고 애쓴다. / 우리를 위해 무언가 해 주도록 / ("여보, 나 오늘 무척 스트레스가 심한 하루를 보냈는데 / 아이를 재우고 설거지를 해 줄래요?")
We attempt to get our kids to clean up their rooms.
우리는 아이들이 방을 치우게 하려고 시도한다.
We try to induce our neighbors / to help out with a neighborhood party.
우리는 이웃을 유도하려고 노력한다. / 동네 파티를 도와주도록
Whatever our official job descriptions, / we are all part-time motivators.
우리의 공식적인 직업에 대한 묘사가 무엇이든 간에, / 우리는 모두 시간제 동기부여자이다.

우리는 우리 삶의 CEO들이다. 우리는 일어나 직장에 가고 매일 해야 할 일을 하도록 스스로를 자극하려고 열심히 노력한다. 또한 우리를 위해 일하고 우리와 함께 일하는 사람들, 우리와 거래하고 있는 사람들, 심지어 우리를 통제하는 사람들을 격려하기 위해 노력한다. 우리는 사적인 삶에서도 이런 행동을 한다. 아주 어릴 때부터 아이들은 성공의 정도는 각기 다르지만 부모가 무언가를 해 주도록 설득하려고 노력한다("아빠, 저 너무 무서워서 이거 못 하겠어요!"). 성인으로서 우리는 우리의 배우자가 우리를 위해 무언가 해 주도록 격려하려고 애쓴다("여보, 나 오늘 무척 스트레스가 심한 하루를 보냈는데 아이를 재우고 설거지를 해 줄래요?"). 우리는 아이들이 방을 치우게 하려고 시도한다. 우리는 이웃이 동네 파티를 도와주도록 유도하려고 노력한다. 우리의 공식적인 직업에 대한 묘사가 무엇이든 간에, 우리는 모두 시간제 동기부여자이다.

Why? 왜 정답일까?

'We work hard to urge ourselves to get up and go to work and do what we must do day after day. We also try to encourage the people

working for and with us, those who are doing business with us, and even those who regulate us.'에서 우리는 스스로 해야 할 일을 하도록 스스로를 격려할 뿐 아니라 주변 사람들 또한 어떤 행동을 해 주도록 끊임없이 격려한다고 하므로, 빈칸에 들어갈 말로 가장 적절한 것은 이를 비유적으로 나타낸 ② '동기부여자'이다.

- **urge** ⓥ 자극하다, 촉구하다
- **regulate** ⓥ 통제하다
- **varying** ⓐ 각기 다른, 변하는
- **do the dishes** 설거지를 하다
- **induce** ⓥ 설득하다, 유도하다
- **do business with** ~와 거래하다
- **persuade** ⓥ 설득하다
- **significant other** 배우자, 남편, 아내, 애인
- **attempt** ⓥ 시도하다

구문 풀이

1행 We work hard / to urge ourselves to get up and (to 생략) go to work and (to 생략) do what we must do day after day.
(urge의 목적격 보어1 / 목적격 보어2 / 목적격 보어3 / 관계대명사(~것))

★★ 문제 해결 꿀~팁 ★★

▶ 많이 틀린 이유는?
빈칸 문장을 제외한 부분이 거의 예문으로만 이루어져 있기에 주제를 나타내는 키워드가 바로 눈에 보이지 않아 틀리기 쉬운 문제였다. 오답률은 비교적 고르게 분포해 있는데, 이는 이 문제를 매력적인 오답 때문에 틀렸다기보다 지문의 내용 자체가 와닿지 않아 틀린 수험생이 많았다는 점을 시사한다.
▶ 문제 해결 방법은?
이 문제의 경우 선택지를 먼저 보고서 지문과 같은 내용이 전개될 수 있는지를 체크하면 오답을 가려낼 수 있다. ①의 '재판관'은 잘잘못을 가려내는 사람이므로, ①이 답이었다면 우리가 평소 시시비비를 가리고 따진다는 내용이 주로 나왔을 것이다. ③ '발명가'의 경우에는 우리가 일상에서 창조적인 영감을 받아 무언가를 만들어보거나 창작하기를 좋아한다는 내용이 전개되었을 것이다.

★★★ 1등급 대비 고난도 3점 문제

11 다수가 항상 옳지는 않음을 이해하기 — 정답률 28% | 정답 ⑤

다음 빈칸에 들어갈 말로 가장 적절한 것을 고르시오. [3점]

① majority rule should be founded on fairness
다수결의 법칙은 공정함에 바탕을 둬야 한다
② the crowd is generally going in the right direction
군중은 일반적으로 맞는 쪽으로 향한다
③ the roles of leaders and followers can change at any time
리더와 팔로워의 역할은 어느 때든 바뀔 수 있다
④ people behave in a different fashion to others around them
사람들은 자기 주변의 다른 사람들과 다른 방식으로 행동한다
✔ there is a huge difference between acceptance and intelligence
수용과 지성 사이에 큰 차이가 있다

Many people look for safety and security / in popular thinking.
많은 사람이 안전과 안심을 찾는다. / 대중적인 사고에서
They figure / that if a lot of people are doing something, / then it must be right.
그들은 생각한다. / 만약 많은 사람이 뭔가 하고 있다면 / 그것은 틀림없이 옳을 것이라고
It must be a good idea.
그것은 좋은 생각임이 틀림없다.
If most people accept it, / then it probably represents fairness, equality, compassion, and sensitivity, / right?
만약 대부분의 사람들이 그것을 받아들인다면, / 그것은 아마도 공정함, 평등함, 동정심, 그리고 민감성을 상징할 것이다. / 그렇지 않은가?
Not necessarily.
꼭 그렇지는 않다.
Popular thinking said / the earth was the center of the universe, / yet Copernicus studied the stars and planets / and proved mathematically / that the earth and the other planets in our solar system / revolved around the sun.
대중적인 사고는 말했지만, / 지구가 우주의 중심이라고 / Copernicus는 별과 행성을 연구했고 / 수학적으로 증명했다. / 지구와 태양계의 다른 행성들이 / 태양 주위를 돈다는 것을
Popular thinking said / surgery didn't require clean instruments, / yet Joseph Lister studied the high death rates in hospitals / and introduced antiseptic practices / that immediately saved lives.
대중적인 사고는 말했지만, / 수술에 깨끗한 도구가 필요하지 않다고 / Joseph Lister는 병원에서의 높은 사망률을 연구했고 / 멸균법을 소개했다. / 즉시 생명을 구한
Popular thinking said / that women shouldn't have the right to vote, / yet people like Emmeline Pankhurst and Susan B. Anthony / fought for and won that right.
대중적인 사고는 말했지만 / 여성들이 투표권을 가져선 안 된다고 / Emmeline Pankhurst와 Susan B. Anthony 같은 사람들은 / 그 권리를 위해 싸웠고 쟁취했다.
We must always remember / there is a huge difference / between acceptance and intelligence.
우리는 항상 기억해야 한다. / 큰 차이가 있다는 것을 / 수용과 지성 사이에
People may say / that there's safety in numbers, / but that's not always true.
사람들은 말할지도 모르지만, / 수가 많은 편이 더 안전하다고 / 그것이 항상 사실이진 않다.

많은 사람이 대중적인 사고에서 안전과 안심을 찾는다. 그들은 만약 많은 사람이 뭔가 하고 있다면 그것은 틀림없이 옳을 것이라 생각한다. 그것은 좋은 생각임이 틀림없다. 만약 대부분의 사람들이 그것을 받아들인다면, 그것은 아마도 공정함, 평등함, 동정심, 그리고 민감성을 상징할 것이다, 그렇지 않은가? 꼭 그렇지는 않다. 대중적인 사고는 지구가 우주의 중심이라고 했지만, Copernicus는 별과 행성을 연구했고 지구와 태양계의 다른 행성들이 태양 주위를 돈다는 것을 수학적으로 증명했다. 대중적인 사고는 수술에 깨끗한 도구가 필요하지 않다고 말했지만, Joseph Lister는 병원에서의 높은 사망률을 연구했고 즉시 생명을 구한 멸균법을 소개했다. 대중적인 사고는 여성들이 투표권을 가져선 안 된다고 했지만, Emmeline Pankhurst와 Susan B. Anthony 같은 사람들은 그 권리를 위해 싸웠고 쟁취했다. 우리는 항상 수용과 지성 사이에 큰 차이가 있다는 것을 기억해야 한다. 사람들은 수가 많은 편이 더 안전하다고 말할지도 모르지만, 그것이 항상 사실이진 않다.

Why? 왜 정답일까?
많은 사람들이 '받아들이고' 있다고 해서 '합당하고, 공정하고, 맞는' 사실은 아닐 수도 있다(**If most people accept it, then it probably represents fairness, equality, compassion, and sensitivity, right? Not necessarily.**)는 내용이다. 따라서 빈칸에 들어갈 말로 가장 적절한 것은 ⑤ '수용과 지성 사이에 큰 차이가 있다'이다.

- **fairness** ⓝ 공정
- **antiseptic** ⓐ 멸균의
- **surgery** ⓝ 수술
- **be founded on** ~에 근거를 두다

구문 풀이

10행 Popular thinking said (that) surgery didn't require clean instruments, yet Joseph Lister studied the high death rates in hospitals and introduced antiseptic practices [that immediately saved lives].
(생략(접속사) / 동사1 / 동사2 / 선행사 / 주격 관·대)

★★ 문제 해결 꿀~팁 ★★

▶ 많이 틀린 이유는?
글의 핵심은 사람들이 보통 주변 사람들의 사고와 행동을 따르지만, 지식의 발견은 이를 거스를 때 이뤄질 수도 있다는 것이다. 즉 대중적 사고와 진짜 지식이 다를 수 있음을 이해하는 게 중요하다는 것이다. ④를 빈칸에 넣어보면, '사람들이 주변 사람들과 다르게 행동한다'는 것을 기억하라는 의미인데, 이것은 앞서 소개한 사람들의 행동 경향과 반대되며, 지식 발견에 관한 내용과도 무관하다.
▶ 문제 해결 방법은?
정답인 ⑤는 '대중적 사고'를 **acceptance**로 재진술했고, 예시로 든 '과학적 발견과 투표권 쟁취'를 **intelligence**로 일반화했다. 이렇듯 지문 표현을 그대로 반복하는 선택지보다 적절히 재진술하고 일반화한 표현이 답일 확률이 높다.

★★★ 1등급 대비 고난도 3점 문제

12 스타트업의 작동 원칙 — 정답률 32% | 정답 ①

다음 빈칸에 들어갈 말로 가장 적절한 것을 고르시오. [3점]

✔ stay small enough so that you actually can
실제로 그렇게 할 수 있도록 충분히 작은 규모를 유지할
② give yourself challenges as often as possible
스스로에게 가능한 한 자주 도전과제를 줄
③ outperform rival businesses in other countries
다른 국가의 라이벌 기업을 뛰어넘을
④ employ the efficient system of big enterprises
대기업의 효율적 시스템을 이용할
⑤ control the organization with consistent policies
일관적인 정책으로 조직을 통제할

New technology tends to come from new ventures / — startups.
신기술은 새로운 벤처 기업에서 생겨나는 경향이 있다. / 즉 스타트업
From the Founding Fathers in politics / to the Royal Society in science / to Fairchild Semiconductor's "traitorous eight" in business, / small groups of people / bound together by a sense of mission / have changed the world for the better.
정치 분야의 Founding Fathers부터 / 과학 분야의 Royal Society와 / 경영 분야의 Fairchild

Semiconductor의 '8명의 배신자'에 이르기까지, / 소집단의 사람들이 / 사명감에 의해 함께 뭉쳐진 / 세상을 더 나은 방향으로 변화시켜 왔다.

The easiest explanation for this is negative: / it's hard to develop new things in big organizations, / and it's even harder to do it by yourself.
이것에 대한 가장 쉬운 설명은 부정적인 것인데, / 큰 규모의 조직에서는 새로운 것을 개발하기가 어렵고, / 혼자 힘으로 해내기는 훨씬 더 어렵다는 것이다.

Bureaucratic hierarchies move slowly, / and entrenched interests shy away from risk.
관료적인 계급 구조는 느리게 움직이고, / 굳어진 이해관계는 위험을 피하려 한다.

In the most dysfunctional organizations, / signaling that work is being done / becomes a better strategy for career advancement / than actually doing work.
가장 제대로 기능을 하지 않는 조직에서는, / 일이 진행되고 있음을 알리는 것이 / 승진을 위한 더 나은 전략이 된다. / 실제로 일을 진행하는 것보다

At the other extreme, / a lone genius might create a classic work of art or literature, / but he could never create an entire industry.
반대 극단에서는, / 혼자인 천재는 최고 수준의 예술이나 문학 작품을 만들어 낼지는 모르지만, / 절대 산업 전체를 창출해 낼 수는 없다.

Startups operate on the principle / that you need to work with other people / to get stuff done, / but you also need to stay small enough / so that you actually can.
스타트업은 원칙에 따라 작동한다. / 당신이 다른 사람들과 함께 일해야 하지만, / 일을 끝내기 위해 / 충분히 작은 규모를 유지할 필요가 있다는 / 또한 실제로 그렇게 할 수 있도록

신기술은 새로운 벤처 기업, 즉 스타트업에서 생겨나는 경향이 있다. 정치 분야의 Founding Fathers부터 과학 분야의 Royal Society와 경영 분야의 Fairchild Semiconductor의 '8명의 배신자'에 이르기까지, 사명감에 의해 함께 뭉쳐진 소집단의 사람들이 세상을 더 나은 방향으로 변화시켜 왔다. 이것에 대한 가장 쉬운 설명은 부정적인 것인데, 큰 규모의 조직에서는 새로운 것을 개발하기가 어렵고, 혼자 힘으로 해내기는 훨씬 더 어렵다는 것이다. 관료적인 계급 구조는 느리게 움직이고, 굳어진 이해관계는 위험을 피하려 한다. 가장 제대로 기능을 하지 않는 조직에서는, 일이 진행되고 있음을 알리는 것이 실제로 일을 진행하는 것보다 승진을 위한 더 나은 전략이 된다. 반대 극단에서는, 혼자인 천재는 최고 수준의 예술이나 문학 작품을 만들어 낼지는 모르지만, 절대 산업 전체를 창출해 낼 수는 없다. 스타트업은 일을 끝내기 위해 다른 사람들과 함께 일해야 하지만, 또한 실제로 그렇게 할 수 있도록 충분히 작은 규모를 유지할 필요가 있다는 원칙에 따라 작동한다.

Why? 왜 정답일까?

스타트업에서 혁신이 비롯되는 이유를 설명한 글로, '~ small groups of people bound together by a sense of mission have changed the world for the better.'에서 소집단의 강점을 언급한 뒤 대규모 집단과 개인을 소집단과 대비시키고 있다. 'Bureaucratic hierarchies move slowly ~' 이하로 대규모 집단은 위험을 피하고 실제 일을 진행하는 것보다 일을 진행하고 있다고 알리는 데 주력한다는 내용이 나온 데 이어, 'At the other extreme, a lone genius ~' 이하로는 개인의 경우 천재라고 할지라도 산업 전체를 창출하기에는 역부족임을 언급하고 있다. 이를 주제와 연결시키면, 스타트업은 대규모 조직도 개인도 아닌 소규모 집단으로 구성되어 실제적인 혁신을 창출한다는 내용이 빈칸에 들어가야 한다. 따라서 답으로 가장 적절한 것은 ① '실제로 그렇게 할 수 있도록 충분히 작은 규모를 유지할'이다.

- traitorous ⓐ 배신하는
- hierarchy ⓝ 계급, 위계
- dysfunctional ⓐ 제대로 기능하지 않는
- principle ⓝ 원칙
- enterprise ⓝ 기업, 회사
- bureaucratic ⓐ 관료주의의
- shy away from ~을 피하다
- career advancement 승진
- outperform ⓥ 뛰어넘다, 능가하다

구문 풀이

15행 Startups(주어) operate(동사) on the principle [that(동격 접속사) you need to work(동사1) with other people to get stuff done(~하기 위해), but you also need to stay small(동사2) enough so that(부사절 접속사(~하도록)) you actually can].

★★ 문제 해결 꿀~팁 ★★

▶ 많이 틀린 이유는?
스타트업이 작동하는 원리로 소규모 집단의 강점을 설명하고 대규모 집단과 개인을 대비시켜 언급한 뒤 그리하여 스타트업은 소규모를 유지하며 작동한다는 결론을 내린 글이다. 핵심 키워드는 '소집단'인데 최다 오답인 ②는 이를 누락하고 있다.

▶ 문제 해결 방법은?
글의 전체 구조와 핵심 개념을 주의 깊게 파악해야 한다. 스타트업과 소집단의 관계를 이해하면 답을 쉽게 찾을 수 있다.

DAY 08 빈칸 추론 08

01 ①	02 ②	03 ②	04 ④	05 ①
06 ③	07 ①	08 ①	09 ②	10 ②
11 ②	12 ①			

01 생물학적인 경쟁과 경제학적 경쟁의 유사성

정답률 58% | 정답 ①

다음 빈칸에 들어갈 말로 가장 적절한 것을 고르시오. [3점]

✔ similar – 비슷한
② confusing – 혼란스러운
③ unrealistic – 비현실적인
④ conventional – 전통적인
⑤ complex – 복잡한

When Charles Darwin developed his theory of natural selection, / he created a picture of the evolutionary process / in which organismic adaptation was ultimately caused / by competition for survival and reproduction.
Charles Darwin이 자연 선택 이론을 전개했을 때, / 그는 진화 과정 묘사를 만들어냈다. / 유기체의 적응이 결국 야기되는 / 생존과 번식을 위한 경쟁에 의해

This biological "struggle for existence" / bears considerable resemblance / to the human struggle between businessmen / who are striving for economic success in competitive markets.
이 생물학상의 '생존 경쟁'은 / 상당히 닮았다. / 사업자들 간에 일어나는 인간의 분투와 / 경쟁 시장에서 경제적 성공을 얻기 위해 애쓰는

Long before Darwin published his work, / social scientist Adam Smith had already considered / that in business life, / competition is the driving force / behind economic efficiency and adaptation.
Darwin이 연구를 발표하기 오래 전에, / 사회 과학자 Adam Smith는 이미 생각했다. / 사업에서 / 경쟁이 추진력이라고 / 경제적 효율과 적응 이면에 있는

It is indeed very striking / how similar the ideas are / on which the founders of modern theory / in evolutionary biology and economics / based their main thoughts.
정말 매우 놀랍다. / 사상이 얼마나 비슷한가는 / 근대 이론 창시자들이 / 진화 생물학과 경제학의 / 주된 견해의 근거로 둔

Charles Darwin이 자연 선택 이론을 전개했을 때, 그는 유기체의 적응이 결국 생존과 번식을 위한 경쟁에 의해 야기되는 진화 과정을 묘사했다. 이 생물학상의 '생존 경쟁'은 경쟁 시장에서 경제적 성공을 얻기 위해 애쓰는 사업자들 간에 일어나는 인간의 분투와 상당히 닮았다. Darwin이 연구를 발표하기 오래 전에, 사회 과학자 Adam Smith는 이미 사업에서 경쟁이 경제적 효율과 적응 이면에 있는 추진력이라고 생각했다. 진화 생물학과 경제학의 근대 이론 창시자들이 주된 견해의 근거로 둔 사상이 얼마나 비슷한가는 정말 매우 놀랍다.

Why? 왜 정답일까?

'This biological "struggle for existence" bears considerable resemblance to the human struggle between businessmen who are striving for economic success in competitive markets.'에서 생물학의 생존 경쟁 개념은 시장에서 일어나는 인간끼리의 경쟁과 그 양태가 '닮아있다'고 이야기하므로, 빈칸에 들어갈 말로 가장 적절한 것은 ① '비슷한'이다.

- develop ⓥ 전개하다
- organismic ⓐ 유기체의, 생물의
- ultimately ad 결국, 궁극적으로
- struggle ⓥ 투쟁하다
- publish ⓥ 발표하다, 출시하다
- efficiency ⓝ 효율(성)
- natural selection 자연 선택
- adaptation ⓝ 적응
- reproduction ⓝ 번식, 재생
- strive ⓥ 분투하다
- driving force 추진력
- evolutionary ⓐ 진화의

구문 풀이

4행 This biological "struggle for existence" bears considerable(동반 생략 가능) resemblance to(~을 닮다) the human struggle between businessmen [who(주격 관계대명사) are striving for economic success in competitive markets].

02 텍스트성의 확장으로 인한 읽기의 대상 확대

정답률 70% | 정답 ②

다음 빈칸에 들어갈 말로 가장 적절한 것을 고르시오.

① knowledge acquisition – 지식 습득

✔ word recognition – 단어 인식
③ imaginative play – 창의적인 놀이
④ subjective interpretation – 주관적인 해석
⑤ image mapping – 이미지 맵핑

Over the last decade / the attention given to how children learn to read / has foregrounded the nature of *textuality*, / and of the different, interrelated ways / in which readers of all ages make texts mean.
지난 10년 동안 / 어린이가 읽기를 배우는 방법에 관한 관심은 / *텍스트성*의 본질을 전면으로 불러왔다. / 그리고 여러 상호 연관된 방식의 본질을 / 모든 연령대의 독자가 텍스트에 의미를 부여하는
'Reading' now applies to a greater number of representational forms / than at any time in the past: / pictures, maps, screens, design graphics and photographs / are all regarded as text.
'읽기'는 이제 훨씬 더 많은 표현 형식에 적용되어서, / 과거 그 어느 시대보다 / 그림, 지도, 화면, 디자인 그래픽, 사진이 / 모두 텍스트로 여겨진다.
In addition to the innovations / made possible in picture books by new printing processes, / design features also predominate in other kinds, / such as books of poetry and information texts.
혁신에 더해, / 새로운 인쇄 공정으로 그림책에서 가능해진 / 다른 종류에서도 디자인적 특징이 두드러진다. / 시집이나 정보 텍스트와 같은
Thus, / reading becomes a more complicated kind of interpretation / than it was / when children's attention was focused on the printed text, / with sketches or pictures as an adjunct.
이처럼, / 읽기는 더 복잡한 종류의 해석이 된다. / 그것이 그랬던 것보다 / 어린이들의 주의 집중이 인쇄된 텍스트에 집중되던 때 / 스케치나 그림이 부속물로 있고
Children now learn from a picture book / that words and illustrations complement and enhance each other.
이제 어린이들은 그림책을 통해 배운다. / 글과 삽화가 서로를 보완하고 향상시킨다는 것을
Reading is not simply word recognition.
읽기는 단순히 단어 인식이 아니다.
Even in the easiest texts, / what a sentence 'says' is often not what it means.
아무리 쉬운 텍스트에서도 / 흔히 문장이 '말하는' 바가 곧 그 문장의 의미인 것은 아니다.

지난 10년 동안 어린이가 읽기를 배우는 방법에 관한 관심은 *텍스트성*의 본질, 그리고 모든 나이의 독자가 텍스트에 의미를 부여하는 여러 상호 연관된 방식의 본질을 전면으로 불러왔다. '읽기'는 이제 과거 그 어느 시대보다 훨씬 더 많은 표현 형식에 적용되어서, 그림, 지도, 화면, 디자인 그래픽, 사진이 모두 텍스트로 여겨진다. 새로운 인쇄 공정으로 그림책에서 가능해진 혁신에 더해, 시집이나 정보 텍스트와 같은 다른 종류에서도 디자인적 특징이 두드러진다. 이처럼, 읽기는 어린이들의 주의 집중이 인쇄된 텍스트에 집중되고 스케치나 그림이 부속물일 때보다 더 복잡한 종류의 해석이 된다. 이제 어린이들은 그림책을 통해 글과 삽화가 서로를 보완하고 향상시킨다는 것을 배운다. 읽기는 단순히 단어 인식이 아니다. 아무리 쉬운 텍스트에서도 흔히 문장이 '말하는' 바가 곧 그 문장의 의미인 것은 아니다.

Why? 왜 정답일까?

읽기의 범주가 글뿐만 아니라 그림, 지도, 그래픽, 사진 등까지 다양하게 아우르게 되면서('Reading' now applies to a greater number of representational forms ~ pictures, maps, screens, design graphics and photographs are all regarded as text.) 단순히 '문장을 있는 그대로 읽는 것'이 읽기로 여겨지지 않게 되었다(what a sentence 'says' is often not what it means)는 내용이다. 따라서 빈칸에 들어갈 말로 가장 적절한 것은 ② '단어 인식'이다.

- foreground ⓥ 전면에 내세우다
- interrelated ⓐ 상호 연관된
- representational ⓐ 표현의, 나타내는
- in addition to ~에 더해
- poetry ⓝ 시, 운문
- interpretation ⓝ 이해, 해석
- illustration ⓝ 삽화
- enhance ⓥ 향상하다
- recognition ⓝ 인식, 식별
- textuality ⓝ 텍스트성
- apply to ~에 적용되다
- be regarded as ~로 간주되다
- predominate ⓥ 두드러지다, 지배적이다
- complicated ⓐ 복잡한
- adjunct ⓝ 부속물
- complement ⓥ 보완하다
- acquisition ⓝ 습득
- subjective ⓐ 주관적인

구문 풀이

1행 Over the last decade(기간 부사구) the attention(주어) (given(과거분사) to how children learn to read) has foregrounded(동사(현재완료)) the nature of *textuality*, and of the different, interrelated ways(선행사) [in which(「전치사+관·대」) readers of all ages make texts mean].

03 명목 수익을 중시했던 관행의 종식

정답률 49% | 정답 ②

다음 빈칸에 들어갈 말로 가장 적절한 것을 고르시오.

① simplified the Web design process
웹 디자인 과정을 단순화했지만
✔ resulted in no additional cash inflow
부가적인 현금 유입을 초래하지 않았지만
③ decreased the salaries of the employees
직원들의 임금을 떨어뜨렸지만
④ intensified competition among companies
회사들 간 경쟁을 심화시켰지만
⑤ triggered conflicts on the content of Web ads
웹 광고 내용에 관한 갈등을 촉발했지만

Many early dot-com investors focused / almost entirely on revenue growth / instead of net income.
초기의 많은 닷컴 투자자들은 집중했다. / 거의 전적으로 수익 증가에만 / 순이익 대신
Many early dot-com companies / earned most of their revenue / from selling advertising space on their Web sites.
초기의 많은 닷컴 회사들은 / 자신들의 수익 대부분을 벌어들였다. / 웹사이트에 광고를 게재하는 공간을 판매하여
To boost reported revenue, / some sites began exchanging ad space.
보고되는 수익을 끌어올리기 위해, / 몇몇 사이트는 광고 게재 공간을 서로 주고받기 시작했다.
Company A would put an ad for its Web site / on company B's Web site, / and company B would put an ad for its Web site / on company A's Web site.
A 회사는 자기 회사의 웹 사이트 광고를 게시하곤 했고, / B 회사의 웹 사이트에 / B 회사는 자기 회사의 웹 사이트 광고를 게시하곤 했다. / A 회사의 웹 사이트에
No money ever changed hands, / but each company recorded revenue / (for the value of the space / that it gave up on its site) / and expense / (for the value of its ad / that it placed on the other company's site).
돈은 다른 회사에게로 전혀 넘어가지 않았지만, / 각 회사는 수익을 보고했다. / (광고 게재 공간의 가치에 대한 / 그곳이 자기 웹 사이트에서 포기한) / 그리고 비용을 / (광고의 가치에 대한 / 그곳이 타 회사의 사이트에 게재한)
This practice did little to boost net income / and resulted in no additional cash inflow / — but it did boost *reported* revenue.
이러한 관행은 순이익을 끌어올리는 데 거의 효과가 없었고 / 부가적인 현금 유입을 초래하지 않았다 / 그러나 *보고되는* 수익은 정말로 끌어올렸다.
This practice was quickly put to an end / because accountants felt / that it did not meet the criteria of the revenue recognition principle.
이 관행은 빠르게 종식되었다. / 회계사들이 생각했기 때문에 / 이러한 관행이 수익 인식 기준을 충족시키지 못한다고

초기의 많은 닷컴 투자자들은 거의 전적으로 순이익 대신 수익 증가에만 집중했다. 초기의 많은 닷컴 회사들은 수익 대부분을 자신들의 웹사이트에 광고를 게재하는 공간을 판매하여 벌어들였다. *보고되는* 수익을 끌어올리기 위해, 몇몇 사이트는 광고 게재 공간을 서로 주고받기 시작했다. A 회사는 자기 회사의 웹 사이트 광고를 B 회사의 웹 사이트에 게시하곤 했고, B 회사는 자기 회사의 웹 사이트 광고를 A 회사의 웹 사이트에 게시하곤 했다. 돈은 다른 회사에게로 전혀 넘어가지 않았지만, 각 회사는 (자기 웹 사이트에서 포기한 광고 게재 공간의 가치에 대한) 수익과 (타 회사의 사이트에 게재한 광고의 가치에 대한) 비용을 보고했다. 이러한 관행은 순이익을 끌어올리는 데 거의 효과가 없었고 부가적인 현금 유입을 초래하지 않았지만, *보고되는* 수익은 정말로 끌어올렸다. 회계사들이 이러한 관행은 수익 인식 기준을 충족시키지 못한다고 생각했기 때문에 이 관행은 빠르게 종식되었다.

Why? 왜 정답일까?

과거 웹 사이트 회사들이 광고 공간을 팔아 수익을 내다가, 명목상의 수익을 부풀리기 위해 서로 광고 공간을 주고받았던 관행을 설명하는 글이다. 이렇듯 공간을 주고받는 것은 돈의 실제적 이동을 수반하지 않았으며(No money ever changed hands), 순이익의 증가도 이끌어내지 않았다(did little to boost net income)는 설명으로 보아, 빈칸에 들어갈 말로 가장 적절한 것은 '실제적 이득이 없었다'는 의미를 완성하는 ② '부가적인 현금 유입을 초래하지 않았지만'이다.

- investor ⓝ 투자자
- revenue ⓝ 수익
- earn ⓥ 벌다
- put an ad for ~을 위한 광고를 싣다
- do little to ~하는 데 거의 효과가 없다
- accountant ⓝ 회계사
- principle ⓝ 원리
- intensify ⓥ 강화하다
- entirely ad 전적으로
- net income 순이익
- boost ⓥ 신장시키다, 높이다
- give up on ~을 포기하다, 단념하다
- put to an end ~을 끝내다
- criterion ⓝ 기준
- inflow ⓝ 유입
- trigger ⓥ 촉발하다

구문 풀이

4행 To boost reported revenue,(목적(~하려면)) some sites began exchanging(목적어(동명사)) ad space.

04 고객 정보가 가장 중요해진 오늘날 기업들

정답률 42% | 정답 ④

다음 빈칸에 들어갈 말로 가장 적절한 것을 고르시오. [3점]

① its success relies on the number of its innovative products
기업의 성공은 혁신적인 제품의 수에 달려있기
② more customers come through word-of-mouth marketing
더 많은 고객이 입소문 마케팅을 통해 오기
③ it has come to realize the importance of offline stores
기업은 오프라인 매장의 중요성을 깨닫게 되었기
④ the customers are themselves the new value-creation devices
고객 자체가 새로운 가치 창출 장치이기
⑤ questions are raised on the effectiveness of the capitalist system
자본주의 체제의 효율성에 관해 의문이 제기되기

Even companies / that sell physical products to make profit / are forced by their boards and investors / to reconsider their underlying motives / and to collect as much data as possible from consumers.
기업조차도 / 수익을 내기 위해 물적 제품을 판매하는 / 이사회와 투자자에 의해 어쩔 수 없이 ~하게 된다. / 자신의 근원적인 동기를 재고하게 되고 / 고객에게서 가능한 한 많은 정보를 수집하게

Supermarkets no longer make all their money / selling their produce and manufactured goods.
슈퍼마켓은 더 이상 자신의 모든 돈을 버는 것이 아니다. / 자신의 농산물과 제조된 물품을 판매해서

They give you loyalty cards / with which they track your purchasing behaviors precisely.
그들은 고객 우대 카드를 여러분에게 준다. / 여러분의 구매 행동을 정밀하게 추적하게 해 주는

Then supermarkets sell this purchasing behavior / to marketing analytics companies.
그러고 나서 슈퍼마켓은 이 구매 행위를 판매한다. / 마케팅 분석 기업에

The marketing analytics companies / perform machine learning procedures, / slicing the data in new ways, / and resell behavioral data back to product manufacturers / as marketing insights.
마케팅 분석 기업은 / 기계 학습 절차를 수행하고 / 그 정보를 새로운 방식으로 쪼개서 / 행동 정보를 제품 제조 기업에 다시 되판다. / 통찰력 있는 마케팅 정보로

When data and machine learning / become currencies of value in a capitalist system, / then every company's natural tendency / is to maximize its ability / to conduct surveillance on its own customers / because the customers are themselves the new value-creation devices.
정보와 기계 학습이 / 자본주의 체제에서 가치 있는 통화가 될 때, / 모든 기업의 자연스러운 경향은 / 그들의 능력을 최대화하는 것이다. / 자신의 고객을 관찰하는 / 고객 자체가 새로운 가치 창출 장치이기 때문에

수익을 내기 위해 물적 제품을 판매하는 기업조차도 이사회와 투자자에 의해 어쩔 수 없이 자신의 근원적인 동기를 재고하게 되고 고객에게서 가능한 한 많은 정보를 수집하게 된다. 슈퍼마켓은 더 이상 자신의 농산물과 제조된 물품을 판매해서 자신의 모든 돈을 버는 것이 아니다. 그들은 여러분의 구매 행동을 정밀하게 추적하게 해 주는 고객 우대 카드를 여러분에게 준다. 그러고 나서 슈퍼마켓은 이 구매 행위를 마케팅 분석 기업에 판매한다. 마케팅 분석 기업은 기계 학습 절차를 수행하고 그 정보를 새로운 방식으로 쪼개서 행동 정보를 제품 제조 기업에 통찰력 있는 마케팅 정보로 다시 되판다. 정보와 기계 학습이 자본주의 체제에서 가치 있는 통화가 될 때, 고객 자체가 새로운 가치 창출 장치이기 때문에 모든 기업의 자연스러운 경향은 자신의 고객을 관찰하는 능력을 최대화하는 것이다.

Why? 왜 정답일까?

첫 두 문장에서 오늘날 기업들은 가급적 고객 정보를 많이 수집할 수밖에 없는 상황에 처해 있는데 더 이상 제품을 팔아 돈을 버는 시대가 아니기 때문이라고 언급하고 있다. 세 번째 문장부터는 고객의 구매 행위 정보를 추적하고 이를 다시 마케팅 분석에 활용하는 과정이 이루지면서 고객을 관찰하는 행위 자체가 기업의 중대 과업이 되었다는 내용이 이어지고 있다. 이에 근거할 때, 빈칸에 들어갈 말로 가장 적절한 것은 고객 자체가 정보적 가치를 갖게 되었기 때문에 기업들로서는 고객을 관찰하는 능력을 최대화하는 것이 당연하다는 의미를 완성하는 ④ '고객 자체가 새로운 가치 창출 장치이기'이다.

- make profit 수익을 내다
- reconsider ⓥ 재고하다
- underlying ⓐ 근본적인, 기저에 있는
- manufacture ⓥ 제조하다, 생산하다
- precisely ad 정밀하게, 정확히
- analytics ⓝ 분석 (정보)
- procedure ⓝ 절차
- behavioral ⓐ 행동의
- capitalist ⓝ 자본주의(자)
- conduct ⓥ 수행하다
- word-of-mouth ⓐ 구두의, 구전의
- effectiveness ⓝ 효과성

구문 풀이

1행 Even companies [that sell physical products to make profit] (주어, 주격 관계대명사) are forced by their boards and investors to reconsider their underlying motives and to collect as much data as possible from consumers.
「be forced + to부정사1 + to부정사2 : 어쩔 수 없이 ~하고 …하게 되다」

05 새로운 자금 조달 방법이 필요한 사회적 기업

정답률 50% | 정답 ①

다음 빈칸에 들어갈 말로 가장 적절한 것을 고르시오. [3점]

① alternatives to the traditional forms of financing
금융의 전통적 형태들의 대안
② guidelines for promoting employee welfare
직원 복지를 증진시키기 위한 지침
③ measures to protect employees' privacy
직원들의 사생활 보호를 위한 조치
④ departments for better customer service
더 나은 고객 서비스를 위한 부서
⑤ incentives to significantly increase productivity
생산성을 현저히 증가시키는 장려금

In the current landscape, / social enterprises tend to rely / either on grant capital (e.g., grants, donations, or project funding) / or commercial financing products (e.g., bank loans).
현재 상황에서 / 사회적 기업들은 의존하는 경향이 있다. / 보조금 자본(예를 들어, 보조금, 기부금, 혹은 프로젝트 기금) / 또는 상업 금융 상품(예를 들어, 은행 대출)에

Ironically, / many social enterprises / at the same time / report of significant drawbacks / related to each of these two forms of financing.
아이러니하게도, / 많은 사회적 기업들은 / 동시에 / 중대한 결점을 보고한다. / 이러한 자금 조달의 두 가지 형태 각각에 관련된

Many social enterprises are for instance reluctant / to make use of traditional commercial finance products, / fearing / that they might not be able to pay back the loans.
예를 들어, 많은 사회적 기업들은 꺼린다. / 전통적인 상업 금융 상품들을 이용하는 것을 / 두려워하여 / 그들이 대출금을 상환하지 못할 수 있다는 것을

In addition, / a significant number of social enterprise leaders report / that relying too much on grant funding / can be a risky strategy / since individual grants are time limited / and are not reliable in the long term.
게다가 / 상당히 많은 사회적 기업 리더들은 말한다. / 보조금 조달에 너무 많이 의존하는 것은 / 위험한 전략일 수 있다고 / 개별적 보조금들은 시간 제한적이고 / 장기적으로는 신뢰할 수 없으므로

Grant funding can also lower the incentive / for leaders and employees / to professionalize the business aspects, / thus leading to unhealthy business behavior.
보조금 조달은 또한 동기를 낮출 수 있고, / 리더들과 직원들이 / 사업적인 면들을 전문화하려는 / 그로 인해 건강하지 않은 사업 행위를 초래한다.

In other words, / there seems to be a substantial need / among social enterprises / for alternatives to the traditional forms of financing.
다시 말해서, / 상당한 필요가 있는 것처럼 보인다. / 사회적 기업들 사이에서 / 금융의 전통적 형태들의 대안에 대한

현재 상황에서 사회적 기업들은 보조금 자본(예를 들어, 보조금, 기부금, 혹은 프로젝트 기금) 또는 상업 금융 상품(예를 들어, 은행 대출)에 의존하는 경향이 있다. 아이러니하게도, 많은 사회적 기업들은 동시에 이러한 자금 조달의 두 가지 형태 각각에 관련된 중대한 결점을 보고한다. 예를 들어, 많은 사회적 기업들은 대출금을 상환하지 못할 수 있다는 것을 두려워하여 전통적인 상업 금융 상품들을 이용하는 것을 꺼린다. 게다가 개별적 보조금들은 시간 제한적이고 장기적으로는 신뢰할 수 없으므로 상당히 많은 사회적 기업 리더들은 보조금 조달에 너무 많이 의존하는 것은 위험한 전략일 수 있다고 말한다. 보조금 조달은 또한 리더들과 직원들이 사업적인 면들을 전문화하려는 동기를 낮출 수 있고, 그로 인해 건강하지 않은 사업 행위를 초래한다. 다시 말해서, 사회적 기업들 사이에서 금융의 전통적 형태들의 대안에 대한 상당한 필요가 있는 것처럼 보인다.

Why? 왜 정답일까?

'Ironically, many social enterprises at the same time report of significant drawbacks related to each of these two forms of financing.'에 따르면 사회적 기업들은 두 가지 전통적인 자금 조달 형태에 중대한 결점이 있음을 지적한다고 한다. 이를 근거로 할 때, 빈칸에 들어갈 말로 가장 적절한 것은 새로운 자금 조달 형태가 필요할 것이라는 의미를 완성하는 ① '금융의 전통적 형태들의 대안'이다.

- enterprise ⓝ 기업
- ironically ad 반어적으로
- significant ⓐ 중대한, 중요한, 상당한
- drawback ⓝ 결점
- reluctant ⓐ 꺼리는, 마지못해 하는
- rely on ~에 의존하다
- reliable ⓐ 신뢰할 수 있는
- professionalize ⓥ 전문화하다
- substantial ⓐ 상당한
- alternative ⓝ 대안
- welfare ⓝ 복지
- productivity ⓝ 생산성

구문 풀이

9행 In addition, a significant number of social enterprise leaders (주어「a + (형용사) + number of + 복수 명사 : (~하게) 많은 …」) report (동사(복수)) that (접속사(~것)) relying too much on grant funding (동명사구 주어) can be (동사) a risky strategy (주격 보어) since (접속사(~이기 때문에)) individual grants are time limited and are not reliable in the long term.

06 마시멜로를 이용한 행동 통제 실험

정답률 52% | 정답 ③

다음 빈칸에 들어갈 말로 가장 적절한 것을 고르시오. [3점]

① change their habit – 자신의 습관을 바꾸기
② get more things done – 더 많은 일을 해내기
③ regulate their behavior – 자신의 행동을 통제하기
④ build their self-esteem – 자존감을 형성하기
⑤ improve their speaking skills – 말하기 능력을 향상시키기

In one experiment, children were told / they could have one marshmallow treat / if they chose to eat it immediately, / but two treats if they waited.
한 실험에서 아이들은 말을 들었다. / 마시멜로 과자 하나를 먹을 수 있지만, / 그들이 그것을 즉시 먹기로 선택하면 / 그들이 기다리면 두 개를 먹을 수 있다는

Most of the children, who ranged in age from 4 to 8, / chose to wait, / but the strategies they used differed significantly.
4세에서 8세에 이르는 아이 대부분은 / 기다리는 것을 선택했지만, / 그들이 사용한 전략은 상당히 달랐다.

The 4-year-olds often chose / to look at the marshmallows while waiting, / a strategy that was not terribly effective.
4세 아이들은 흔히 선택했다. / 기다리면서 마시멜로를 쳐다보는 것을 / (그것은) 그다지 효과적이지는 않은 전략(이었다.)

In contrast, 6- and 8-year-olds used language / to help overcome temptation, / although in different ways.
그에 반해서, 6세와 8세 아이들은 언어를 사용했다. / 유혹을 이겨내는 데 도움을 얻기 위해 / 방법은 서로 달랐어도

The 6-year-olds spoke and sang to themselves, / reminding themselves / they would get more treats if they waited.
6세 아이들은 혼잣말을 하고 노래를 흥얼거렸다. / 자신에게 상기시키며, / 기다리면 더 많은 과자를 얻게 될 거라

The 8-year-olds focused on aspects of the marshmallows / unrelated to taste, such as appearance, / which helped them to wait.
8세 아이들은 마시멜로의 측면들에 집중했는데, / 겉모습과 같이 맛과 무관한 / 이것은 그들이 기다리는 데 도움을 주었다.

In short, / children used "self-talk" to regulate their behavior.
요컨대, / 아이들은 자신의 행동을 통제하기 위해 '혼잣말'을 사용했다.

한 실험에서 아이들은 마시멜로 과자를 즉시 먹기로 선택하면 과자 하나를 먹을 수 있지만, 기다리면 두 개를 먹을 수 있다는 말을 들었다. 4세에서 8세에 이르는 아이 대부분은 기다리는 것을 선택했지만, 그들이 사용한 전략은 상당히 달랐다. 4세 아이들은 기다리면서 마시멜로를 쳐다보는 것을 흔히 선택했는데, 그 전략은 그다지 효과적이지는 않았다. 그에 반해서, 6세와 8세 아이들은 방법은 서로 달랐어도 유혹을 이겨내는 데 도움을 얻기 위해 언어를 사용했다. 6세 아이들은 기다리면 더 많은 과자를 얻게 될 거라 자신에게 상기시키며, 혼잣말을 하고 노래를 흥얼거렸다. 8세 아이들은 겉모습과 같이 맛과 무관한 마시멜로의 측면들에 집중했는데, 이것은 그들이 기다리는 데 도움을 주었다. 요컨대, 아이들은 자신의 행동을 통제하기 위해 '혼잣말'을 사용했다.

Why? 왜 정답일까?

'**In contrast, 6- and 8-year-olds used language to help overcome temptation, although in different ways.**'에서 마시멜로 실험에 참가한 아이들은 (마시멜로를 먹고 싶은) 유혹을 참기 위해, 즉 먹는 행동을 막고 기다리는 행동을 지속하기 위해 언어를 사용했다고 말하므로, 빈칸에 들어갈 말로 가장 적절한 것은 ③ '자신의 행동을 통제하기'이다.

- **strategy** ⓝ 전략
- **significantly** ad 상당히
- **overcome** ⓥ 이겨 내다, 극복하다
- **temptation** ⓝ 유혹
- **remind** ⓥ 상기시키다
- **aspect** ⓝ 측면, 국면, 양상
- **unrelated** ⓐ 관련 없는
- **self-talk** 혼잣말

구문 풀이

8행 In contrast, 6- and 8-year-olds used language / to help(부사적 용법(목적)) overcome(원형부정사) temptation, / although(양보 접속사(비록 ~일지라도)) (they did)(생략) in different ways.

07 경험에 따라 발달하는 뇌

정답률 48% | 정답 ①

다음 빈칸에 들어갈 말로 가장 적절한 것을 고르시오. [3점]

① sculpted by our own history of experiences
우리 자신의 경험 이력에 의해 만들어진다
② designed to maintain their initial structures
그것의 최초의 구조를 유지하도록 설계된다
③ geared toward strengthening recent memories
최근의 기억을 강화하도록 조정된다
④ twinned with the development of other organs
다른 기관의 발달과 밀접히 연결된다
⑤ portrayed as the seat of logical and creative thinking
논리적이고 창의적인 사고가 일어나는 장소로 그려진다

Thanks to newly developed neuroimaging technology, / we now have access to the specific brain changes / that occur during learning.
새롭게 개발된 신경 촬영 기술 덕분에, / 우리는 이제 특정한 뇌 변화에 접근할 수 있게 되었다. / 학습 중에 일어나는

Even though all of our brains contain the same basic structures, / our neural networks are as unique as our fingerprints.
모든 뇌는 같은 기본 구조를 가지고 있음에도 불구하고, / 우리의 신경망은 우리의 지문만큼이나 독특하다.

The latest developmental neuroscience research has shown / that the brain is much more malleable throughout life / than previously assumed; / it develops in response to its own processes, / to its immediate and distant "environments," / and to its past and current situations.
가장 최신의 발달 신경 과학 연구는 보여 주는데, / 뇌가 평생 동안 훨씬 더 순응성이 있다는 것을 / 이전에 가정된 것보다도 / 뇌는 자기만의 처리 과정에 반응하여 발달한다. / 자신에게 인접한 '환경'과 멀리 떨어진 '환경'에, / 그리고 자신의 과거와 현재의 상황에

The brain seeks to create meaning / through establishing or refining existing neural networks.
뇌는 의미를 창조하려고 한다. / 기존의 신경망을 확립하거나 개선하여

When we learn a new fact or skill, / our neurons communicate to form networks of connected information.
우리가 새로운 사실이나 기술을 배울 때, / 우리의 뉴런들은 연결된 정보망을 형성하기 위해 소통한다.

Using this knowledge or skill / results in structural changes / to allow similar future impulses / to travel more quickly and efficiently than others.
이러한 지식이나 기술을 사용하는 것은 / 구조적 변화를 가져온다. / 앞으로 유사한 자극이 ~하게 하는 / 다른 것들보다 더 빠르고 효율적으로 이동할 수 있게

High-activity synaptic connections are stabilized and strengthened, / while connections with relatively low use are weakened and eventually pruned.
고활동성 시냅스 연결이 안정화되고 강화된다. / 상대적으로 적게 사용되는 연결은 약해져서 결국에는 잘리는 반면

In this way, / our brains are sculpted by our own history of experiences.
이런 식으로, / 우리의 뇌는 우리 자신의 경험 이력에 의해 만들어진다.

새롭게 개발된 신경 촬영 기술 덕분에, 우리는 이제 학습 중에 일어나는 특정한 뇌 변화에 접근할 수 있게 되었다. 모든 뇌는 같은 기본 구조를 가지고 있음에도 불구하고, 우리의 신경망은 우리의 지문만큼이나 독특하다. 가장 최신의 발달 신경 과학 연구는 이전에 가정된 것보다도 뇌가 평생 동안 훨씬 더 순응성이 있다는 것을 보여 주는데, 뇌는 자기만의 처리 과정에, 자신에게 인접한 '환경'과 멀리 떨어진 '환경'에, 자신의 과거와 현재의 상황에 반응하여 발달한다. 뇌는 기존의 신경망을 확립하거나 개선하여 의미를 창조하려고 한다. 우리가 새로운 사실이나 기술을 배울 때, 우리의 뉴런들은 연결된 정보망을 형성하기 위해 소통한다. 이러한 지식이나 기술을 사용하는 것은 앞으로 유사한 자극이 다른 것들보다 더 빠르고 효율적으로 이동할 수 있게 하는 구조적 변화를 가져온다. 고활동성 시냅스 연결이 안정화되고 강화되는 반면에, 상대적으로 적게 사용되는 연결은 약해져서 결국에는 잘린다. 이런 식으로, 우리의 뇌는 우리 자신의 경험 이력에 의해 만들어진다.

Why? 왜 정답일까?

세 번째 문장과 네 번째 문장에서 뇌는 특유의 처리 과정과 환경과 과거 및 현재 상황에 맞추어 발달하며, 기존의 신경망을 확립하거나 개선하는 방식으로 의미를 창조한다(**The brain seeks to create meaning through establishing or refining existing neural networks.**)고 설명하고 있다. 이를 근거로 볼 때, 뇌가 지문만큼이나 고유해지는 이유는 결국 우리 각자의 경험이 반영되기 때문이라는 결론을 내릴 수 있다. 따라서 빈칸에 들어갈 말로 가장 적절한 것은 ① '우리 자신의 경험 이력에 의해 만들어진다'이다.

- **neural** ⓐ 신경의
- **previously** ad 이전에
- **establish** ⓥ 확립하다
- **refine** ⓥ 개선하다
- **existing** ⓐ 기존의
- **impulse** ⓝ 자극
- **stabilize** ⓥ 안정화하다
- **sculpt** ⓥ 조각하다, 형상을 만들다
- **geared A toward B** A를 B에 맞춰 조정하다

구문 풀이

5행 The latest developmental neuroscience research(주어1) has shown(동사1) that(접속사(~것)) the brain is much(비교급 강조(훨씬)) more malleable(보어(비교급 형용사)) throughout life than previously assumed; it(주어2) develops(동사2) in response to(~에 반응하여) its own processes, (in response)(생략) to its immediate and distant "environments," and (in response)(생략) to its past and current situations.

★★★ 1등급 대비 고난도 2점 문제

08 다른 사람의 도움이 자존감에 해가 되는 순간 정답률 44% | 정답 ①

다음 빈칸에 들어갈 말로 가장 적절한 것을 고르시오.

① make you feel bad about yourself
당신이 스스로를 안 좋게 느끼도록 만들
② improve your ability to deal with challenges
어려움에 대처하는 능력을 높여줄
③ be seen as a way of asking for another favor
또 다른 부탁을 하는 방법으로 여겨질
④ trick you into thinking that you were successful
스스로 성공했다고 착각하게 할
⑤ discourage the person trying to model your behavior
당신의 행동을 본보기로 삼으려는 사람을 낙담시킬

There are several reasons / why support may not be effective.
몇몇 이유들이 있다. / 도움이 효과적이지 않을 수 있는

One possible reason is / that receiving help could be a blow to self-esteem.
한 가지 가능한 이유는 / 도움을 받는 것이 자존감에 타격이 될 수 있다는 것이다.

A recent study by Christopher Burke and Jessica Goren at Lehigh University / examined this possibility.
Lehigh 대학의 Christopher Burke와 Jessica Goren에 의한 최근 한 연구는 / 이 가능성을 조사했다.

According to the threat to self-esteem model, / help can be perceived as supportive and loving, / or it can be seen as threatening / if that help is interpreted as implying incompetence.
자존감 위협 모델 이론에 따르면, / 도움은 협력적이고 애정 있는 것으로 여겨질 수도 있고, / 혹은 그것은 위협적으로 보여질 수도 있다. / 만약 그 도움이 무능함을 암시하는 것으로 해석된다면

According to Burke and Goren, / support is especially likely to be seen as threatening / if it is in an area that is self-relevant or self-defining / — that is, in an area / where your own success and achievement are especially important.
Burke와 Goren에 따르면 / 도움은 특히 위협으로 보여질 가능성이 있다. / 그것이 자기 연관적이거나 자기 정의적인 영역 안에 있는 경우 / 다시 말해, 영역에서 / 자신의 성공과 성취가 특히 중요한

Receiving help with a self-relevant task / can make you feel bad about yourself, / and this can undermine the potential positive effects of the help.
자기 연관적인 일로 도움을 받는 것은 / 당신이 스스로를 안 좋게 느끼도록 만들 수 있고, / 이것은 도움의 잠재적인 긍정적 영향에 해를 줄 수 있다.

For example, / if your self-concept rests, in part, on your great cooking ability, / it may be a blow to your ego / when a friend helps you prepare a meal for guests / because it suggests / that you're not the master chef you thought you were.
예를 들어, / 만약 당신의 자아 개념이 훌륭한 요리 실력에 일부 기초한다면, / 이는 당신의 자아에 타격이 될 수 있는데 / 친구가 당신이 손님들을 위해 식사를 준비하는 것을 도울 때 / 이는 암시하기 때문이다. / 당신이 생각했던 만큼 유능한 요리사가 아니라는 것을

도움이 효과적이지 않을 수 있는 몇몇 이유들이 있다. 한 가지 가능한 이유는 도움을 받는 것이 자존감에 타격이 될 수 있다는 것이다. Lehigh 대학의 Christopher Burke와 Jessica Goren에 의한 최근 한 연구는 이 가능성을 조사했다. 자존감 위협 모델 이론에 따르면, 도움은 협력적이고 애정 있는 것으로 여겨질 수도 있고, 혹은 만약 그 도움이 무능함을 암시하는 것으로 해석된다면 위협적으로 보여질 수 있다. Burke와 Goren에 따르면 도움이 자기 연관적이거나 자기 정의적인 영역 — 다시 말해, 자신의 성공과 성취가 특히 중요한 영역 — 안에 있는 경우, 그것은 특히 위협으로 보여질 가능성이 있다. 자기 연관적인 일로 도움을 받는 것은 당신이 스스로를 안 좋게 느끼도록 만들 수 있고, 이것은 도움의 잠재적인 긍정적 영향에 해를 줄 수 있다. 예를 들어, 만약 당신의 자아 개념이 훌륭한 요리 실력에 일부 기초한다면, 친구가 당신이 손님들을 위해 식사를 준비하는 것을 도울 때 이는 당신의 자아에 타격이 될 수 있는데 이는 당신이 생각했던 만큼 유능한 요리사가 아니라는 뜻이기 때문이다.

Why? 왜 정답일까?

도움이 효과적이지 않은 순간 중 하나는 도움이 자존감에 타격을 줄 때(One possible reason is that receiving help could be a blow to self-esteem.)임을 설명하는 글이므로, 빈칸에 들어갈 말로 가장 적절한 것은 ① '당신이 스스로를 안 좋게 느끼도록 만들'이다.

- blow ⓝ 타격, 충격
- threat ⓝ 위협
- self-relevant ⓐ 자아 관련의
- self-concept ⓝ 자아 개념
- trick A into B A를 속여 B하게 하다
- self-esteem ⓝ 자아 존중감
- incompetence ⓝ 무능
- undermine ⓥ 손상시키다
- rest on ~에 놓여 있다
- discourage ⓥ 낙담시키다

구문 풀이

17행 ~ it may be a blow to your ego when a friend helps you prepare a meal for guests because it suggests that you're not the master chef [(you thought) you were]. [ ]: 형용사절
선행사 / 삽입절 / (were의 보어가 없는 불완전한 절)

★★ 문제 해결 꿀~팁 ★★

▶ 많이 틀린 이유는?

'~ support is especially likely to be seen as threatening ~' 문장에서 과업의 자기 관련성이 높은(self-relevant or self-defining) 경우 타인의 도움이 오히려 위협으로 여겨질 수 있다고 한다. ②의 경우, 이런 과업에서 타인의 도움을 받으면 위기 대처 능력이 '향상된다'는 의미이므로 주제와 정반대된다. ④는 자기 관련성이 높은 과업에서 타인의 도움을 받을 때 '우리가 성공했다는 착각에 빠질 수 있다'는 의미인데, 성공에 대한 착각은 글에서 언급되지 않았다.

▶ 문제 해결 방법은?

마지막 문장의 a blow to your ego를 ①에서 feel bad abour yourself로 바꾸었다.

★★★ 1등급 대비 고난도 2점 문제

09 생물 다양성에 대한 인식을 돕는 유전 공학 정답률 32% | 정답 ②

다음 빈칸에 들어갈 말로 가장 적절한 것을 고르시오.

① ecological systems are genetically programmed
생태계는 유전적으로 프로그램되어 있다
② we should avoid destroying natural ecosystems
우리가 자연 생태계를 파괴하는 것을 피해야 한다
③ we need to stop creating genetically modified organisms
우리가 유전자 변형 유기체를 만드는 것을 중단할 필요가 있다
④ artificial organisms can survive in natural environments
인위적인 유기체는 자연환경에서 생존할 수 있다
⑤ living things adapt themselves to their physical environments
살아있는 것들은 자신의 물리적 환경에 적응한다

Genetic engineering followed by cloning / to distribute many identical animals or plants / is sometimes seen as a threat to the diversity of nature.
복제로 이어지는 유전 공학은 / 많은 똑같은 동물이나 식물을 퍼뜨리기 위한 / 때때로 자연의 다양성에 대한 위협으로 여겨진다.

However, / humans have been replacing diverse natural habitats / with artificial monoculture / for millennia.
그러나 / 인간은 다양한 자연 서식지를 대체해 오고 있다. / 인위적인 단일 경작으로 / 수천 년 동안

Most natural habitats in the advanced nations / have already been replaced / with some form of artificial environment / based on mass production or repetition.
선진국 자연 서식지의 대부분은 / 이미 대체되었다. / 어떤 형태의 인위적인 환경으로 / 대량 생산 또는 반복에 기반을 둔

The real threat to biodiversity / is surely the need to convert ever more of our planet into production zones / to feed the ever-increasing human population.
생물 다양성에 대한 진정한 위협은 / 지구의 더욱더 많은 부분을 생산지대로 전환해야 할 필요성임이 확실하다. / 계속 늘어나는 인구에 식량을 공급하기 위해서

The cloning and transgenic alteration of domestic animals / makes little difference to the overall situation.
가축의 복제와 이식 유전자에 의한 변형은 / 전반적인 상황에 거의 변화를 주지 않는다.

Conversely, / the renewed interest in genetics / has led to a growing awareness / that there are many wild plants and animals with interesting or useful genetic properties / that could be used for a variety of as-yet-unknown purposes.
반대로, / 유전학에 관한 새로워진 관심은 / 인식을 점점 키웠다. / 흥미롭거나 유용한 유전 특성을 가진 많은 야생 동식물이 있다는 / 아직 알려지지 않은 다양한 목적을 위해서 이용될 수 있는

This has led in turn to a realization / that we should avoid destroying natural ecosystems / because they may harbor tomorrow's drugs against cancer, malaria, or obesity.
이것은 결국 깨닫게 해 주었다. / 우리가 자연 생태계를 파괴하는 것을 피해야 한다는 것을 / 자연 생태계가 암, 말라리아 또는 비만을 치료하는 미래의 약을 품고 있을 수도 있기 때문에

많은 똑같은 동물이나 식물을 퍼뜨리기 위한 복제로 이어지는 유전 공학은 때때로 자연의 다양성에 대한 위협으로 여겨진다. 그러나 인간은 수천 년 동안 인위적인 단일 경작으로 다양한 자연 서식지를 대체해 오고 있다. 선진국 자연 서식지의 대부분은 대량 생산 또는 반복에 기반을 둔 어떤 형태의 인위적인 환경으로 이미 대체되었다. 생물 다양성에 대한 진정한 위협은 계속 늘어나는 인구에 식량을 공급하기 위해서 지구의 더욱더 많은 부분을 생산지대로 전환해야 할 필요성임이 확실하다. 가축의 복제와 이식 유전자에 의한 변형은 전반적인 상황에 거의 변화를 주지 않는다. 반대로, 유전학에 관한 새로워진 관심은 아직 알려지지 않은 다양한 목적을 위해서 이용될 수 있는 흥미롭거나 유용한 유전 특성을 가진 많은 야생 동식물이 있다는 인식을 점점 키웠다. 이것은 결국 자연 생태계가 암, 말라리아 또는 비만을 치료하는 미래의 약을 품고 있을 수도 있기 때문에 우리가 자연 생태계를 파괴하는 것을 피해야 한다는 것을 깨닫게 해 주었다.

DAY 08

[문제편 p.054]

Why? 왜 정답일까?

첫 문장에서 유전 공학의 발전은 흔히 생물 다양성에 대한 위협으로 인식된다는 통념을 제시한 후 이를 반박한 글이다. 특히 'Conversely, the renewed interest in genetics has led to a growing awareness that there are many wild plants and animals with interesting or useful genetic properties that could be used for a variety of as-yet-unknown purposes.'에서는 유전학에 대한 관심이 커지면서 오히려 인간은 아직 알려지지 못한 유용한 생물 종들이 있음을 인식하게 된다고 설명하는 것으로 볼 때, 빈칸에는 유전 공학이 발전함에 따라 '생물 다양성에 대한 사람들의 인식이 높아질 수 있다'는 내용이 들어가야 한다. 따라서 빈칸에 들어갈 말로 가장 적절한 것은 '생물 다양성 보존'을 '생태계 파괴 방지'라는 말로 바꾸어 표현한 ② '우리가 자연 생태계를 파괴하는 것을 피해야 한다'이다.

- genetic ⓐ 유전학의, 유전적인
- distribute ⓥ 퍼뜨리다, 분배하다
- artificial ⓐ 인위적인
- biodiversity ⓝ 생물 다양성
- transgenic ⓐ 이식 유전자를 가진
- property ⓝ 특성
- harbor ⓥ (계획이나 생각을) 품다
- clone ⓥ 복제하다
- identical ⓐ 똑같은, 동일한
- mass production ⓝ 대량 생산
- ever-increasing ⓐ 계속 늘어나는
- alteration ⓝ 변형
- as-yet-unknown ⓐ 아직 알려지지 않은
- obesity ⓝ 비만

구문 풀이

13행 Conversely, the renewed interest in genetics has led to a growing awareness that there are many wild plants and animals with interesting or useful genetic properties [that could be used for a variety of as-yet-unknown purposes].
(that: 동격(= awareness) / are: 동사 / many wild plants and animals: 주어(복수) / genetic properties: 선행사 / that: 주격 관계대명사)

★★ 문제 해결 꿀~팁 ★★

▶ 많이 틀린 이유는?
이 글은 통념과는 달리 유전 공학이 발전하면 사람들이 여태까지 미지의 영역 안에 있었던 다양한 생물군에 대해 알게 되면서 오히려 생물 다양성의 가치에 대한 인식을 높일 수 있다는 내용을 다루고 있다. ③은 '유전자 변형 생물의 생산 중단'을 언급하고 있는데, 이는 유전 공학 기술을 부정적으로 보는 시각과 더 관련되어 있어 답으로 적절치 않다. ④의 '인공 유기체의 생존'에 관해서는 글에서 언급되지 않았다.
▶ 문제 해결 방법은?
Conversely 이하로 필자의 핵심 주장이 전개된다. 유전 공학의 발전은 도리어 다양한 생물에 대한 관심을 일깨운다는 내용으로 볼 때, 사람들이 '다양한 생물 종을 보존해야 한다=생태계 파괴를 멈춰야 한다'는 결론에 이르게 된다는 내용이 이어져야 한다.

★★★ 1등급 대비 고난도 3점 문제

10 아이의 혼자 있을 수 있는 능력의 발달 정답률 26% | 정답 ②

다음 빈칸에 들어갈 말로 가장 적절한 것을 고르시오. [3점]

① Hardship – 고난
✔ Attachment – 애착
③ Creativity – 창의력
④ Compliment – 칭찬
⑤ Responsibility – 책임감

Children develop the capacity for solitude / in the presence of an attentive other.
아이들은 혼자 있을 수 있는 능력을 발달시킨다. / 관심을 가져주는 타인이 있을 때
Consider the silences that fall / when you take a young boy on a quiet walk in nature.
다가오는 고요를 생각해 보아라. / 여러분이 어린 아이를 자연에서 조용히 산책시킬 때
The child comes to feel increasingly aware / of what it is to be alone in nature, / supported by being "with" someone / who is introducing him to this experience.
그 아이는 점점 알아 간다고 느끼게 된다. / 자연 속에서 혼자 있는 것이 어떤 것인지에 대해 / 누군가와 '함께' 있다는 것에 도움을 받아, / 그에게 이러한 경험을 처음으로 하게 한
Gradually, the child takes walks alone.
점차적으로, 그 아이는 혼자 산책한다.
Or imagine a mother / giving her two-year-old daughter a bath, / allowing the girl's reverie with her bath toys / as she makes up stories / and learns to be alone with her thoughts, / all the while knowing her mother is present and available to her.
또는 엄마를 생각해 보아라. / 또는 두 살짜리 딸아이를 목욕시키는 / 아이가 목욕 장난감을 가지고 공상에 잠길 수 있게 하는 것을 / 아이가 이야기를 만들고 / 생각을 하며 혼자 있는 법을 배우면서 / 딸이 엄마가 함께 있고 자신에게 시간을 내어줄 수 있다는 것을 내내 아는 상태로
Gradually, the bath, taken alone, / is a time when the child is comfortable with her imagination.
점차적으로, 혼자서 하는 목욕은 / 그 아이가 상상을 하며 편안해 하는 시간이 된다.
Attachment enables solitude.
애착은 혼자 있는 것을 가능하게 한다.

아이들은 관심을 가져주는 타인이 있을 때 혼자 있을 수 있는 능력을 발달시킨다. 여러분이 어린 아이를 자연에서 조용히 산책시킬 때 다가오는 고요를 생각해 보아라. 그 아이는, 그에게 이러한 경험을 처음으로 하게 한 누군가와 '함께' 있다는 것에 도움을 받아, 자연 속에서 혼자 있는 것이 어떤 것인지에 대해 점점 알아 간다고 느끼게 된다. 점차적으로, 그 아이는 혼자 산책한다. 또는 두 살짜리 딸아이를 목욕시키는 엄마가, 딸이 엄마가 함께 있고 자신에게 시간을 내어줄 수 있다는 것을 내내 아는 상태로 이야기를 만들고 생각을 하며 혼자 있는 법을 배우면서 목욕 장난감을 가지고 공상에 잠길 수 있게 하는 것을 생각해 보아라. 점차적으로, 혼자서 하는 목욕은 그 아이가 상상을 하며 편안해 하는 시간이 된다. 애착은 혼자 있는 것을 가능하게 한다.

Why? 왜 정답일까?

첫 문장인 'Children develop the capacity for solitude in the presence of an attentive other.'에서 아이들은 관심을 주는 타인이 있을 때 혼자 있을 수 있게 된다는 핵심 내용이 제시되므로, 빈칸에 들어갈 말로 가장 적절한 것은 ② '애착'이다.

- solitude ⓝ 혼자 있음, 고독
- attentive ⓐ 관심을 가져주는
- gradually ad 점차적으로
- presence ⓝ 존재
- increasingly ad 점점
- available ⓐ (사람이) 시간이 있는

구문 풀이

7행 Or imagine a mother giving her two-year-old daughter a bath, allowing the girl's reverie with her bath toys as she makes up stories and learns to be alone with her thoughts, all the while knowing (that) her mother is present and available to her.
(명령문「imagine+목적어+현재분사 : ~이 …하는 것을 상상하다」 / allowing: 분사구문1(a mother 설명) / as: ~하면서 / makes up: 동사1 / learns: 동사2 / knowing: 분사구문2(the girl 설명) / (that): 접속사(생략))

★★ 문제 해결 꿀~팁 ★★

▶ 많이 틀린 이유는?
글 중간의 예시에 주목하면 ③ '창의력'이 답처럼 보일 수 있다. 하지만 주제문인 첫 문장에서 관심 있는 타인의 존재를 중요하게 언급하는 것으로 볼 때 이는 답으로 부적절하다.
▶ 문제 해결 방법은?
빈칸 문제에서 빈칸은 글의 주제와 관련되어 있다. 따라서 이 글처럼 '주제 – 예시' 구조로 이루어진 글에서는 주제문인 첫 문장을 근거로 답을 찾아야 한다. 또한, 예시에서도 'being "with" someone'이라는 키워드를 제시하고 있다.

★★★ 1등급 대비 고난도 3점 문제

11 인간의 인지 작용 정답률 33% | 정답 ②

다음 빈칸에 들어갈 말로 가장 적절한 것을 고르시오. [3점]

① tend to favor learners with great social skills
사교성이 뛰어난 학습자를 선호하는 경향이 있다
✔ are marked by a steady elimination of information
정보의 지속적인 제거로 특징지어진다
③ require an external aid to support our memory capacity
우리 기억력을 보조하고자 외부의 도움을 필요로 한다
④ are determined by the accuracy of incoming information
유입되는 정보의 정확성에 의해 결정된다
⑤ are facilitated by embracing chaotic situations as they are
혼돈의 상황을 있는 그대로 받아들이는 것으로부터 촉진된다

Much of human thought / is designed to screen out information / and to sort the rest into a manageable condition.
인간 사고의 많은 부분은 / 정보를 걸러내도록 설계된다. / 그리고 나머지는 처리하기 쉬운 상태로 분류하도록
The inflow of data from our senses / could create an overwhelming chaos, / especially given the enormous amount of information / available in culture and society.
우리 감각에서 오는 데이터의 유입은 / 압도적인 혼란을 낳을 수 있다. / 특히 엄청난 양의 정보를 고려할 때, / 문화와 사회에서 이용할 수 있는
Out of all the sensory impressions and possible information, / it is vital / to find a small amount / that is most relevant to our individual needs / and to organize that into a usable stock of knowledge.
모든 감각적 인상과 가능한 정보 중에서, / 중요하다. / 적은 양을 찾는 것이 / 우리의 개인적인 필요와 가장 관련이 있는 / 그리고 그것을 사용 가능한 지식체로 구성하는 것이
Expectancies accomplish some of this work, / helping to screen out information / that is irrelevant to what is expected, / and focusing our attention on clear contradictions.

예상들은 이 작업의 일부를 수행하여 / 정보를 걸러내는 데 도움이 되고, / 예상되는 것과 무관한 / 명확한 모순에 우리의 주의를 집중시킨다.

The processes of learning and memory / are marked by a steady elimination of information.
학습과 기억의 과정은 / 정보의 지속적인 제거로 특징지어진다.

People notice only a part of the world around them.
사람들은 그들 주변 세계의 일부분만을 인지한다.

Then, / only a fraction of what they notice / gets processed and stored into memory.
그런 다음, / 그들이 알아차린 것의 일부만 / 처리되어 기억에 저장된다.

And / only part of what gets committed to memory / can be retrieved.
그리고 / 기억에 넘겨진 것의 일부만 / 생각해 낼 수 있다.

인간 사고의 많은 부분은 정보를 걸러내고 나머지는 처리하기 쉬운 상태로 분류하도록 설계된다. 특히 문화와 사회에서 이용할 수 있는 엄청난 양의 정보를 고려할 때, 우리 감각에서 오는 데이터의 유입은 압도적인 혼란을 낳을 수 있다. 모든 감각적 인상과 가능한 정보 중에서, 우리의 개인적인 필요와 가장 관련된 적은 양을 찾아서 그것을 사용 가능한 지식체로 구성하는 게 중요하다. 예상들은 이 작업의 일부를 수행하여 예상되는 것과 무관한 정보를 걸러내는 데 도움이 되고, 명확한 모순에 우리의 주의를 집중시킨다. 학습과 기억의 과정은 정보의 지속적인 제거로 특징지어진다. 사람들은 그들 주변 세계의 일부분만을 인지한다. 그런 다음, 그들이 알아차린 것의 일부만 처리되어 기억에 저장된다. 그리고 기억에 넘겨진 것의 일부만 생각해 낼 수 있다.

Why? 왜 정답일까?

빈칸 뒤에서 우리는 세계의 일부만 인지하고, 인지한 것 중 일부만 저장하고, 저장된 것의 일부만 회상할 수 있다고 한다. 말인즉 정보를 점점 줄여가는 것이 우리의 인지 과정이라는 것이므로, 빈칸에 들어갈 말로 가장 적절한 것은 ② '정보의 지속적인 제거로 특징지어진다'이다.

- screen out 차단하다
- inflow ⓝ 유입
- chaos ⓝ 혼돈
- vital ⓐ 매우 중요한
- accomplish ⓥ 해내다, 성취하다
- contradiction ⓝ 모순
- commit A to memory A를 기억하다
- accuracy ⓝ 정확성
- manageable ⓐ 처리하기 쉬운
- overwhelming ⓐ 압도적인
- enormous ⓐ 막대한
- stock ⓝ 저장, 축적 ⓥ 저장하다, 보관하다
- irrelevant ⓐ 무관한
- fraction ⓝ 부분
- retrieve ⓥ 생각해 내다
- facilitate ⓥ 촉진하다

구문 풀이

6행 Out of all the sensory impressions and possible information, (~ 중에서) it (가주어) is vital to find (진주어1) a small amount (선행사) [that (주격 관·대) is most relevant to our individual needs] and to organize (진주어2) that (대명사(= the small amount)) into a usable stock of knowledge.

★★ 문제 해결 꿀~팁 ★★

▶ 많이 틀린 이유는?
외부에서 들어오는 데이터나 정보를 차단하고 줄여야 한다는 내용 때문에 '기억력을 외부에서 보조해줘야 한다'는 의미의 ③을 고르게 될 수도 있다. 하지만 '외부의 보조'에 관해서는 전혀 언급되지 않았다.

▶ 문제 해결 방법은?
빈칸 뒤가 인간의 인지적 과정을 잘 요약하고 있다. 주변 정보를 선별적으로 받아들이고, 받아들인 정보 중 일부만을 저장하고, 저장된 정보 중 일부만을 기억하게 된다는 것은 결국 '계속 정보를 지워간다'는 의미와 같다. 본문의 screen out이 ②의 elimination과 연결된다.

★★★ 1등급 대비 고난도 3점 문제

12 찰나의 인식에 의해 형성되는 직감 정답률 46% | 정답 ①

다음 빈칸에 들어갈 말로 가장 적절한 것을 고르시오. [3점]

✔ result of our cognitive processing system
우리의 인지 처리 체계의 결과
② instance of discarding negative memories
부정적 기억을 버리는 것의 예시
③ mechanism of overcoming our internal conflicts
우리의 내적 갈등을 극복하는 기제
④ visual representation of our emotional vulnerability
우리의 정서적 취약성의 시각적 표현
⑤ concrete signal of miscommunication within the brain
뇌 속의 의사소통 오류에 대한 구체적 신호

We might think / that our gut instinct is just an inner feeling / — a secret interior voice — / but in fact it is shaped / by a perception of something visible around us, / such as a facial expression or a visual inconsistency / so fleeting that often we're not even aware we've noticed it.
우리는 생각할지도 모르지만, / 우리의 직감이 단지 내면의 느낌이라고 / 즉 비밀스러운 내적 목소리 / 사실 그것은 형성된다. / 우리 주변의 가시적인 무언가에 대한 인식에 의해 / 얼굴 표정 또는 시각적 불일치와 같이 / 너무 빨리 지나가서 보통 우리가 그것을 알아차렸음을 의식하지도 못하는

Psychologists now think of this moment / as a 'visual matching game'.
오늘날 심리학자들은 이러한 순간을 생각한다. / '시각적 연결시키기 게임'으로

So / a stressed, rushed or tired person / is more likely to resort to this visual matching.
그렇다면 / 스트레스를 받거나, 서두르고 있거나 피곤한 사람이 / 이 시각적 연결시키기에 의존할 가능성이 더 높다.

When they see a situation in front of them, / they quickly match it to a sea of past experiences / stored in a mental knowledge bank / and then, based on a match, / they assign meaning to the information in front of them.
그들이 눈앞의 상황을 볼 때 / 그들은 과거 경험의 바다와 그것을 재빨리 연결해 보고, / 정신의 지식 저장고 안에 보관된 / 그다음 연결에 기초하여 / 그들은 앞에 있는 정보에 의미를 부여한다.

The brain then sends a signal to the gut, / which has many hundreds of nerve cells.
그러고 나서 뇌가 창자로 신호를 보내는데 / 이것은 수백 개의 신경세포를 가지고 있다.

So / the visceral feeling we get in the pit of our stomach / and the butterflies we feel / are a result of our cognitive processing system.
따라서 / 우리가 우리의 뱃속에서 받는 본능적인 느낌과 / 우리가 느끼는 긴장감은 / 우리의 인지 처리 체계의 결과이다.

우리는 우리의 직감이 단지 내면의 느낌, 즉 비밀스러운 내적 목소리라고 생각할지도 모르지만, 사실 그것은 얼굴 표정 또는 시각적 불일치와 같이 너무 빨리 지나가서 보통 우리가 그것을 알아차렸음을 의식하지도 못하는, 우리 주변의 가시적인 무언가에 대한 인식에 의해 형성된다. 오늘날 심리학자들은 이러한 순간을 '시각적 연결시키기 게임'으로 생각한다. 그렇다면 스트레스를 받거나, 서두르고 있거나 피곤한 사람이 이 시각적 연결시키기에 의존할 가능성이 더 높다. 그들이 눈앞의 상황을 볼 때 정신의 지식 저장고 안에 보관된 과거 경험의 바다와 그것을 재빨리 연결해 보고, 그다음 연결에 기초하여 앞에 있는 정보에 의미를 부여한다. 그러고 나서 뇌가 창자로 신호를 보내는데 이것은 수백 개의 신경세포를 가지고 있다. 따라서 우리가 뱃속에서 받는 본능적인 느낌과 우리가 느끼는 긴장감은 우리의 인지 처리 체계의 결과이다.

Why? 왜 정답일까?

첫 문장에서 우리의 직감은 단지 내면의 느낌에 불과한 것이 아니라 아주 찰나에 이루어지는, 주변 정보에 대한 처리에 기반하여 형성된다(~ shaped by a perception ~ so fleeting that often we're not even aware we're notice it.)고 한다. 이를 가리켜 '시각적 연결시키기 게임'이라고 정리한 후 예시가 이어지고, 빈칸은 예시의 결론 부분에 있으므로 첫 문장의 주제와 동일한 내용일 것이다. 따라서 빈칸에 들어갈 말로 가장 적절한 것은 ① '우리의 인지 처리 체계의 결과'이다.

- instinct ⓝ 본능, 직감
- inconsistency ⓝ 불일치, 모순
- assign A to B A를 B에 부여하다
- vulnerability ⓝ 취약성, 연약함
- interior ⓐ 내부의
- fleeting ⓐ 순식간의, 잠깐 동안의
- discard ⓥ 버리다
- concrete ⓐ 구체적인

구문 풀이

1행 We might think that our gut instinct is just an inner feeling — a secret interior voice (동격) — but in fact it is shaped by a perception of something visible around us (-thing + 형용사), such as a facial expression or a visual inconsistency (선행사) [(which is) (생략) so fleeting that often we're not even aware we've noticed it]. 「so ~ that ⋯ : 너무 ~해서 ⋯하다」

★★ 문제 해결 꿀~팁 ★★

▶ 많이 틀린 이유는?
글에 따르면 직감은 그저 느낌이 아니라, 우리도 모르는 새에 스쳐간 정보를 재빨리 분석한 결과이다. 이 일련의 과정은 '시각적 연결시키기 게임'과 비슷하다고 하는데, 이는 정보 분석의 과정을 비유하는 설명일 뿐 직감 자체가 시각적 표현이라는 의미는 아니다. 따라서 ④는 빈칸에 적합하지 않다.

▶ 문제 해결 방법은?
빈칸이 마지막 문장에 있으면 앞에 제시된 요지를 반복하거나 예시를 일반화하는 말을 답으로 골라야 한다. 이 문제에서도 예시 앞의 주제인 첫 문장이 가장 큰 힌트이다.

DAY 08

[문제편 p.056]

DAY 09 빈칸 추론 09

01 ③	02 ②	03 ①	04 ③	05 ④
06 ⑤	07 ①	08 ④	09 ①	10 ⑤
11 ④	12 ①			

01 기억의 사회적 공유

정답률 54% | 정답 ③

다음 빈칸에 들어갈 말로 가장 적절한 것을 고르시오.

① biased – 편향된 ② illegal – 불법적인
✔ repetitive – 반복되는 ④ temporary – 일시적인
⑤ rational – 합리적인

Finkenauer and Rimé investigated the memory / of the unexpected death of Belgium's King Baudouin in 1993 / in a large sample of Belgian citizens.
Finkenauer와 Rimé는 기억을 조사했다. / 1993년 벨기에 왕 Baudouin의 예기치 못한 죽음에 대한 / 표본으로 추출된 많은 벨기에 시민들을 대상으로
The data revealed / that the news of the king's death / had been widely socially shared.
그 자료는 나타냈다. / 왕의 죽음에 대한 소식이 / 널리 사회적으로 공유되었다는 것을
By talking about the event, / people gradually constructed / a social narrative and a collective memory / of the emotional event.
그 사건에 관해 이야기함으로써 / 사람들은 서서히 구축했다. / 사회적 이야기와 집단 기억을 / 그 감정적 사건의
At the same time, / they consolidated their own memory of the personal circumstances / in which the event took place, / an effect known as "flashbulb memory."
동시에 / 그들은 개인적 상황에 대한 자신들의 기억을 공고히 했는데, / 그 사건이 발생했던 / 그것은 '섬광 기억'으로 알려진 효과이다.
The more an event is socially shared, / the more it will be fixed in people's minds.
한 사건이 사회적으로 더 많이 공유되면 될수록, / 그것은 사람들 마음속에 더 많이 고착될 것이다.
Social sharing may in this way help / to counteract some natural tendency / people may have.
사회적 공유는 이런 식으로 도움이 될 수도 있다. / 어떤 자연적인 성향을 중화시키는 데 / 사람들이 갖고 있을 수 있는
Naturally, / people should be driven / to "forget" undesirable events.
자연스럽게 / 사람들은 이끌릴 것이다. / 바람직하지 않은 사건을 '잊도록'
Thus, / someone who just heard a piece of bad news / often tends initially to deny what happened.
그래서 / 방금 어떤 나쁜 소식을 들은 어떤 사람은 / 발생한 일을 처음에는 흔히 부인하고 싶어 한다.
The repetitive social sharing of the bad news / contributes to realism.
나쁜 소식의 반복되는 사회적 공유는 / 현실성에 기여한다.

Finkenauer와 Rimé는 표본으로 추출된 많은 벨기에 시민들을 대상으로 1993년 벨기에 왕 Baudouin의 예기치 못한 죽음에 대한 기억을 조사했다. 그 자료는 왕의 죽음에 대한 소식이 널리 사회적으로 공유되었다는 것을 나타냈다. 그 사건에 관해 이야기함으로써 사람들은 서서히 그 감정적 사건의 사회적 이야기와 집단 기억을 구축했다. 동시에 그들은 그 사건이 발생했던 개인적 상황에 대한 자신들의 기억을 공고히 했는데, 그것은 '섬광 기억'으로 알려진 효과이다. 한 사건이 사회적으로 더 많이 공유되면 될수록, 그것은 사람들 마음속에 더 많이 고착될 것이다. 사회적 공유는 이런 식으로 사람들이 갖고 있을 수 있는 어떤 자연적인 성향을 중화시키는 데 도움이 될 수도 있다. 자연스럽게 사람들은 바람직하지 않은 사건을 '잊도록' 이끌릴 것이다. 그래서 방금 어떤 나쁜 소식을 들은 어떤 사람은 발생한 일을 처음에는 흔히 부인하고 싶어 한다. 나쁜 소식의 반복되는 사회적 공유는 현실성에 기여한다.

Why? 왜 정답일까?

'**The more an event is socially shared, the more it will be fixed in people's minds.**'에서 한 사건에 대한 기억은 더 많이 공유될수록 더 공고해진다고 이야기하므로, 빈칸에 들어갈 말로 가장 적절한 것은 ③ '반복되는'이다.

- **unexpected** ⓐ 예기치 못한
- **gradually** ad 서서히
- **flashbulb memory** 섬광 기억
- **tendency** ⓝ 성향, 경향
- **undesirable** ⓐ 바람직하지 않은
- **deny** ⓥ 부인하다, 부정하다
- **realism** ⓝ 현실성, 현실주의
- **reveal** ⓥ 드러내다, 밝히다
- **consolidate** ⓥ 굳히다, 공고히 하다
- **counteract** ⓥ 중화시키다, 대항하다
- **naturally** ad 당연히, 자연스럽게
- **initially** ad 처음에
- **contribute to** ~에 기여하다
- **biased** ⓐ 편향된

구문 풀이

7행 At the same time, they consolidated their own memory of the personal circumstances [in which the event took place], (which is) an effect [known as "flashbulb memory."]
(선행사: the personal circumstances / in which = where / 자동사: took place / 생략(계속적 용법): which is / known as: ~라고 알려진)

02 예측 불가능한 자극이 있을 때 일어나는 학습

정답률 57% | 정답 ②

다음 빈칸에 들어갈 말로 가장 적절한 것을 고르시오.

① audible – 잘 들리는지 ✔ predictable – 예측 가능한지
③ objective – 객관적인지 ④ countable – 셀 수 있는지
⑤ recorded – 녹음된 것인지

No learning is possible / without an error signal.
어떤 학습도 가능하지 않다. / 오류 신호 없이는
Organisms only learn / when events violate their expectations.
유기체는 오로지 학습한다. / 사건이 기대에 어긋날 때
In other words, / surprise is one of the fundamental drivers of learning.
다시 말해 / 놀람은 학습의 근본적인 동력 중 하나이다.
Imagine hearing a series of identical notes, AAAAA.
일련의 똑같은 음인 AAAAA를 듣는 것을 상상해 보라.
Each note draws out a response / in the auditory areas of your brain / — but as the notes repeat, / those responses progressively decrease.
각각의 음은 반응을 끌어내지만, / 여러분의 뇌의 청각 영역에서 / 음이 반복되면서 / 그 반응은 점진적으로 감소한다.
This is called "adaptation," / a deceptively simple phenomenon / that shows / that your brain is learning to anticipate the next event.
이것은 '적응'이라 불리며, / 현혹될 정도로 단순해 보이는 현상이다. / 알려주는 / 뇌가 다음 사건을 예상하는 법을 배울 것임을
Suddenly, the note changes: AAAAA#.
문득, 그 음이 AAAAA#으로 바뀐다.
Your primary auditory cortex / immediately shows a strong surprise reaction: / not only does the adaptation fade away, / but additional neurons begin to vigorously fire / in response to the unexpected sound.
당신의 일차 청각 피질은 / 즉시 강한 놀람의 반응을 보이는데, / 즉 적응이 점차 사라질 뿐만 아니라 / 추가적인 뉴런이 힘차게 활성화되기 시작한다. / 예상치 못한 소리에 대한 반응으로
And it is not just repetition / that leads to adaptation: / what matters is / whether the notes are predictable.
그리고 단순한 반복이 아니라, / 적응을 유발하는 것은 / 중요한 것은 ~이다. / 그 음이 예측 가능한지이다.
For instance, / if you hear an alternating set of notes, / such as ABABA, / your brain gets used to this alternation, / and the activity in your auditory areas / again decreases.
예를 들어 / 만약 당신이 일련의 교차하는 음을 듣는다면, / ABABA와 같이 / 당신의 뇌는 이 교차에 익숙해지고, / 당신의 청각 영역 내 활동은 / 다시 감소한다.
This time, however, / it is an unexpected repetition, / such as ABABB, / that triggers a surprise response.
그러나 이번에는 / 바로 예상치 못한 반복이다. / ABABB와 같은 / 놀람의 반응을 일으키는 것은

어떤 학습도 오류 신호 없이는 가능하지 않다. 유기체는 사건이 기대에 어긋날 때에만 학습한다. 다시 말해 놀람은 학습의 근본적인 동력 중 하나이다. 일련의 똑같은 음인 AAAAA를 듣는 것을 상상해 보라. 각각의 음은 여러분의 뇌의 청각 영역에서 반응을 끌어내지만, 음이 반복되면서 그 반응은 점진적으로 감소한다. 이것은 '적응'이라 불리며, 뇌가 다음 사건을 예상하는 법을 배울 것임을 알려주는 현혹될 정도로 단순해 보이는 현상이다. 문득, 그 음이 AAAAA#으로 바뀐다. 당신의 일차 청각 피질은 즉시 강한 놀람의 반응을 보이는데, 즉 적응이 점차 사라질 뿐만 아니라 예상치 못한 소리에 대한 반응으로 추가적인 뉴런이 힘차게 활성화되기 시작한다. 그리고 적응을 유발하는 것은 단순한 반복이 아니며, 중요한 것은 그 음이 예측 가능한지이다. 예를 들어 만약 당신이 ABABA와 같이 일련의 교차하는 음을 듣는다면, 당신의 뇌는 이 교차에 익숙해지고, 당신의 청각 영역 내 활동은 다시 감소한다. 그러나 이번에는 놀람의 반응을 일으키는 것은 바로 ABABB와 같은 예상치 못한 반복이다.

Why? 왜 정답일까?

첫 세 문장에서 학습이 가능한 것은 오류 신호, 즉 '예측을 벗어나는 놀람'이 있을 때라고 한다(**Organisms only learn when events violate their expectations. In other words, surprise is one of the fundamental drivers of learning.**). 이어서 우리 뇌는 자극에 '적응하는' 능력을 지니고 있기에 반복되는 패턴에 주의를 덜 기울이고, 예측에 벗어나는 변칙이 주어질 때 '놀라면서' 비로소 학습하려 한다는 설명이 제시된다. 따라서 빈칸에 들어갈 말로 가장 적절한 것은 ② '예측 가능한지'이다.

- violate ⓥ 위반하다
- identical ⓐ 동일한
- draw out ~을 끌어내다
- progressively ad 점진적으로
- phenomenon ⓝ 현상
- primary ⓐ 1차의, 주요한, 기본적인
- fade away 흐려지다, 옅어지다
- alternate ⓥ 번갈아 나오다, 교대로 나오다
- predictable ⓐ 예측 가능한
- fundamental ⓐ 근본적인
- note ⓝ 음
- auditory ⓐ 청각의
- deceptively ad 현혹될 정도로
- anticipate ⓥ 기대하다, 예상하다
- cortex ⓝ (대뇌의) 피질
- vigorously ad 힘차게
- audible ⓐ 잘 들리는, 들을 수 있는

구문 풀이

11행 Your primary auditory cortex immediately shows a strong surprise reaction: not only does the adaptation fade away, but 「부정어구+조동사+주어+동사원형 : 도치 구문」 additional neurons begin to vigorously fire in response to the unexpected sound.

03 가상 세계를 지탱하는 군중의 힘

정답률 46% | 정답 ①

다음 빈칸에 들어갈 말로 가장 적절한 것을 고르시오. [3점]

✔ be a large enough group to be considered a society
사회로 여겨질 정도로 충분히 큰 규모의 집단이어야
② have historical evidence to make it worth believing
그것을 믿을 가치가 있게 만들어주는 역사적 증거가 있어야
③ apply their individual values to all of their affairs
그들의 개인적 가치관을 그들의 모든 일에 적용해야
④ follow a strict order to enhance their self-esteem
그들의 자존감을 높이기 위해 엄격한 질서를 따라야
⑤ get approval in light of the religious value system
종교적 가치 체계의 관점에서 승인을 받아야

Scholars of myth have long argued / that myth gives structure and meaning to human life; / that meaning is amplified / when a myth evolves into a world.
신화 학자들은 오랫동안 주장해 왔다. / 신화가 인간의 삶에 구조와 의미를 부여한다고 / 그 의미는 증폭된다. / 하나의 신화가 하나의 세상으로 진화할 때
A virtual world's ability to fulfill needs / grows / when lots and lots of people believe in the world.
욕구를 충족시킬 수 있는 가상 세계의 능력이 / 커진다. / 수많은 사람이 그 세상의 존재를 믿을 때
Conversely, / a virtual world cannot be long sustained / by a mere handful of adherents.
이와 반대로, / 가상 세계는 오래 지속될 수 없다. / 단지 몇 명뿐인 추종자들에 의해서는
Consider the difference / between a global sport / and a game I invent with my nine friends and play regularly.
차이를 고려해 보라. / 전 세계적인 스포츠와 / 내가 내 친구 9명과 만들어 정기적으로 하는 게임 사이의
My game might be a great game, / one that is completely immersive, / one that consumes all of my group's time and attention.
나의 게임은 훌륭한 게임이고 / 완전히 몰입하게 하는 게임이며, / 내 집단의 시간과 관심 모두를 소모하는 게임일 수 있다.
If its reach is limited to the ten of us, / though, / then it's ultimately just a weird hobby, / and it has limited social function.
그것이 미치는 범위가 우리 10명으로 제한된다면, / 하지만 / 그것은 최종적으로 그저 이상한 취미일 뿐이고, / 그것은 제한된 사회적 기능을 가진다.
For a virtual world / to provide lasting, wide-ranging value, / its participants must be a large enough group / to be considered a society.
가상 세계가 / 지속적이고 넓은 범위에 퍼지는 가치를 제공하려면 / 그 참여자들이 충분히 큰 규모의 집단이어야 한다. / 사회로 여겨질 정도로
When that threshold is reached, / psychological value can turn into wide-ranging social value.
그 기준점에 도달했을 때, / 심리적 가치가 넓은 범위에 퍼지는 사회적 가치로 변할 수 있다.

신화(를 연구하는) 학자들은 신화가 인간의 삶에 구조와 의미를 부여한다고 오랫동안 주장해 왔다. 그 의미는 하나의 신화가 하나의 세상으로 진화할 때 증폭된다. 욕구를 충족시킬 수 있는 가상 세계의 능력은 수많은 사람이 그 세상의 존재를 믿을 때 커진다. 이와 반대로, 가상 세계는 단지 몇 명뿐인 추종자들에 의해서는 오래 지속될 수 없다. 전 세계적인 스포츠와 내가 내 친구 9명과 만들어 정기적으로 하는 게임의 차이를 고려해 보라. 나의 게임은 훌륭한 게임이고 완전히 몰입하게 하는 게임이며, 내 집단의 시간과 관심 모두를 소모하는 게임일 수 있다. 하지만 그것이 미치는 범위가 우리 10명으로 제한된다면, 그것은 최종적으로 그저 이상한 취미일 뿐이고, 제한된 사회적 기능을 가진다. 가상 세계가 지속적이고 넓은 범위에 퍼지는 가치를 제공하려면 그 참여자들이 사회로 여겨질 정도로 충분히 큰 규모의 집단이어야 한다. 그 기준점에 도달했을 때, 심리적 가치가 넓은 범위에 퍼지는 사회적 가치로 변할 수 있다.

Why? 왜 정답일까?

신화, 게임, 혹은 다른 어떤 가상 세계가 지속적인 영향력을 갖기 위해서는 '많은 사람'이 필요하다(A virtual world's ability to fulfill needs grows when lots and lots of people believe in the world.)는 내용의 글이다. 따라서 빈칸에 들어갈 말로 가장 적절한 것은 ① '사회로 여겨질 정도로 충분히 큰 규모의 집단이어야'이다.

- scholar ⓝ 학자
- amplify ⓥ 증폭하다
- conversely ad 반대로
- adherent ⓝ 추종자
- attention ⓝ 주의, 관심
- wide-ranging ⓐ 광범위한
- affair ⓝ 일, 사건
- enhance ⓥ 향상시키다
- in light of ~의 관점에서, ~을 고려하여
- myth ⓝ 신화
- fulfill ⓥ 충족하다, 이루다
- sustain ⓥ 지탱하다
- immersive ⓐ 몰입시키는
- weird ⓐ 이상한
- threshold ⓝ 기준점
- strict ⓐ 엄격한
- self-esteem ⓝ 자존감

구문 풀이

13행 For a virtual world to provide lasting, wide-ranging value, its participants must be a large enough group to be considered a society.
(의미상 주어 / 부사적 용법(~하려면) / 「형/부+enough ~ to 부정사 : ~할 정도로 충분히 …한 ~」)

04 음악이 기억 회상에 미치는 영향

정답률 56% | 정답 ③

다음 빈칸에 들어갈 말로 가장 적절한 것을 고르시오.

① analyzing memories of the event thoroughly
사건에 대한 기억을 면밀히 분석하는 것
② increasing storage space for recalling the event
사건을 기억하기 위한 저장 공간을 늘리는 것
✔ re-hearing the same music associated with the event
그 사건과 연관된 바로 그 음악을 다시 듣는 것
④ reconstructing the event in the absence of background music
배경 음악 없이 사건을 재구성하는 것
⑤ enhancing musical competence to deliver emotional messages
감정적인 메시지를 전달하는 음악적 능력을 향상시키는 것

One of the primary ways / by which music is able to take on significance in our inner world / is by the way it interacts with memory.
주요한 방법 중 하나는 / 음악이 우리의 내면세계에서 중요성을 가질 수 있는 / 그것이 기억과 상호작용하는 방식에 의해서이다.
Memories associated with important emotions / tend to be more deeply embedded in our memory / than other events.
중요한 감정과 연관된 기억들은 / 우리 기억 속에 더욱 깊이 박혀 있는 경향이 있다. / 다른 사건들보다
Emotional memories / are more likely to be vividly remembered / and are more likely to be recalled with the passing of time / than neutral memories.
감정적인 기억들은 / 생생히 기억될 가능성이 더 크고 / 시간이 지나도 기억될 가능성이 더 크다. / 중립적인 기억들보다
Since music can be extremely emotionally evocative, / key life events can be emotionally heightened by the presence of music, / ensuring that memories of the event become deeply encoded.
음악이 감정을 엄청나게 불러일으킬 수 있기 때문에 / 삶의 중요한 사건들은 음악의 존재에 의해 감정적으로 고조될 수 있고, / 이는 그 사건에 대한 기억들이 확실히 깊이 부호화되도록 해 준다.
Retrieval of those memories / is then enhanced by contextual effects, / in which a recreation of a similar context / to that in which the memories were encoded / can facilitate their retrieval.
그러한 기억들의 회복은 / 그러고 나서 맥락 효과에 의해 강화되는데, / 이 맥락 효과에서는 비슷한 맥락의 재창조가 / 그 기억들이 부호화되었던 것과 / 그것들의 회복을 촉진시킬 수 있다.
Thus, / re-hearing the same music associated with the event / can activate intensely vivid memories of the event.
따라서 / 그 사건과 연관된 바로 그 음악을 다시 듣는 것이 / 그 사건에 대한 강렬하게 생생한 기억들을 활성화할 수 있다.

음악이 우리의 내면세계에서 중요성을 가질 수 있는 주요한 방법 중 하나는 그것이 기억과 상호작용하는 방식에 의해서이다. 중요한 감정과 연관된 기억들은 다른 사건들보다 우리 기억 속에 더욱 깊이 박혀 있는 경향이 있다. 감정적인 기억들은 생생히 기억될 가능성이 더 크고 중립적인 기억들보다 시간이 지나도 기억될 가능성이 더 크다. 음악이 감정을 엄청나게 불러일으킬 수 있기 때문에 삶의 중요한 사건들은 음악의 존재에 의해 감정적으로 고조될 수 있고, 이는 그 사건에 대한 기억들이 확실히 깊이 부호화되도록 해 준다. 그러고 나서 그러한 기억들의 회복은 맥락 효과에 의해 강화되는데, 그 기억들이 부호화되었던 맥락과 비슷한 맥락의 재창조가 기억의 회복을 촉진시킬 수 있다. 따라서 그 사건과 연관된 바로 그 음악을 다시 듣는 것이 그 사건에 대한 강렬하게 생생한 기억들을 활성화할 수 있다.

Why? 왜 정답일까?

음악은 듣는 이의 감정을 고조시키고, 감정적인 기억은 더 생생히 저장되게 하는 경향이 있기 때문에, 어떤 사건이 일어날 때 특정한 음악을 듣고 있었다면 나중에 그 음악을 다시

DAY 09

듣는 '맥락'이 조성될 때 관련된 사건을 기억해내기가 훨씬 쉬워진다(~ a recreation of a similar context to that in which the memories were encoded can facilitate their retrieval.)는 내용의 글이다. 따라서 빈칸에 들어갈 말로 가장 적절한 것은 ③ '그 사건과 연관된 바로 그 음악을 다시 듣는 것'이다.

- take on (특징 등을) 띠다, (일을) 맡다
- significance ⓝ 중요성
- with the passing of time 시간이 지남에 따라
- neutral ⓐ 중립적인
- extremely ⓐⓓ 극도로
- heighten ⓥ 고조시키다
- presence ⓝ 존재
- encode ⓥ 부호화하다
- enhance ⓥ 강화하다
- facilitate ⓥ 용이하게 하다
- activate ⓥ 활성화하다
- intensely ⓐⓓ 강렬하게, 매우
- thoroughly ⓐⓓ 면밀하게, 철저하게
- in the absence of ~이 없을 때
- competence ⓝ 능력, 능숙함

구문 풀이

11행 Retrieval of those memories is then enhanced by
주어 / 동사구(수동태)
contextual effects, in which a recreation of a similar context to that
선행사 / =where / 주어 / 지시대명사(= context)
[in which the memories were encoded] can facilitate their retrieval.
= where / 동사

05 기억을 개선하고 보존할 방법 정답률 54% | 정답 ④

다음 빈칸에 들어갈 말로 가장 적절한 것을 고르시오.

① keep your body and mind healthy – 몸과 마음을 건강하게 유지해야
② calm your mind in stressful times – 스트레스를 받을 때 마음을 가라앉혀야
③ concentrate on one thing at a time – 한 번에 한 가지 일에 집중해야
✔ work on all functions of your brain – 뇌의 모든 기능을 작동시켜야
⑤ share what you learn with other people – 배우는 것을 다른 사람과 공유해야

When you're driving a car, / your memory of how to operate the vehicle / comes from one set of brain cells; / the memory of how to navigate the streets / to get to your destination / springs from another set of neurons; / the memory of driving rules and following street signs / originates from another family of brain cells; / and the thoughts and feelings / you have about the driving experience itself, / including any close calls with other cars, / come from yet another group of cells.
여러분이 자동차를 운전할 때, / 차량을 조작하는 방법에 관한 기억은 / 일련의 뇌세포에서 나오고, / 도로를 주행하는 방법에 관한 기억은 / 목적지에 도착하기 위해 / 또 다른 일련의 신경 세포로부터 발생하며, / 운전 규칙에 관한 기억과 도로 표지를 따르는 것에 관한 기억은 / 또 다른 뇌세포 집단으로부터 생기고, / 생각과 느낌은 / 운전 경험 자체에 대해 여러분이 가지고 있는 / 다른 자동차와의 위기일발을 포함하여 / 또 다른 세포 집단에서 나온다.

You do not have conscious awareness / of all these separate mental plays and cognitive neural firings, / yet they somehow work together in beautiful harmony / to synthesize your overall experience.
여러분은 의식적인 인지를 하고 있지는 않지만, / 이 모든 별개의 정신적 활동과 인지적 신경 활성화에 관한 / 그것들은 아름다운 조화를 이루며 어떻게든 함께 작동한다. / 여러분의 전반적인 경험을 종합하기 위해

In fact, / we don't even know the real difference / between how we remember and how we think.
사실, / 우리는 진정한 차이를 알지도 못한다. / 우리가 기억하는 방식과 우리가 생각하는 방식 사이의

But, / we do know they are strongly intertwined.
하지만, / 우리는 그것들이 강력하게 뒤얽혀 있다는 것을 정말로 안다.

That is why / truly improving memory / can never simply be about using memory tricks, / although they can be helpful / in strengthening certain components of memory.
그것이 ~한 이유이다. / 진정으로 기억력을 향상시키는 것은 / 결코 단지 기억력 기술을 사용하는 것에 관한 것일 수 없는 / 그것들이 도움이 될 수 있다 하더라도, / 기억력의 특정 구성 요소를 강화하는 데

Here's the bottom line:
여기 요점이 있다.

To improve and preserve memory at the cognitive level, / you have to work on all functions of your brain.
인지적 수준에서 기억력을 개선하고 보존하기 위해서는 / 여러분은 뇌의 모든 기능을 작동시켜야 한다.

자동차를 운전할 때, 차량을 조작하는 방법에 관한 기억은 일련의 뇌세포에서 나오고, 목적지에 도착하기 위해 도로를 주행하는 방법에 관한 기억은 또 다른 일련의 신경 세포로부터 발생하며, 운전 규칙에 관한 기억과 도로 표지를 따르는 것에 관한 기억은 또 다른 뇌세포 집단으로부터 생기고, 다른 자동차와의 위기일발을 포함하여 운전 경험 자체에 대해 여러분이 가지고 있는 생각과 느낌은 또 다른 세포 집단에서 나온다. 여러분은 이 모든 별개의 정신적 활동과 인지적 신경 활성화에 관한 의식적으로 인지하고 있지는 않지만, 그것들은 여러분의 전반적인 경험을 종합하기 위해 아름다운 조화를 이루며 어떻게든 함

께 작동한다. 사실, 우리가 기억하는 방식과 우리가 생각하는 방식 사이의 진정한 차이를 우리는 알지도 못한다. 하지만, 우리는 그것들이 강력하게 뒤얽혀 있다는 것을 정말로 안다. 그런 이유로 기억력 기술이 기억력의 특정 구성 요소를 강화하는 데 도움이 될 수 있다 하더라도, 진정으로 기억력을 향상시키는 것은 결코 단지 기억력 기술의 사용에 관한 것일 수 없다. 요컨대, 인지적 수준에서 기억력을 개선하고 보존하기 위해서는 뇌의 모든 기능을 작동시켜야 한다.

Why? 왜 정답일까?

정신적 활동은 서로 밀접하게 연결된(strongly intertwined) 여러 기능이 함께 작동하여(work together) 이루어진다는 설명으로 보아, 기억력을 높이기 위해서는 단지 기억에 관련된 요소만을 사용하기 보다 뇌를 전방위적으로 사용할 필요가 있다는 결론을 내릴 수 있다. 따라서 빈칸에 들어갈 말로 가장 적절한 것은 ④ '뇌의 모든 기능을 작동시켜야'이다.

- spring from ~로부터 일어나다, 비롯되다
- originate from ~에서 기원하다
- conscious ⓐ 의식적인
- awareness ⓝ 인식, 앎
- synthesize ⓥ 종합하다, 합성하다
- strengthen ⓥ 강화하다
- the bottom line 가장 중요한 점, 핵심
- concentrate on ~에 집중하다

구문 풀이

1행 When you're driving a car, your memory of {how to operate
주어1 / { } : 명사구(how + to부정사 : ~하는 방법)
the vehicle} comes from one set of brain cells; the memory of {how to
동사1 / 주어2
navigate the streets to get to your destination} springs from another
동사2
set of neurons; the memory of driving rules and following street signs
주어3
originates from another family of brain cells; and the thoughts and
동사3 / 주어4(복수)
feelings [(that) you have about the driving experience itself], (including
생략(목적격 관·대)
any close calls with other cars), come from yet another group of cells.
삽입구 / 동사4

06 마케팅과 발명의 통합의 필요성을 깨달은 에디슨 정답률 63% | 정답 ⑤

다음 빈칸에 들어갈 말로 가장 적절한 것을 고르시오. [3점]

① consider the likelihood of mass production – 대량 생산의 가능성을 고려하고
② simplify the design of his inventions – 그의 발명품의 디자인을 단순화하고
③ work with other inventors regularly – 다른 발명가들과 정기적으로 작업하고
④ have knowledge of law in advance – 법을 미리 알고
✔ put the customers' needs first – 고객의 요구를 우선시하고

Thomas Edison was indeed a creative genius, / but it was not until he discovered / some of the principles of marketing / that he found increased success.
토마스 에디슨은 정말 창의적인 천재였지만 / 그가 발견한 후에야 / 어떠한 마케팅 원칙을 / 그는 비로소 큰 성공에 도달했다.

One of his first inventions was, / although much needed, a failure.
그의 최초 발명품 중 하나는 / 매우 필요함에도 불구하고, 실패였다.

In 1869, he created and patented an electronic vote recorder, / which recorded and totalled the votes / in the Massachusetts state legislature / faster than the chamber's old manual system.
1869년에 그는 전자식 투표 기록 장치를 만들어 특허를 얻었는데, / 이것은 투표를 더 빠르게 기록하고 합계를 냈다. / Massachusetts 주 의회에서의 / 의회의 오래된 수기 시스템보다

To Edison's astonishment, it failed.
에디슨으로서는 놀랍게도 그것은 실패했다.

Edison had not taken into account legislators' habits.
에디슨은 의원들의 습관을 고려하지 않았다.

They didn't like to vote quickly and efficiently.
그들은 빠르고 효율적으로 투표하는 것을 원하지 않았다.

They liked to lobby their fellow legislators / as voting took place.
그들은 자신의 동료 의원에게 로비하는 것을 원했다. / 투표가 진행될 때

Edison had a great idea, / but he completely misunderstood the needs of his customers.
에디슨은 훌륭한 아이디어를 가졌으나 / 그는 자신의 고객의 요구를 완전히 잘못 이해했다.

He learned from his failure / the relationship between invention and marketing.
그는 자신의 실패로부터 배웠다. / 발명과 마케팅의 관계를

Edison learned / that marketing and invention must be integrated.
에디슨은 알게 되었다. / 마케팅과 발명이 통합되어야 함을

"Anything that won't sell, / I don't want to invent," / he said.
"팔리지 않을 어떤 것도 / 나는 발명하고 싶지 않다."라고 / 그가 말했다.

"Its sale is proof of utility, / and utility is success."
"그것의 판매량이 유용성의 증거이며, / 유용성이 성공이다."

He realized / he needed to put the customers' needs first / and tailor his thinking accordingly.
그는 깨달았다. / 자신이 고객의 요구를 우선시하고 / 자신의 생각을 그에 따라 맞출 필요가 있다는 것을

토마스 에디슨은 정말 창의적인 천재였지만 어떠한 마케팅 원칙을 발견한 후에야 그는 비로소 큰 성공에 도달했다. 매우 필요함에도 불구하고, 그의 최초 발명품 중 하나는 실패였다. 1869년에 그는 전자식 투표 기록 장치를 만들어 특허를 얻었는데, 이것은 Massachusetts 주 의회에서의 투표를 의회의 오래된 수기 시스템보다 더 빠르게 기록하고 합계를 냈다. 에디슨으로서는 놀랍게도 그것은 실패했다. 에디슨은 의원들의 습관을 고려하지 않았다. 그들은 빠르고 효율적으로 투표하는 것을 원하지 않았다. 투표가 진행될 때 그들은 자신의 동료 의원에게 로비하는 것을 원했다. 에디슨은 훌륭한 아이디어를 가졌으나 자신의 고객의 요구를 완전히 잘못 이해했다. 그는 자신의 실패로부터 발명과 마케팅의 관계를 배웠다. 에디슨은 마케팅과 발명이 통합되어야 함을 알게 되었다. "팔리지 않을 어떤 것도 나는 발명하고 싶지 않다."라고 그가 말했다. "그것의 판매량이 유용성의 증거이며, 유용성이 성공이다." 그는 자신이 고객의 요구를 우선시하고 자신의 생각을 그에 따라 맞출 필요가 있다는 것을 깨달았다.

Why? 왜 정답일까?

'He learned from his failure ~ that marketing and invention must be integrated.'에서 에디슨은 고객의 요구를 잘못 파악하여 발명품 판매에 실패했으며, 그 실패로부터 마케팅과 발명이 통합되어야 한다는 사실을 배웠다고 진술한다. 이에 비추어 볼 때, 빈칸에 들어갈 말로 가장 적절한 것은 고객의 요구를 고려하여 발명품을 만들어야 한다는 뜻을 완성하는 ⑤ '고객의 요구를 우선시하고'이다.

- genius ⓝ 천재
- manual ⓐ 손으로 하는, 수기의
- take into account ~을 고려하다
- integrate ⓥ 통합시키다
- accordingly ad 그에 따라
- legislature ⓝ 의회
- astonishment ⓝ 놀람
- efficiently ad 효율적으로
- tailor ⓥ ~에 맞추다
- mass production 대량 생산

구문 풀이

1행 Thomas Edison was indeed a creative genius, but it was not until he discovered some of the principles of marketing 「it is not until ~ that he found increased success.
that+주어+동사 : ~한 후에야 비로소 …하다」

07 과거 신용 거래가 활성화되지 않았던 이유
정답률 40% | 정답 ①

다음 빈칸에 들어갈 말로 가장 적절한 것을 고르시오. [3점]

✔ it never got any bigger – 그것은 절대 조금도 더 커지지 않았다
② its value changed in time – 그것의 가치는 이윽고 변했다
③ it made everybody wealthier – 그것은 모두를 더 부유하게 해 주었다
④ there always was another pie – 항상 또 하나의 파이가 있었다
⑤ everyone could get an even share of it – 모두가 동일한 몫을 가질 수 있었다

Credit arrangements of one kind or another / have existed / in all known human cultures.
이런저런 종류의 신용 거래는 / 존재해 왔다. / 모든 알려진 인류 문화에

The problem in previous eras was not / that no one had the idea / or knew how to use it.
이전 시대의 문제는 아니었다. / 아무도 그 생각을 못했거나, / 그것을 사용하는 방법을 몰랐던 것이

It was / that people seldom wanted to extend much credit / because they didn't trust / that the future would be better than the present.
문제였다. / 사람들이 많은 신용 거래를 원하는 경우가 좀처럼 없었던 것이 / 믿지 않았기 때문에 / 미래가 현재보다 더 나을 것으로

They generally believed / that times past had been better than their own times / and that the future would be worse.
그들은 대체로 믿었다. / 지나간 시간이 자신들의 시간(현재)보다 더 나았으며, / 미래는 더 나쁠 것이라고

To put that in economic terms, / they believed / that the total amount of wealth was limited.
그것을 경제 용어로 바꾸어 말하면, / 그들은 믿었다. / 부의 총량이 제한되어 있다고

People therefore considered it a bad bet to assume / that they would be producing more wealth / ten years down the line.
그러므로 사람들은 추정하는 것은 나쁜 선택이라고 생각했다. / 자신들이 더 많은 부를 만들어 낼 것으로 / 십 년이 지난 후

Business looked like a zero-sum game.
사업은 제로섬 게임과 같아 보였다.

Of course, / the profits of one particular bakery / might rise, / but only at the expense of the bakery next door.
물론, / 한 특정 빵집의 수익이 / 오를 수 있었지만, / 이웃 빵집의 희생을 통해서만 가능했다.

The king of England might enrich himself, / but only by robbing the king of France.
영국의 왕이 부자가 될 수 있었지만, / 프랑스 왕을 약탈함으로써만 가능했다.

You could cut the pie in many different ways, / but it never got any bigger.
많은 다양한 방법으로 파이를 자를 수 있었지만, / 그것은 절대 조금도 더 커지지 않았다.

이런저런 종류의 신용 거래는 모든 알려진 인류 문화에 존재해 왔다. 이전 시대의 문제는 아무도 그 생각을 못했거나, 그것을 사용하는 방법을 몰랐던 것이 아니었다. 미래가 현재보다 더 나을 것으로 믿지 않았기 때문에 사람들이 많은 신용 거래를 원하는 경우가 좀처럼 없었던 것이었다. 그들은 대체로 지나간 시간이 자신들의 시간(현재)보다 더 나았으며, 미래는 더 나쁠 것이라고 믿었다. 그것을 경제 용어로 바꾸어 말하면, 그들은 부의 총량이 제한되어 있다고 믿었다. 그러므로 사람들은 십 년이 지난 후 자신들이 더 많은 부를 만들어 낼 것으로 추정하는 것은 나쁜 짐작이라고 생각했다. 사업은 제로섬 게임과 같아 보였다. 물론, 한 특정 빵집의 수익이 오를 수 있었지만, 이웃 빵집의 희생을 통해서만 가능했다. 영국의 왕이 부자가 될 수 있었지만, 프랑스 왕을 약탈함으로써만 가능했다. 많은 다양한 방법으로 파이를 자를 수 있었지만, 그것은 절대 조금도 더 커지지 않았다.

Why? 왜 정답일까?

과거에 신용 거래가 많이 이루어지지 않았던 이유를 설명하는 글이다. **'To put that in economic terms, they believed that the total amount of wealth was limited.'**에서 이전 시대의 사람들은 부의 양이 한정되어 있다고 믿었다는 내용을 언급한 데 이어, **'Business looked like a zero-sum game.'**에서는 그리하여 사업이 제로섬 게임처럼 여겨졌다는 비유를 제시한다. 즉 과거 사람들은 시간이 지나도 창출될 수 있는 부의 총량이 제한되어 있다고 보았기에 어딘가에서 수익이 생기면 다른 어딘가에서 손해가 날 것으로 기대하며, 결국에는 현재보다 나쁜 상태가 이어질 것으로 보았다는 것이다. 따라서 빈칸에 들어갈 말로 가장 적절한 것은 ① '그것은 절대 조금도 더 커지지 않았다'이다.

- era ⓝ 시대
- extend credit 신용 거래를 하다
- wealth ⓝ 부, 재산, 부유함
- profit ⓝ 이익, 수익
- at the expense of ~의 희생으로
- rob ⓥ 약탈하다, 빼앗다
- seldom ad 좀처럼 ~않는
- present ⓝ 현재, 지금
- bet ⓝ 짐작, 추측, 내기
- particular ⓐ 특정한
- enrich ⓥ 풍요롭게 하다
- in time 이윽고, 마침내

구문 풀이

10행 People therefore considered(5형식 동사) it(가목적어) a bad bet(목적격 보어(명사)) to assume {that they would be producing more wealth ten years down the line}.(진목적어)
{ }: 명사절

★★★ 1등급 대비 고난도 2점 문제

08 새롭고 예기치 못한 사건과 정보를 잘 기억하는 뇌
정답률 32% | 정답 ④

다음 빈칸에 들어갈 말로 가장 적절한 것을 고르시오.

① Awareness of social responsibility – 사회적 책임에 대한 인식
② Memorization of historical facts – 역사적 사실의 암기
③ Competition with rivals – 라이벌과의 경쟁
✔ Preference for novelty – 새로움에 대한 선호
⑤ Fear of failure – 실패에 대한 두려움

Our brains have evolved to remember unexpected events / because basic survival depends on the ability / to perceive causes and predict effects.
우리의 뇌는 예상치 못한 사건들을 기억하도록 진화해 왔는데, / 왜냐하면 기본적인 생존이 능력에 달려 있기 때문이다. / 원인을 인식하고 결과를 예측하는

If the brain predicts one event and experiences another, / the unusualness will be especially interesting / and will be encoded accordingly.
만약 뇌가 어떤 사건을 예측하고 다른 사건을 경험한다면, / 그 특이함은 특히 흥미로울 것이고 / 그에 따라 입력될 것이다.

Neurologist and classroom teacher Judith Willis has claimed / that surprise in the classroom / is one of the most effective ways of teaching / with brain stimulation in mind.
신경학자이자 학급 교사인 Judith Willis는 주장했다. / 교실에서의 놀라움은 / 가르치는 가장 효과적인 방법 중 하나라고 / 뇌 자극을 염두에 두고

If students are exposed to new experiences / via demonstrations / or through the unexpected enthusiasm of their teachers or peers, / they will be much more likely to connect with the information that follows.

[문제편 p.060]

학생들이 새로운 경험에 노출되면, / 실연을 통해 / 혹은 교사나 또래 친구의 예상치 못한 열의를 통해 / 그들은 뒤따르는 정보와 연결될 가능성이 훨씬 더 클 것이다.

Willis has written / that encouraging active discovery in the classroom / allows students to interact with new information, / moving it beyond working memory to be processed in the frontal lobe, / which is devoted to advanced cognitive functioning.

Willis는 기술했는데, / 교실에서 능동적인 발견을 장려하는 것이 / 학생들로 하여금 새로운 정보와 상호 작용하게 해 주어서, / 그것이 작업 기억을 넘어 전두엽에서 처리되도록 한다고 / 이 전두엽은 고도의 인지 기능을 전담한다.

Preference for novelty sets us up for learning / by directing attention, / providing stimulation to developing perceptual systems, / and feeding curious and exploratory behavior.

새로움에 대한 선호는 우리를 학습하도록 준비시킨다. / 주의를 이끌고, / 지각 체계를 발전시키는 데 자극을 제공하며, / 호기심 많고 탐구적인 행동을 충족함으로써

우리의 뇌는 예상치 못한 사건들을 기억하도록 진화해 왔는데, 왜냐하면 기본적인 생존이 원인을 인식하고 결과를 예측하는 능력에 달려 있기 때문이다. 만약 뇌가 어떤 사건을 예측하고 (그것과) 다른 사건을 경험한다면, 그 특이함은 특히 흥미로울 것이고 그에 따라 (뇌 속의 정보로) 입력될 것이다. 신경학자이자 학급 교사인 Judith Willis는 교실에서의 놀라움은 뇌 자극을 염두에 두고 가르치는 가장 효과적인 방법 중 하나라고 주장했다. 학생들이 실연, 혹은 교사나 또래 친구의 예상치 못한 열의를 통해 새로운 경험에 노출되면, 그들은 뒤따르는 정보와 연결될 가능성이 훨씬 더 클 것이다. Willis는 교실에서 능동적인 발견을 장려하는 것이 학생들로 하여금 새로운 정보와 상호 작용하게 해 주어서, 그것(새로운 정보)이 작업 기억을 넘어 전두엽에서 처리되도록 한다고 기술했는데, 이 전두엽은 고도의 인지 기능을 전담한다. 새로움에 대한 선호는 주의를 이끌고, 지각 체계를 발전시키는 데 자극을 제공하며, 호기심 많고 탐구적인 행동을 충족함으로써 우리를 학습하도록 준비시킨다.

Why? 왜 정답일까?

'Our brains have evolved to remember unexpected events because basic survival depends on the ability to perceive causes and predict effects.'에서 우리 뇌는 기본적인 생존을 위해 '예기치 못한' 사건을 기억하도록 진화해 왔다고 언급하는 것으로 볼 때, 빈칸에 들어갈 말로 가장 적절한 것은 ④ '새로움에 대한 선호'이다. 본문의 unexpected, unusualness, surprise, new 등이 novelty로 재진술되었다.

- unexpected ⓐ 예상치 못한
- predict ⓥ 예측하다
- encode ⓥ 부호화하다
- stimulation ⓝ 자극
- enthusiasm ⓝ 열정
- exploratory ⓐ 탐구적인
- perceive ⓥ 인지하다
- unusualness ⓝ 특이함
- accordingly ad 그에 따라
- demonstration ⓝ (사용법에 대한) 실연
- be devoted to ~에 전념하다
- novelty ⓝ 새로움

구문 풀이

13행 Willis has written that encouraging active discovery in the classroom allows students to interact with new information, moving it beyond working memory to be processed in the frontal lobe, which is devoted to advanced cognitive functioning.
- that: 접속사(~것)
- encouraging active discovery: 동명사구 주어
- allows students to interact: 「allow+목적어+to부정사 : ~이 …하게 해주다」
- moving it beyond ...: 분사구문(그리고 ~하다)
- the frontal lobe: 선행사
- which: 관·대 계속적 용법

★★ 문제 해결 꿀~팁 ★★

▶ 많이 틀린 이유는?

뇌는 새롭고 예기치 못한 사건이나 정보를 더 잘 기억한다는 내용의 글이다. 역사적 사실을 단순 암기하는 것에 관해서는 언급되지 않으므로 ②는 답으로 부적절하다.

▶ 문제 해결 방법은?

첫 두 문장에서 주제를 제시한 뒤 연구 내용을 예시로 들고 마지막 문장에서 주제를 한 번 더 정리하고 있으므로, 글 서두의 내용과 상통하는 내용의 선택지를 답으로 골라야 한다.

★★★ 1등급 대비 고난도 3점 문제

09 반항 경향을 이용한 마케팅 — 정답률 45% | 정답 ①

다음 빈칸에 들어갈 말로 가장 적절한 것을 고르시오. [3점]

✔ reversal – 반전
② imitation – 모방
③ repetition – 반복
④ conformity – 순응
⑤ collaboration – 협력

Rebels may think they're rebels, / but clever marketers influence them / just like the rest of us.

반항자들은 자기가 반항자라고 생각할지도 모르지만, / 영리한 마케터들은 그들에게 영향을 준다. / 나머지 우리에게 그러듯이

Saying, "Everyone is doing it" / may turn some people off from an idea.

"모두가 그렇게 하고 있다."라고 말하는 것은 / 일부 사람들이 어떤 생각에 흥미를 잃게 할지도 모른다.

These people will look for alternatives, / which (if cleverly planned) can be / exactlywhat a marketer or persuader wants you to believe.

이 사람들은 대안을 찾을 것이고, / 그것은 (만약 영리하게 계획된다면) ~일 수 있다. / 정확히 마케터나 설득자가 여러분이 믿기를 원하는 것

If I want you to consider an idea, / and know you strongly reject popular opinion / in favor of maintaining your independence and uniqueness, / I would present the majority option first, / which you would reject in favor of my actual preference.

만약 내가 여러분이 어떤 아이디어를 고려하길 바라는데, / 여러분이 대중적인 의견을 강하게 거부한다는 것을 안다면, / 독립성과 고유성을 유지하기 위해서 / 나는 대다수가 선택하는 것을 먼저 제시할 것이고, / 여러분은 내 실제 선호에 따라 그것을 거부할 것이다.

We are often tricked / when we try to maintain a position of defiance.

우리는 종종 속는다. / 우리가 반항의 입장을 유지하려 할 때

People use this reversal / to make us independently" choose an option / which suits their purposes.

사람들은 이러한 반전을 사용한다. / 우리가 선택지를 '독자적으로' 택하도록 만들기 위해 / 그들의 목적에 맞는

Some brands have taken full effect of our defiance towards the mainstream / and positioned themselves as rebels; / which has created even stronger brand loyalty.

일부 브랜드들은 주류에 대한 우리의 반항을 온전히 활용해 / 반항자로 자리 잡았으며, / 이는 훨씬 더 강력한 브랜드 충성도를 만들어 왔다.

반항자들은 자기가 반항자라고 생각할지도 모르지만, 영리한 마케터들은 나머지 우리에게 그러듯이 그들에게 영향을 준다. "모두가 그렇게 하고 있다."라고 말하는 것은 일부 사람들이 어떤 생각에 흥미를 잃게 할지도 모른다. 이 사람들은 대안을 찾을 것이고, 그것은 (만약 영리하게 계획된다면) 정확히 마케터나 설득자가 여러분이 믿기를 원하는 것일 수 있다. 만약 내가 여러분이 어떤 아이디어를 고려하길 바라는데, 여러분이 독립성과 고유성을 유지하기 위해서 대중적인 의견을 강하게 거부한다는 것을 안다면, 나는 대다수가 선택하는 것을 먼저 제시할 것이고, 여러분은 내 실제 선호에 따라 그것을 거부할 것이다. 우리는 반항의 입장을 유지하려 할 때 종종 속는다. 사람들은 우리가 그들의 목적에 맞는 선택지를 '독자적으로' 택하도록 만들기 위해 이러한 반전을 사용한다. 일부 브랜드들은 주류에 대한 우리의 반항을 온전히 활용해 반항자로 자리 잡았으며, 이는 훨씬 더 강력한 브랜드 충성도를 만들어 왔다.

Why? 왜 정답일까?

반항자들을 대상으로 한 마케팅 기법을 소개하고 있다. 반항자들은 스스로의 독립성과 고유성을 중시하기 때문에, 대중의 생각을 제시받으면 그에 반감을 보이고, 실은 그 '반감 형성'이 마케터들의 의도라는 것이다. (Some brands have taken full effect of our defiance towards the mainstream and positioned themselves as rebels; which has created even stronger brand loyalty.)따라서 반항적인 행동 경향을 '역이용'하여 본래의 마케팅 목적을 달성한다는 의미로, 빈칸에 들어갈 말로 가장 적절한 것은 ① '반전'이다.

- rebel ⓝ 반항아
- turn off ~을 지루하게 만들다
- reject ⓥ 거부하다
- independence ⓝ 독립
- majority ⓝ 대다수
- defiance ⓝ 반항
- mainstream ⓝ 주류
- repetition ⓝ 반복
- clever ⓐ 영리한
- alternative ⓝ 대안
- in favor of ~을 위해
- uniqueness ⓝ 고유성
- trick ⓥ 속이다
- suit ⓥ ~에 맞추다
- loyalty ⓝ 충성도
- conformity ⓝ 순응

구문 풀이

6행 If I want you to consider an idea, and know {(that) you strongly reject popular opinion in favor of maintaining your independence and uniqueness}, I would present the majority option first, which you would reject in favor of my actual preference.
- If: 접속사(~라면)
- want: 동사1
- know: 동사2
- (that): 접속사
- the majority option: 선행사
- which: 계속적 용법

★★ 문제 해결 꿀~팁 ★★

▶ 많이 틀린 이유는?

'누구나 다 하고 있다'는 인용구만 보면 남들을 '따라 한다'는 의미의 ②를 고르기 쉽다. 하지만 글에서 언급된 반항자들은 대중의 의견을 따르기보다는 '반대하는' 사람들이므로 '모방'이라는 단어는 적절하지 않다.

▶ 문제 해결 방법은?
대중적인 의견에 반대하려는 성향을 '오히려 이용해서' 브랜드에 대한 강한 충성도를 형성한다는 내용을 요약하는 단어가 필요하다.

★★★ 1등급 대비 고난도 3점 문제

10 모르는 것을 질문하는 일의 중요성 정답률 40% | 정답 ⑤

다음 빈칸에 들어갈 말로 가장 적절한 것을 고르시오. [3점]

① showing caring attitudes to others
타인에게 배려하는 태도를 보여주는
② admitting you are less than perfect
당신이 결코 완벽하지 않다는 것을 인정하는
③ wanting to feel triumph over reality
현실감보다 승리감을 느끼고 싶어 하는
④ arguing against any opposing opinion
그 어떤 반대 의견이든 맞서는
⑤ pretending to know more than you do
당신이 알고 있는 것보다 더 많이 아는 척하는

Confident leaders are not afraid / to ask the basic questions: / the questions to which you may feel embarrassed / about not already knowing the answers.
자신감 있는 리더들은 두려워하지 않는다. / 기본적인 질문을 하는 것을 / 당신이 창피하게 느낄 수도 있는 질문 / 아직 답을 알지 못한다는 데 대해
When you don't know something, / admit it as quickly as possible / and immediately take action / — ask a question.
당신이 뭔가를 알지 못한다면, / 이를 가능한 빨리 인정하고 / 즉시 조치를 취하라. / 즉, 질문을 하라.
If you have forgotten who the governor is / or how many hydrogen atoms are in a molecule of water, / quietly ask a friend / but one way or the other, / quit hiding, and take action.
만약 당신이 주지사가 누구인지 잊어버렸다면, / 혹은 물 분자 한 개에 수소 원자가 얼마나 있는지를 / 친구에게 조용히 물어보고, / 그러나 어떤 식으로든 / 그만 감추고, 조치를 취하라.
Paradoxically, when you ask basic questions, / you will more than likely be perceived by others / to be smarter.
역설적이게도, 당신이 기본적인 질문을 할 때, / 당신은 다른 사람들에 의해 인식될 가능성이 높다. / 더 똑똑하다고
And more importantly, / you'll end up knowing far more over your lifetime.
그리고 더 중요하게는, / 당신은 결국 일생에 걸쳐 훨씬 더 많은 것을 알게 될 것이다.
This approach will cause you to be more successful / than you would have been / had you employed the common practice / of pretending to know more than you do.
이러한 접근법은 당신이 더 많이 성공하게 할 것이다. / 당신이 그러했을 것보다 / 만약 당신이 흔한 관행을 취했다면 / 당신이 알고 있는 것보다 더 많이 아는 척하는
To make good leaders, / effective teachers encourage, invite, and even force their students / to ask those fundamental questions.
훌륭한 리더를 만들어 내기 위해서 / 유능한 교사들은 학생들에게 격려하고 권유하며, 심지어 강요도 한다. / 그러한 기본적인 질문을 하도록

자신감 있는 리더들은 아직 답을 알지 못한다는 데 대해 창피하게 느낄 수도 있는 기본적인 질문을 하는 것을 두려워하지 않는다. 뭔가를 알지 못한다면, 이를 가능한 빨리 인정하고 즉시 조치를 취하라. 즉, 질문을 하라. 만약 당신이 주지사가 누구인지 혹은 물 분자 한 개에 수소 원자가 얼마나 있는지를 잊어버렸다면, 친구에게 조용히 어떻게든 물어보고, 그만 감추고, 조치를 취하라. 역설적이게도, 당신이 기본적인 질문을 할 때, 당신은 다른 사람들에 의해 더 똑똑하다고 인식될 가능성이 높다. 그리고 더 중요하게는, 결국 일생에 걸쳐 훨씬 더 많은 것을 알게 될 것이다. 이러한 접근법은 만약 당신이 알고 있는 것보다 더 많이 아는 척하는 흔한 관행을 취했다면 이뤘을 성공보다 더 많이 성공하게 할 것이다. 훌륭한 리더를 만들어 내기 위해서 유능한 교사들은 학생들이 그러한 기본적인 질문을 하도록 격려하고 권유하며, 심지어 강요도 한다.

Why? 왜 정답일까?

'When you don't know something, admit it as quickly as possible and immediately take action — ask a question.'에서 뭔가를 알지 못한다면 이를 가능한 한 빨리 인정하고 질문을 하라고 권하는데, 빈칸 문장은 '~을 할 경우보다 질문을 많이 할 경우에 더 많은 성공을 이룰 수 있다'는 뜻이다. 결국 빈칸에는 질문을 하는 경우와는 반대되는 말이 들어가야 하므로, 답으로 가장 적절한 것은 ⑤ '당신이 알고 있는 것보다 더 많이 아는 척하는'이다.

- confident ⓐ 자신감 있는
- admit ⓥ 인정하다
- take action 조치를 취하다
- hydrogen ⓝ 수소
- one way or the other 어떻게든
- embarrassed ⓐ 창피한, 당황한
- immediately ad 즉시, 바로
- governor ⓝ (미국에서) 주지사
- molecule ⓝ 분자
- paradoxically ad 역설적으로
- perceive ⓥ 인식하다
- practice ⓝ 관행, 관습
- fundamental ⓐ 기본적인
- employ ⓥ 이용하다
- invite ⓥ 권유하다, 요청하다
- attitude ⓝ 태도, 자세, 행동

구문 풀이

1행 Confident leaders are not afraid to ask the basic questions: [the questions {to which you may feel embarrassed about not already knowing the answers}].
(are not afraid to: ~하는 것을 두려워하다 / [ ]: the basic questions와 동격 / to which: 전치사+관계대명사 / about: 전치사 / not already knowing: 동명사 부정형)

★★ 문제 해결 꿀~팁 ★★

▶ 많이 틀린 이유는?
주제는 쉽게 파악되지만 빈칸에는 주제와 반대되는 말을 넣어야 하기에 어려운 문제였다. 최다 오답인 ②는 주제를 그대로 나타낸 말이어서 빈칸에 넣고 해석하면 '자신이 불완전하다고 인정할 때보다 (질문을 많이 할 때) 더 성공적이게 된다'라는 뜻이 되는데, '불완전하다고 인정하는 것=질문을 많이 하는 것'이므로 비교 자체가 불가능하며 문장의 전체적인 의미 또한 성립되지 않는다.
▶ 문제 해결 방법은?
빈칸 문장의 의미가 '~한 경우보다 질문을 하는 경우가 이득이 된다'임을 이해하고 빈칸 부분에는 '질문을 하지 않는 경우'에 해당하는 말을 넣어야 함을 파악한다.

★★★ 1등급 대비 고난도 3점 문제

11 문화적 산물이 사람들에게 미치는 영향 정답률 40% | 정답 ④

다음 빈칸에 들어갈 말로 가장 적절한 것을 고르시오. [3점]

① can provide many valuable views
여러 가치 있는 시각을 제공해줄 수 있다
② reflects the idea of the sociologists
사회학자들의 생각을 반영한다
③ forms prejudices to certain characters
특정 캐릭터에 대한 편견을 형성한다
④ will have the same effect on everyone
모든 사람에게 똑같은 영향을 줄 것이라
⑤ might resolve social conflicts among people
사람들 사이의 사회적 갈등을 해결해줄지 모른다

Sociologists have proven / that people bring their own views and values / to the culture they encounter; / books, TV programs, movies, and music / may affect everyone, / but they affect different people in different ways.
사회학자들은 입증해 왔는데, / 사람들이 자신만의 관점이나 가치를 가져온다는 것을 / 그들이 직면하는 문화로 / 책, TV 프로그램, 영화, 음악은 / 모두에게 영향을 줄지도 모르지만 / 그것들은 다양한 사람들에게 다양한 방식으로 영향을 준다.
In a study, / Neil Vidmar and Milton Rokeach / showed episodes of the sitcom *All in the Family* / to viewers with a range of different views on race.
한 연구에서, / Neil Vidmar와 Milton Rokeach는 / 시트콤 *All in the Family*의 에피소드들을 보여주었다. / 인종에 관한 다양한 관점을 가진 시청자들에게
The show centers on a character named Archie Bunker, / an intolerant bigot / who often gets into fights with his more progressive family members.
이 쇼는 Archie Bunker라는 인물에 초점을 맞춘다. / 편협한 고집쟁이인 / 보다 진보적인 가족 구성원들과 자주 싸움에 휘말리는
Vidmar and Rokeach found / that viewers who didn't share Archie Bunker's views / thought the show was very funny / in the way it made fun of Archie's absurd racism / — in fact, this was the producers' intention.
Vidmar와 Rokeach는 발견했는데, / Archie Bunker의 관점을 공유하지 않는 시청자들이 / 그 쇼가 아주 재미있다고 생각했다는 것을 / Archie의 어처구니없는 인종 차별주의를 비웃는 방식에 있어 / 실은 이것이 제작자의 의도였다.
On the other hand, though, / viewers who were themselves bigots / thought Archie Bunker was the hero of the show / and that the producers meant to make fun of his foolish family!
그러나 반면에, / 스스로가 고집쟁이인 시청자들은 / Archie Bunker가 그 쇼의 영웅이라고 생각했고, / 제작자가 Bunker의 어리석은 가족들을 비웃으려 한다고 생각했다!
This demonstrates / why it's a mistake to assume / that a certain cultural product will have the same effect on everyone.
이것은 보여준다. / 왜 가정하는 것이 잘못인지를 / 특정 문화적 산물이 모든 사람에게 똑같은 영향을 줄 것이라고

사회학자들은 사람들이 그들 자신의 관점이나 가치를 그들이 직면하는 문화로 가져온다는 것을 입증해 왔는데, 책, TV 프로그램, 영화, 음악은 모두에게 영향을 줄지도 모르지만 다양한 사람들에게 다양한 방식으로 영향을 준다. 한 연구에서, Neil Vidmar와 Milton Rokeach는 인종에 관한 다양한 관점을 가진 시청자들에게 시트콤 *All in the Family*의 에피소드들을 보여주었다. 이 쇼는 보다 진보적인 가족 구성원들과 자주 싸움에 휘말리는 편협한 고집쟁이 Archie

Bunker라는 인물에 초점을 맞춘다. Vidmar와 Rokeach는 Archie Bunker의 관점을 공유하지 않는 시청자들이 Archie의 어처구니없는 인종 차별주의를 비웃는 방식에 있어 그 쇼가 아주 재미있다고 생각했다는 것을 발견했는데, 실은 이것이 제작자의 의도였다. 그러나 반면에, 스스로가 고집쟁이인 시청자들은 Archie Bunker가 그 쇼의 영웅이라고 생각했고, 제작자가 Bunker의 어리석은 가족들을 비웃으려 한다고 생각했다! 이것은 왜 특정 문화적 산물이 모든 사람에게 똑같은 영향을 줄 것이라고 가정하는 것이 잘못인지를 보여준다.

Why? 왜 정답일까?

첫 문장인 '~ **books, TV programs, movies, and music may affect everyone, but they affect different people in different ways.**'에서 책, TV 프로, 영화, 음악 등은 모두에게 영향을 주기는 하지만 그 영향의 대상과 양상은 다양하다는 주제를 제시하고 있다. 이를 근거로 할 때, 어느 시각이 '잘못된' 것인지를 지적하는 빈칸에는 주제와는 반대로 모두에게 같은 영향이 갈 것으로 생각한다는 내용이 들어가야 하므로, 답으로 가장 적절한 것은 ④ '모든 사람에게 똑같은 영향을 줄 것이라'이다.

- encounter ⓥ 직면하다, 마주치다
- progressive ⓐ 진보적인
- racism ⓝ 인종 차별주의
- assume ⓥ 가정하다
- have an effect on ~에게 영향을 주다
- intolerant ⓐ 편협한
- absurd ⓐ 어처구니없는, 불합리한
- demonstrate ⓥ 분명히 보여주다
- prejudice ⓝ 편견
- resolve ⓥ 해결하다

구문 풀이

17행 **This demonstrates why it's a mistake to assume that a certain cultural product will have the same effect on everyone.**
(why: 의문부사 / it's: 가주어 / to assume: 진주어 / that: 접속사(~것))

★★ 문제 해결 꿀~팁 ★★

▶ 많이 틀린 이유는?

첫 문장에 따르면 각종 문화적 산물이 사람마다 미치는 영향이 다른데, 이는 사람들이 문화적 산물을 접할 때 각기 자기만의 견해와 가치관을 투영하기 때문이다. 이를 근거로 할 때, 문화적 산물이 사람들에게 가치로운 견해를 '주는' 입장이라고 서술한 ①은 글의 내용과 맞지 않다. ③ 또한 문화적 산물을 특정 캐릭터들에 대한 편견을 형성시키는 주체로 보고 있어 답으로 부적절하다.

▶ 문제 해결 방법은?

첫 문장에서 주제를 제시한 후 이를 뒷받침하는 연구의 내용을 후술한 글이다. 따라서 연구의 결론을 나타내는 빈칸 문장은 첫 문장과 동일한 내용일 것임을 예측할 수 있다.

★★★ 1등급 대비 고난도 3점 문제

12 인간성 정의에 도움을 주는 인공 지능 정답률 45% | 정답 ①

다음 빈칸에 들어갈 말로 가장 적절한 것을 고르시오. [3점]

① AIs will help define humanity
AI가 인간성을 정의하는 데 도움을 줄 것이라는
② humans could also be like AIs
사람도 AI와 같아질 수 있다는
③ humans will be liberated from hard labor
사람은 힘든 노동으로부터 해방될 것이라는
④ AIs could lead us in resolving moral dilemmas
AI는 도덕적 딜레마 해결에서 우리를 이끌 수 있다는
⑤ AIs could compensate for a decline in human intelligence
AI는 인간의 지능 감퇴를 보완해줄 수 있다는

Over the past 60 years, / as mechanical processes have replicated behaviors and talents / we thought were unique to humans, / we've had to change our minds about what sets us apart.
지난 60년 동안 / 기계식 공정이 행동과 재능을 복제해왔기 때문에, / 우리가 생각하기에 인간에게만 있는 / 우리는 우리를 다르게 만드는 것에 관한 생각을 바꿔야만 했다.

As we invent more species of AI, / we will be forced to surrender more / of what is supposedly unique about humans.
더 많은 종의 AI를 발명하면서, / 우리는 더 많은 것을 내줘야만 할 것이다. / 아마도 인간에게만 있는 것 중

Each step of surrender / — we are not the only mind / that can play chess, fly a plane, make music, or invent a mathematical law — / will be painful and sad.
매번 내주는 일은 / (우리가 유일한 존재가 아니라는 것) / 체스를 둘 줄 알거나, 비행기를 날릴 줄 알거나, 음악을 만들거나, 아니면 수학 법칙을 발명할 줄 아는 / 고통스럽고 슬플 것이다.

We'll spend the next three decades — indeed, perhaps the next century — / in a permanent identity crisis, / continually asking ourselves what humans are good for.
우리는 앞으로 다가올 30년(사실, 어쩌면 앞으로 다가올 한 세기)을 보내며, / 영속적인 정체성 위기 속에서 / 계속 스스로에게 인간이 무슨 소용이 있는지를 질문하게 될 것이다.

If we aren't unique toolmakers, or artists, or moral ethicists, / then what, if anything, makes us special?
우리가 유일한 도구 제작자나 예술가, 또는 도덕 윤리학자가 아니라면, / 도대체 무엇이 우리를 특별하게 만드는가?

In the grandest irony of all, / the greatest benefit of an everyday, utilitarian AI / will not be increased productivity / or an economics of abundance / or a new way of doing science / — although all those will happen.
가장 아이러니하게도, / 일상적이고도 실용적인 AI의 가장 큰 이점은, / 생산성 증가나 / 풍요의 경제학, / 혹은 과학을 행하는 새로운 방식이 아닐 것이다. / 비록 이 모든 일이 일어난다 할지라도

The greatest benefit of the arrival of artificial intelligence is / that AIs will help define humanity.
인공 지능의 도래가 주는 가장 큰 이점은 / AI가 인간성을 정의하는 데 도움을 줄 것이라는 점이다.

지난 60년 동안 기계식 공정이 우리가 생각하기에 인간에게만 있는 행동과 재능을 복제해왔기 때문에, 우리는 우리를 다르게 만드는 것에 관한 생각을 바꿔야만 했다. 더 많은 종의 AI(인공지능)를 발명하면서, 우리는 아마도 인간에게만 있는 것 중 더 많은 것을 내줘야만 할 것이다. 매번 내주는 일(우리가 체스를 둘 줄 알거나, 비행기를 날릴 줄 알거나, 음악을 만들거나, 아니면 수학 법칙을 발명할 줄 아는 유일한 존재가 아니라는 것)은 고통스럽고 슬플 것이다. 우리는 앞으로 다가올 30년(사실, 어쩌면 앞으로 다가올 한 세기)을 영속적인 정체성 위기 속에서 보내며, 계속 스스로에게 인간이 무슨 소용이 있는지를 질문하게 될 것이다. 우리가 유일한 도구 제작자나 예술가, 또는 도덕 윤리학자가 아니라면, 도대체 무엇이 우리를 특별하게 만드는가? 가장 아이러니하게도, 일상적이고도 실용적인 AI의 가장 큰 이점은, 비록 이 모든 일이 일어난다 할지라도, 생산성 증가나 풍요의 경제학, 혹은 과학을 행하는 새로운 방식이 아닐 것이다. 인공 지능의 도래가 주는 가장 큰 이점은 AI가 인간성을 정의하는 데 도움을 줄 것이라는 점이다.

Why? 왜 정답일까?

기존에 인간에게만 있는 것이라고 생각해 왔던 것들을 기계식 공정이 복제해내고 정교한 **AI**가 만들어지게 되면서 인간의 고유성에 대한 문제의식이 커지게 되었는데, '아이러니하게도' 여기에 **AI**가 도움을 줄 수 있다는 내용을 다룬 글이다. 따라서 빈칸에 들어갈 말로 가장 적절한 것은 ① '**AI**가 인간성을 정의하는 데 도움을 줄 것이라는'이다.

- replicate ⓥ 복제하다
- surrender ⓥ 내어주다, 항복하다
- permanent ⓐ 영속적인, 영구적인
- abundance ⓝ 풍요, 풍부
- compensate for ~을 보완하다, 보상하다
- set apart 다르게 하다, 구별시키다
- supposedly ⓐⓓ 아마
- utilitarian ⓐ 실용적인, 공리주의의
- liberate ⓥ 해방시키다, 자유롭게 하다

구문 풀이

1행 **Over the past 60 years, as mechanical processes have replicated behaviors and talents (we thought) were unique to humans, / we've had to change our minds about [what sets us apart].**
(Over the past 60 years: 기간 부사구 / as: 접속사(~ 때문에) / have replicated: 현재완료 / (주격 관계대명사 생략))

★★ 문제 해결 꿀~팁 ★★

▶ 많이 틀린 이유는?

답과 바로 대응될만한 표현이 지문에 등장하지 않고 '유추'를 통해 답을 찾아야 했다는 점에서 난이도가 높은 문항이었다.

오답률은 대동소이했는데 이는 매력적인 오답 선택지가 있었다기보다는, 지문의 내용 자체를 파악하는 데 어려움을 느낀 수험생이 많았다는 사실을 보여준다.

▶ 문제 해결 방법은?

'**AI**'라는 핵심 소재와 첫 문장에서 제시한 '인간성의 정의'가 어떤 식으로 연관이 되어야 하는지를 능동적으로 유추해보도록 한다.

AI는 정교화되면서 인간의 많은 행위를 따라하게 되고, 이에 따라 인간은 과연 **AI**와 인간을 구별해주는 특성이 무엇일지 고민하게 된다는 내용이 나오는데, 여기서 '아이러니하게도'라는 말이 등장하여 흐름을 반전시킨다. 이는 **AI**가 인간의 정체성 고민을 '촉발'시키는 존재였지만 동시에 '해결'을 해 주기도 한다는 '역설적인' 내용을 설명하기 위해 등장한 부사어이다.

DAY 10 빈칸 추론 10

01 ①	02 ①	03 ⑤	04 ③	05 ②
06 ④	07 ②	08 ②	09 ②	10 ①
11 ①	12 ②			

01 세부 사항에 대한 기억

정답률 35% | 정답 ①

다음 빈칸에 들어갈 말로 가장 적절한 것을 고르시오.

✔ identical - 동일하다　② beneficial - 이롭다
③ alien - 맞지 않다　④ prior - 우선하다
⑤ neutral - 중립적이다

When you begin to tell a story again / that you have retold many times, / what you retrieve from memory / is the index to the story itself.
당신이 이야기를 다시 하기 시작할 때, / 당신이 여러 번 반복하여 말했던 / 기억에서 불러오는 것은 / 이야기 자체에 대한 지표이다.
That index can be embellished in a variety of ways.
그 지표는 다양한 방식으로 윤색될 수 있다.
Over time, even the embellishments become standardized.
시간이 흐르면서, 그 윤색된 것들조차도 표준화된다.
An old man's story that he has told hundreds of times / shows little variation, / and any variation that does exist / becomes part of the story itself, / regardless of its origin.
한 노인이 수백 번 말한 이야기는 / 변형을 거의 보이지 않으며, / 어떤 변형이든 실제로 존재하는 것이면 / 이야기 자체의 일부가 된다. / 그것의 기원에 관계없이
People add details to their stories / that may or may not have occurred.
사람들은 세부 사항을 자신들의 이야기에 덧붙인다. / 일어났을 수도, 또는 일어나지 않았을 수도 있는
They are recalling indexes and reconstructing details.
그들은 지표들을 기억해 내고 세부 사항들을 재구성하고 있는 것이다.
If at some point they add a nice detail, / not really certain of its validity, / telling the story with that same detail a few more times / will ensure its permanent place in the story index.
만약 어떤 시점에 그들이 어떤 멋진 세부 사항을 덧붙이고, / 그것의 타당성에 대해 정말로 확신하지 못한 채 / 동일한 그 세부 사항과 함께 몇 번 더 그 이야기를 말하는 것은 / 이야기 지표에서 영구적인 위치를 확보할 것이다.
In other words, the stories we tell time and again / are identical to the memory / we have of the events that the story relates.
다시 말해 우리가 되풀이해서 말하는 이야기는 / 기억과 동일하다. / 그 이야기가 전달하는 사건들에 대해 우리가 가지고 있는

여러 번 반복하여 말했던 이야기를 다시 하기 시작할 때, 기억에서 불러오는 것은 이야기 자체에 대한 지표이다. 그 지표는 다양한 방식으로 윤색될 수 있다. 시간이 흐르면서, 그 윤색된 것들조차도 표준화된다. 한 노인이 수백 번 말한 이야기는 변형을 거의 보이지 않으며, 어떤 변형이든 실제로 존재하는 것이면 그것의 기원에 관계없이 이야기 자체의 일부가 된다. 사람들은 일어났을 수도, 또는 일어나지 않았을 수도 있는 세부 사항을 자신들의 이야기에 덧붙인다. 그들은 지표들을 기억해 내고 세부 사항들을 재구성하고 있는 것이다. 만약, 어떤 시점에 그들이 어떤 멋진 세부 사항의 타당성에 대해 정말로 확신하지 못한 채 그것을 덧붙이고, 동일한 그 세부 사항과 함께 몇 번 더 그 이야기를 말하다보면 그것은 이야기 지표에서 영구적인 위치를 확보할 것이다. 다시 말해 우리가 되풀이해서 말하는 이야기는 그 이야기가 전달하는 사건들에 대해 우리가 가지고 있는 기억과 동일하다.

Why? 왜 정답일까?

우리는 어떤 이야기를 기억할 때 이야기의 모든 세부 사항이 아닌 지표를 기억하는 것이며, 세부 사항은 지표에 맞게 재구성되는데, 시간이 흐르며 반복적으로 언급된 세부 사항은 기원에 관계없이 이야기의 일부가 되며(~ **any variation that does exist becomes part of the story itself**, ~), 즉 이야기 지표에서 영구적인 입지를 확보하게 된다(~ **ensure its permanent place in the story index.**)는 내용의 글이다. 다시 말해 어떤 세부 사항이 실제로 일어났는지 여부에 상관없이 이야기를 재구성하는 데 반복적으로 포함되다 보면 기억의 일부가 된다는 내용이 핵심이므로, 빈칸에 들어갈 말로 가장 적절한 것은 ① '동일하다'이다.

- **standardize** ⓥ 표준화하다
- **regardless of** ~에 관계없이
- **relate** ⓥ 이야기하다, 말하다, 관련시키다
- **alien to** ~에 맞지 않는
- **variation** ⓝ 변형, 변주
- **certain of** ~을 확신하는
- **identical to** ~와 동일한
- **prior to** ~에 우선하는

구문 풀이

5행 An old man's story [that he has told hundreds of times] shows little variation, and any variation [that does exist] becomes part of the story itself, regardless of its origin.
(주어1 / 목적격 관계대명사 / 동사1 / 주어2 / 주격 관·대 / 동사 강조 / 동사2 / 강조 / ~에 관계없이)

02 행동의 연쇄 반응

정답률 61% | 정답 ①

다음 빈칸에 들어갈 말로 가장 적절한 것을 고르시오.

✔ isolation - 고립　② comfort - 위안
③ observation - 관찰　④ fairness - 공정함
⑤ harmony - 조화

The tendency / for one purchase to lead to another one / has a name: / the Diderot Effect.
경향에는 / 한 구매가 또 다른 구매로 이어지는 / 이름이 있는데, / 바로 Diderot 효과이다.
The Diderot Effect states / that obtaining a new possession / often creates a spiral of consumption / that leads to additional purchases.
Diderot 효과는 말한다. / 새로운 소유물을 얻는 것이 / 종종 소비의 소용돌이를 만든다고 / 추가적인 구매들로 이어지는
You can spot this pattern everywhere.
당신은 이러한 경향을 어디서든지 발견할 수 있다.
You buy a dress / and have to get new shoes and earrings to match.
당신은 드레스를 사고 / 어울리는 새 신발과 귀걸이를 사야 한다.
You buy a toy for your child / and soon find yourself purchasing all of the accessories / that go with it.
당신은 아이를 위해 장난감을 사고 / 곧 모든 액세서리들을 구매하는 자신을 발견한다. / 그것과 어울리는
It's a chain reaction of purchases.
이것은 구매의 연쇄 반응이다.
Many human behaviors follow this cycle.
많은 인간의 행동들은 이 순환을 따른다.
You often decide what to do next / based on what you have just finished doing.
당신은 종종 다음에 무엇을 할지 결정한다. / 당신이 방금 끝낸 것에 근거하여
Going to the bathroom / leads to washing and drying your hands, / which reminds you / that you need to put the dirty towels in the laundry, / so you add laundry detergent to the shopping list, and so on.
화장실에 가는 것은 / 손을 씻고 말리는 것으로 이어지고, / 이는 당신으로 하여금 생각이 들게 하고, / 당신이 더러운 수건을 세탁실에 넣을 필요가 있다는 / 그래서 당신은 쇼핑 목록에 세탁 세제를 더하고, 기타 등등을 한다.
No behavior happens in isolation.
고립되어 일어나는 행동은 없다.
Each action becomes a cue / that triggers the next behavior.
각 행동은 신호가 된다. / 다음 행동을 유발하는

한 구매가 또 다른 구매로 이어지는 경향에는 이름이 있는데, 바로 Diderot 효과이다. Diderot 효과는 새로운 소유물을 얻는 것이 종종 추가적인 구매들로 이어지는 소비의 소용돌이를 만든다고 말한다. 당신은 이러한 경향을 어디서든지 발견할 수 있다. 당신은 드레스를 사고 어울리는 새 신발과 귀걸이를 사야 한다. 당신은 아이를 위해 장난감을 사고 곧 그것과 어울리는 모든 액세서리들을 구매하는 자신을 발견한다. 이것은 구매의 연쇄 반응이다. 많은 인간의 행동들은 이 순환을 따른다. 당신은 종종 당신이 방금 끝낸 것에 근거하여 다음에 무엇을 할지 결정한다. 화장실에 가는 것은 손을 씻고 말리는 것으로 이어지고, 이로 인해 당신은 더러운 수건을 세탁실에 넣을 필요가 있다는 생각이 들고, 그래서 당신은 쇼핑 목록에 세탁 세제를 더하고, 기타 등등을 한다. 고립되어 일어나는 행동은 없다. 각 행동은 다음 행동을 유발하는 신호가 된다.

Why? 왜 정답일까?

마지막 문장인 '**Each action becomes a cue that triggers the next behavior.**'에서 한 행동은 다음 행동을 유발하는 신호가 된다고 언급하는 것으로 보아, 빈칸이 포함된 문장은 그 어떤 행동도 '따로' 일어나지 않는다는 의미를 나타내야 한다. 따라서 빈칸에 들어갈 말로 가장 적절한 것은 ① '고립'이다.

- **state** ⓥ 진술하다
- **possession** ⓝ 소유물
- **consumption** ⓝ 소비
- **spot** ⓥ 발견하다
- **go with** ~와 어울리다
- **remind** ⓥ 상기시키다
- **detergent** ⓝ 세제
- **isolation** ⓝ 고립
- **obtain** ⓥ 얻다, 입수하다
- **spiral** ⓝ 소용돌이
- **additional** ⓐ 추가의
- **pattern** ⓝ (정형화된) 양식, 패턴, 경향
- **chain reaction** 연쇄 반응
- **laundry** ⓝ 세탁실
- **trigger** ⓥ 유발하다
- **fairness** ⓝ 공정함, 공평함

DAY 10

구문 풀이

1행 The tendency for one purchase to lead to another one has a name: the Diderot Effect.
(The tendency: 주어 / for one purchase: 의미상 주어 / to lead: 형용사적 용법 / has: 동사(단수) / the Diderot Effect: 동격(= a name))

03 탈진실이 일어나는 이유

정답률 47% | 정답 ⑤

다음 빈칸에 들어갈 말로 가장 적절한 것을 고르시오. [3점]

① to hold back our mixed feelings
우리의 혼재된 감정들을 억누를
② that balances our views on politics
정치에 관한 우리의 견해들의 균형을 잡는
③ that leads us to give way to others in need
우리가 어려운 처지의 타인에게 양보하게 하는
④ to carry the constant value of absolute truth
절대적 진리의 변치 않는 가치를 지닐
⑤ that is more important to us than the truth itself
진실 그 자체보다 우리에게 더 중요한

If one looks at the Oxford definition, / one gets the sense / that post-truth is not so much a claim / that truth *does not exist* / as that *facts are subordinate to our political point of view*.
Oxford 사전의 정의를 보면, / 우리는 알게 된다. / 탈진실이란 주장이 아니라, / 진실이 *존재하지 않는다는* / *사실이 우리의 정치적 관점에 종속되어 있다*는 주장임을

The Oxford definition focuses on "*what*" post-truth is: / the idea that feelings sometimes matter more than facts.
Oxford 사전의 정의는 탈진실이란 '*무엇인가*'에 초점을 둔다. / 즉 때로는 감정이 사실보다 더 중요하다는 생각에

But just as important is the next question, / which is *why* this ever occurs.
하지만 그다음 질문은 그에 못지않게 중요한데, / 그것은 도대체 *왜* 이런 일이 일어나는가이다.

Someone does not argue against an obvious or easily confirmable fact / for no reason; / he or she does so / when it is to his or her advantage.
어떤 사람은 분명하거나 쉽게 확인할 수 있는 사실에 반대하는 게 아니며, / 아무런 이유 없이 / 그 사람은 그렇게 한다. / 그렇게 하는 것이 자신의 이익에 부합할 때

When a person's beliefs are threatened by an "inconvenient fact," / sometimes it is preferable to challenge the fact.
어떤 사람의 믿음이 '불편한 사실'에 의해 위협받을 때, / 때로는 그 사실에 이의를 제기하는 것이 선호된다.

This can happen at either a conscious or unconscious level / (since sometimes the person we are seeking to convince / is ourselves), / but the point is / that this sort of post-truth relationship to facts occurs / only when we are seeking to assert something / that is more important to us than the truth itself.
이것은 의식적인 수준이나 무의식적인 수준에서 일어날 수 있지만, / (때로는 우리가 납득시키려고 추구하는 사람이 / 우리 자신이기 때문에) / 핵심은 / 사실에 대한 이러한 종류의 탈진실적 관계가 일어난다는 것이다. / 우리가 어떤 것을 주장하려고 할 때에만 / 진실 그 자체보다 우리에게 더 중요한

Oxford 사전의 정의를 보면, 탈진실이란 진실이 *존재하지 않는다는* 주장이 아니라, *사실이 우리의 정치적 관점에 종속되어 있다*는 주장임을 알게 된다. Oxford 사전의 정의는 탈진실이란 '*무엇인가*', 즉 때로는 감정이 사실보다 더 중요하다는 생각에 초점을 둔다. 하지만 그다음 질문은 그에 못지않게 중요한데, 그것은 도대체 *왜* 이런 일이 일어나는가이다. 어떤 사람은 아무런 이유 없이 분명하거나 쉽게 확인할 수 있는 사실에 반대하는 게 아니며, 그렇게 하는 것이 자신의 이익에 부합할 때 그렇게 한다. 어떤 사람의 믿음이 '불편한 사실'에 의해 위협받을 때, 때로는 그 사실에 이의를 제기하는 것이 선호된다. 이것은 (때로는 우리가 납득시키려고 추구하는 사람이 우리 자신이기 때문에) 의식적인 수준이나 무의식적인 수준에서 일어날 수 있지만, 핵심은 사실에 대한 이러한 종류의 탈진실적 관계가 우리가 진실 그 자체보다 우리에게 더 중요한 어떤 것을 주장하려고 할 때에만 일어난다는 것이다.

Why? 왜 정답일까?

'~ **he or she does so when it is to his or her advantage.**'에서 탈진실 현상, 즉 사실이 개인의 정치적 관점에 종속되는 현상이 일어나는 까닭은 그것이 그 개인의 이익에 부합하기 때문임을 설명한다. 따라서 빈칸에 들어갈 말로 가장 적절한 것은 사실보다도 개인의 이익이 중시된다는 의미를 나타낸 ⑤ '진실 그 자체보다 우리에게 더 중요한'이다.

- **definition** ⓝ 정의, 의미
- **argue against** ~에 반대하다
- **to one's advantage** ~에게 이득이 되는
- **preferable** ⓐ 선호되는
- **unconscious** ⓐ 무의식적인
- **ourselves** pron 우리 자신[스스로]
- **assert** ⓥ 주장하다
- **give way to** ~에 못 이기다, 양보하다
- **post-truth** 탈진실
- **confirmable** ⓐ 확인할 수 있는
- **inconvenient** ⓐ 불편한
- **challenge** ⓥ 이의를 제기하다
- **convince** ⓥ 납득시키다
- **sort of** 종류의
- **hold back** 억누르다
- **in need** 어려운 처지의

구문 풀이

12행 This can happen at either a conscious or unconscious level (since sometimes the person [we are seeking to convince] is ourselves), / but the point is that this sort of post-truth relationship to facts occurs only when we are seeking to assert something [that is more important to us than the truth itself].
(can happen: 자동사 / 「either + A + or + B : A, B 둘 중 하나」 / since: ~이기 때문에 / the point is that: 핵심은 ~이다 / this sort of post-truth relationship: 주어 / occurs: 자동사 / only when: 오로지 ~할 때에만 / that: 주격 관계대명사 / itself: 강조)

04 스스로 운이 나쁘다고 믿는 사람들의 특성

정답률 44% | 정답 ③

다음 빈칸에 들어갈 말로 가장 적절한 것을 고르시오. [3점]

① instructions should be followed at all costs
어떤 희생을 치르더라도 지시 사항은 준수되어야 한다
② their mission was impossible to complete
그들의 임무는 완수하기 불가능한 것이었다
③ other options were passing them by
다른 선택 사항들이 그들을 지나쳐가고 있다
④ counting was such a demanding task
수를 세는 것은 너무도 힘든 과업이었다
⑤ efforts would pay off in the long run
노력하면 결국에 성과가 있을 것이다

In the early 2000s, / British psychologist Richard Wiseman / performed a series of experiments with people / who viewed themselves as either 'lucky' / (they were successful and happy, / and events in their lives seemed to favor them) / or 'unlucky' / (life just seemed to go wrong for them).
2000년대 초반에, / 영국의 심리학자 Richard Wiseman은 / 사람들을 대상으로 일련의 실험을 수행했다. / 스스로 '운이 좋다'라고 생각하는 / (그들은 성공했고 행복하며, / 그들의 삶에서 일어난 일들은 그들에게 우호적인 것처럼 보였다) / 혹은 '운이 나쁘다'라고 / (삶은 그저 잘 풀리지 않는 것처럼 보였다).

What he found was / that the 'lucky' people were good at spotting opportunities.
그가 발견한 것은 / '운이 좋은' 사람들은 기회를 발견하는 데 능숙하다는 것이었다.

In one experiment he told both groups / to count the number of pictures in a newspaper.
한 실험에서 그는 두 집단에게 시켰다. / 신문에 있는 그림의 수를 세도록

The 'unlucky' diligently ground their way through the task; / the 'lucky' usually noticed / that the second page contained an announcement / that said: / "Stop counting — there are 43 photographs in this newspaper."
'운이 나쁜' 집단은 자신의 과업을 열심히 수행했고, / '운이 좋은' 집단은 대체적으로 알아차렸다. / 두 번째 페이지에 안내가 포함되어 있다는 것을 / 적혀 있는 / "숫자 세기를 멈추세요. 이 신문에는 43개의 사진이 있습니다."라고

On a later page, / the 'unlucky' were also too busy counting images / to spot a note reading: / "Stop counting, / tell the experimenter you have seen this, / and win $250."
나중 페이지에서 / '운이 나쁜' 집단은 역시 그림의 개수를 세는 데 너무 바쁜 나머지 / 안내를 발견하지 못했다. / "숫자 세는 것을 멈추고, / 실험자에게 당신이 이것을 봤다고 말하고, / 250달러를 받아가시오."라는

Wiseman's conclusion was / that, when faced with a challenge, / 'unlucky' people were less flexible.
Wiseman의 결론은, / 도전 과제에 직면했을 때 / '운이 나쁜' 사람들은 융통성을 덜 발휘한다는 것이었다.

They focused on a specific goal, / and failed to notice that other options were passing them by.
그들은 특정한 목표에 초점을 맞추어, / 다른 선택 사항들이 그들을 지나쳐가고 있다는 것을 알지 못했다.

2000년대 초반에, 영국의 심리학자 Richard Wiseman은 스스로 '운이 좋다'(그들은 성공했고 행복하며, 그들의 삶에서 일어난 일들은 그들에게 우호적인 것처럼 보였다) 혹은 '운이 나쁘다'(삶은 그저 잘 풀리지 않는 것처럼 보였다)라고 생각하는 사람들을 대상으로 일련의 실험을 수행했다. 그가 발견한 것은 '운이 좋은' 사람들은 기회를 발견하는 데 능숙하다는 것이었다. 한 실험에서 그는 두 집단에게 신문에 있는 그림의 수를 세게 했다. '운이 나쁜' 집단은 자신의 과업을 열심히 수행했고, '운이 좋은' 집단은 두 번째 페이지에 "숫자 세기를 멈추세요. 이 신문에는 43개의 사진이 있습니다."라고 적혀 있는 안내가 포함되어 있다는 것을 대체적으로 알아차렸다. 나중 페이지에서 '운이 나쁜' 집단은 역시 그림의 개수를 세는 데 너무 바쁜 나머지 "숫자 세는 것을 멈추고, 실험자에게 당신이 이것(문구)을 봤다고 말하고, 250달러를 받아가시오."라는 안내를 발견하지 못했다. Wiseman의 결론은, '운이 나쁜' 사람들은 도전 과제에 직면했을 때 융통성을 덜 발휘한다는 것이었다. 그들은 특정한 목표에 초점을 맞추어, 다른 선택 사항들이 그들을 지나쳐가고 있다는 것을 알지 못했다.

Why? 왜 정답일까?

실험의 예를 들어 스스로 운이 좋다고 생각하는 사람들과 운이 나쁘다고 생각하는 사람들의 인지적 특성을 대조한 글이다. '**What he found was that the 'lucky' people were good at spotting opportunities.**'와 **Wiseman's conclusion was**

that, when faced with a challenge, 'unlucky' people were less flexible.' 에서 스스로 운이 좋다고 믿는 사람들은 문제 해결을 도와줄 수 있는 새로운 기회를 더 잘 발견하는 인지적 융통성이 있지만, 스스로 운이 나쁘다고 믿는 사람들은 그러한 기회를 발견할 수 있는 융통성이 덜하다는 결론을 소개한다. 따라서 빈칸에 들어갈 말로 가장 적절한 것은 ③ '다른 선택 사항들이 그들을 지나쳐가고 있다'이다.

- **view** ⓥ (~을 …라고) 생각하다, 여기다
- **spot** ⓥ 알아채다
- **faced with** ~에 직면한
- **at all costs** 어떤 희생을 치르더라도
- **pay off** 성과를 올리다, 성공하다
- **favor** ⓥ 호의를 보이다, 찬성하다
- **diligently** ad 열심히, 부지런히
- **specific** ⓐ 특정한, 구체적인
- **demanding** ⓐ 까다로운, 어려운
- **in the long run** 결국에는

구문 풀이

9행 The 'unlucky'(주어1) diligently ground(동사1(갈다, 연마하다)) their way through the task; / the 'lucky'(주어2) usually noticed(동사2) {that(접속사) the second page contained an announcement [that said: "Stop counting(주격 관·대 / ~하기를 멈추다) — there are 43 photographs in this newspaper."]}

05 접근 가능한 정보의 확장과 창의성의 증가

정답률 47% | 정답 ②

다음 빈칸에 들어갈 말로 가장 적절한 것을 고르시오. [3점]

① the number of rich people increased
부유한 사람들의 수가 증가하였기
✔② information became more widely accessible
정보가 더욱 널리 접근 가능하게 되었기
③ people were able to learn Latin more easily
사람들이 라틴을 더 쉽게 배울 수 있게 되었기
④ education provided equal opportunities for all
교육이 모두에게 평등한 기회를 제공하였기
⑤ new methods of scientific research were introduced
새로운 과학적 연구 방법이 도입되었기

For many centuries / European science, and knowledge in general, was recorded in Latin / — a language that no one spoke any longer / and that had to be learned in schools.
수 세기 동안, / 유럽의 과학과 일반적인 지식은 라틴어로 기록되었는데, / 그 언어는 아무도 더 이상 말하지 않고 / 학교에서 배워야 하는 언어였다.

Very few individuals, probably less than one percent, / had the means to study Latin / enough to read books in that language / and therefore to participate in the intellectual discourse of the times.
어쩌면 1퍼센트도 안 되는 아주 극소수의 사람들만이 / 라틴어를 공부할 수단을 지녔다. / 그 언어로 된 책을 읽고 / 그리하여 당시의 지적인 담화에 참여할 만큼 충분히

Moreover, few people had access to books, / which were handwritten, scarce, and expensive.
게다가, 책에 접근할 수 있는 사람은 거의 없었는데, / 그 책들은 손으로 쓰였고 아주 희귀하며 비쌌다.

The great explosion of scientific creativity in Europe / was certainly helped by the sudden spread of information / brought about by Gutenberg's use of movable type in printing / and by the legitimation of everyday languages, / which rapidly replaced Latin as the medium of discourse.
유럽에서 과학적 창의성의 폭발적 증가는 / 갑작스런 정보의 확산에 의해 확실히 도움을 받았고 / 인쇄술에서 구텐베르크의 가동 활자 사용과 / 일상 언어의 합법적 인정에 의해 생겨난 / 그것은 담화의 수단으로서 라틴어를 빠르게 대체했다.

In sixteenth-century Europe / it became much easier to make a creative contribution / not necessarily because more creative individuals were born then / than in previous centuries / or because social supports became more favorable, / but because information became more widely accessible.
16세기 유럽에서 / 창의적인 기여를 하는 것이 훨씬 더 쉬워졌다. / 반드시 그때 더 많은 창의적인 사람들이 태어났거나 / 이전 시대보다 / 사회적인 지원이 좀 더 호의적이었기 때문이 아니라, / 정보가 더욱 널리 접근 가능하게 되었기 때문에

수 세기 동안, 유럽의 과학과 일반적인 지식은 라틴어로 기록되었는데, 그 언어는 아무도 더 이상 말하지 않고 학교에서 배워야 하는 언어였다. 어쩌면 1퍼센트도 안 되는 아주 극소수의 사람들만이 그 언어로 된 책을 읽고 그리하여 당시의 지적인 담화에 참여할 만큼 충분히 라틴어를 공부할 수단을 지녔다. 게다가, 책에 접근할 수 있는 사람은 거의 없었는데, 그 책들은 손으로 쓰였고 아주 희귀하며 비쌌다. 인쇄술에서 구텐베르크의 가동 활자 사용과 일상 언어의 합법적 인정에 의해 생겨난 갑작스런 정보의 확산이 유럽에서 과학적 창의성의 폭발적 증가를 확실히 도왔고, 그것은 담화의 수단으로서 라틴어를 빠르게 대체했다. 이전 시대보다 반드시 그때 더 많은 창의적인 사람들이 태어났거나 사회적인 지원이 좀 더 호의적이었기 때문이 아니라, 정보가 더욱 널리 접근 가능하게 되었기 때문에 16세기 유럽에서 창의적인 기여를 하는 것이 훨씬 더 쉬워졌다.

Why? 왜 정답일까?

'The great explosion of scientific creativity in Europe was certainly helped by the sudden spread of information brought about by Gutenberg's use of movable type in printing and by the legitimation of everyday languages, ~'에서 인쇄술에서의 가동 활자 사용과 일상 언어의 합법화로 '정보의 확산'이 일어나면서 과학적 창의성이 폭발적으로 증가할 수 있게 되었다는 내용을 설명하므로, 빈칸에 들어갈 말로 가장 적절한 것은 ② '정보가 더욱 널리 접근 가능하게 되었기'이다.

- **intellectual** ⓐ 지적인, 교양 있는
- **have access to** ~에 접근하다
- **explosion** ⓝ 폭발적 증가, 폭발
- **legitimation** ⓝ 합법화
- **necessarily** ad 반드시, 필연적으로
- **discourse** ⓝ 담화
- **scarce** ⓐ 희귀한, 드문
- **spread** ⓝ 확산, 퍼짐
- **contribution** ⓝ 기여, 공헌
- **accessible** ⓐ 접근 가능한

구문 풀이

9행 The great explosion(주어) of scientific creativity in Europe was certainly helped(수동태) by the sudden spread of information [brought about(과거분사구(생겨난, 야기된)) by Gutenberg's use(전명구1) of movable type in printing and by the legitimation(전명구2) of everyday languages], which(계속적 용법) rapidly replaced Latin as(~로서) the medium of discourse.

06 사회주의 폴란드의 신발 공장에서 있었던 일

정답률 53% | 정답 ④

다음 빈칸에 들어갈 말로 가장 적절한 것을 고르시오. [3점]

① improve the working environment for employees
직원을 위한 업무 환경을 개선할
② simplify the production process to reduce costs
비용을 절감하기 위해 생산 과정을 단순화할
③ increase the number of factories to make more profit
더 많은 수익을 내기 위해 공장의 수를 늘릴
✔④ produce shoes in various sizes that met people's needs
사람들의 필요를 충족하는 다양한 크기의 신발을 생산할
⑤ adopt new technology to compete against foreign shoes
외국 신발과 경쟁하기 위해 신기술을 받아들일

This true story is / about a government-owned shoe factory in Poland / in the days when the country had a much more socialist economy.
이 실화는 / 폴란드에 있었던 정부 소유의 신발 공장에 관한 이야기이다. / 폴란드가 훨씬 더 사회주의적인 경제 체제였던 시절에

Every month, / the Polish government gave the factory materials, / and the manager was told / to produce a fixed number of shoes.
매달 / 폴란드 정부는 공장에 재료를 주었고 / 공장 관리자는 지시받았다. / 정해진 수량의 신발을 생산하도록

Because there was no profit motive involved, / the manager's basic goal / was to meet the quota in the easiest possible way / — by producing only small shoes.
수익 창출을 위한 동기가 없었기 때문에 / 관리자의 기본 목적은 / 할 수 있는 가장 쉬운 방법으로 할당량을 충족시키는 것이었다. / 즉 작은 신발만을 생산하여서

This production strategy created a problem / for people who had big feet, / and so the government revised the system.
이러한 생산 전략은 문제가 되었고, / 발이 큰 사람들에게는 / 그래서 정부는 체계를 수정했다.

Now the factory received the same amount of materials, / but instead of producing a fixed number of shoes, / the factory was expected / to produce a fixed number of tons of shoes.
이제 그 공장은 똑같은 양의 재료를 받지만, / 정해진 수량의 신발을 생산하는 대신 / 공장은 기대되었다. / 정해진 톤의 신발을 생산하도록

In other words, / the factory's output would now be weighed / rather than counted.
다시 말해, / 그 공장의 생산품은 이제 무게로 측정될 것이었다. / 수가 세어지는 대신에

And again, / the factory's manager responded in the most efficient way, / by producing nothing but huge shoes.
이제 다시 / 공장 관리자는 가장 효율적인 방법으로 이에 대응하였다. / 즉 아주 큰 크기의 신발만을 생산하여

In either situation, / the government's strategy did not provide any motivation / to produce shoes in various sizes / that met people's needs.
둘 중 어느 상황에서든, / 정부의 전략은 그 어떤 동기도 부여하지 못했다. / 다양한 크기의 신발을 생산할 / 사람들의 필요를 충족하는

이 실화는 폴란드가 훨씬 더 사회주의적인 경제 체제였던 시절에 폴란드에 있었던 정부 소유의 신발 공장에 관한 이야기이다. 매달 폴란드 정부는 공장에 재료를 주었고 공장 관리자는 정해진 수량의 신발을 생산하도록 지시받았다. 수익 창출을 위한 동기가 없었기 때문에 관리자의 기본 목적은 할 수 있는 가장 쉬운 방법, 즉 작은 신발만을 생산하여서 할당량을 충족시키는 것이었다.

이러한 생산 전략은 발이 큰 사람들에게는 문제가 되었고, 그래서 정부는 체계를 수정했다. 이제 그 공장은 똑같은 양의 재료를 받지만, 정해진 수량의 신발을 생산하는 대신 정해진 톤의 신발을 생산하도록 요구받았다. 다시 말해, 그 공장의 생산품은 이제 수량이 아닌 무게로 측정될 것이었다. 이제 다시 공장 관리자는 가장 효율적인 방법, 즉 아주 큰 크기의 신발만을 생산하여 이에 대응하였다. 둘 중 어느 상황에서든, 정부의 전략은 사람들의 필요를 충족하는 다양한 크기의 신발을 생산할 그 어떤 동기도 부여하지 못했다.

Why? 왜 정답일까?

'~ **the manager's basic goal was to meet the quota in the easiest possible way — by producing only small shoes.**'와 '**And again, the factory's manager responded in the most efficient way, by producing nothing but huge shoes.**'에서 신발 생산 할당량을 수량에 따라 정하건 무게에 따라 정하건, 공장에서는 가장 쉽게 할당량을 맞출 수 있는 방법, 즉 작은 신발만을 생산하거나 큰 신발만을 생산하는 방식으로 할당량을 맞추었다고 한다. 이는 결국 어느 경우에서든 사람들의 다양한 필요를 맞추는 쪽으로 생산을 하도록 이끌어내지는 못했다는 뜻으로 받아들일 수 있으므로, 빈칸에 들어갈 말로 가장 적절한 것은 ④ '사람들의 필요를 충족하는 다양한 크기의 신발을 생산할'이다.

- socialist ⓝ 사회주의자
- quota ⓝ 한도, 할당량
- weigh ⓥ 무게를 달다
- huge ⓐ 큰, 거대한
- material ⓝ 재료, 자재
- revise ⓥ 수정하다
- efficient ⓐ 효율적인
- strategy ⓝ 전략

구문 풀이

10행 Now the factory received the same amount of materials, but (instead of producing a fixed number of shoes), the factory was expected to produce a fixed number of tons of shoes.

주어1 / 동사1 / 병렬 / 전치사(~ 대신에) 동명사(~것) / 주어2 / 동사2 「be expected + to부정사 : ~하도록 기대되다」

07 정보의 해석으로 구성되는 인간의 주관적 세계 — 정답률 46% | 정답 ②

다음 빈칸에 들어갈 말로 가장 적절한 것을 고르시오. [3점]

① the reality placed upon us through social conventions
사회적 관습을 통해 우리에게 자리 잡은 현실
② the one we know as a result of our own interpretations ✔
우리 자신의 해석의 결과로 알고 있는 세계
③ the world of images not filtered by our perceptual frame
우리의 인지적 틀을 통해 걸러지지 않은 이미지의 세계
④ the external world independent of our own interpretations
우리 자신의 해석과는 별개인 외부 세계
⑤ the physical universe our own interpretations fail to explain
우리 자신의 해석이 설명하지 못하는 물리적 우주

Modern psychological theory states / that the process of understanding is a matter of construction, not reproduction, / which means that the process of understanding takes the form of the interpretation of data / coming from the outside and generated by our mind.
현대의 심리학 이론에서 말하는데, / 이해의 과정은 재생이 아니라 구성의 문제라고 / 그것은 이해의 과정이 정보를 해석하는 형태를 취한다는 말이다. / 외부로부터 들어오고 우리 마음에서 생성되는

For example, / the perception of a moving object as a car / is based on an interpretation of incoming data / within the framework of our knowledge of the world.
예를 들어 / 움직이는 물체를 차라고 인식하는 것은 / 들어오는 정보를 해석하는 데 근거한다. / 세상에 대한 우리의 지식이라는 틀 안에서

While the interpretation of simple objects is usually an uncontrolled process, / the interpretation of more complex phenomena, / such as interpersonal situations, / usually requires active attention and thought.
간단한 물체의 해석은 대개 통제되지 않는 과정이지만, / 더 복잡한 현상에 대한 해석은 / 대인 관계 상황 같은 / 대개 적극적인 주의 집중과 사고를 필요로 한다.

Psychological studies indicate / that it is knowledge possessed by the individual / that determines / which stimuli become the focus of that individual's attention, / what significance he or she assigns to these stimuli, / and how they are combined into a larger whole.
심리학 연구에서는 보여준다. / 바로 그 개인이 소유하고 있는 지식이라는 점을 / 결정하는 것은 / 어떤 자극이 개인의 주의에 초점이 되는지, / 그 사람이 이 자극에 어떤 의미를 부여하는지, / 그리고 그 자극들이 어떻게 결합되어 더 커다란 전체를 이루는지를

This subjective world, / interpreted in a particular way, / is for us the "objective" world; / we cannot know any world / other than the one / we know as a result of our own interpretations.
이 주관적 세계는 / 특정한 방식으로 해석되는 / 우리에게 있어 '객관적인' 세계인데, / 우리는 그 어떤 세계도 알 수 없다. / 세계 외에는 / 우리 자신의 해석의 결과로 알고 있는

현대의 심리학 이론에서 이해의 과정은 재생이 아니라 구성의 문제라고 말하는데, 그것은 이해의 과정이 외부로부터 들어오고 우리 마음에서 생성되는 정보를 해석하는 형태를 취한다는 말이다. 예를 들어 움직이는 물체를 차라고 인식하는 것은 세상에 대한 우리의 지식이라는 틀 안에서, 들어오는 정보를 해석하는 데 근거한다. 간단한 물체의 해석은 대개 통제되지 않는 과정이지만, 대인 관계 상황 같은 더 복잡한 현상에 대한 해석은 대개 적극적인 주의 집중과 사고를 필요로 한다. 심리학 연구에서는 어떤 자극이 개인의 주의에 초점이 되는지, 그 사람이 이 자극에 어떤 의미를 부여하는지, 그리고 그 자극들이 어떻게 결합되어 더 커다란 전체를 이루는지를 결정하는 것은 바로 그 개인이 소유하고 있는 지식이라는 점을 보여준다. 특정한 방식으로 해석되는 이 주관적 세계는 우리에게 있어 '객관적인' 세계인데, 우리는 우리 자신의 해석의 결과로 알고 있는 세계 외에는 그 어떤 세계도 알 수 없다.

Why? 왜 정답일까?

'~ **the process of understanding is a matter of construction, not reproduction, which means that the process of understanding takes the form of the interpretation of data coming from the outside and generated by our mind.**'에서 현대 심리학에 따르면 인간은 외부의 정보를 그대로 재생하기보다 마음속에서 해석하여 구성한다고 하는데, 이는 인간이 인지하는 세계가 '주관적일' 수밖에 없다는 의미를 나타낸다. 따라서 빈칸에 들어갈 말로 가장 적절한 것은 ② '우리 자신의 해석의 결과로 알고 있는 세계'이다.

- construction ⓝ 구성, 이해
- generate ⓥ 생성하다, 만들어내다
- uncontrolled ⓐ 통제되지 않는
- assign ⓥ 부여하다, 할당하다
- independent of ~와는 별개인, 독립적인
- interpretation ⓝ 해석, 이해, 설명
- perception ⓝ 인식, 인지
- phenomenon ⓝ 현상
- subjective ⓐ 주관적인

구문 풀이

1행 Modern psychological theory states {that the process of understanding is a matter of construction, not reproduction}, which means that the process of understanding takes the form of the interpretation of data [coming from the outside and generated by our mind].

{ }: 명사절(선행사) / 계속적 용법 / ~의 형태를 취하다 / 분사구1 / 분사구2

★★★ 1등급 대비 고난도 2점 문제

08 소비자의 행동에 따라 좌우되는 재화 간 관계 — 정답률 52% | 정답 ②

다음 빈칸에 들어갈 말로 가장 적절한 것을 고르시오.

① interaction with other people – 다른 사람들과의 상호 작용
② individual consumer's behavior – 개별 소비자의 행동 ✔
③ obvious change in social status – 사회적 지위의 명백한 변화
④ innovative technological advancement – 혁신적인 기술 진보
⑤ objective assessment of current conditions – 현재 상황에 대한 객관적 평가

Are the different types of mobile device, / smartphones and tablets, / substitutes or complements?
다른 유형의 모바일 기기인 / 스마트폰과 태블릿은 / 대체재인가 또는 보완재인가?

Let's explore this question / by considering the case of Madeleine and Alexandra, / two users of these devices.
이 질문을 탐구해보자. / Madeleine과 Alexandra의 사례를 생각하면서 / 이 기기들의 두 사용자인

Madeleine uses her tablet / to take notes in class.
Madeleine은 자신의 태블릿을 사용한다. / 수업 중에 필기하기 위해

These notes are synced to her smartphone wirelessly, / via a cloud computing service, / allowing Madeleine to review her notes on her phone / during the bus trip home.
이 필기는 무선으로 스마트폰에 동기화되어 / 클라우드 컴퓨팅 서비스를 통해 / Madeleine이 전화기로 자신의 필기를 복습하도록 해준다. / 집으로 버스를 타고 가는 동안

Alexandra uses both her phone and tablet / to surf the Internet, write emails and check social media.
Alexandra는 자신의 전화기와 태블릿을 둘 다 사용한다. / 인터넷을 검색하고, 이메일을 쓰고, 소셜 미디어를 확인하기 위해

Both of these devices / allow Alexandra to access online services / when she is away from her desktop computer.
이러한 두 기기 모두 / Alexandra가 온라인 서비스에 접근하도록 해준다. / 그녀가 데스크톱 컴퓨터로부터 떨어져 있을 때

For Madeleine, smartphones and tablets are *complements*.
Madeleine에게 스마트폰과 태블릿은 *보완재*이다.

She gets greater functionality out of her two devices / when they are used together.
그녀는 그녀의 두 기기로부터 더 큰 기능성을 얻는다. / 그것들이 함께 사용될 때

For Alexandra, they are *substitutes*.
Alexandra에게 그것들은 *대체재*이다.

Both smartphones and tablets / fulfill more or less the same function in Alexandra's life.
스마트폰과 태블릿 둘 다 / Alexandra의 생활에서 거의 같은 기능을 수행한다.

This case illustrates the role / that an individual consumer's behavior plays / in determining the nature of the relationship / between two goods or services.
이 사례는 역할을 보여준다. / 개별 소비자의 행동이 행하는 / 관계의 속성을 결정하는 데 있어 / 두 개의 상품 또는 서비스 사이의

다른 유형의 모바일 기기인 스마트폰과 태블릿은 대체재인가, 보완재인가? 이 기기들의 두 사용자인 Madeleine과 Alexandra의 사례를 생각하면서 이 질문을 탐구해보자. Madeleine은 수업 중에 필기하기 위해 자신의 태블릿을 사용한다. 이 필기는 클라우드 컴퓨팅 서비스를 통해 무선으로 스마트폰에 동기화되어 Madeleine이 집으로 버스를 타고 가는 동안 전화기로 자신의 필기를 복습하도록 해준다. Alexandra는 인터넷을 검색하고, 이메일을 쓰고, 소셜 미디어를 확인하기 위해 자신의 전화기와 태블릿을 둘 다 사용한다. 이러한 두 기기 모두 Alexandra가 데스크톱 컴퓨터로부터 떨어져 있을 때 그녀가 온라인 서비스에 접근하도록 해준다. Madeleine에게 스마트폰과 태블릿은 *보완재*이다. 두 기기가 함께 사용될 때, 그녀는 그것들로부터 더 큰 기능성을 얻는다. Alexandra에게 그것들은 *대체재*이다. 스마트폰과 태블릿 둘 다 Alexandra의 생활에서 거의 같은 기능을 수행한다. 이 사례는 개별 소비자의 행동이 두 개의 상품 또는 서비스 사이의 관계의 속성을 결정하는 데 있어 행하는 역할을 보여준다.

Why? 왜 정답일까?

첫 문장인 주제문을 완성하는 빈칸 문제로, 빈칸 앞의 예시를 적절히 일반화하여 빈칸에 들어갈 말을 추론해야 한다. 두 번째 문장 이후로 **Madeleine**와 **Alexandra**의 예를 통해, 스마트폰과 태블릿이 사용자에 따라 보완재 또는 대체재로 모두 이용될 수 있음을 보여주고 있다. 따라서 빈칸에 들어갈 말로 가장 적절한 것은 똑같은 두 상품이 각 사용자의 사용 행위 패턴에 따라 서로 다른 관계에 놓일 수 있다는 뜻을 완성하는 ② '개별 소비자의 행동'이다.

- **substitute** ⓝ 대체재, 대체물
- **be synced to** ~에 동기화되다
- **via** prep ~을 통해
- **functionality** ⓝ 기능성
- **more or less** 거의, 대략
- **nature** ⓝ 속성, 본질
- **complement** ⓝ 보완재, 보충물
- **wirelessly** ad 무선으로
- **access** ⓥ 접속하다
- **fulfill** ⓥ 수행하다, 달성하다
- **illustrate** ⓥ 분명히 보여주다
- **assessment** ⓝ 평가

구문 풀이

17행 This case illustrates the role [that an individual consumer's behavior plays in determining the nature of the relationship between two goods or services].
(the role: 선행사 / that: 목적격 관계대명사 / in determining: ~함에 있어)

★★ 문제 해결 꿀~팁 ★★

▶ 많이 틀린 이유는?
글에서 태블릿과 스마트폰이 언급되기는 하지만, 이는 같은 두 재화 사이의 관계가 사용자의 행위 유형에 따라 달라질 수 있음을 보여주기 위한 예시이다. 두 단어만 보고 ④의 '기술적 진보'에 관한 글이라고 오해하지 않도록 한다.

▶ 문제 해결 방법은?
앞에 나오는 예시를 읽고 직접 요약된 결론을 도출해야 하는 빈칸 문제이므로, **Madeleine**과 **Alexandra**의 '차이'에 집중하여 글 전체를 주의 깊게 읽어야 한다.

★★★ 1등급 대비 고난도 3점 문제

09 약간의 도약에서 출발한 위대한 수학적 발견 — 정답률 38% | 정답 ②

다음 빈칸에 들어갈 말로 가장 적절한 것을 고르시오. [3점]

① calculus was considered to be the study of geniuses
미적분학은 천재들의 학문이라고 여겨졌기
② it was not a huge leap from what was already known
그것은 이미 알려진 것으로부터의 큰 도약은 아니었기
③ it was impossible to make a list of the uses of calculus
미적분학의 용도를 목록으로 만드는 것은 불가능했기
④ they pioneered a breakthrough in mathematic calculations
그들은 수학적 계산에서 중대한 발견을 선도했기
⑤ other mathematicians didn't accept the discovery as it was
다른 수학자들은 그 발견을 있는 그대로 받아들이지 않았기

The whole history of mathematics / is one long sequence / of taking the best ideas of the moment / and finding new extensions, variations, and applications.
수학의 모든 역사는 / 하나의 긴 연속적인 사건들이다. / 그 순간의 가장 좋은 생각들을 취하여 / 새로운 확장, 변이, 그리고 적용을 찾아가는

Our lives today are totally different / from the lives of people three hundred years ago, / mostly owing to scientific and technological innovations / that required the insights of calculus.
오늘날 우리의 삶은 전적으로 다르다. / 300년 전 사람들의 삶과는 / 주로 과학적이고 기술적인 혁신 때문에 / 미적분학의 통찰을 요구하는

Isaac Newton and Gottfried von Leibniz / independently discovered calculus / in the last half of the seventeenth century.
Isaac Newton과 Gottfried von Leibniz는 / 각기 독자적으로 미적분학을 발견하였다. / 17세기 후반에

But a study of the history reveals / that mathematicians had thought of all the essential elements of calculus / before Newton or Leibniz came along.
하지만 역사 연구는 보여준다. / 수학자들이 미적분학의 모든 주요한 요소들에 대해 생각했었다는 것을 / Newton 또는 Leibniz가 나타나기 전에

Newton himself acknowledged this flowing reality / when he wrote, / "If I have seen farther than others / it is because I have stood on the shoulders of giants."
Newton 스스로도 이러한 흘러가는 현실을 인정하였다. / 그가 썼을 때 / "만약 내가 다른 사람들보다 더 멀리 보았다면 / 그것은 내가 거인들의 어깨 위에 섰기 때문이다."라고

Newton and Leibniz came up with their brilliant insight / at essentially the same time / because it was not a huge leap / from what was already known.
Newton과 Leibniz는 그들의 뛰어난 통찰력을 내놓았는데 / 본질적으로 동시대에 / 왜냐하면 그것은 큰 도약은 아니었기 때문이었다. / 이미 알려진 것으로부터의

All creative people, / even ones who are considered geniuses, / start as nongeniuses / and take baby steps from there.
모든 창의적인 사람들은, / 심지어 천재라고 여겨지는 사람들조차, / 천재가 아닌 사람으로 시작하여 / 거기에서부터 아기 걸음마를 뗀다.

수학의 모든 역사는 그 순간의 가장 좋은 생각들을 취하여 새로운 확장, 변이, 그리고 적용을 찾아가는 하나의 긴 연속적인 사건들이다. 오늘날 우리의 삶은 주로 미적분학의 통찰을 요구하는 과학적이고 기술적인 혁신 때문에 300년 전 사람들의 삶과는 전적으로 다르다. Isaac Newton과 Gottfried von Leibniz는 17세기 후반에 각기 독자적으로 미적분학을 발견하였다. 하지만 역사 연구는 수학자들이 Newton 또는 Leibniz가 나타나기 전에 미적분학의 모든 주요한 요소들에 대해 생각했었다는 것을 보여준다. Newton 스스로도 "만약 내가 다른 사람들보다 더 멀리 보았다면 그것은 내가 거인들의 어깨 위에 섰기 때문이다."라고 썼을 때 이러한 흘러가는 현실을 인정하였다. Newton과 Leibniz는 본질적으로 동시대에 그들의 뛰어난 통찰력을 내놓았는데 왜냐하면 그것은 이미 알려진 것으로부터의 큰 도약은 아니었기 때문이었다. 모든 창의적인 사람들은, 심지어 천재라고 여겨지는 사람들조차, 천재가 아닌 사람으로 시작하여 거기에서부터 아기 걸음마를 뗀다.

Why? 왜 정답일까?

Newton과 Leibniz는 흔히 미적분학을 발견한 사람들로 회자되지만, 실은 미적분학에 대한 논의가 이들이 나타나기 이전부터 있었다(~ **mathematicians had thought of all the essential elements of calculus before Newton or Leibniz came along.**)는 언급을 통해, 위대한 발견은 완전한 무에서 이룩되지 않으며 기존의 것을 크게 뛰어넘는 것이라기보다는 약간 더 멀리 보는 관점에서 비롯되는 것이라는 내용을 유추할 수 있다. 마지막 문장인 '**All creative people, even ones who are considered geniuses, start as nongeniuses and take baby steps from there.**'에서 심지어 후에 천재로 여겨진 사람들조차 처음에는 천재가 아닌 존재로서 작은 걸음, 즉 아기 걸음마를 떼는 것으로부터 시작하여 위대한 성과를 이룩하였다는 결론을 제시하고 있다. 따라서 빈칸에 들어갈 말로 가장 적절한 것은 ② '그것은 이미 알려진 것으로부터의 큰 도약은 아니었기'이다.

- **sequence** ⓝ 연속적인 사건들, 순서
- **variation** ⓝ 변이, 변화
- **owing to** ~ 때문에
- **essential** ⓐ 본질적인, 필수적인
- **come along** 나타나다
- **come up with** ~을 떠올리다
- **leap** ⓝ 도약, 뜀
- **breakthrough** ⓝ 돌파구, 획기적 발견
- **extension** ⓝ 확장
- **application** ⓝ 응용, 적용
- **insight** ⓝ 통찰력
- **element** ⓝ 요소
- **acknowledge** ⓥ 인정하다
- **brilliant** ⓐ 뛰어난, 훌륭한
- **pioneer** ⓥ 선도하다

구문 풀이

4행 Our lives today are totally different from the lives of people three hundred years ago, / mostly owing to scientific and technological innovations [that required the insights of calculus].
(Our lives today: 주어 / are: 동사 / different from: ~와 다른 / owing to: 전치사(~ 때문에) / scientific and technological innovations: 목적어 / that: 주격 관계대명사)

DAY 10

★★ 문제 해결 꿀~팁 ★★

▶ 많이 틀린 이유는?

미적분학의 발견을 예로 들어 수학적 발견이 어떻게 이루어지는지에 관해 설명한 글로, 소재가 낯설어 이해하기 까다롭다. 최다 오답인 ④의 경우 calculation(계산)과 calculus(미적분학)가 형태상 유사하기 때문에 혼동을 유발했을 수 있다. 하지만 본문에서 '계산'과 관련된 내용은 언급되지 않았다.

▶ 문제 해결 방법은?

빈칸이 글의 중후반부에 나오면 주로 답의 근거는 뒤에 있다. '~ start as nongeniuses and take baby steps from there.'에서 중요한 표현은 baby steps이고, 이는 ②의 'not a huge leap'에 대응된다.

★★★ 1등급 대비 고난도 3점 문제

10 Theodore Roosevelt의 개인 홍보 전략 정답률 30% | 정답 ①

다음 빈칸에 들어갈 말로 가장 적절한 것을 고르시오. [3점]

✔ understood and made intelligent use of personal promotion
개인 홍보를 이해하고 영리하게 활용했다
② made public policies that were beneficial to his people
자신의 국민들에게 이익을 주는 공공 정책을 만들었다
③ knew when was the right time for him to leave office
자신이 관직을 떠날 적절한 시점이 언제인지를 알았다
④ saw the well-being of his supporters as the top priority
자신을 지지하는 사람들의 행복을 최고 우선순위로 생각했다
⑤ didn't appear before the public in an arranged setting
연출된 상황 속에서 대중 앞에 모습을 드러내지는 않았다

When the late Theodore Roosevelt came back from Africa, / just after he left the White House in 1909, / he made his first public appearance / at Madison Square Garden.
고(故) Theodore Roosevelt는 아프리카에서 돌아왔을 때 / 1909년에 백악관을 떠난 직후 / 처음으로 대중에 모습을 드러냈다. / Madison Square Garden에서

Before he would agree to make the appearance, / he carefully arranged for nearly one thousand *paid applauders* / to be scattered throughout the audience / to applaud his entrance on the platform.
모습을 드러내는 데 동의하기 전에 / 그는 거의 1,000명에 달하는 돈을 받은 *박수 부대*를 세심하게 준비했다. / 청중들 사이에 흩어져 있도록 / 자신이 연단에 입장할 때 박수갈채를 보내줄

For more than 15 minutes, / these paid hand-clappers / made the place ring with their enthusiasm.
15분이 넘게 / 돈을 받은 이 박수 부대들은 / 그 장소에 자신들의 열광이 울려 퍼지게 했다.

The rest of the audience took up the suggestion / and joined in for another quarter hour.
나머지 청중도 그 유도에 호응하여 / 15분 더 그 열광에 동참했다.

The newspaper men present were literally swept off their feet / by the tremendous applause given the American hero, / and his name was emblazoned / across the headlines of the newspapers / in letters two inches high.
참석한 신문 기자들은 문자 그대로 열광했고, / 그 미국 영웅에게 보내는 엄청난 박수갈채에 / 그의 이름은 선명히 새겨졌다. / 각종 신문의 헤드라인에 / 2인치 크기의 글자로

Roosevelt understood and made intelligent use of personal promotion.
Roosevelt는 개인 홍보를 이해하고 영리하게 활용했다.

고(故) Theodore Roosevelt는 1909년에 백악관을 떠난 직후 아프리카에서 돌아왔을 때 Madison Square Garden에서 처음으로 대중에 모습을 드러냈다. 모습을 드러내는 데 동의하기 전에 그는 자신이 연단에 입장할 때 박수갈채를 보내줄 거의 1,000명에 달하는 *돈을 받은 박수 부대*가 청중들 사이에 흩어져 있도록 세심하게 준비했다. 돈을 받은 이 박수 부대들은 15분이 넘게 그 장소에 자신들의 열광이 울려 퍼지게 했다. 나머지 청중도 그 유도에 호응하여 15분 더 그 열광에 동참했다. 참석한 신문 기자들은 문자 그대로 그 미국 영웅(Roosevelt)에게 보내는 엄청난 박수갈채에 열광했고, 그의 이름은 각종 신문의 헤드라인에 2인치 크기의 글자로 선명히 새겨졌다. Roosevelt는 개인 홍보를 이해하고 영리하게 활용했다.

Why? 왜 정답일까?

미국 전 대통령인 Roosevelt가 돈을 주고 고용한 '박수 부대'를 활용하여 자신의 존재를 대중에게 각인시켰던 전략을 소개한 글이다. 따라서 빈칸에 들어갈 말로 가장 적절한 것은 예시의 결론으로 보기 적합한 ① '개인 홍보를 이해하고 영리하게 활용했다'이다.

- late ⓐ 고(故) ~, 작고한
- arrange ⓥ 준비하다
- scatter ⓥ 흩뜨리다, 흩어지게 만들다
- hand-clapper 박수 치는 사람
- literally ad 문자 그대로
- tremendous ⓐ 엄청난
- make an appearance 모습을 드러내다
- applauder ⓝ 박수 치는 사람
- platform ⓝ 연단
- take up (제의 등을) 받아들이다
- sweep ~ off one's feet ~을 열광시키다

구문 풀이

1행 When the late Theodore Roosevelt came back from Africa, / (just after he left the White House in 1909), / he made his first public appearance at Madison Square Garden.
(시간 접속사(~할 때) / 막 ~하고 나서 / ( ): 시점 부연 설명 / 주어 / 동사)

★★ 문제 해결 꿀~팁 ★★

▶ 많이 틀린 이유는?

지문의 다른 부분에서 '개인 홍보'라는 핵심 소재가 직접 언급되지 않지만, 돈을 주고 고용한 '박수 부대'가 결국에는 Roosevelt 대통령의 이미지를 제고하기 위한 장치였음을 이해한다면 ①을 답으로 고를 수 있다. 최다 오답은 ②였는데 글에서 '공공 정책'의 예는 언급된 바가 없다. 또 다른 오답 ⑤는 글의 정황과 반대되는 내용을 나타낸다.

▶ 문제 해결 방법은?

일화 형식의 글을 기반으로 한 문제이므로 주제문을 중심으로 간략하게 읽기보다는 이야기의 전반적인 흐름을 따라가며 통독할 필요가 있다.

★★★ 1등급 대비 고난도 3점 문제

11 우리가 고지방 음식을 찾는 이유 정답률 35% | 정답 ①

다음 빈칸에 들어갈 말로 가장 적절한 것을 고르시오. [3점]

✔ actually be our body's attempt to stay healthy
실제로 건강을 유지하려는 우리 몸의 시도일
② ultimately lead to harm to the ecosystem
궁극적으로 생태계에 대한 피해를 낳을
③ dramatically reduce our overall appetite
우리의 전반적 식욕을 극적으로 줄일
④ simply be the result of a modern lifestyle
단지 현대 생활 방식의 결과일
⑤ partly strengthen our preference for fresh food
신선 식품에 대한 우리의 선호를 부분적으로 강화할

Deep-fried foods are tastier than bland foods, / and children and adults develop a taste for such foods.
기름에 튀긴 음식은 싱거운 음식보다 더 맛있고, / 어린이와 어른들은 그런 음식에 대한 취향을 발달시킨다.

Fatty foods cause the brain to release oxytocin, / a powerful hormone with a calming, antistress, and relaxing influence, / said to be the opposite of adrenaline, / into the blood stream; / hence the term "comfort foods."
지방이 많은 음식은 뇌로 하여금 옥시토신을 분비하게 하고 / 진정, 항스트레스와 진정 효과를 가진 강한 호르몬인, / 아드레날린의 반대로 알려진 / 혈류에 / 그로 인해 '위안을 주는 음식'이란 용어가 있다.

We may even be genetically programmed / to eat too much.
심지어 우리는 유전적으로 프로그램되어 있을지도 모른다. / 너무 많이 먹도록

For thousands of years, / food was very scarce.
수천 년 동안, / 음식은 매우 부족했다.

Food, along with salt, carbs, and fat, / was hard to get, / and the more you got, the better.
소금, 탄수화물, 지방이 있는 음식은 / 구하기 어려웠고, / 더 많이 구할수록 더 좋았다.

All of these things are necessary nutrients in the human diet, / and when their availability was limited, / you could never get too much.
이러한 모든 것은 인간의 식단에 필수적 영양소이고, / 그것들의 이용 가능성이 제한되었을 때, / 여러분은 아무리 많이 먹어도 지나침은 없었다.

People also had to hunt down animals or gather plants / for their food, / and that took a lot of calories.
사람들은 또한 동물을 사냥하거나 식물을 채집해야 했고, / 음식을 위해 / 그것은 많은 칼로리를 필요로 했다.

It's different these days.
오늘날은 이와 다르다.

We have food at every turn / — lots of those fast-food places / and grocery stores with carry-out food.
우리에게는 도처에 음식이 있다. / 많은 패스트푸드점과 / 포장음식이 있는 식료품점과 같이

But that ingrained "caveman mentality" says / that we can't ever get too much to eat.
하지만 그 뿌리 깊은 '원시인 사고방식'은 말한다. / 우리가 너무 많아 못 먹는 만큼을 구할 수는 없다고

So / craving for "unhealthy" food / may actually be our body's attempt to stay healthy.
그래서 / '건강하지 않은' 음식에 대한 갈망은 / 실제로 건강을 유지하려는 우리 몸의 시도일 수 있다.

기름에 튀긴 음식은 싱거운 음식보다 더 맛있고, 어린이와 어른들은 그런 음식에 대한 취향을 발달시킨다. 지방이 많은 음식은 뇌로 하여금 진정, 항스트레스와 진정 효과를 가진 강한 호르몬인, 아드레날린의 반대로 알려진 옥시토신을 혈류에 분비하게 하고 그로 인해 '위안을 주는 음식'이란 용어가 있다. 심지어 우리는 너무 많이 먹도록 유전적으로 프로그램되어 있을지도 모른다. 수천 년 동안, 음식은 매우 부족했다. 소금, 탄수화물, 지방이 있는 음식은 구하기

[문제편 p.067]

어려웠고, 더 많이 구할수록 더 좋았다. 이러한 모든 것은 인간의 식단에 필수적 영양소이고, 이용 가능성이 제한되었을 때, 아무리 많이 먹어도 지나침은 없었다. 사람들은 또한 음식을 위해 동물을 사냥하거나 식물을 채집해야 했고, 그것은 많은 칼로리를 필요로 했다. 오늘날은 이와 다르다. 많은 패스트푸드점의 음식과 식료품점의 포장음식과 같이 도처에 음식이 있다. 하지만 그 뿌리 깊은 '원시인 사고방식'은 우리가 너무 많아 못 먹는 만큼을 구할 수는 없다고 말한다. 그래서 '건강하지 않은' 음식에 대한 갈망은 실제로 건강을 유지하려는 우리 몸의 시도일 수 있다.

Why? 왜 정답일까?

'It's different these days.' 앞에서 아주 오랫동안 음식은 매우 부족했고, 어떤 영양소든 먹어두는 것이 다 필요하고 좋았기에 지나친 섭취라는 개념이 없었다고 언급한다. 오늘날에는 상황이 비록 달라졌지만, **'But that ingrained "caveman mentality" says that we can't ever get too much to eat.'**에 따르면 우리의 사고방식은 여전히 음식이 부족하던 시대에 머물러 있다고 한다. 즉 우리가 고지방 음식을 찾는 것은 옛날 관점에서 생각하면 '필요하게' 여겨지는 행위일 수 있다는 것이다. 따라서 빈칸에 들어갈 말로 가장 적절한 것은 ① '실제로 건강을 유지하려는 우리 몸의 시도일'이다.

- bland ⓐ 싱거운, 담백한, 특징 없는
- calming ⓐ 진정시키는
- genetically [ad] 유전적으로
- carry-out food 포장음식
- ultimately [ad] 궁극적으로
- strengthen ⓥ 강화하다
- release ⓥ 분비하다
- comfort food 위안을 주는 음식
- scarce ⓐ 드문
- mentality ⓝ 사고방식
- dramatically [ad] 극적으로

구문 풀이

9행 Food, (along with salt, carbs, and fat), was hard to get, and the more you got, the better.
주어 / ( ): 삽입구 / 동사
「the+비교급 ~, the+비교급 …: ~할수록 더 …하다」

★★ 문제 해결 꿀~팁 ★★

▶ 많이 틀린 이유는?
우리가 기름진 음식을 선호하는 이유로 우리 뇌가 아직 과거에 머물러 있기 때문(caveman mentality)이라는 내용을 다룬 글이다. 글에 따르면 과거에는 식량이 부족해서 음식을 구하는 대로 다 먹어두면 좋았지만, 오늘날에는 식량이 풍부해졌고, 따라서 기름진 음식이 '건강하지 않게' 여겨지게 되었음에도 우리의 몸은 계속해서 기름진 음식을 찾는다고 하였다. 최다 오답인 ④에서는 우리가 기름진 음식을 찾는 까닭이 현대적 생활 방식(a modern lifestyle)에 있다고 하는데, 이는 정답의 주요 근거인 'caveman mentality'라는 표현과 정반대된다.
▶ 문제 해결 방법은?
더 이상 건강하게 여겨지지 않는 기름진 음식이 과거에는 사람이 살아남고 건강을 유지하는 데 도움이 되는 것이었기에, 그 시절 사고방식이 아직 박혀 있는 인간으로서는 '건강을 유지하기 위해' 기름진 음식을 찾는 것이라는 내용을 완성시키는 말이 빈칸에 들어가야 한다.

★★★ 1등급 대비 고난도 3점 문제

12 해석의 방향에 따라 다른 의미를 갖는 수치 　정답률 30% | 정답 ②

다음 빈칸에 들어갈 말로 가장 적절한 것을 고르시오. [3점]

① be influenced by the data collection strategy
자료 수집 전략에 영향을 받을
② be cited as a cause for celebration or shame
축하 혹은 애석한 일의 원인으로 인용될
③ be obtained from different experimental data
다양한 실험 데이터로부터 얻어질
④ cause various social problems in many cases
많은 경우 다양한 사회 문제를 야기할
⑤ trigger minimum wage protests across the U.S.
미국 전역에 최저 임금 항의 운동을 촉발시킬

It's possible to lie with numbers, / even those that are accurate, / because numbers rarely speak for themselves.
숫자를 가지고서도 거짓말을 하는 것은 가능한데 / 심지어 정확한 숫자를 / 왜냐하면 숫자들은 좀처럼 스스로를 대변하지 않기 때문이다.
They need to be interpreted by writers.
숫자는 필자에 의해 해석되어야만 한다.
And writers almost always have purposes / that shape the interpretations.
그리고 필자들은 거의 항상 목적을 가진다. / 그 해석의 방향을 정하는
For example, / you might want to announce the good news / that unemployment in the United States / stands at just a little over 5 percent.
예컨대 / 당신은 기쁜 소식을 알리고 싶을 수 있다. / 미국의 실업률이 / 5퍼센트를 단지 살짝 넘긴 상태에 있다는
That means / 95 percent of Americans have jobs, / an employment rate much higher / than that of most other industrial nations.
이는 뜻한다. / 95퍼센트의 미국인들이 직업을 가지고 있다는 것, / 즉 고용률이 훨씬 높다는 것을 / 다른 대부분의 산업 국가보다
But let's spin the figure another way.
그러나 그 수치를 다른 방식으로 제시해 보자.
In a country as populous as the United States, / unemployment at 5 percent means / that millions of Americans don't earn a daily wage.
미국만큼 인구가 많은 나라에서 / 5퍼센트의 실업률은 의미한다. / 수백만 명의 미국인들이 일당을 벌지 못한다는 것을
Indeed, / one out of every twenty adults / who wants work can't find it.
실제로 / 일자리를 원하는 20명의 성인들 중 한 명이 / 일을 찾지 못한다.
Suddenly that's a sobering number.
별안간 이는 정신이 확 들게 하는 숫자가 된다.
And, as you can see, / the same statistic can be cited / as a cause for celebration or shame.
그리고 당신이 보는 것처럼, / 똑같은 통계 수치가 인용될 수 있다. / 축하 혹은 애석한 일의 원인으로

심지어 정확한 숫자를 가지고서도 거짓말을 하는 것은 가능한데 왜냐하면 숫자들은 좀처럼 스스로를 대변하지 않기 때문이다. 숫자는 필자에 의해 해석되어야만 한다. 그리고 필자들은 거의 항상 그 해석의 방향을 정하는 목적을 가진다. 예컨대 당신은 미국의 실업률이 5퍼센트를 단지 살짝 넘긴 상태에 있다는 기쁜 소식을 알리고 싶을 수 있다. 이는 95퍼센트의 미국인들이 직업을 가지고 있다는 것, 즉 다른 대부분의 산업 국가보다 고용률이 훨씬 높다는 것을 뜻한다. 그러나 그 수치를 다른 방식으로 제시해 보자. 미국만큼 인구가 많은 나라에서 5퍼센트의 실업률은 수백만 명의 미국인들이 일당을 벌지 못한다는 것을 의미한다. 실제로 일자리를 원하는 20명의 성인들 중 한 명이 일을 찾지 못한다. 별안간 이는 정신이 확 들게 하는 숫자가 된다. 그리고 당신이 보는 것처럼, 똑같은 통계 수치가 축하 혹은 애석한 일의 원인으로 인용될 수 있다.

Why? 왜 정답일까?

'It's possible to lie with numbers, even those that are accurate, because numbers rarely speak for themselves.'에서 숫자 자체는 정확한 값을 나타내기는 하지만 (글에 인용되는 등의 경우) 이는 스스로 어떤 의미를 갖는다기보다 '해석'되어야 한다는 것을 이야기한다. 이어서 **For example** 뒤에서는 '미국 실업률 **5**퍼센트'라는 동일한 수치를 고용률이 **95**퍼센트라는 의미로 해석하는가, 혹은 미국 인구 중 **5**퍼센트에 해당하는 수백만 명의 인원이 일자리를 얻지 못한다는 의미로 해석하는가에 따라 같은 숫자가 긍정적 또는 부정적인 의미를 모두 나타낼 수 있다는 점을 제시한다. 따라서 빈칸에 들어갈 말로 가장 적절한 것은 예시의 결론을 보다 구체적인 표현으로 제시한 ② '축하 혹은 애석한 일의 원인으로 인용될'이다.

- accurate ⓐ 정확한
- interpret ⓥ 해석하다
- unemployment ⓝ 실업
- populous ⓐ 인구가 많은
- statistic ⓝ 통계 (수치)
- speak for ~을 대변하다
- shape ⓥ (진로나 방향을) 정하다
- spin ⓥ (특정한 방향으로) 제시하다
- earn ⓥ 벌다, 얻다

구문 풀이

1행 It's possible to lie with numbers, even those [that are accurate], / because numbers rarely speak for themselves.
가주어 / 진주어 / =numbers 주격 관계대명사 / 접속사(~이기 때문에) / 스스로

★★ 문제 해결 꿀~팁 ★★

▶ 많이 틀린 이유는?
보통의 빈칸 문제와 같이 주제문만 읽고 일부 표현을 바꾸어 빈칸에 넣는 경우가 아니라 예시 부분을 일반화한 말을 답으로 골라야 하기에 어려운 문제였다. 오답으로 ①, ③이 많이 나왔는데 두 선택지 모두 본문의 주된 내용과는 무관하다. '자료 수집 전략', '다양한 실험' 등의 단어는 본문에 언급된 바 없다.
▶ 문제 해결 방법은?
예시의 세부사항에 주목하기보다는 '그래서 결론이 무엇인지'를 빨리 파악해야 한다. '실업률 5퍼센트'라는 수치를 95%의 고용률로 보는 것은 긍정적인 해석이고, 수백만 명의 실업 상태를 나타낸다고 보는 것은 부정적인 해석이다. 마찬가지로 정답인 ②에서는 '축하'라는 긍정적인 의미의 단어와 '애석한 일'이라는 부정적 의미의 단어를 모두 포함하여 한 가지 숫자가 좋게, 혹은 나쁘게 받아들여질 수 있다는 내용을 고루 나타낸다.

DAY 11 글의 순서 01

01 ②	02 ④	03 ②	04 ②	05 ②
06 ⑤	07 ③	08 ⑤	09 ②	10 ⑤
11 ③	12 ④			

01 의도하지 않은 결과의 법칙

정답률 69% | 정답 ②

주어진 글 다음에 이어질 글의 순서로 가장 적절한 것을 고르시오.

① (A) − (C) − (B)
② (B) − (A) − (C)
③ (B) − (C) − (A)
④ (C) − (A) − (B)
⑤ (C) − (B) − (A)

When evaluating a policy, / people tend to concentrate / on how the policy will fix some particular problem / while ignoring or downplaying other effects it may have.
정책을 평가할 때, / 사람들은 집중하는 경향이 있다 / 그것이 어떤 특정한 문제를 어떻게 해결할 것인가에 / 그 정책이 가질 수 있는 다른 효과는 무시하거나 경시하는 한편

Economists often refer to this situation / as *The Law of Unintended Consequences*.
경제학자들은 종종 이 상황을 부른다. / *의도하지 않은 결과의 법칙*이라고

(B) For instance, / suppose / that you impose a tariff on imported steel / in order to protect the jobs of domestic steelworkers.
예를 들어, / 가정해 보자. / 당신이 수입된 철강에 관세를 부과한다고 / 국내 철강 노동자들의 일자리를 보호하기 위해

If you impose a high enough tariff, / their jobs will indeed be protected / from competition by foreign steel companies.
만약 당신이 충분히 높은 관세를 부과한다면, / 그들의 일자리는 실제로 보호될 것이다. / 외국 철강 회사들과의 경쟁으로부터

(A) But / an unintended consequence is / that the jobs of some autoworkers will be lost to foreign competition.
그러나 / 한 가지 의도하지 않은 결과는 ~이다. / 일부 자동차 노동자들의 일자리를 외국 경쟁사에 빼앗기게 된다는 것

Why?
왜일까?

The tariff that protects steelworkers / raises the price of the steel / that domestic automobile makers need / to build their cars.
철강 노동자들을 보호하는 관세는 / 철강의 가격을 높인다. / 국내 자동차 제조업체들이 필요로 하는 / 자동차를 만들기 위해

(C) As a result, / domestic automobile manufacturers / have to raise the prices of their cars, / making them relatively less attractive / than foreign cars.
그 결과, / 국내 자동차 제조업체들은 / 자동차 가격을 인상해야 하고, / 국산 차를 상대적으로 덜 매력적이게 만든다. / 외제 차에 비해

Raising prices tends to reduce domestic car sales, / so some domestic autoworkers lose their jobs.
가격을 올리는 것은 국산 차 판매를 줄이는 경향이 있어서, / 일부 국내 자동차 노동자들은 일자리를 잃는다.

정책을 평가할 때, 사람들은 그것이 어떤 특정한 문제를 어떻게 해결할 것인가에 집중하는 경향이 있으며, 그 정책이 가질 수 있는 다른 효과는 무시하거나 경시한다. 경제학자들은 종종 이 상황을 *의도하지 않은 결과의 법칙*이라고 부른다.

(B) 예를 들어, 국내 철강 노동자들의 일자리를 보호하기 위해 수입된 철강에 관세를 부과한다고 가정해 보자. 만약 당신이 충분히 높은 관세를 부과한다면, 그들의 일자리는 실제로 외국 철강 회사들과의 경쟁으로부터 보호될 것이다.

(A) 그러나 한 가지 의도하지 않은 결과는 일부 자동차 노동자들의 일자리를 외국 경쟁사에 빼앗기게 된다는 것이다. 왜일까? 철강 노동자들을 보호하는 관세는 국내 자동차 제조업체들이 자동차를 만드는 데 필요한 철강의 가격을 높인다.

(C) 그 결과, 국내 자동차 제조업체들은 자동차 가격을 인상해야 하고, 국산 차를 외제 차에 비해 상대적으로 덜 매력적이게 만든다. 가격을 올리는 것은 국산 차 판매를 줄이는 경향이 있어서, 일부 국내 자동차 노동자들은 일자리를 잃는다.

Why? 왜 정답일까?

'의도하지 않은 결과의 법칙'을 소개하는 주어진 글 뒤로, 국내 철강 회사를 보호하기 위한 무역 조치를 예로 드는 **(B)**, 이 조치의 '의도하지 않은 결과'에 관해 언급하는 **(A)**, 그 최종 영향을 설명하는 **(C)**가 차례로 연결되어야 한다. 따라서 글의 순서로 가장 적절한 것은 ② **'(B) − (A) − (C)'**이다.

- **evaluate** ⓥ 평가하다
- **downplay** ⓥ 경시하다
- **refer to A as B** A를 B라고 부르다
- **consequence** ⓝ 결과
- **tariff** ⓝ 관세
- **raise** ⓥ 올리다
- **attractive** ⓐ 매력적인
- **concentrate on** ~에 집중하다
- **economist** ⓝ 경제학자
- **unintended** ⓐ 의도되지 않은
- **autoworker** ⓝ 자동차 업체 근로자
- **steelworker** ⓝ 철강 노동자
- **import** ⓥ 수입하다

구문 풀이

1행 When evaluating a policy, people tend to concentrate on {how the policy will fix some particular problem} while ignoring or downplaying other effects [it may have.]
(When evaluating: 분사구문(= When they evaluate ~) / on: 전치사 / { }: 간접의문문 / while ignoring or downplaying: 분사구문(= while they ignore or downplay ~))

02 환경과 경험의 중요성

정답률 58% | 정답 ④

주어진 글 다음에 이어질 글의 순서로 가장 적절한 것을 고르시오.

① (A) − (C) − (B)
② (B) − (A) − (C)
③ (B) − (C) − (A)
④ (C) − (A) − (B)
⑤ (C) − (B) − (A)

If DNA were the only thing that mattered, / there would be no particular reason / to build meaningful social programs / to pour good experiences into children / and protect them from bad experiences.
만약 DNA가 유일하게 중요한 것이라면, / 특별한 이유가 없을 것이다. / 의미 있는 사회 프로그램을 만들 / 아이들에게 좋은 경험을 제공하고 / 그들을 해로운 경험들로부터 보호하는

(C) But brains require the right kind of environment / if they are to correctly develop.
하지만 뇌는 적절한 종류의 환경을 필요로 한다. / 그것이 제대로 발달하려면

When the first draft of the Human Genome Project / came to completion / at the turn of the millennium, / one of the great surprises was / that humans have only about twenty thousand genes.
Human Genome Project의 첫 번째 초안이 / 완성되었을 때, / 새천년에 들어 / 큰 놀라움 중 하나는 ~이었다. / 인간이 대략 2만 개의 유전자만 갖고 있다는 것

(A) This number came as a surprise to biologists: / given the complexity of the brain and the body, / it had been assumed / that hundreds of thousands of genes would be required.
이 숫자는 생물학자들에게 놀라움으로 다가왔는데, / 뇌와 신체의 복잡성을 고려했을 때 / 추정되어 왔기 때문이었다. / 수십만 개의 유전자가 필요할 것이라고

(B) So how does the massively complicated brain, / with its eighty-six billion neurons, / get built / from such a small recipe book?
그러면 극도로 복잡한 뇌가 어떻게 / 860억 개의 뉴런을 갖고 있는 / 만들어질 수 있었을까? / 그렇게 작은 요리책으로부터

The answer relies on a clever strategy / implemented by the genome: / build incompletely and let world experience refine.
그 해답은 한 영리한 전략에 있다. / 게놈에 의해 실행된 / 즉 불완전하게 만들고 세상 경험으로 정교하게 다듬는다는 것

만약 DNA가 유일하게 중요한 것이라면, 아이들에게 좋은 경험을 제공하고 해로운 경험들로부터 보호하는 의미 있는 사회 프로그램을 만들 특별한 이유가 없을 것이다.

(C) 하지만 뇌는 제대로 발달하려면 적절한 종류의 환경을 필요로 한다. Human Genome Project의 첫 번째 초안이 새천년에 들어 완성되었을 때, 큰 놀라움 중 하나는 인간이 대략 2만 개의 유전자만 갖고 있다는 것이었다.

(A) 이 숫자는 생물학자들에게 놀라움으로 다가왔는데, 뇌와 신체의 복잡성을 고려했을 때 수십만 개의 유전자가 필요할 것이라고 추정되어 왔기 때문이었다.

(B) 그러면 860억 개의 뉴런을 갖고 있는 극도로 복잡한 뇌가 어떻게 그렇게 작은 요리책으로부터 만들어질 수 있었을까? 그 해답은 게놈에 의해 실행된 한 영리한 전략, 즉 불완전하게 만들고 세상 경험으로 정교하게 다듬는다는 데 있다.

Why? 왜 정답일까?

만일 **DNA**만 중요하다면 경험과 환경의 의미가 약해질 것이라는 주어진 글 뒤로, '하지

만' 뇌 발달에는 적절한 환경이 중요하다는 내용의 (C)가 먼저 연결된다. 한편 (C)의 후반부에서 인간의 유전자는 대략 2만 개에 불과하다고 하는데, (A)는 '이 숫자'가 생각보다 너무 적어서 과학자들이 놀랐다는 설명을 이어 간다. 마지막으로 (B)는 이렇게 턱없이 부족한 유전자만 갖고도 뇌가 그토록 복잡해질 수 있는 까닭은 '경험' 때문이라는 결론을 적절히 제시한다. 따라서 글의 순서로 가장 적절한 것은 ④ '(C) – (A) – (B)'이다.

- matter ⓥ 중요하다
- meaningful ⓐ 의미 있는
- protect A from B A를 B로부터 보호하다
- given prep ~을 고려할 때
- hundreds of thousands of 수십만의
- billion ⓝ 10억
- recipe book 요리책
- implement ⓥ 실행하다
- refine ⓥ 다듬다, 정제하다
- come to completion 완수되다
- millennium ⓝ 새천년
- particular ⓐ 특정한, 특별한
- pour ⓥ 쏟아붓다
- come as a surprise 놀라움으로 다가오다
- gene ⓝ 유전자
- massively ad 엄청나게
- neuron ⓝ 뉴런, 신경 세포
- clever ⓐ 영리한
- incompletely ad 불완전하게
- first draft 초안
- at the turn of ~의 전환기에

구문 풀이

6행 ~ given the complexity of the brain and the body, it had been assumed that hundreds of thousands of genes would be required.

(given: 분사구문(~을 고려하면) / had been assumed: 과거완료 수동태 / that: 접속사(~것))

03 좌석표 만들기

정답률 65% | 정답 ②

주어진 글 다음에 이어질 글의 순서로 가장 적절한 것을 고르시오.

① (A) – (C) – (B)
② (B) – (A) – (C) ✔
③ (B) – (C) – (A)
④ (C) – (A) – (B)
⑤ (C) – (B) – (A)

One of the first things / I did in each classroom in South Milwaukee / was to draw a diagram of the students' desks, / labelled with their names, / as an aid to recognizing them.
첫 번째 일 중 하나는 / 내가 South Milwaukee의 각 교실에서 했던 / 학생들의 좌석표를 그리는 일이었다. / 그들의 이름을 적은, / 학생들을 알아보기 위한 보조물로

(B) At lunch in the first grade classroom / the first day I was present, / a group of students came over, / saw the diagram, / and began finding their names on my picture.
1학년 교실에서 점심시간에 / 내가 들어간 첫째 날 / 한 무리의 학생들이 다가와 / 좌석표를 보고는 / 내가 그린 그림에서 자신의 이름을 찾기 시작했다.

(A) One said, / "Where's your name?" / and was not satisfied / until I included a sketch of the chair / by the bookcase / where I was sitting, / labelled with my name.
한 학생이 말하더니, / "선생님 이름은 어디 있어요?"라고 / 비로소 흡족해했다. / 의자 그림을 내가 포함하고 나서야 / 책장 옆 / 내가 앉아 있던 / 내 이름을 적은

It had not occurred to me / that I needed to be included: / after all, / I knew where I was sitting, / and knew my name.
나는 생각을 하지 못했었다. / 내가 포함될 필요가 있다는 / 어쨌든 / 나는 내가 어디 앉아 있는지 알고 있었고, / 내 이름을 알고 있었다.

(C) But to her, / my presence in the classroom / was the newest, most noteworthy thing / that had occurred that day, / and it was logical to include me.
하지만 그녀에게는 / 교실에서의 나의 존재가 / 가장 새롭고 가장 주목할 만한 일이었으며, / 그날 일어난 / 나를 포함시키는 것이 타당했다.

Her point of view was different from mine, / and resulted in a different diagram of the classroom.
그녀의 관점은 내 관점과 달랐고, / 그 결과 교실의 좌석표가 달라졌다.

내가 South Milwaukee의 각 교실에서 처음 한 일 중 하나는 학생들을 알아보기 위한 보조물로 학생들의 이름을 적은 좌석표를 그리는 것이었다.

(B) 내가 들어간 첫째 날 1학년 교실에서 점심시간에 한 무리의 학생들이 다가와 좌석표를 보고는 내가 그린 그림에서 자신의 이름을 찾기 시작했다.

(A) 한 학생이 "선생님 이름은 어디 있어요?"라고 말하더니, 내가 책장 옆 내가 앉아 있던 의자 그림을 포함시키고 내 이름을 적고 나서야 비로소 흡족해했다. 나는 내가 포함될 필요가 있다는 생각을 하지 못했었다. 어쨌든 나는 내가 어디 앉아 있는지 알고 있었고, 내 이름을 알고 있었다.

(C) 하지만 그녀에게는 교실에서의 나의 존재가 그날 일어난 가장 새롭고 가장 주목할 만한 일이었으며, 나를 포함시키는 것이 타당했다. 그녀의 관점은 내 관점과 달랐고, 그 결과 교실의 좌석표가 달라졌다.

Why? 왜 정답일까?

선생님인 필자가 아이들의 좌석표를 만들었다는 내용의 주어진 글 뒤에는, 학생들이 좌석표를 보고 자신의 이름을 찾기 시작했다는 내용의 (B), 한 학생이 선생님 이름은 어디에 있는지 물었다는 내용의 (A), 그 학생에게는 선생님 또한 좌석표에 포함되어야 할 일원처럼 여겨졌기에 결국 교실의 좌석표가 선생님의 이름을 넣은 것으로 바뀌었다는 내용의 (C)가 차례로 이어지는 것이 자연스럽다. 따라서 글의 순서로 가장 적절한 것은 ② '(B) – (A) – (C)'이다.

- diagram ⓝ 도표
- label ⓥ 라벨을 붙이다, 표시하다
- bookcase ⓝ 책장
- after all 어쨌든
- newest ⓐ 최신의
- noteworthy ⓐ 주목할 만한
- point of view 관점
- aid ⓝ 보조물, 도움
- satisfied ⓐ 만족한
- occur to ~에게 (…라는) 생각이 떠오르다
- present ⓐ 있는, 참석한
- presence ⓝ 존재, 있음
- logical ⓐ 타당한, 논리적인

구문 풀이

8행 It had not occurred to me {that I needed to be included}: / after all, I knew where I was sitting, and knew my name.

({ }: 명사절 수동 부정사(~되는 것) / knew: 동사1 / where: 의문부사 / knew: 동사2)

04 황색 저널리즘의 태동

정답률 42% | 정답 ②

주어진 글 다음에 이어질 글의 순서로 가장 적절한 것을 고르시오.

① (A) – (C) – (B)
② (B) – (A) – (C) ✔
③ (B) – (C) – (A)
④ (C) – (A) – (B)
⑤ (C) – (B) – (A)

During the late 1800s, / printing became cheaper and faster, / leading to / an explosion in the number of newspapers and magazines / and the increased use of images in these publications.
1800년대 후반 동안 / 인쇄가 더 저렴해지고 더 빨라지면서 / 이어졌다. / 신문과 잡지 수에서의 급증과 / 이러한 출판물들에서의 이미지 사용 증가로

(B) Photographs, / as well as woodcuts and engravings of them, / appeared in newspapers and magazines.
사진도 / 목판화와 판화뿐만 아니라 / 신문과 잡지에 등장했다.

The increased number of newspapers and magazines / created greater competition / — driving some papers to print more salacious articles / to attract readers.
늘어난 수의 신문과 잡지는 / 더 큰 경쟁을 만들어 냈는데, / 몇몇 신문들이 더 외설적인 기사들을 찍어내도록 만들었다. / 독자를 끌어들이기 위해

(A) This "yellow journalism" / sometimes took the form of gossip about public figures, / as well as about socialites / who considered themselves private figures, / and even about those / who were not part of high society / but had found themselves involved in a scandal, crime, or tragedy / that journalists thought would sell papers.
이러한 '황색 저널리즘'은 / 때때로 공인들에 대한 가십의 형태를 취했다. / 사교계 인물들뿐만 아니라 / 자신을 사적인 인물로 여기는 / 그리고 심지어 사람들 / 고위층에 속하지는 않지만, / 스캔들, 범죄 또는 비극적인 일에 연루된 것으로 밝혀진 / 기자들이 생각했을 때 신문을 잘 팔리게 할 수 있는

(C) Gossip was of course nothing new, / but the rise of mass media / in the form of widely distributed newspapers and magazines / meant that gossip moved / from limited (often oral only) distribution / to wide, printed dissemination.
가십이 물론 새로운 것은 아니었지만, / 대중 매체의 증가는 / 널리 배포된 신문과 잡지 형태의 / 가십이 이동했다는 것을 의미했다. / 제한된 유포(흔히 구두로만)에서 / 광범위한 인쇄된 형태의 보급으로

1800년대 후반 동안 인쇄가 더 저렴해지고 더 빨라진 것은 신문과 잡지 수의 급증과 이러한 출판물들에서 이미지의 사용 증가로 이어졌다.

(B) 목판화와 판화뿐만 아니라 사진도 신문과 잡지에 등장했다. 늘어난 수의 신문과 잡지는 더 큰 경쟁을 야기했고, 몇몇 신문들이 독자를 끌어들이기 위해 더 외설적인 기사들을 찍어내도록 만들었다.

(A) 이러한 "황색 저널리즘"은 때때로 자신을 사적인 인물로 여기는 사교계 인물들뿐만 아니라 공인들, 그리고 심지어 고위층에 속하지는 않지만 기자들이 생각했을 때 신문을 잘 팔리게 할 수 있는 스캔들이나 범죄 또는 비극적인 일에 연루된 것으로 밝혀진 사람들에 대한 가십의 형태를 취했다.

(C) 가십이 물론 새로운 것은 아니었지만, 널리 배포되는 신문과 잡지 형태의 대중 매체의 증가는 가십이 (흔히 구두로만) 제한된 유포에서 광범위한 인쇄된 형태의 보급으로 이동했다는 것을 의미했다.

Why? 왜 정답일까?

1800년대 후반 인쇄비가 저렴해지면서 신문과 잡지 수가 늘어나고 출판물에서 이미지가 사용되는 경우도 늘어났다는 내용의 주어진 글 뒤에는, 이로 인해 신문사와 잡지사들 간의 경쟁이 심해져 더 자극적인 기사들이 쏟아져 나오는 결과가 생겼다는 내용의 (B), 이를 '황색 저널리즘'이라는 용어로 설명하는 (A), 이 황색 저널리즘은 가십의 형태를 주로 취한다는 내용의 (C)가 차례로 이어지는 것이 자연스럽다. 따라서 글의 순서로 가장 적절한 것은 ② '(B) – (A) – (C)'이다.

- explosion ⓝ 폭발, 급증
- take the form of ~의 형태를 취하다
- tragedy ⓝ 비극
- woodcut ⓝ 목판화
- woodcut ⓝ 목판화
- publication ⓝ 출판, 출판물
- socialite ⓝ 사교계 명사
- paper ⓝ 신문
- appear ⓥ (신문 등에) 나다
- distribute ⓥ 배포하다, 분포시키다

구문 풀이

5행 This "yellow journalism" sometimes took the form of gossip about public figures, as well as about socialites [who considered themselves private figures], and even about those [who were not part of high society but had found themselves involved in a scandal, crime, or tragedy {that (journalists thought) would sell papers}].

전명구1 / 전명구2 / 전명구3 / 동사1 / 동사2 / 목적어 / 목적격 보어 / 선행사 / 주격 관·대 / ( ): 삽입절 / 동사

05 사업가의 성격적 특성 　정답률 63% | 정답 ②

주어진 글 다음에 이어질 글의 순서로 가장 적절한 것을 고르시오.

① (A) – (C) – (B)　✔(B) – (A) – (C)
③ (B) – (C) – (A)　④ (C) – (A) – (B)
⑤ (C) – (B) – (A)

Studies show / that no one is "born" to be an entrepreneur / and that everyone has the potential to become one.
여러 연구에서는 보여 준다. / 어느 누구도 사업가가 되도록 '타고난' 것은 아니며 / 모든 사람은 사업가가 될 잠재력이 있다는 것을

(B) Whether someone does or doesn't / is a function of environment, life experiences, and personal choices.
어떤 사람이 사업가가 되느냐 되지 않느냐에는 / 환경, 인생 경험, 그리고 개인적인 선택이 작용한다.

However, there are personality traits and characteristics / commonly associated with entrepreneurs.
그러나 성격 특성과 특징이 있다. / 사업가와 흔히 연관되어 있는

(A) These traits are developed over time / and evolve from an individual's social context.
이런 특성은 시간이 경과하면서 드러나고 / 개인의 사회적 환경으로부터 서서히 발달한다.

For example, / people with parents who were self-employed / are more likely to become entrepreneurs.
예를 들어, / 자영업을 하는 부모를 가진 사람은 / 사업가가 될 가능성이 더 높다.

(C) After witnessing a father's or mother's independence in the workplace, / an individual is more likely to find independence appealing.
아버지나 어머니가 직장에서 독립적으로 일하는 것을 보고 나면 / 개인은 독립이 매력적이라고 생각할 가능성이 더 높다.

Similarly, people who personally know an entrepreneur / are more than twice as likely / to be involved in starting a new firm / as those with no entrepreneur acquaintances or role models.
마찬가지로, 개인적으로 사업가를 알고 있는 사람이 / 가능성이 두 배가 넘게 높다. / 새로운 회사를 시작하는 일에 관여할 / 사업가인 지인이나 롤 모델이 없는 사람보다

여러 연구에서는 어느 누구도 사업가가 되도록 '타고난' 것은 아니며 모든 사람은 사업가가 될 잠재력이 있다는 것을 보여 준다.

(B) 어떤 사람이 사업가가 되느냐 되지 않느냐에는 환경, 인생 경험, 그리고 개인적인 선택이 작용한다. 그러나 사업가와 흔히 연관되어 있는 성격 특성과 특징이 있다.

(A) 이런 특성은 시간이 경과하면서 드러나고 개인의 사회적 환경으로부터 서서히 발달한다. 예를 들어, 자영업을 하는 부모를 가진 사람은 사업가가 될 가능성이 더 높다.

(C) 아버지나 어머니가 직장에서 독립적으로 일하는 것을 보고 나면 개인은 독립이 매력적이라고 생각할 가능성이 더 높다. 마찬가지로, 개인적으로 사업가를 알고 있는 사람이 사업가인 지인이나 롤 모델이 없는 사람보다 새로운 회사를 시작하는 일에 관여할 가능성이 두 배가 넘게 높다.

Why? 왜 정답일까?

주어진 글에서 타고나는 사업가의 특성이 있다기보다는 모두가 사업가가 될 잠재력이 있다는 내용을 언급한 데 이어, (B)에서는 환경, 인생 경험, 개인적 선택 등이 개인이 사업가가 되는 데 영향을 미칠 수 있다는 내용을 말한다. 한편 (B)의 마지막에서는 그럼에도 불구하고 사업가와 흔히 연관되는 성격적 특성이 있음을 말하는데 (A)에서는 '이런 특성'이 시간이 지나며 발현된다고 설명하며 예시를 든다. (C) 또한 (A)에 이어 예시를 다루는 단락이다. 따라서 글의 순서로 가장 적절한 것은 ② '(B) – (A) – (C)'이다.

- potential ⓝ 잠재력
- trait ⓝ 특성
- self-employed 자영업을 하는
- personality ⓝ 성격, 인성
- witness ⓥ 목격하다, 보다
- appealing ⓐ 매력적인, 호소하는
- acquaintance ⓝ 지인
- entrepreneur ⓝ 사업가, 기업가
- evolve ⓥ 서서히 발달하다
- function ⓝ 작용, 역할, 기능
- characteristic ⓝ 특징
- independence ⓝ 독립
- involved in ~에 연루되는, ~에 관여하는

구문 풀이

15행 Similarly, / people [who personally know an entrepreneur] are more than twice as likely to be involved in starting a new firm as those [with no entrepreneur acquaintances or role models].

~ 이상인 / 「배수사+as+원급+ as : ~의 …배인」

06 원인 파악 오류 　정답률 73% | 정답 ⑤

주어진 글 다음에 이어질 글의 순서로 가장 적절한 것을 고르시오. [3점]

① (A) – (C) – (B)　② (B) – (A) – (C)
③ (B) – (C) – (A)　④ (C) – (A) – (B)
✔(C) – (B) – (A)

Once we recognize the false-cause issue, / we see it everywhere.
일단 잘못 파악한 원인 문제를 우리가 인식하면, / 우리는 그것을 어디에서나 보게 된다.

For example, / a recent long-term study of University of Toronto medical students / concluded / that medical school class presidents lived an average of 2.4 years less / than other medical school graduates.
예를 들어, / 토론토 대학의 의대생들에 대한 최근의 장기 연구는 / 결론을 내렸다. / 의대 학년 대표들이 평균 2.4년 더 적게 살았다는 / 다른 의대 졸업생들보다

(C) At first glance, / this seemed to imply / that being a medical school class president is bad for you.
처음 언뜻 봐서는, / 이것은 의미하는 것처럼 보였다. / 의대 학년 대표인 것이 여러분에게 해롭다는 것을

Does this mean / that you should avoid being medical school class president at all costs?
이것은 의미하는가? / 여러분이 무슨 수를 써서라도 의대 학년 대표가 되는 것을 피해야 한다는 것을

(B) Probably not.
아마도 그렇지는 않을 것이다.

Just because being class president is correlated with shorter life expectancy / does not mean / that it *causes* shorter life expectancy.
단지 학년 대표인 것이 더 짧은 평균 수명과 서로 관련된다고 해서 / 의미는 아니다. / 그것이 더 짧은 평균 수명을 *유발한다는*

In fact, / it seems likely / that the sort of person / who becomes medical school class president / is, on average, extremely hard-working, serious, and ambitious.
사실, / 아마도 ~한 것 같다. / 그런 부류의 사람은 / 의대 학년 대표가 되는 / 평균적으로 몹시 열심히 공부하고, 진지하며, 야망이 있는

(A) Perhaps this extra stress, / and the corresponding lack of social and relaxation time / — rather than being class president per se — / contributes to lower life expectancy.
아마도 이러한 가중된 스트레스와 / 그에 상응하는 사교와 휴식 시간의 부족이 / 의대 학년 대표인 것 그 자체보다, / 더 짧은 평균 수명의 원인인 것 같다.

If so, / the real lesson of the study is / that we should all relax a little / and not let our work take over our lives.
만약 그렇다면, / 이 연구의 진정한 교훈은 / 우리 모두가 약간의 휴식을 취해야 하고 / 우리의 일이 우리의 삶을 장악하게 해서는 안 된다는 것이다.

일단 잘못 파악한 원인 문제를 우리가 인식하면, 우리는 그것을 어디에서나 보게 된다. 예를 들어, 토론토 대학의 의대생들에 대한 최근의 장기 연구는 의대 학년 대표들이 다른 의대 졸업생들보다 평균 2.4년 더 적게 살았다는 결론을 내렸다.

(C) 처음 언뜻 봐서는, 이것은 의대 학년 대표인 것이 여러분에게 해롭다는 것을 의미하는 것처럼 보였다. 이것은 여러분이 무슨 수를 써서라도 의대 학년 대표가 되는 것을 피해야 한다는 것을 의미하는가?

(B) 아마도 그렇지는 않을 것이다. 단지 학년 대표인 것이 더 짧은 평균 수명과 서로 관련된다고 해서 그것이 더 짧은 평균 수명을 *유발한다*는 의미는 아니다. 사실, 아마도 의대 학년 대표가 되는 그런 부류의 사람은 평균적으로 몹시 열심히 공부하고, 진지하며, 야망이 있는 것 같다.

(A) 의대 학년 대표인 것 그 자체보다, 아마도 이러한 가중된 스트레스와 그에 상응하는 사교와 휴식 시간의 부족이 더 짧은 평균 수명의 원인인 것 같다. 만약 그렇다면, 이 연구의 진정한 교훈은 우리 모두가 약간의 휴식을 취해야 하고 우리의 일이 우리의 삶을 장악하게 해서는 안 된다는 것이다.

Why? 왜 정답일까?

주어진 글에서 원인 파악 오류를 화제로 언급하며, 의대생 학년 대표들이 다른 의대 졸업생보다 평균적으로 2.4년 더 적게 산다는 연구 결과를 예시로 들고 있다. (C)는 이 연구 결과를 '처음 언뜻 보면' 의대 학년 대표를 맡는 것이 수명에 해롭다는 의미로 해석할 수 있는데, 그렇다면 이 결과로부터 의대 학년 대표가 되는 것을 피해야 한다는 의미까지 도출할 수 있는지 자문한다. (B)는 이 질문에 'Probably not'이라는 부정의 답을 제시하며, 의대 학년 대표가 평균 수명이 더 적은 경향이 있다는 연구 결과만으로 의대 학년 대표가 되는 것 자체가 건강에 부정적 영향을 끼치는 원인이라는 결론을 내릴 수는 없다고 설명한다. (A)는 (B)의 후반부에 이어서 의대 학년 대표들의 어떤 다른 특성들이 실제로 수명에 부정적 영향을 끼친 원인으로 분석될 수 있는지를 보충 설명한다. 따라서 글의 순서로 가장 적절한 것은 ⑤ '(C) – (B) – (A)'이다.

- corresponding ⓐ 상응하는, 해당하는
- be correlated with ~와 서로 관련되다
- ambitious ⓐ 야망 있는
- at all costs 무슨 수를 써서라도, 기어코
- life expectancy 기대 수명, 평균 수명
- extremely ad 극도로, 몹시
- at first glance 처음 언뜻 보면

구문 풀이

13행 {Just because being class president is correlated with shorter life expectancy} does not mean that it *causes* shorter life expectancy.
(being class president: 동명사구 주어 / is correlated: 동사(수동태) / { }: 주어 역할 / does not mean: 동사 / that: 접속사(~것))

07 네트워크 시장에서 역사의 중요성
정답률 64% | 정답 ③

주어진 글 다음에 이어질 글의 순서로 가장 적절한 것을 고르시오. [3점]

① (A) – (C) – (B) ② (B) – (A) – (C)
✔(B) – (C) – (A) ④ (C) – (A) – (B)
⑤ (C) – (B) – (A)

One interesting feature of network markets / is that "history matters."
네트워크 시장의 한 가지 흥미로운 특징은 / '역사가 중요하다'라는 것이다.
A famous example is the QWERTY keyboard / used with your computer.
한 가지 유명한 예는 QWERTY 키보드이다. / 컴퓨터와 함께 사용되는
(B) You might wonder / why this particular configuration of keys, / with its awkward placement of the letters, / became the standard.
당신은 의아해할지도 모른다. / 이 독특한 키의 배열이 왜 / 어색한 문자 배치를 가진, / 표준이 되었는지
The QWERTY keyboard in the 19th century was developed / in the era of manual typewriters with physical keys.
19세기 QWERTY 키보드는 개발되었다. / 물리적 키가 있는 수동 타자기 시대에
(C) The keyboard was designed / to keep frequently used keys (like E and O) physically separated / in order to prevent them from jamming.
그 키보드는 설계되었다. / 자주 사용되는 (E와 O 같은) 키가 물리적으로 떨어져 있도록 / 그것들이 걸리는 것을 막기 위해
By the time the technology for electronic typing evolved, / millions of people had already learned / to type on millions of QWERTY typewriters.
전자 타이핑 기술이 발전했을 무렵, / 수백만 명의 사람들이 이미 배운 상태였다. / 수백만 개의 QWERTY 타자기에서 타자 치는 법을
(A) Replacing the QWERTY keyboard with a more efficient design / would have been both expensive and difficult to coordinate.
QWERTY 키보드를 더 효율적인 디자인으로 교체하는 것은 / 비용이 많이 들고 조정하기 어려웠을 것이다.
Thus, / the placement of the letters / stays with the obsolete QWERTY / on today's English-language keyboards.
따라서, / 문자의 배치는 / 구식 QWERTY로 남아 있다. / 오늘날의 영어 키보드에서

네트워크 시장의 한 가지 흥미로운 특징은 '역사가 중요하다'라는 것이다. 한 가지 유명한 예는 컴퓨터와 함께 사용되는 QWERTY 키보드이다.

(B) 당신은 문자 배치가 어색한 이 독특한 키의 배열이 왜 표준이 되었는지 의아해할지도 모른다. 19세기 QWERTY 키보드는 물리적 키가 있는 수동 타자기 시대에 개발되었다.

(C) 그 키보드는 자주 사용되는 (E와 O 같은) 키가 걸리는 것을 막기 위해 물리적으로 떨어져 있도록 설계되었다. 전자 타이핑 기술이 발전했을 무렵, 수백만 명의 사람들이 이미 수백만 개의 QWERTY 타자기에서 타자 치는 법을 배운 상태였다.

(A) QWERTY 키보드를 더 효율적인 디자인으로 교체하는 것은 비용이 많이 들고 조정하기 어려웠을 것이다. 따라서, 오늘날의 영어 키보드에서 문자의 배치는 구식 QWERTY로 남아 있다.

Why? 왜 정답일까?

네트워크 시장에서 역사가 중요하다는 일반적인 내용과 함께 QWERTY 키보드의 사례를 언급하는 주어진 글 뒤로, 이 독특한 키보드가 수동 타자기 시대에 개발되었다는 배경을 설명하는 (B)가 먼저 연결된다. 이어서 (C)는 QWERTY 배열이 왜 특이하게 설계되었는지를 설명한 후, 전자 타이핑 기술이 발전했을 무렵에는 이미 QWERTY 키보드가 너무 많이 쓰이고 있었음을 언급하고, (A)는 그래서 QWERTY가 계속 그대로 쓰이게 되었다는 결론을 제시한다. 따라서 글의 순서로 가장 적절한 것은 ③ '(B) – (C) – (A)'이다.

- coordinate ⓥ 조정하다
- letter ⓝ 문자
- awkward ⓐ 어색한
- manual ⓐ 수동의
- prevent A from B A가 B하지 못하게 하다
- placement ⓝ 배열
- particular ⓐ 독특한
- standard ⓝ 표준
- typewriter ⓝ 타자기
- jam ⓥ 걸리다, 움직이지 않게 하다

구문 풀이

4행 Replacing the QWERTY keyboard with a more efficient design would have been both expensive and difficult to coordinate.
(동명사구 주어 / 「would have + 과거분사 : ~했을 것이다(과거 추측)」)

08 문화에 대한 인간의 인식
정답률 58% | 정답 ⑤

주어진 글 다음에 이어질 글의 순서로 가장 적절한 것을 고르시오. [3점]

① (A) – (C) – (B) ② (B) – (A) – (C)
③ (B) – (C) – (A) ④ (C) – (A) – (B)
✔(C) – (B) – (A)

When we think of culture, / we first think of human cultures, / of *our* culture.
우리가 문화에 대해 생각할 때, / 우리는 먼저 인간의 문화를 생각한다. / 즉 *우리의* 문화를
We think of computers, airplanes, fashions, teams, and pop stars.
우리는 컴퓨터, 비행기, 패션, 팀, 그리고 팝 스타를 생각한다.
For most of human cultural history, / none of those things existed.
대부분의 인간 문화의 역사에서 / 그러한 것들 중 어느 것도 존재하지 않았다.
(C) For hundreds of thousands of years, / no human culture had a tool with moving parts.
수십만 년 동안, / 어떤 인간의 문화도 움직이는 부품들이 있는 도구를 가지지 않았다.
Well into the twentieth century, / various human foraging cultures / retained tools of stone, wood, and bone.
20세기까지도 / 다양한 인간의 수렵 채집 문화는 / 돌, 나무, 그리고 뼈로 된 도구를 보유했다.
We might pity human hunter-gatherers for their stuck simplicity, / but we would be making a mistake.
우리는 수렵 채집인들을 그들의 꽉 막힌 단순함 때문에 동정할지도 모르지만, / 우리는 실수를 범하고 있는 것일 수 있다.
(B) They held extensive knowledge, / knew deep secrets of their lands and creatures.
그들은 광범위한 지식을 가졌고 / 그들의 땅과 생명체의 깊은 비밀을 알았다.
And they experienced rich and rewarding lives; / we know so / because when their ways were threatened, / they fought to hold on to them, to the death.
그리고 그들은 풍요롭고 가치 있는 삶을 경험했는데, / 우리는 그것을 알고 있다. / 그들의 (삶의) 방식이 위협받았을 때 ~했기 때문에 / 그것을 고수하기 위해 죽을 때까지 그들이 싸웠기
(A) Sadly, this remains true / as the final tribal peoples get overwhelmed / by those who value money above humanity.
슬프게도 이것은 여전히 사실이다. / 마지막 부족민들이 제압당할 때도 / 인간성보다 돈을 가치 있게 여기는 사람들에 의해
We are living in their end times / and, to varying extents, / we're all contributing to those endings.
우리는 그들의 종말의 시대에 살고 있고, / 다양한 정도로 / 우리는 모두 그러한 종말에 원인이 되고 있다.
Ultimately our values may even prove self-defeating.
결국 우리의 가치들이 스스로를 파괴하고 있다는 것을 증명하는 것일 수도 있다.

우리가 문화에 대해 생각할 때, 우리는 먼저 인간의 문화, 우리의 문화를 생각한다. 우리는 컴퓨터, 비행기, 패션, 팀, 그리고 팝 스타를 생각한다. 그러한 것들 중 어느 것도 대부분의 인간 문화의 역사에서 존재하지 않았다.

(C) 수십만 년 동안, 어떤 인간의 문화도 움직이는 부품들이 있는 도구를 가지지 않았다. 20세기까지도 다양한 인간의 수렵 채집 문화는 돌, 나무, 그리고 뼈로 된 도구를 보유했다. 우리는 수렵 채집인들을 그들의 꽉 막힌 단순함 때문에 동정할지도 모르지만, 우리는 실수를 범하고 있는 것일 수 있다.

(B) 그들은 광범위한 지식을 가졌고 그들의 땅과 생명체의 깊은 비밀을 알았다. 그리고 그들은 풍요롭고 가치 있는 삶을 경험했는데, 그들의 (삶의) 방식이 위협받았을 때 그것을 고수하기 위해 죽을 때까지 그들이 싸웠기 때문에 우리는 그것을 알고 있다.

(A) 슬프게도 인간성보다 돈을 가치 있게 여기는 사람들에 의해 마지막 부족민들이 제압당할 때도 이것은 여전히 사실이다. 우리는 그들의 종말의 시대에 살고 있고, 다양한 정도로 우리는 모두 그러한 종말에 원인이 되고 있다. 결국 우리의 가치들이 스스로를 파괴하고 있다는 것을 증명하는 것일 수도 있다.

Why? 왜 정답일까?

주어진 글에서 인간은 '문화'라는 말을 들으면 '현대 우리의' 문화를 떠올리는 경향이 있지만 사실 현대 문화의 역사는 매우 짧다고 언급한 데 이어, **(C)**에서는 수십만 년 동안 현대의 '움직이는 부품'은 존재하지 않았으며 20세기까지만 해도 수렵 채집 문화에서는 돌, 나무, 뼈 등을 사용했다는 부연 설명을 이어간다. 특히 **(C)**의 후반부에서는 현대의 우리가 수렵채집 문화권의 사람들을 단순하다고 동정하는 것이 실수일 수 있다고 지적하는데, **(B)**에서는 '수렵채집인'들을 **They**로 받으며 이들이 광범위한 지식을 지니고 있었다는 점과 풍요롭고 가치로운 삶 또한 누렸다는 점을 보충 설명한다. **(A)**는 '슬프게도' 우리가 이들이 종말을 맞는 시대에 살고 있으며, 이로 인해 우리 자신의 가치를 파괴하는 과정에 있는 것지도 모른다는 결론을 제시한다. 따라서 글의 순서로 가장 적절한 것은 ⑤ '**(C) – (B) – (A)**'이다.

- tribal ⓐ 부족의
- varying ⓐ 다양한, 바뀌는
- self-defeating ⓐ 스스로를 파괴하는
- rewarding ⓐ 가치 있는, 보람 있는
- retain ⓥ 보유하다
- overwhelm ⓥ 압도하다, 제압하다
- ultimately ad 결국, 궁극적으로
- extensive ⓐ 광범위한
- hold on to ~을 고수하다
- simplicity ⓝ 단순함

구문 풀이

6행 Sadly, this remains true as the final tribal peoples get overwhelmed by those [who value money above humanity].
(remains: 2형식 동사, true: 형용사 보어, as: 접속사(~할 때), those: 선행사, who: 주격 관계대명사)

09 환경세 부과의 배경과 결과

정답률 66% | 정답 ②

주어진 글 다음에 이어질 글의 순서로 가장 적절한 것을 고르시오.

① (A) – (C) – (B)
✔ (B) – (A) – (C)
③ (B) – (C) – (A)
④ (C) – (A) – (B)
⑤ (C) – (B) – (A)

According to the market response model, / it is increasing prices / that drive providers to search for new sources, / innovators to substitute, / consumers to conserve, / and alternatives to emerge.
시장 반응 모형에 따르면, / 바로 가격의 인상이다. / 공급자가 새로운 공급원을 찾게 하고, / 혁신가가 대용하게 하고, / 소비자가 아껴 쓰게 하고, / 대안이 생기게 하는 것은

(B) Taxing certain goods or services, / and so increasing prices, / should result in either decreased use of these resources / or creative innovation of new sources or options.
특정 재화나 서비스에 과세하여 / 가격을 인상시키는 것은 / 이러한 자원의 사용이 줄어드는 결과를 낳을 것이다. / 혹은 새로운 공급원 또는 선택사항의 창조적 혁신을

The money raised through the tax / can be used directly by the government / either to supply services or to search for alternatives.
세금을 통해 조성된 돈은 / 정부에 의해 직접 사용될 수 있다. / 서비스를 공급하거나 대안을 모색하는 데

(A) Many examples of such "green taxes" exist.
그러한 '환경세'의 많은 예가 존재한다.

Facing landfill costs, / labor expenses, / and related costs in the provision of garbage disposal, / for example, / some cities have required households / to dispose of all waste in special trash bags, / purchased by consumers themselves, / and often costing a dollar or more each.
쓰레기 매립 비용에 직면한 / 인건비에 / 그리고 쓰레기 처리를 준비하는 데 관련된 비용에 / 예를 들어, / 일부 도시는 가정에 요구했는데, / 모든 폐기물을 특별 쓰레기 봉투에 담아서 처리하도록 / 이는 소비자가 직접 구입하는 것이며 / 한 장당 1달러 이상의 비용이 드는 것이었다.

(C) The results have been greatly increased recycling / and more careful attention by consumers to packaging and waste.
그 결과는 재활용을 크게 증가시켰다. / 그리고 포장과 폐기물에 대한 소비자의 더 세심한 주의(를 낳았다)

By internalizing the costs of trash to consumers, / there has been an observed decrease / in the flow of garbage from households.
소비자에게 쓰레기 비용을 자기 것으로 만들게 함으로써, / 감소가 관찰되었다. / 가정에서 나오는 쓰레기 흐름의

시장 반응 모형에 따르면, 공급자가 새로운 공급원을 찾게 하고, 혁신가가 대용하게 하고, 소비자가 아껴 쓰게 하고, 대안이 생기게 하는 것은 바로 가격의 인상이다.

(B) 특정 재화나 서비스에 과세하여 가격이 인상되면 이러한 자원의 사용이 줄거나 새로운 공급원 또는 선택사항의 창조적 혁신을 낳을 것이다. 세금을 통해 조성된 돈은 정부가 직접 서비스를 공급하거나 대안을 모색하는 데 사용할 수 있다.

(A) 그러한 '환경세'의 많은 예가 존재한다. 예를 들어, 쓰레기 매립 비용, 인건비, 쓰레기 처리를 준비하는 데 관련된 비용에 직면한 일부 도시는 가정이 모든 폐기물을 특별 쓰레기 봉투에 담아서 처리하도록 요구했는데, 이는 소비자가 직접 구입하는 것이며 한 장당 1달러 이상의 비용이 드는 것이었다.

(C) 그 결과 재활용이 크게 증가했고 소비자가 포장과 폐기물에 더 세심한 주의를 기울이게 되었다. 소비자에게 쓰레기 비용을 자기 것으로 만들게 함으로써, 가정에서 나오는 쓰레기 흐름의 감소가 관찰되었다.

Why? 왜 정답일까?

주어진 글에서 어떤 것을 아껴 쓰게 하거나 그 대안을 찾게 하려면 비용을 증가시키면 된다고 언급한 데 이어, **(B)**에서는 보다 구체적으로 특정 재화나 서비스에 '과세'를 하여 비용을 증가시키면 혁신이 일어날 수 있다고 설명한다. 이어서 **(A)**는 '환경세'의 다양한 예를 들고, **(C)**에서는 다양한 환경세를 부과한 결과 사람들이 재활용과 쓰레기 처리에 더 주의하는 결과가 나타났음을 제시한다. 따라서 글의 순서로 가장 적절한 것은 ② '**(B) – (A) – (C)**'이다.

- substitute ⓥ 대체하다
- emerge ⓥ 생겨나다, 나타나다
- expense ⓝ 비용
- result in ~을 초래하다
- conserve ⓥ 아끼다, 보존하다
- landfill ⓝ 쓰레기 매립지
- disposal ⓝ (없애기 위한) 처리
- internalize ⓥ 내재화하다

구문 풀이

5행 Facing landfill costs, labor expenses, and related costs in the provision of garbage disposal, for example, some cities have required households to dispose of all waste in special trash bags, (which are) purchased by consumers themselves, and often costing a dollar or more each.
(Facing: 분사구문, some cities: 주어, have required: 5형식 동사, households: 목적어, to dispose of: 목적격 보어, special trash bags: 선행사, (which are): 생략(계속적 용법), purchased: 보어1, costing: 보어2)

★★★ **1등급 대비 고난도 2점 문제**

10 광고를 하는 이유

정답률 33% | 정답 ⑤

주어진 글 다음에 이어질 글의 순서로 가장 적절한 것을 고르시오.

① (A) – (C) – (B)
② (B) – (A) – (C)
③ (B) – (C) – (A)
④ (C) – (A) – (B)
✔ (C) – (B) – (A)

If you drive down a busy street, / you will find many competing businesses, / often right next to one another.
만약 여러분이 번화한 거리를 운전한다면, / 여러분은 경쟁하는 많은 업체들을 발견할 것이다. / 흔히 바로 서로 옆에서

For example, / in most places / a consumer in search of a quick meal / has many choices, / and more fast-food restaurants appear all the time.
예를 들어, / 대부분의 장소에서 / 간단한 식사를 찾는 소비자에게는 / 선택권이 많고, / 항상 여러 패스트푸드 식당들이 눈에 띈다.

(C) These competing firms advertise heavily.
이 경쟁 업체들은 광고를 많이 한다.

The temptation is / to see advertising as driving up the price of a product / without any benefit to the consumer.
유혹은 ~이다. / 광고가 제품의 가격을 올린다고 본다는 것 / 소비자에게 어떤 혜택도 없이

(B) However, / this misconception doesn't account for / why firms advertise.
그러나 / 이러한 오해는 설명해주지 않는다. / 회사들이 광고하는 이유를

In markets / where competitors sell slightly differentiated products, / advertising enables firms / to inform their customers about new products and services.
시장에서, / 경쟁사들이 약간씩 차별화된 제품들을 판매하는 / 광고는 회사들이 ~할 수 있게 해 준다. / 소비자들에게 새로운 제품과 서비스를 알릴

(A) Yes, costs rise, / but consumers also gain information / to help make purchasing decisions.
물론 가격이 상승하기는 하지만, / 소비자들은 도움이 되는 정보도 얻는다. / 구매 결정을 내리는 데
Consumers also benefit from added variety, / and we all get a product / that's pretty close to our vision of a perfect good / — and no other market structure delivers that outcome.
또한 소비자들은 추가된 다양성으로부터 혜택을 얻고, / 우리 모두는 제품을 얻는데, / 완벽한 제품에 대한 우리의 상상에 매우 근접한 / 다른 어떤 시장 구조도 그러한 결과를 제공하지 않는다.

만약 여러분이 번화한 거리를 운전한다면, 여러분은 바로 서로 옆에서 경쟁하는 많은 업체들을 흔히 발견할 것이다. 예를 들어, 대부분의 장소에서 간단한 식사를 찾는 소비자에게는 선택권이 많고, 항상 여러 패스트푸드 식당들이 눈에 띈다.

(C) 이 경쟁 업체들은 광고를 많이 한다. 광고라고 하면 소비자에게 어떤 혜택도 없이 제품의 가격을 올린다고 보기 쉽다.

(B) 그러나 이러한 오해는 회사들이 광고하는 이유를 설명해주지 않는다. 경쟁사들이 약간씩 차별화된 제품들을 판매하는 시장에서, 광고는 회사들이 소비자들에게 새로운 제품과 서비스를 알릴 수 있게 해 준다.

(A) 물론 가격이 상승하기는 하지만, 소비자들은 구매 결정을 내리는 데 도움이 되는 정보도 얻는다. 또한 소비자들은 추가된 다양성으로 혜택을 얻고, 우리 모두는 완벽한 제품에 대한 우리의 상상에 매우 근접한 제품을 얻는데, 다른 어떤 시장 구조도 그러한 결과를 제공하지 않는다.

Why? 왜 정답일까?

주어진 글은 우리가 일상에서 경쟁 관계에 있는 업체들을 많이 볼 수 있다는 내용이고, **(C)**는 '이 업체들'이 살아남기 위해 광고를 한다는 내용이다. 특히 **(C)**의 후반부는 우리가 광고 때문에 제품 가격이 올라간다고 여기기 쉽다고 하는데, **(B)**는 이런 '오해'가 광고의 이유를 설명해주지 못한다면서 광고의 효과를 설명하기 시작한다. **(A)** 또한 **(B)**에 이어 광고의 이득과 효과를 언급하므로, 글의 순서로 가장 적절한 것은 ⑤ '**(C) – (B) – (A)**'이다.

- in search of ~을 찾아서
- benefit from ~에서 이득을 보다
- vision ⓝ 상상
- misconception ⓝ 오해
- advertise ⓥ 광고하다
- differentiate ⓥ 차별(화)하다, 구별하다
- temptation ⓝ 유혹
- quick meal 간단한 식사
- variety ⓝ 다양성, 품종
- deliver ⓥ (결과를) 내놓다, 산출하다
- account for ~을 설명하다
- slightly ad 약간
- heavily ad 많이, 심하게
- drive up (값 등을) 끌어올리다

구문 풀이

13행 In markets [where competitors sell slightly differentiated products], advertising enables firms to inform their customers about new products and services.
(장소 선행사 / 관계부사절 / 「enable + 목적어 + to부정사 : ~이 …할 수 있게 해주다」)

★★ 문제 해결 꿀~팁 ★★

▶ 많이 틀린 이유는?
(C)의 driving up the price of a product 다음에 (A)의 Yes, costs rise가 와도 자연스러워 보이지만, (A) 다음 (B)가 자연스럽지 않다. (A)에서 '오해'로 볼 만한 내용이 언급되지 않기 때문이다.
▶ 문제 해결 방법은?
(C)의 see advertising as driving up the price of a product without any benefit to the consumer가 (B)의 this misconception으로 연결되고, also가 포함된 (A)에서 광고의 이점에 대한 내용을 추가하는 흐름이다.

★★★ 1등급 대비 고난도 2점 문제

11 쌍둥이가 유전자 연구에 기여하는 바 — 정답률 41% | 정답 ③

주어진 글 다음에 이어질 글의 순서로 가장 적절한 것을 고르시오.

① (A) – (C) – (B) ② (B) – (A) – (C)
③ (B) – (C) – (A) ④ (C) – (A) – (B)
⑤ (C) – (B) – (A)

Twins provide a unique opportunity / to study genes.
쌍둥이는 특별한 기회를 제공한다. / 유전자를 연구할
Some pairs of twins are identical: / they share the exact same genes in their DNA.
어떤 쌍둥이들은 일란성인데, / 즉 이들은 DNA 속에 정확히 똑같은 유전자를 공유한다.
(B) Other pairs are fraternal, / sharing only half of their genes on average.
다른 쌍둥이들은 이란성으로, / 평균적으로 그들 유전자의 절반만을 공유한다.
Differences in genetic similarity / turn out to be a powerful natural experiment, / allowing us to estimate / how much genes influence a given trait.
유전적 유사성의 차이가 / 강력한 자연적 실험인 것으로 밝혀지면서, / 우리로 하여금 추정하게 해 준다. / 유전자가 특정 특성에 얼마나 많이 영향을 미치는지를
(C) For example, / identical twins almost always have the same eye color, / but fraternal twins often do not.
예를 들어, / 일란성 쌍둥이는 거의 항상 눈 색깔이 똑같지만, / 이란성 쌍둥이는 종종 그렇지 않다.
This suggests / that genes play a role in eye color, / and in fact / geneticists have identified several specific genes / that are involved.
이것은 암시하고, / 유전자가 눈 색깔에 있어 어떤 역할을 한다는 것을 / 실제로 / 유전학자들은 몇 가지 특정 유전자를 찾아냈다. / 이와 관련된
(A) In the same way, / scientists can estimate the role / genes play in any other trait / by comparing the similarity of identical twins / to the similarity of fraternal twins.
마찬가지로, / 과학자들은 역할을 추정할 수 있다. / 그 어떤 다른 특성에서 유전자가 하는 / 일란성 쌍둥이의 유사성을 비교하여 / 이란성 쌍둥이의 유사성과
If there is a difference, / then the magnitude of the difference gives a clue / as to how much genes are involved.
만약 어떤 차이가 있다면, / 그 차이의 크기는 단서를 제공한다. / 유전자가 얼마나 많이 관련되어 있는지에 대한

쌍둥이는 유전자를 연구할 특별한 기회를 제공한다. 어떤 쌍둥이들은 일란성인데, 즉 이들은 DNA 속에 정확히 똑같은 유전자를 공유한다.

(B) 다른 쌍둥이들은 이란성으로, 평균적으로 그들 유전자의 절반만을 공유한다. 유전적 유사성의 차이가 강력한 자연적 실험인 것으로 밝혀지면서, 우리로 하여금 유전자가 특정 특성에 얼마나 많이 영향을 미치는지를 추정하게 해 준다.

(C) 예를 들어, 일란성 쌍둥이는 거의 항상 눈 색깔이 똑같지만, 이란성 쌍둥이는 종종 그렇지 않다. 이것은 유전자가 눈 색깔에 있어 어떤 역할을 한다는 것을 암시하고, 실제로 유전학자들은 이와 관련된 몇 가지 특정 유전자를 찾아냈다.

(A) 마찬가지로, 과학자들은 일란성 쌍둥이의 유사성과 이란성 쌍둥이의 유사성을 비교하여 그 어떤 다른 특성에서 유전자가 하는 역할을 추정할 수 있다. 만약 어떤 차이가 있다면, 그 차이의 크기는 유전자가 얼마나 많이 관련되어 있는지에 대한 단서를 제공한다.

Why? 왜 정답일까?

쌍둥이 연구는 유전자 연구에 있어 특별한 기회를 제공한다는 내용 뒤로 일란성 쌍둥이는 유전자 구성이 서로 똑같다는 내용을 설명한 주어진 글 뒤에는, 이와 달리 이란성 쌍둥이는 서로 유전자 구성이 다르기 때문에 일란성과 이란성을 비교하면 유전자가 어떤 특성에 얼마나 관여하는지를 알 수 있게 된다고 말한 **(B)**가 이어지는 것이 적절하다. 뒤에는 **For example**로 시작하여 눈 색깔 연구라는 구체적인 예를 들기 시작하는 **(C)**, **In the same way**로 시작하며 이뿐 아니라 다른 특성에도 비슷한 연구를 할 수 있다는 결론을 내린 **(A)**가 차례로 이어지는 것이 자연스럽다. 따라서 주어진 글 다음에 이어질 글의 순서로 가장 적절한 것은 ③ '**(B) – (C) – (A)**'이다.

- gene ⓝ 유전자
- estimate ⓥ 추정하다
- fraternal ⓐ (쌍둥이가) 이란성인, 이란성의
- experiment ⓝ 실험
- identical ⓐ (쌍둥이가) 일란성인, 일란성의
- trait ⓝ 특성, 특징
- magnitude ⓝ 크기, 정도, 규모
- specific ⓐ 특정한, 구체적인

구문 풀이

7행 If there is a difference, / then the magnitude of the difference gives a clue as to [how much genes are involved]. [ ] : as to의 목적어
(조건 접속사(~한다면) / 주어 / 동사 / ~에 대한 / 의문사)

★★ 문제 해결 꿀~팁 ★★

▶ 많이 틀린 이유는?
①을 제외한 ②, ④, ⑤의 오답률이 비슷했는데 이는 수험생들이 지문의 내용 파악 자체를 어려워했다는 뜻이다. 과학이나 경제 내용을 다루는 지문에서 이런 현상이 흔히 있는데, 해당 지문도 쌍둥이 연구에 관한 '유전과학' 내용을 다루고 있어 이해하기가 다소 까다로웠다.
▶ 문제 해결 방법은?
순서 문항인 만큼 모든 문장 내용을 속속들이 파악하기보다는 지시사 및 연결어를 중심으로 대략적인 단락의 내용만을 파악할 필요가 있다. 주어진 글에서 '쌍둥이'를

이야기한 후 '일란성 쌍둥이'를 언급하므로, 뒤에는 '이란성 쌍둥이'를 소개하는 (B)를 먼저 배치하여 '쌍둥이'라는 큰 주제를 대략적으로 마무리한다. 이어서 (A)와 (C)의 순서를 정해야 하는데, (A)의 In the same way는 '마찬가지로'라는 뜻이어서 앞에서 한 가지 예가 나오고 뒤에 다른 예나 결론을 추가적으로 언급할 때 쓴다. 그러므로 For example로 시작하여 예 하나를 먼저 소개하는 (C)가 먼저 나오고 (A)가 이어지는 것이 적절하다. 이렇게 (B) – (C) – (A) 배치를 끝낸 후, 빠르게 훑으며 흐름이 자연스러운지 확인한다.

★★★ 1등급 대비 고난도 3점 문제

12 과학에서의 획기적 발견 정답률 53% | 정답 ④

주어진 글 다음에 이어질 글의 순서로 가장 적절한 것을 고르시오. [3점]

① (A) − (C) − (B)
② (B) − (A) − (C)
③ (B) − (C) − (A)
④ (C) − (A) − (B)
⑤ (C) − (B) − (A)

Like the physiological discoveries of the late nineteenth century, / today's biological breakthrough / has fundamentally altered our understanding / of how the human organism works / and will change medical practice fundamentally and thoroughly.
19세기 후반 생리학의 발견처럼, / 오늘날 생물학의 획기적인 발견은 / 우리의 이해를 근본적으로 바꿔놓았고, / 인간 유기체가 작동하는 방식에 대한 / 의료 행위를 본질적이면서도 철저하게 변화시킬 것이다.
(C) The word "breakthrough," however, / seems to imply in many people's minds / an amazing, unprecedented revelation / that, in an instant, makes everything clear.
그러나 '획기적인 발견'이라는 말은 / 많은 사람들의 마음속에서는 의미하는 것처럼 보인다. / 놀랍고 전례 없는 발견을 / 순식간에 모든 것을 명확하게 만드는
Science doesn't actually work that way.
사실 과학은 그런 방식으로 작동하지 않는다.
(A) Remember the scientific method, / which you probably first learned / about back in elementary school?
과학적 방법을 기억하는가? / 여러분이 아마 처음 배웠을 / 대략 초등학교 때
It has a long and difficult process / of observation, hypothesis, experiment, testing, modifying, retesting, / and retesting again and again and again.
그것은 길고 어려운 과정을 지닌다. / 관찰, 가설, 실험, 검증, 수정, 재검증, / 그리고 재차 반복되는 재검증이라는
(B) That's how science works, / and the breakthrough understanding of the relationship / between our genes and chronic disease / happened in just that way, / building on the work of scientists / from decades — even centuries — ago.
그것이 과학이 작동하는 방식이고, / 관계에 대한 획기적 이해도 / 우리 유전자와 만성 질환 사이의 / 바로 그러한 방식으로 일어났다. / 과학자들의 연구를 기반으로 하여 / 수십 년, 심지어 수백 년 전으로부터의
In fact, it is still happening; / the story continues to unfold / as the research presses on.
사실, 그 이야기는 여전히 일어나고 있으며 / 그것은 계속 펼쳐진다. / 연구가 계속되는 한

19세기 후반 생리학의 발견처럼, 오늘날 생물학의 획기적인 발견은 인간 유기체가 작동하는 방식에 대한 우리의 이해를 근본적으로 바꿔놓았고, 의료 행위를 본질적이면서도 철저하게 변화시킬 것이다.

(C) 그러나 '획기적인 발견'이라는 말은 많은 사람들의 마음속에서는 순식간에 모든 것을 명확하게 만드는 놀랍고 전례 없는 발견을 의미하는 것처럼 보인다. 사실 과학은 그런 방식으로 작동하지 않는다.

(A) 여러분이 대략 초등학교 때 아마 처음 배웠을 과학적 방법을 기억하는가? 그것은 관찰, 가설, 실험, 검증, 수정, 재검증, 그리고 재차 반복되는 재검증이라는 길고 어려운 과정을 지닌다.

(B) 그것이 과학이 작동하는 방식이고, 우리 유전자와 만성 질환 사이의 관계에 대한 획기적 이해도 수십 년, 심지어 수백 년 전으로부터의 과학자들의 연구를 기반으로 하여 바로 그러한 방식으로 일어났다. 사실, 그것은 여전히 일어나고 있으며 연구가 계속되는 한 그 이야기는 계속 펼쳐진다.

Why? 왜 정답일까?

오늘날 생물학의 획기적 발견을 화두로 제시하는 주어진 글 뒤에는, however로 흐름을 반전시키며 사실 과학에는 순식간에 모든 것을 정리해주는 '획기적 발견'이라는 것이 존재하지 않는다고 언급하는 (C)가 먼저 이어진다. 이어서 (A)는 과학이 관찰, 가설, 실험, 검증, 수정, 재검증 등의 길고 복잡한 과정을 통해 이루어진다는 점을 상기시키고, (B)는 그러한 긴 과정이 곧 과학의 진정한 작동 방식이라는 결론을 제시한다. 따라서 글의 순서로 가장 적절한 것은 ④ '(C) – (A) – (B)'이다.

- physiological ⓐ 생리학적인
- fundamentally ad 근본적으로
- hypothesis ⓝ 가설
- chronic ⓐ 만성의
- unprecedented ⓐ 전례 없는
- breakthrough ⓝ 획기적 발견
- thoroughly ad 철저히
- modify ⓥ 수정하다
- unfold ⓥ 펼쳐지다, 펴다
- revelation ⓝ 발견

구문 풀이

12행 That's how science works, and the breakthrough understanding of the relationship between our genes and chronic disease happened in just that way, building on the work of scientists from decades — even centuries — ago.
(how: 관계부사(~하는 방법) / the breakthrough understanding: 주어 / happened: 동사 / building: 분사구문(~하면서))

★★ 문제 해결 꿀~팁 ★★

▶ 많이 틀린 이유는?
(C)와 (B)에 나오는 breakthrough만 보고 (C) – (B)를 곧장 연결시켜서는 안 된다. (C)는 'Science doesn't actually work that way.'로 끝나는데, 이 뒤에 (B)의 'That's how science works, ~'가 이어지면 '과학은 그런 식으로 작동하지 않는다. vs. 바로 그렇게 과학이 작동한다.'와 같이 상충되는 의미의 두 문장이 역접의 연결어 없이 이어져 버린다.
▶ 문제 해결 방법은?
맥락상 (C) 뒤에 관찰, 가설, 실험, 검증, 수정, 재검증 등을 언급하며 과학의 작동 원리를 설명하는 (A)가 먼저 나오고, 이것이 바로 과학의 작동 원리가 맞다고 확인해주는 (B)가 연결되어야 적절한 흐름이 완성된다.

DAY 12 글의 순서 02

01 ④	02 ②	03 ②	04 ⑤	05 ④
06 ②	07 ③	08 ⑤	09 ②	10 ②
11 ②	12 ⑤			

01 나쁜 습관을 '깬다'는 언어 표현

정답률 53% | 정답 ④

주어진 글 다음에 이어질 글의 순서로 가장 적절한 것을 고르시오.

① (A) − (C) − (B)
② (B) − (A) − (C)
③ (B) − (C) − (A)
④ (C) − (A) − (B) ✔
⑤ (C) − (B) − (A)

Like positive habits, / bad habits exist / on a continuum of easy-to-change and hard-to-change.
긍정적인 습관과 마찬가지로, / 나쁜 습관은 존재한다. / 바꾸기 쉽다와 바꾸기 어렵다의 연속체에

(C) When you get toward the "hard" end of the spectrum, / note the language you hear / — *breaking* bad habits and *battling* addiction.
여러분이 그 연속체의 '어려운 쪽' 끝에 가까워질 때, / 여러분이 듣는 언어에 주목하라. / 즉 나쁜 습관을 *깨는 것*과 중독과 *싸우는 것*

It's as if an unwanted behavior is a nefarious villain / to be aggressively defeated.
바람직하지 못한 행동은 마치 사악한 악당인 것 같다. / 격렬히 패배시켜야 할

(A) But / this kind of language / (and the approaches it spawns) / frames these challenges / in a way that isn't helpful or effective.
그러나 / 이러한 종류의 언어는 / (그리고 그것이 낳는 접근법) / 이러한 도전에 틀을 씌운다. / 도움이 되지 않거나 효과적이지 않은 방식으로

I specifically hope / we will stop using this phrase: / "break a habit."
특히 나는 바란다. / 우리가 이 문구를 그만 사용하기를 / '습관을 깨다'라는

This language misguides people.
이 언어는 사람들을 잘못된 길로 이끈다.

The word "break" sets the wrong expectation / for how you get rid of a bad habit.
'깨다'라는 단어는 잘못된 기대를 형성한다. / 여러분이 나쁜 습관을 없애는 방법에 대해

(B) This word implies / that if you input a lot of force in one moment, / the habit will be gone.
이 단어는 의미를 담는다. / 여러분이 한순간에 많은 힘을 가하면 / 그 습관이 없어질 거라는

However, that rarely works, / because you usually cannot get rid of an unwanted habit / by applying force one time.
하지만 그것은 거의 효과가 없는데, / 대체로 여러분이 바람직하지 못한 습관을 없앨 수 없기 때문이다. / 한 번 힘을 가하는 것으로

긍정적인 습관과 마찬가지로, 나쁜 습관은 바꾸기 쉽다와 바꾸기 어렵다의 연속체에 존재한다.

(C) 그 연속체의 '어려운 쪽' 끝에 가까워질 때, 여러분이 듣는 언어, 즉 나쁜 습관을 *깨는 것*과 중독과 *싸우는 것*에 주목하라. 바람직하지 못한 행동은 마치 격렬히 패배시켜야 할 사악한 악당인 것 같다.

(A) 그러나 이러한 종류의 언어(와 그것이 낳는 접근법)는 도움이 되지 않거나 효과적이지 않은 방식으로 이러한 도전에 틀을 씌운다. 특히 나는 우리가 '습관을 깨다'라는 문구를 그만 사용하기를 바란다. 이 언어는 사람들을 잘못된 길로 이끈다. '깨다'라는 단어는 나쁜 습관을 없애는 방법에 대해 잘못된 기대를 형성한다.

(B) 이 단어는 여러분이 한순간에 많은 힘을 가하면 그 습관이 없어질 거라는 의미를 담는다. 하지만 그것은 거의 효과가 없는데, 대체로 여러분이 한 번 힘을 가하는 것으로 바람직하지 못한 습관을 없앨 수 없기 때문이다.

Why? 왜 정답일까?

습관이 바꾸기 쉽다와 어렵다라는 연속체 안에 존재한다는 주어진 글 뒤로, '연속체'를 다시 언급하며 사람들이 흔히 습관을 '깬다'는 표현을 사용한다고 언급하는 **(C)**가 먼저 연결된다. 이어서 **But**으로 시작하는 **(A)**는 이런 식의 언어, 즉 '습관을 깬다'고 말하는 것이 사람들에게 잘못된 기대를 품게 한다는 내용을 전개한다. 마지막으로 **(B)**는 **(A)**에서 언급된 **The word "break"**를 **This word**라는 지시어로 가리키며 왜 이 표현에 담긴 의미가 현실성이 없는지 설명한다. 따라서 주어진 글의 순서로 가장 적절한 것은 ④ '**(C) − (A) − (B)**'이다.

- **continuum** ⓝ 연속체
- **spawn** ⓥ 낳다
- **frame** ⓥ (특정한 방식으로) 표현하다
- **get rid of** ~을 제거하다
- **addiction** ⓝ 중독
- **villain** ⓝ 악당
- **break a habit** (흔히 나쁜) 습관을 고치다
- **input** ⓥ 투입하다
- **nefarious** ⓐ 사악한
- **aggressively** ⓐⓓ 맹렬하게, 격렬하게

구문 풀이

16행 It's as if an unwanted behavior is a nefarious villain to be aggressively defeated.
(It's as if: 마치 ~인 것 같다(비유) / to be: 형용사적 용법)

02 식품 생산의 책임에 관한 개념의 차이

정답률 64% | 정답 ②

주어진 글 다음에 이어질 글의 순서로 가장 적절한 것을 고르시오.

① (A) − (C) − (B)
② (B) − (A) − (C) ✔
③ (B) − (C) − (A)
④ (C) − (A) − (B)
⑤ (C) − (B) − (A)

Regarding food production, / under the British government, / there was a different conception of responsibility / from that of French government.
식품 생산과 관련하여 / 영국 정부하에서는 / 다른 책임 개념이 있었다. / 프랑스 정부의 그것과는

In France, / the responsibility for producing good food / lay with the producers.
프랑스에서 / 좋은 식품을 생산하는 것에 대한 책임은 / 생산자들에게 있었다.

(B) The state would police their activities / and, if they should fail, / would punish them / for neglecting the interests of its citizens.
정부가 그들의 활동들을 감시하곤 했고, / 만약 그들이 실패했다면, / 그들을 처벌했을 것이다. / 시민들의 이익을 등한시한 이유로

By contrast, / the British government / — except in extreme cases — / placed most of the responsibility with the individual consumers.
대조적으로 / 영국 정부는 / 극단적인 경우들을 제외하고 / 그 책임의 대부분을 개인 소비자들에게 두었다.

(A) It would be unfair / to interfere with the shopkeeper's right / to make money.
부당했을 것이다. / 가게 주인의 권리를 침해하는 것은 / 돈을 벌기 위한

In the 1840s, / a patent was granted for a machine / designed for making fake coffee beans out of chicory, / using the same technology / that went into manufacturing bullets.
1840년대에 / 기계에 특허권이 승인되었다. / 치커리로부터 가짜 커피콩을 만들어 내기 위해 고안된 / 똑같은 기술을 이용해서 / 총알을 제조하는 데 들어갔던

(C) This machine was clearly designed / for the purposes of swindling, / and yet the government allowed it.
이 기계는 분명히 고안되었지만 / 사기의 목적으로 / 그런데도 정부는 그것을 허가했다.

A machine for forging money / would never have been licensed, / so why this?
돈을 위조하기 위한 기계였다면 / 결코 허가를 받을 수 없었을 텐데 / 그렇다면 이것은 왜 허가됐을까?

As one consumer complained, / the British system of government / was weighted against the consumer / in favour of the swindler.
한 소비자가 불평했던 것처럼 / 영국의 정부 체제는 / 소비자에게는 불리하도록 치우쳐 있었다. / 사기꾼의 편을 들고

식품 생산과 관련하여 영국 정부하에서는 프랑스 정부의 책임의 개념과는 다른 개념이 있었다. 프랑스에서 좋은 식품을 생산하는 것에 대한 책임은 생산자들에게 있었다.

(B) 정부가 그들의 활동들을 감시하곤 했고, 만약 그들이 실패했다면, 시민들의 이익을 등한시한 이유로 그들을 처벌했을 것이다. 대조적으로 영국 정부는 극단적인 경우들을 제외하고 그 책임의 대부분을 개인 소비자들에게 두었다.

(A) 돈을 벌기 위한 가게 주인의 권리를 침해하는 것은 부당했을 것이다. 1840년대에, 총알을 제조하는 데 들어갔던 똑같은 기술을 이용해서 치커리로부터 가짜 커피콩을 만들어 내기 위해 고안된 기계에 특허권이 승인되었다.

(C) 이 기계는 분명히 사기의 목적으로 고안되었지만 정부는 그것을 허가했다. 돈을 위조하기 위한 기계였다면 결코 허가를 받을 수 없었을 텐데, 그렇다면 이것은 왜 허가됐을까? 한 소비자가 불평했던 것처럼 영국의 정부 체제는 사기꾼의 편을 들고 소비자에게는 불리하도록 치우쳐 있었다.

Why? 왜 정답일까?

프랑스에서 좋은 식품 생산에 대한 책임은 생산자에 있었다는 내용의 주어진 글 뒤로, **(B)**에서는 정부가 이들을 감독했다는 설명을 덧붙인 뒤 영국 정부를 대조적 사례로 언급한다. 이어서 **(A)**는 총알 제조 기술을 이용해 치커리로 가짜 커피콩을 만드는 기계를 영국 정부가 승인했다는 예를 들고, **(C)**는 이 허가 행위를 통해 영국 정부가 생산자보다도

[문제편 p.077]

소비자에 책임론을 돌리는 입장이었음을 알 수 있다고 한다. 따라서 글의 순서로 가장 적절한 것은 ② '(B) – (A) – (C)'이다.

- conception ⓝ 개념
- shopkeeper ⓝ 가게주인
- patent ⓝ 특허
- manufacture ⓥ 생산하다, 제조하다
- police ⓥ 감시하다
- neglect ⓥ 등한시하다
- except prep 제외하고는
- swindle ⓥ 사기 치다
- license ⓥ 허가하다
- weigh against ~에 불리하다
- unfair ⓐ 부당한
- right ⓝ 권리
- grant ⓥ (공식적으로) 주다
- bullet ⓝ 총알
- punish ⓥ 처벌하다
- by contrast 그와 대조적으로, 그에 반해서
- clearly ad 분명히
- forge ⓥ 위조하다
- complain ⓥ 불평하다

구문 풀이

19행 A machine for forging money would never have been licensed, so why this?
「would have p.p. : ~했을 것이다(과거에 대한 추측)」

03 기계식 시계의 발명과 그 영향

정답률 52% | 정답 ②

주어진 글 다음에 이어질 글의 순서로 가장 적절한 것을 고르시오.

① (A) – (C) – (B) ✔② (B) – (A) – (C)
③ (B) – (C) – (A) ④ (C) – (A) – (B)
⑤ (C) – (B) – (A)

The invention of the mechanical clock / was influenced by monks / who lived in monasteries / that were the examples of order and routine.
기계식 시계의 발명은 / 수도사들에 의해 영향을 받았다. / 수도원에 살았던 / 질서와 규칙적인 일상의 예시인
(B) They had to keep accurate time / so that monastery bells could be rung at regular intervals / to announce the seven hours of the day / reserved for prayer.
그들은 정확한 시간을 지켜야 했다. / 수도원의 종이 규칙적인 간격으로 울릴 수 있도록 / 하루의 일곱 시간을 알리기 위해 / 기도를 위해 지정된
Early clocks were nothing more than a weight / tied to a rope wrapped around a revolving drum.
초기의 시계들은 무게추에 불과했다. / 회전하는 드럼통 주위에 감긴 줄에 묶인
(A) Time was determined / by watching the length of the weighted rope.
시간은 정해졌다. / 무게를 단 줄의 길이를 관찰하여
The discovery of the pendulum in the seventeenth century / led to the widespread use of clocks and enormous public clocks.
17세기의 흔들리는 추의 발견은 / 시계와 큰 대중 시계의 광범위한 사용으로 이어졌다.
Eventually, / keeping time turned into serving time.
마침내, / 시간을 지키는 것은 시간에 복종하는 것이 되었다.
(C) People started to follow the mechanical time of clocks / rather than their natural body time.
사람들은 기계식 시계의 시간을 따르기 시작했다. / 그들의 자연적 생체 시간보다는
They ate at meal time, / rather than when they were hungry, / and went to bed when it was time, / rather than when they were sleepy.
그들은 식사 시간에 먹었고, / 그들이 배고플 때보다는 / 시간이 되었을 때 자러 갔다. / 그들이 졸릴 때보다는
Even periodicals and fashions became "yearly."
심지어 정기 간행물들과 패션들도 '연간으로' 되었다.
The world had become orderly.
세상은 질서 정연해졌다.

기계식 시계의 발명은 질서와 규칙적인 일상의 예시인 수도원에 살았던 수도사들에 의해 영향을 받았다.

(B) 그들은 기도를 위해 지정된 하루의 일곱 시간을 알리기 위해 수도원의 종이 규칙적인 간격으로 울릴 수 있도록 정확한 시간을 지켜야 했다. 초기의 시계들은 회전하는 드럼통 주위에 감긴 줄에 묶인 무게추에 불과했다.

(A) 시간은 무게를 단 줄의 길이를 관찰하여 정해졌다. 17세기의 흔들리는 추의 발견은 시계와 큰 대중 시계의 광범위한 사용으로 이어졌다. 마침내, 시간을 지키는 것은 시간에 복종하는 것이 되었다.

(C) 사람들은 그들의 자연적 생체 시간보다는 기계식 시계의 시간을 따르기 시작했다. 그들은, 그들이 배고플 때보다는 식사 시간에 먹었고, 졸릴 때보다는 시간이 되었을 때 자러 갔다. 심지어 정기 간행물들과 패션들도 '연간으로' 되었다. 세상은 질서 정연해졌다.

Why? 왜 정답일까?

기계식 시계의 발명이 수도원의 수도사들로 인해 영향을 받았다는 내용의 주어진 글 뒤에는 수도사들을 They로 받아 이들이 기도하기 위해 시간을 잘 지켜 종을 울려야 했다는 설명을 제시하는 (B)가 연결된다. 이어서 (A)는 (B) 후반부에 이어 초기 시계의 특징을 설명하고, (C)는 시계추의 발견 이후 시계가 보다 자리잡고 그 사용이 널리 이루어지면서 사람들이 생체 시간보다는 기계식 시간을 따르게 되었다는 결과를 언급한다. 따라서 글의 순서로 가장 적절한 것은 ② '(B) – (A) – (C)'이다.

- invention ⓝ 발명
- monk ⓝ 수도사, 승려
- enormous ⓐ 거대한, 엄청난
- interval ⓝ 간격
- orderly ⓐ 질서 정연한
- mechanical ⓐ 기계의
- widespread ⓐ 널리 퍼진
- accurate ⓐ 정확한
- periodical ⓝ 정기 간행물

구문 풀이

9행 They had to keep accurate time so that monastery bells could be rung at regular intervals to announce the seven hours of the day reserved for prayer.
목적(~하도록) / 조동사 수동태 / 목적(~하기 위해) / 명사구 / 과거분사구

04 탐구 주도형 교실에서 내용 이해를 평가할 필요성

정답률 48% | 정답 ⑤

주어진 글 다음에 이어질 글의 순서로 가장 적절한 것을 고르시오.

① (A) – (C) – (B) ② (B) – (A) – (C)
③ (B) – (C) – (A) ④ (C) – (A) – (B)
✔⑤ (C) – (B) – (A)

Testing strategies / relating to direct assessment of content knowledge / still have their value in an inquiry-driven classroom.
테스트 전략은 / 내용 지식에 대한 직접 평가와 관련된 / 탐구 주도형 교실에서 여전히 그 가치를 지닌다.
(C) Let's pretend for a moment / that we wanted to ignore content / and only assess a student's skill with investigations.
잠시 가정해 보자. / 우리가 내용을 무시하고 / 연구를 통해 학생의 기술만을 평가하기를 원한다고
The problem is / that the skills and the content are interconnected.
문제는 / 기술과 내용이 서로 연결되어 있다는 것이다.
When a student fails at pattern analysis, / it could be because they do not understand / how to do the pattern analysis properly.
학생이 패턴 분석에 실패하면 / 그것은 학생이 이해하지 못하기 때문일 수 있다. / 패턴 분석을 적절히 수행하는 방법을
(B) However, it also could be / that they did not understand the content / that they were trying to build patterns with.
그러나 ~일 수도 있다. / 그들은 내용을 이해하지 못한 것 / 그들이 패턴을 만드는 데 사용하는
Sometimes students will understand the processes of inquiry well, / and be capable of skillfully applying social studies disciplinary strategies, / yet fail to do so / because they misinterpret the content.
때때로 학생들은 탐구 과정을 잘 이해하고 / 사회 교과의 전략을 능숙하게 적용할 수 있지만 / 그렇게 하지 못할 것이다. / 내용을 잘못 해석하기 때문에
(A) For these reasons, / we need a measure of a student's content understanding.
이러한 이유로 / 우리는 학생의 내용 이해에 대한 측정이 필요하다.
To do this right, / we need to make sure / our assessment is getting us accurate measures / of whether our students understand the content / they use in an inquiry.
이것을 제대로 하기 위해서 / 우리는 확실하게 할 필요가 있다. / 우리의 평가가 정확한 측정을 하게 하는지 / 학생들이 내용을 이해했는지 여부에 대한 / 그들이 탐구에서 사용하는

내용 지식에 대한 직접 평가와 관련된 테스트 전략은 탐구 주도형 교실에서 여전히 그 가치를 지닌다.

(C) 우리가 내용을 무시하고 연구를 통해 학생의 기술만을 평가하기를 원한다고 잠시 가정해 보자. 문제는 기술과 내용이 서로 연결되어 있다는 것이다. 학생이 패턴 분석에 실패하면 그것은 학생이 패턴 분석을 적절히 수행하는 방법을 이해하지 못하기 때문일 수 있다.

(B) 그러나 그들은 패턴을 만드는 데 사용하는 내용을 이해하지 못한 것일 수도 있다. 때때로 학생들은 탐구 과정을 잘 이해하고 사회 교과의 전략을 능숙하게 적용할 수 있지만 내용을 잘못 해석하기 때문에 그렇게 하지 못할 것이다.

(A) 이러한 이유로 우리는 학생의 내용 이해에 대한 측정이 필요하다. 이것을 제대로 하기 위해서 우리의 평가가 학생들이 탐구에서 사용하는 내용을 이해했는지 여부에 대한 정확한 측정을 하게 하는지 확실하게 할 필요가 있다.

Why? 왜 정답일까?

탐구 주도형 교실에서도 여전히 내용 지식에 대한 직접 평가 전략이 가치를 지닌다는 내용의 주어진 글 뒤에는, 내용을 무시하고 기술만 평가할 때의 한계점을 지적하며 패턴 분석에 실패하는 학생의 예를 드는 (C), 예를 이어서 설명하는 (B), 앞의 근거로 인해 내용 이해에 대한 정확한 측정이 필요하다는 결론을 정리하는 (A)가 차례로 이어져야 자연스럽다. 따라서 글의 순서로 가장 적절한 것은 ⑤ '(C) – (B) – (A)'이다.

- strategy ⓝ 전략
- inquiry ⓝ 탐구
- skillfully ad 능숙하게
- misinterpret ⓥ 잘못 해석하다
- for a moment 잠시 동안, 당장 그때만
- interconnected ⓐ 서로 연결된
- properly ad 적절히
- assessment ⓝ 평가
- accurate ⓐ 정확한
- disciplinary ⓐ 교과의
- pretend ⓥ ~인 척하다, ~라고 가장하다
- investigation ⓝ 연구
- analysis ⓝ 분석

구문 풀이

5행 To do this right, we need to make sure (that) our assessment is getting us accurate measures of whether our students understand the content [they use in an inquiry].

(To do: ~하기 위해 / make sure: ~을 확실히 하다 / (that): 접속사(생략) / is getting: 4형식 동사 / us: 간접 목적어 / accurate measures: 직접 목적어 / of: 전치사 / whether ~: 명사절 접속사(~인지 아닌지) / the content: 선행사)

05 버스 운전사보다 해마가 더 큰 택시 운전사

정답률 76% | 정답 ④

주어진 글 다음에 이어질 글의 순서로 가장 적절한 것을 고르시오.

① (A) – (C) – (B)
② (B) – (A) – (C)
③ (B) – (C) – (A)
④ (C) – (A) – (B)
⑤ (C) – (B) – (A)

Both taxi and bus drivers / use a part of their brain / called the hippocampus / to navigate routes / that can sometimes be very complicated.
택시 운전사와 버스 운전사 둘 다 / 뇌의 한 부분을 사용한다. / 해마라 불리는 / 경로를 찾기 위해 / 때때로 매우 복잡할 수 있는

Who would you guess has the larger hippocampus: / the taxi driver or bus driver?
누가 더 큰 해마를 가지고 있을 것이라 추측하는가? / 택시 운전사인가, 버스 운전사인가?

(C) The answer is the taxi driver.
정답은 택시 운전사이다.

This is because / taxi drivers need to take new routes quite often.
이는 ~ 때문이다. / 택시 운전사들이 상당히 자주 새로운 경로로 가야 하기

To do this, / they use their hippocampus intensively / to memorize all kinds of routes / and figure out the quickest way to reach their destinations.
이렇게 하기 위해 / 그들은 해마를 집중적으로 사용한다. / 모든 종류의 경로를 기억하고 / 목적지에 도달할 가장 빠른 경로를 찾아내기 위해

(A) In contrast, / most bus drivers follow the same route every day / and therefore do not stimulate their hippocampus as much.
반면에, / 대부분의 버스 운전사는 매일 똑같은 경로를 따라가고 / 그렇기에 해마 부분을 그만큼 많이 자극하지는 않는다.

Over time, / the taxi driver's role triggers a growth / of neurons and synapses in the hippocampus, / resulting in its increased size.
시간이 흐르면서, / 택시 운전사의 역할은 성장을 유발하여 / 해마에 있는 뉴런과 시냅스의 / 해마의 크기가 커지도록 한다.

(B) Brain changes like this are the basis / for seeing improvement in mental performance.
이와 같은 뇌의 변화는 토대가 된다. / 지적 수행 능력의 향상을 이해하기 위한

So if you put away your satellite navigation system / and regularly use your memory instead, / you may end up with a larger hippocampus / and perhaps a better memory, too.
그래서 만일 당신이 위성 네비게이션 시스템을 치우고 / 대신에 꾸준히 기억력을 사용한다면 / 당신은 결국 해마가 더 커지고 / 아마 기억력 또한 더 좋아질 것이다.

택시 운전사와 버스 운전사 둘 다 때때로 매우 복잡할 수 있는 경로를 찾기 위해 해마라 불리는 뇌의 한 부분을 사용한다. 누가 더 큰 해마를 가지고 있을 것이라 추측하는가? 택시 운전사인가, 버스 운전사인가?

(C) 정답은 택시 운전사이다. 이는 택시 운전사들이 상당히 자주 새로운 경로로 가야 하기 때문이다. 이렇게 하기 위해 그들은 모든 종류의 경로를 기억하고 목적지에 도달할 가장 빠른 경로를 찾아내기 위해 해마를 집중적으로 사용한다.

(A) 반면에, 대부분의 버스 운전사는 매일 똑같은 경로를 따라가기 때문에 해마 부분을 그만큼 많이 자극하지는 않는다. 시간이 흐르면서, 택시 운전사의 역할은 해마에 있는 뉴런과 시냅스의 성장을 유발하여 해마의 크기가 커지도록 한다.

(B) 이와 같은 뇌의 변화는 지적 수행 능력의 향상을 이해하는 데 토대가 된다. 그래서 만일 당신이 위성 네비게이션 시스템을 치우고 대신에 꾸준히 기억력을 사용한다면 결국 해마가 더 커지고 아마 기억력 또한 더 좋아질 것이다.

Why? 왜 정답일까?

택시 운전사와 버스 운전사 중 누구의 해마가 더 클까를 묻는 주어진 글 뒤에는, 택시 운전사의 해마가 더 크다는 답과 이유를 설명하는 (C), 버스 운전사를 비교하여 설명하는 (A), 우리도 네비게이션 시스템 대신 우리 자신의 기억력을 사용하면 해마가 더 커지게 된다는 결론을 제시하는 (B)가 차례로 나오는 것이 자연스럽다. 따라서 글의 순서로 가장 적절한 것은 ④ '(C) – (A) – (B)'이다.

- complicated ⓐ 복잡한
- trigger ⓥ 유발하다
- result in (그 결과) ~하게 되다
- improvement ⓝ 향상, 발전, 증진
- regularly ad 꾸준히, 규칙적으로
- intensively ad 집중적으로
- destination ⓝ 목적지
- stimulate ⓥ 자극하다
- growth ⓝ 성장
- basis ⓝ 토대, 기초
- put away ~을 치우다, ~을 집어넣다
- end up with 결국 ~하게 되다
- memorize ⓥ 기억하다, 외우다, 암기하다

구문 풀이

1행 Both taxi and bus drivers use a part of their brain (which is 생략) [called the hippocampus] / to navigate routes [that can sometimes be very complicated].

(Both A and B : A와 B 둘 다 / use: 동사(복수) / their brain: 선행사 / called: 과거분사 / to navigate: 부사적 용법(~하기 위해) / that: 주격 관계대명사)

06 파란색이 청바지에 자주 사용된 이유

정답률 69% | 정답 ②

주어진 글 다음에 이어질 글의 순서로 가장 적절한 것을 고르시오.

① (A) – (C) – (B)
② (B) – (A) – (C)
③ (B) – (C) – (A)
④ (C) – (A) – (B)
⑤ (C) – (B) – (A)

Calling your pants "blue jeans" almost seems redundant / because practically all denim is blue.
바지를 '파란 청바지'라 부르는 것은 거의 표현이 중복된 것처럼 보인다. / 거의 모든 데님이 파란색이기 때문에

While jeans are probably the most versatile pants in your wardrobe, / blue actually isn't a particularly neutral color.
청바지가 아마도 당신의 옷장 속에 있는 가장 활용도가 높은 바지이지만, / 사실 파란색이 특별히 무난한 색은 아니다.

(B) Ever wonder why it's the most commonly used hue?
왜 파란색이 (청바지에) 가장 흔하게 사용되는 색상인지 궁금했던 적이 있는가?

Blue was the chosen color for denim / because of the chemical properties of blue dye.
파란색은 데님의 색깔로 선택되었다. / 청색 염료의 화학적 특성 때문에

Most dyes will permeate fabric in hot temperatures, / making the color stick.
대부분의 염료는 높은 온도에서 스며들게 된다. / 색이 천에 들러붙게 하며

(A) The natural indigo dye used in the first jeans, / on the other hand, / would stick only to the outside of the threads.
최초의 청바지에 사용되었던 천연 남색 염료는 / 반면에 / 옷감의 바깥쪽에만 들러붙었다.

When the indigo-dyed denim is washed, / tiny amounts of that dye get washed away, / and the thread comes with them.
남색으로 염색된 데님을 빨 때, / 그 염료 중 소량은 씻겨나가게 되고 / 실이 염료와 함께 나오게 된다.

(C) The more denim was washed, / the softer it would get, / eventually achieving that worn-in, made-just-for-me feeling / you probably get with your favorite jeans.
데님을 더 많이 빨수록 / 더 부드러워지게 되고, / 마침내 닳아 해어지고, 나만을 위해 만들어졌다는 느낌이 생기게 된다. / 당신이 가장 좋아하는 청바지로부터 아마도 받을

That softness made jeans / the trousers of choice for laborers.
이 부드러움은 청바지를 만들었다. / 노동자들이 가장 많이 선택하는 바지로

거의 모든 데님이 파란색이기 때문에 바지를 '파란 청바지'라 부르는 것은 거의 표현이 중복된 것처럼 보인다. 청바지가 아마도 당신의 옷장 속에 있는 가장 활용도가 높은 바지이지만, 사실 파란색이 특별히 무난한 색은 아니다.

(B) 왜 파란색이 (청바지에) 가장 흔하게 사용되는 색상인지 궁금했던 적이 있는가? 파란색은 청색 염료의 화학적 특성 때문에 데님의 색깔로 선택되었다. 대부분의 염료는 높은 온도에서 색이 천에 들러붙게 하며 스며들게 된다.

[문제편 p.079]

(A) 반면에 최초의 청바지에 사용되었던 천연 남색 염료는 옷감의 바깥쪽에만 들러붙었다. 남색으로 염색된 데님을 빨 때, 그 염료 중 소량은 씻겨나가게 되고 실이 염료와 함께 나오게 된다.

(C) 데님을 더 많이 빨수록 더 부드러워지게 되고, 마침내 당신이 가장 좋아하는 청바지로부터 아마도 받을, 닳아 해어지고, 나만을 위해 만들어졌다는 느낌이 생기게 된다. 이 부드러움 때문에 청바지는 노동자들이 가장 많이 선택하는 바지가 되었다.

Why? 왜 정답일까?

파란색이 청바지에 자주 사용되기는 하지만 사실 파란색이 특별히 무난한 색은 아님을 언급하는 주어진 글 뒤에는, 그럼에도 불구하고 왜 파란색이 유독 자주 사용되는지 본격적으로 물음을 던지는 **(B)**, 고온에서 색이 천에 들러붙게 하며 스며드는 다른 염료들과는 달리 파란색은 바깥쪽에만 들러붙는 특성이 있음을 설명하는 **(A)**, 설명을 마무리하는 **(C)**가 차례로 이어지는 것이 자연스럽다. 따라서 글의 순서로 가장 적절한 곳은 ② **'(B) – (A) – (C)'**이다.

- **redundant** ⓐ (표현이) 중복되는
- **wardrobe** ⓝ 옷장
- **dye** ⓝ 염료
- **property** ⓝ 특성
- **laborer** ⓝ 노동자, 인부
- **versatile** ⓐ 활용도가 높은, 다용도의
- **neutral** ⓐ 무난한
- **thread** ⓝ 실, 가닥
- **worn-in** (옷을 자주 입어) 닳은, 해어진

구문 풀이

16행 The more denim was washed, the softer it would get, / 「the+비교급 ~, the+비교급 ⋯ : ~할수록 더 ⋯하다」 eventually achieving(분사구문) that worn-in, made-just-for-me feeling [you probably get with your favorite jeans].

07 기계와 알고리즘을 이용한 '창의적' 작업

정답률 43% | 정답 ③

주어진 글 다음에 이어질 글의 순서로 가장 적절한 것을 고르시오. [3점]

① (A) – (C) – (B) ② (B) – (A) – (C)
✔③ (B) – (C) – (A) ④ (C) – (A) – (B)
⑤ (C) – (B) – (A)

Architects might say / a machine can never design an innovative or impressive building / because a computer cannot be "creative."
건축가들은 말할지도 모른다. / 기계는 결코 혁신적이거나 인상적인 건물을 디자인하지 못한다고 / 컴퓨터는 '창의적일' 수 없기 때문에

Yet consider the Elbphilharmonie, / a new concert hall in Hamburg, / which contains a remarkably beautiful auditorium / composed of ten thousand interlocking acoustic panels.
그러나 Elbphilharmonie를 생각해보라. / Hamburg에 있는 새로운 콘서트 홀인 / 이곳에는 놀랍도록 아름다운 강당이 있다. / 1만 개의 서로 맞물리는 음향 패널로 구성된

(B) It is the sort of space / that makes one instinctively think / that only a human being / — and a human with a remarkably refined creative sensibility, at that — / could design something so aesthetically impressive.
그것은 부류의 공간이다. / 우리를 본능적으로 생각하게 만드는 / 인간만이, / 그것도 놀랍도록 세련된 창의적 감수성을 가진 인간만이 / 그토록 미적으로 인상적인 것을 디자인할 수 있을 거라고

Yet the auditorium was, / in fact, / designed algorithmically, / using a technique known as "parametric design."
하지만 그 강당은 / 사실 / 알고리즘 방식으로 설계되었다. / '파라메트릭 디자인'이라고 알려진 기술을 사용해

(C) The architects gave the system a set of criteria, / and it generated a set of possible designs / for the architects to choose from.
건축가들은 그 시스템에 일련의 기준을 부여했고, / 그것은 일련의 가능한 디자인을 만들어냈다. / 건축가들이 선택할 수 있는

Similar software has been used / to design lightweight bicycle frames and sturdier chairs, / among much else.
비슷한 소프트웨어가 이용돼 왔다. / 경량 자전거 프레임과 더 튼튼한 의자를 디자인할 목적으로 / 다른 많은 것들보다도

(A) Are these systems behaving "creatively"?
이러한 시스템들은 '창의적으로' 작동하고 있는가?

No, / they are using lots of processing power / to blindly generate varied possible designs, / working in a very different way from a human being.
아니다. / 그것들은 많은 처리 능력을 사용해 / 여러 가능한 디자인을 닥치는 대로 만들면서, / 인간과는 매우 다른 방식으로 일하고 있다.

건축가들은 컴퓨터는 '창의적일' 수 없기 때문에 기계는 결코 혁신적이거나 인상적인 건물을 디자인하지 못한다고 말할지도 모른다. 그러나 Hamburg에 있는 새로운 콘서트 홀인 Elbphilharmonie를 생각해보라. 이곳에는 1만 개의 서로 맞물리는 음향 패널로 구성된 놀랍도록 아름다운 강당이 있다.

(B) 그것은 인간만이, 그것도 놀랍도록 세련된 창의적 감수성을 가진 인간만이 그토록 미적으로 인상적인 것을 디자인할 수 있을 거라고 본능적으로 생각하게 만드는 부류의 공간이다. 하지만 사실 그 강당은 '파라메트릭 디자인'이라고 알려진 기술을 사용해 알고리즘 방식으로 설계되었다.

(C) 건축가들은 그 시스템에 일련의 기준을 부여했고, 그것은 건축가들이 선택할 수 있는 일련의 가능한 디자인을 만들어냈다. 다른 많은 것들보다도 경량 자전거 프레임과 더 튼튼한 의자를 디자인할 목적으로 비슷한 소프트웨어가 이용돼 왔다.

(A) 이러한 시스템들은 '창의적으로' 작동하고 있는가? 아니다, 그것들은 많은 처리 능력을 사용해 여러 가능한 디자인을 닥치는 대로 만들면서, 인간과는 매우 다른 방식으로 일하고 있다.

Why? 왜 정답일까?

주어진 글에서 언급된 콘서트 홀(**Elbphilharmonie**)을 **(B)**에서는 **It**으로 가리키며 이것이 알고리즘에 의해 디자인됐다고 설명한다. 이어서 **(C)**는 건축가들이 이 콘서트홀을 만들었던 과정을 설명한 뒤, 경량 자전거 프레임 등 다른 분야에도 이런 식의 소프트웨어가 이용되고 있다고 한다. **(A)**는 '이런 시스템들'이 진정한 의미로 '창의적'이지는 않지만, 인간과는 매우 다른 방식으로 작업을 이어간다는 내용이다. 따라서 글의 순서로 가장 적절한 것은 ③ **'(B) – (C) – (A)'**이다.

- **interlock** ⓥ 서로 맞물리다
- **instinctively** ad 본능적으로
- **sensibility** ⓝ 감수성
- **architect** ⓝ 건축가
- **sturdy** ⓐ 튼튼한, 견고한
- **generate** ⓥ 만들어내다, 생성하다
- **refine** ⓥ 개선하다
- **aesthetically** ad 미적으로
- **criterion** (*pl.* **criteria**) ⓝ 기준

구문 풀이

3행 Yet consider the Elbphilharmonie, a new concert hall in Hamburg(동격(선행사)), which contains(계속적 용법) a remarkably beautiful auditorium (composed(과거분사구) of ten thousand interlocking acoustic panels).

08 올바른 식이요법

정답률 54% | 정답 ⑤

주어진 글 다음에 이어질 글의 순서로 가장 적절한 것을 고르시오. [3점]

① (A) – (C) – (B) ② (B) – (A) – (C)
③ (B) – (C) – (A) ④ (C) – (A) – (B)
✔⑤ (C) – (B) – (A)

Some fad diets / might have you running a caloric deficit, / and while this might encourage weight loss, / it has no effect on improving body composition, / and it could actually result in a loss of muscle mass.
일시적으로 유행하는 (체중 감량 목적의) 식이요법은 / 여러분을 열량 부족 상태로 만들지도 모르는데, / 이것이 체중 감량을 촉진할 수는 있지만 / 체성분을 향상시키는 데는 아무런 효과가 없으며 / 실제로 근육량의 손실을 초래할 수도 있다.

(C) Calorie restriction / can also cause your metabolism to slow down, / and significantly reduce energy levels.
열량 제한은 / 신진대사가 느려지게 할 수도 있고, / 에너지 수준을 상당히 감소시킬 수 있다.

Controlling caloric intake / to deliver the proper amount of calories / so that the body has the energy / it needs to function and heal / is the only proper approach.
열량 섭취를 조절하는 것이 / 적당한 양의 열량을 전달하기 위해 / 신체가 에너지를 가질 수 있도록 / 기능하고 치유되는 데 필요한 / 유일한 올바른 접근법이다.

(B) Your body also needs / the right balance of key macronutrients / to heal and grow stronger.
여러분의 신체는 필요하다. / 주요 다량 영양소의 알맞은 균형도 / 치유되고 더 강해지기 위해서

These macronutrients, / which include protein, carbohydrates, and healthy fats, / can help your body maximize its ability / to repair, rebuild, and grow stronger.
이러한 다량 영양소는 / 단백질, 탄수화물 그리고 건강에 좋은 지방을 포함하는 / 여러분의 신체가 능력을 최대화하는 데 도움이 될 수 있다. / 치료되고 회복되며 더 강해질 수 있는

(A) Timing is also important.
시기도 중요하다.

By eating the right combinations / of these key macronutrients / at strategic intervals throughout the day, / we can help / our bodies heal and grow even faster.
알맞은 조합으로 섭취함으로써 / 이러한 주요 다량 영양소를 / 하루 중에 전략적인 간격으로 / 우리는 도울 수 있다. / 신체가 치유되고 훨씬 더 빠르게 성장하도록

일시적으로 유행하는 (체중 감량 목적의) 식이요법은 여러분을 열량 부족 상태로 만들지도 모르는데, 이것이 체중 감량을 촉진할 수는 있지만 체성분을 향상시키는 데는 아무런 효과가 없으며 실제로 근육량의 손실을 초래할 수도 있다.

(C) 열량 제한은 신진대사가 느려지게 할 수도 있고 에너지 수준을 상당히 감소시킬 수 있다. 신체가 기능하고 치유되는 데 필요한 에너지를 가질 수 있도록 적당한 양의 열량을 전달하기 위해 열량 섭취를 조절하는 것이 유일한 올바른 접근법이다.

(B) 여러분의 신체는 치유되고 더 튼튼해지기 위해서 주요 다량 영양소의 알맞은 균형도 필요하다. 단백질, 탄수화물 그리고 건강에 좋은 지방을 포함하는 이러한 다량 영양소는 여러분의 신체가 치료되고 회복되며 더 튼튼해질 수 있는 능력을 최대화하는 데 도움이 될 수 있다.

(A) 시기도 중요하다. 하루 중에 전략적인 간격으로 이러한 주요 다량 영양소를 알맞은 조합으로 섭취함으로써 우리는 신체가 치유되고 훨씬 더 빠르게 성장하도록 도울 수 있다.

Why? 왜 정답일까?

유행하는 식이요법으로 체중 감량을 시도하는 것은 실제로 감량으로 이어질 수 있기는 하지만 건강 면에서 이득이 없거나 도리어 손실을 야기할 수 있다는 내용의 주어진 글 뒤에는, 신체가 기능하는 데 적당한 열량이 유지될 수 있도록 열량 섭취를 적절히 조절하는 것이 유일한 정도라는 내용의 **(C)**, 영양소의 균형이 또한 중요하다는 내용의 **(B)**, 이에 더불어 섭취 시기도 함께 생각해야 한다는 내용의 **(A)**가 차례로 이어지는 것이 적절하다. 따라서 글의 순서로 가장 적절한 것은 ⑤ '**(C) – (B) – (A)**'이다.

- **fad diet** 과학적 근거 없이 체중 감량을 약속하는, 매우 제한적이고 특이한 유행성 식이요법
- **deficit** ⓝ 결핍, 부족
- **improve** ⓥ 향상시키다, 개선하다
- **body composition** 체성분, 신체 조성
- **interval** ⓝ 간격
- **carbohydrate** ⓝ 탄수화물
- **rebuild** ⓥ 증강하다, 보강하다, 재건하다
- **restriction** ⓝ 제한, 제약
- **metabolism** ⓝ 신진대사
- **significantly** ad 상당히, 크게, 유의미하게
- **intake** ⓝ 섭취(량)

구문 풀이

1행 **Some fad diets might have you running a caloric deficit, / and while this might encourage weight loss, it has no effect on improving body composition, and it could actually result in a loss of muscle mass.**
(주어1 / 동사1(사역동사) 목적어 목적격 보어(현재분사) / ~하는 반면 / 주어2 동사2(~에 영향이 없다) / 주어3 동사3(~을 야기하다))

09 습관의 형성 과정

정답률 69% | 정답 ②

주어진 글 다음에 이어질 글의 순서로 가장 적절한 것을 고르시오. [3점]

① (A) – (C) – (B)
② (B) – (A) – (C)
③ (B) – (C) – (A)
④ (C) – (A) – (B)
⑤ (C) – (B) – (A)

Most habits are probably good / when they are first formed.
대부분의 습관들은 아마 좋은 습관일 것이다. / 그것들이 처음 형성될 때는

That is, for many of the habits / that you do not create intentionally, / there must have been some value / to performing that particular behavior.
즉, 많은 습관에 대해서, / 당신이 의도적으로 만들지 않은 / 분명 어떤 가치가 있었을 것이다. / 그 특정한 행동을 하게 된 데

(B) That value is / what causes you to repeat the behavior / often enough to create the habit.
그 가치가 / 그 행동을 반복하게 하는 것이다. / 그 습관이 형성될 만큼 충분히 자주

Some habits become bad, / because a behavior / that has rewarding elements to it at one time / also has negative consequences / that may not have been obvious / when the habit began.
몇몇 습관은 나빠지기도 하는데, / 그 이유는 행동이 / 한때 보상적 요소를 가진 / 부정적인 영향을 또한 가지고 있기 때문이다. / 명확하지 않았을지도 모를 / 그 습관이 시작되었을 때는

(A) Overeating is one such habit.
과식이 그런 습관이다.

You may know conceptually / that eating too much is a problem.
당신은 머릿속으로는 / 과식이 문제라는 걸 알고 있을 것이다.

But when you actually overeat, / there are few really negative consequences in the moment.
그러나 당신이 실제로 과식을 할 때, / 바로 그 순간에는 부정적인 영향이 거의 없다.

(C) So you do it again and again.
그래서 당신은 그 행동을 반복한다.

Eventually, though, you'll start to gain weight.
그러나 결국 당신은 살이 찌기 시작할 것이다.

By the time you really notice this, / your habit of eating too much / is deeply rooted.
당신이 이것을 인지할 때쯤에는 / 당신의 과식 습관은 / 깊이 뿌리를 내리게 된다.

대부분의 습관들은 아마 처음 형성될 때는 좋은 습관일 것이다. 즉, 당신이 의도적으로 만들지 않은 많은 습관에 대해서, 그 특정한 행동을 하게 된 데 분명 어떤 가치가 있었을 것이다.

(B) 그 가치가 그 습관이 형성될 만큼 충분히 자주 그 행동을 반복하게 하는 것이다. 몇몇 습관은 나빠지기도 하는데, 그 이유는 한때 보상적 요소를 가진 행동이 그 습관이 시작되었을 때는 명확하지 않았을지도 모를 부정적인 영향을 또한 가지고 있기 때문이다.

(A) 과식이 그런 습관이다. 당신은 머릿속으로는 과식이 문제라는 걸 알고 있을 것이다. 그러나 실제로 과식을 할 때, 바로 그 순간에는 부정적인 영향이 거의 없다.

(C) 그래서 당신은 그 행동을 반복한다. 그러나 결국 당신은 살이 찌기 시작할 것이다. 이것을 인지할 때쯤에는 당신의 과식 습관은 깊이 뿌리를 내리게 된다.

Why? 왜 정답일까?

대개의 습관은 처음 형성될 때는 어떤 '가치'를 주는 좋은 행동이었을 것이라고 말한 주어진 글 뒤에는, 바로 '그 가치(**that value**)'가 특정 행동을 반복하는 요인으로 기능하지만 시간이 흐를수록 잠재되어 있던 부정적 영향이 드러나게 된다는 내용의 **(B)**, 과식을 예로 들어 설명하기 시작하는 **(A)**, 처음에는 부정적인 영향이 없어 과식이 반복되지만 그 악영향이 드러날 때쯤에는 이미 그것이 습관화된 뒤일 것임을 지적하는 **(C)**가 차례로 이어져야 자연스럽다. 따라서 주어진 글 다음에 이어질 글의 순서로 가장 적절한 것은 ② '**(B) – (A) – (C)**'이다.

- **create** ⓥ 만들다, 창조하다
- **intentionally** ad 의도적으로
- **perform** ⓥ 수행하다
- **particular** ⓐ 특정한
- **conceptually** ad 머릿속으로, 개념적으로
- **negative** ⓐ 부정적인
- **consequence** ⓝ 결과
- **rewarding** ⓐ 보상을 주는, 보람 있는
- **eventually** ad 결국
- **gain weight** 살이 찌다
- **by the time** ~할 때쯤, ~할 무렵

구문 풀이

2행 **That is, for many of the habits [that you do not create intentionally], / there must have been some value to performing that particular behavior.**
(접속부사(즉) / ~에 대해 / 목적격 관계대명사(생략 가능) / ~었음에 틀림없다 / 전치사 동명사)

★★★ 1등급 대비 고난도 2점 문제

10 잊힐 권리

정답률 30% | 정답 ②

주어진 글 다음에 이어질 글의 순서로 가장 적절한 것을 고르시오.

① (A) – (C) – (B)
② (B) – (A) – (C)
③ (B) – (C) – (A)
④ (C) – (A) – (B)
⑤ (C) – (B) – (A)

The right to be forgotten / is a right / distinct from but related to a right to privacy.
잊힐 권리는 / 권리이다. / 사생활 권리와 구별되지만 연관성이 있는

The right to privacy is, / among other things, / the right for information / traditionally regarded as protected or personal / not to be revealed.
사생활 권리는 ~이다. / 무엇보다도 / 정보에 대한 권리이다. / 전통적으로 보호되거나 개인적인 것으로 여겨지는 / 공개되지 않아야 할

(B) The right to be forgotten, / in contrast, / can be applied to information / that has been in the public domain.
잊힐 권리는 / 반면에 / 정보에 적용될 수 있다. / 공공의 영역에 있었던

The right to be forgotten / broadly includes the right of an individual / not to be forever defined by information / from a specific point in time.
잊힐 권리는 / 개인의 권리를 폭넓게 포함한다. / 정보에 의해 영원히 규정되지 않을 / 특정 시점의

(A) One motivation for such a right / is to allow individuals / to move on with their lives / and not be defined by a specific event or period in their lives.
그러한 권리의 한 가지 이유는 / 개인이 ~하도록 해 주는 것이다. / 자기 삶을 영위하고 / 삶의 특정한 사건이나 기간에 의해 한정되지 않도록

For example, / it has long been recognized in some countries, / such as the UK and France, / that even past criminal convictions should eventually be "spent" / and not continue to affect a person's life.

예를 들어, / 일부 국가에서는 오랫동안 인식되어 왔다. / 영국과 프랑스와 같은 / 과거의 범죄 유죄 판결조차도 결국 '다 소모되어야'한다고 / 그리고 한 사람의 삶에 계속 영향을 미치지 않아야 한다고

(C) Despite the reason / for supporting the right to be forgotten, / the right to be forgotten / can sometimes come into conflict with other rights.
이유에도 불구하고, / 잊힐 권리를 지지하는 / 잊힐 권리는 / 다른 권리와 때때로 충돌할 수 있다.

For example, / formal exceptions are sometimes made / for security or public health reasons.
예를 들어, / 공식적인 예외가 때때로 생겨난다. / 안보와 공공 보건의 이유로 인해

잊힐 권리는 사생활 권리와 구별되지만 연관성이 있는 권리이다. 사생활 권리는 무엇보다도 전통적으로 보호되거나 공개되지 않아야 할 개인적인 것으로 여겨지는 정보에 대한 권리이다.

(B) 반면에 잊힐 권리는 공공의 영역에 있었던 정보에 적용될 수 있다. 잊힐 권리는 개인이 특정 시점의 정보에 의해 영원히 규정되지 않을 권리를 폭넓게 포함한다.

(A) 그러한 권리의 한 가지 이유는 개인이 자기 삶을 영위하고 삶의 특정한 사건이나 기간에 의해 한정되지 않도록 해 주는 것이다. 예를 들어, 영국과 프랑스와 같은 일부 국가에서는 과거의 범죄 유죄 판결조차도 결국 '다 소모되고' 한 사람의 삶에 계속 영향을 미치지 않아야 한다고 오랫동안 인식되어 왔다.

(C) 잊힐 권리를 지지하는 이유에도 불구하고, 잊힐 권리는 다른 권리와 때때로 충돌할 수 있다. 예를 들어, 공식적인 예외가 안보와 공공 보건의 이유로 인해 때때로 생겨난다.

Why? 왜 정답일까?

잊힐 권리의 개념과 필요성을 설명하는 글이다. 주어진 글에서 '사생활 권리'를 잊힐 권리와 대비되는 개념으로 언급한 후, **in contrast**로 시작하는 **(B)**는 잊힐 권리로 다시 돌아와 예시와 함께 의미를 설명한다. **(A)**에서는 잊힐 권리가 왜 필요한지 이유를 설명하고, **(C)**에서는 그런 이유에도 불구하고 가끔 예외 상황은 생길 수 있음을 덧붙인다. 따라서 글의 순서로 가장 적절한 것은 ② '**(B) – (A) – (C)**'이다.

- **right to be forgotten** 잊힐 권리
- **reveal** ⓥ 드러내다, 폭로하다
- **criminal** ⓐ 형사상의, 범죄의
- **spent** ⓐ 소모된, 영향력이 없어진
- **formal** ⓐ 공식적인
- **public health** 공중 보건
- **right to privacy** 사생활 권리
- **define** ⓥ 규정하다, 한정짓다
- **conviction** ⓝ 유죄 판결
- **domain** ⓝ 영역
- **security** ⓝ 안보

구문 풀이

2행 The right to privacy is, (among other things), the right for information traditionally regarded as protected or personal not to be revealed.
(is: 동사 / ( ): 삽입구 / the right: 주격 보어 / regarded as: ~라고 여겨지는)

★★ 문제 해결 꿀~팁 ★★

▶ 많이 틀린 이유는?
주어진 글과 **(B)**를 연결하고 난 다음이 문제이다. **(B)**의 마지막은 '잊힐 권리'의 범위(**includes ~**)를 언급하며 끝나는데, **(A)**는 이 권리가 필요한 이유를, **(C)**는 이 권리가 다른 권리와 충돌을 일으킨다는 내용을 각각 다룬다. 즉 **(C)**에서 글의 흐름이 전환되고 있으므로 **(B) – (C)**를 바로 연결하는 ③은 답으로 적절치 않다.

▶ 문제 해결 방법은?
(A)의 **motivation**이 바로 '이유'를 말하는 표현이다. **(B)**에서 잊힐 권리의 개념과 범위를 소개한 뒤, 이런 권리를 지지하는 '한 가지 이유'를 말하는 **(A)**가 먼저 나오고, '그런 이유에도 불구하고' 권리 충돌이 발생한다는 내용의 **(C)**가 마지막에 나와야 적절하다.

★★★ 1등급 대비 고난도 3점 문제

11 겸손을 길러주는 근거와 주장 　　정답률 46% | 정답 ②

주어진 글 다음에 이어질 글의 순서로 가장 적절한 것을 고르시오. [3점]

① (A) – (C) – (B)
② (B) – (A) – (C)
③ (B) – (C) – (A)
④ (C) – (A) – (B)
⑤ (C) – (B) – (A)

One benefit of reasons and arguments is / that they can foster humility.
근거와 주장의 한 가지 이점은 ~이다. / 겸손을 기를 수 있다는 점

If two people disagree without arguing, / all they do is yell at each other.
만약에 두 사람이 논쟁 없이 의견만 다르다면, / 그들이 하는 것은 서로에게 고함을 지르는 것뿐이다.

No progress is made.
어떠한 발전도 없다.

(B) Both still think that they are right.
양측은 여전히 자신이 옳다고 생각한다.

In contrast, / if both sides give arguments / that articulate reasons for their positions, / then new possibilities open up.
대조적으로, / 양측이 주장을 제시한다면, / 자신의 입장에 대한 이유를 분명하게 말하는 / 새로운 가능성이 열린다.

One of the arguments gets refuted / — that is, it is shown to fail.
이러한 주장 중 한쪽이 반박된다. / 즉, 틀렸다는 것이 드러난다.

In that case, / the person who depended on the refuted argument / learns that he needs to change his view.
이런 경우에 / 반박된 주장에 의지했던 사람은 / 자신의 관점을 바꿀 필요가 있다는 것을 배운다.

(A) That is one way to achieve humility / — on one side at least.
이것은 겸손을 얻는 한 가지 방식이다. / 적어도 한쪽에서는

Another possibility is / that neither argument is refuted.
또 다른 가능성은 ~이다. / 어떤 주장도 반박되지 않는 것

Both have a degree of reason on their side.
둘 다 자기 입장에 대해 어느 정도 근거가 있다.

Even if neither person involved is convinced by the other's argument, / both can still come to appreciate the opposing view.
두 대화자 모두 상대의 주장에 설득되지 않더라도, / 양측은 그럼에도 불구하고 반대 견해를 이해하게 된다.

(C) They also realize / that, even if they have some truth, / they do not have the whole truth.
또한 그들은 인식하게 된다. / 자신이 약간의 진실은 갖고 있더라도 / 그들이 완전한 진실은 가지고 있지 않다는 점을

They can gain humility / when they recognize and appreciate the reasons / against their own view.
그들은 겸손을 얻을 수 있다. / 그들이 근거를 인식하고 이해할 때 / 자신의 견해에 반대되는

근거와 주장의 한 가지 이점은 겸손을 기를 수 있다는 점이다. 만약에 두 사람이 논쟁 없이 의견만 다르다면, 그들이 하는 것은 서로에게 고함을 지르는 것뿐이다. 어떠한 발전도 없다.

(B) 양측은 여전히 자신이 옳다고 생각한다. 대조적으로, 양측이 자신의 입장에 대한 이유를 분명하게 말하는 주장을 제시한다면, 새로운 가능성이 열린다. 이러한 주장 중 한쪽이 반박된다. 즉, 틀렸다는 것이 드러난다. 이런 경우에 반박된 주장에 의지했던 사람은 자신의 관점을 바꿀 필요가 있다는 것을 배운다.

(A) 이것은 적어도 한쪽에서는 겸손을 얻는 한 가지 방식이다. 또 다른 가능성은 어떤 주장도 반박되지 않는 것이다. 둘 다 자기 입장에 대해 어느 정도 근거가 있다. 두 대화자 모두 상대의 주장에 설득되지 않더라도, 양측은 그럼에도 불구하고 반대 견해를 이해하게 된다.

(C) 또한 그들은 자신이 약간의 진실은 몰라도 완전한 진실은 가지고 있지 않다는 점을 인식하게 된다. 그들은 자신의 견해에 반대되는 근거를 인식하고 이해할 때 겸손을 얻을 수 있다.

Why? 왜 정답일까?

근거와 주장은 겸손에 도움이 될 수 있다는 내용과 함께 서로 의견 차이를 좁히지 못하는 두 사람의 예를 드는 주어진 글 뒤에는, 양쪽이 적절한 근거를 들어 말하다가 한쪽의 결함이 드러나는 경우를 설명하는 **(B)**가 먼저 연결된다. 이어서 **(A)**는 두 주장에 모두 합당한 근거가 있는 '또 다른' 경우를 언급하고, **(C)**는 이들 또한 각자 주장이 '온전히' 맞지 않음을 수긍하며 겸손을 배울 수 있게 된다고 설명한다. 따라서 글의 순서로 가장 적절한 것은 ② '**(B) – (A) – (C)**'이다.

- **yell at** ~에게 소리 지르다
- **refute** ⓥ 반박하다
- **appreciate** ⓥ 제대로 이해하다
- **whole** ⓐ 온전한, 전체의
- **progress** ⓝ 진전, 진행
- **a degree of** 어느 정도의
- **opposing** ⓐ 반대되는, 상충하는

구문 풀이

14행 One of the arguments gets refuted — that is, it is shown to fail.
(「be shown + to부정사 : ~함이 드러나다」)

★★ 문제 해결 꿀~팁 ★★

▶ 많이 틀린 이유는?
(B)를 자세히 읽어보면, 견해가 다른 두 사람 중 한쪽의 주장이 반박당하는 경우를 설명하고 있다. 하지만 **(C)**는 '둘 중 아무도 온전한 진실을 갖고 있지 않은 경우'를 다

루므로 (B)와 연결되지 않는다. 이때 (A)가 '둘 중 어느 주장도 반박되지 않는 경우'를 말하고 있으므로, 이 상황에 대한 보충 설명이 (C)임을 알 수 있다.

▶ 문제 해결 방법은?

단순히 지시어나 연결어 등 형태적인 힌트에만 의존하면 답을 찾기 어렵다. 다른 쉬운 문제(심경, 도표, 안내문 등)를 빨리 풀고 남은 시간을 투자해 단락별 내용을 깊이 파악해야 한다.

★★★ 1등급 대비 고난도 3점 문제

12 온라인 공간의 특성 정답률 44% | 정답 ⑤

주어진 글 다음에 이어질 글의 순서로 가장 적절한 것을 고르시오. [3점]

① (A) − (C) − (B)
② (B) − (A) − (C)
③ (B) − (C) − (A)
④ (C) − (A) − (B)
⑤ (C) − (B) − (A)

The online world is an artificial universe / — entirely human-made and designed.
온라인 세상은 인공의 세계이다. / 완전히 사람에 의해 만들어지고 설계된
The design of the underlying system shapes / how we appear / and what we see of other people.
그 근본적인 시스템의 디자인은 형성한다. / 우리가 어떻게 보이고 / 우리가 다른 사람들에게서 무엇을 보는지를
(C) It determines / the structure of conversations / and who has access to what information.
그것은 결정한다. / 대화의 구조와, / 누가 어떤 정보에 접근할 수 있는지를
Architects of physical cities determine / the paths people will take / and the sights they will see.
물리적인 도시의 건축가들은 결정한다. / 사람들이 가게 될 길과 / 그들이 보게 될 광경을
They affect people's mood / by creating / cathedrals that inspire awe / and schools that encourage playfulness.
그들은 사람들의 기분에 영향을 미친다. / 지어서 / 경외감을 불러일으키는 대성당들과 / 명랑함을 북돋는 학교들을
(B) Architects, however, do not control / how the residents of those buildings present themselves / or see each other / — but the designers of virtual spaces do, / and they have far greater influence / on the social experience of their users.
그러나, 건축가들이 통제하지는 않는 반면, / 그러한 건물들의 거주자들이 어떻게 자신들을 나타내는지 / 또는 서로를 어떻게 바라보는지를 / 가상공간의 설계자들은 그렇게 하며, / 그들은 훨씬 더 큰 영향을 준다. / 사용자들의 사회적 경험에
(A) They determine / whether we see each other's faces / or instead know each other only by name.
그들은 결정한다. / 우리가 서로의 얼굴을 볼지 / 아니면 대신 이름만으로 서로를 알지를
They can reveal the size and makeup of an audience, / or provide the impression / that one is writing intimately to only a few, / even if millions are in fact reading.
그들은 구독자의 규모와 구성을 드러낼 수 있거나, / 인상을 줄 수 있다. / 한 사람이 오직 소수에게만 친밀하게 글을 쓰고 있다는 / 실제로는 수백 만 명이 읽고 있을지라도

온라인 세상은 완전히 사람에 의해 만들어지고 설계된 인공의 세계이다. 그 근본적인 시스템의 디자인은 우리가 어떻게 보이고 우리가 다른 사람들에게서 무엇을 보는지를 형성한다.

(C) 그것은 대화의 구조와, 누가 어떤 정보에 접근할 수 있는지를 결정한다. 물리적인 도시의 건축가들은 사람들이 가게 될 길과 그들이 보게 될 광경을 결정한다. 그들은 경외감을 불러일으키는 대성당들과 명랑함을 북돋는 학교들을 지어 사람들의 기분에 영향을 미친다.

(B) 그러나, 건축가들이 그러한 건물들의 거주자들이 어떻게 자신들을 나타내는지 또는 서로를 어떻게 바라보는지를 통제하지는 않는 반면, 가상공간의 설계자들은 그렇게 하며, 그들은 사용자들의 사회적 경험에 훨씬 더 큰 영향을 준다.

(A) 그들은 우리가 서로의 얼굴을 볼지 아니면 대신 이름만으로 서로를 알지를 결정한다. 그들은 구독자의 규모와 구성을 드러낼 수 있거나, 실제로는 수백 만 명이 읽고 있을지라도 한 사람이 오직 소수에게만 친밀하게 글을 쓰고 있다는 인상을 줄 수 있다.

Why? 왜 정답일까?

주어진 글에서 온라인 세상은 기본적으로 인간이 만들고 설계한 인공적 세계임을 말한 데 이어, (C)에서는 실제 물리적인 세계를 대조의 대상으로 언급한다. (B)에서는 however로 흐름을 뒤집으며 사이버 공간에 다시 주목하고, (A)는 문두의 대명사 They를 통해 (B)의 'the designers of virtual spaces'를 가리키며 (B)와 동일한 이야기 흐름을 이어 간다. 따라서 글의 순서로 가장 적절한 것은 ⑤ '(C) − (B) − (A)'이다.

- artificial ⓐ 인공적인, 인위적인
- determine ⓥ 결정하다
- impression ⓝ 인상
- influence ⓝ 영향(력)
- have access to ~에 접근하다
- cathedral ⓝ 대성당
- underlying ⓐ 근본적인, 기저에 있는
- makeup ⓝ 구성, 구조
- intimately ad 친밀하게
- structure ⓝ 구조
- architect ⓝ 건축가
- playfulness ⓝ 명랑함, 우스꽝스러움, 재미

구문 풀이

6행 They can reveal(동사1) the size and makeup of an audience, / or provide(동사2) the impression {that(접속사) one is writing intimately to only a few(몇 안 되는 (사람들)), / even if(비록 ~일지라도) millions are in fact reading}.
{ }: 동격 명사절

★★ 문제 해결 꿀~팁 ★★

▶ 많이 틀린 이유는?

(A), (B)의 순서를 제대로 잡는 것이 올바른 문제 풀이의 관건이다. (C)에서 가상 공간을 설계하는 사람과 대비되는 개념으로 물리적인 공간의 건축가를 언급하므로, 이들을 연이어 언급하는 (B)가 먼저 나오고, 이어서 다시 가상 공간 설계자들을 언급하며 주제를 정리하는 (A)가 마지막에 나오는 것이 적절하다.

▶ 문제 해결 방법은?

(A)의 They, (B)의 however 등 지시사와 접속부사에 주목하도록 한다. They 앞에는 반드시 복수의 명사가 지시 대상으로 나오게 되며, However 앞에는 반드시 뒤와 상반되는 내용이 미리 제시되어야 한다.

DAY 13 글의 순서 03

01 ③	02 ②	03 ⑤	04 ③	05 ③
06 ②	07 ⑤	08 ③	09 ④	10 ③
11 ⑤	12 ③			

01 멸종에 취약한 단일 지역 토착종

정답률 58% | 정답 ③

주어진 글 다음에 이어질 글의 순서로 가장 적절한 것을 고르시오.

① (A) − (C) − (B) ② (B) − (A) − (C)
✔(B) − (C) − (A) ④ (C) − (A) − (B)
⑤ (C) − (B) − (A)

Species that are found in only one area / are called endemic species / and are especially vulnerable to extinction.
오직 한 지역에서만 발견되는 종들은 / 토착종이라고 불리고 / 특히 멸종에 취약하다.
(B) They exist on islands and in other unique small areas, / especially in tropical rain forests / where most species are highly specialized.
그들은 섬들과 다른 독특한 작은 지역에 있다. / 특히 열대 우림인 / 대부분의 종이 매우 특화된
One example is the brilliantly colored golden toad / once found only in a small area of lush rain forests / in Costa Rica's mountainous region.
한 가지 예는 번쩍이는 색깔의 황금 두꺼비이다. / 무성한 열대 우림의 작은 지역에서만 한때 발견되었던, / 코스타리카의 산악 지역에 있는
(C) Despite living in the country's well-protected Monteverde Cloud Forest Reserve, / by 1989, / the golden toad had apparently become extinct.
그 나라의 잘 보존된 Monteverde Cloud Forest Reserve에서 살았음에도 불구하고, / 1989년 즈음에 / 황금 두꺼비는 멸종된 것으로 보였다.
Much of the moisture / that supported its rain forest habitat / came in the form of moisture-laden clouds / blowing in from the Caribbean Sea.
습기의 많은 부분은 / 그것의 열대 우림 서식지를 지탱해 준 / 습기를 실은 구름의 형태에서 왔다. / 카리브해에서 불어 들어오는
(A) But warmer air from global climate change / caused these clouds to rise, / depriving the forests of moisture, / and the habitat for the golden toad and many other species / dried up.
하지만 세계적 기후 변화로 인한 더 따뜻한 공기가 / 이러한 구름들을 상승하게 했고, / 숲에서 습기를 제거하였으며, / 황금 두꺼비와 많은 다른 종들의 서식지가 / 완전히 말라 버렸다.
The golden toad / appears to be one of the first victims of climate change / caused largely by global warming.
황금 두꺼비는 / 기후 변화의 첫 희생양들 중 하나인 것 같다. / 대체로 지구 온난화로 인한

오직 한 지역에서만 발견되는 종들은 토착종이라고 불리고 특히 멸종에 취약하다.

(B) 그들은 섬들과 특히 대부분의 종이 매우 특화된 열대 우림인 다른 독특한 작은 지역에 있다. 한 가지 예는 코스타리카의 산악 지역에 있는 무성한 열대 우림의 작은 지역에서만 한때 발견되었던, 번쩍이는 색깔의 황금 두꺼비이다.

(C) 그 나라의 잘 보존된 Monteverde Cloud Forest Reserve에서 살았음에도 불구하고, 1989년 즈음에 황금 두꺼비는 멸종된 것으로 보였다. 그것의 열대 우림 서식지를 지탱해 준 습기의 많은 부분은 카리브해에서 불어 들어오는 습기를 실은 구름의 형태에서 왔다.

(A) 하지만 세계적 기후 변화로 인한 더 따뜻한 공기가 이러한 구름들을 상승하게 했고, 숲에서 습기를 제거하였으며, 황금 두꺼비와 많은 다른 종들의 서식지가 완전히 말라 버렸다. 황금 두꺼비는 주로 지구 온난화로 인한 기후 변화의 첫 희생양들 중 하나인 것 같다.

Why? 왜 정답일까?

한 가지 서식지에만 있는 생물 종은 멸종에 취약하다는 일반적인 내용의 주어진 글 뒤로, 황금 두꺼비라는 구체적 예를 언급하는 **(B)**가 먼저 연결된다. 이어서 **(C)**는 이들이 **1989**년 무렵 멸종되었다는 내용과 함께 서식지 환경에 관해 설명하고, **(A)**는 이 환경이 지구 온난화 때문에 '변하면서' 결국 두꺼비가 멸종되었다고 언급한다. 따라서 글의 순서로 가장 적절한 것은 ③ '(B) − (C) − (A)'이다.

- **endemic** ⓐ 토착의, 풍토의, 고유의
- **vulnerable to** ~에 취약한
- **extinction** ⓝ 멸종
- **deprive A of B** A에게서 B를 빼앗다
- **habitat** ⓝ 서식지
- **victim** ⓝ 희생자
- **brilliantly** ad 눈부시게
- **lush** ⓐ 무성한, 우거진
- **mountainous** ⓐ 산악의
- **reserve** ⓝ 보호 구역
- **apparently** ad 겉보기에, 분명히
- **moisture-laden** ⓐ 습기 찬

구문 풀이

16행 Despite living in the country's well-protected Monteverde Cloud Forest Reserve, by 1989, the golden toad had apparently become extinct.
(Despite: 전치사, living: 동명사, had apparently become: 동사(과거완료), extinct: 주격 보어)

02 행동을 억제하거나 형성할 수 있는 과세

정답률 42% | 정답 ②

주어진 글 다음에 이어질 글의 순서로 가장 적절한 것을 고르시오.

① (A) − (C) − (B) ✔(B) − (A) − (C)
③ (B) − (C) − (A) ④ (C) − (A) − (B)
⑤ (C) − (B) − (A)

We commonly argue about the fairness of taxation / — whether this or that tax / will fall more heavily on the rich or the poor.
우리는 흔히 과세의 공정성에 관해 논한다. / 즉 이런저런 세금이 / 부자들에게 더 과중하게 부과될 것인지 아니면 가난한 사람들에게 그럴 것인지
(B) But the expressive dimension of taxation / goes beyond debates about fairness, / to the moral judgements societies make / about which activities are worthy of honor and recognition, / and which ones should be discouraged.
그러나 과세의 표현적 차원은 / 공정성에 대한 논쟁을 넘어, / 사회가 내리는 도덕적 판단에까지 이른다. / 어떤 활동이 명예와 인정을 받을 가치가 있고 / 어떤 활동이 억제되어야 하는지에 대해
Sometimes, these judgements are explicit.
때때로 이러한 판단은 명백하다.
(A) Taxes on tobacco, alcohol, and casinos / are called "sin taxes" / because they seek to discourage activities / considered harmful or undesirable.
담배, 술, 그리고 카지노에 대한 세금은 / '죄악세'라고 불린다. / 그것들이 활동들을 억제하려고 하기 때문에 / 해롭거나 바람직하지 않은 것으로 간주되는
Such taxes express society's disapproval of these activities / by raising the cost of engaging in them.
그런 세금은 이러한 활동에 대한 사회의 반대를 표현한다. / 그것을 하는 데 드는 비용을 증가시킴으로써
Proposals to tax sugary sodas (to combat obesity) / or carbon emissions (to address climate change) / likewise seek to change norms and shape behavior.
(비만을 퇴치하기 위해) 설탕이 든 탄산음료에 세금을 부과하는 제안은 / 또는 (기후 변화에 대처하기 위해) 탄소 배출에 / 마찬가지로 규범을 바꾸고 행동을 형성하려 한다.
(C) Not all taxes have this aim.
모든 세금이 이런 목적을 가진 것은 아니다.
We do not tax income / to express disapproval of paid employment / or to discourage people from engaging in it.
우리는 소득에 세금을 부과하는 것은 아니다. / 유급 고용에 대한 반대를 표명하거나 / 혹은 사람들이 그것을 하는 것을 막기 위해
Nor is a general sales tax intended / as a deterrent to buying things.
일반 판매세 역시 의도된 것이 아니다. / 물건을 사는 것의 억제책으로서
These are simply ways of raising revenue.
이것들은 단순히 세입을 올리는 방법이다.

우리는 흔히 과세의 공정성, 즉 이런저런 세금이 부자들에게 더 과중하게 부과될 것인지 아니면 가난한 사람들에게 그럴 것인지에 관해 논한다.

(B) 그러나 과세의 표현적 차원은 공정성에 대한 논쟁을 넘어, 어떤 활동이 명예와 인정을 받을 가치가 있고 어떤 활동이 억제되어야 하는지에 대해 사회가 내리는 도덕적 판단에까지 이른다. 때때로 이러한 판단은 명백하다.

(A) 담배, 술, 그리고 카지노에 대한 세금은 해롭거나 바람직하지 않은 것으로 간주되는 활동들을 억제하려고 하기 때문에 '죄악세'라고 불린다. 그런 세금은 이러한 활동을 하는 데 드는 비용을 증가시킴으로써 그것에 대한 사회의 반대를 표현한다. 마찬가지로 (비만을 퇴치하기 위해) 설탕이 든 탄산음료에 세금을 부과하는 제안이나 (기후 변화에 대처하기 위해) 탄소 배출에 세금을 부과하는 제안은 규범을 바꾸고 행동을 형성하려 한다.

(C) 모든 세금이 이런 목적을 가진 것은 아니다. 우리는 유급 고용에 대한 반대를 표명하거나 사람들이 그것을 하는 것을 막기 위해 소득에 세금을 부과하는 것은 아니다. 일반 판매세 역시 물건을 사는 것의 억제책으로서 의도된 것이 아니다. 이것들은 단순히 세입을 올리는 방법이다.

Why? 왜 정답일까?

과세의 공정성에 관한 논의를 화제로 제시한 주어진 글 뒤에는 이러한 논의가 특정 행위에 대한 사회의 도덕적 판단에 이를 수 있다고 언급하는 **(B)**가 먼저 연결된다. 이어서

(A)는 담배, 술, 카지노 등에 부과되는 세금을 예로 들며, 이러한 행위를 사회에서 '바람직하지 않다'고 보고 억제하려는 시각이 반영된 결과로서 세금이 부과된다는 보충 설명을 제시한다. 마지막으로 **(C)**는 모든 세금이 '이러한 목적', 즉 **(A)**에서 언급한 대로 '사람들의 행동을 바꾸려는' 목적으로 매겨지는 것은 아니라고 언급하며 소득세, 일반 판매세 등 다른 세금의 예를 든다. 따라서 글의 순서로 가장 적절한 것은 ② '**(B) – (A) – (C)**'이다.

- **fairness** ⓝ 공정함
- **fall on** (부담이) ~에게 떨어지다
- **undesirable** ⓐ 바람직하지 않은
- **combat** ⓥ 방지하다, 퇴치하다, 싸우다
- **emission** ⓝ 배출(량)
- **explicit** ⓐ 명백한
- **taxation** ⓝ 과세, 조세
- **discourage** ⓥ 낙담시키다
- **disapproval** ⓝ 반대, 못마땅함
- **obesity** ⓝ 비만
- **address** ⓥ 해결하다, 대처하다, 다루다
- **revenue** ⓝ 수입

구문 풀이

20행 Nor is a general sales tax intended as a deterrent to buying things.
「부정어구+be+주어+p.p.: 도치 구문(~도 또한 아니다)」

03 변화를 받아들이고 놓아주는 법을 배우기

정답률 60% | 정답 ⑤

주어진 글 다음에 이어질 글의 순서로 가장 적절한 것을 고르시오.

① (A) – (C) – (B) ② (B) – (A) – (C)
③ (B) – (C) – (A) ④ (C) – (A) – (B)
⑤ (C) – (B) – (A)

When an important change takes place in your life, / observe your response.
중요한 변화가 당신의 삶에서 일어났을 때, / 당신의 반응을 관찰해라.

If you resist accepting the change / it is because you are afraid; / afraid of losing something.
만약 당신이 이 변화를 받아들이는 것을 저항한다면 / 그것은 당신이 두려워하기 때문인데, / 즉 무언가를 잃을까 두려워하기 때문이다.

(C) Perhaps you might lose / your position, property, possession, or money.
아마도 당신은 잃을지도 모른다. / 당신의 지위, 재산, 소유물, 혹은 돈을

The change might mean / that you lose privileges or prestige.
이 변화는 의미할지도 모른다. / 당신이 특권이나 명성을 잃는 것을

Perhaps with the change / you lose the closeness of a person or a place.
아마도 이 변화로 / 당신은 어떤 사람이나 장소의 친밀함을 잃게 된다.

(B) In life, / all these things come and go / and then others appear, / which will also go.
인생에서 / 이러한 모든 것들은 있다가 없어지고 / 그러고 나서 다른 것들이 나타나며 / 그것 또한 사라진다.

It is like a river in constant movement.
그것은 끊임없이 움직이는 강과 같다.

If we try to stop the flow, / we create a dam; / the water stagnates / and causes a pressure / which accumulates inside us.
만약 우리가 그 흐름을 멈추려고 노력한다면, / 우리는 댐을 만들고, / 물은 고여서 / 압박을 유발한다. / 우리 안에 축적되는

(A) To learn to let go, / to not cling / and allow the flow of the river, / is to live without resistances; / being the creators of constructive changes / that bring about improvements / and widen our horizons.
놓아주는 법을 배우는 것, / 즉 집착하지 않고 / 강물의 흐름을 허용하는 것은 / 저항 없이 살아가는 것이며, / 건설적인 변화의 창조자가 되는 것이다. / 개선을 가져오고 / 우리의 시야를 넓히는

당신의 삶에서 중요한 변화가 일어났을 때, 당신의 반응을 관찰해라. 당신이 이 변화를 받아들이는 것을 저항한다면 그것은 당신이 두려워하기 때문인데, 즉 무언가를 잃을까 두려워하기 때문이다.

(C) 아마도 당신은 당신의 지위, 재산, 소유물, 혹은 돈을 잃을지도 모른다. 이 변화는 당신이 특권이나 명성을 잃는 것을 의미할지도 모른다. 아마도 이 변화로 당신은 어떤 사람이나 장소의 친밀함을 잃게 된다.

(B) 인생에서 이러한 모든 것들은 있다가 없어지고 그러고 나서 다른 것들이 나타났다가 또한 사라진다. 그것은 끊임없이 움직이는 강과 같다. 만약 우리가 그 흐름을 멈추려고 노력한다면, 우리는 댐을 만들고, 물은 고여서 우리 안에 축적되는 압박을 유발한다.

(A) 놓아주는 법을 배우는 것, 즉 집착하지 않고 강물의 흐름을 허용하는 것은 저항 없이 살아가는 것이며, 개선을 가져오고 우리의 시야를 넓히는 건설적인 변화의 창조자가 되는 것이다.

Why? 왜 정답일까?

우리가 어떤 중요한 변화를 받아들이기 어려운 까닭은 손실에 대한 두려움 때문임을 언급한 주어진 글 뒤에는, 이 손실이 지위, 재산, 소유물, 돈, 혹은 특권이나 명성과 관련되어 있을지도 모른다는 설명으로 주어진 글을 뒷받침하는 **(C)**가 먼저 연결된다. 이어서 **(B)**는 **(C)**에서 열거된 대상을 **all these things**로 가리키며 인생은 끊임없이 흐르는 강물과 같아서 모든 것이 왔다 사라진다는 내용을 덧붙인다. 마지막으로 **(A)**는 놓아주는 법을 배우고 생의 '흐름'을 받아들이라는 결론을 제시한다. 따라서 글의 순서로 가장 적절한 것은 ⑤ '**(C) – (B) – (A)**'이다.

- **cling** ⓥ 집착하다, 고수하다
- **constructive** ⓐ 건설적인
- **improvement** ⓝ 개선, 향상
- **accumulate** ⓥ 축적되다
- **possession** ⓝ 소유물
- **prestige** ⓝ 명성, 위신
- **resistance** ⓝ 저항
- **bring about** ~을 가져오다
- **constant** ⓐ 끊임없는
- **property** ⓝ 재산, 특성
- **privilege** ⓝ 특권

구문 풀이

5행 To learn to let go, to not cling and allow the flow of the river, is to live without resistances; being the creators of constructive changes [that bring about improvements and widen our horizons].
(To learn to let go: 동사(단수) / to not cling and allow …: 부정사구 주어 — 주어 동격 / is: 동사(단수) / to live …: 주격 보어 / changes: 선행사(복수) / that: 주격 관·대 / bring about: 동사1 / widen: 동사2)

04 연꽃 식물의 잎 정화 원리를 이용한 페인트 개발

정답률 71% | 정답 ③

주어진 글 다음에 이어질 글의 순서로 가장 적절한 것을 고르시오.

① (A) – (C) – (B) ② (B) – (A) – (C)
③ (B) – (C) – (A) ④ (C) – (A) – (B)
⑤ (C) – (B) – (A)

The lotus plant (a white water lily) / grows in the dirty, muddy bottom of lakes and ponds, / yet despite this, / its leaves are always clean.
연꽃 식물(흰 수련)은 / 호수와 연못의 더럽고 진흙투성이인 바닥에서 성장하지만, / 그러함에도 불구하고 / 그것의 잎은 항상 깨끗하다.

(B) That is because / whenever the smallest particle of dust lands on the plant, / it immediately waves the leaf, / directing the dust particles to one particular spot.
그것은 ~ 때문이다. / 먼지 같은 가장 작은 입자가 그 식물에 떨어질 때마다, / 그것이 즉시 잎을 흔들어서 / 먼지 입자들을 어떠한 특정 장소로 향하도록 하기 (때문이다.)

Raindrops falling on the leaves / are sent to that same place, / to thus wash the dirt away.
잎에 떨어지는 빗방울들이 / 그 동일한 장소로 보내져 / 먼지를 씻어낸다.

(C) This property of the lotus / led researchers to design a new house paint.
연꽃의 이러한 특성은 / 연구자들이 새로운 주택용 페인트를 고안하도록 이끌었다.

Researchers began working on how to develop paints / that wash clean in the rain, / in much the same way as lotus leaves do.
연구자들은 페인트를 어떻게 개발할지에 대한 연구를 시작했다. / 비가 올 때 깨끗하게 씻기는 / 연꽃잎이 하는 것과 대체로 똑같이

(A) As a result of this investigation, / a German company produced a house paint.
이 연구의 결과로 / 한 독일 회사가 주택용 페인트를 생산했다.

On the market in Europe and Asia, / the product even came with a guarantee / that it would stay clean for five years without detergents or sandblasting.
유럽과 아시아의 시장에서 / 이 제품은 심지어 보증했다 / 그것이 세제나 모래 분사 세척 없이 5년 동안 깨끗한 상태로 유지된다고

연꽃 식물(흰 수련)은 호수와 연못의 더럽고 진흙투성이인 바닥에서 성장하지만, 그러함에도 불구하고 그것의 잎은 항상 깨끗하다.

(B) 그것은 먼지 같은 가장 작은 입자가 그 식물에 떨어질 때마다, 즉시 잎을 흔들어서 먼지 입자들을 어떠한 특정 장소로 향하도록 하기 때문이다. 잎에 떨어지는 빗방울들이 그 동일한 장소로 보내져 먼지를 씻어낸다.

(C) 연꽃의 이러한 특성은 연구자들이 새로운 주택용 페인트를 고안하도록 이끌었다. 연구자들은 연꽃잎이 하는 것과 대체로 똑같이 비가 올 때 깨끗하게 씻기는 페인트를 어떻게 개발할지에 대한 연구를 시작했다.

(A) 이 연구의 결과로 한 독일 회사가 주택용 페인트를 생산했다. 유럽과 아시아의 시장에서 이 제품은 심지어 세제나 모래 분사 세척 없이 5년 동안 깨끗한 상태로 유지된다고 보증했다.

Why? 왜 정답일까?

연꽃 식물이 더러운 환경에서 자람에도 잎은 늘 깨끗하다고 설명한 주어진 글 뒤에는, 주어진 글의 내용을 **That**으로 받아 그 이유를 설명하는 **(B)**가 먼저 이어져야 한다. **(B)**에서는 먼지 같은 입자가 떨어질 때마다 연꽃이 잎을 즉시 흔들어서 입자들을 다른 곳으로 보낸다는 점을 언급하는데, **(C)**는 이를 **This property of the lotus**로 가리키며, 이 특성을 접목하여 탄생한 것이 새로운 주택용 페인트임을 설명한다. **(A)**에서는 **(C)**의 후

DAY 13

[문제편 p.084]
반부에 이어 페인트 개발에 관한 연구와 그 결과를 언급하고 있다. 따라서 글의 순서로 가장 적절한 것은 ③ '(B) – (C) – (A)'이다.

- lotus ⓝ 연꽃, 수련
- guarantee ⓝ 보증 ⓥ 보장하다
- sandblasting ⓝ 모래 분사
- property ⓝ 특성
- investigation ⓝ 연구, 조사
- detergent ⓝ 세제
- particle ⓝ 입자

구문 풀이

15행 Researchers began working on how to develop paints [that wash clean in the rain], in much the same way as lotus leaves do.

(「how+to부정사 : 어떻게 ~할지」 / 선행사 / 주격 관계대명사 / ~와 대체로 똑같이 / =wash clean)

05 효과적인 퍼스널브랜딩

정답률 60% | 정답 ③

주어진 글 다음에 이어질 글의 순서로 가장 적절한 것을 고르시오.

① (A) – (C) – (B) ② (B) – (A) – (C)
✔③ (B) – (C) – (A) ④ (C) – (A) – (B)
⑤ (C) – (B) – (A)

Your story is what makes you special.
당신의 이야기는 당신을 특별하게 만드는 것이다.
But the tricky part is showing how special you are / without talking about yourself.
그러나 까다로운 부분은 당신이 얼마나 특별한지를 보여주는 것이다. / 당신 자신에 대한 이야기를 하지 않고
Effective personal branding / isn't about talking about yourself all the time.
효과적인 퍼스널브랜딩은 / 항상 당신 자신에 대해 이야기하는 것이 아니다.
(B) Although everyone would like to think / that friends and family are eagerly waiting by their computers / hoping to hear some news about what you're doing, / they're not.
모든 사람들은 생각하고 싶겠지만, / 친구들이나 가족이 컴퓨터 옆에서 간절히 기다린다고 / 당신이 무엇을 하고 있는지에 대한 소식을 듣기를 희망하며 / 그렇지 않다.
(C) Actually, they're hoping / you're sitting by your computer, / waiting for news about them.
사실, 그들은 희망한다. / 당신이 컴퓨터 옆에 앉아있기를 / 자신들에 대한 소식을 기다리며
The best way to build your personal brand / is to talk more about other people, events, and ideas / than you talk about yourself.
당신의 퍼스널브랜드를 구축하는 최선의 방법은 / 타인, (그들의) 사건, 그리고 (그들의) 생각에 대한 이야기를 더 많이 하는 것이다. / 당신 자신에 대한 이야기를 하는 것보다
(A) By doing so, / you promote their victories and their ideas, / and you become an influencer.
그렇게 하여 / 당신은 다른 사람들의 성취와 생각을 추켜 세워주고, / 영향을 주는 사람이 된다.
You are seen as someone / who is not only helpful, but is also a valuable resource.
당신은 누군가로 여겨진다. / 도움이 될 뿐 아니라, 귀중한 자원이 되는
That helps your brand more / than if you just talk about yourself over and over.
그것은 당신의 브랜드에 더 도움이 된다. / 당신이 스스로의 이야기를 반복해서 하는 것보다

당신의 이야기는 당신을 특별하게 만드는 것이다. 그러나 까다로운 부분은 당신 자신에 대한 이야기를 하지 않고 당신이 얼마나 특별한지를 보여주는 것이다. 효과적인 퍼스널브랜딩은 항상 당신 자신에 대해 이야기하는 것이 아니다.

(B) 모든 사람들은 친구들이나 가족이 당신이 무엇을 하고 있는지에 대한 소식을 듣기를 희망하며 컴퓨터 옆에서 간절히 기다린다고 생각하고 싶겠지만, 그렇지 않다.

(C) 사실, 그들은 당신이 자신들에 대한 소식을 기다리며 컴퓨터 옆에 앉아있기를 희망한다. 당신의 퍼스널브랜드를 구축하는 최선의 방법은 당신 자신에 대한 이야기를 하는 것보다 타인, (그들의) 사건, 그리고 (그들의) 생각에 대한 이야기를 더 많이 하는 것이다.

(A) 그렇게 하여 당신은 다른 사람들의 성취와 생각을 추켜 세워주고, 영향을 주는 사람이 된다. 당신은 도움이 되는 사람일 뿐 아니라, 귀중한 자원이 되는 사람으로 여겨진다. 그것은 당신이 스스로의 이야기를 반복해서 하는 것보다 당신의 브랜드에 더 도움이 된다.

Why? 왜 정답일까?

퍼스널브랜딩은 자신에 대해 말하기만 하는 것이 아니라고 지적한 주어진 글 뒤에는, 모든 타인이 사실 '나'에 대한 이야기를 기다리고 있지 않다는 내용의 (B), 그러므로 오히려 '나'보다는 타인의 이야기를 하는 것이 효과적이라는 내용의 (C), 그렇게 하면 브랜드에 도움이 될 수 있다는 내용의 (A)가 차례로 이어지는 것이 적절하다. 따라서 글의 순서로 가장 적절한 것은 ③ '(B) – (C) – (A)'이다.

- tricky ⓐ 교묘한, 까다로운, 곤란한
- promote ⓥ 촉진하다, 홍보하다
- valuable ⓐ 소중한, 귀중한
- effective ⓐ 효과적인
- influencer ⓝ 영향력을 행사하는 사람
- eagerly ad 간절히, 열망하여

구문 풀이

10행 Although everyone would like to think {that friends and family are eagerly waiting by their computers / hoping to hear some news about what you're doing}, / they're not (eagerly waiting ~).

(양보 접속사 / 동사(현재진행) / ~ 옆에서 / 분사구문(~하면서) / 의문사(무엇) / 생략)

06 소방 스프링클러 시스템의 개발

정답률 66% | 정답 ②

주어진 글 다음에 이어질 글의 순서로 가장 적절한 것을 고르시오. [3점]

① (A) – (C) – (B) ✔② (B) – (A) – (C)
③ (B) – (C) – (A) ④ (C) – (A) – (B)
⑤ (C) – (B) – (A)

James Francis was born in England / and emigrated to the United States at age 18.
James Francis는 영국에서 태어나 / 열여덟 살에 미국으로 이주했다.
One of his first contributions to water engineering / was the invention of the sprinkler system / now widely used in buildings for fire protection.
물공학에 대한 그의 첫 공헌 중 하나는 / 스프링클러 시스템의 발명이었다. / 현재 소방 목적으로 건물에서 널리 이용되는
(B) Francis's design involved a series of perforated pipes / running throughout the building.
Francis의 디자인은 일련의 구멍 낸 파이프를 포함했다. / 건물 전체에 뻗어 있는
It had two defects: / it had to be turned on manually, / and it had only *one* valve.
여기에는 두 가지 결점이 있었는데, / 밸브를 손으로 열어야만 한다는 것과 / 밸브가 단 *한 개*만 있다는 것이었다.
(A) Once the system was activated by opening the valve, / water would flow out everywhere.
밸브를 열어 일단 시스템이 작동되면, / 물이 사방에서 쏟아져 나왔다.
If the building did not burn down, / it would certainly be completely flooded.
건물은 불에 타지 않는다면 / 그것은 완전히 물에 잠기게 될 것이었다.
(C) Only some years later, / when other engineers perfected the kind of sprinkler heads / in use nowadays, / did the concept become popular.
몇 년이 지나고 / 다른 엔지니어들이 스프링클러 헤드를 완성했을 때에야 / 오늘날 사용되는 종류의 / 비로소 그 개념은 대중화되었다.
They turned on automatically / and were activated only where actually needed.
이는 자동으로 켜지고 / 실제로 필요한 곳에서만 작동되었다.

James Francis는 영국에서 태어나 열여덟 살에 미국으로 이주했다. 물공학에 대한 그의 첫 공헌 중 하나는 현재 소방 목적으로 건물에서 널리 이용되는 스프링클러 시스템을 발명한 것이었다.

(B) Francis의 디자인은 건물 전체에 뻗어 있는, 일련의 구멍 낸 파이프를 포함했다. 여기에는 두 가지 결점이 있었는데, 밸브를 손으로 열어야만 한다는 것과 밸브가 단 *한 개*만 있다는 것이었다.

(A) 밸브를 열어 일단 시스템이 작동되면, 물이 사방에서 쏟아져 나왔다. 건물은 불에 타지 않는다면 완전히 물에 잠기게 될 것이었다.

(C) 몇 년이 지나고 다른 엔지니어들이 오늘날 사용되는 종류의 스프링클러 헤드를 완성했을 때에야 비로소 그 개념은 대중화되었다. 이는 자동으로 켜지고 실제로 필요한 곳에서만 작동되었다.

Why? 왜 정답일까?

주어진 글에서 James Francis가 방화 목적의 스프링클러를 개발했다고 이야기하는 데 (B)에서는 Francis의 초기 디자인이 한계를 지니고 있었음을 설명한다. 특히 (B)의 마지막 부분에 밸브가 수동인 데다 개수도 하나만 있어 불편함이 따랐다는 언급이 있는 데 (A)에서는 실제로 이 밸브를 열었을 때 물이 너무 많이 나와서 건물이 타 버리거나 수장되거나 둘 중 하나의 결말을 맞이할 지경이었다는 내용을 이어서 설명한다. (C)에서는 '몇 년 후'로 시점을 옮겨 이 디자인이 보완되면서 비로소 소방용 스프링클러의 대중화가 이루어졌음을 이야기한다. 따라서 주어진 글 다음에 이어질 글의 순서로 가장 적절한 것은 ② '(B) – (A) – (C)'이다.

- emigrate ⓥ 이주하다, 이민 가다
- invention ⓝ 발명
- activate ⓥ 작동시키다, 활성화하다
- contribution ⓝ 공헌, 기여
- fire protection 소방, 방화
- flow out 쏟아져 나오다, 흘러나오다

- completely [ad] 완전히
- defect ⓝ 결점, 단점
- perfect ⓥ 완벽하게 하다
- flood ⓥ 물에 잠기다, 침수되다
- manually [ad] 손으로, 수동으로
- automatically [ad] 자동으로

구문 풀이

14행 Only some years later, [when other engineers perfected the kind of sprinkler heads in use nowadays], did the concept become popular.
「only+부사구+」 관계부사 do/does/did+주어+동사원형: 부정어구의 도치」

07 생태계의 회복력

정답률 51% | 정답 ⑤

주어진 글 다음에 이어질 글의 순서로 가장 적절한 것을 고르시오. [3점]

① (A) – (C) – (B) ② (B) – (A) – (C)
③ (B) – (C) – (A) ④ (C) – (A) – (B)
⑤ (C) – (B) – (A)

Because we are told that the planet is doomed, / we do not register the growing number of scientific studies / demonstrating the resilience of other species.
우리는 지구가 운이 다한 것이라고 듣기 때문에 / 우리는 증가하는 수의 과학적 연구를 기억하지 않는다. / 다른 종의 회복력을 증명하는
For instance, / climate-driven disturbances / are affecting the world's coastal marine ecosystems / more frequently and with greater intensity.
예를 들어 / 기후로 인한 교란이 / 세계 해안의 해양 생태계에 영향을 미치고 있다. / 더 자주, 더 큰 강도로
(C) This is a global problem / that demands urgent action.
이것은 세계적인 문제이다. / 긴급한 조치를 요구하는
Yet, as detailed in a 2017 paper in *BioScience*, / there are also instances / where marine ecosystems show remarkable resilience / to acute climatic events.
하지만 *BioScience*의 2017년 논문에서 자세히 설명된 것처럼, / 경우들이 또한 있다. / 해양 생태계가 놀라운 회복력을 보여주는 / 극심한 기후의 사건들에
(B) In a region in Western Australia, for instance, / up to 90 percent of live coral was lost / when ocean water temperatures rose, / causing what scientists call coral bleaching.
예를 들어 Western Australia의 한 지역에서 / 살아 있는 산호의 90퍼센트까지 소실되어 / 바닷물 온도가 상승했을 때, / 과학자들이 산호 백화라 부르는 것을 야기했다.
Yet in some sections of the reef surface, / 44 percent of the corals recovered within twelve years.
하지만 암초 표면의 몇몇 부분에서 / 산호의 44퍼센트가 12년 이내에 회복했다.
(A) Similarly, / kelp forests hammered by intense El Niño water-temperature / increases recovered within five years.
마찬가지로 / 극심한 엘니뇨 수온 상승에 의해 강타당한 켈프 숲이 / 5년 이내에 회복했다.
By studying these "bright spots," / situations where ecosystems persist / even in the face of major climatic impacts, / we can learn what management strategies help / to minimize destructive forces and nurture resilience.
이러한 '밝은 지점들'을 연구함으로써 / 즉 생태계가 지속되는 상황들을 / 중대한 기후의 영향에 직면한 순간에도 / 우리는 어떠한 관리 전략들이 도움이 되는지를 배울 수 있다. / 파괴적인 힘을 최소화하고 회복력을 키우는 데

우리는 지구가 운이 다한 것이라고 듣기 때문에 다른 종의 회복력을 증명하는 과학적 연구의 증가를 기억하지 않는다. 예를 들어 기후로 인한 교란이 세계 해안의 해양 생태계에 더 자주, 더 큰 강도로 영향을 미치고 있다.

(C) 이것은 긴급한 조치를 요구하는 세계적인 문제이다. 하지만 *BioScience*의 2017년 논문에서 자세히 설명된 것처럼, 해양 생태계가 극심한 기후의 사건들에 놀라운 회복력을 보여주는 경우들이 또한 있다.

(B) 예를 들어 Western Australia의 한 지역에서 바닷물 온도가 상승했을 때, 살아 있는 산호의 90퍼센트까지 소실되어 과학자들이 산호 백화라 부르는 것을 야기했다. 하지만 암초 표면의 몇몇 부분에서 산호의 44퍼센트가 12년 이내에 회복했다.

(A) 마찬가지로 극심한 엘니뇨 수온 상승에 의해 강타당한 켈프 숲이 5년 이내에 회복했다. 이러한 '밝은 지점들', 즉 중대한 기후의 영향에 직면한 순간에도 생태계가 지속되는 상황들을 연구함으로써, 우리는 어떠한 관리 전략들이 파괴적인 힘을 최소화하고 회복력을 키우는 데 도움이 되는지를 배울 수 있다.

Why? 왜 정답일까?

해양 생태계가 기후 교란에 큰 영향을 받고 있음을 언급하는 주어진 글 뒤로 **(C)**는 '이것'이 세계적 문제임을 언급한 후, 희망적이게도 해양 생태계의 회복력에 관한 사례들이 존재함을 상기시킨다. **for instance**로 연결되는 **(B)**는 산호의 회복 사례를 언급하고, **Similarly**로 시작되는 **(A)**는 켈프 숲 회복 사례를 추가로 열거한다. 따라서 글의 순서로 가장 적절한 것은 ⑤ **'(C) – (B) – (A)'**이다.

- register ⓥ 기억하다
- disturbance ⓝ 교란
- persist ⓥ 지속되다
- destructive ⓐ 파괴적인
- bleaching ⓝ 표백
- remarkable ⓐ 놀라운, 주목할 만한
- demonstrate ⓥ 입증하다
- intensity ⓝ 강도
- in the face of ~에 직면하여
- nurture ⓥ 양성하다, 키우다
- reef ⓝ 암초

구문 풀이

1행 Because we are told {that the planet is doomed}, we do not register the growing number of scientific studies demonstrating the resilience of other species.
동사(4형식 수동태) { }: 목적어 현재분사

08 아이의 고유한 경험을 가로막을 수 있는 교육

정답률 50% | 정답 ③

주어진 글 다음에 이어질 글의 순서로 가장 적절한 것을 고르시오. [3점]

① (A) – (C) – (B) ② (B) – (A) – (C)
③ (B) – (C) – (A) ④ (C) – (A) – (B)
⑤ (C) – (B) – (A)

A little boy sees and hears birds with delight.
한 어린 소년이 즐겁게 새들을 보고 새 소리를 듣는다.
Then the "good father" comes along / and feels / he should "share" the experience / and help his son "develop."
그때 '좋은 아버지'가 와서, / 느낀다. / 자신이 그 경험을 '공유하고' / 아들이 '발전하도록' 도와야겠다고
(B) He says: / "That's a jay, and this is a sparrow."
그는 말한다. / "저건 어치야, 그리고 이건 참새야."라고
The moment the little boy is concerned with / which is a jay / and which is a sparrow, / he can no longer see the birds / or hear them sing.
그 어린 소년이 관심을 두는 순간, / 어느 것이 어치이고, / 어느 것이 참새인지에 대해 / 그는 더 이상 새들을 보거나 / 새들이 노래하는 것을 들을 수 없다.
He has to see and hear them / the way the father wants him to.
그는 새들을 보고 들어야 한다. / 아버지가 원하는 방식으로
(C) Father has good reasons on his side, / since few people can go through life / listening to the birds sing, / and the sooner the boy starts his "education" / the better.
아버지의 입장에서는 합당한 이유가 있는데, / 인생을 살아갈 수 있는 사람은 거의 없고, / 새들이 노래하는 것에 귀를 기울이며 / 그 소년이 자신의 '교육'을 빨리 시작하면 할수록 / 더 좋기 때문이다.
Maybe he will be an ornithologist / when he grows up.
어쩌면 그는 조류학자가 될지도 모른다. / 자라서
A few people, / however, / can still see and hear / in the old way.
몇몇 사람들은 / 그러나 / 여전히 보고 들을 수 있다. / 옛날 방식으로
(A) But / most of the members of the human race / have lost the capacity / to be painters, poets, or musicians, / and are not left the option of seeing and hearing directly / even if they can afford to; / they must get it secondhand.
그러나 / 인류의 구성원 대다수는 / 능력을 잃었고, / 화가, 시인 또는 음악가가 될 수 있는 / 그들에게는 직접 보고 들을 수 있는 선택권이 남겨져 있지 않다. / 할 수 있음에도 불구하고, / 그들은 그것을 간접적으로 받아들여야 한다.

한 어린 소년이 즐겁게 새들을 보고 새 소리를 듣는다. 그때 '좋은 아버지'가 와서, 자신이 그 경험을 '공유하고' 아들이 '발전하도록' 도와야겠다고 느낀다.

(B) 그는 "저건 어치야, 그리고 이건 참새야."라고 말한다. 그 어린 소년이 어느 것이 어치이고, 어느 것이 참새인지에 대해 관심을 두는 순간, 그는 더 이상 새들을 보거나 새들이 노래하는 것을 들을 수 없다. 그는 아버지가 원하는 방식으로 새들을 보고 들어야 한다.

(C) 아버지의 입장에서는 합당한 이유가 있는데, 새들이 노래하는 것에 귀를 기울이며 인생을 살아갈 수 있는 사람은 거의 없고, 그 소년이 자신의 '교육'을 빨리 시작하면 할수록 더 좋기 때문이다. 어쩌면 그는 자라서 조류학자가 될지도 모른다. 그러나 몇몇 사람들은 여전히 옛날 방식으로 보고 들을 수 있다.

(A) 그러나 인류의 구성원 대다수는 화가, 시인 또는 음악가가 될 수 있는 능력을 잃었고, 할 수 있음에도 불구하고, 그들에게는 직접 보고 들을 수 있는 선택권이 남아 있지 않다. 그들은 그것을 간접적으로 받아들여야 한다.

Why? 왜 정답일까?

아들이 새를 구경하는 것을 보고 '좋은 아버지'가 다가와 아들을 도와주어야겠다고 느낀다는 예시로 시작하는 주어진 글 뒤에는, 아버지가 아들에게 자신이 아는 것을 가르쳐주

[문제편 p.086]

면 아들은 더 이상 자기만의 방식으로 새들을 경험할 수 없고 아버지가 알려준 방식대로 경험할 수밖에 없게 된다는 내용의 **(B)**, 아버지가 이러한 교육을 시작하는 이유를 설명하는 **(C)**, 그러한 교육의 이점에도 불구하고 결국에는 아이들이 직접 자신만의 방식으로 보고 들을 수 있는 기회를 잃게 되고 만다는 내용의 **(A)**가 차례로 이어지는 것이 자연스럽다. 따라서 글의 순서로 가장 적절한 것은 ③ '**(B) – (C) – (A)**'이다.

- **delight** ⓝ 기쁨
- **race** ⓝ 인종
- **secondhand** ad 간접적으로, 전해 들어
- **sparrow** ⓝ 참새
- **share** ⓥ 공유하다
- **capacity** ⓝ 능력, 역량
- **jay** ⓝ 어치(까마귓과의 새)
- **go through** ~을 겪다, 통과하다

구문 풀이

4행 But most of the members of the human race have lost the capacity to be painters, poets, or musicians, / and are not left the option of seeing and hearing directly even if they can afford to; they must get it secondhand.
(주어1: most of the members of the human race / 동사1: have lost / 동사2(4형식 수동태): are not left / 직접목적어: the option / 동명사1: seeing / 동명사2: hearing / 비록 ~일지라도: even if / ~할 여유가 있다: can afford to)

09 대상을 분류하고 일반화하는 인간의 능력

정답률 49% | 정답 ④

주어진 글 다음에 이어질 글의 순서로 가장 적절한 것을 고르시오.

① (A) – (C) – (B)
② (B) – (A) – (C)
③ (B) – (C) – (A)
✔④ (C) – (A) – (B)
⑤ (C) – (B) – (A)

The intuitive ability to classify and generalize / is undoubtedly a useful feature of life and research, / but it carries a high cost, / such as in our tendency / to stereotype generalizations about people and situations.
분류하고 일반화하는 직관적인 능력은 / 분명 생활과 연구에 유용한 특징이지만 / 그것은 많은 대가를 수반한다. / 가령 우리의 경향 / 사람과 상황에 대해 일반화를 고착시키는

(C) For most people, / the word stereotype arouses negative connotations: / it implies a negative bias.
사람들 대부분에게 / 고정 관념이라는 단어는 부정적인 함축을 불러일으킨다 / 즉 그것은 부정적인 편견을 암시한다.

But, in fact, / stereotypes do not differ in principle from all other generalizations; / generalizations about groups of people / are not necessarily always negative.
하지만 사실 / 고정 관념은 원칙적으로 모든 다른 일반화와 다르지 않으며, / 집단에 대한 사람들의 일반화가 / 반드시 꼭 부정적인 것은 아니다.

(A) Intuitively and quickly, / we mentally sort things into groups / based on what we perceive the differences between them to be, / and that is the basis for stereotyping.
직관적이고도 신속하게, / 우리는 머릿속에서 사물을 그룹으로 분류하며, / 우리가 그들끼리 차이가 있다고 생각하는 것에 근거해 / 그리고 그것은 고정관념의 기초이다.

Only afterwards / do we examine (or not examine) more evidence / of how things are differentiated, / and the degree and significance of the variations.
그 후에 비로소 / 우리는 더 많은 증거를 조사한다(혹은 조사하지 않는다). / 사물이 어떻게 차별화되는지 / 그리고 그 차이의 정도와 중요성에 대한

(B) Our brain performs these tasks efficiently and automatically, / usually without our awareness.
우리의 뇌는 이런 일을 효율적이고 자동으로 수행한다. / 대개 우리가 인식하지 못하는 사이에

The real danger of stereotypes is not their inaccuracy, / but their lack of flexibility and their tendency to be preserved, / even when we have enough time to stop and consider.
고정 관념이 진정 위험한 것은 그것의 부정확함이 아니라, / 그것의 유연성 부족과 유지되려는 경향이다. / 우리가 곰곰이 생각할 시간이 충분할 때조차

분류하고 일반화하는 직관적인 능력은 분명 생활과 연구에 유용한 특징이지만 많은 대가를 수반하는데, 가령 우리가 사람과 상황에 대해 일반화를 고착시키는 경향 등이 그 예이다.

(C) 사람들 대부분에게 고정 관념이라는 단어는 부정적인 함축을 불러일으킨다. 즉 그것은 부정적인 편견을 암시한다. 하지만 사실 고정 관념은 원칙적으로 모든 다른 일반화와 다르지 않으며, 집단에 대한 사람들의 일반화가 반드시 꼭 부정적인 것은 아니다.

(A) 직관적이고도 신속하게, 우리는 사물끼리 차이가 있다고 생각하는 것에 근거해 머릿속에서 그들을 그룹으로 분류하며, 그것이 고정관념의 기초이다. 그 후에 비로소 우리는 사물이 어떻게 차별화되는지, 그리고 그 차이의 정도와 중요성에 대한 더 많은 증거를 조사한다(혹은 조사하지 않는다).

(B) 우리의 뇌는 대개 우리가 인식하지 못하는 사이에 이런 일을 효율적이고 자동으로 수행한다. 고정 관념이 진정 위험한 것은 그것의 부정확함이 아니라, 그것의 유연성 부족과 유지되려는 경향인데, 이는 우리가 곰곰이 생각할 시간이 충분할 때조차 그렇다.

Why? 왜 정답일까?

분류하고 일반화하는 능력이 '대가'를 낳는다는 주어진 글 뒤로 **(C)**가 연결되어 고정 관념이 항상 나쁘지는 않다고 설명한다. **(A)**에서는 고정 관념이 어떻게 만들어지는지 보충 설명하고, **(B)**는 고정 관념이 '진짜' 위험할 때가 언제인지 구체화한다. 따라서 글의 순서로 가장 적절한 것은 ④ '**(C) – (A) – (B)**'이다.

- **intuitive** ⓐ 직관적인
- **feature** ⓝ 특징
- **stereotype** ⓥ 고정 관념으로 만들다
- **intuitively** ad 직관적으로
- **differentiate** ⓥ 구별하다, 차별화하다
- **inaccuracy** ⓝ 부정확함
- **arouse** ⓥ 불러일으키다
- **imply** ⓥ 시사하다
- **undoubtedly** ad 의심의 여지 없이
- **tendency** ⓝ 경향
- **generalization** ⓝ 일반화
- **examine** ⓥ 조사하다
- **automatically** ad 자동으로
- **preserve** ⓥ 보존하다
- **connotation** ⓝ 함축
- **in principle** 원칙적으로

구문 풀이

9행 Only afterwards do we examine (or not examine) more evidence of [how things are differentiated], and the degree and significance of the variations.
(「도치 구문 : only 부사구+do+주어+동사원형」 / 의문사절(of의 목적어1): how things are differentiated / 명사구(of의 목적어2): the degree and significance of the variations)

★★★ 1등급 대비 고난도 2점 문제

10 발췌본의 유용함과 한계

정답률 29% | 정답 ③

주어진 글 다음에 이어질 글의 순서로 가장 적절한 것을 고르시오.

① (A) – (C) – (B)
② (B) – (A) – (C)
✔③ (B) – (C) – (A)
④ (C) – (A) – (B)
⑤ (C) – (B) – (A)

There is no doubt / that the length of some literary works is overwhelming.
의심의 여지가 없다. / 일부 문학 작품의 길이가 압도적이라는 것에는

Reading or translating a work in class, / hour after hour, week after week, / can be such a boring experience / that many students never want to open a foreign language book again.
수업 시간에 작품을 읽거나 번역하는 것은 / 몇 시간, 몇 주 동안 / 너무나 지루한 경험일 수 있어서 / 많은 학생이 다시는 외국어 서적을 절대 펴고 싶어 하지 않는다.

(B) Extracts provide one type of solution.
발췌본은 한 가지 해결책을 제공한다.

The advantages are obvious: / reading a series of passages from different works / produces more variety in the classroom, / so that the teacher has a greater chance of avoiding monotony, / while still giving learners a taste / at least of an author's special flavour.
장점들은 분명하다. / 다양한 작품에서 가져온 일련의 단락을 읽는 것은 / 교실에서 더 많은 다양성을 만들어 내서 / 교사는 단조로움을 피할 가능성이 더 크다. / 학습자에게 여전히 맛보게 하는 한편 / 최소한이라도 어떤 작가의 특별한 묘미를

(C) On the other hand, / a student / who is only exposed to 'bite-sized chunks' / will never have the satisfaction / of knowing the overall pattern of a book, / which is after all the satisfaction most of us seek / when we read something in our own language.
반면에, / 학생은 / '짧은 토막글'만 접한 / 만족감을 결코 가질 수 없을 것이며, / 책의 전반적인 구성을 안다는 / 결국 그 만족감은 우리 대부분이 찾고자 하는 것이다. / 우리가 모국어로 된 어떤 글을 읽을 때

(A) Moreover, / there are some literary features / that cannot be adequately illustrated by a short excerpt: / the development of plot or character, / for instance, / with the gradual involvement of the reader / that this implies; / or the unfolding of a complex theme / through the juxtaposition of contrasting views.
게다가 / 문학적인 특징이 몇 가지 있다. / 짧은 발췌로는 충분히 설명될 수 없는 / 줄거리나 등장인물의 전개 / 예를 들면 / 독자의 점진적 몰입과 더불어 / 이것이 내포하는 / 또는 복잡한 주제의 전개 / 대조적인 관점의 병치를 통해

일부 문학 작품의 길이가 압도적이라는 데는 의심의 여지가 없다. 수업 시간에 작품을 몇 시간, 몇 주 동안 읽거나 번역하는 것은 너무나 지루한 경험일 수 있어서 많은 학생이 다시는 외국어 서적을 절대 펴고 싶어 하지 않는다.

(B) 발췌본은 한 가지 해결책을 제공한다. 장점들은 분명하다. 즉, 다양한 작품에서 가져온 일련의 단락을 읽는 것은 교실에서 더 많은 다양성을 만들어 내서, 교사는 단조로움을 피할 가능성이 더 큰 한편으로, 여전히 최소한이라도 어떤 작가의 특별한 묘미를 학습자에게 맛보게 한다.

(C) 반면에, '짧은 토막글'만 접한 학생은 책의 전반적인 구성을 아는 만족감을

결코 가질 수 없을 것이며, 결국 그 만족감은 모국어로 된 어떤 글을 읽을 때 우리 대부분이 찾고자 하는 것이다.

(A) 게다가 짧은 발췌로는 충분히 설명될 수 없는 문학적인 특징이 몇 가지 있는데, 예를 들면 줄거리나 등장인물의 전개와 더불어 이것이 내포하는 독자의 점진적 몰입, 또는 대조적인 관점의 병치를 통한 복잡한 주제 전개 등이 있다.

Why? 왜 정답일까?

긴 문학 작품을 다루는 경우를 언급하는 주어진 글 뒤로, 발췌본을 활용하는 것이 해결책이 될 수 있다는 내용의 (B), On the other hand로 흐름을 반전시키며 발췌본에 한계가 있음을 설명하는 (C), Moreover와 함께 한계점을 추가로 열거하는 (A)가 차례로 연결된다. 따라서 글의 순서로 가장 적절한 것은 ③ '(B) – (C) – (A)'이다.

- literary ⓐ 문학의
- translate ⓥ 번역하다
- adequately ad 충분히
- unfolding ⓝ 전개, 펼침
- extract ⓝ 발췌(본) ⓥ 발췌하다, 뽑아내다
- flavour ⓝ 묘미, 맛
- overwhelming ⓐ 압도적인
- feature ⓝ 특징
- gradual ⓐ 점진적인
- contrasting ⓐ 대조되는, 상충하는
- monotony ⓝ 단조로움
- overall ⓐ 전반적인

구문 풀이

2행 Reading or translating a work in class, hour after hour, week after week, can be such a boring experience that many students never want to open a foreign language book again.
(Reading ~ week: 주어(동명사구) / can be: 동사 / 「such ~ that …: 너무 ~해서 …하다」)

★★ 문제 해결 꿀~팁 ★★

▶ 많이 틀린 이유는?
발췌본의 한계를 연이어 설명하는 (C) – (A)의 연결고리를 파악했다면, (B)의 순서를 잡는 것이 관건이다. 주어진 글에서 '발췌본'에 관한 언급이 아예 나오지 않는데, 바로 On the other hand로 시작하는 (C)가 연결되어 발췌본의 한계를 지적하면 글의 흐름이 어색하다. 따라서 (C) 앞에 (B)가 나와 '발췌본'이라는 소재를 등장시켜야 흐름이 매끄러워진다.
▶ 문제 해결 방법은?
주어진 글이 아닌 (B)에서 중심 소재가 등장하므로, 일단 (B)가 전제되어야 나머지 단락을 연결할 수 있다는 점을 파악하도록 한다.

★★★ 1등급 대비 고난도 2점 문제

11 공학 기술로 지식 노동자의 생산성 높이기 정답률 30% | 정답 ⑤

주어진 글 다음에 이어질 글의 순서로 가장 적절한 것을 고르시오.

① (A) – (C) – (B) ② (B) – (A) – (C)
③ (B) – (C) – (A) ④ (C) – (A) – (B)
⑤ (C) – (B) – (A) ✔

According to the consulting firm McKinsey, / knowledge workers spend up to 60 percent of their time / looking for information, responding to emails, and collaborating with others.
컨설턴트 회사 McKinsey에 따르면, / 노동자는 자신들의 시간 중 60퍼센트까지 사용한다. / 지식 정보를 찾고, 이메일에 답장하며, 다른 사람들과 협력하는 데

(C) By using social technologies, / those workers can become up to 25 percent more productive.
사회 공학적 기술을 이용함으로써, / 그런 노동자들은 25퍼센트까지 생산성이 더 높아질 수 있다.

The need for productivity gains / through working harder and longer / has a limit and a human toll.
생산성 증진의 필요성에는 / 더 열심히 그리고 더 오래 일하는 것을 통한 / 한계가 있고 사람들의 희생이 따른다.

(B) The solution is to enable people to work smarter, / not just by saying it, / but by putting smart tools and improved processes in place / so that people can perform at enhanced levels.
해결책은 사람들이 더 스마트하게 일할 수 있게 해 주는 것이다. / 그냥 말만 함으로써가 아니라 / 스마트 기기와 개선된 과정을 가동함으로써 / 사람들이 향상된 수준에서 업무를 할 수 있도록

(A) Think of it / as the robot-assisted human, given superpowers / through the aid of technology.
그것을 생각해 보라. / 막강한 힘을 부여받은, 로봇의 도움을 받는 인간으로 / 기술의 도움으로

Our jobs become enriched / by relying on robots to do the tedious / while we work on increasingly more sophisticated tasks.
우리의 일은 질이 높아지게 된다. / 지루한 일은 로봇이 하리라 믿고 / 그 동안 우리는 점점 더 정교한 과업을 수행함으로써

컨설턴트 회사 McKinsey에 따르면, 지식 노동자는 정보를 찾고, 이메일에 답장하며, 다른 사람들과 협력하는 데 자신들의 시간 중 60퍼센트까지 사용한다.

(C) 사회 공학적 기술을 이용함으로써, 그런 노동자들은 25퍼센트까지 생산성이 더 높아질 수 있다. 더 열심히 그리고 더 오래 일하는 것을 통한 생산성 증진의 필요성에는 한계가 있고 사람들의 희생이 따른다.

(B) 해결책은 사람들이 향상된 수준에서 업무를 할 수 있도록 그냥 말만 함으로써가 아니라 스마트 기기와 개선된 과정을 가동함으로써 사람들이 더 스마트하게 일할 수 있게 해 주는 것이다.

(A) 그것을 기술의 도움으로 막강한 힘을 부여받은, 로봇의 도움을 받는 인간으로 생각해 보라. 지루한 일은 로봇이 하리라 믿고 그 동안 우리는 점점 더 정교한 과업을 수행함으로써 우리의 일은 질이 높아지게 된다.

Why? 왜 정답일까?

주어진 글에서 지식 노동자는 정보를 찾고 이메일에 답장하고 타인과 협력하는 데에만 이미 업무 시간의 60퍼센트를 쓴다는 내용을 말한 데 이어, (C)에서는 사회 공학적 기술의 도움이 있으면 '그런 노동자'들의 생산성이 더 높아질 수 있음을 말한다. 'The solution is ~'로 시작하는 (B)에서는 스마트 기기의 도입과 개선된 (업무) 과정 도입 등이 실질적인 해결책일 것임을 피력하고, (A)에서는 기술이 지루한 일을 대신해 주고 인간이 더 정교한 과업을 수행할 수 있게 되면 업무의 질이 높아질 것이라는 결론을 제시한다. 따라서 글의 순서로 가장 적절한 것은 ⑤ '(C) – (B) – (A)'이다.

- consulting firm 컨설턴트 회사
- collaborate ⓥ 협력하다
- aid ⓝ 도움
- rely ⓥ 의지하다
- smart tool 스마트 기기
- enhance ⓥ 향상시키다
- gain ⓝ 증진, 얻는 것
- respond ⓥ 답장하다
- assist ⓥ 돕다
- enrich ⓥ 질을 높이다, 풍요롭게 하다
- sophisticated ⓐ 정교한
- put ~ in place ~을 가동하다
- productive ⓐ 생산성이 높은, 생산적인
- toll ⓝ 희생

구문 풀이

6행 Our jobs become enriched / by relying on robots to do the tedious / while we work on increasingly more sophisticated tasks.
(「rely on+목적어+to부정사: ~이 …할 것을 믿다」 / while: 시간 접속사(~하는 동안) / more sophisticated: 비교급)

★★ 문제 해결 꿀~팁 ★★

▶ 많이 틀린 이유는?
최다 오답이 ④임을 고려할 때, (B)에 이어 (A)를 연결할 근거를 찾는 것이 문제 풀이의 핵심임을 알 수 있다. (C)에서 '문제' 상황을 언급하므로 이에 대한 해결책을 (B)에서 먼저 제시하고, 구체적인 예를 들어 해결책을 지지하는 (A)를 마지막에 배치하는 것이 적절하다.
▶ 문제 해결 방법은?
학생으로서 생소한 '스마트 워크'의 개념을 다룬 글이지만, '문제–해결'의 흐름, 지시사(C)의 those workers, (A)의 it) 등에 유의한다면 답을 쉽게 찾을 수 있다.

★★★ 1등급 대비 고난도 3점 문제

12 행동에 관한 경제학적 관점 정답률 31% | 정답 ③

주어진 글 다음에 이어질 글의 순서로 가장 적절한 것을 고르시오. [3점]

① (A) – (C) – (B) ② (B) – (A) – (C)
③ (B) – (C) – (A) ✔ ④ (C) – (A) – (B)
⑤ (C) – (B) – (A)

To an economist / who succeeds in figuring out a person's preference structure / — understanding whether the satisfaction gained from consuming one good / is greater than that of another — / explaining behavior / in terms of changes in underlying likes and dislikes / is usually highly problematic.
경제학자에게 있어, / 한 사람의 선호도 구조를 알아내는 것에 성공한 / 즉 한 상품을 소비하여 얻는 만족도가 ~한지 아닌지를 이해하는 데 성공한 / 또 다른 상품을 소비하여 얻는 만족도보다 더 큰지를 / 행동을 설명하는 것은 / 기저에 있는 호불호의 변화 측면에서 / 대체로 아주 문제가 많다.

(B) To argue, / for instance, / that the baby boom and then the baby bust / resulted from an increase and then a decrease / in the public's inherent taste for children, / rather than a change in relative prices / against a background of stable preferences, / places a social scientist in an unsound position.
주장하는 것은 / 예를 들어 / 베이비 붐과 그 이후의 출생률 급락이 / 증가 후 감소에서 비롯되었다고 / 아기에 대한 대중의 내재적 선호의 / 상대적 비용의 변화보다는 / 변동 없는 선호도를 배경으로 한 / 사회과학자를 불안정한 입지에 둔다.

[문제편 p.088]

(C) In economics, / such an argument about birth rates / would be equivalent to saying / that a rise and fall in mortality / could be attributed to an increase / in the inherent desire change for death.
경제학에서 / 출생률에 대한 그러한 주장은 / 말하는 것과 같다. / 사망률의 상승과 하락이 / 증가에서 비롯된다고 / 죽음에 대한 내재적 욕구 변화의
For an economist, / changes in income and prices, / rather than changes in tastes, / affect birth rates.
경제학자에게는 / 소득과 물가의 변화가 / 기호의 변화보다는 / 출생률에 영향을 미친다.
(A) When income rises, / for example, / people want more children / (or, as you will see later, / more satisfaction derived from children), / even if their inherent desire for children / stays the same.
소득이 증가할 때 / 예를 들어 / 사람들은 더 많은 자녀를 원한다. / (또는 여러분이 나중에 알게 되겠지만, / 아이로부터 오는 더 큰 만족감) / 자녀에 대한 내재적 욕구가 / 그대로 유지되더라도

한 사람의 선호도 구조를 알아내는 것, 즉 한 상품을 소비하여 얻는 만족도가 또 다른 상품을 소비하여 얻는 만족도보다 더 큰지를 이해하는 데 성공한 경제학자에게 있어, 행동을 기저에 있는 호불호의 변화 측면에서 설명하는 것은 대체로 아주 문제가 많다.

(B) 예를 들어 베이비 붐과 그 이후의 출생률 급락이 변동 없는 선호도를 배경으로 한 상대적 비용의 변화보다는, 아기에 대한 대중의 내재적 선호가 증가했다가 이후 떨어진 것에서 비롯되었다고 주장하는 것은 사회과학자를 불안정한 입지에 둔다.

(C) 경제학에서 출생률에 대한 그러한 주장은 사망률의 상승과 하락이 죽음에 대한 내재적 욕구 변화의 증가에서 비롯된다고 말하는 것과 같다. 경제학자에게는 기호의 변화보다는 소득과 물가의 변화가 출생률에 영향을 미친다.

(A) 예를 들어 소득이 증가할 때 사람들은 자녀에 대한 내재적 욕구가 그대로 유지되더라도 더 많은 자녀(또는 여러분이 나중에 알게 되겠지만, 아이로부터 오는 더 큰 만족감)를 원한다.

Why? 왜 정답일까?

경제학적으로 볼 때 선호도 변화로 행동을 설명하는 것은 문제가 있다는 주어진 글에 이어, **(B)**는 베이비 붐 시대의 인구 증가와 그 이후 세대의 인구 감소를 설명할 때를 예로 든다. **(C)**는 **(B)**에서 소개되었듯이 아기에 대한 대중의 선호 변화라는 관점에서 인구 증감을 설명하는 '그러한 주장'이 경제학적으로 타당하지 않다는 내용을 제시한다. 마지막으로 **(A)**는 **(C)**의 마지막 부분에서 언급되었듯이, 선호도보다는 '소득'의 변화가 출산율에 영향을 미칠 수 있음을 구체적 사례로 설명한다. 따라서 글의 순서로 가장 적절한 것은 ③ '**(B) – (C) – (A)**'이다.

- **underlying** ⓐ 기저에 있는
- **income** ⓝ 소득, 수입
- **baby boom** 베이비 붐
- **stable** ⓐ 안정된
- **be equivalent to** ~와 같다
- **mortality** ⓝ 사망률
- **like and dislikes** 호불호
- **inherent** ⓐ 내재된
- **baby bust** 출생률 급감
- **unsound** ⓐ 불안정한, 불건전한
- **rise and fall** 증감, 흥망성쇠
- **be attributed to** ~에서 비롯되다

구문 풀이

1행 To an economist [who succeeds in figuring out a person's preference structure] — understanding {whether the satisfaction gained from consuming one good} is greater than that of another — explaining behavior in terms of changes in underlying likes and dislikes is usually highly problematic.
(주격 관계대명사: who / 동명사 주어1: understanding / { }: 명사절(~인지 아닌지) / 동사1: is / 동명사 주어2: explaining / 동사2: is)

★★ 문제 해결 꿀~팁 ★★

▶ 많이 틀린 이유는?
④는 정답과 마찬가지로 **(C) – (A)**를 잘 연결했지만 **(B)**를 맨 뒤에 배치했는데, 이는 적절한 선택이 아니다. 주어진 글에서 '출생률에 관한 주장'을 다루지 않았는데, **(C)**에서는 '그러한 주장'을 언급하기 때문이다. 이 주장을 언급한 단락은 **(B)**이다. 따라서 **(B)**가 먼저 배치된 후 '그러한 주장'에 관해 평가하는 **(C)**를 배치하는 것이 옳다.
▶ 문제 해결 방법은?
어떤 두 단락이 인접하다면, 앞 단락의 마지막 부분에서 언급된 내용이 뒷 단락의 처음 부분에서 다시 언급된다. 가령 **(C)**의 첫 문장에서 '출생률에 관한 그러한 주장'을 언급하려면 앞에 '베이비 붐, 출산율'과 관련된 '주장'을 제시하는 **(B)**가 나와야 하는 식이다.

DAY 14 글의 순서 04

01 ②	02 ④	03 ②	04 ②	05 ⑤
06 ③	07 ②	08 ③	09 ⑤	10 ⑤
11 ①	12 ②			

01 logos와 mythos의 관계

정답률 55% | 정답 ②

주어진 글 다음에 이어질 글의 순서로 가장 적절한 것을 고르시오.

① (A) – (C) – (B)
② (B) – (A) – (C)
③ (B) – (C) – (A)
④ (C) – (A) – (B)
⑤ (C) – (B) – (A)

The ancient Greeks / used to describe two very different ways of thinking / — *logos* and *mythos*.
고대 그리스인들은 / 두 가지의 매우 다른 사고방식을 설명하곤 했다. / *logos*와 *mythos*라는
Logos roughly referred to / the world of the logical, the empirical, the scientific.
*logos*는 대략 ~을 지칭했다. / 논리적, 경험적, 과학적 세계
(B) *Mythos* referred to / the world of dreams, storytelling and symbols.
*mythos*는 ~을 지칭했다. / 꿈, 스토리텔링, 상징의 세계
Like many rationalists today, / some philosophers of Greece prized *logos* / and looked down at *mythos*.
오늘날의 많은 합리주의자처럼, / 그리스의 일부 철학자들은 *logos*를 높이 평가하고 / *mythos*를 경시했다.
Logic and reason, / they concluded, / make us modern; / storytelling and mythmaking are primitive.
논리와 이성은 / 그들은 결론지었다. / 우리를 현대적으로 만들고, / 스토리텔링과 신화 만들기는 원시적이라고
(A) But lots of scholars then and now / — including many anthropologists, sociologists and philosophers today — / see a more complicated picture, / where *mythos* and *logos* are intertwined and interdependent.
그러나 그때나 지금이나 많은 학자는 / 오늘날의 많은 인류학자, 사회학자, 철학자를 포함하여, / 더 복잡하게 상황을 이해하는데, / *mythos*와 *logos*는 뒤얽혀 있고 상호 의존적이라는 것이다.
Science itself, / according to this view, / relies on stories.
과학 자체가 / 이 관점에 따르면 / 이야기에 의존한다.
(C) The frames and metaphors / we use to understand the world / shape the scientific discoveries we make; / they even shape what we see.
생각의 틀과 은유는 / 우리가 세상을 이해하기 위해 사용하는 / 우리가 하는 과학적 발견을 형성하고, / 그것은 심지어 우리가 보는 것을 형성한다.
When our frames and metaphors change, / the world itself is transformed.
우리의 생각의 틀과 은유가 바뀌면 / 세상 자체가 변한다.
The Copernican Revolution / involved more than just scientific calculation; / it involved a new story / about the place of Earth in the universe.
코페르니쿠스 혁명은 / 단순한 과학적 계산보다 더 많은 것을 포함하는데, / 그것은 새로운 이야기를 포함했다. / 우주 속 지구의 위치에 관한

고대 그리스인들은 *logos*와 *mythos*라는 두 가지의 매우 다른 사고방식을 설명하곤 했다. *logos*는 대략 논리적, 경험적, 과학적 세계를 지칭했다.

(B) *mythos*는 꿈, 스토리텔링, 상징의 세계를 지칭했다. 오늘날의 많은 합리주의자처럼, 그리스의 일부 철학자들은 *logos*를 높이 평가하고 *mythos*를 경시했다. 그들은 논리와 이성이 우리를 현대적으로 만들고, 스토리텔링과 신화 만들기를 원시적이라고 결론지었다.

(A) 그러나 오늘날의 많은 인류학자, 사회학자, 철학자를 포함하여, 그때나 지금이나 많은 학자는 더 복잡하게 상황을 이해하는데, *mythos*와 *logos*는 뒤얽혀 있고 상호 의존적이라는 것이다. 이 관점에 따르면 과학 자체가 이야기에 의존한다.

(C) 우리가 세상을 이해하기 위해 사용하는 생각의 틀과 은유는 우리의 과학적 발견을 형성하고, 심지어 우리가 보는 것을 형성한다. 우리 생각의 틀과 은유가 바뀌면 세상 자체가 변한다. 코페르니쿠스 혁명은 단순한 과학적 계산보다 더 많은 것을 포함하는데, 우주 속 지구의 위치에 관한 새로운 이야기를 포함했다.

Why? 왜 정답일까?

주어진 글은 고대 그리스의 **logos**와 **mythos** 개념을 언급한 후, 먼저 **logos**가 무엇을 지칭하는지 설명한다. **(B)**는 이어서 **mythos**가 지칭하는 바를 설명한 뒤, 그리스의 철학자들 사이에서는 **logos**가 중시되고 **mythos**가 격하되었음을 언급한다. 한편 **(A)**는 **But**으로 흐름을 반전시키며, 오늘날 두 개념은 상호 의존적인 관계로 이해됨을 서술한

다. 마지막으로 (C)에서는 (A)의 마지막 문장에서 언급된, '과학 자체가 이야기에 의존한다'는 내용을 보충 설명한다. 따라서 글의 순서로 가장 적절한 것은 ② '(B) – (A) – (C)'이다.

- anthropologist ⓝ 인류학자
- intertwined ⓐ 뒤얽힌
- rely on ~에 의존하다
- look down at ~을 경시하다
- metaphor ⓝ 은유
- complicated ⓐ 복잡한
- interdependent ⓐ 상호 의존적인
- rationalist ⓝ 합리주의자
- primitive ⓐ 원시적인
- calculation ⓝ 계산

구문 풀이

5행 But lots of scholars then and now — (including many anthropologists, sociologists and philosophers today) — see a more complicated picture, where *mythos* and *logos* are intertwined and inter-dependent.
삽입구 / 선행사(공간) / 계속적 용법

02 새로운 정보의 원천이 될 수 있는 약한 유대관계
정답률 61% | 정답 ④

주어진 글 다음에 이어질 글의 순서로 가장 적절한 것을 고르시오.

① (A) – (C) – (B)
② (B) – (A) – (C)
③ (B) – (C) – (A)
✔(④) (C) – (A) – (B)
⑤ (C) – (B) – (A)

Mark Granovetter examined the extent / to which information about jobs / flowed through weak versus strong ties / among a group of people.
Mark Granovetter는 정도를 조사했다. / 직업에 대한 정보가 / 약한 유대관계 대비 강한 유대관계를 통해 유입되는 / 한 무리의 사람들 사이에서

(C) He found / that only a sixth of jobs that came via the network / were from strong ties, / with the rest coming via medium or weak ties; / and with more than a quarter coming via weak ties.
그는 발견했다. / 관계망을 통해 오는 직업의 6분의 1만이 / 강한 유대관계로부터 오며 / 나머지는 중간이나 약한 유대관계를 통해 오고 / 4분의 1 이상이 약한 유대관계로부터 온다는 것을

Strong ties can be more homophilistic.
강한 유대관계는 더 동족친화적일 수 있다.

Our closest friends are often those / who are most like us.
우리의 가장 친한 친구들은 종종 사람들이다. / 우리와 가장 비슷한

(A) This means / that they might have information / that is most relevant to us, / but it also means / that it is information / to which we may already be exposed.
이것은 의미하지만 / 그들이 정보를 가지고 있을지 모른다는 것을 / 우리와 가장 관련 있는 / 또한 이는 의미한다. / 그것이 정보라는 것을 / 우리가 이미 접하고 있을지도 모르는

In contrast, / our weaker relationships are often with people / who are more distant both geographically and demographically.
대조적으로, / 우리의 더 약한 인간 관계는 종종 사람들을 상대로 한다. / 지리적으로나 인구통계학적으로나 더 먼

(B) Their information is more novel.
그들의 정보는 더 새롭다.

Even though we talk to these people less frequently, / we have so many weak ties / that they end up being a sizable source of information, / especially of information to which we don't otherwise have access.
우리는 이러한 사람들과 덜 빈번하게 이야기를 하지만, / 우리는 매우 많은 약한 유대관계를 가지고 있어서 / 결국 그것이 정보의 엄청난 원천이 된다. / 특히 우리가 그렇지 않다면 접근하지 못하는 정보의

Mark Granovetter는 한 무리의 사람들 사이에서 직업에 대한 정보가 약한 유대관계 대비 강한 유대관계를 통해 유입되는 정도를 조사했다.

(C) 그는 관계망을 통해 오는 직업의 6분의 1만이 강한 유대관계로부터 오며 나머지는 중간이나 약한 유대관계를 통해 오고 4분의 1 이상이 약한 유대관계로부터 온다는 것을 발견했다. 강한 유대관계는 더 동족친화적일 수 있다. 우리의 가장 친한 친구들은 종종 우리와 가장 비슷한 사람들이다.

(A) 이것은 그들이 우리와 가장 관련 있는 정보를 가지고 있을지 모른다는 것을 의미하지만 또한 이는 그것이 우리가 이미 접하고 있을지도 모르는 정보라는 것을 의미한다. 대조적으로, 우리의 더 약한 인간관계는 종종 지리적으로나 인구통계학적으로나 더 먼 사람들을 상대로 한다.

(B) 그들의 정보는 더 새롭다. 우리는 이러한 사람들과 덜 빈번하게 이야기를 하지만, 우리는 매우 많은 약한 유대관계를 가지고 있어서 결국 그것이 정보, 특히 우리가 그렇지 않다면 접근하지 못하는 정보의 엄청난 원천이 된다.

Why? 왜 정답일까?

주어진 글에서 한 연구자가 약한 유대관계와 강한 유대관계에서 각각 직업에 관한 정보가 유입되는 정도를 조사했다고 언급한 데 이어, (C)는 연구자를 He로 받으며 그가 밝힌 결과를 제시한다. 특히 (C)의 후반부에서는 결과의 이유를 밝히기 위해 강한 유대관계의 특성부터 설명하며, 흔히 가장 친한 친구들은 자신과 가장 비슷하기 마련이라고 언급하는데, (A)에서는 바로 그렇기 때문에 이들(they)로부터 오는 정보는 우리가 이미 알고 있는 정보일 수 있음을 지적한다. 이어서 (A)의 후반부에서는 약한 인간관계의 특성을 언급하고, (B)에서는 이들을 Their로 받으며 이들이 우리와 더 '멀기' 때문에 이들이 가진 정보가 오히려 더 새롭다는 점을 상기시킨다. 따라서 글의 순서로 가장 적절한 것은 ④ '(C) – (A) – (B)'이다.

- examine ⓥ 조사하다
- geographically ad 지리적으로
- frequently ad 자주
- otherwise ad 그렇지 않으면
- relevant ⓐ 관련 있는
- novel ⓐ 새로운, 신기한
- sizable ⓐ (크기 등이) 상당한
- have access to ~에 접근하다

구문 풀이

10행 Even though we talk to these people less frequently, we have so many weak ties that they end up being a sizable source of information, especially of information [to which we don't otherwise have access].
접속사(~에도 불구하고) / 「so ~ that …: 너무 ~해서 …하다」 / 결국 ~하게 되다 / 선행사 / 「전치사+관계대명사」

03 환경 변화에 따른 순응 작용
정답률 74% | 정답 ②

주어진 글 다음에 이어질 글의 순서로 가장 적절한 것을 고르시오.

① (A) – (C) – (B)
✔(②) (B) – (A) – (C)
③ (B) – (C) – (A)
④ (C) – (A) – (B)
⑤ (C) – (B) – (A)

When a change in the environment occurs, / there is a relative increase or decrease in the rate / at which the neurons fire, / which is how intensity is coded.
환경에서 변화가 일어날 때, / 속도에서의 상대적인 증가나 감소가 있는데, / 뉴런이 발화하는 / 이것이 강도가 암호화되는 방법이다.

Furthermore, / relativity operates / to calibrate our sensations.
게다가 / 상대성은 작용한다. / 우리의 감각을 조정하기 위해

(B) For example, / if you place one hand in hot water / and the other in iced water / for some time / before immersing them both / into lukewarm water, / you will experience conflicting sensations of temperature / because of the relative change in the receptors / registering hot and cold.
예를 들어, / 만약 당신이 한 손을 뜨거운 물에 넣고, / 다른 한 손을 얼음물에 담가두면, / 얼마간 / 두 손을 담가두기 전 / 미지근한 물에 / 당신은 온도 감각이 상충하는 것을 경험할 것이다. / 수용체들의 상대적인 변화 때문에 / 뜨거운 것과 차가운 것을 인식하는

(A) Although both hands are now in the same water, / one feels / that it is colder / and the other feels warmer / because of the relative change / from prior experience.
비록 지금은 두 손이 같은 물속에 있지만, / 한 손은 느낀다 / 더 차갑게 / 그리고 다른 손은 더 따뜻하게 느낀다. / 상대적인 변화 때문에 / 이전 경험으로부터의

This process, called *adaptation*, / is one of the organizing principles / operating throughout the central nervous system.
*순응*이라고 불리는 이 과정은 / 작동 원리 중 하나이다. / 중추신경계 전반에 걸쳐 작용하는

(C) It explains / why you can't see well inside a dark room / if you have come in from a sunny day.
그것은 설명한다. / 당신이 왜 어두운 방 안에서 잘 볼 수 없는지를 / 당신이 햇볕이 쨍쨍한 날에 실내로 들어온다면

Your eyes have to become accustomed / to the new level of luminance.
당신의 눈은 익숙해져야 한다. / 새로운 수준의 밝기에

Adaptation explains / why apples taste sour / after eating sweet chocolate / and why traffic seems louder in the city / if you normally live in the country.
순응은 설명한다. / 왜 사과가 신맛이 나는지 / 달콤한 초콜릿을 먹은 후 / 그리고 왜 도시에서 교통이 더 시끄러운 것 같은지를 / 만약 당신이 보통 때는 시골에 산다면

환경에서 변화가 일어날 때, 뉴런이 발화하는 속도에서의 상대적인 증가나 감소가 있는데, 이것이 강도가 암호화되는 방법이다. 게다가 상대성은 우리의 감각을 조정하기 위해 작용한다.

(B) 예를 들어, 당신이 두 손을 미지근한 물에 담그기 전 얼마간 한 손을 뜨거운 물에, 다른 한 손을 얼음물에 담가두면, 뜨거운 것과 차가운 것을 인식하는 수용체들의 상대적인 변화 때문에 온도 감각이 상충하는 것을 경험할 것이다.

(A) 비록 지금은 두 손이 같은 물속에 있지만, 이전 경험으로부터의 상대적인 변화 때문에 한 손은 더 차갑게 느끼고 다른 손은 더 따뜻하게 느낀다. 순응

이라고 불리는 이 과정은 중추신경계 전반에 걸쳐 작용하는 작동 원리 중 하나이다.

(C) 그것은 당신이 햇볕이 쨍쨍한 날에 실내로 들어온다면, 왜 어두운 방 안에서 잘 볼 수 없는지를 설명한다. 당신의 눈은 새로운 수준의 밝기에 익숙해져야 한다. 순응은 달콤한 초콜릿을 먹은 후 왜 사과가 신맛이 나는지와 만약 당신이 보통 때는 시골에 산다면 왜 도시에서 교통이 더 시끄러운 것 같은지를 설명한다.

Why? 왜 정답일까?

환경에 변화가 일어날 때 우리의 감각을 조정하고자 상대성이 작용하기 시작한다는 내용을 언급한 주어진 글 뒤에는, 두 손을 똑같이 미지근한 물에 넣기 전 한 손은 차가운 물에, 다른 손은 뜨거운 물에 담가두었다면 서로 다른 감각을 느낄 것이라는 내용의 (B)가 연결된다. 이어서 (A)는 이전 경험의 차이로 인해 같은 대상도 다르게 경험하게 되는 이러한 현상을 '순응'이라는 용어로 정리할 수 있다고 설명한다. 마지막으로 (C)에서는 순응의 다양한 예를 추가로 들고 있다. 따라서 글의 순서로 가장 적절한 것은 ② '(B) – (A) – (C)'이다.

- intensity ⓝ 강도
- sensation ⓝ (자극을 받아서 느끼는) 감각
- immerse ⓥ (액체 속에) 담그다
- conflicting ⓐ 상충하는, 모순되는
- register ⓥ 인식하다, 알아채다, 등록하다
- normally ⓐ𝖽 보통
- relativity ⓝ 상대성
- adaptation ⓝ 순응, 적응
- lukewarm ⓐ 미지근한
- receptor ⓝ 수용체
- accustomed to ~에 익숙한

구문 풀이

1행 When a change in the environment occurs, there is
접속사(~할 때) 주어 자동사 동사(단수)
a relative increase or decrease in the rate [at which the neurons
주어 선행사 「전치사+관·대」
fire], which is how intensity is coded.
계속적 용법(주절 보충)

04 성인의 비형식적 학습 정답률 64% | 정답 ②

주어진 글 다음에 이어질 글의 순서로 가장 적절한 것을 고르시오.

① (A) – (C) – (B) ✔(B) – (A) – (C)
③ (B) – (C) – (A) ④ (C) – (A) – (B)
⑤ (C) – (B) – (A)

A researcher in adult education at the University of Toronto, / Allen Tough wrote a paper / called "The Iceberg of Informal Adult Learning."
Toronto 대학에서 성인 교육 연구자인 / Allen Tough가 논문을 썼다. / '비형식적 성인 학습의 빙산'이라는

Tough formulated a reverse 20/80 rule / for adult learning.
Tough는 정반대의 20/80 규칙을 만들어 냈다. / 성인 학습에 대해

(B) Twenty percent of an adult learner's efforts were formal, / organized by an institution.
성인 학습자들의 노력의 20퍼센트는 형식적인 것이었다. / 기관에 의해 조직된

Eighty percent was informal, / organized by the learner.
80퍼센트는 비형식적인 것이었다. / 학습자에 의해 조직된

He used the metaphor of an iceberg / to describe the large portion of learning, informal learning, / that remains invisible.
그는 빙산의 비유를 사용했다. / 학습의 커다란 부분인 비형식적 학습을 설명하기 위해 / 눈에 보이지 않은 채로 남아 있는

(A) Tough researched the reasons / why people chose to learn on their own / rather than attend a class.
Tough는 이유를 연구했다. / 사람들이 스스로 학습하는 것을 선택한 / 수업을 듣는 것보다

"People seem to want to be in control," he wrote.
"사람들은 주도권을 잡고 싶어 하는 것처럼 보인다."라고 그는 썼다.

"They want to set their own pace / and use their own style of learning; / they want to keep it flexible."
"그들은 자신만의 속도를 정하고 / 자신만의 학습 스타일을 사용하고 싶어 하며, / 그것을 융통성 있게 유지하고 싶어 한다."

(C) People also seem to consider informal learning / experiential and social.
사람들은 또한 비형식적 학습을 간주하는 것처럼 보인다. / 경험적이고 사회적인 것으로

Lifelong learning organized around one's interests / might be seen as a new form of recreation.
한 사람의 관심사에 맞춰 조직된 평생의 학습은 / 오락 활동의 새로운 형태로 보일지도 모른다.

Toronto 대학에서 성인 교육 연구자인 Allen Tough가 '비형식적 성인 학습의 빙산'이라는 논문을 썼다. Tough는 성인 학습에 대해 정반대의 20/80 규칙을 만들어 냈다.

(B) 성인 학습자들의 노력의 20퍼센트는 기관에 의해 조직된 형식적인 것이었다. 80퍼센트는 학습자에 의해 조직된 비형식적인 것이었다. 그는 눈에 보이지 않은 채로 남아 있는, 학습의 커다란 부분인 비형식적 학습을 설명하기 위해 빙산의 비유를 사용했다.

(A) Tough는 사람들이 수업을 듣는 것보다 스스로 학습하는 것을 선택한 이유를 연구했다. "사람들은 주도권을 잡고 싶어 하는 것처럼 보인다."라고 그는 썼다. "그들은 자신만의 속도를 정하고 자신만의 학습 스타일을 사용하고 싶어 하며, 그것을 융통성 있게 유지하고 싶어 한다."

(C) 사람들은 또한 비형식적 학습을 경험적이고 사회적인 것으로 간주하는 것처럼 보인다. 한 사람의 관심사에 맞춰 조직된 평생의 학습은 오락 활동의 새로운 형태로 보일지도 모른다.

Why? 왜 정답일까?

주어진 글에서 성인 학습과 관련한 20/80 규칙을 언급한 데 이어, (B)에서는 20과 80이 각각 형식적 학습, 비형식적 학습과 관련된 수치임을 설명한다. (A)에서는 본격적으로 연구의 구체적인 내용으로서 사람들이 비형식적 학습을 선택한 이유를 설명하고, (C)에서는 also라는 부사를 통해 비형식적 학습에 대한 사람들의 생각 내용을 덧붙여 나간다. 따라서 글의 순서로 가장 적절한 것은 ② '(B) – (A) – (C)'이다.

- iceberg ⓝ 빙산
- formulate ⓥ (공식 등을) 만들다
- attend ⓥ 참석하다, 출석하다
- metaphor ⓝ 비유, 은유
- invisible ⓐ 눈에 보이지 않는, 비가시적인
- informal ⓐ 비형식적인, 비공식적인
- reverse ⓐ 정반대의
- in control 주도권을 잡고 있는
- organize ⓥ 조직하다, 준비하다, 정리하다
- experiential ⓐ 경험적인

구문 풀이

5행 Tough researched the reasons [why people chose {to learn
관계부사
on their own} rather than {attend a class}].
「{A} rather than {B} : B라기보다 A」

05 직감을 기반으로 한 주식 투자 선택 정답률 50% | 정답 ⑤

주어진 글 다음에 이어질 글의 순서로 가장 적절한 것을 고르시오.

① (A) – (C) – (B) ② (B) – (A) – (C)
③ (B) – (C) – (A) ④ (C) – (A) – (B)
✔(C) – (B) – (A)

Many years ago / I visited the chief investment officer of a large financial firm, / who had just invested some tens of millions of dollars / in the stock of the ABC Motor Company.
수년 전에 / 나는 한 큰 금융회사의 최고 투자 책임자를 방문했는데, / 그는 수천만 달러 상당의 돈을 투자했었다. / ABC Motor Company의 주식에

(C) When I asked how he had made that decision, / he replied / that he had recently attended an automobile show / and had been impressed.
내가 어떻게 그가 그러한 결정을 하게 되었는지를 묻자, / 그는 대답했다. / 그가 최근에 자동차 쇼에 참석했고 / 깊은 인상을 받았다고

He said, / "Boy, they do know how to make a car!"
그는 말했다. / "세상에, 그들은 자동차를 만드는 법을 알더라니까!"라고

(B) His response made it very clear / that he trusted his gut feeling / and was satisfied with himself and with his decision.
그의 반응은 분명히 했다. / 그가 자신의 직감을 믿으며, / 스스로와 자기 결정에 만족한다는 것을

I found it remarkable / that he had apparently not considered the one question / that an economist would call relevant: Is the ABC stock currently underpriced?
나는 놀랍다고 생각했다. / 그가 한 가지 질문을 명백하게도 고려하지 않았다는 것이 / 경제학자들이 적절하다고 할 만한 / 'ABC 주식이 현재 저평가되었는가?'

(A) Instead, he had listened to his intuition; / he liked the cars, he liked the company, / and he liked the idea of owning its stock.
대신에, 그는 그의 직감을 믿었는데, / 그는 자동차를 좋아하고, 그 회사를 좋아하며, / 그 회사의 주식을 소유한다는 생각이 좋았다.

From what we know about the accuracy of stock picking, / it is reasonable to believe / that he did not know what he was doing.
주식 선택의 정확성에 대해 우리가 알고 있는 것에 비추어볼 때, / 믿는 것이 당연하다. / 그가 자신이 무엇을 하고 있는지를 몰랐다고

수년 전에 나는 한 큰 금융회사의 최고 투자 책임자를 방문했는데, 그는 ABC Motor Company의 주식에 수천만 달러 상당의 돈을 투자했었다.

(C) 내가 어떻게 그가 그러한 결정을 하게 되었는지를 묻자, 그는 최근에 자동차 쇼에 참석했고 깊은 인상을 받았다고 대답했다. 그는 "세상에, 그들은 자동차를 만드는 법을 알더라니까!"라고 말했다.

(B) 그의 반응은 그가 자신의 직감을 믿으며, 스스로와 자기 결정에 만족한다는 것을 분명히 했다. 나는 그가 경제학자들이 적절하다고 할 만한 한 가지 질문인, 'ABC 주식이 현재 저평가되었는가?'를 명백하게도 고려하지 않았다는 것이 놀랍다고 생각했다.

(A) 대신에, 그는 그의 직감을 믿었는데, 그는 자동차를 좋아하고, 그 회사를 좋아하며, 그 회사의 주식을 소유한다는 생각이 좋았다. 주식 선택의 정확성에 대해 우리가 알고 있는 것에 비추어볼 때, 그가 자신이 무엇을 하고 있는지를 몰랐다고 믿는 것이 당연하다.

Why? 왜 정답일까?

필자가 특정 자동차 회사 주식에 큰돈을 투자한 적이 있는 금융회사 사람을 만났다는 내용의 주어진 글 뒤에는, 필자가 그에게 투자의 이유에 관해 묻는 (C), 그가 중요한 경제학적 질문을 고려하지 않았음을 언급하는 (B), 대신에 그는 직감에 바탕을 두고 투자 결정을 했었음을 밝히는 (A)가 차례로 이어지는 것이 적절하다. 따라서 글의 순서로 가장 적절한 것은 ⑤ '(C) – (B) – (A)'이다.

- investment ⓝ 투자
- own ⓥ 소유하다
- accuracy ⓝ 정확성
- satisfied ⓐ 만족한
- apparently ad 명백하게
- relevant ⓐ 적절한, 관련 있는
- underpriced ⓐ 가격이 너무 낮은, 제값을 못 받는
- intuition ⓝ 직감, 직관
- stock ⓝ 저장품
- reasonable ⓐ 타당한, 사리에 맞는
- remarkable ⓐ 놀라운, 놀랄만한
- economist ⓝ 경제학자
- currently ad 현재, 지금

구문 풀이

12행 I found it remarkable that he had apparently not considered the one question [that an economist would call relevant]: {Is the ABC stock currently underpriced?}

가목적어 / 목적격 보어 / 접속사 / 선행사 / 동사 / 목적격 보어 / { }: one question과 동격

06 이성적 판단 이면의 감정

정답률 65% | 정답 ③

주어진 글 다음에 이어질 글의 순서로 가장 적절한 것을 고르시오. [3점]

① (A) – (C) – (B)
② (B) – (A) – (C)
③ (B) – (C) – (A)
④ (C) – (A) – (B)
⑤ (C) – (B) – (A)

A common but incorrect assumption / is / that we are creatures of reason / when, in fact, we are creatures of both reason and emotion.
일반적이지만 잘못된 가정은 / ~이다 / 우리가 이성의 피조물이라는 것 / 사실 우리는 이성과 감정 둘 다의 피조물이다.

We cannot get by on reason alone / since any reason always eventually leads to a feeling.
우리는 이성만으로 살아갈 수 없다. / 어떤 이성도 항상 결국 감정으로 이어지기 때문에

Should I get a wholegrain cereal or a chocolate cereal?
내가 통곡물 시리얼을 선택해야 할까, 혹은 초콜릿 시리얼을 선택해야 할까?

(B) I can list all the reasons I want, / but the reasons have to be based on something.
나는 내가 원하는 모든 이유를 열거할 수 있지만, / 그 이유는 뭔가에 근거해야 한다.

For example, / if my goal is to eat healthy, / I can choose the wholegrain cereal, / but what is my reason / for wanting to be healthy?
예를 들어 / 나의 목표가 건강하게 먹는 것이라면 / 나는 통곡물 시리얼을 선택할 수 있지만, / 내 근거는 무엇일까? / 건강해지고 싶다는 것을 뒷받침하는

(C) I can list more and more reasons / such as wanting to live longer, / spending more quality time with loved ones, etc., / but what are the reasons / for those reasons?
나는 더 많은 이유를 나열할 수 있지만, / 더 오래 살고 싶은 것과 같은 / 사랑하는 사람들과 양질의 시간을 더 많이 보내고 싶은 것 등 / 이유는 무엇인가? / 그러한 이유를 뒷받침하는

You should be able to see by now / that reasons are ultimately based on non-reason / such as values, feelings, or emotions.
여러분은 이제 알 수 있을 것이다. / 이유가 궁극적으로 비이성에 근거한다는 것을 / 가치, 느낌, 또는 감정과 같은

(A) These deep-seated values, feelings, and emotions we have / are rarely a result of reasoning, / but can certainly be influenced by reasoning.
우리가 가진 이러한 뿌리 깊은 가치, 느낌, 감정은 / 추론의 산물인 경우가 거의 없지만, / 물론 추론의 영향을 받을 수 있다.

We have values, feelings, and emotions / before we begin to reason / and long before we begin to reason effectively.
우리는 가치, 느낌, 감정을 갖는다. / 우리가 추론을 시작하기 전에, / 우리가 추론을 효과적으로 시작하기 훨씬 전에

일반적이지만 잘못된 가정은 우리가 이성의 피조물이라는 것이지만, 사실 우리는 이성과 감정 둘 다의 피조물이다. 어떤 이성도 항상 결국 감정으로 이어지기 때문에 우리는 이성만으로 살아갈 수 없다. 내가 통곡물 시리얼을 선택해야 할까, 혹은 초콜릿 시리얼을 선택해야 할까?

(B) 나는 내가 원하는 모든 이유를 열거할 수 있지만, 그 이유는 뭔가에 근거해야 한다. 예를 들어 건강하게 먹는 것이 나의 목표라면 통곡물 시리얼을 선택할 수 있지만, 건강해지고 싶다는 것을 뒷받침하는 내 근거는 무엇일까?

(C) 나는 더 오래 살고 싶은 것, 사랑하는 사람들과 양질의 시간을 더 많이 보내고 싶은 것 등과 같은 더 많은 이유를 나열할 수 있지만, 그러한 이유를 뒷받침하는 이유는 무엇인가? 여러분은 이유가 궁극적으로 가치, 느낌, 또는 감정과 같은 비이성에 근거한다는 것을 이제 알 수 있을 것이다.

(A) 우리가 가진 이러한 뿌리 깊은 가치, 느낌, 감정은 추론의 산물인 경우가 거의 없지만, 물론 추론의 영향을 받을 수 있다. 우리는 추론을 시작하기 전에, (더 정확히는) 추론을 효과적으로 시작하기 훨씬 전에 가치, 느낌, 감정을 갖는다.

Why? 왜 정답일까?

주어진 글은 우리가 이성과 동시에 감정도 가진 존재임을 언급하며 선택의 상황을 예로 든다. 이어서 (B)는 주어진 글에서 언급된 선택 상황에 대해 근거를 생각해보자고 언급하고, (C)는 근거를 열거하다 보면 결국 그 이면에 '비이성'이 있다는 것을 알게 된다고 말한다. (A)는 (C) 후반부에서 언급된 비이성적 요소, 즉 가치관이나 느낌, 감정 등을 다시 언급하며 이런 것들이 우리가 이성적 추론을 시작하기 훨씬 앞서 자리잡고 있던 것임을 설명한다. 따라서 글의 순서로 가장 적절한 것은 ③ '(B) – (C) – (A)'이다.

- incorrect ⓐ 부정확한
- wholegrain ⓝ 통곡물
- effectively ad 효과적으로
- loved one 사랑하는 사람
- get by on ~로 그럭저럭 살아가다
- deep-seated ⓐ 뿌리 깊은
- live long 장수하다

구문 풀이

1행 A common but incorrect assumption is that we are creatures of reason when, (in fact), we are creatures of both reason and emotion.

접속사(~것) / 접속사(~할 때) / ( ): 삽입구

07 캐나다 이누이트족의 민족 정신 유지

정답률 43% | 정답 ②

주어진 글 다음에 이어질 글의 순서로 가장 적절한 것을 고르시오. [3점]

① (A) – (C) – (B)
② (B) – (A) – (C)
③ (B) – (C) – (A)
④ (C) – (A) – (B)
⑤ (C) – (B) – (A)

When trying to sustain an independent ethos, / cultures face a problem of critical mass.
독립적인 민족(사회) 정신을 유지하려고 할 때, / 문화는 임계 질량의 문제에 직면한다.

No single individual, / acting on his or her own, / can produce an ethos.
어떤 한 개인도 / 자신 혼자서 행동하는 / 민족 정신을 만들어 낼 수 없다.

(B) Rather, / an ethos results from the interdependent acts of many individuals.
오히려 / 민족 정신은 많은 개인의 상호의존적인 행위에서 비롯된다.

This cluster of produced meaning / may require some degree of insulation / from larger and wealthier outside forces.
생성된 의미의 이러한 군집은 / 어느 정도의 단절을 필요로 할 수 있다. / 더 크고 더 부유한 외부 세력으로부터

The Canadian Inuit maintain their own ethos, / even though they number no more than twenty-four thousand.
캐나다 이누이트족은 그들만의 민족 정신을 유지하고 있다. / 그들이 수는 비록 2만 4천 명에 불과하지만

(A) They manage this feat / through a combination of trade, / to support their way of life, / and geographic isolation.
그들은 이러한 업적을 해낸다. / 무역의 조합을 통해 / 그들의 삶을 유지하기 위해 / 지리적 고립과

The Inuit occupy remote territory, / removed from major population centers of Canada.
이누이트족은 멀리 떨어진 영토를 차지하고 있다. / 캐나다의 주요 인구 중심지에서 따로 떨어진

If cross-cultural contact were to become sufficiently close, / the Inuit ethos would disappear.
만약 문화 간 접촉이 충분히 긴밀해진다면, / 이누이트인들의 민족 정신이 사라지게 될 것이다.

(C) Distinct cultural groups of similar size do not, / in the long run, / persist in downtown Toronto, Canada, / where they come in contact with many outside influences / and pursue essentially Western paths for their lives.
비슷한 규모의 다른 문화 집단은 ~하지 않는데, / 결국 / 캐나다 토론토 도심에서는 지속되지 / 여기서 그들은 많은 외부 영향과 접촉하고 / 살아가기 위해 본질적으로 서구적 방식을 추구한다.

DAY 14

독립적인 민족(사회) 정신을 유지하려고 할 때, 문화는 임계 질량(바람직한 결과를 얻기 위해 필요한 양)의 문제에 직면한다. 자신 혼자서 행동하는 어떤 한 개인도 민족 정신을 만들어 낼 수 없다.

(B) 오히려 민족 정신은 많은 개인의 상호의존적인 행위에서 비롯된다. 생성된 의미의 이러한 군집은 더 크고 더 부유한 외부 세력으로부터 어느 정도의 단절을 필요로 할 수 있다. 캐나다 이누이트족은 비록 2만 4천 명에 불과하지만 그들만의 민족 정신을 유지하고 있다.

(A) 그들은 삶을 유지하기 위해 무역과 지리적 고립의 조합을 통해 이러한 업적을 해낸다. 이누이트족은 캐나다의 주요 인구 중심지에서 따로 멀리 떨어진 영토를 차지하고 있다. 만약 문화 간 접촉이 충분히 긴밀해진다면, 이누이트인들의 민족 정신이 사라지게 될 것이다.

(C) 비슷한 규모의 다른 문화 집단은 캐나다 토론토 도심에서는 결국 지속되지 않는데, 여기서 그들은 많은 외부 영향과 접촉하고 본질적으로 서구적 생활 방식을 추구한다.

Why? 왜 정답일까?

주어진 글에서는 독립적인 민족 정신을 유지하는 데 있어 임계 질량의 문제가 있다고 언급하며, 한 명의 구성원만 가지고는 민족 정신이 유지되지 않는다고 설명한다. 여기에 Rather로 연결되는 (B)는 한 명이 아닌 많은 개인의 상호의존적 행위가 필요하다고 언급하며 2만 4천 명 규모의 캐나다 이누이트족을 예로 든다. (A)는 이누이트족들이 어떻게 민족 정신을 유지하는지 설명한다. 마지막으로 (C)는 비슷한 규모의 다른 문화 집단은 이누이트족과는 달리 민족 정신을 유지하지 못하고 있음을 대비시켜 언급한다. 따라서 글의 순서로 가장 적절한 것은 ② '(B) – (A) – (C)'이다.

- sustain ⓥ 지속하다
- critical mass 임계 질량
- combination ⓝ 조합
- geographic ⓐ 지리적인
- occupy ⓥ 차지하다, 점유하다
- territory ⓝ 지역, 영토
- sufficiently ad 충분히
- cluster ⓝ 군집, 무리
- insulation ⓝ 단절, 절연
- persist ⓥ 지속하다
- pursue ⓥ 추구하다
- path ⓝ (행동) 계획[방식]
- independent ⓐ 독립된
- feat ⓝ 위업, 공적
- trade ⓝ 거래, 무역
- isolation ⓝ 고립
- remote ⓐ 외진, 외딴
- cross-cultural 여러 문화가 섞인
- disappear ⓥ (눈앞에서) 사라지다
- require ⓥ 필요[요구]하다, 필요로 하다
- distinct ⓐ 구별되는, 다른
- come in contact with ~와 접촉하다
- essentially ad 본질적으로

구문 풀이

8행 **If cross-cultural contact were to become sufficiently close,**
「if + 주어 + were to + 동사원형 ~
the Inuit ethos would disappear.
주어 + 조동사 과거형 + 동사원형 : 가정법 미래(가능성이 없거나 희박한 일 가정)」

08 운동 기술의 처리 및 내면화

정답률 43% | 정답 ③

주어진 글 다음에 이어질 글의 순서로 가장 적절한 것을 고르시오. [3점]

① (A) – (C) – (B)
② (B) – (A) – (C)
③ (B) – (C) – (A)
④ (C) – (A) – (B)
⑤ (C) – (B) – (A)

Brain research provides a framework / for understanding / how the brain processes and internalizes athletic skills.
뇌 연구는 틀을 제공한다. / 이해하기 위한 / 뇌가 어떻게 운동 기술을 처리하고 내면화하는지를

(B) In practicing a complex movement / such as a golf swing, / we experiment / with different grips, positions and swing movements, / analyzing each in terms of the results it yields.
복잡한 움직임을 연습할 때, / 골프채 휘두르기와 같은 / 우리는 실험하면서 / 다양한 잡기, 자세, 그리고 휘두르는 움직임으로 / 그것이 산출하는 결과의 관점에서 각각을 분석한다.

This is a conscious, left-brain process.
이것은 의식적인 좌뇌 과정이다.

(C) Once we identify those elements of the swing / that produce the desired results, / we rehearse them over and over again / in an attempt to record them permanently in "muscle memory."
일단 우리가 휘두르기의 그러한 요소들을 확인하면, / 원하는 결과를 만들어내는 / 우리는 그것들을 반복적으로 연습한다. / "근육 기억" 속에 그것들을 영구적으로 기록하려 시도하며

In this way, / we internalize the swing / as a kinesthetic feeling that we trust / to recreate the desired swing on demand.
이러한 방식으로, / 우리는 휘두르기를 내면화한다. / 우리가 의존하는 운동감각의 느낌으로서 / 필요할 때마다 언제든지 원하는 휘두르기를 다시 해내기 위해

(A) This internalization transfers the swing / from a consciously controlled left-brain function / to a more intuitive or automatic right-brain function.
이러한 내면화는 휘두르기를 전이시킨다. / 의식적으로 통제되는 좌뇌 기능에서 / 더 직관적이거나 자동화된 우뇌 기능으로

This description, / despite being an oversimplification of the actual processes involved, / serves as a model for the interaction / between conscious and unconscious actions in the brain, / as it learns to perfect an athletic skill.
이러한 설명은 / 관련된 실제 과정의 과도한 단순화에도 불구하고, / 상호 작용을 위한 모델로서 기능한다. / 뇌 속의 의식과 무의식 활동 사이의 / 그것이 운동 기술을 완벽히 하는 법을 배울 때

뇌 연구는 뇌가 어떻게 운동 기술을 처리하고 내면화하는지를 이해하기 위한 틀을 제공한다.

(B) 골프채 휘두르기와 같은 복잡한 움직임을 연습할 때, 우리는 다양한 잡기, 자세, 그리고 휘두르는 움직임으로 실험하면서 그것이 산출하는 결과의 관점에서 각각을 분석한다. 이것은 의식적인 좌뇌 과정이다.

(C) 일단 우리가 원하는 결과를 만들어내는 휘두르기의 그러한 요소들을 확인하면, 우리는 "근육 기억" 속에 그것들을 영구적으로 기록하려 시도하며 그것들을 반복적으로 연습한다. 이러한 방식으로, 우리는 필요할 때마다 언제든지 원하는 휘두르기를 다시 해내기 위해 우리가 의존하는 운동감각의 느낌으로서 휘두르기를 내면화한다.

(A) 이러한 내면화는 의식적으로 통제되는 좌뇌 기능에서 더 직관적이거나 자동화된 우뇌 기능으로 휘두르기를 전이시킨다. 관련된 실제 과정의 과도한 단순화에도 불구하고, 이러한 설명은 뇌가 운동 기술을 완벽히 하는 법을 배울 때 뇌 속의 의식과 무의식 활동 사이에 일어나는 상호 작용을 위한 모델로서 기능한다.

Why? 왜 정답일까?

운동 기술의 처리 및 내면화 과정을 화두로 제시한 주어진 글 뒤에는, 처음에 기술을 습득할 때에는 과정이 좌뇌에서 의식적으로 처리된다는 내용의 (B), 과정의 내면화를 위한 반복적인 연습이 일어난다는 내용의 (C), 내면화를 통해 기능이 우뇌로 전이된다는 내용의 (A)가 차례로 이어져야 한다. 따라서 글의 순서로 가장 적절한 것은 ③ '(B) – (C) – (A)'이다.

- internalize ⓥ 내면화하다
- transfer ⓥ 전이시키다, 옮기다
- intuitive ⓐ 직관적인
- serve as ~로 기능하다, ~의 역할을 하다
- experiment ⓥ 실험하다
- identify ⓥ 확인하다, 동일시하다
- on demand 요구만 있으면 (언제든)
- athletic ⓐ 운동의, 육상의
- consciously ad 의식적으로
- oversimplification ⓝ 과도한 단순화
- interaction ⓝ 상호작용
- yield ⓥ 산출하다
- permanently ad 영구적으로

구문 풀이

6행 **This description, despite being an oversimplification of the actual processes involved, serves as a model for the interaction between conscious and unconscious actions in the brain, as it learns to perfect an athletic skill.**
주어 / 전치사 / 동명사 / 동사(~로 기능하다) / 「between + A + and + B : A와 B 사이의」 / ~할 때, ~함에 따라

09 진화론을 뒷받침하고 검증하는 화석 기록

정답률 46% | 정답 ⑤

주어진 글 다음에 이어질 글의 순서로 가장 적절한 것을 고르시오.

① (A) – (C) – (B)
② (B) – (A) – (C)
③ (B) – (C) – (A)
④ (C) – (A) – (B)
⑤ (C) – (B) – (A)

The fossil record provides evidence of evolution.
화석 기록은 진화의 증거를 제공한다.

The story the fossils tell / is one of change.
화석이 전하는 이야기는 / 변화에 관한 것이다.

Creatures existed in the past / that are no longer with us.
생물들이 과거에는 존재했다. / 더는 우리와 함께하지 않는

Sequential changes are found in many fossils / showing the change of certain features over time from a common ancestor, / as in the case of the horse.
많은 화석에서 일련의 변화가 발견된다. / 시간이 지남에 따라 공통의 조상으로부터 특정 특징의 변화를 보여주는 / 말의 경우에서처럼

(C) Apart from demonstrating that evolution did occur, / the fossil record also provides tests of the predictions / made from evolutionary theory.
진화가 진짜 일어났다는 것을 증명하는 것 외에도, / 화석 기록은 또한 예측에 대한 테스트를 제공한다. / 진화론에서 만들어진

For example, / the theory predicts / that single-celled organisms evolved before multicelled organisms.
예를 들어, / 진화론은 예측한다. / 단세포 생물이 다세포 생물 이전에 진화했다고
(B) The fossil record supports this prediction / — multicelled organisms are found in layers of earth / millions of years after the first appearance of single-celled organisms.
화석 기록은 이 예측을 뒷받침하는데, / 다세포 생물은 지구 지층에서 발견된다. / 단세포 생물이 최초로 출현한 수백만 년 후
Note that the possibility always remains / that the opposite could be found.
가능성은 항상 남아 있다는 점에 주목하라. / 그 반대가 발견될 수 있는
(A) If multicelled organisms were indeed found / to have evolved before single-celled organisms, / then the theory of evolution would be rejected.
다세포 생물이 정말로 밝혀진다면, / 단세포 생물보다 먼저 진화한 것으로 / 진화론은 거부될 것이다.
A good scientific theory / always allows for the possibility of rejection.
좋은 과학 이론은 / 항상 거부의 가능성을 허용한다.
The fact that we have not found such a case / in countless examinations of the fossil record / strengthens the case for evolutionary theory.
그러한 경우를 발견하지 못했다는 사실은 / 화석 기록에 대한 수많은 조사에서 / 진화론을 위한 논거를 강화한다.

화석 기록은 진화의 증거를 제공한다. 화석이 전하는 이야기는 변화에 관한 것이다. 더는 우리와 함께하지 않는 생물들이 과거에는 존재했다. 말의 경우에서처럼, 시간이 지남에 따라 공통의 조상으로부터 특정 특징의 변화를 보여주는 많은 화석에서 일련의 변화가 발견된다.

(C) 진화가 진짜 일어났다는 것을 증명하는 것 외에도, 화석 기록은 또한 진화론에서 했던 예측에 대한 테스트를 제공한다. 예를 들어, 진화론은 단세포 생물이 다세포 생물 이전에 진화했다고 예측한다.

(B) 화석 기록은 이 예측을 뒷받침하는데, 다세포 생물은 단세포 생물이 최초로 출현한 수백만 년 후 지구 지층에서 발견된다. 그 반대가 발견될 수 있는 가능성은 항상 남아 있다는 점에 주목하라.

(A) 다세포 생물이 단세포 생물보다 먼저 진화한 것으로 정말로 밝혀진다면, 진화론은 거부될 것이다. 좋은 과학 이론은 항상 거부의 가능성을 허용한다. 화석 기록에 대한 수많은 조사에서 그러한 경우를 발견하지 못했다는 사실은 진화론을 위한 논거를 강화한다.

Why? 왜 정답일까?

화석 기록은 진화를 뒷받침한다는 주어진 글 뒤로, (C)는 '이외에도' 화석 기록이 진화론의 예측을 검증한다는 내용과 함께 단세포 생물이 다세포 생물에 선행했다는 예측을 예로 들기 시작한다. (B)는 (C)에서 언급한 예측을 this prediction으로 받으며, 화석 증거가 이를 뒷받침한다고 설명하고, (A)는 이것의 반론 가능성에 관해 언급한다. 따라서 글의 순서로 가장 적절한 것은 ⑤ '(C) – (B) – (A)'이다.

- evidence ⓝ 증거
- ancestor ⓝ 조상
- single-celled organism 단세포 생물
- countless ⓐ 수없이 많은
- evolutionary ⓐ 진화의
- layer ⓝ 지층
- apart from ~ 이외에도, ~와는 별개로
- occur ⓥ 일어나다, 발생하다
- sequential ⓐ 일련의, 연속적인
- multicelled organism 다세포 생물
- reject ⓥ 거부하다
- examination ⓝ 조사
- prediction ⓝ 예측
- appearance ⓝ 출현
- demonstrate ⓥ 입증하다

★★★ 1등급 대비 고난도 2점 문제

10 협상에서 근원적인 이해관계 살피기 정답률 29% | 정답 ⑤

주어진 글 다음에 이어질 글의 순서로 가장 적절한 것을 고르시오.

① (A) – (C) – (B)　② (B) – (A) – (C)
③ (B) – (C) – (A)　④ (C) – (A) – (B)
✔⑤ (C) – (B) – (A)

Consider the story of two men / quarreling in a library.
두 사람의 이야기를 생각해 보자. / 도서관에서 싸우는
One wants the window open / and the other wants it closed.
한 사람은 창문을 열고 싶어 하고 / 다른 사람은 그것을 닫고 싶어 한다.
They argue back and forth / about how much to leave it open: / a crack, halfway, or three-quarters of the way.
그들은 옥신각신한다. / 그것을 얼마나 많이 열어 둘지에 대해 / 즉 조금, 절반, 혹은 4분의 3 정도 중
(C) No solution satisfies them both.
어떤 해결책도 둘 다를 만족시키지 못한다.
Enter the librarian.
사서를 투입하라.
She asks one why he wants the window open:
사서는 한 명에게 왜 그가 창문을 열고 싶어 하는지 묻는다.
"To get some fresh air."
"신선한 공기를 쐬기 위해서."
She asks the other why he wants it closed:
사서는 다른 사람에게도 왜 창문을 닫고 싶어 하는지 묻는다.
"To avoid a draft."
"외풍을 피하기 위해서."
(B) After thinking a minute, / she opens wide a window in the next room, / bringing in fresh air without a draft.
잠시 생각한 후, / 그녀는 옆방의 창문을 활짝 열고, / 외풍 없이 신선한 공기를 들여온다.
This story is typical of many negotiations.
이 이야기는 많은 협상의 전형이다.
Since the parties' problem / appears to be a conflict of positions, / they naturally tend to talk about positions / — and often reach an impasse.
당사자들의 문제가 / 입장 충돌로 보이기 때문에, / 그들은 자연스레 입장을 말하는 경향이 있고, / 흔히 막다른 상황에 이른다.
(A) The librarian could not have invented the solution she did / if she had focused only on the two men's stated positions / of wanting the window open or closed.
사서는 자신이 생각해 낸 해결책을 생각해 낼 수 없었을 것이다. / 만약 그녀가 말로 언급된 두 사람의 입장에만 집중했다면 / 창문을 열거나 닫기를 원하는
Instead, / she looked to their underlying interests / of fresh air and no draft.
대신에, / 그녀는 그들의 근본적인 이해관계를 살펴보았다. / 신선한 공기가 있고 외풍이 없어야 한다는

두 사람이 도서관에서 싸우는 이야기를 생각해 보자. 한 사람은 창문을 열고 싶어 하고 다른 사람은 그것을 닫고 싶어 한다. 그들은 얼마나 많이, 즉 조금, 절반, 혹은 4분의 3 정도 중 얼마나 열어 둘지에 대해 옥신각신한다.

(C) 어떤 해결책도 둘 다를 만족시키지 못한다. 사서를 투입하라. 사서는 한 명에게 왜 창문을 열고 싶어 하는지 묻는다. "신선한 공기를 쐬기 위해서."(라는 답이 돌아온다.) 사서는 다른 사람에게도 왜 창문을 닫고 싶어 하는지 묻는다. "외풍을 피하기 위해서."(라는 답이 돌아온다.)

(B) 잠시 생각한 후, 사서는 옆방의 창문을 활짝 열고, 외풍 없이 신선한 공기를 들여온다. 이 이야기는 많은 협상의 전형이다. 당사자들의 문제가 입장 충돌로 보이기 때문에, 그들은 자연스레 (자신의) 입장을 말하는 경향이 있고, 흔히 막다른 상황에 이른다.

(A) 만약 창문을 열거나 닫기를 원하는, 말로 언급된 두 사람의 입장에만 집중했다면 사서는 자신이 생각해 낸 해결책을 생각해 낼 수 없었을 것이다. 대신에, 사서는 신선한 공기가 있고 외풍이 없어야 한다는 그들의 근본적인 이해관계를 살펴보았다.

Why? 왜 정답일까?

주어진 글은 도서관에 있는 두 사람 중 한 사람은 창문을 열고 싶어 하고 다른 사람은 창문을 닫고 싶어 하여 충돌이 일어나는 상황을 소개한다. 이어서 (C)는 주어진 글에서 언급되듯이 창문을 약간만 열든, 절반만 열든, 4분의 3을 열든 두 사람 모두를 만족시키기는 어렵기 때문에, 사서를 투입해서 이유를 들어본다고 언급한다. (B)에서는 두 사람의 이야기를 모두 들어본 사서가 잠시 생각한 뒤 옆방 창문을 열어 문제를 해결한다고 설명하고, (A)에서는 이것이 양쪽 입장의 근원적인 욕구에 집중하여 문제를 해결한 사례임을 정리한다. 따라서 글의 순서로 가장 적절한 것은 ⑤ '(C) – (B) – (A)'이다.

- quarrel ⓥ 싸우다
- crack ⓝ (좁은) 틈, (갈라진) 금
- invent ⓥ 발명하다, ~을 지어내다
- underlying ⓐ 근본적인, 기저에 있는
- negotiation ⓝ 협상
- argue back and forth 옥신각신하다
- librarian ⓝ (도서관의) 사서
- state ⓥ 언급하다, 말하다
- typical ⓝ 전형 ⓐ 전형적인
- conflict ⓝ 충돌, 갈등

구문 풀이

6행 The librarian could not have invented the solution she did
「주어+조동사 과거형+have p.p. ~」
if she had focused only on the two men's stated positions of
「if+주어+had p.p. ~ : 가정법 과거완료(과거 사실의 반대 가정)」
wanting the window open or closed.

★★ 문제 해결 꿀~팁 ★★

▶ 많이 틀린 이유는?
도서관에서 싸우는 두 사람을 중재시킨 사서의 예를 통해 협상의 기본 원칙을 보여주는 글로, (C) 이후 나머지 두 단락의 순서를 파악하는 것이 관건이다. (A)의 첫 문장을 살펴보면, 사서가 만일 두 사람이 말로 표현한 입장에만 치중했다면 '그 해결책(the solution)'을 고안할 수 없었을 것이라는 의미이다. 하지만 (C)에서는 아직 해

결책이 언급되지 않으므로, (C) 뒤에 (A)를 연결하면 the solution으로 가리킬 내용이 앞에 없어 흐름이 어색해진다.

▶ 문제 해결 방법은?

(B)에서 사서가 옆방 창문을 열어 외풍 없이 신선한 공기를 들여왔다고 하는데, 바로 이 내용을 (A)에서 the solution으로 받았다.

★★★ 1등급 대비 고난도 3점 문제

11 환경 보호와 일자리 창출의 양립 가능성 정답률 38% | 정답 ①

주어진 글 다음에 이어질 글의 순서로 가장 적절한 것을 고르시오. [3점]

✔(A) − (C) − (B) ② (B) − (A) − (C)
③ (B) − (C) − (A) ④ (C) − (A) − (B)
⑤ (C) − (B) − (A)

For years / business leaders and politicians / have portrayed environmental protection and jobs / as mutually exclusive.
수년간 / 기업주들과 정치인들은 / 환경 보호와 일자리를 묘사해 왔다. / 상호 배타적인 것으로

(A) Pollution control, / protection of natural areas and endangered species, / and limits on use of nonrenewable resources, / they claim, / will choke the economy / and throw people out of work.
공해 방지와, / 자연 구역 및 멸종 위기 종 보호, / 재생 불가한 자원의 사용 제한 등이 / 그들은 주장한다. / 경제를 억압하고 / 사람들을 실직하게 할 것이라고

Ecological economists dispute this claim, however.
하지만 생태 경제학자들은 이 주장에 이의를 제기한다.

(C) Their studies show / that only 0.1 percent of all large-scale layoffs / in the United States in recent years / were due to government regulations.
그들의 연구에서는 보여준다. / 대규모 해고 중 단 0.1퍼센트만이 / 최근 수년간 미국에서 / 정부 규제로 인한 것이었음을

Environmental protection, they argue, / not only is necessary for a healthy economic system, / but it actually creates jobs and stimulates business.
그들이 주장하기로 환경 보호는 / 건강한 경제 시스템을 위해 필요할 뿐만 아니라 / 그것은 실제로 일자리를 창출하며 사업을 촉진시킨다.

(B) Recycling, for instance, / makes more new jobs / than extracting raw materials.
예를 들면 재활용은 / 새 일자리를 더 많이 만들어낸다. / 원자재를 추출해 내는 경우보다

This doesn't necessarily mean / that recycled goods are more expensive / than those from raw resources.
이는 꼭 ~하다는 뜻은 아니다. / 재활용된 상품들이 더 비싸다는 / 원자재에서 나온 상품들보다

We're simply substituting labor in the recycling center / for energy and huge machines / used to extract new materials in remote places.
우리는 재활용 센터의 노동력으로 대체하고 있을 뿐이다. / 에너지와 거대한 기계들을 / 먼 지역에서 새로운 자재를 추출하기 위해 사용되던

수년간 기업주들과 정치인들은 환경 보호와 일자리가 상호 배타적인 것으로 묘사해 왔다.

(A) 그들은 공해 방지와, 자연 구역 및 멸종 위기 종 보호, 재생 불가한 자원의 사용 제한 등이 경제를 억압하고 사람들을 실직하게 할 것이라고 주장한다. 하지만 생태 경제학자들은 이 주장에 이의를 제기한다.

(C) 그들의 연구에서는 최근 수년간의 미국 내 대규모 해고 중 단 0.1퍼센트만이 정부 규제로 인한 것이었음을 보여준다. 그들이 주장하기로 환경 보호는 건강한 경제 시스템을 위해 필요할 뿐만 아니라 실제로 일자리를 창출하며 사업을 촉진시킨다.

(B) 예를 들면 재활용은 원자재를 추출해 내는 경우보다 새 일자리를 더 많이 만들어낸다. 이는 재활용된 상품들이 원자재에서 나온 상품들보다 꼭 더 비싸다는 뜻은 아니다. 우리는 먼 지역에서 새로운 자재를 추출하기 위해 사용되던 에너지와 거대한 기계들을 재활용 센터의 노동력으로 대체하고 있을 뿐이다.

Why? 왜 정답일까?

수년간 기업주들과 정치인들은 환경 보호와 일자리가 양립할 수 없다고 말해 왔다는 내용을 제시한 주어진 글 뒤에는, '기업주와 정치가'를 they로 나타내며 이들이 많은 환경 보호 정책으로 인해 경제가 억압되고 실직이 발생할 것이라 주장해 왔다는 흐름을 그대로 잇는 (A)가 나오는 것이 적절하다. 한편 (A)의 말미에서는 생태 경제학자들이 이런 주장을 '반박'했다고 이야기하는데, (C)는 이 생태 경제학자들을 Their로 나타내며 실제로 미국에서 있었던 대규모 해고에서 환경과 관련된 정부 규제로 인한 해고는 극히 미미한 비율만을 차지하였다는 내용을 설명한다. 마지막으로 (B)는 도리어 환경을 보호하는 재활용 등의 정책이 새 일자리를 '창출'하는 데 기여할 수 있다는 내용을 뒷받침하는 구체적인 예를 든다. 따라서 글의 순서로 가장 적절한 것은 ① '(A) − (C) − (B)'이다.

- politician ⓝ 정치인
- mutually exclusive 상호 배타적인
- nonrenewable ⓐ 재생 불가능한
- dispute ⓥ 반박하다
- raw material 원자재, 원료
- labor ⓝ 노동(력)
- regulation ⓝ 규제, 통제
- portray ⓥ 묘사하다, 그리다
- endangered ⓐ 멸종 위기에 처한
- ecological ⓐ 생태학의, 생태학적인
- extract ⓥ 추출하다
- substitute ⓥ 대체하다
- layoff ⓝ 해고
- stimulate ⓥ 촉진하다, 고무시키다

구문 풀이

4행 Pollution control(주어1), protection(주어2) [of natural areas and endangered species], and limits(주어3) on use of nonrenewable resources, (they claim,) will(미래 조동사) choke(동사원형1) the economy and throw(동사원형2) people out of work.
( ): 삽입절(원래 문두)

★★ 문제 해결 꿀~팁 ★★

▶ 많이 틀린 이유는?

(A)의 대명사 they를 주어진 글의 business leaders and politicians로 연결시킬 수 있는지에 따라 답을 바로 고를 수도 있고 그렇지 못할 수도 있는 문제였다. 오답으로 ②가 많이 나왔는데 이는 순서 문제에서 ①이 답으로 나오는 경우가 드물다는 선입견에도 영향을 받은 것으로 보인다.

▶ 문제 해결 방법은?

(A)와 (C)에 3인칭 복수대명사인 they와 their가 나오지만 가리키는 대상은 판이하게 다르다. (A)의 they는 환경 보호 정책이 '실직'을 이끌 것이라고 보는 입장의 사람들을 나타내는 것으로 보아 주어진 글의 '기업주 및 정치인'이고, (C)의 their는 환경 보호 정책의 일환인 재활용이 일자리 '창출'에 기여할 수 있다고 보는 입장을 취하는 (A) 말미의 '생태 경제학자들'이다. 두 주장의 내용이 서로 대조된다는 것을 알면 (A)와 (C)가 (A) 마지막에 나온 'however'로 연결되는 관계임을 파악할 수 있다.

★★★ 1등급 대비 고난도 3점 문제

12 농경 이후 사회의 인구 정답률 37% | 정답 ②

주어진 글 다음에 이어질 글의 순서로 가장 적절한 것을 고르시오. [3점]

① (A) − (C) − (B) ✔(B) − (A) − (C)
③ (B) − (C) − (A) ④ (C) − (A) − (B)
⑤ (C) − (B) − (A)

Regardless of whether the people existing after agriculture / were happier, healthier, or neither, / it is undeniable that there were more of them.
농경 이후에 존재했던 사람들이 / 더 행복했든, 더 건강했든, 아니면 둘 다 아니었든 간에 관계없이, / 더 많은 수의 사람들이 있었다는 것은 부인할 수 없다.

Agriculture both supports and requires / more people to grow the crops / that sustain them.
농경은 더 많은 사람을 부양하는 동시에, 필요로 한다. / 농작물을 기를 더 많은 사람을 / 그들을 지탱해 주는

(B) Estimates vary, of course, / but evidence points to an increase in the human population / from 1-5 million people worldwide to a few hundred million / once agriculture had become established.
물론, 추정치는 다양하지만, / 증거는 인구의 증가를 보여준다. / 전 세계적으로 1 ~ 5백만 명에서 수억 명으로 / 농경이 확립된 후

(A) And a larger population / doesn't just mean increasing the size of everything, / like buying a bigger box of cereal for a larger family.
그리고 더 많은 인구는 / 단지 모든 것의 규모를 확장하는 것을 의미하지는 않는다. / 더 큰 가족을 위해 더 큰 상자의 시리얼을 사는 것 같이

It brings qualitative changes / in the way people live.
그것은 질적인 변화를 가져온다. / 사람들이 사는 방식에

(C) For example, / more people means more kinds of diseases, / particularly when those people are sedentary.
예를 들어 / 더 많은 사람은 더 많은 종류의 질병을 의미하는데, / 특히 그 사람들이 한 곳에 정착해 있을 때 그렇다.

Those groups of people / can also store food for long periods, / which creates a society with haves and have-nots.
그러한 사람들의 집단은 / 또한 음식을 장기간 보관할 수 있고, / 이것은 가진 자와 가지지 못한 자가 있는 사회를 만들어 낸다.

농경 이후에 존재했던 사람들이 더 행복했든, 더 건강했든, 아니면 둘 다 아니었든 간에 관계없이, 더 많은 수의 사람들이 있었다는 것은 부인할 수 없다. 농경은 더 많은 사람을 부양하는 동시에, 그들을 지탱해 주는 농작물을 기를 더 많은 사람을 필요로 한다.

(B) 물론, 추정치는 다양하지만, 증거에 따르면 농경이 확립된 후 전 세계적으로 인구가 1 ~ 5백만 명에서 수억 명으로 증가했다.

(A) 그리고 더 많은 인구는 더 큰 가족을 위해 더 큰 상자의 시리얼을 사는 것 같이 단지 모든 것의 규모를 확장하는 것을 의미하지는 않는다. 그것은 사람들의 생활 방식에 질적인 변화를 가져온다.

(C) 예를 들어 더 많은 사람은 더 많은 종류의 질병을 의미하는데, 특히 그 사람들이 한 곳에 정착해 있을 때 그렇다. 그러한 사람들의 집단은 또한 음식을 장기간 보관할 수 있고, 이것은 가진 자와 가지지 못한 자가 있는 사회를 만들어 낸다.

Why? 왜 정답일까?

농경 이후 사회의 인구는 이전보다 더 많아졌다는 내용을 제시하는 주어진 글 뒤에는, 농경 이후의 인구 증가를 수치로 보여주는 (B), 농경이 사람들의 생활 방식에 질적인 변화를 가져왔다는 내용의 (A), 질적 변화에 대한 예를 드는 (C)가 차례로 이어져야 한다. 따라서 글의 순서로 가장 적절한 것은 ② '(B) – (A) – (C)'이다.

- regardless of ~에 관계없이
- undeniable ⓐ 부인할 수 없는
- qualitative ⓐ 질적인
- vary ⓥ 다양하다, 다르다
- established ⓐ 확립된
- agriculture ⓝ 농경
- population ⓝ 인구
- estimate ⓝ 추정치 ⓥ 추정하다
- point to ~을 보여주다, 시사하다

구문 풀이

[10행] Estimates vary, of course, but evidence points to an increase
주어1 └동사1(자동사) 주어2 동사2(~을 시사하다)
in the human population from 1-5 million people worldwide to a few
「from + A + to + B : A에서 B까지」
hundred million / once agriculture had become established.
일단 ~한 후에 과거완료

★★ 문제 해결 꿀~팁 ★★

▶ 많이 틀린 이유는?
(B)는 농경 이후 세계 인구가 1 ~ 5백만에서 수억까지 증가했다는 내용으로 끝나는데 (C)는 사람들이 많아지면 질병도 많아진다는 내용으로 이어지고 있어 두 단락 사이에 논리적 연관성이 없다. 따라서 (B) 뒤로 '사람들이 많아지면 삶에서 단순히 양적인 변화뿐 아니라 질적인 변화도 야기된다'는 내용을 제시하는 (A)가 먼저 나온 후 '질적인 변화'를 부가 설명하는 (C)가 연결되어야 한다.

▶ 문제 해결 방법은?
For example 등 연결어는 순서 문제 풀이에 큰 힌트를 제공한다. 여기서도 (C)의 For example 뒤로 소개되는 예시가 (A)와 (B) 중 어느 단락과 연결되는지를 중점적으로 파악해보면 정답을 찾을 수 있다.

DAY 15 　　　　글의 순서 05

01 ⑤	02 ③	03 ⑤	04 ⑤	05 ⑤
06 ③	07 ⑤	08 ③	09 ②	10 ④
11 ③	12 ⑤			

01 촉감 수용체의 분포
정답률 47% | 정답 ⑤

주어진 글 다음에 이어질 글의 순서로 가장 적절한 것을 고르시오.

① (A) – (C) – (B)　　　　② (B) – (A) – (C)
③ (B) – (C) – (A)　　　　④ (C) – (A) – (B)
✔ (C) – (B) – (A)

Touch receptors are spread over all parts of the body, / but they are not spread evenly.
촉감 수용체는 신체 곳곳에 퍼져 있지만 / 그것들은 골고루 퍼져 있지는 않다.
Most of the touch receptors / are found in your fingertips, tongue, and lips.
대부분의 촉감 수용체는 / 손가락 끝, 혀, 그리고 입술에서 발견된다.
(C) On the tip of each of your fingers, for example, / there are about five thousand separate touch receptors.
예를 들어, 각각의 손가락 끝에는 / 약 5천 개의 서로 떨어져 있는 촉감 수용체가 있다.
In other parts of the body / there are far fewer.
몸의 다른 부분에서는 / 훨씬 더 적다.
In the skin of your back, / the touch receptors may be as much as 2 inches apart.
당신의 등 피부에는, / 촉감 수용체가 2인치만큼 떨어져 있을 수도 있다.
(B) You can test this for yourself.
당신은 스스로 이것을 테스트해 볼 수 있다.
Have someone poke you in the back with one, two, or three fingers / and try to guess how many fingers the person used.
누군가에게 당신의 등을 한 손가락, 두 손가락, 또는 세 손가락으로 찌르게 하고 / 그 사람이 얼마나 많은 손가락을 사용했는지 추측해 보라.
If the fingers are close together, / you will probably think it was only one.
만약 손가락이 서로 가까이 붙어 있다면, / 당신은 아마 그것이 한 개라고 생각할 것이다.
(A) But if the fingers are spread far apart, / you can feel them individually.
하지만 만약 손가락끼리 멀리 떨어져 있다면, / 당신은 그것들을 각각 느낄 수 있다.
Yet if the person does the same thing on the back of your hand / (with your eyes closed, / so that you don't see how many fingers are being used), / you probably will be able to tell easily, / even when the fingers are close together.
하지만 만약 그 사람이 당신의 손등에 똑같이 해보면 / (당신의 눈을 감은 채로 / 몇 개의 손가락이 사용되고 있는지 당신이 모르도록) / 당신은 아마 쉽게 구별할 수 있을 것이다. / 손가락이 서로 가까이 있을 때조차도

촉감 수용체는 신체 곳곳에 퍼져 있지만 골고루 퍼져 있지는 않다. 대부분의 촉감 수용체는 손가락 끝, 혀, 그리고 입술에서 발견된다.

(C) 예를 들어, 각각의 손가락 끝에는 별개의 촉감 수용체가 약 5천 개있다. 몸의 다른 부분에는 훨씬 더 적다. 당신의 등 피부에는 촉감 수용체가 2인치만큼 떨어져 있을 수도 있다.

(B) 당신은 스스로 이것을 테스트해 볼 수 있다. 누군가에게 당신의 등을 한 손가락, 두 손가락, 또는 세 손가락으로 찌르게 하고 그 사람이 손가락을 몇 개 사용했는지 추측해 보라. 만약 손가락이 서로 가까이 붙어 있다면, 당신은 아마 그것이 한 개라고 생각할 것이다.

(A) 하지만 만약 손가락끼리 멀리 떨어져 있다면, 당신은 그것들을 각각 느낄 수 있다. 하지만 만약 그 사람이 당신의 손등에 똑같이 해보면(몇 개의 손가락이 사용되고 있는지 모르도록 눈을 감은 채로), 당신은 아마 손가락이 서로 가까이 있을 때조차도 쉽게 구별할 수 있을 것이다.

Why? 왜 정답일까?

촉감 수용체의 분포에 관해 언급하는 주어진 글 뒤로, 손가락 끝과 다른 부분을 예를 들어 비교하는 (C), 촉감 수용체를 테스트하는 과정에 대한 설명으로 넘어가는 (B), 설명을 이어 가는 (A)가 차례로 이어져야 자연스럽다. 따라서 글의 순서로 가장 적절한 것은 ⑤ '(C) – (B) – (A)'이다.

- receptor ⓝ 수용체
- individually ⓐⓓ 개별적으로
- poke ⓥ 쿡 찌르다
- back ⓝ 등, 허리
- fingertip ⓝ 손가락 끝
- for oneself 스스로, 혼자 힘으로
- separate ⓐ 각각의, 별개의 ⓥ 분리하다

[문제편 p.094]

구문 풀이

6행 Yet if the person does the same thing on the back of your hand (with your eyes closed, so that you don't see how many fingers are being used), you probably will be able to tell easily, even when the fingers are close together.

Yet: 접속사(조건) / does: 동사(현재) / with your eyes closed: 「with+명사+분사: ~한 채로」 / so that: 접속사(조건: ~하도록) / will be able to tell: 동사(미래)

02 질문의 프레이밍이 답변에 미치는 영향

정답률 64% | 정답 ③

주어진 글 다음에 이어질 글의 순서로 가장 적절한 것을 고르시오.

① (A) − (C) − (B)
② (B) − (A) − (C)
③ (B) − (C) − (A) ✔
④ (C) − (A) − (B)
⑤ (C) − (B) − (A)

In one survey, / 61 percent of Americans said / that they supported the government / spending more on 'assistance to the poor'.
한 조사에서, / 61%의 미국인들이 말했다. / 그들이 정부를 지지한다고 / '빈곤층 지원'에 더 많은 돈을 쓰는

(B) But when the same population was asked / whether they supported spending more government money on 'welfare', / only 21 percent were in favour.
그러나 같은 모집단이 질문을 받았을 때, / 그들이 '복지'에 더 많은 정부 예산을 쓰는 것을 지지하느냐는 / 단지 21%만이 찬성했다.

In other words, / if you ask people about individual welfare programmes / — such as giving financial help to people / who have long-term illnesses / and paying for school meals / for families with low income / — people are broadly in favour of them.
다시 말해, / 만약 당신이 개별 복지 프로그램에 관해 사람들에게 질문한다면, / 즉 사람들에게 재정적 도움을 주고 / 오랫동안 병을 앓은 / 학교 급식비를 내주는 것 같은 / 저소득층 가정을 위해 / 사람들은 대체로 그것들에 찬성한다.

(C) But if you ask about 'welfare' / — which refers to those exact same programmes / that you've just listed / — they're against it.
그러나 만약 당신이 '복지'에 관해서 질문한다면 / 정확히 똑같은 프로그램을 가리키는, / 당신이 방금 열거한 것과 / 사람들은 그것에 반대한다.

The word 'welfare' has negative connotations, / perhaps because of the way / many politicians and newspapers portray it.
'복지'라는 단어는 부정적인 함축을 가지고 있다. / 방식 때문일지 몰라도 / 많은 정치인들과 신문들이 그것을 묘사하는

(A) Therefore, / the framing of a question / can heavily influence the answer in many ways, / which matters / if your aim is to obtain / a 'true measure' of what people think.
따라서, / 질문의 프레이밍은 / 여러 가지 방식으로 답변에 큰 영향을 미칠 수 있으며, / 이는 중요하다. / 당신의 목표가 얻는 것이라면 / 사람들이 생각하는 것에 대한 '진정한 척도'를

And next time you hear a politician say / 'surveys prove that the majority of the people agree with me', / be very wary.
그리고 다음번에 어느 정치인이 말하는 것을 듣게 되면, / '설문조사를 통해 대다수 국민들이 제게 동의한다는 점이 입증됩니다'라고 / 아주 조심하라.

한 조사에서, 61%의 미국인들이 '빈곤층 지원'에 더 많은 돈을 쓰는 정부를 지지한다고 말했다.

(B) 같은 모집단이 '복지'에 더 많은 정부 예산을 쓰는 것을 지지하느냐는 질문을 받았을 때, 단지 21%만이 찬성했다. 다시 말해, 만약 당신이 개별 복지 프로그램, 즉 오랫동안 병을 앓은 사람들에게 재정적 도움을 주고 저소득층 가정을 위해 학교 급식비를 내주는 것 같은 프로그램에 관해 사람들에게 질문한다면, 사람들은 대체로 그것들에 찬성한다.

(C) 그러나 만약 당신이 방금 열거한 것과 정확히 똑같은 프로그램을 가리키는, '복지'에 관해서 질문한다면 사람들은 그것에 반대한다. '복지'라는 단어는 많은 정치인들과 신문들이 그것을 묘사하는 방식 때문일지 몰라도 부정적인 함축을 가지고 있다.

(A) 따라서, 질문의 프레이밍은 여러 가지 방식으로 답변에 큰 영향을 미칠 수 있으며, 이는 당신의 목표가 사람들이 생각하는 것에 대한 '진정한 척도'를 얻는 것이라면 중요하다. 그리고 다음번에 어느 정치인이 '설문조사를 통해 대다수 국민들이 제게 동의한다는 점이 입증됩니다'라고 말하는 것을 듣게 되면, 아주 조심하라.

Why? 왜 정답일까?

현안이나 문제를 어떤 말로 묘사하는지가 사람들의 응답에 영향을 미칠 수 있다는 내용의 글이다. 주어진 글에서 미국인들의 61%가 '빈곤층 지원'에 정부 예산을 사용하는 데 호의적이라는 예를 제시한 데 이어, **(B)**는 만일 빈곤층 지원이라는 단어를 '복지'라는 말로 바꾸면 21%만이 호의적인 태도를 보인다는 내용을 대비하여 제시한다. 이어서 **(B)**의 마지막 문장과 **(C)**의 첫 번째 문장은 앞서 언급된 내용을 더 자세한 예로 풀어서, 사람들이 '병원비 또는 저소득층 급식비 지원'에는 찬성하면서도 '복지'라는 단어에는 반대할 수 있다고 설명한다. **(A)**는 예시를 토대로 질문의 프레이밍, 즉 질문의 언어 표현 방식이 여러모로 답변에 영향을 미친다는 결론을 내린다. 따라서 글의 순서로 가장 적절한 것은 ③ '**(B) − (C) − (A)**'이다.

- assistance ⓝ 도움, 원조
- influence ⓥ 영향을 미치다 ⓝ 영향
- welfare ⓝ 복지
- illness ⓝ 병, 질환
- negative ⓐ 부정적인
- framing ⓝ 프레이밍, (특정한 방식의) 표현
- politician ⓝ 정치인
- financial ⓐ 재정의
- refer to ~을 나타내다
- portray ⓥ 묘사하다

구문 풀이

4행 Therefore, the framing of a question can heavily influence the answer in many ways, which matters if your aim is to obtain a 'true measure' of what people think.

which: 계속적 용법(앞 문장) / if: 접속사(만약 ~라면) / what: 관계대명사(~것)

03 돈의 기능

정답률 51% | 정답 ⑤

주어진 글 다음에 이어질 글의 순서로 가장 적절한 것을 고르시오.

① (A) − (C) − (B)
② (B) − (A) − (C)
③ (B) − (C) − (A)
④ (C) − (A) − (B)
⑤ (C) − (B) − (A) ✔

Without money, people could only barter.
돈이 없다면, 사람들은 물물 교환만 할 수 있을 것이다.

Many of us barter to a small extent, / when we return favors.
우리 대다수는 작은 규모에서 물물 교환을 한다. / 우리가 호의에 보답할 때

(C) A man might offer to mend his neighbor's broken door / in return for a few hours of babysitting, / for instance.
한 사람은 이웃의 고장 난 문을 수리해주겠다고 제안할지도 모른다. / 몇 시간 동안 아기를 돌봐준 것에 대한 보답으로 / 예를 들어

Yet it is hard to imagine these personal exchanges / working on a larger scale.
그러나 이러한 개인적인 교환들을 상상하기 어렵다. / 더 큰 규모로 작동하는

(B) What would happen / if you wanted a loaf of bread / and all you had to trade was your new car?
어떤 일이 일어날까? / 만약 당신이 빵 한 덩어리를 원하고 / 교환하기 위해 가지고 있는 전부가 새 자동차뿐이라면

Barter depends on the double coincidence of wants, / where not only does the other person happen to have what I want, / but I also have what he wants.
물물 교환은 필요의 이중적 우연의 일치에 달려있는데, / 이는 다른 사람이 내가 원하는 것을 우연히 가지고 있을 뿐만 아니라 / 또한 나도 그가 원하는 것을 가지고 있는 경우이다.

Money solves all these problems.
돈은 이러한 모든 문제를 해결한다.

(A) There is no need to find someone / who wants what you have to trade; / you simply pay for your goods with money.
누군가를 찾을 필요가 없다. / 당신이 교환하기 위해 가지고 있는 것을 원하는 / 당신은 단순히 돈으로 물건 값을 지불하면 된다.

The seller can then take the money / and buy from someone else.
그러면 판매자는 돈을 받고 / 다른 누군가로부터 구매할 수 있다.

Money is transferable and deferrable / — the seller can hold on to it / and buy when the time is right.
돈은 이동 가능하고 (지불을) 연기할 수 있다 / 판매자는 그것을 쥐고 있다가 / 시기가 적절한 때에 구매할 수 있다.

돈이 없다면, 사람들은 물물 교환만 할 수 있을 것이다. 우리 대다수는 호의에 보답할 때 작은 규모에서 물물 교환을 한다.

(C) 예를 들어, 한 사람은 (이웃이) 몇 시간 동안 아기를 돌봐준 것에 대한 보답으로 이웃의 고장 난 문을 수리해주겠다고 제안할지도 모른다. 그러나 이러한 개인적인 교환들이 더 큰 규모로 작동하는 것을 상상하기 어렵다.

(B) 만약 당신이 빵 한 덩어리를 원하고 교환하기 위해 가지고 있는 전부가 새 자동차뿐이라면 어떤 일이 일어날까? 물물 교환은 필요의 이중적 우연의 일치에 달려있는데, 이는 다른 사람이 내가 원하는 것을 우연히 가지고 있을 뿐만 아니라 또한 나도 그가 원하는 것을 가지고 있는 경우이다. 돈은 이러한 모든 문제를 해결한다.

(A) 당신이 교환하기 위해 가지고 있는 것을 원하는 누군가를 찾을 필요가 없다. 당신은 단순히 돈으로 물건 값을 지불하면 된다. 그러면 판매자는 돈을 받고 다른 누군가로부터 구매할 수 있다. 돈은 이동 가능하고 (지불을)

연기할 수 있다 — 판매자는 그것을 쥐고 있다가 시기가 적절한 때에 구매할 수 있다.

Why? 왜 정답일까?

돈이 없다면 사람들은 물물 교환밖에 할 수 없다는 내용의 주어진 글 뒤에는, 물물교환의 예시를 드는 (C), 물물교환을 성립하게 하는 요인으로서 필요의 이중적 우연의 일치를 언급하는 (B), 이 이중적 우연의 일치가 성립하지 않을 때 문제를 해결해주는 것이 돈임을 설명하는 (A)가 차례로 이어져야 한다. 따라서 글의 순서로 가장 적절한 것은 ⑤ '(C) – (B) – (A)'이다.

- **trade** ⓥ 교환하다
- **deferrable** ⓐ 연기할 수 있는
- **loaf** ⓝ 빵 한 덩이
- **want** ⓝ 필요한 것, 원하는 것, 결핍
- **scale** ⓝ 규모
- **transferable** ⓐ 이동 가능한
- **hold on to** 계속 보유하다
- **coincidence** ⓝ 우연의 일치
- **mend** ⓥ 수리하다

구문 풀이

10행 Barter depends on the double coincidence of wants, where not only does the other person happen to have what I want, but I also have what he wants.

(wants: 선행사 / where: 관계부사 / not only does the other person happen: 「부정어구+조동사+주어+동사원형 : 도치 구문」 / what: 관계대명사 / what: 관계대명사)

04 대체재와 보완재의 개념

정답률 54% | 정답 ⑤

주어진 글 다음에 이어질 글의 순서로 가장 적절한 것을 고르시오.

① (A) – (C) – (B)
② (B) – (A) – (C)
③ (B) – (C) – (A)
④ (C) – (A) – (B)
✔ (C) – (B) – (A)

Suppose that the price of frozen yogurt falls.
냉동 요거트의 가격이 떨어진다고 가정해 보자.
The law of demand says / that you will buy more frozen yogurt.
수요의 법칙은 말한다. / 당신은 더 많은 냉동 요거트를 사게 될 것이라고
At the same time, you will probably buy less ice cream.
동시에 아마도 아이스크림은 더 적게 살 것이다.
(C) This is because ice cream and frozen yogurt / are both cold and sweet desserts, / satisfying similar desires.
그 이유는 아이스크림과 냉동 요거트는 / 둘 다 차갑고 달콤한 디저트여서 / 비슷한 욕구를 충족시키기 때문이다.
When a fall in the price of one good / reduces the demand for another good, / the two goods are called substitutes.
한 재화의 가격 하락이 / 다른 재화의 수요를 감소시킬 때, / 이 두 재화는 대체재라 불린다.
(B) They are often pairs of goods / that are used in place of each other, / like hot dogs and hamburgers.
이는 종종 재화의 쌍이다. / 서로를 대신하여 이용되는 / 핫도그와 햄버거처럼
Now suppose / that the price of chocolate topping falls.
이제 상상해 보자. / 초콜릿 토핑의 가격이 하락한다고
According to the law of demand, / you will buy more chocolate topping.
수요의 법칙에 따르면 / 당신은 더 많은 초콜릿 토핑을 살 것이다.
(A) Yet, in this case, / you will likely buy more ice cream as well, / since ice cream and topping are often used together.
그러나 이 경우에는 / 아마 아이스크림도 더 많이 사게 될 것인데, / 왜냐하면 아이스크림과 토핑은 종종 함께 이용되기 때문이다.
When a fall in the price of one good / raises the demand for another good, / the two goods are called complements.
한 재화의 가격 하락이 / 다른 재화의 수요를 상승시킬 때 / 이 두 재화는 보완재라 불린다.

냉동 요거트의 가격이 떨어진다고 가정해 보자. 수요의 법칙에 따르면 당신은 더 많은 냉동 요거트를 사게 될 것이다. 동시에 아마도 아이스크림은 더 적게 살 것이다.

(C) 그 이유는 아이스크림과 냉동 요거트 모두 차갑고 달콤한 디저트여서 비슷한 욕구를 충족시키기 때문이다. 한 재화의 가격 하락이 다른 재화의 수요를 감소시킬 때, 이 두 재화는 대체재라 불린다.

(B) 이는 핫도그와 햄버거처럼 종종 서로를 대신하여 이용되는 재화의 쌍이다. 이제 초콜릿 토핑의 가격이 하락한다고 상상해 보자. 수요의 법칙에 따르면 당신은 더 많은 초콜릿 토핑을 살 것이다.

(A) 그러나 이 경우에는 아마 아이스크림도 더 많이 사게 될 것인데, 왜냐하면 아이스크림과 토핑은 종종 함께 이용되기 때문이다. 한 재화의 가격 하락이 다른 재화의 수요를 상승시킬 때 이 두 재화는 보완재라 불린다.

Why? 왜 정답일까?

주어진 문장에서 냉동 요거트의 가격이 떨어지면 요거트는 더 사고 아이스크림은 더 적게 사게 된다고 말한 데 이어 (C)에서는 '그 이유'로 두 재화가 서로 비슷한 욕구를 충족시키는 대체재 관계에 있기 때문임을 이야기한다. (B)는 (C)의 마지막에 나온 **substitutes**를 **They**로 나타내며 대체재란 서로를 대신하여 이용되는 재화의 쌍임을 말하고, 초콜릿 토핑과 아이스크림을 또 다른 예로 들기 시작한다. (A)에서는 이 경우 두 재화의 수요가 함께 증가하는데 이 관계를 보완재라는 말로 나타낸다고 설명한다. 따라서 주어진 글 다음에 이어질 글의 순서로 가장 적절한 것은 ⑤ '(C) – (B) – (A)'이다.

- **demand** ⓝ 수요
- **likely** ad 아마 ⓐ ~할 것 같은
- **in place of** ~을 대신하여
- **satisfy** ⓥ 충족시키다, 만족시키다
- **reduce** ⓥ 감소시키다, 줄이다
- **probably** ad 아마
- **complement** ⓝ 보완재, 보완, 보충
- **according to** ~에 따라
- **desire** ⓝ 욕구
- **substitute** ⓝ 대체재, 대체

구문 풀이

15행 This is because ice cream and frozen yogurt are both cold and sweet desserts, / satisfying similar desires.

(This is because: 「this is because+원인 : 이것이 ~한 이유이다」 / both ... and: 「both A and B : A와 B 모두」 / satisfying: 분사구문)

05 감각 정보의 의미 해석에 영향을 주는 머릿속 개념

정답률 48% | 정답 ⑤

주어진 글 다음에 이어질 글의 순서로 가장 적절한 것을 고르시오.

① (A) – (C) – (B)
② (B) – (A) – (C)
③ (B) – (C) – (A)
④ (C) – (A) – (B)
✔ (C) – (B) – (A)

Your concepts are a primary tool / for your brain to guess the meaning of incoming sensory inputs.
당신의 개념은 주요한 도구이다. / 뇌가 입력되는 감각 정보의 의미를 추측하게 하는
(C) For example, concepts give meaning / to changes in sound pressure / so you hear them as words or music / instead of random noise.
예를 들어, 개념은 의미를 부여하므로, / 음압의 변화에 / 당신은 그 변화를 말이나 음악으로 듣는다. / 마구잡이의 소음 대신에
In Western culture, / most music is based on an octave / divided into twelve equally spaced pitches: / the equal-tempered scale / codified by Johann Sebastian Bach in the 17th century.
서구 문화에서 / 대부분의 음악은 하나의 옥타브를 기본으로 하는데, / 12개의 동일한 간격을 가지고 있는 음의 높낮이로 나누어진 / 이것은 평균율 음계이다. / 17세기의 Johann Sebastian Bach가 체계화한
(B) All people of Western culture with normal hearing / have a concept for this ubiquitous scale, / even if they can't explicitly describe it.
정상적인 듣기 능력을 가지고 있는 서구 문화의 모든 사람들은 / 이 흔한 음계에 대한 개념을 가지고 있다. / 비록 명시적으로 설명할 수 없을지라도
Not all music uses this scale, however.
그러나 모든 음악이 이 음계를 사용하는 것은 아니다.
(A) When Westerners hear Indonesian gamelan music for the first time, / which is based on seven pitches per octave / with varied tunings, / it's more likely to sound like noise.
인도네시아 가믈란 음악을 서구인들이 처음 들었을 때 / 한 옥타브당 7개의 음의 높낮이를 기본으로 한 / 다양한 음의 조율과 더불어 / 이는 소음처럼 들릴 가능성이 더 높다.
A brain that's been wired by listening to twelve-tone scales / doesn't have a concept for that music.
12음계를 들으며 고정된 뇌는 / 그 음악에 대한 개념을 가지고 있지 않다.

당신의 개념은 뇌가 입력되는 감각 정보의 의미를 추측하게 하는 주요한 도구이다.

(C) 예를 들어, 개념은 음압의 변화에 의미를 부여하므로, 당신은 그 변화를 마구잡이의 소음 대신에 말이나 음악으로 듣는다. 서구 문화에서 대부분의 음악은 12개의 동일한 간격을 가지고 있는 음의 높낮이로 나누어진 하나의 옥타브를 기본으로 하는데, 이것은 17세기의 Johann Sebastian Bach가 체계화한 평균율 음계이다.

(B) 정상적인 듣기 능력을 가지고 있는 서구 문화의 모든 사람들은 비록 명시적으로 설명할 수 없을지라도 이 흔한 음계에 대한 개념을 가지고 있다. 그러나 모든 음악이 이 음계를 사용하는 것은 아니다.

(A) 다양한 음의 조율과 더불어 한 옥타브당 7개의 음의 높낮이를 기본으로 한 인도네시아 가믈란 음악을 서구인들이 처음 들었을 때 이는 소음처럼 들릴 가능성이 더 높다. 12음계를 들으며 고정된 뇌는 그 음악에 대한 개념을 가지고 있지 않다.

[문제편 p.096]

Why? 왜 정답일까?

음계를 예로 들어 머릿속 개념이 감각 정보를 해석하는 데 영향을 미친다는 내용을 설명한 글이다. 주제를 일반적으로 제시한 주어진 글 뒤에는, 12음계의 예를 처음 언급하는 (C), 12음계가 매우 흔히 쓰이지만 모든 음악이 이 음계를 사용하지는 않는다는 내용을 제시하는 (B), 인도네시아의 음악을 대조하여 언급하는 (A)가 차례로 이어지는 것이 자연스럽다. 따라서 글의 순서로 가장 적절한 것은 ⑤ '(C) – (B) – (A)'이다.

- gamelan ⓝ 가믈란
- varied ⓐ 다양한
- scale ⓝ 음계
- explicitly [ad] 명시적으로
- pitch ⓝ 음높이
- wired ⓐ 고정되어있는
- ubiquitous ⓐ 흔한, 어디에나 있는
- codify ⓥ 체계화하다, 성문화하다

구문 풀이

3행 When Westerners hear Indonesian gamelan music for the first time, [which is based on seven pitches per octave with varied tunings], / it's more likely to sound like noise.
(선행사 / ~을 기본으로 하다 / 「be likely+to부정사 : ~할 가능성이 높다」)

06 동물과 인간의 차이

정답률 51% | 정답 ③

주어진 글 다음에 이어질 글의 순서로 가장 적절한 것을 고르시오. [3점]

① (A) – (C) – (B)
② (B) – (A) – (C)
③ (B) – (C) – (A) ✔
④ (C) – (A) – (B)
⑤ (C) – (B) – (A)

Heat is lost at the surface, / so the more surface area you have relative to volume, / the harder you must work to stay warm.
열은 표면에서 손실되므로, / 당신이 체적에 대비하여 더 많은 표면적을 가질수록 / 당신은 따뜻함을 유지하기 위해 더 열심히 움직여야 한다.
That means / that little creatures have to produce heat / more rapidly than large creatures.
그것은 의미한다. / 작은 생물이 열을 생산해야 함을 / 큰 생물보다 더 빠르게
(B) They must therefore lead completely different lifestyles.
그러므로 그들은 완전히 다른 생활방식으로 살아가야만 한다.
An elephant's heart beats just thirty times a minute, / a human's sixty, / a cow's between fifty and eighty, / but a mouse's beats six hundred times a minute / — ten times a second.
코끼리의 심장은 1분에 단 30회를 뛰고 / 인간은 60회, / 소는 50회에서 80회를 뛰지만, / 생쥐는 1분에 600회를 뛴다. / 즉 1초에 10회
Every day, just to survive, / the mouse must eat about 50 percent of its own body weight.
매일 단지 살아남기 위해 / 생쥐는 자신의 몸무게의 약 50퍼센트를 먹어야 한다.
(C) We humans, / by contrast, / need to consume only about 2 percent of our body weight / to supply our energy requirements.
우리 인간은 / 대조적으로 / 우리 체중의 단지 약 2퍼센트만 먹으면 된다. / 에너지 요구량을 공급하기 위해
One area where animals are curiously uniform / is with the number of heartbeats / they have in a lifetime.
동물이 기묘하게도 동일한 하나의 영역은 / 심박수라는 부분이다. / 동물이 평생 동안 갖는
(A) Despite the vast differences in heart rates, / nearly all mammals have about 800 million heartbeats in them / if they live an average life.
심박수의 엄청난 차이에도 불구하고 / 거의 모든 포유동물은 약 8억 회의 심장 박동 수를 갖는다. / 만약 그들이 평균수명을 산다면
The exception is humans.
예외는 인간이다.
We pass 800 million heartbeats after twenty-five years, / and just keep on going for another fifty years / and 1.6 billion heartbeats or so.
우리는 25년 이후 8억 회를 넘어서고 / 또 다른 50년 동안 계속해서 심장이 뛰어 / 약 16억 회 정도의 심박수를 갖는다.

열은 표면에서 손실되므로, 당신이 체적에 대비하여 더 많은 표면적을 가질수록 당신은 따뜻함을 유지하기 위해 더 열심히 움직여야 한다. 그것은 작은 생물이 큰 생물보다 더 빠르게 열을 생산해야 함을 의미한다.

(B) 그러므로 그들은 완전히 다른 생활방식으로 살아가야만 한다. 코끼리의 심장은 1분에 단 30회를 뛰고 인간은 60회, 소는 50회에서 80회를 뛰지만, 생쥐는 1분에 600회, 즉 1초에 10회를 뛴다. 매일 단지 살아남기 위해 생쥐는 자신의 몸무게의 약 50퍼센트를 먹어야 한다.

(C) 대조적으로 우리 인간은 에너지 요구량을 공급하기 위해 우리 체중의 단지 약 2퍼센트만 먹으면 된다. 동물이 기묘하게도 동일한 하나의 영역은 동물이 평생 동안 뛰는 심박수라는 부분이다.

(A) 심박수의 엄청난 차이에도 불구하고 거의 모든 포유동물은 만약 그들이 평균수명을 산다면 약 8억 회의 심장 박동 수를 갖는다. 예외는 인간이다. 우리는(태어나고) 25년 이후 8억 회를 넘어서고 또 다른 50년 동안 계속해서 심장이 뛰어 약 16억 회 정도의 심박수를 갖는다.

Why? 왜 정답일까?

작은 생물은 큰 생물에 비해 열을 더 많이 생산해내야 체온을 유지한다는 내용의 주어진 글 뒤로, (B)는 그리하여 작은 생물과 큰 생물의 삶의 방식이 아예 다르다고 설명한다. (C)는 (B)에서 언급된 동물들과 대비되는 예로 인간을 언급한 후, 서로 다른 동물들끼리 비슷한 점이 하나 있다고 말하며 심박수를 언급한다. (A)는 심박수에 대한 내용을 이어간다. 따라서 글의 순서로 가장 적절한 것은 ③ '(B) – (C) – (A)'이다.

- surface ⓝ 표면, 지면
- volume ⓝ 부피, 체적
- rapidly [ad] 빠르게
- vast ⓐ 큰, 방대한
- heartbeat ⓝ 심장 박동
- requirement ⓝ 필요, 요구
- curiously [ad] 기묘하게도
- lifetime ⓝ 일생, 평생
- relative to ~에 비해
- creature ⓝ 생명이 있는 존재, 생물
- despite [prep] …에도 불구하고
- nearly [ad] 거의
- completely [ad] 완전히
- supply ⓥ 공급[제공]하다
- uniform ⓐ 동일한

구문 풀이

1행 Heat is lost at the surface, so the more surface area you have relative to volume, the harder you must work to stay warm.
(「the+비교급 ~, the+비교급 … : ~할수록 더 …하다」)

07 습관화의 장단점

정답률 50% | 정답 ⑤

주어진 글 다음에 이어질 글의 순서로 가장 적절한 것을 고르시오. [3점]

① (A) – (C) – (B)
② (B) – (A) – (C)
③ (B) – (C) – (A)
④ (C) – (A) – (B)
⑤ (C) – (B) – (A) ✔

Habits create the foundation for mastery.
습관은 숙달의 토대를 만든다.
In chess, / it is only after the basic movements of the pieces / have become automatic / that a player can focus on the next level of the game.
체스에서 / 오직 말의 기본적인 움직임이 / 자동적으로 이루어지고 나서이다. / 체스를 두는 사람이 게임의 다음 레벨에 집중할 수 있게 되는 것은
Each chunk of information that is memorized / opens up the mental space for more effortful thinking.
암기된 각각의 정보 덩어리는 / 더 노력이 필요한 사고를 할 수 있도록 정신적 공간을 열어준다.
(C) This is true for anything you attempt.
이것은 여러분이 시도하는 어떤 것에도 적용된다.
When you know the simple movements so well / that you can perform them without thinking, / you are free to pay attention to more advanced details.
여러분이 간단한 동작을 매우 잘 알고 있어서 / 그것을 생각하지 않고도 할 수 있을 때, / 여러분은 더 높은 수준의 세부 사항에 자유롭게 집중하게 된다.
In this way, / habits are the backbone of any pursuit of excellence.
이런 식으로, / 습관은 그 어떤 탁월함을 추구할 때도 중추적인 역할을 한다.
(B) However, the benefits of habits come at a cost.
그러나 습관의 이점에는 대가가 따른다.
At first, each repetition develops fluency, speed, and skill.
처음에, 각각의 반복은 유창함, 속도, 그리고 기술을 발달시킨다.
But then, as a habit becomes automatic, / you become less sensitive to feedback.
그러나 그 다음에 습관이 자동화되면서 / 여러분은 피드백에 덜 민감해지게 된다.
(A) You fall into mindless repetition.
여러분은 아무 생각 없이 하는 반복으로 빠져든다.
It becomes easier to let mistakes slide.
실수를 대수롭지 않게 여기기가 더 쉬워진다.
When you can do it "good enough" automatically, / you stop thinking about how to do it better.
여러분이 저절로 '충분히 잘' 할 수 있을 때, / 여러분은 그것을 더 잘 할 수 있는 방법에 대해 생각하기를 멈춘다.

습관은 숙달의 토대를 만든다. 체스에서 체스를 두는 사람이 게임의 다음 레벨에 집중할 수 있게 되는 것은 오직 말의 기본적인 움직임이 자동적으로 이루어지고 나서이다. 암기된 각각의 정보 덩어리는 더 노력이 필요한 사고를 할 수 있도록 정신적 공간을 열어준다.

(C) 이것은 여러분이 시도하는 어떤 것에도 적용된다. 간단한 동작을 매우 잘 알고 있어서 생각하지 않고도 할 수 있을 때, 더 높은 수준의 세부 사항에

[문제편 p.097]

자유롭게 집중하게 된다. 이런 식으로, 습관은 그 어떤 탁월함을 추구할 때도 중추적인 역할을 한다.

(B) 그러나 습관의 이점에는 대가가 따른다. 처음에, 각각의 반복은 유창함, 속도, 그리고 기술을 발달시킨다. 그러나 그 다음에 습관이 자동화되면서 여러분은 피드백에 덜 민감해지게 된다.

(A) 여러분은 아무 생각 없이 하는 반복으로 빠져든다. 실수를 대수롭지 않게 여기기가 더 쉬워진다. 여러분이 저절로 '충분히 잘' 할 수 있을 때, 그것을 더 잘 할 수 있는 방법에 대해 생각하기를 멈춘다.

Why? 왜 정답일까?

습관이 숙달의 토대가 된다며 체스 두는 사람의 예를 드는 주어진 글 뒤에는, 다른 예에도 이 명제가 적용된다는 내용의 **(C)**, 습관의 이점에는 대가가 따른다는 반전된 내용으로 연결되는 **(B)**, 습관이 자동화되면 우리는 무의식적인 반복에 빠져들며 더 잘하려고 고민하지 않게 된다는 내용의 **(A)**가 차례로 이어져야 한다. 따라서 글의 순서로 가장 적절한 것은 ⑤ **'(C) – (B) – (A)'**이다.

- **foundation** ⓝ 토대, 기초
- **mindless** ⓐ 아무 생각 없이 하는
- **let ~ slide** ~을 되어가는 대로 내버려 두다
- **automatically** ad 저절로, 자동적으로
- **sensitive** ⓐ 민감한
- **backbone** ⓝ 중추, 근간
- **effortful** ⓐ 노력이 필요한
- **repetition** ⓝ 반복
- **come at a cost** 대가가 따르다
- **fluency** ⓝ 유창함
- **attempt** ⓥ 시도하다
- **pursuit** ⓝ 추구

구문 풀이

15행 When you know the simple movements so well that you can perform them without thinking, you are free to pay attention to more advanced details.
「so ~ that … : 너무 ~해서 …하다」 / 자유롭게 ~하다

08 플라시보 버튼 현상의 예시와 개념 소개

정답률 53% | 정답 ③

주어진 글 다음에 이어질 글의 순서로 가장 적절한 것을 고르시오. [3점]

① (A) − (C) − (B)
② (B) − (A) − (C)
✔(B) − (C) − (A)
④ (C) − (A) − (B)
⑤ (C) − (B) − (A)

Crossing the street in Los Angeles / is a tricky business, / but luckily, at the press of a button, / we can stop traffic.
로스앤젤레스에서 도로를 건너는 것은 / 까다로운 일이지만, / 다행히도 버튼을 눌러 / 우리는 차량의 통행을 멈출 수 있다.
Or can we?
과연 그럴까?
(B) The button's real purpose / is to make us believe / we have an influence on the traffic lights, / and thus we're better able to endure the wait / for the signal to change / with more patience.
그 버튼의 실제 목적은 / 우리가 믿게 하는 데 있고, / 우리는 신호등에 영향을 끼칠 수 있다고 / 그리하여 우리는 기다리는 것을 더 잘 참을 수 있다. / 신호가 바뀌기를 / 더 많은 인내심을 갖고
(C) The same goes for "door-open" and "door-close" buttons in elevators:
엘리베이터의 "문 열림", "문 닫힘" 버튼도 마찬가지이다.
Many are not even connected to the electrical panel.
많은 버튼이 전기 패널에 연결조차 되어 있지 않다.
Such tricks are also designed in offices:
이러한 속임수는 사무실에도 설계되어 있다.
For some people / it will always be too hot, / for others, too cold.
어떤 사람들에게는 / 사무실이 언제나 너무 더울 것이고 / 다른 이들에게는 너무 추울 것이다.
(A) Clever technicians create the illusion of control / by installing fake temperature dials.
영리한 기술자들은 통제에 관한 환상을 만들어낸다. / 가짜 온도 조절 다이얼을 설치하여
This reduces energy bills — and complaints.
이는 에너지 이용 요금과 불평을 줄여준다.
Such tricks are called "placebo buttons" / and they are being pushed in all sorts of contexts.
그러한 속임수들은 "플라세보 버튼"이라고 불리며 / 그것들은 온갖 상황에서 눌려지고 있다.

로스앤젤레스에서 도로를 건너는 것은 까다로운 일이지만, 다행히도 우리는 버튼을 눌러 차량의 통행을 멈출 수 있다. 과연 그럴까?

(B) 그 버튼의 실제 목적은 우리가 신호등에 영향을 끼칠 수 있다고 믿게 하는 데 있고, 그리하여 우리는 더 많은 인내심을 갖고 신호가 바뀌기를 기다리는 과정을 더 잘 참을 수 있다.

(C) 엘리베이터의 "문 열림", "문 닫힘" 버튼도 마찬가지이다. 많은 버튼이 전기 패널에 연결조차 되어 있지 않다. 이러한 속임수는 사무실에도 설계되어 있다. 어떤 사람들에게는 사무실이 언제나 너무 더울 것이고 다른 이들에게는 너무 추울 것이다.

(A) 영리한 기술자들은 가짜 온도 조절 다이얼을 설치하여 통제에 관한 환상을 만들어낸다. 이는 에너지 이용 요금과 불평을 줄여준다. 그러한 속임수들은 "플라세보 버튼"이라고 불리며 온갖 상황에서 눌려지고 있다.

Why? 왜 정답일까?

신호등을 조절할 수 있는 버튼 이야기를 처음 꺼낸 주어진 글 뒤에는, 그 버튼의 실제 목적에 대해 이야기하는 **(B)**, 비슷한 예로 엘리베이터의 문 버튼과 사무실의 온도 조절 다이얼을 언급하는 **(C)**, 온도 다이얼 이야기를 마무리하며 이 모든 예가 '플라세보 버튼' 현상을 설명한다고 말하는 **(A)**가 차례로 이어져야 자연스럽다. 따라서 주어진 글 다음에 이어질 글의 순서로 가장 적절한 것은 ③ **'(B) – (C) – (A)'**이다.

- **tricky** ⓐ 까다로운, 곤란한
- **install** ⓥ 설치하다
- **have an influence on** ~에 영향을 미치다
- **patience** ⓝ 인내심
- **illusion** ⓝ 환상
- **context** ⓝ 맥락, 상황
- **endure** ⓥ 견디다, 참다
- **be connected to** ~에 연결되다

구문 풀이

9행 The button's real purpose is to make us believe (that 생략) we have an influence on the traffic lights, / and thus we're better able to endure the wait for the signal to change with more patience.
주어1 / 동사1 / 주격 보어(~것) / ~에 영향을 미치다 / 주어2 / 동사2(~할 수 있다) / 의미상 주어 / 형용사적 용법

09 중력의 강도에 영향을 미치는 요소

정답률 45% | 정답 ②

주어진 글 다음에 이어질 글의 순서로 가장 적절한 것을 고르시오. [3점]

① (A) − (C) − (B)
✔(B) − (A) − (C)
③ (B) − (C) − (A)
④ (C) − (A) − (B)
⑤ (C) − (B) − (A)

You know that forks don't fly off to the Moon / and that neither apples nor anything else on Earth / cause the Sun to crash down on us.
여러분은 포크가 달로 날아가지 않는다는 것을 알고 있다. / 사과나 지구상의 다른 어떤 것도 / 태양이 우리에게 추락하게 만들지 않는다는 것을
(B) The reason these things don't happen is / that the strength of gravity's pull depends on two things.
이런 일들이 일어나지 않는 이유는 / 중력의 당기는 힘의 강도가 두 가지에 따라 달라지기 때문이다.
The first is the mass of the object.
첫째는 물체의 질량이다.
The apple is very small, / and doesn't have much mass, / so its pull on the Sun is absolutely tiny, / certainly much smaller than the pull of all the planets.
사과는 매우 작아 / 큰 질량을 가지고 있지 않아서 / 이것이 태양에 작용하는 인력은 분명히 매우 작은데, / 확실히 모든 행성의 인력보다 훨씬 작다.
(A) The Earth has more mass than tables, trees, or apples, / so almost everything in the world / is pulled towards the Earth.
지구는 탁자, 나무, 또는 사과보다 더 큰 질량을 가지고 있어서 / 지구상의 거의 모든 것이 / 지구를 향해 당겨진다.
That's why apples fall from trees.
그것이 나무에서 사과가 떨어지는 이유다.
Now, you might know / that the Sun is much bigger than Earth / and has much more mass.
이제 여러분은 알고 있을 것이다. / 태양이 지구보다 훨씬 크고 / 훨씬 더 많은 질량을 가지고 있다는 것을
(C) So why don't apples fly off towards the Sun?
그렇다면 왜 사과는 태양을 향해 날아가지 않을까?
The reason is / that the pull of gravity also depends on the distance / to the object doing the pulling.
이유는 / 중력의 당기는 힘이 거리에 따라 또한 달라지기 때문이다. / 잡아당기는 물체와의
Although the Sun has much more mass than the Earth, / we are much closer to the Earth, / so we feel its gravity more.
태양이 지구보다 훨씬 더 많은 질량을 가지고 있지만 / 우리는 지구에 훨씬 가까워서 / 지구의 중력을 더 많이 느낀다.

여러분은 포크가 달로 날아가지 않으며 사과나 지구상의 다른 어떤 것도 태양이 우리에게 추락하게 만들지 않는다는 것을 알고 있다.

(B) 이런 일들이 일어나지 않는 이유는 중력의 당기는 힘의 강도가 두 가지에 따라 달라지기 때문이다. 첫째는 물체의 질량이다. 사과는 매우 작아 큰

질량을 가지고 있지 않아서 이것이 태양에 작용하는 인력은 분명히 매우 작은데, 확실히 모든 행성의 인력보다 훨씬 작다.

(A) 지구는 탁자, 나무, 또는 사과보다 더 큰 질량을 가지고 있어서 지구상의 거의 모든 것이 지구를 향해 당겨진다. 그것이 나무에서 사과가 떨어지는 이유다. 이제 여러분은 태양이 지구보다 훨씬 크고 훨씬 더 많은 질량을 가지고 있다는 것을 알고 있을 것이다.

(C) 그렇다면 왜 사과는 태양을 향해 날아가지 않을까? 이유는 중력의 당기는 힘이 잡아당기는 물체와의 거리에 따라 또한 달라지기 때문이다. 태양이 지구보다 훨씬 더 많은 질량을 가지고 있지만 우리는 지구에 훨씬 가까워서 지구의 중력을 더 많이 느낀다.

Why? 왜 정답일까?

지구에 있는 포크가 달로 날아가거나 태양이 중력에 의해 지구로 끌려올 일이 없다는 것을 우리 모두 알고 있다는 내용의 주어진 글 뒤에는, 이러한 일이 일어나지 않는 두 가지 이유가 있다고 설명하며 먼저 물체의 질량을 언급하는 (B), 지구는 지구상의 대부분의 물체보다 질량이 크기 때문에 물체의 중력에 의해 끌려오지 않는다는 예를 드는 (A), 중력의 당기는 힘은 또한 물체의 거리에도 영향을 받음을 추가로 설명하는 (C)가 차례로 이어져야 자연스럽다. 따라서 글의 순서로 가장 적절한 것은 ② '(B) – (A) – (C)'이다.

- fly off 날아가 버리다
- mass ⓝ 질량
- absolutely ad 분명히, 절대적으로
- planet ⓝ 행성
- crash down on ~로 추락하다
- gravity ⓝ 중력
- certainly ad 확실히

구문 풀이

1행 You know that forks don't fly off to the Moon and that neither apples nor anything else on Earth cause the Sun to crash down on us.
(접속사1, 접속사2 / 「neither+A+nor+B : A도 B도 아닌」 / 「cause+목적어+to부정사 : ~이 …하도록 야기하다」)

10 적당한 스트레스가 초래하는 긍정적 결과

정답률 62% | 정답 ④

주어진 글 다음에 이어질 글의 순서로 가장 적절한 것을 고르시오.

① (A) – (C) – (B)
② (B) – (A) – (C)
③ (B) – (C) – (A)
✔ ④ (C) – (A) – (B)
⑤ (C) – (B) – (A)

Studies of people / struggling with major health problems / show / that the majority of respondents report / they derived benefits from their adversity.
사람들에 대한 연구는 / 중대한 건강 문제를 해결하려고 노력하는 / 보여준다. / 대다수의 응답자가 보고한다는 것을 / 자신이 겪은 역경에서 이익을 얻었다고

Stressful events sometimes force people / to develop new skills, / reevaluate priorities, / learn new insights, / and acquire new strengths.
스트레스를 주는 사건들은 때때로 사람들에게 ~하게 한다. / 새로운 기술을 개발하고, / 우선순위를 재평가하고, / 새로운 통찰을 배우고 / 새로운 강점을 얻게

(C) In other words, / the adaptation process initiated by stress / can lead to personal changes for the better.
다시 말해, / 스트레스에 의해 시작된 적응 과정은 / 더 나은 쪽으로의 개인적 변화를 가져올 수 있다.

One study / that measured participants' exposure to thirty-seven major negative events / found a curvilinear relationship / between lifetime adversity and mental health.
한 연구는 / 참가자들의 서른일곱 가지 주요 부정적인 사건 경험을 측정한 / 곡선 관계를 발견했다. / 생애에서 겪은 역경과 정신 건강 사이의

(A) High levels of adversity / predicted poor mental health, as expected, / but people who had faced intermediate levels of adversity / were healthier than those / who experienced little adversity, / suggesting that moderate amounts of stress can foster resilience.
높은 수준의 역경은 / 예상대로 나쁜 정신 건강을 예측했지만, / 중간 수준의 역경에 직면했던 사람들은 / 사람들보다 더 건강했는데, / 역경을 거의 경험하지 않았던 / 이것은 적당한 양의 스트레스가 회복력을 촉진할 수 있음을 보여준다.

A follow-up study found a similar link / between the amount of lifetime adversity / and subjects' responses to laboratory stressors.
후속 연구는 비슷한 관계를 발견했다. / 생애에서 겪은 역경의 양과 / 실험 중 주어진 스트레스 요인에 대한 피실험자들의 반응 사이에서

(B) Intermediate levels of adversity / were predictive of the greatest resilience.
중간 수준의 역경이 / 가장 큰 회복력을 예측했다.

Thus, having to deal with a moderate amount of stress / may build resilience in the face of future stress.
따라서 적당한 양의 스트레스를 해결해야 하는 것은 / 미래에 스트레스를 직면할 때의 회복력을 기를 수도 있다.

중대한 건강 문제를 해결하려고 노력하는 사람들에 대한 연구는 대다수의 응답자가 자신이 겪은 역경에서 이익을 얻었다고 보고한다는 것을 보여준다. 스트레스를 주는 사건들은 때때로 사람들이 새로운 기술을 개발하고, 우선순위를 재평가하고, 새로운 통찰을 배우고 새로운 강점을 얻게 한다.

(C) 다시 말해, 스트레스에 의해 시작된 적응 과정은 더 나은 쪽으로의 개인적 변화를 가져올 수 있다. 참가자들의 서른일곱 가지 주요 부정적인 사건 경험을 측정한 한 연구는 생애에서 겪은 역경과 정신 건강 사이의 곡선 관계를 발견했다.

(A) 높은 수준의 역경은 예상대로 나쁜 정신 건강을 예측했지만, 중간 수준의 역경에 직면했던 사람들은 역경을 거의 경험하지 않았던 사람들보다 더 건강했는데, 이것은 적당한 양의 스트레스가 회복력을 촉진할 수 있음을 보여준다. 후속 연구는 생애에서 겪은 역경의 양과 실험 중 주어진 스트레스 요인에 대한 피실험자들의 반응 사이에서 비슷한 관계를 발견했다.

(B) 중간 수준의 역경이 가장 큰 회복력을 예측했다. 따라서 적당한 양의 스트레스를 해결해야 하는 것은 미래에 스트레스를 직면할 때의 회복력을 기를 수도 있다.

Why? 왜 정답일까?

사람들이 역경에서 도리어 이익을 얻을 수 있다는 내용을 제시하는 주어진 글 뒤에는, In other words 뒤로 스트레스에 의해 시작되는 적응 과정이 긍정적인 개인적 변화를 가져올 수 있다고 풀어서 설명하는 (C)가 먼저 연결된다. 이어서 (A)는 (C)의 후반부에서 처음 언급된 역경과 정신 건강에 관한 연구를 상술하고, (B)는 후속 연구, 즉 역경의 양과 스트레스 회복력을 연관시킨 연구에 관해 부연한다. 따라서 글의 순서로 가장 적절한 것은 ④ '(C) – (A) – (B)'이다.

- adversity ⓝ 역경
- acquire ⓥ 얻다, 습득하다
- foster ⓥ 촉진하다, 키우다
- adaptation ⓝ 적응
- curvilinear ⓐ 곡선의
- reevaluate ⓥ 재평가하다
- moderate ⓐ 중간의, 온건한
- predictive of ~을 예측하는
- initiate ⓥ 착수시키다

구문 풀이

7행 High levels of adversity predicted poor mental health, as expected, but people [who had faced intermediate levels of adversity] were healthier than those [who experienced little adversity], suggesting that moderate amounts of stress can foster resilience.
(주어1, 동사1, 주어2, 과거완료, 동사2, 선행사, 분사구문, 접속사(~것), 「비교급+than : 더 ~한/하게」)

★★★ 1등급 대비 고난도 2점 문제

11 판매와 마케팅의 차이

정답률 45% | 정답 ③

주어진 글 다음에 이어질 글의 순서로 가장 적절한 것을 고르시오.

① (A) – (C) – (B)
② (B) – (A) – (C)
✔ ③ (B) – (C) – (A)
④ (C) – (A) – (B)
⑤ (C) – (B) – (A)

The difference between selling and marketing / is very simple.
판매와 마케팅 사이의 차이는 / 아주 간단하다.

Selling focuses mainly on the firm's desire / to sell products for revenue.
판매는 주로 회사의 요구에 초점을 맞춘다. / 수익을 위해 제품을 판매하고자 하는

(B) Salespeople and other forms of promotion / are used / to create demand for a firm's current products.
판매원 및 다른 형태의 판촉이 / 사용된다. / 회사의 현재 제품에 대한 수요를 창출하기 위해

Clearly, the needs of the seller are very strong.
분명히 판매자의 요구가 아주 강하다.

(C) Marketing, however, / focuses on the needs of the consumer, / ultimately benefiting the seller as well.
그러나 마케팅은 / 소비자의 요구에 초점을 맞추면서 / 궁극적으로 판매자 또한 이득을 얻게 한다.

When a product or service is truly marketed, / the needs of the consumer are considered / from the very beginning of the new product development process, / and the product-service mix is designed / to meet the unsatisfied needs of the consuming public.
제품이나 서비스가 진정으로 마케팅될 때, / 소비자의 요구가 고려되며, / 신제품 개발 과정의 아주 초기부터 / 제품과 서비스의 결합이 기획된다. / 소비하는 대중들의 충족되지 않은 요구에 부응할 목적으로

(A) When a product or service is marketed in the proper manner, / very little selling is necessary / because the consumer need already exists / and the product or service is merely being produced / to satisfy the need.

제품이나 서비스가 적절한 방식으로 마케팅될 때, / 판매 활동은 거의 필요하지 않다. / 소비자의 요구가 이미 존재하고 / 제품이나 서비스가 그저 만들어지고 있는 것이기에 / 그 요구를 충족시키기 위해

판매와 마케팅 사이의 차이는 아주 간단하다. 판매는 주로 수익을 위해 제품을 판매하고자 하는 회사의 요구에 초점을 맞춘다.

(B) 회사의 현재 제품에 대한 수요를 창출하기 위해 판매원 및 다른 형태의 판촉이 사용된다. 분명히 판매자의 요구가 아주 강하다.

(C) 그러나 마케팅은 소비자의 요구에 초점을 맞추면서 궁극적으로 판매자 또한 이득을 얻게 한다. 제품이나 서비스를 진정으로 마케팅할 때, 신제품 개발 과정의 아주 초기부터 소비자의 요구가 고려되며, 소비하는 대중들의 충족되지 않은 요구에 부응할 목적으로 제품과 서비스의 결합이 기획된다.

(A) 적절한 방식으로 제품이나 서비스를 마케팅할 때, 소비자의 요구가 이미 존재하고 그 요구를 충족시키기 위해 제품이나 서비스가 그저 만들어지고 있는 것이기에 판매 활동은 거의 필요하지 않다.

Why? 왜 정답일까?

주어진 글은 판매와 마케팅의 차이를 글의 주된 소재로 제시하며 먼저 '판매'의 개념을 설명하고, **(B)**는 이에 이어서 판매란 판매자의 요구가 아주 강한 과정임을 언급한다. **(C)**는 역접의 연결어로 흐름을 전환하며 마케팅에 관해 이야기하기 시작하고, **(A)** 또한 마케팅에 관해 언급한다. 따라서 주어진 글 다음에 이어질 글의 순서로 가장 적절한 것은 ③ **'(B) – (C) – (A)'**이다.

- **desire** ⓝ 욕구
- **proper** ⓐ 적절한, 알맞은
- **satisfy** ⓥ 충족시키다, 만족시키다
- **current** ⓐ 현재의
- **benefit** ⓥ ~을 이롭게 하다
- **design** ⓥ 기획하다, 고안하다
- **public** ⓝ 대중
- **revenue** ⓝ 수익, 수입
- **merely** [ad] 단지
- **promotion** ⓝ 판촉, 홍보
- **ultimately** [ad] 궁극적으로
- **process** ⓝ 과정
- **meet the needs of** ~의 요구에 부응하다

구문 풀이

4행 When a product or service is marketed in the proper manner, very / little selling is necessary / because the consumer need already exists and the product or service is merely being produced to satisfy the need.

(little: 거의 없는 / selling: 주어 / is: 동사 / because: 접속사(~이기 때문에) / the consumer need: 주어1 / exists: 동사1 / the product or service: 주어2 / is merely being produced: 동사2(현재진행 수동태) / to satisfy: 부사적 용법(~하기 위해))

★★ 문제 해결 꿀~팁 ★★

▶ 많이 틀린 이유는?

서로 다른 두 개념을 비교하는 글이기에 '대조'가 시작되는 **(C)**의 위치를 어디로 잡을지 아는 것이 풀이의 관건이다. 오답으로 ④가 많이 나왔는데 이는 주어진 글이 판매와 마케팅을 모두 언급한 뒤 판매를 설명하면서 끝났기 때문에 바로 이어서 마케팅을 대조하는 단락이 와야 한다고 판단한 것이다. 하지만 **(B)**가 판매자 중심의 '판매' 개념을 이어서 설명하고 있기에 이 이야기가 마무리된 뒤 비로소 **(C)**가 이어질 수 있다는 점을 파악해야 한다.

▶ 문제 해결 방법은?

순서 문제에서 상반된 두 개념을 설명하는 지문은 단골로 등장하는데, 글의 흐름이 반전되는 포인트가 분명하기 때문이다. 인접한 두 단락은 역접의 연결사 없이는 서로 다른 내용을 말할 수 없으므로 한 개념에 대한 설명이 어디까지 이어지는지를 분명히 파악하여야 한다.

★★★ 1등급 대비 고난도 3점 문제

12 **편향의 영향력을 제한하기 위한 노력** 정답률 39% | 정답 ⑤

주어진 글 다음에 이어질 글의 순서로 가장 적절한 것을 고르시오. [3점]

① (A) – (C) – (B)
② (B) – (A) – (C)
③ (B) – (C) – (A)
④ (C) – (A) – (B)
✔(C) – (B) – (A)

Since we know we can't completely eliminate our biases, / we need to try to limit the harmful impacts / they can have on the objectivity and rationality / of our decisions and judgments.
우리는 우리의 편향을 완전히 없앨 수 없다는 것을 알고 있기 때문에, / 우리는 해로운 영향들을 제한하도록 노력할 필요가 있다. / 편향이 객관성과 합리성에 끼칠 수 있는 / 우리의 결정과 판단의

(C) It is important / that we are aware / when one of our cognitive biases is activated / and make a conscious choice to overcome that bias.
중요하다. / 우리가 인지하고, / 언제 우리의 인지적 편향 중 하나가 활성화되는지를 / 그 편향을 극복하기 위한 의식적 결정을 내리는 것이

We need to be aware of the impact / the bias has on our decision making process and our life.
우리는 영향력을 인지할 필요가 있다. / 편향이 우리의 의사 결정 과정과 삶에 끼치는

(B) Then we can choose an appropriate de-biasing strategy / to combat it.
그때 우리 적절한 반(反) 편향 전략을 선택할 수 있다. / 편향과 싸우기 위해

After we have implemented a strategy, / we should check in again / to see if it worked in the way we had hoped.
우리가 전략을 실행해 본 이후에, / 우리는 한 번 더 확인해야 한다. / 그것이 우리가 희망했던 방식대로 작동했는지를 보기 위해

(A) If it did, / we can move on / and make an objective and informed decision.
만약 그러했다면, / 우리는 넘어가서 / 객관적이고 정보에 근거한 결정을 내릴 수 있다.

If it didn't, / we can try the same strategy again / or implement a new one / until we are ready to make a rational judgment.
만약 그러지 않았다면, / 우리는 똑같은 전략을 다시 시도하거나 / 새로운 것을 실행할 수 있다. / 우리가 이성적 판단을 내릴 준비가 될 때까지

우리는 우리의 편향을 완전히 없앨 수 없다는 것을 알고 있기 때문에, 우리는 편향이 우리의 결정과 판단의 객관성과 합리성에 끼칠 수 있는 해로운 영향들을 제한하도록 노력할 필요가 있다.

(C) 우리가 언제 우리의 인지적 편향 중 하나가 활성화되는지를 인지하고, 그 편향을 극복하기 위한 의식적 결정을 내리는 것이 중요하다. 우리는 편향이 우리의 의사 결정 과정과 삶에 끼치는 영향력을 인지할 필요가 있다.

(B) 그때 우리는 편향과 싸우기 위해 적절한 반(反) 편향 전략을 선택할 수 있다. 우리가 전략을 실행해 본 이후에, 우리는 그것이 우리가 희망했던 방식대로 작동했는지를 보기 위해 한 번 더 확인해야 한다.

(A) 만약 그러했다면, 우리는 넘어가서 객관적이고 정보에 근거한 결정을 내릴 수 있다. 만약 그러지 않았다면, 우리는 우리가 이성적 판단을 내릴 준비가 될 때까지 똑같은 전략을 다시 시도하거나 새로운 것을 실행할 수 있다.

Why? 왜 정답일까?

편향의 영향력을 제한하기 위해 노력할 필요가 있다는 내용의 주어진 글 뒤에는, 우리가 편향이 언제 작용하는지를 이해하고 이를 극복하기 위한 의식적인 결정을 내릴 수 있어야 한다는 설명으로 주어진 글의 내용을 뒷받침하는 **(C)**가 먼저 연결된다. 이어서 **(B)**는 **(C)**의 후반부 내용을 받아 '편향이 삶에 미치는 영향력을 우리가 인지할 때' 바로 반 편향 전략 사용으로 나아갈 수 있다는 내용을 제시한다. 마지막으로 **(A)**는 **(B)**의 후반부 내용을 받아 전략이 우리가 기대한 대로 작용했는지 그렇지 못했는지에 따라 이어지는 결과를 소개하고 있다. 따라서 글의 순서로 가장 적절한 것은 ⑤ **'(C) – (B) – (A)'**이다.

- **eliminate** ⓥ 없애다, 제거하다
- **harmful** ⓐ 해로운
- **rationality** ⓝ 합리성
- **implement** ⓥ 실행하다
- **combat** ⓥ 싸우다
- **overcome** ⓥ 극복하다
- **bias** ⓝ 편향, 편견
- **objectivity** ⓝ 객관성
- **informed** ⓐ 정보에 근거한
- **appropriate** ⓐ 적절한
- **cognitive** ⓐ 인지적인

구문 풀이

10행 After we have implemented a strategy, we should check in again to see if it worked in the way [we had hoped].

(After: 접속사(~한 이후에) / have implemented: 현재완료 / to see: 목적(~하기 위해) / if: 접속사(~인지 아닌지) / had hoped: 과거완료(worked보다 먼저 일어남))

★★ 문제 해결 꿀~팁 ★★

▶ 많이 틀린 이유는?

(C)에 이어 **(A)**와 **(B)** 중 어느 단락이 이어질지 파악하는 것이 풀이의 관건이다. **(C)** 뒤에 **(A)**가 바로 이어질 경우, '편견이 우리의 의사 결정에 영향을 미친다면 우리가 객관적이고 정보에 근거한 판단을 내릴 수 있다'는 의미가 완성되어 맥락에 부합하지 않는다.

▶ 문제 해결 방법은?

(B) 후반부의 **'if it worked in the way we had hoped'**를 **(A)**에서 **'if it did ~'**와 **'if it didn't ~'**로 나누어 설명하고 있음을 파악하면 쉽게 답을 고를 수 있다.

DAY 15

[문제편 p.102]

DAY 16 문장 삽입 01

01 ④	02 ⑤	03 ③	04 ⑤	05 ④
06 ④	07 ③	08 ③	09 ③	10 ④
11 ⑤	12 ③			

01 뇌의 연료 자원 사용

정답률 54% | 정답 ④

글의 흐름으로 보아, 주어진 문장이 들어가기에 가장 적절한 곳을 고르시오.

The brain is a high-energy consumer of glucose, / which is its fuel.
뇌는 포도당의 고에너지 소비자이다. / 자기 연료인

Although the brain accounts for merely 3 percent of a person's body weight, / it consumes 20 percent of the available fuel.
비록 뇌는 사람 체중의 단지 3퍼센트를 차지하지만, / 그것은 사용 가능한 연료의 20퍼센트를 소비한다.

① Your brain can't store fuel, however, / so it has to "pay as it goes."
하지만 여러분의 뇌는 연료를 저장할 수 없고, / 따라서 '활동하는 대로 대가를 지불'해야 한다.

② Since your brain is incredibly adaptive, / it economizes its fuel resources.
여러분의 뇌는 놀라울 정도로 적응력이 뛰어나기 때문에, / 그것의 연료 자원을 경제적으로 사용한다.

③ Thus, / during a period of high stress, / it shifts away from the analysis of the nuances of a situation / to a singular and fixed focus on the stressful situation at hand.
따라서, / 극심한 스트레스를 받는 중이라면, / 뇌는 상황의 미묘한 차이를 분석하는 것으로부터 옮겨 간다. / 눈에 닥친 스트레스 상황에 대한 단일하고 고정된 집중으로

✔You don't sit back / and speculate about the meaning of life / when you are stressed.
여러분은 앉아서 / 삶의 의미에 대해 사색하지 않는다. / 여러분이 스트레스를 받을 때

Instead, / you devote all your energy / to trying to figure out what action to take.
대신에, / 여러분은 모든 에너지를 쏟는다. / 어떤 행동을 취해야 할지 알아내려고 노력하는 데

⑤ Sometimes, however, / this shift from the higher-thinking parts of the brain / to the automatic and reflexive parts of the brain / can lead you / to do something too quickly, without thinking.
그러나 때때로 / 이런 식으로 뇌의 고차원적 사고 영역에서 이동하는 것은 / 뇌의 자동적이고 반사적인 영역으로 / 여러분이 ~하도록 이끌 수 있다. / 무언가를 생각 없이 너무 빨리 하도록

뇌는 자기 연료인 포도당의 고에너지 소비자이다. 비록 뇌는 사람 체중의 단지 3퍼센트를 차지하지만, 사용 가능한 연료의 20퍼센트를 소비한다. ① 하지만 여러분의 뇌는 연료를 저장할 수 없고, 따라서 '활동하는 대로 대가를 지불'해야 한다. ② 여러분의 뇌는 놀라울 정도로 적응력이 뛰어나기 때문에, 그것의 연료 자원을 경제적으로 사용한다. ③ 따라서, 극심한 스트레스를 받는 중이라면, 뇌는 상황의 미묘한 차이를 분석하는 것으로부터 눈에 닥친 스트레스 상황에 대한 단일하고 고정된 집중으로 옮겨 간다. ④ 여러분은 스트레스를 받을 때 앉아서 삶의 의미에 대해 사색하지 않는다. 대신에, 여러분은 어떤 행동을 취해야 할지 알아내려고 노력하는 데 모든 에너지를 쏟는다. ⑤ 그러나 때때로 이런 식으로 뇌의 고차원적 사고 영역에서 자동적이고 반사적인 영역으로 이동하는 것은 여러분이 무언가를 생각 없이 너무 빨리 하도록 이끌 수 있다.

Why? 왜 정답일까?

④ 앞에서 극도로 스트레스를 받는 상황을 제시하며, 이때 우리 뇌는 상황의 미묘한 차이까지 관심을 기울이기보다는 눈에 닥친 것들에 주목하게 된다고 한다. 이어서 주어진 문장은 우리가 스트레스 상황일 때 삶의 의미를 생각하지는 않는다고 하고, ④ 뒤의 문장은 '그 대신(Instead)' 우리가 '(이 상황에서 지금) 뭘 할지'에 초점을 맞추게 된다고 설명한다. 따라서 주어진 문장이 들어가기에 가장 적절한 곳은 ④이다.

- glucose ⓝ 포도당
- merely ad 단지, 그저
- incredibly ad 놀라울 정도로
- economize ⓥ 절약하다, 아끼다
- nuance ⓝ 미묘한 차이
- at hand 당면한, 눈앞에 있는
- automatic ⓐ 자동적인
- fuel ⓝ 연료 ⓥ 부추기다
- body weight 체중
- adaptive ⓐ 적응하는
- analysis ⓝ 분석
- fixed ⓐ 고정된
- devote A to B A를 B에 바치다
- reflexive ⓐ 반사적인

구문 풀이

12행 Instead, you devote all your energy to trying to figure out {what action to take}.
「devote+A+to -ing : A를 ~하는 데 바치다」
「what+명사+to부정사 : 어떤 ~할지」

02 과학자들이 생각을 전달하는 수단의 변화

정답률 38% | 정답 ⑤

글의 흐름으로 보아, 주어진 문장이 들어가기에 가장 적절한 곳을 고르시오.

In the early stages of modern science, / scientists communicated their creative ideas / largely by publishing books.
현대 과학의 초기 단계에서 / 과학자들은 자신의 창의적인 생각을 전달했다. / 주로 책을 출판하여

① This modus operandi is illustrated / not only by Newton's *Principia*, / but also by Copernicus' *On the Revolutions of the Heavenly Spheres*, / Kepler's *The Harmonies of the World*, / and Galileo's *Dialogues Concerning the Two New Sciences*.
이런 작업 방식은 설명된다. / 뉴턴의 *Principia*로뿐만 아니라 / 코페르니쿠스의 *On the Revolutions of the Heavenly Spheres*와 / 케플러의 *The Harmonies of the World*, / 갈릴레오의 *Dialogues Concerning the Two New Sciences*로도

② With the advent of scientific periodicals, / such as the *Transactions of the Royal Society of London*, / books gradually yielded ground / to the technical journal article / as the chief form of scientific communication.
과학 정기 간행물의 출현과 함께, / *Transactions of the Royal Society of London* 같은 / 책은 점차 자리를 내주었다. / 전문 학술지 논문에 / 과학적 의사소통의 주요한 형식으로

③ Of course, / books were not abandoned altogether, / as Darwin's *Origin of Species* shows.
물론 / 책이 완전히 버려진 것은 아니었다. / 다윈의 *Origin of Species*가 보여주듯이

④ Even so, / it eventually became possible for scientists / to establish a reputation for their creative contributions / without publishing a single book-length treatment of their ideas.
그렇다고 하더라도, / 결국 과학자들로서는 가능해졌다. / 자신이 창의적으로 기여한 바에 대한 명성을 세우는 것이 / 자기 생각을 다룬 책 한 권 길이의 출간물을 내지 않고도

✔For instance, / the revolutionary ideas / that earned Einstein his Nobel Prize / — concerning the special theory of relativity and the photoelectric effect — / appeared as papers in the *Annalen der Physik*.
예를 들어, / 혁명적인 생각들은 / 아인슈타인에게 노벨상을 안겨 준, / 특수 상대성 이론과 광전 효과에 관한 / *Annalen der Physik*에 논문으로 등장했다.

His status as one of the greatest scientists of all time / does not depend on the publication of a single book.
역사상 가장 위대한 과학자 중 한 명이라는 그의 지위는 / 단 한 권의 책의 출간에 달려 있지는 않다.

현대 과학의 초기 단계에서 과학자들은 주로 책을 출판하여 자신의 창의적인 생각을 전달했다. ① 이런 작업 방식은 뉴턴의 *Principia*뿐만 아니라 코페르니쿠스의 *On the Revolutions of the Heavenly Spheres*와 케플러의 *The Harmonies of the World*, 갈릴레오의 *Dialogues Concerning the Two New Sciences*로도 설명된다. ② *Transactions of the Royal Society of London* 같은 과학 정기 간행물의 출현과 함께, 책은 과학적 의사소통의 주요한 형식으로 전문 학술지 논문에 점차 자리를 내주었다. ③ 물론 다윈의 *Origin of Species*가 보여주듯이, 책이 완전히 버려진 것은 아니었다. ④ 그렇다고 하더라도, 과학자들은 자기 생각을 다룬 책 한 권 길이의 출간물을 내지 않고도 자신이 창의적으로 기여한 바에 대한 명성을 세우는 것이 결국 가능해졌다. ⑤ 예를 들어, 아인슈타인에게 노벨상을 안겨 준, 특수 상대성 이론과 광전 효과에 관한 혁명적인 생각들은 *Annalen der Physik*에 논문으로 등장했다. 역사상 가장 위대한 과학자 중 한 명이라는 그의 지위는 단 한 권의 책의 출간에 달려 있지는 않다.

Why? 왜 정답일까?

현대 과학 초기에 과학자들은 책을 출판해 자신의 생각을 세상에 알렸지만, 시간이 흐르며 책보다 짧은 학술 논문의 형태로 생각을 발표하게 되었다는 내용의 글이다. ⑤ 앞에서 책 한 권 길이의 출간물 없이도 과학자들이 자신의 업적을 드러낼 수 있게 되었다고 설명한 데 이어, 주어진 문장에서는 책 대신 '논문'을 활용한 과학자의 예로 아인슈타인을 언급한다. 이어서 ⑤ 뒤에서는 아인슈타인을 His로 지칭하며, '그'의 입지가 책 출간 여부에 좌우되지는 않는다고 부연한다. 따라서 주어진 문장이 들어가기에 가장 적절한 곳은 ⑤이다.

- revolutionary ⓐ 혁명적인
- special theory of relativity 특수 상대성 이론
- photoelectric effect 광전 효과
- communicate ⓥ 전달하다
- publish ⓥ 출판하다
- periodical ⓝ 정기 간행물
- yield ground to ~에 자리를 내주다
- abandon ⓥ 버리다
- establish ⓥ 세우다, 확립하다
- contribution ⓝ 기여, 공헌
- status ⓝ 지위, 상태
- concerning prep ~에 관하여
- paper ⓝ 논문
- largely ad 주로, 대개
- advent ⓝ 출현
- gradually ad 점차로
- journal ⓝ 학술지
- altogether ad 완전히, 전적으로
- reputation ⓝ 명성
- treatment ⓝ 취급, 대우
- depend on ~에 달려 있다

구문 풀이

17행 Even so, it eventually became possible for scientists to establish a reputation for their creative contributions without publishing a single book-length treatment of their ideas.
가주어 / 2형식 동사 / 보어 / 의미상 주어 / 진주어(~것) / ~하지 않은 채

03 소유권/이용권 공유 서비스

정답률 58% | 정답 ③

글의 흐름으로 보아, 주어진 문장이 들어가기에 가장 적절한 곳을 고르시오.

Car-sharing is now a familiar concept, / but creative companies are making it possible / for their clients to share / ownership and access to just about everything, / such as villas, handbags and even diamond necklaces.
자동차 공유는 지금 익숙한 개념이지만 / 창의적인 회사들은 가능하게 하고 있다. / 그들의 고객들이 공유하는 것을 / 거의 모든 것에 대한 소유권과 이용권을 / 별장, 핸드백, 그리고 심지어 다이아몬드 목걸이와 같은

① According to a Portuguese saying, / "You should never have a yacht; / you should have a friend with a yacht."
포르투갈의 한 속담에 따르면, / '여러분은 절대 요트를 가져서는 안 되고 / 요트가 있는 친구를 가져야 한다.'

② By joining a yacht sharing service, / members can live the Portuguese dream / by sharing a yacht with up to seven other people.
요트 공유 서비스에 가입함으로써, / 회원들은 포르투갈인들의 꿈을 성취할 수 있다. / 최대 7명의 다른 사람들과 한 대의 요트를 공유함으로써

✔In describing the service, / a recent newspaper article warned consumers / that sharing the yacht means / "there is no guarantee / you will always be able to use it when you want."
그 서비스를 설명하면서, / 최근 한 신문 기사는 소비자에게 경고했다. / 요트를 공유하는 것은 의미한다고 / '보장은 없다'는 것을 / '여러분이 원할 때 그것을 항상 이용할 수 있을 것이라는'

This apparent limitation is / precisely what helps consumers make it a treat.
이 외견상의 제한이 / 바로 소비자들이 그것을 큰 기쁨으로 만들도록 돕는 것이다.

④ Limiting your access to everything / from sandwiches to luxury cars / helps to reset your cheerometer.
모든 것에 여러분의 이용권을 제한하는 것이 / 샌드위치부터 고급 자동차까지 / 여러분의 활기 온도계를 재설정하도록 돕는다.

⑤ That is, / knowing you can't have access to something all the time / may help you appreciate it more / when you do.
즉, / 어떤 것에 여러분이 항상 이용권을 가질 수는 없다는 것을 아는 것이 / 그것에 대해 더 감사하도록 도울 것이다. / 여러분이 이용권을 가질 때

자동차 공유는 지금 익숙한 개념이지만 창의적인 회사들은 그들의 고객들이 별장, 핸드백, 그리고 심지어 다이아몬드 목걸이와 같은 거의 모든 것에 대한 소유권과 이용권을 공유하는 것을 가능하게 하고 있다. ① 포르투갈의 한 속담에 따르면, '여러분은 절대 요트를 가져서는 안 되고 요트가 있는 친구를 가져야 한다.' ② 요트 공유 서비스에 가입함으로써, 회원들은 최대 7명의 다른 사람들과 한 대의 요트를 공유함으로써 포르투갈인들의 꿈을 성취할 수 있다. ③ 그 서비스를 설명하면서, 최근 한 신문 기사는 요트를 공유하는 것은 '여러분이 원할 때 여러분이 그것을 항상 이용할 수 있을 것이라는 보장은 없다'는 것을 의미한다고 소비자에게 경고했다. 이 외견상의 제한이 바로 소비자들이 그것을 큰 기쁨으로 만들도록 돕는 것이다. ④ 샌드위치부터 고급 자동차까지 모든 것에 여러분의 이용권을 제한하는 것이 여러분의 활기 온도계를 재설정하도록 돕는다. ⑤ 즉, 어떤 것에 여러분이 항상 이용권을 가질 수는 없다는 것을 아는 것이 여러분이 이용권을 가질 때 그것에 대해 더 감사하도록 도울 것이다.

Why? 왜 정답일까?

③ 앞에서 요트 공유 서비스를 예로 들어 거의 모든 재화에 대한 소유권 및 이용권 공유가 활발히 이루어지고 있는 상황을 제시하는데, ③ 뒤에서는 공유 서비스의 '외견상 제한'을 언급하고 있다. 즉 ③ 앞뒤로 공유 서비스에 대한 논조가 상반되어 논리적 공백이 생겨나므로, 주어진 문장이 들어가기에 가장 적절한 곳은 ③이다.

- guarantee ⓝ 보장 ⓥ 보장하다
- ownership ⓝ 소유권
- apparent ⓐ 외견상의, 겉보기의
- limitation ⓝ 제한
- precisely ad 정확히, 꼭
- reset ⓥ 다시 맞추다
- cheerometer ⓝ 활기 온도계
- appreciate ⓥ 감사하다

구문 풀이

5행 Car-sharing is now a familiar concept, but creative companies are making it possible for their clients to share ownership and access to just about everything, such as villas, handbags and even diamond necklaces.
「make + 가목적어 + 목적격 보어 + 의미상 주어 + 진목적어 : ~이 …하는 것을 ~하게 만들다」

04 사랑과 나눔의 힘을 보여주는 사례

정답률 56% | 정답 ⑤

글의 흐름으로 보아, 주어진 문장이 들어가기에 가장 적절한 곳을 고르시오.

The world can be a different and better place / if, while you are here, you give of yourself.
세상은 다르고 더 좋은 곳이 될 수 있다. / 이 세상에 있는 동안 여러분이 자신을 헌신한다면

This concept became clear to Azim one day / when he was watching television at an airport terminal / while waiting for a flight.
이런 생각은 어느 날 Azim에게 분명해졌다. / 그가 공항에서 TV 시청을 하고 있었을 때 / 비행기를 기다리며

A priest was sharing a story about newborn twins, / one of whom was ill.
한 성직자가 갓 태어난 쌍둥이 이야기를 해 주었는데, / 그중 한 명은 아팠다.

① The twins were in separate incubators, / as per hospital rules.
그 쌍둥이는 별개의 인큐베이터에 있었다. / 병원 규칙대로

② A nurse on the floor repeatedly suggested / that the twins be kept together in one incubator.
그 층의 간호사는 반복해서 제안했다. / 쌍둥이를 한 인큐베이터에 두어야 한다고

③ The doctors finally agreed to try this.
의사들은 마침내 이를 시도하는 데 동의했다.

④ When the twins were brought into contact with each other, / the healthy twin immediately put his arms around his sick brother.
쌍둥이들이 서로 접촉하게 되었을 때, / 건강한 쌍둥이가 아픈 형제를 즉시 껴안았다.

✔This instinctive exchange / gradually helped the sick twin / to recover and regain his health.
이러한 본능적인 교감은 / 서서히 아픈 아이를 도와주었다. / 회복하고 건강을 찾도록

The babies' family and the doctors / witnessed the intangible force of love and the incredible power of giving.
아이들의 가족과 의사들은 / 만질 수 없는 사랑의 힘과 믿을 수 없는 나눔의 힘을 목격하였다.

이 세상에 있는 동안 여러분이 자신을 헌신한다면 세상은 다르고 더 좋은 곳이 될 수 있다. 이런 생각은 어느 날 Azim이 비행기를 기다리며 공항에서 TV 시청을 하고 있었을 때 분명해졌다. 한 성직자가 갓 태어난 쌍둥이 이야기를 해 주었는데, 그중 한 명은 아팠다. ① 그 쌍둥이는 병원 규칙대로 별개의 인큐베이터에 있었다. ② 그 층의 간호사는 쌍둥이를 한 인큐베이터에 두어야 한다고 반복해서 제안했다. ③ 의사들은 마침내 이를 시도하는 데 동의했다. ④ 쌍둥이들이 서로 접촉하게 되었을 때, 건강한 쌍둥이가 아픈 형제를 즉시 껴안았다. ⑤ 이러한 본능적인 교감은 아픈 아이가 서서히 회복하고 건강을 찾도록 도와주었다. 아이들의 가족과 의사들은 만질 수 없는 사랑의 힘과 믿을 수 없는 나눔의 힘을 목격하였다.

Why? 왜 정답일까?

⑤ 앞의 문장에서 각각의 인큐베이터에 따로 놓여있던 쌍둥이가 마침내 같은 인큐베이터에 있게 되었을 때 건강한 아이가 아픈 아이를 즉시 껴안았음을 이야기하는데, 주어진 문장은 이를 '본능적인 교감'이라는 말로 나타내며 이런 행동이 아픈 아이가 건강을 회복하게 도왔다고 설명한다. ⑤ 뒤의 문장에서는 이를 통해 쌍둥이의 가족들과 의사들이 사랑과 나눔의 힘을 직접 목도하게 되었다는 결과를 이야기한다. 따라서 주어진 문장이 들어가기에 가장 적절한 곳은 ⑤이다.

- instinctive ⓐ 본능적인
- exchange ⓝ 주고받음
- gradually ad 서서히
- regain ⓥ 되찾다, 회복하다
- priest ⓝ 성직자
- newborn ⓐ 갓 태어난, 신생아의
- separate ⓐ 별개의, 개별적인
- as per ~대로, ~에 따라
- repeatedly ad 반복적으로
- bring into contact with ~와 접촉시키다
- witness ⓥ 목격하다
- intangible ⓐ 만질 수 없는, 무형의

구문 풀이

5행 The world can be a different and better place / if, (while you are here), you give of yourself.
주격 보어(The world 설명) / 접속사(~한다면) / 접속사(~하는 동안) / 헌신하다, 할 수 있는 것을 다하다

05 심장 이식의 시작

정답률 60% | 정답 ④

글의 흐름으로 보아, 주어진 문장이 들어가기에 가장 적절한 곳을 고르시오. [3점]

Of all the medical achievements of the 1960s, / the most widely known was the first heart transplant, / performed by the South African surgeon Christiaan Barnard in 1967.
1960년대의 모든 의학적 성취 중에서 / 가장 널리 알려진 것은 최초의 심장 이식이었다. / 1967년 남아프리카 공화국의 외과 의사 Christiaan Barnard에 의해서 행해진

① The patient's death 18 days later / did not weaken the spirits of those / who welcomed a new era of medicine.

18일 후 그 환자의 사망이 / 사람들의 사기를 떨어뜨리지 않았다. / 의학의 새로운 시대를 환영하는

② The ability to perform heart transplants / was linked to the development of respirators, / which had been introduced to hospitals in the 1950s.
심장 이식을 할 수 있는 능력은 / 인공호흡기의 개발과 관련이 있었는데, / 이것은 1950년대에 병원에 도입되었다.

③ Respirators could save many lives, / but not all those whose hearts kept beating / ever recovered any other significant functions.
인공호흡기는 많은 생명을 구할 수 있었지만, / 심장이 계속해서 뛰는 사람들 모두가 / 어떤 다른 중요한 기능을 회복한 것은 아니었다.

✔ In some cases, / their brains had ceased to function altogether.
어떤 경우에는 / 그들의 뇌가 완전히 기능을 멈추었다.

The realization / that such patients could be a source of organs for transplantation / led to the setting up of the Harvard Brain Death Committee, / and to its recommendation / that the absence of all "discernible central nervous system activity" / should be "a new criterion for death".
그 인식이 / 그러한 환자들이 이식용 장기 공급자가 될 수 있다는 / 하버드 뇌사 위원회의 설립으로 이어졌고, / 그 위원회의 권고로 이어졌다. / 모든 '식별 가능한 중추 신경계 활동'의 부재는 / '사망의 새로운 기준'이 되어야 한다는

⑤ The recommendation has since been adopted, with some modifications, / almost everywhere.
그 권고는 그 후 일부 수정을 거쳐 받아들여졌다. / 거의 모든 곳에서

1960년대의 모든 의학적 성취 중에서 가장 널리 알려진 것은 1967년 남아프리카 공화국의 외과 의사 Christiaan Barnard에 의해서 행해진 최초의 심장 이식이었다. ① 18일 후에 그 환자가 사망한 것이 의학의 새로운 시대를 환영하는 사람들의 사기를 떨어뜨리지 않았다. ② 심장 이식을 할 수 있는 능력은 인공호흡기의 개발과 관련이 있었는데, 이것은 1950년대에 병원에 도입되었다. ③ 인공호흡기는 많은 생명을 구할 수 있었지만, 심장이 계속해서 뛰는 사람들이 모두 다 어떤 다른 중요한 기능을 회복한 것은 아니었다. ④ 어떤 경우에는 그들의 뇌가 완전히 기능을 멈추었다. 그러한 환자들이 이식용 장기 공급자가 될 수 있다는 인식으로 인해 하버드 뇌사 위원회가 설립되었고, 모든 '식별 가능한 중추 신경계 활동'의 부재는 '사망의 새로운 기준'이 되어야 한다는 그 위원회의 권고로 이어졌다. ⑤ 그 권고는 그 후 일부 수정을 거쳐 거의 모든 곳에서 받아들여졌다.

Why? 왜 정답일까?

심장 이식의 시작을 소재로 다룬 글이다. ④ 앞의 두 문장에서 심장 이식은 인공호흡기의 개발로 가능해졌는데, 이 인공호흡기는 많은 생명을 구할 수 있기는 했지만 모든 이가 온전히 기능을 회복하게 해주는 것은 아니었다는 내용을 제시한다. 주어진 문장은 인공호흡기로 인해 심장이 계속 뛰게 된 환자들 중 일부를 **their**로 받으며 때때로 이들의 뇌 기능이 완전히 정지되기도 했다는 내용을 언급한다. ④ 뒤의 문장은 뇌 기능이 멈춘 환자들을 다시 **such patients**로 받으며 이들의 장기를 이식하기 위한 뇌사 위원회가 설립되었다고 설명한다. 따라서 주어진 문장이 들어가기에 가장 적절한 곳은 ④이다.

- **cease** ⓥ 멈추다
- **transplant** ⓝ 이식
- **realization** ⓝ 인식, 깨달음
- **absence** ⓝ 부재
- **altogether** ad 완전히
- **significant** ⓐ 중요한
- **recommendation** ⓝ 권고, 추천
- **modification** ⓝ 수정

구문 풀이

3행 Of all the medical achievements of the 1960s, the most widely known was the first heart transplant, (which was) performed by the South African surgeon Christiaan Barnard in 1967.
(모든 ~들 중에서 / 「보어+동사+주어 : 도치 구문」 / 생략)

06 창의성과 생산성의 관계

정답률 47% | 정답 ④

글의 흐름으로 보아, 주어진 문장이 들어가기에 가장 적절한 곳을 고르시오. [3점]

Creativity can have an effect on productivity.
창의성은 생산성에 영향을 미칠 수 있다.

Creativity leads some individuals to recognize problems / that others do not see, / but which may be very difficult.
창의성은 어떤 이들이 문제들을 인식하게 하지만, / 남들은 보지 못하는 / 이는 매우 어려울 수도 있다.

① Charles Darwin's approach to the speciation problem / is a good example of this; / he chose a very difficult and tangled problem, speciation, / which led him / into a long period of data collection and deliberation.
종 분화 문제에 대한 찰스 다윈의 접근이 / 이것의 좋은 예시인데, / 그는 매우 어렵고 복잡한 문제인 종 분화를 선택했고, / 이것은 그를 이끌었다. / 오랜 자료 수집과 심사숙고의 기간으로

② This choice of problem / did not allow for a quick attack or a simple experiment.
이러한 문제 선택은 / 빠른 착수나 간단한 실험을 허용하지 않았다.

③ In such cases / creativity may actually decrease productivity / (as measured by publication counts) / because effort is focused on difficult problems.
이 경우, / 창의성은 사실 생산성을 감소시킬 수 있다. / (출판물의 수로 측정되듯) / 노력은 어려운 문제에 집중되기 때문에

✔ For others, / whose creativity is more focused on methods and technique, / creativity may lead to solutions / that drastically reduce the work / necessary to solve a problem.
다른 이들의 경우, / 창의성이 방법과 기술에 더 집중돼 있는 / 창의성은 해결책으로 이어질 수 있다. / 작업을 극적으로 줄이는 / 문제 해결에 필요한

We can see an example / in the development of the polymerase chain reaction (PCR) / which enables us to amplify small pieces of DNA in a short time.
우리는 한 예를 볼 수 있다. / 중합 효소 연쇄 반응(PCR)의 개발에서 / 작은 DNA 조각들을 짧은 시간에 증폭시켜 주는

⑤ This type of creativity / might reduce the number of steps / or substitute steps / that are less likely to fail, / thus increasing productivity.
이러한 유형의 창의성은 / 단계의 수를 줄이거나 / 단계로 대체해주고, / 실패할 가능성이 더 낮은 / 그리하여 생산성을 높일 수도 있다.

창의성은 생산성에 영향을 미칠 수 있다. 창의성은 어떤 이들이 남들은 보지 못하는 문제들을 인식하게 하지만, 이는 매우 어려울 수도 있다. ① 종 분화 문제에 대한 찰스 다윈의 접근이 이것의 좋은 예시인데, 그는 매우 어렵고 복잡한 문제인 종 분화를 선택했고, 이것은 그를 오랜 자료 수집과 심사숙고의 기간으로 이끌었다. ② 이러한 문제 선택은 빠른 착수나 간단한 실험을 허용하지 않았다. ③ 이 경우, 노력은 어려운 문제에 집중되기 때문에 창의성은 (출판물의 수로 측정되듯) 사실 생산성을 감소시킬 수 있다. ④ 창의성이 방법과 기술에 더 집중돼 있는 다른 이들의 경우, 창의성은 문제 해결에 필요한 작업을 극적으로 줄이는 해결책으로 이어질 수 있다. 우리는 작은 DNA 조각들을 짧은 시간에 증폭시켜 주는 중합 효소 연쇄 반응(PCR)의 개발에서 한 예를 볼 수 있다. ⑤ 이러한 유형의 창의성은 단계의 수를 줄이거나 실패할 가능성이 더 낮은 단계로 대체해주고, 그리하여 생산성을 높일 수도 있다.

Why? 왜 정답일까?

창의성이 생산성에 부정적 또는 긍정적 영향을 끼친다는 내용으로, ④ 앞에서는 창의성으로 인해 생산성이 떨어지는 예시를, ④ 뒤에서는 생산성이 오르는 사례를 보여주고 있다. 따라서 생산성의 긍정적 영향에 관한 설명으로 넘어가는 주어진 문장이 들어가기에 가장 적절한 곳은 ④이다.

- **lead to** ~로 이어지다
- **productivity** ⓝ 생산성
- **tangled** ⓐ 복잡한, 뒤엉킨
- **publication** ⓝ 출판(물)
- **polymerase chain reaction** 중합 효소 연쇄 반응
- **amplify** ⓥ 증폭하다
- **drastically** ad 극적으로
- **speciation** ⓝ 종(種) 분화
- **deliberation** ⓝ 숙고
- **development** ⓝ 개발, 발전, 전개
- **substitute** ⓥ 대체하다

구문 풀이

1행 For others, whose creativity is more focused on methods and technique, creativity may lead to solutions [that drastically reduce the work necessary to solve a problem]. [ ] : 형용사절(solutions 수식)
(선행사 / 소유격 관계대명사 / 형용사구)

07 조수간만의 차

정답률 35% | 정답 ③

글의 흐름으로 보아, 주어진 문장이 들어가기에 가장 적절한 곳을 고르시오. [3점]

The difference in the Moon's gravitational pull / on different parts of our planet / effectively creates a "stretching force."
달 중력의 차이는 / 우리 행성의 여러 부분에 대한 / 효과적으로 '잡아 늘리는 힘'을 만든다.

① It makes our planet / slightly stretched out along the line of sight to the Moon / and slightly compressed along a line perpendicular to that.
그것은 우리 행성을 ~하게 만든다. / 달이 보이는 쪽으로 약간 늘어나고, / 그것에 직각을 이루는 선을 따라 약간 눌리게

② The tidal stretching / caused by the Moon's gravity / affects our entire planet, / including both land and water, inside and out.
조수의 팽창은 / 달의 중력으로 발생하는 / 우리 행성 전체에 영향을 미친다. / 땅과 물을 포함한 안팎으로

✔ However, / the rigidity of rock means / that land rises and falls with the tides / by a much smaller amount than water, / which is why we notice only the ocean tides.
하지만 / 암석의 단단함은 의미한다 / 땅이 조수와 함께 오르락내리락한다는 것을 / 물보다는 훨씬 적은 양만큼 / 이 이유로 우리는 오로지 바다의 조수만을 알아차리게 된다.

The stretching also explains / why there are generally *two* high tides / (and two low tides) / in the ocean each day.
또한, 그 팽창은 설명한다. / 왜 일반적으로 *두 번의* 만조가 발생하는지 / (그리고 두 번의 간조) / 매일 바다에서
④ Because Earth is stretched / much like a rubber band, / the oceans bulge out / both on the side facing toward the Moon / and on the side facing away from the Moon.
지구가 늘어나기 때문에, / 고무줄처럼 / 바다는 팽창해 나간다. / 달을 향하는 쪽에서도, / 달에서 멀어지는 쪽에서도
⑤ As Earth rotates, / we are carried through both of these tidal bulges each day, / so we have high tide / when we are in each of the two bulges / and low tide / at the midpoints in between.
지구가 자전함에 따라 / 우리는 매일 이 두 개의 조수 팽창부를 통과하게 된다 / 그래서 우리는 만조를 겪는다. / 우리가 각각 두 개의 팽창부에 있을 때 / 그리고 간조를 / 그 사이 중간 지점에서

우리 행성의 여러 부분에 대한 달 중력의 차이는 효과적으로 '잡아 늘리는 힘'을 만든다. ① 그것은 우리 행성이 달이 보이는 쪽으로 약간 늘어나고, 그것에 직각을 이루는 선을 따라 약간 눌리게 만든다. ② 달의 중력으로 발생하는 조수의 팽창은 땅과 물을 포함한 우리 행성 전체에 안팎으로 영향을 미친다. ③ 하지만 암석의 단단함은 땅이 물보다는 훨씬 적은 양만큼 조수와 함께 오르락내리락한다는 것을 의미하며, 이 이유로 우리는 오로지 바다의 조수만을 알아차리게 된다. 또한, 그 팽창은 왜 일반적으로 매일 바다에서 *두 번의* 만조(그리고 두 번의 간조)가 발생하는지 설명한다. ④ 지구가 고무줄처럼 늘어나기 때문에, 바다는 달을 향하는 쪽에서도, 달에서 멀어지는 쪽에서도 팽창해 나간다. ⑤ 지구가 자전함에 따라 우리는 매일 이 두 개의 조수 팽창부를 통과하게 되어서, 우리가 각각 두 개의 팽창부에 있을 때 만조를 겪고 그 사이 중간 지점에 있을 때 간조를 겪는다.

Why? 왜 정답일까?

조수간만의 차가 발생하는 이유를 설명하는 글이다. 달의 중력은 지구의 영역마다 다르게 작용하기 때문에 지구는 달을 보는 쪽을 따라 늘어나고, 이와 직각을 이루는 지점에서는 줄어든다는 배경 설명이 ③ 앞까지 이어진다. 이때 주어진 문장은 암석으로 이뤄진 지구의 땅은 팽창과 수축이 덜 드러나는 반면, 바다의 물은 보다 크게 차이를 보인다고 설명한다. also로 시작하는 ③ 뒤의 문장부터는 조수간만의 차가 일어나는 횟수에 관해 언급하며 앞과 내용상 달라진다. 따라서 주어진 문장이 들어가기에 가장 적절한 곳은 ③이다.

- rigidity ⓝ 단단함
- gravitational ⓐ 중력의
- compress ⓥ 압축하다, 수축하다
- inside and out 안팎으로
- bulge ⓥ 팽창하다 ⓝ 튀어나온 것
- midpoint ⓝ 중간 지점
- tide ⓝ 조수, 밀물과 썰물
- slightly ad 약간
- perpendicular ⓐ 직각을 이루는
- rubber band 고무줄
- carry through 헤쳐나가다, 달성하다
- in between 사이에

구문 풀이

1행 However, the rigidity of rock means that land rises and falls with the tides by a much smaller amount than water, which is why we notice only the ocean tides.
(선행사(문장) / 계속적 용법)

★★★ 1등급 대비 고난도 2점 문제

08 지중해 사람들이 더 건강한 이유 — 정답률 39% | 정답 ③

글의 흐름으로 보아, 주어진 문장이 들어가기에 가장 적절한 곳을 고르시오.

Why do people in the Mediterranean live longer / and have a lower incidence of disease?
왜 지중해 지역의 사람들은 더 오래 살고 / 질병 발생률이 더 낮을까?
Some people say / it's because of what they eat.
몇몇의 사람들은 말한다. / 그것이 그들이 먹는 것 때문이라고
Their diet is full of fresh fruits, fish, vegetables, whole grains, and nuts.
그들의 식단은 신선한 과일, 생선, 채소, 통곡물, 견과류로 가득하다.
Individuals in these cultures / drink red wine / and use great amounts of olive oil.
이러한 문화권의 사람들은 / 적포도주를 마시고 / 많은 양의 올리브유를 사용한다.
Why is that food pattern healthy?
왜 그러한 음식 패턴이 건강에 좋을까?
① One reason is / that they are eating a palette of colors.
한 가지 이유는 ~이다. / 그들이 다양한 색깔을 먹고 있다는 것
② More and more research is surfacing / that shows us the benefits / of the thousands of colorful "phytochemicals" (*phyto*=plant) / that exist in foods.
점점 더 많은 연구가 부상하고 있다. / 우리에게 이점을 보여주는 / 수천 가지의 다채로운 '생화학 물질'(*phyto*=식물)의 / 식품에 존재하는

✔These healthful, non-nutritive compounds in plants / provide color and function to the plant / and add to the health of the human body.
식물에 있는 이 건강에 좋은 비영양성 이 화합물들은 / 식물에 색과 기능을 제공하고 / 인체의 건강에 보탬이 된다.
Each color connects to a particular compound / that serves a specific function in the body.
각각의 색깔은 특정 화합물과 연결된다. / 몸에서 특정 기능을 하는
④ For example, / if you don't eat purple foods, / you are probably missing out on anthocyanins, / important brain protection compounds.
예를 들어, / 만약 당신이 보라색 음식을 먹지 않는다면, / 당신은 안토시아닌을 아마도 놓치고 있는 것이다. / 중요한 뇌 보호 화합물인
⑤ Similarly, / if you avoid green-colored foods, / you may be lacking chlorophyll, / a plant antioxidant / that guards your cells from damage.
마찬가지로, / 만약 당신이 녹색 음식을 피한다면, / 당신에게는 엽록소가 부족할 수도 있다. / 식물 산화 방지제인 / 세포가 손상되는 것을 막아주는

왜 지중해 지역의 사람들은 더 오래 살고 질병 발생률이 더 낮을까? 몇몇의 사람들은 그것이 그들이 먹는 것 때문이라고 말한다. 그들의 식단은 신선한 과일, 생선, 채소, 통곡물, 견과류로 가득하다. 이러한 문화권의 사람들은 적포도주를 마시고 많은 양의 올리브유를 사용한다. 왜 그러한 음식 패턴이 건강에 좋을까? ① 한 가지 이유는 그들이 다양한 색깔을 먹고 있기 때문이다. ② 식품에 존재하는 수천 가지의 다채로운 '생화학 물질'(*phyto*=식물)의 이점을 보여주는 점점 더 많은 연구가 부상하고 있다. ③ 식물에 있는 이 건강에 좋은 비영양성 화합물들은 식물에 색과 기능을 제공하고 인체의 건강에 보탬이 된다. 각각의 색깔은 몸에서 특정 기능을 하는 특정 화합물과 연결된다. ④ 예를 들어, 만약 당신이 보라색 음식을 먹지 않는다면, 당신은 중요한 뇌 보호 화합물인 안토시아닌을 아마도 놓치고 있는 것이다. ⑤ 마찬가지로, 만약 당신이 녹색 음식을 피한다면, 세포가 손상되는 것을 막아주는 식물 산화 방지제인 엽록소가 부족할 수도 있다.

Why? 왜 정답일까?

③ 앞에서 다채로운 생화학 물질이 연구되고 있다고 하는데, 주어진 문장에서는 이 생화학 물질을 These healthful, non-nutritive compounds로 지칭하며 보충 설명한다. ③ 뒤로는 색깔마다 어떤 기능의 화합물과 연관되는지 구체적으로 열거하는 내용이 일관성 있게 제시된다. 따라서 주어진 문장이 들어가기에 가장 적절한 곳은 ③이다.

- Mediterranean ⓐ 지중해의
- miss out on ~을 놓치다
- incidence ⓝ (사건의) 발생
- antioxidant ⓝ 산화 방지제

구문 풀이

18행 Similarly, if you avoid green-colored foods, you may be lacking chlorophyll, a plant antioxidant [that guards your cells from damage].
(동격(= chlorophyll) / 주격 관·대)

★★ 문제 해결 꿀~팁 ★★

▶ 많이 틀린 이유는?
④ 앞에 a particular compound가 나오고, 주어진 문장에도 compounds가 나오기 때문에 얼핏 보면 연결되는 것처럼 보인다. 하지만 'these ~ compounds'는 엄밀히 따지면 복수의 지시어이므로, 앞에 '복수 명사'가 나와야 사용 가능하다.
▶ 문제 해결 방법은?
주어진 문장의 These healthful, non-nutritive compounds가 가리킬 만한 말이 ③ 앞의 복수 명사 phytochemicals 뿐이다. 따라서 아무리 ③ 앞뒤가 내용상 자연스러워 보여도, 지시어로 인해 발생하는 논리적 공백을 메꾸기 위해 ③에 주어진 문장을 넣어야 한다.

★★★ 1등급 대비 고난도 2점 문제

09 오랜 역사를 지닌 아미노산 결핍의 문제 — 정답률 35% | 정답 ③

글의 흐름으로 보아, 주어진 문장이 들어가기에 가장 적절한 곳을 고르시오.

The problem of amino acid deficiency / is not unique to the modern world / by any means.
아미노산 결핍의 문제가 / 현대 세계에 유일한 것은 아니다. / 결코
① Preindustrial humanity / probably dealt with protein and amino acid insufficiency / on a regular basis.
산업화 이전의 인류는 / 아마 단백질과 아미노산의 부족에 대처했을 것이다. / 정기적으로
② Sure, / large hunted animals / such as mammoths / provided protein and amino acids aplenty.
물론, / 거대한 사냥한 동물들이 / 매머드와 같은 / 단백질과 아미노산을 많이 제공했다.

✔ However, / living off big game / in the era before refrigeration / meant humans had to endure / alternating periods of feast and famine.
하지만, / 거대한 사냥감에 의존해서 사는 것은 / 냉장 보관 이전 시대에 / 사람들이 견뎌야 했다는 것을 의미했다. / 성찬과 기근이 교대로 일어나는 시기를

Droughts, forest fires, superstorms, and ice ages / led to long stretches of difficult conditions, / and starvation was a constant threat.
가뭄, 산불, 슈퍼스톰 그리고 빙하기는 / 장기적인 어려움의 상황으로 이어졌고, / 굶주림은 지속적인 위협이었다.

④ The human inability to synthesize / such basic things as amino acids / certainly worsened those crises / and made surviving on whatever was available / that much harder.
인간이 합성할 수 없다는 것이 / 아미노산과 같은 기본적인 것들을 / 확실히 그러한 위기들을 악화시켰고 / 구할 수 있는 무엇이든 먹으며 생존하는 것을 / 그만큼 훨씬 더 힘들게 했다.

⑤ During a famine, / it's not the lack of calories / that is the ultimate cause of death; / it's the lack of proteins / and the essential amino acids / they provide.
기근 동안, / 열량 부족이 아니라, / 죽음의 궁극적인 원인은 / 바로 단백질과 / 필수 아미노산의 부족이다. / 그것이 제공하는

아미노산 결핍의 문제가 결코 현대 세계에 유일한 것은 아니다. ① 산업화 이전의 인류는 아마 단백질과 아미노산의 부족에 정기적으로 대처했을 것이다. ② 물론, 매머드와 같은 사냥으로 잡은 거대한 동물들이 단백질과 아미노산을 많이 제공했다. ③ 하지만, 냉장 보관 이전 시대에 거대한 사냥감에 의존해서 사는 것은 사람들이 성찬과 기근이 교대로 일어나는 시기를 견뎌야 했다는 것을 의미했다. 가뭄, 산불, 초강력 태풍 그리고 빙하기는 장기적인 어려움의 상황으로 이어졌고, 굶주림은 지속적인 위협이었다. ④ 아미노산과 같은 기본적인 것들을 인간이 합성할 수 없다는 것은 확실히 그러한 위기들을 악화시켰고 구할 수 있는 무엇이든 먹으며 생존하는 것을 그만큼 훨씬 더 힘들게 했다. ⑤ 기근 동안 죽음의 궁극적인 원인은 열량 부족이 아니라, 바로 단백질과 그것이 제공하는 필수 아미노산의 부족이다.

Why? 왜 정답일까?

이 글은 아미노산 결핍의 문제가 현대 인류뿐 아니라 산업화 이전의 인류 또한 겪었던 문제임을 설명하고 있다. ③ 앞에서 산업화 이전의 인류는 매머드와 같은 거대한 사냥감을 통해 아미노산 부족의 문제를 해결했을 것임을 언급한 데 이어, 주어진 문장은 However로 흐름을 반전시키며 냉장 기술이 있기 이전의 세대는 (사냥감을 오래 저장 또는 보관할 수 없었기에) 성찬과 기근을 교대로 경험할 수밖에 없었다는 내용을 제시한다. ③ 뒤에서는 가뭄, 산불, 초강력 태풍, 빙하기 등으로 인해 어려운 상황이 이어지고 굶주림이 장기화되면 스스로 아미노산을 합성할 능력이 없는 인간은 기근의 위기 속에서 고전할 수밖에 없었다는 설명을 이어 간다. 따라서 주어진 문장이 들어가기에 가장 적절한 곳은 ③이다.

- live off ~에 의지해서 살다
- refrigeration ⓝ 냉장
- feast ⓝ 성찬, 포식, 마음껏 먹음
- deficiency ⓝ 결핍
- preindustrial ⓐ 산업화 이전의
- aplenty ⓐ 많은 [ad] 많이
- starvation ⓝ 굶주림, 기아
- worsen ⓥ 악화시키다
- ultimate ⓐ 궁극적인
- era ⓝ 시대
- alternate ⓥ 교대로 나오다, 교차하다
- famine ⓝ 기근
- not ~ by any means 결코 ~않다
- insufficiency ⓝ 부족, 불충분
- superstorm ⓝ 초강력 태풍
- inability ⓝ 무능, 할 수 없음
- survive on ~을 먹고 살다

구문 풀이

11행 The human inability to synthesize such basic things as
　　　　주어　　　　　형용사적 용법(~할 능력이 없음)
amino acids certainly worsened those crises and made surviving on
　　　　　　　　　　동사1　　　　　　　　　동사2　　목적어
{whatever was available} that much harder.
　[]: 명사절(~한 무엇이든지)　　목적격 보어

★★ 문제 해결 꿀~팁 ★★

▶ 많이 틀린 이유는?
인간은 스스로 단백질 및 필수 아미노산을 합성할 수 없어 사냥감에 의존해야 하고, 시절이 좋지 않아 먹을 것을 구하기 쉽지 않으면 주기적으로 아사의 위기에 처했다는 내용을 다룬 글이다. 내용과 구문이 모두 까다로워 난이도가 높지만, 선택지 앞뒤로 논리적 공백이 발생하는 부분을 찾는 데 주력하면 어렵지 않게 풀 수 있는 문제이기도 하다.

▶ 문제 해결 방법은?
③의 앞뒤를 보면 '큰 사냥감들이 아미노산을 풍부하게 제공해주었다 vs. 기근은 지속적인 위험이었다'라는 내용이 서로 대조를 이루고 있다. 이는 바로 ③에 역접 연결어가 필요함을 암시한다.

★★★ 1등급 대비 고난도 2컷 문제

10 여윳돈 비축의 중요성 　　정답률 52% | 정답 ④

글의 흐름으로 보아, 주어진 문장이 들어가기에 가장 적절한 곳을 고르시오.

If you apply all your extra money to paying off debt / without saving for the things / that are guaranteed to happen, / you will feel like you've failed / when something does happen.
만약 당신이 모든 여윳돈을 빚을 갚는 데 다 쓴다면, / 일에 대비하여 모아 놓지 않고 / 반드시 일어나게 되어 있는 / 당신은 당신이 도산한 기분을 느낄 것이다. / 어떤 일이 실제로 발생할 때

You will end up going further into debt.
당신은 결국 더 많은 빚을 지게 될 것이다.

① Let's use an example of an unexpected auto repair bill of $500.
예기치 못한 500달러짜리 차 수리 청구서를 예로 생각해 보자.

② If you don't save for this, / you'll end up with another debt to pay off.
만약 이 일을 위해 돈을 모아 놓지 않는다면, / 당신은 결국 갚아야 할 또 다른 빚을 지게 될 것이다.

③ You'll feel frustrated / that you have been working so hard to pay things off / and yet you just added more debt to your list.
당신은 좌절감을 느낄 것이다. / 당신이 빚을 갚기 위해 열심히 일해 왔지만, / 빚 목록에 빚을 더 추가했을 뿐이라는 데 대해

✔ On the other hand, / if you are saving for auto repairs / and pay down your debt a little slower, / you will feel proud / that you planned for the auto repair.
반면에, / 만약 당신이 차 수리를 위해 돈을 모으고 있고 / 빚을 좀 더 천천히 줄여 가고 있다면, / 당신은 자부심을 느낄 것이다. / 당신이 차 수리에 대한 대책을 세웠다는 데

You will have cash to pay for it, / and you are still paying down your debt / uninterrupted and on schedule.
당신은 거기 지불할 돈을 가지고 있으면서도 / 여전히 빚을 줄여 가고 있을 것이다. / 방해받지 않고 예정대로

⑤ Instead of frustration and disappointment / from the unexpected auto repair, / you feel proud and excited.
좌절과 실망 대신에, / 예상치 못한 차 수리로 인한 / 당신은 자랑스럽고 신나는 기분이 들 것이다.

만약 당신이 모든 여윳돈을 반드시 일어날 일에 대비하여 모아 놓지 않고 빚을 갚는 데 다 쓴다면, 어떤 일이 실제로 발생했을 때 도산한 기분을 느낄 것이다. 당신은 결국 더 많은 빚을 지게 될 것이다. ① 예기치 못한 500달러짜리 차 수리 청구서를 예로 생각해 보자. ② 만약 이 일을 위해 돈을 모아 놓지 않는다면, 당신은 결국 갚아야 할 또 다른 빚을 지게 될 것이다. ③ 당신은 빚을 갚기 위해 열심히 일해 왔지만, 빚 목록에 빚을 더 추가했을 뿐이라는 데 대해 좌절감을 느낄 것이다. ④ 반면에, 만약 당신이 차 수리를 위해 돈을 모으고 있고 빚은 좀 더 천천히 줄여 가고 있다면, 당신은 차 수리에 대한 대책을 세웠다는 데 자부심을 느낄 것이다. 당신은 거기 지불할 돈을 가지고 있으면서도 방해받지 않고 예정대로 여전히 빚을 줄여 가고 있을 것이다. ⑤ 예상치 못한 차 수리로 인한 좌절과 실망 대신에, 당신은 자랑스럽고 신나는 기분이 들 것이다.

Why? 왜 정답일까?

④ 앞에서 여윳돈을 모아두지 않고 계속 빚을 갚아버리면 예기치 못한 지출에 대비하지 못하여 좌절감이 들게 된다고 이야기하는데, 주어진 문장은 On the other hand로 흐름을 뒤집으며 돈을 조금씩 모아둔다면 갑작스런 상황이 생겨도 대책을 세웠다는 느낌이 들 것이라고 설명한다. ④ 뒤에서는 주어진 문장의 흐름을 이어 여윳돈이 있다면 차 수리에 지불할 돈이 있으면서도 빚도 줄여가게 된다는 것을 상기시킨다. 따라서 주어진 문장이 들어가기에 가장 적절한 곳은 ④이다.

- debt ⓝ 빚, 채무
- guarantee ⓥ 보장하다
- unexpected ⓐ 예기치 못한
- uninterrupted ⓐ 방해받지 않는
- instead of ~ 대신에
- pay off (빚 등을) 갚다, 정산하다
- end up 결국 ~하게 되다
- frustrated ⓐ 좌절한
- on schedule 예정대로, 예정대로인
- disappointment ⓝ 실망

구문 풀이

4행 If you apply all your extra money to paying off debt
「apply + A + to + B(동명사): A를 B에 쓰다」
without saving for the things [that are guaranteed to happen], / you
~하지 않고　　　　　　　　　　반드시 ~하게 되다
will feel like you've failed when something does happen.
~처럼 느끼다　　　　　　　　　「do/does/did + 동사원형: 강조」

★★ 문제 해결 꿀~팁 ★★

▶ 많이 틀린 이유는?
'경제' 관련 내용을 소재로 한다는 점, 예시가 쉽게 와닿지 않는 내용으로 구성되어 있다는 점으로 인해 혼란이 생기기 쉬운 문제였다. 주어진 문장에 On the other hand가 있으므로 흐름 반전의 포인트를 찾는 것이 풀이의 핵심이다.

최다 오답인 ③의 경우 아직 여윳돈을 평소에 챙겨두지 않다가 빚만 더 늘어나서 좌절하는 예시의 내용을 ③ 앞에 이어서 설명하고 있기에 답이 되기에 부적절하다. 반면 ④의 뒤에서는 앞과는 달리 돈도 있고 빚도 줄어드는 '좋은' 상황에 대해 이야기하고 있어서, ④ 자리에 '역접'의 연결어가 나와 흐름의 전환을 유도해야만 ④ 앞뒤로 상반되는 내용 전개가 가능해진다.

▶ 문제 해결 방법은?

도식화를 통해 쉽게 내용을 파악하도록 한다. ④ 앞은 대략 '여유 자금(−), 빚(+)'로 정리되지만, 주어진 문장과 ④ 뒤의 문장은 '여유 자금(+), 빚(−)'로 정리된다.

★★★ 1등급 대비 고난도 3점 문제

11 임무가 종료된 인공 위성의 처리 문제 정답률 41% | 정답 ⑤

글의 흐름으로 보아, 주어진 문장이 들어가기에 가장 적절한 곳을 고르시오. [3점]

The United Nations asks / that all companies remove their satellites from orbit / within 25 years / after the end of their mission.
국제연합은 요청하고 있다. / 모든 기업들이 위성을 궤도에서 제거해 줄 것을 / 25년 이내에 / 인공위성의 임무 종료 후

This is tricky to enforce, though, / because satellites can (and often do) fail.
하지만 이것은 시행하기에 까다롭다. / 인공위성이 작동하지 않을 수 있기(그리고 종종 정말로 작동하지 않기) 때문에

① To tackle this problem, / several companies around the world / have come up with novel solutions.
이 문제를 해결하기 위해 / 전세계의 몇몇 회사들이 / 새로운 해결책을 내놓았다.

② These include / removing dead satellites from orbit / and dragging them back into the atmosphere, / where they will burn up.
이것은 포함하는데, / 수명이 다한 인공위성을 궤도에서 제거하고, / 대기권으로 다시 끌어들이는 것을 / 여기서 그것은 다 타 버리게 될 것이다.

③ Ways we could do this / include / using a harpoon to grab a satellite, / catching it in a huge net, / using magnets to grab it, / or even firing lasers to heat up the satellite, / increasing its atmospheric drag / so that it falls out of orbit.
우리가 이렇게 할 수 있는 방법은 / 포함한다. / 작살을 이용해서 위성을 잡거나, / 거대한 그물로 그것을 잡거나, / 자석을 이용하여 위성을 잡거나, / 혹은 레이저를 발사하여 위성을 가열하는 것을 / 그것의 대기 항력을 증가시키면서 / 그것이 궤도에서 떨어져 나오도록

④ However, / these methods are only useful / for large satellites orbiting Earth.
하지만, / 이러한 방법은 오직 유용하다. / 지구 궤도를 도는 큰 위성들에게만

✔ There isn't really a way for us / to pick up smaller pieces of debris / such as bits of paint and metal.
우리로서는 방법이 정말로 없다. / 작은 잔해물을 치울 수 있는 / 페인트 조각이나 금속 같은

We just have to wait for them / to naturally re-enter Earth's atmosphere.
우리는 그것들을 기다려야 할 뿐이다. / 자연적으로 지구의 대기로 다시 들어오기를

국제연합은 모든 기업들이 인공위성의 임무 종료 후 25년 이내에 위성을 궤도에서 제거해 줄 것을 요청하고 있다. 하지만 인공위성이 작동하지 않을 수 있기(그리고 종종 정말로 작동하지 않기) 때문에 이것은 시행하기에 까다롭다. ① 이 문제를 해결하기 위해 전세계의 몇몇 회사들이 새로운 해결책을 내놓았다. ② 이것은 수명이 다한 인공위성을 궤도에서 제거하고, 대기권으로 다시 끌어들이는 것을 포함하는데, 여기서 그것은 다 타 버리게 될 것이다. ③ 우리가 이렇게 할(인공위성을 대기권으로 끌고 들어올) 수 있는 방법은 위성이 궤도에서 떨어져 나오도록 대기 항력을 증가시키면서 위성을 작살을 이용해서 잡거나, 거대한 그물로 잡거나, 자석을 이용하여 잡거나, 레이저를 발사하여 가열하는 것을 포함한다. ④ 하지만, 이러한 방법은 오직 지구 궤도를 도는 큰 위성들에게만 유용하다. ⑤ 우리가 페인트 조각이나 금속 같은 작은 잔해물을 치울 수 있는 방법은 정말로 없다. 우리는 그것들이 자연적으로 지구의 대기로 다시 들어오기를 기다려야 할 뿐이다.

Why? 왜 정답일까?

⑤ 앞의 문장에서 임무가 종료된 인공위성을 대기권으로 끌어들여 태우는 방법은 지구 궤도를 도는 큰 위성들에게만 유용하다고 언급한다. 주어진 문장은 우리가 '작은' 잔해물을 처리할 방법이 없다고 언급하며 ⑤ 앞의 문장 내용을 보충 설명한다. ⑤ 뒤의 문장은 주어진 문장에서 언급된 **smaller pieces of debris**를 **them**으로 받으며, 작은 잔해물은 알아서 대기로 들어오기를 바랄 수밖에 없다고 언급한다. 따라서 주어진 문장이 들어가기에 가장 적절한 곳은 ⑤이다.

- **debris** ⓝ 잔해
- **orbit** ⓝ 궤도
- **tricky** ⓐ 까다로운
- **satellite** ⓝ 인공위성
- **mission** ⓝ 임무
- **enforce** ⓥ 시행하다
- **tackle** ⓥ 다루다, 해결하다
- **novel** ⓐ 새로운, 신기한
- **atmosphere** ⓝ (지구의) 대기
- **magnet** ⓝ 자석, 자철
- **fall out of** ~을 빠져나오다, 떨어져 나오다
- **come up with** ~을 떠올리다
- **drag** ⓝ 항력, 끌림
- **burn up** 타 버리다
- **heat up** 데우다, 열을 가하다
- **method** ⓝ 방법

구문 풀이

11행 Ways [we could do this] include using a harpoon to grab a satellite, catching it in a huge net, using magnets to grab it, or even firing lasers to heat up the satellite, increasing its atmospheric drag so that it falls out of orbit.
(Ways: 주어(복수) / include: 동사 / using ~: 목적어1 / catching ~: 목적어2 / using magnets ~: 목적어3 / firing lasers ~: 목적어4 / increasing ~: 분사구문(~하면서) / so that: 접속사(~하도록, ~하기 위해))

★★ 문제 해결 꿀~팁 ★★

▶ 많이 틀린 이유는?

수명이 다한 인공위성의 사후 처리에 관한 글로, 대명사 힌트를 잘 활용하면 오답을 쉽게 소거할 수 있다. ③ 앞에서 인공위성을 다시 대기로 끌어들여 없애는 방법을 언급한 데 이어, ③ 뒤이자 ④ 앞의 문장에서는 이를 **do this**로 가리킨다. 또한 이 문장의 '**using ~, catching ~, using ~, or even firing ~**'을 ④ 뒤에서 **these methods**로 가리킨다. 즉 ③, ④ 앞뒤에서 대명사 사용이 모두 적절하기 때문에 주어진 문장은 이 두 곳에 들어갈 수 없다.

▶ 문제 해결 방법은?

정답을 골라내는 데에도 대명사 힌트가 큰 역할을 한다. ⑤ 앞의 문장에서는 대기로 끌어당기는 갖가지 방법이 큰 인공위성(**large satellites**)에만 적용될 수 있다고 하는데, ⑤ 뒤의 문장은 '이 방법을 사용하지 못하고 그저 자연스럽게 지구로 다시 오기를 기다려야 하는' 대상을 **them**으로 가리키고 있다. 즉 **them**이 **large satellites**와 일치하지 않으므로, 주어진 문장이 ⑤에 들어가야 함을 알 수 있다.

★★★ 1등급 대비 고난도 3점 문제

12 생각과 행동의 전파 정답률 50% | 정답 ③

글의 흐름으로 보아, 주어진 문장이 들어가기에 가장 적절한 곳을 고르시오. [3점]

In the late twentieth century, / researchers sought to measure / how fast and how far news, rumours or innovations moved.
20세기 후반 / 연구자들은 측정하고자 했다. / 뉴스, 소문, 혁신이 얼마나 빨리 그리고 얼마나 멀리 이동하는지를

① More recent research has shown / that ideas — even emotional states and conditions — / can be transmitted through a social network.
더 최근의 연구는 보여주었다. / 생각, 즉 감정 상태와 상황까지도 / 사회 관계망을 통해 전파될 수 있다는 것을

② The evidence of this kind of contagion / is clear:
이러한 종류의 전염의 증거는 / 분명하다.

'Students with studious roommates / become more studious.
즉 '학구적인 룸메이트와 함께 하는 학생들은 / 더욱 학구적이 된다.

Diners sitting next to heavy eaters / eat more food.'
폭식하는 사람 옆에 앉아 식사하는 사람은 / 더 많은 음식을 먹는다.'

✔ However, according to Christakis and Fowler, / we cannot transmit ideas and behaviours / much beyond our friends' friends' friends / (in other words, across just three degrees of separation).
그러나 Christakis와 Fowler에 따르면 / 우리는 생각과 행동을 전파할 수 없다. / 우리의 친구의 친구의 친구를 훨씬 넘어서서, / (다시 말해 고작 세 단계의 분절을 건너서는)

This is because the transmission and reception of an idea or behaviour / requires a stronger connection / than the relaying of a letter / or the communication that a certain employment opportunity exists.
이것은 생각이나 행동의 전파와 수용이 / 더 강한 연결을 요구하기 때문이다. / 편지를 전달하는 것보다 / 혹은 어떤 고용 기회가 있다는 말의 전달이나

④ Merely knowing people is not the same / as being able to influence them to study more or over-eat.
단지 사람을 아는 것은 같지 않다. / 그들이 더 공부하거나 과식하도록 영향을 미칠 수 있는 것과는

⑤ Imitation is indeed the sincerest form of flattery, / even when it is unconscious.
모방은 실로 가장 순수한 형태의 아첨이다. / 그것이 무의식적일 때조차도

20세기 후반 연구자들은 뉴스, 소문, 혁신이 얼마나 빨리 그리고 얼마나 멀리 이동하는지를 측정하고자 했다. ① 더 최근의 연구는 생각, 즉 감정 상태와 상황까지도 사회 관계망을 통해 전파될 수 있다는 것을 보여주었다. ② 이러한 종류의 전염의 증거는 분명한데, '학구적인 룸메이트와 함께 하는 학생들은 더욱 학구적이 되고, 폭식하는 사람 옆에 앉아 식사하는 사람은 더 많은 음식을 먹는다.' ③ 그러나 Christakis와 Fowler에 따르면 우리는 우리의 친구의 친구

의 친구를 훨씬 넘어서서(다시 말해 고작 세 단계의 분절을 건너서는) 생각과 행동을 전파할 수 없다. 이것은 생각이나 행동의 전파와 수용이 편지나 어떤 고용 기회가 있다는 말을 전달하는 것보다 더 강한 연결을 요구하기 때문이다. ④ 단지 사람을 아는 것은 그들이 더 공부하거나 과식하도록 영향을 미칠 수 있는 것과는 같지 않다. ⑤ 모방은 그것이 무의식적일 때조차도 실로 가장 순수한 형태의 아첨이다.

Why? 왜 정답일까?

③ 앞에서 뉴스, 소문, 혁신뿐 아니라 감정 상태나 상황 또한 흔히 사람들 간에 전염처럼 번질 수 있다고 언급한 데 이어, 주어진 문장은 친구의 친구의 친구, 즉 세 단계를 걸쳐 아는 사람들을 넘어서면 그 전파력이 잘 발휘되지 않는다는 상반된 내용을 제시한다. ③ 뒤의 문장은 주어진 문장 내용을 This로 받으며, 생각이나 행동의 전파 또는 수용이 편지나 정보를 단순히 전달하는 경우보다 더 강한 유대나 연결을 요구하기 때문이라는 이유를 제시한다. 따라서 주어진 문장이 들어가기에 가장 적절한 곳은 ③이다.

- transmit ⓥ 전달하다
- innovation ⓝ 혁신
- studious ⓐ 학구적인
- relaying ⓝ (정보나 뉴스 등의) 전달
- unconscious ⓐ 무의식적인
- separation ⓝ 단절, 분리
- contagion ⓝ 전염
- reception ⓝ 수용
- merely ad 단지, 그저

구문 풀이

7행 More recent research has shown that ideas — (even emotional states and conditions) — can be transmitted through a social network.
(that: 접속사(~것) / ideas: 주어 / ( ): 삽입구 / can be transmitted: 조동사 수동태)

★★ 문제 해결 꿀~팁 ★★

▶ 많이 틀린 이유는?

④ 앞에서 생각이나 행동을 전파할 때는 단순히 소식이나 정보를 전달할 때보다 더 강한 연결이 필요하다고 설명한다. 이어서 ④ 뒤의 문장에서는 단지 사람을 안다고 해서 그 사람의 행동에 영향을 미칠 수 있다고 볼 수는 없다고 언급한다. 즉 ④ 앞뒤로 생각이나 행동에 영향을 미치려면 '알고 있는 것 이상'의 강한 연결고리가 필요하다는 내용이 일관성 있게 제시되므로, 주어진 문장은 ④에 들어갈 수 없다.

▶ 문제 해결 방법은?

③ 앞뒤로 '생각 · 행동이 사회 관계망을 통해 전파되는 경우 vs. 그 전파가 어려운 경우'가 대비되고 있음을 파악하도록 한다.

DAY 17 문장 삽입 02

01 ②	02 ④	03 ④	04 ③	05 ④
06 ④	07 ③	08 ④	09 ②	10 ⑤
11 ⑤	12 ②			

01 창의력 지수

정답률 52% | 정답 ②

글의 흐름으로 보아, 주어진 문장이 들어가기에 가장 적절한 곳을 고르시오.

The holy grail of the first wave of creativity research / was a personality test / to measure general creativity ability, / in the same way that IQ measured general intelligence.
창의성 연구의 첫 번째 물결의 성배는 / 성격 검사였다. / 전반적인 창의력을 측정하기 위한 / IQ가 전반적인 지능을 측정했던 것과 같은 방식으로

① A person's creativity score should tell us / his or her creative potential in any field of endeavor, / just like an IQ score is not limited to physics, math, or literature.
한 사람의 창의성 점수는 우리에게 알려줄 것이었다. / 노력하는 어떤 분야에서든 그 사람의 창의적 잠재력을 / IQ 점수가 물리학, 수학 또는 문학에 국한되지 않는 것과 마찬가지로

✔ But by the 1970s, / psychologists realized / there was no such thing as a general "creativity quotient."
그러나 1970년대에, / 심리학자들은 깨달았다. / 전반적인 '창의성 지수' 같은 것은 없음을

Creative people aren't creative in a general, universal way; / they're creative in a specific sphere of activity, / a particular domain.
창의적인 사람들은 전반적이고 보편적으로 창의적인 것은 아니어서, / 이들은 활동의 특정 범위에서 창의적이다. / 즉 특정 영역

③ We don't expect a creative scientist / to also be a gifted painter.
우리는 창의적인 과학자에게 기대하지 않는다. / 재능 있는 화가도 될 것이라고

④ A creative violinist may not be a creative conductor, / and a creative conductor may not be very good / at composing new works.
창의적인 바이올린 연주자는 창의적인 지휘자가 아닐 수도 있고, / 창의적인 지휘자는 매우 뛰어나지 않을 수도 있다. / 새로운 곡을 작곡하는 데

⑤ Psychologists now know / that creativity is domain specific.
심리학자들은 이제 안다. / 창의성이 특정 영역에만 한정된 것이라는 것을

창의성 연구의 첫 번째 급증의 궁극적 목표는 IQ가 전반적인 지능을 측정했던 것과 같은 방식으로 전반적인 창의력을 측정하기 위한 성격 검사였다. ① 한 사람의 창의성 점수는 IQ 점수가 물리학, 수학 또는 문학에 국한되지 않는 것과 마찬가지로, 그 사람이 노력하는 어떤 분야에서든 그 사람의 창의적 잠재력을 우리에게 알려줄 것이었다. ② 그러나 1970년대에, 심리학자들은 전반적인 '창의성 지수' 같은 것은 없음을 깨달았다. 창의적인 사람들은 전반적이고 보편적으로 창의적인 것은 아니어서, 이들은 활동의 특정 범위, 즉 특정 영역에서 창의적이다. ③ 우리는 창의적인 과학자가 재능 있는 화가도 되리라고 기대하지 않는다. ④ 창의적인 바이올린 연주자는 창의적인 지휘자가 아닐 수도 있고, 창의적인 지휘자는 새로운 곡을 작곡하는 데 매우 뛰어나지 않을 수도 있다. ⑤ 심리학자들은 이제 창의성이 특정 영역에만 한정된 것이라는 것을 안다.

Why? 왜 정답일까?

창의적 연구 초창기에는 전반적인 창의력을 측정하고자 했다는 내용이 ② 앞에 나오는데, 주어진 문장은 But으로 흐름을 전환시키며 1970년대부터 전반적인 창의력 지수라는 것은 없다는 인식이 생겨났다고 설명한다. ② 뒤에서는 창의적인 사람들이 전반적 또는 보편적으로 창의적인 것은 아니라는 보충 설명으로 주어진 문장 내용을 뒷받침한다. 따라서 주어진 문장이 들어가기에 가장 적절한 곳은 ②이다.

- realize ⓥ 깨닫다
- personality test 성격 검사
- endeavor ⓝ 노력
- literature ⓝ 문학
- sphere ⓝ 범위, 영역
- conductor ⓝ 지휘자
- quotient ⓝ 지수
- intelligence ⓝ 지능
- physics ⓝ 물리학
- universal ⓐ 보편적인
- domain ⓝ 영역
- compose ⓥ 작곡하다

구문 풀이

3행 The holy grail of the first wave of creativity research was a personality test to measure general creativity ability, in the same way that IQ measured general intelligence.
(The holy grail: 주어 / was: 동사(단수) / a personality test: 주격 보어 / to measure: 형용사적 용법 / in the same way that: ~와 같은 방법으로)

02 영역 특수 지식과 일반적 지식의 구별 정답률 61% | 정답 ④

글의 흐름으로 보아, 주어진 문장이 들어가기에 가장 적절한 곳을 고르시오.

There are different kinds of knowledge.
다양한 종류의 지식이 있다.

Some is domain-specific knowledge / that relates to a particular task or subject.
어떤 것은 영역 특수 지식이다. / 특정한 과업이나 주제와 관련된

For example, / knowing that the shortstop plays between second and third base / is specific to the domain of baseball.
예를 들어, / 유격수가 2루와 3루 사이를 맡고 있음을 아는 것은 / 야구라는 영역에 한정된다.

① Some knowledge, on the other hand, is general — / it applies to many different situations.
반면에 어떤 지식은 일반적이다. / 그것은 많은 다른 상황에 적용된다.

② For example, / general knowledge / about how to read or write or use a computer / is useful both in and out of school.
예를 들어, / 일반적 지식은 / 읽거나 쓰는 방법 또는 컴퓨터를 사용하는 방법에 관한 / 학교 안팎 모두에서 유용하다.

③ Of course, / there is no absolute line / between general and domain-specific knowledge.
물론, / 절대적인 경계선은 없다. / 일반적 지식과 영역 특수 지식 사이에

✔ When you were first learning to read, / you may have studied specific facts / about the sounds of letters.
당신이 처음 읽기를 배웠을 때 / 당신은 특정한 사실들을 배웠을 것이다. / 철자 소리에 관한

At that time, / knowledge about letter sounds / was specific to the domain of reading.
당시에는 / 철자 소리에 관한 지식이 / 읽기 영역에 한정되었다.

⑤ But now / you can use both knowledge about sounds / and the ability to read / in more general ways.
하지만 이제 / 당신은 소리에 관한 지식을 사용할 수 있다. / 그리고 읽는 능력을 둘 다 / 보다 일반적인 방식으로

다양한 종류의 지식이 있다. 어떤 것은 특정한 과업이나 주제와 관련된 영역 특수 지식이다. 예를 들어 유격수가 2루와 3루 사이를 맡고 있음을 아는 것은 야구라는 영역에 한정된다. ① 반면에 어떤 지식은 일반적이어서, 많은 다른 상황에 적용된다. ② 예를 들어, 읽거나 쓰는 방법 또는 컴퓨터를 사용하는 방법에 관한 일반적 지식은 학교 안팎 모두에서 유용하다. ③ 물론, 일반적 지식과 영역 특수 지식 사이에 절대적인 경계선은 없다. ④ 당신이 처음 읽기를 배웠을 때 당신은 철자 소리에 관한 특정한 사실들을 배웠을 것이다. 당시에는 철자 소리에 관한 지식이 읽기 영역에 한정되었다. ⑤ 하지만 이제 당신은 소리에 관한 지식과 읽는 능력 모두를 보다 일반적인 방식으로 사용할 수 있다.

Why? 왜 정답일까?

④ 앞에서 영역 특수 지식은 어느 특정 과업 및 주제와 연관되어 있고 일반적 사실은 보다 넓은 범위에 적용되는 지식이지만, 둘 사이의 경계는 절대적이지 않다는 내용을 말하는데, 주어진 문장은 '읽기'를 처음 배우는 구체적인 경우를 예로 들어 우리가 처음 철자의 소리를 배울 때에는 하나하나 특정한 사실을 배우는 것부터 시작하였음을 설명한다. 이에 이어서 ④ 뒤의 두 문장에서는, 비록 그때는 읽기에 관한 지식이 영역 특수 지식이었지만, 이제는 '소리 지식, 읽기 능력'이라는 일반적 지식이 되어 보다 일반적인 방식으로 이 지식이 활용될 수 있다는 결론을 낸다. 따라서 주어진 문장이 들어가기에 가장 적절한 곳은 ④이다.

- **specific** ⓐ 특정적인, 구체적인
- **domain** ⓝ 영역
- **general** ⓐ 일반적인
- **absolute** ⓐ 절대적인
- **knowledge** ⓝ 지식
- **relate to** ~에 관련되다
- **apply to** ~에 적용되다

구문 풀이

1행 When you were first learning to read, / you
접속사(~할 때) ┗→ 동사(과거진행형) ←┛
may have studied specific facts about the sounds of letters.
「may have + 과거분사 : ~했을 것이다(과거에 대한 약한 추측)」

03 재능보다 노력을 칭찬해 주기 정답률 58% | 정답 ④

글의 흐름으로 보아, 주어진 문장이 들어가기에 가장 적절한 곳을 고르시오.

A child bounces up to you holding her school work; / perhaps she's your daughter, cousin, or neighbour.
한 아이가 자신의 학교 과제를 손에 들고 당신에게 뛰어 오른다. / 어쩌면 그 애는 당신의 딸, 사촌, 또는 이웃일 것이다.

① She proudly shows you a big red A / at the bottom of her test paper.
그녀는 자랑스럽게 당신에게 큼지막하게 붉은 색으로 쓰인 A를 보여준다. / 자기 시험지 아래에

② How do you praise her?
당신은 그녀를 어떻게 칭찬할 것인가?

③ For decades, people have been told / that praise is vital for happy and healthy children / and that the most important job in raising a child / is nurturing her self-esteem.
수십 년 간, 사람들은 이야기를 들어왔다. / 아이가 행복하고 건강하기 위해서는 칭찬이 필수적이며, / 아이를 기를 때 가장 중요한 것은 / 아이의 자존감을 길러주는 것이라는

✔ Recently, however, some researchers found / that how people are praised is very important.
그러나 최근에 몇몇 연구자들은 발견했다. / 사람들이 칭찬 받는 방식이 매우 중요하다는 것을

They discovered / that if you say "What a very clever girl you are!" / to the child showing you an A, / you may cause her more harm than good.
연구자들은 발견했다. / 만약 당신이 "넌 정말 똑똑한 아이야!"라고 칭찬을 한다면, / A를 보여주는 아이에게 / 당신이 그 아이에게 득보다는 해를 끼칠 수도 있다는 것을

⑤ For your children to succeed and be happy, / you need to convince them / that success comes from effort, / not from some talent / that they're born with or without.
당신의 아이가 성공하고 행복해지려면, / 당신은 그들에게 확신시킬 필요가 있다. / 성공은 노력에서 오는 것이지, / 약간의 재능에서 오는 것은 아니라는 것을 / 그들이 타고 났거나 타고 나지 않은

한 아이가 자신의 학교 과제를 손에 들고 당신에게 뛰어 오른다. 어쩌면 그 애는 당신의 딸, 사촌, 또는 이웃일 것이다. ① 그녀는 자랑스럽게 당신에게 시험지 아래에 큼지막하게 붉은색으로 쓰인 A를 보여준다. ② 당신은 그녀를 어떻게 칭찬할 것인가? ③ 수십 년 간, 사람들은 아이가 행복하고 건강하기 위해서는 칭찬이 필수적이며, 아이를 기를 때 가장 중요한 것은 아이의 자존감을 길러주는 것이라는 이야기를 들어왔다. ④ 그러나 최근에 몇몇 연구자들은 사람들이 칭찬 받는 방식이 매우 중요하다는 것을 발견했다. 연구자들은 만약 당신이 A를 보여주는 아이에게 "넌 정말 똑똑한 아이야!"라고 칭찬을 한다면, 당신이 그 아이에게 득보다는 해를 끼칠 수도 있다는 것을 발견했다. ⑤ 당신의 아이가 성공하고 행복해지려면, 성공은 노력에서 오는 것이지, 타고 났거나 타고 나지 않은 약간의 재능에서 오는 것은 아니라는 것을 확신시킬 필요가 있다.

Why? 왜 정답일까?

아이를 칭찬할 때는 성공에 대한 재능보다 노력을 언급해주는 것이 중요하다는 내용을 다룬 글이다. ④ 앞에서는 아이를 칭찬하여 자존감을 높여주는 것이 중요하다고 말하는데, 주어진 문장에서는 그 칭찬 방식에도 신경을 써야 한다는 점을 언급한다. ④ 뒤의 두 문장에서는 아이의 '똑똑함' 등 타고난 능력을 칭찬해주면 도리어 아이에게 해가 될 수도 있다는 내용을 이야기한다. 따라서 주어진 문장이 들어가기에 가장 적절한 곳은 ④이다.

- **bounce up** 펄쩍 뛰다
- **proudly** ⓐⓓ 자랑스럽게
- **vital** ⓐ 필수적인
- **nurture** ⓥ 양육하다, 보살피다
- **harm** ⓝ 해
- **cousin** ⓝ 사촌
- **praise** ⓥ 칭찬하다
- **raise** ⓥ 늘리다
- **self-esteem** 자존감, 자아 존중감
- **convince** ⓥ 확신시키다

구문 풀이

12행 For your children to succeed and (to) be happy, you need to
의미상 주어 ~하기 위해서
convince them {that success comes from effort, not from some talent
간접 목적어
[that they're born with or without]}.
목적격 관계대명사 { }: 직접 목적어

04 에세이를 쓸 때 소리 내어 읽기 정답률 46% | 정답 ③

글의 흐름으로 보아, 주어진 문장이 들어가기에 가장 적절한 곳을 고르시오.

It can be helpful / to read your own essay aloud / to hear how it sounds, / and it can sometimes be even more beneficial / to hear someone else read it.
도움이 될 수 있고, / 여러분 자신의 에세이를 큰 소리로 읽는 것이 / 어떻게 들리는지 들어 보기 위해서 / 때로 훨씬 더 이로울 수 있다. / 다른 누군가가 그것을 읽는 것을 듣는 것이

① Either reading will help you to hear things / that you otherwise might not notice / when editing silently.
어느 쪽의 읽기든 당신이 듣는 데 도움이 될 것이다. / 그렇게 하지 않을 경우에 알아채지 못할지도 모르는 것들을 / 조용히 편집할 때

② If you feel uncomfortable / having someone read to you, / however, / or if you simply don't have someone / you can ask to do it, / you can have your computer read your essay to you.
불편하거나, / 누군가가 당신에게 읽어 주도록 하는 것이 / 하지만 / 누군가가 단순히 없다면, / 그것을 요청할 수 있는 / 컴퓨터가 여러분의 에세이를 여러분에게 읽어 주도록 할 수 있다.

✔ Granted, / it's not quite the same thing, / and the computer is not going to tell you / when something doesn't "sound right."

[문제편 p.110]

물론, / 그것은 완전히 똑같은 것은 아니고, / 컴퓨터는 여러분에게 이를 말해 주지 않을 것이다. / 어떤 것이 '맞는 것처럼 들리지' 않을 때

The computer also won't stumble over things / that are awkward / — it will just plow right on through.

컴퓨터는 또한 더듬거리지도 않을 것이며, / 어색한 것들에 대해서 / 그저 끝까지 계속해 나갈 것이다.

④ But / hearing the computer read your writing / is a very different experience / from reading it yourself.

하지만 / 컴퓨터가 여러분의 글을 읽는 것을 듣는 것은 / 매우 다른 경험이다. / 여러분이 그것을 직접 읽는 것과는

⑤ If you have never tried it, / you might find / that you notice areas for revision, editing, and proofreading / that you didn't notice before.

여러분이 그것을 시도해 본 적이 없다면, / 알게 될 것이다. / 수정, 편집 및 교정이 필요한 부분들을 알아차리게 된다는 것을 / 이전에 알아채지 못했던

여러분 자신의 에세이가 어떻게 들리는지 들어 보기 위해서 그것을 큰 소리로 읽는 것이 도움이 될 수 있고, 때때로 다른 누군가가 그것을 읽는 것을 듣는 것이 훨씬 더 유익할 수 있다. ① 어느 쪽의 읽기든 그렇게 하지 않을 경우에 당신이 조용히 편집할 때 알아채지 못할지도 모르는 것들을 듣는 데 도움이 될 것이다. ② 하지만 누군가가 당신에게 읽어 주도록 하는 것이 불편하거나, 그것을 요청할 수 있는 누군가가 없다면, 컴퓨터가 여러분의 에세이를 여러분에게 읽어 주도록 할 수 있다. ③ 물론, 그것은 완전히 똑같은 것은 아니고, 컴퓨터는 여러분에게 어떤 것이 '맞는 것처럼 들리지' 않을 때 이를 말해 주지 않을 것이다. 컴퓨터는 또한 어색한 것들에 대해서 더듬거리지도 않을 것이며, 그저 끝까지 애써 계속해 나갈 것이다. ④ 하지만 컴퓨터가 여러분의 글을 읽는 것을 듣는 것은 여러분이 그것을 직접 읽는 것과는 매우 다른 경험이다. ⑤ 여러분이 그것을 시도해 본 적이 없다면, 이전에 알아채지 못했던 수정, 편집 및 교정이 필요한 부분들을 알아차리게 된다는 것을 깨달을 것이다.

Why? 왜 정답일까?

첫 두 문장에서 에세이를 쓸 때 직접 소리 내어 읽어보거나 다른 사람에게 읽어달라고 청하여 들어보는 것이 좋다고 말한 데 이어, ③ 앞의 문장에서는 만일 상황이 여의치 않은 경우 컴퓨터의 힘을 빌릴 수도 있음을 언급하는데, 주어진 문장은 '물론'이라는 뜻의 **Granted**로 시작하며 컴퓨터와 사람의 읽기 방식에는 차이가 존재한다는 점을 상기시키고 있다. ③ 뒤에서는 주어진 문장에 이어서 컴퓨터 특유의 읽기 방식을 부연하고 있다. 따라서 주어진 문장이 들어가기에 가장 적절한 곳은 ③이다.

- **beneficial** ⓐ 이로운, 도움이 되는
- **silently** ad 조용히
- **plow through** 고생하며 나아가다
- **proofreading** ⓝ (책 또는 원고의) 교정
- **notice** ⓥ 알아채다
- **awkward** ⓐ 어색한, 곤란한
- **revision** ⓝ 수정, 검토, 변경

구문 풀이

6행 Either reading will help you to hear things [that you otherwise might not notice when editing silently].

(「either+단수명사 : (둘 중) 어느 하나」 / will help: 준사역동사 / you: 목적어 / to hear: 목적격 보어 / that: 목적격 관계대명사 / when editing: 분사구문(~할 때))

05 건물 스타일의 지역적 제한 정답률 57% | 정답 ④

글의 흐름으로 보아, 주어진 문장이 들어가기에 가장 적절한 곳을 고르시오. [3점]

In the US, / regional styles of speech have always been associated / with regional styles of building: / the Midwestern farmhouse, the Southern plantation mansion, and the Cape Cod cottage / all have their equivalent in spoken dialect.

미국에서는 / 말투의 지역적 스타일이 항상 연결되어 왔다. / 건물의 지역적 스타일과 함께 / 중서부의 농장 주택, 남부의 대농장 저택, 그리고 Cape Cod 지역의 오두막 / 모두가 구어 방언에서 그에 상응하는 것을 가진다.

① These buildings may be old and genuine, / or they may be recent reproductions, / the equivalent of an assumed rather than a native accent.

이 건물들은 오래되고 진품일 수도 있고 / 또는 최근의 복제품일 수도 있다. / 그 지방 고유의 방언이라기보다는 꾸며진 방언에 상응하는 것인

② As James Kunstler says, / "half-baked versions of Scarlett O'Hara's Tara / now stand replicated in countless suburban subdivisions / around the United States."

James Kunstler가 말한 것처럼, / "Scarlett O'Hara의 Tara의 어설픈 변형들이 / 요즘 수없이 많은 교외 지역에 복제되어 세워져 있다. / 미국 전역의"

③ In some cities and towns, / especially where tourism is an important part of the economy, / zoning codes may make a sort of artificial authenticity compulsory.

몇몇 도시와 마을에서는 / 특히 관광 사업이 경제의 중요한 일부분인 / 지역제(地域制) 규칙이 일종의 인위적인 진정성을 의무로 정할 수 있다.

✔ Houses in the historic district of Key West, Florida, for example, / whether new or remodeled, / must be built of wood in a traditional style, / and there are only a few permissible colors of paint, / white being preferred.

예를 들어, 플로리다 주 Key West의 역사적으로 유명한 지역에 있는 주택들은 / 신축이거나 리모델링이거나 / 전통적 양식에 따라 목재로 지어져야만 하고, / 허용되는 페인트의 색깔이 몇 가지 뿐이며, / 흰색이 선호되고 있다.

From the street / these houses may look / like the simple sea captains' mansions they imitate.

거리에서 보면 / 이 주택들은 보일 수도 있다. / 그것들이 모방하고 있는 단순한 선장의 저택처럼

⑤ Inside, however, / where zoning does not reach, / they often contain modern lighting and state-of-the-art kitchens and bathrooms.

그러나, 내부에는, / 지역제가 미치지 않는 / 그것들은 흔히 현대적인 조명과 최신식 부엌과 욕실을 포함하고 있다.

미국에서는 말투의 지역적 스타일이 건물의 지역적 스타일과 함께 항상 연결되어 왔다. 중서부의 농장 주택, 남부의 대농장 저택, 그리고 Cape Cod 지역의 오두막 모두가 구어 방언에서 그에 상응하는 것을 가진다. ① 이 건물들은 오래되고 진품일 수도 있고 또는 그 지방 고유의 방언이라기보다는 꾸며진 방언에 상응하는 것인 최근의 복제품일 수도 있다. ② James Kunstler가 말한 것처럼, "Scarlett O'Hara의 Tara의 어설픈 변형들이 요즘 미국 전역의 수없이 많은 교외 지역에 복제되어 세워져 있다." ③ 특히 관광 사업이 경제의 중요한 일부분인 몇몇 도시와 마을에서는 지역제(地域制) 규칙이 일종의 인위적인 진정성을 의무로 정할 수 있다. ④ 예를 들어, 플로리다 주 Key West의 역사적으로 유명한 지역에 있는 주택들은 신축이거나 리모델링이거나 전통적 양식에 따라 목재로 지어져야만 하고, 허용될 수 있는 페인트의 색깔이 몇 가지 뿐이며, 흰색이 선호되고 있다. 거리에서 보면 이 주택들은 그것들이 모방하고 있는 단순한 선장의 저택처럼 보일 수도 있다. ⑤ 그러나, 지역제가 미치지 않는 내부에는, 그것들은 흔히 현대적인 조명과 최신식 부엌과 욕실을 포함하고 있다.

Why? 왜 정답일까?

④ 앞에서 건물 스타일의 지역제 규칙이 특정 지역 내의 주택 건축 양식을 의무로 정할 수 있다고 언급한 데 이어, **for example**이 포함된 주어진 문장은 **Key West** 지역의 주택들을 예로 제시한다. ④ 뒤의 문장은 주어진 문장에 언급된 주택들을 **these houses**로 언급한다. 따라서 주어진 문장이 들어가기에 가장 적절한 곳은 ④이다.

- **district** ⓝ 지역
- **plantation** ⓝ 대농장
- **cottage** ⓝ 오두막
- **dialect** ⓝ 방언
- **replicate** ⓥ 복제하다
- **authenticity** ⓝ 진정성
- **state-of-the-art** 최신식의
- **permissible** ⓐ 허용 가능한
- **mansion** ⓝ 저택
- **equivalent** ⓐ 상응하는
- **genuine** ⓐ 진품의, 진짜인
- **artificial** ⓐ 인공의
- **compulsory** ⓐ 의무적인, 필수의

구문 풀이

1행 Houses in the historic district of Key West, Florida, for example, whether new or remodeled, must be built of wood in a traditional style, and there are only a few permissible colors of paint, white being preferred.

(Houses: 주어1 / 「whether+A+or+B : A이든 B이든」 / must be built: 동사1(조동사 수동태) / are: 동사2 / colors: 주어2 / white: 의미상 주어 / white being preferred: 분사구문(그리고 ~되고 있다))

06 몰입의 원인 정답률 47% | 정답 ④

글의 흐름으로 보아, 주어진 문장이 들어가기에 가장 적절한 곳을 고르시오. [3점]

Much research has been carried out on the causes of engagement, / an issue that is important / from both a theoretical and practical standpoint: / identifying the drivers of work engagement / may enable us / to manipulate or influence it.

몰입의 원인에 대한 많은 연구가 수행되었는데, / 이는 중요한 문제이다. / 이론적 및 실제적 둘 다의 관점에서 / 업무 몰입의 동기를 알아내는 것은 / 우리가 ~할 수 있게 할 것이다. / 우리가 그것을 조작하거나 그것에 영향을 줄

① The causes of engagement fall into two major camps: / situational and personal.

몰입의 원인은 두 가지 주요한 분야로 나뉜다. / 상황적인 것과 개인적인 것이라는

② The most influential situational causes / are job resources, feedback and leadership, / the latter, of course, / being responsible for job resources and feedback.

가장 영향력 있는 상황적 원인은 / 직무 자원, 피드백, 그리고 리더십이며, / 후자는 당연하게도 / 직무 자원과 피드백에 대한 책임이다.

③ Indeed, / leaders influence engagement / by giving their employees / honest and constructive feedback on their performance, / and by providing them with the necessary resources / that enable them to perform their job well.

실제로 / 리더들은 몰입에 영향을 미친다. / 직원들에게 제공해서 / 수행에 대한 솔직하고 건설적인 피드백을 / 그리고 직원들에게 필요한 자원을 제공하여 / 그들이 자기 직무를 잘 수행할 수 있도록

✔ It is, however, noteworthy / that although engagement drives job performance, / job performance also drives engagement.

그러나 주목할 점은 / 몰입이 직무 수행의 동기가 되지만, / 직무 수행도 몰입의 동기가 된다는 것이다.
In other words, / when employees are able to do their jobs well / — to the point that they match or exceed their own expectations and ambitions — / they will engage more, / be proud of their achievements, / and find work more meaningful.
즉, / 직원들이 직무를 잘 수행할 수 있을 때 / 자기 기대와 포부에 부합하거나 그것을 능가할 정도로 / 직원들은 더 많이 몰입하고, / 자기 성과를 자랑스러워하며, / 업무를 더 의미 있게 생각할 것이다.
⑤ This is especially evident / when people are employed in jobs / that align with their values.
이것은 특히 분명하다. / 사람들이 직무에 종사했을 때 / 자기 가치와 일치하는

몰입의 원인에 대한 많은 연구가 수행되었는데, 이는 이론적 및 실제적 둘 다의 관점에서 중요한 문제이다. 업무 몰입의 동기를 알아내는 것은 우리가 그것을 조작하거나 그것에 영향을 줄 수 있게 할 것이다. ① 몰입의 원인은 상황적인 것과 개인적인 것이라는 두 가지 주요한 분야로 나뉜다. ② 가장 영향력 있는 상황적 원인은 직무 자원, 피드백, 그리고 리더십이며, 후자는 당연하게도 직무 자원과 피드백에 대한 책임이다. ③ 실제로 리더들은 직원들에게 수행에 대한 솔직하고 건설적인 피드백을 제공하고 직원들이 자기 직무를 잘 수행할 수 있도록 필요한 자원을 제공하여 몰입에 영향을 미친다. ④ 그러나 주목할 점은 몰입이 직무 수행의 동기가 되지만, 직무 수행도 몰입의 동기가 된다는 것이다. 즉, 직원들이 자기 기대와 포부에 부합하거나 그것을 능가할 정도로 직무를 잘 수행할 수 있을 때 직원들은 더 많이 몰입하고, 자기 성과를 자랑스러워하며, 업무를 더 의미 있게 생각할 것이다. ⑤ 이것은 사람들이 자기 가치와 일치하는 직무에 종사했을 때 특히 분명하다.

Why? 왜 정답일까?

④ 앞에서 리더들이 직원의 수행에 대해 주는 피드백이 업무에 대한 몰입을 촉진할 수 있다고 한다. 이에 대해 주어진 문장은 거꾸로 '수행' 역시 몰입의 원인이 될 수 있다고 설명하고, ④ 뒤의 문장은 직무 수행력이 좋아졌을 때 직원의 업무 몰입이 상승할 수도 있다는 말로 주어진 문장 내용을 다시 풀어(In other words) 설명한다. 따라서 주어진 문장이 들어가기에 가장 적절한 곳은 ④이다.

- noteworthy ⓐ 주목할 만한
- carry out 수행하다
- standpoint ⓝ 관점, 견지
- manipulate ⓥ 조작하다
- be employed in ~에 종사하다
- engagement ⓝ 몰입, 참여
- theoretical ⓐ 이론적인
- identify ⓥ 식별하다, 알아내다
- evident ⓐ 분명한
- align with ~과 일치하다

구문 풀이

10행 The most influential situational causes are job resources, feedback and leadership, the latter(의미상 주어), of course, being responsible for(분사구문) job resources and feedback.

07 어둠 속에서의 식물 생장 정답률 57% | 정답 ③

글의 흐름으로 보아, 주어진 문장이 들어가기에 가장 적절한 곳을 고르시오. [3점]

Scientists who have observed plants growing in the dark / have found / that they are vastly different in appearance, form, and function / from those grown in the light.
어둠 속에서 식물이 자라는 것을 관찰해 온 과학자들은 / 발견해 왔다. / 그것들이 생김새, 형태, 기능 면에서 상당히 다르다는 것을 / 빛 속에서 길러진 것들과
① This is true / even when the plants in the different light conditions / are genetically identical / and are grown under identical conditions of temperature, water, and nutrient level.
이것은 적용된다. / 다른 빛 조건에 있는 식물들이 ~할 때에도 / 유전적으로 같고, / 동일한 온도, 물, 영양소 수준의 조건에서 길러질
② Seedlings grown in the dark / limit the amount of energy going to organs / that do not function at full capacity in the dark, / like cotyledons and roots, / and instead initiate elongation of the seedling stem / to propel the plant out of darkness.
어둠 속에서 길러진 묘목은 / 기관으로 가는 에너지의 양을 제한하고, / 어둠 속에서 완전히 기능하지 않는 / 떡잎이나 뿌리처럼, / 대신 묘목 줄기의 연장을 시작한다. / 그 식물을 어둠 바깥으로 나아가게 하기 위하여
✔ In full light, / seedlings reduce the amount of energy / they allocate to stem elongation.
충분한 빛 속에서 / 묘목은 에너지의 양을 줄인다. / 그것들이 줄기 연장에 배분하는
The energy is directed / to expanding their leaves / and developing extensive root systems.
그 에너지는 향한다. / 그것들의 잎을 확장하고 / 광범위한 근계(根系)를 발달시키는 데로
④ This is a good example of phenotypic plasticity.
이것이 표현형 적응성의 좋은 예이다.
⑤ The seedling adapts to distinct environmental conditions / by modifying its form / and the underlying metabolic and biochemical processes.
묘목은 별개의 환경 조건에 적응한다. / 그것의 형태를 바꿈으로써 / 그리고 근원적인 신진대사 및 생화학적 과정을

어둠 속에서 식물이 자라는 것을 관찰해 온 과학자들은 그것들이 빛 속에서 길러진 것들과 생김새, 형태, 기능 면에서 상당히 다르다는 것을 발견해 왔다. ① 이것은 다른 빛 조건에 있는 식물들이 유전적으로 같고, 동일한 온도, 물, 영양소 수준의 조건에서 길러질 때에도 적용된다. ② 어둠 속에서 길러진 묘목은 떡잎이나 뿌리처럼, 어둠 속에서 완전히 기능하지 않는 기관으로 가는 에너지의 양을 제한하고, 대신 그 식물을 어둠 바깥으로 나아가게 하기 위하여 묘목 줄기를 연장하기 시작한다. ③ 충분한 빛 속에서 묘목은 줄기 연장에 배분하는 에너지의 양을 줄인다. 그 에너지는 잎을 확장하고 광범위한 근계(根系)를 발달시키는 데로 향한다. ④ 이것이 표현형 적응성의 좋은 예이다. ⑤ 묘목은 형태와 근원적인 신진대사 및 생화학적 과정을 바꿈으로써 별개의 환경 조건에 적응한다.

Why? 왜 정답일까?

어둠 속에서 길러진 묘목이 떡잎이나 뿌리로 가는 에너지 양을 줄이고 줄기를 연장시킨다는 ③ 앞의 내용에 이어, 주어진 문장은 빛이 충분해지면 줄기 연장에 할당되는 에너지 양이 다시 줄어듦을 설명한다. 이어서 ③ 뒤의 문장은 대신에 에너지가 묘목의 잎을 확장하고 뿌리를 확장시키는 쪽으로 이용됨을 설명한다. 따라서 주어진 문장이 들어가기에 가장 적절한 곳은 ③이다.

- seedling ⓝ 묘목
- stem ⓝ 줄기
- genetically ad 유전적으로
- nutrient ⓝ 영양소
- propel ⓥ 나아가게 하다, 추진시키다
- distinct ⓐ 별개의, 다른
- allocate ⓥ 할당하다
- vastly ad 상당히, 대단히, 엄청나게
- identical ⓐ 동일한
- initiate ⓥ 시작하다
- extensive ⓐ 광범위한
- underlying ⓐ 기저의, 근본적인

구문 풀이

9행 Seedlings(주어) grown(과거분사) in the dark limit(동사1) the amount of energy going to organs(선행사) [that(주격 관·대) do not function at full capacity in the dark, like cotyledons and roots], and instead initiate(동사2) elongation of the seedling stem to propel(부사적 용법(~하기 위해)) the plant out of darkness.

08 살충제 사용에 관한 생각의 변화 정답률 50% | 정답 ④

글의 흐름으로 보아, 주어진 문장이 들어가기에 가장 적절한 곳을 고르시오.

Simply maintaining yields at current levels / often requires new cultivars and management methods, / since pests and diseases continue to evolve, / and aspects of the chemical, physical, and social environment / can change over several decades.
수확량을 단지 현재 수준으로 유지하는 것만 해도 / 보통 새로운 품종과 관리 기법을 필요로 하는데, / 해충과 질병이 계속 진화하고 있고 / 그리고 화학적, 물리적, 사회적 환경 양상은 / 수십 년에 걸쳐 변할 수 있기 때문이다.
① In the 1960s, / many people considered pesticides / to be mainly beneficial to mankind.
1960년대에 / 많은 사람은 살충제를 여겼다. / 사람들에게 대체로 유익한 것으로
② Developing new, broadly effective, and persistent pesticides / often was considered to be the best way / to control pests on crop plants.
새롭고 널리 효과를 거두고 지속하는 살충제를 개발하는 것은 / 흔히 최고의 방법으로 여겨졌다. / 농작물 해충을 통제하는
③ Since that time, / it has become apparent / that broadly effective pesticides / can have harmful effects on beneficial insects, / which can negate their effects in controlling pests, / and that persistent pesticides / can damage non-target organisms in the ecosystem, / such as birds and people.
그 이후로, / 분명해졌다. / 널리 효과를 거두는 살충제가 / 유익한 곤충에 해로운 영향을 미칠 수 있어서 / 해충 통제 효과를 무효화할 수 있으며, / 그 끈질긴 살충제가 / 생태계 속 목표 외 생물에게 해가 될 수 있다는 점이 / 새와 사람 같은
✔ Also, / it has become difficult for companies / to develop new pesticides, / even those / that can have major beneficial effects and few negative effects.
또한, / 기업들로서는 어려워졌다. / 새로운 살충제를 개발하는 것이 / 그것들조차 / 주된 이로운 효과가 있고 부작용이 거의 없는
Very high costs are involved in following all of the procedures / needed to gain government approval for new pesticides.
모든 절차를 따르는 데 아주 높은 비용이 수반된다. / 새로운 살충제에 정부 승인을 얻는 데 필요한
⑤ Consequently, / more consideration is being given / to other ways to

manage pests, / such as incorporating greater resistance to pests into cultivars / by breeding and using other biological control methods.
결과적으로, / 더 많은 고려가 이루어지고 있다. / 해충을 관리하는 다른 방법들에 대해 / 품종에 더 강한 해충 내성을 포함시키는 것 같은 / 다른 생물학적 통제 기법을 개량해 사용하여

수확량을 단지 현재 수준으로 유지하는 것만 해도 보통 새로운 품종과 관리 기법을 필요로 하는데, 해충과 질병이 계속 진화하고 있고 화학적, 물리적, 사회적 환경 양상이 수십 년에 걸쳐 변할 수 있기 때문이다. ① 1960년대에 많은 사람은 살충제가 사람들에게 대체로 유익한 것으로 여겼다. ② 새롭고 널리 효과가 있고 지속하는 살충제를 개발하는 것은 흔히 농작물 해충을 통제하는 최고의 방법으로 여겨졌다. ③ 그 이후로, 널리 효과가 있는 살충제가 유익한 곤충에게 해로운 영향을 미칠 수 있어서 해충 통제 효과를 무효화할 수 있으며, 그 끈질긴 살충제가 새와 사람 등, 생태계 속 목표 외 생물에게 해가 될 수 있다는 점이 분명해졌다. ④ 또한, 기업들이 새로운 살충제를 개발하는 것이 어려워져서, 주된 이로운 효과가 있고 부작용이 거의 없는 것들조차 만들기 어렵게 되었다. 새로운 살충제에 정부 승인을 얻는 데 필요한 모든 절차를 따르는 데 아주 높은 비용이 수반된다. ⑤ 결과적으로, 해충을 관리하는 다른 방법들, 말하자면 다른 생물학적 통제 기법을 개량해 사용하여 (재배 중인) 품종에 더 강한 해충 내성을 포함시키는 것 등이 더 고려되고 있다.

Why? 왜 정답일까?

④ 앞에서 살충제는 1960년대만 해도 각광을 받았으나 이후 분명한 부작용이 밝혀졌음을 언급하고 있다. 이어서 Also로 연결되는 주어진 문장은 새로운 살충제를 기업에서 개발하기도 어려워졌음을 보태어 설명한다. ④ 뒤의 문장에서는 비용 문제가 따른다는 것을 언급하며 주어진 문장 내용을 뒷받침한다. 따라서 주어진 문장이 들어가기에 가장 적절한 곳은 ④이다.

- pesticide ⓝ 살충제
- method ⓝ 방법
- disease ⓝ 질병
- decade ⓝ 십 년
- broadly ad 광범위하게
- crop plant 농작물
- insect ⓝ 곤충
- non-target 목표 외의
- approval ⓝ 승인
- resistance ⓝ 내성, 저항
- cultivar ⓝ 품종
- pest ⓝ 해충
- aspect ⓝ 양상
- mankind ⓝ 사람들
- persistent ⓐ 지속력 있는, 끈질긴
- apparent ⓐ 분명한
- negate ⓥ 무효화하다, 효력이 없게 만들다
- procedure ⓝ 과정, 절차
- consequently ad 결과적으로
- breed ⓥ 개량하다

구문 풀이

1행 Also, it has become difficult for companies to develop new pesticides, even those [that can have major beneficial effects and few negative effects].
(it: 가주어 / for companies: 의미상 주어 / to develop ~: 진주어 / those: 대명사(=pesticides) ← 주격 관·대)

★★★ 1등급 대비 고난도 2점 문제

09 물고기의 전기 신호 정답률 30% | 정답 ②

글의 흐름으로 보아, 주어진 문장이 들어가기에 가장 적절한 곳을 고르시오.

Electric communication is mainly known in fish.
전기적 의사소통은 주로 물고기에서 알려져 있다.
The electric signals are produced / in special electric organs.
전기 신호는 생성된다. / 특수 전기 기관에서
When the signal is discharged / the electric organ will be negatively loaded / compared to the head / and an electric field is created around the fish.
신호가 방출되면 / 전기 기관이 음전하를 띠고 / 머리에 대해 / 물고기 주위에 전기장이 생긴다.
① A weak electric current is created / also in ordinary muscle cells / when they contract.
약한 전류가 발생한다. / 일반 근육 세포 안에서도 / 그것이 수축할 때
✔ In the electric organ / the muscle cells are connected in larger chunks, / which makes the total current intensity larger / than in ordinary muscles.
전기 기관 안에서 / 근육 세포는 더 큰 덩어리로 연결되어 있으며, / 이는 총 전류 강도를 더 크게 만든다. / 일반 근육에서보다
The fish varies the signals / by changing the form of the electric field / or the frequency of discharging.
물고기는 신호를 다양하게 한다. / 전기장의 형태를 변화시켜 / 혹은 방출 주파수를
③ The system is only working over small distances, / about one to two meters.
이 체계는 짧은 거리에서만 작동한다. / 약 1~2미터 정도의
④ This is an advantage / since the species using the signal system / often live in large groups / with several other species.
이것은 이점이 있다. / 신호 체계를 사용하는 종들은 ~때문에 / 흔히 큰 무리를 지어 살기 / 다른 여러 종과 함께
⑤ If many fish send out signals at the same time, / the short range decreases the risk of interference.
많은 물고기가 동시에 신호를 보내면, / 짧은 범위는 전파 방해의 위험을 줄여 준다.

전기적 의사소통은 주로 물고기에서 알려져 있다. 전기 신호는 특수 전기 기관에서 생성된다. 신호가 방출되면 머리에 대해 전기 기관이 음전하를 띠고 물고기 주위에 전기장이 생긴다. ① 일반 근육 세포가 수축할 때 약한 전류가 그 안에서도 발생한다. ② 전기 기관 안에서 근육 세포는 더 큰 덩어리로 연결되어 있으며, 이는 일반 근육에서보다 총 전류 강도를 더 크게 만든다. 물고기는 전기장의 형태나 방출 주파수를 변화시켜 신호를 다양하게 한다. ③ 이 체계는 약 1~2미터 정도의 짧은 거리에서만 작동한다. ④ 신호 체계를 사용하는 종들은 흔히 큰 무리를 지어 다른 여러 종과 함께 살기 때문에 이것은 이점이 있다. ⑤ 많은 물고기가 동시에 신호를 보내면, 짧은 (도달 가능) 범위는 전파 방해의 위험을 줄여 준다.

Why? 왜 정답일까?

물고기가 사용하는 전기적 의사소통 과정을 소개하는 글이다. ② 앞에서 전기 신호는 특수 전기 기관에서 생성되거나, 일반 근육 세포에서도 미세하게 발생할 수 있다고 언급하는데, 주어진 문장은 전기 기관에서는 근육 세포가 더 큰 덩어리로 연결돼 있어 전류 강도가 더 크다고 설명한다. 이어서 ③ 뒤부터는 물고기가 신호를 다양하게 만들어낼 수 있다는 것과 이 신호가 작동하는 범위에 관해 주로 설명하고 있다. 따라서 근육 세포에서 만들어진 신호에 관한 설명을 마무리하는 주어진 문장이 들어가기에 가장 적절한 곳은 ②이다.

- chunk ⓝ 덩어리
- discharge ⓥ 방출하다, 내보내다
- contract ⓥ 수축하다
- interference ⓝ 전파 방해, 간섭
- intensity ⓝ 강도
- load ⓥ (짐, 부담을) 실어주다
- frequency ⓝ 주파수

구문 풀이

1행 In the electric organ the muscle cells are connected in larger chunks, which makes the total current intensity larger than in ordinary muscles.
(chunks: 선행사(문장) / which: 계속적 용법)

★★ 문제 해결 꿀~팁 ★★

▶ 많이 틀린 이유는?
④가 만일 정답이면, ④ 뒤의 This가 앞 문장과 이어지지 않아 논리적 공백이 생길 것이다. 하지만 여기서는 This 자리에 앞 문장 내용을 넣어서 읽어도 흐름이 어색하지 않다. 즉 '전기 신호 체계가 짧은 거리에 작용한다는 사실'이 물고기에게 이점이 맞고, 그 이유를 설명하는 문장이 'since ~'와 ⑤ 뒤의 문장이므로 흐름상 어색하지 않다.
▶ 문제 해결 방법은?
② 앞과 주어진 문장은 둘 다 전기 강도와 근육 세포를 언급한다. ② 뒤를 보면 근육에 대한 언급은 없고 바로 신호 종류가 다양하다는 새로운 내용으로 넘어간다. 따라서 전류가 '어디서 발생하는지'에 대한 이야기는 ②에서 마무리되어야 한다.

★★★ 1등급 대비 고난도 2점 문제

10 인터넷 쿠키 파일의 장단점 정답률 43% | 정답 ⑤

글의 흐름으로 보아, 주어진 문장이 들어가기에 가장 적절한 곳을 고르시오.

Favorite websites sometimes greet users / like old friends.
즐겨찾기 웹 사이트는 때때로 사용자들을 맞이한다. / 오랜 친구처럼
Online bookstores welcome their customers by name / and suggest new books / they might like to read.
온라인 서점은 이름으로 고객들을 환영하며 / 새로운 도서를 제안해 준다. / 고객이 읽고 싶어 할 수도 있는
① Real estate sites tell their visitors about new properties / that have come on the market.
부동산 사이트는 방문자들에게 새로운 부동산에 대해 알려 준다. / 시장에 나온
② These tricks are made possible by cookies, / small files / that an Internet server stores inside individuals' web browsers / so it can remember them.
이러한 기술은 쿠키 파일에 의해서 가능한데, / 이는 작은 파일이다. / 인터넷 서버가 개인의 웹 브라우저 안에 저장해 두는 / 그것이 사용자를 기억해 낼 수 있도록
③ Therefore, cookies can greatly benefit individuals.
그러므로 쿠키 파일은 개인에게 매우 도움이 될 수 있다.
④ For example, / cookies save users the chore / of having to enter names and addresses into e-commerce websites / every time they make a purchase.
예컨대, / 쿠키 파일은 사용자에게 귀찮은 일을 덜어 준다. / 전자상거래 사이트에 이름과 주소를 입력해야만 하는 / 그들이 구매를 할 때마다

✔However, concerns have been raised / that cookies, / which can track what people do online, / may be violating privacy / by helping companies or government agencies / accumulate personal information.
하지만, 우려가 제기되어 왔다. / 쿠키 파일은 / 사람들이 온라인에서 무엇을 하는지 추적할 수 있는 / 사생활을 침해할 수도 있다는 / 기업체나 정부기관을 도와주어서 / 개인 정보를 모으도록

Security is another concern:
보안은 또 다른 걱정거리이다.

Cookies make shared computers far less secure / and offer hackers many ways to break into systems.
쿠키 파일은 공유된 컴퓨터를 훨씬 덜 안전하게 만들고 / 해커들에게 시스템에 침입해 들어올 많은 방법을 제공한다.

즐겨찾기 웹 사이트는 때때로 사용자들을 오랜 친구처럼 맞이한다. 온라인 서점은 이름으로 고객들을 환영하며 고객이 읽고 싶어 할 수도 있는 새로운 도서를 제안해 준다. ① 부동산 사이트는 방문자들에게 시장에 나온 새로운 부동산에 대해 알려 준다. ② 이러한 기술은 쿠키 파일에 의해서 가능한데, 이는 인터넷 서버가 사용자를 기억해 낼 수 있도록 개인의 웹 브라우저 안에 저장해 두는 작은 파일이다. ③ 그러므로 쿠키 파일은 개인에게 매우 도움이 될 수 있다. ④ 예컨대, 쿠키 파일은 사용자가 구매를 할 때마다 전자상거래 사이트에 이름과 주소를 입력해야만 하는 귀찮은 일을 덜어 준다. ⑤ 하지만, 사람들이 온라인에서 무엇을 하는지 추적할 수 있는 쿠키 파일은 기업체나 정부기관이 개인 정보를 모으는 것을 도와주어서 사생활을 침해할 수도 있다는 우려가 제기되어 왔다. 보안은 또 다른 걱정거리이다. 쿠키 파일은 공유된 컴퓨터를 훨씬 덜 안전하게 만들고 해커들에게 시스템에 침입해 들어올 많은 방법을 제공한다.

Why? 왜 정답일까?

⑤ 앞의 문장에서 쿠키 파일은 사람들이 온라인에서 물건을 살 때마다 매번 정보를 입력해야 하는 귀찮음을 덜어줄 수 있는 장점을 지닌다고 설명하는데, However로 시작하는 주어진 문장은 쿠키 파일이 기업체나 정부 기관의 개인 정보 수집을 도와 사생활 침해를 일으킬 수도 있음을 제시한다. ⑤ 뒤의 문장에서는 쿠키 파일이 보안 취약의 문제와도 연결될 수 있음을 추가로 지적한다. 따라서 주어진 문장이 들어가기에 가장 적절한 곳은 ⑤이다.

- concern ⓝ 우려, 걱정거리
- track ⓥ 추적하다
- accumulate ⓥ 모으다, 축적하다
- real estate 부동산
- make a purchase 구매하다
- break into ~에 침입하다
- raise ⓥ (문제 등을) 제기하다
- violate ⓥ 침해하다, 위반하다
- greet ⓥ 맞다, 환영하다
- property ⓝ 부동산, 재산, 소유물
- security ⓝ 보안, 안전

구문 풀이

1행 However, concerns have been raised [that cookies, (which can track what people do online), may be violating privacy / by helping companies or government agencies accumulate personal information].
(concerns: 주어 / have been raised: 동사(현재완료 수동태) / that: 접속사(동격) / which: 주격 관계대명사 / what: 관계대명사(~것) / by helping: 「by+동명사 : ~함으로써」 / companies or government agencies: helping의 목적어 / accumulate personal information: 목적격 보어(원형부정사))

★★ 문제 해결 꿀~팁 ★★

▶ 많이 틀린 이유는?
'쿠키'라는 익숙한 소재가 '음식'으로서의 쿠키가 아닌 '인터넷 임시 파일'을 나타내므로, 지문을 이해할 때 혼동이 생길 수 있는 문제였다. 오답으로 ④가 많이 나왔는데, ④에 주어진 문장을 넣고 나면 ⑤ 앞뒤로 역접의 연결어 없이 서로 반대되는 내용의 문장이 이어지게 되므로 글의 일관성이 저해된다.

▶ 문제 해결 방법은?
상반된 두 문장이 앞뒤에 놓이기 위해서는 중간에 반드시 역접의 연결어가 있어야 한다. ⑤ 앞뒤의 문장은 '쿠키의 장점 vs. 쿠키의 단점'을 언급하여 내용상 충돌을 일으키므로 '하지만'으로 시작하는 주어진 문장이 반드시 사이에 위치하여 흐름을 전환한다는 신호를 주어야 한다.

★★★ 1등급 대비 고난도 2점 문제

11 다른 매질보다 음파를 더 잘 전달하는 고체 | 정답률 45% | 정답 ⑤

글의 흐름으로 보아, 주어진 문장이 들어가기에 가장 적절한 곳을 고르시오.

Tap your finger on the surface of a wooden table or desk, / and observe the loudness of the sound you hear.
손가락으로 나무 탁자나 책상의 표면 위를 두드리고 / 당신이 듣는 소리의 크기를 관찰하라.

Then, place your ear flat on top of the table or desk.
그런 다음, 귀를 탁자나 책상의 표면에 바싹 댄다.

① With your finger about one foot away from your ear, / tap the table top / and observe the loudness of the sound you hear again.
손가락을 귀로부터 대략 1피트 정도 떨어지게 놓고, / 다시 탁자 표면을 두드리고 / 당신이 듣는 소리의 크기를 관찰한다.

② The volume of the sound / you hear with your ear on the desk / is much louder than with it off the desk.
소리의 크기는 / 당신이 책상 위에 귀를 대고 듣는 / 책상으로부터 귀를 떼고 듣는 소리보다 훨씬 크다.

③ Sound waves are capable of traveling through many solid materials / as well as through air.
음파는 많은 고체 물질을 통해 이동할 수 있다. / 공기를 통해서뿐만 아니라

④ Solids, like wood for example, / transfer the sound waves much better / than air typically does / because the molecules in a solid substance / are much closer and more tightly packed together / than they are in air.
예를 들어 나무와 같은 고체는 / 훨씬 더 잘 전달하는데 / 공기가 보통 음파를 전달하는 것보다 / 왜냐하면 고체 물체의 분자들이 / 훨씬 더 가깝고 더 촘촘하게 함께 뭉쳐있기 때문이다. / 공기 중에서보다

✔This allows the solids to carry the waves more easily and efficiently, / resulting in a louder sound.
이것이 고체로 하여금 그 파장을 더 쉽고 효율적으로 이동시키게 해서, / 더 큰 소리를 만들어 낸다.

The density of the air itself / also plays a determining factor / in the loudness of sound waves passing through it.
또한 공기의 밀도는 / 결정하는 요소로 작용한다. / 그것을 통과하는 음파의 크기를

손가락으로 나무 탁자나 책상의 표면 위를 두드리고 당신이 듣는 소리의 크기를 관찰하라. 그런 다음, 귀를 탁자나 책상의 표면에 바싹 댄다. ① 손가락을 귀로부터 대략 1피트 정도 떨어지게 놓고, 다시 탁자 표면을 두드리고 당신이 듣는 소리의 크기를 관찰한다. ② 당신이 책상 위에 귀를 대고 듣는 소리의 크기는 책상으로부터 귀를 떼고 듣는 소리보다 훨씬 크다. ③ 음파는 공기를 통해서뿐만 아니라 많은 고체 물질을 통해 이동할 수 있다. ④ 예를 들어 나무와 같은 고체는 공기가 보통 음파를 전달하는 것보다 훨씬 더 잘 전달하는데 왜냐하면 공기 중에서보다 고체 물체의 분자들이 훨씬 더 가깝고 더 촘촘하게 함께 뭉쳐있기 때문이다. ⑤ 이것이 고체로 하여금 그 파장을 더 쉽고 효율적으로 이동시키게 해서, 더 큰 소리를 만들어 낸다. 또한 공기의 밀도는 그것을 통과하는 음파의 크기를 결정하는 요소로 작용한다.

Why? 왜 정답일까?

고체가 음파를 더 잘 전달하는 이유에 관해 설명한 글이다. ⑤ 앞의 문장에서 고체 물체의 분자들이 더 촘촘하게 뭉쳐있음을 언급한 데 이어, 주어진 문장은 '바로 이 이유로' 고체가 음파를 더 잘 이동시켜 더 큰 소리를 만들어내게 된다고 설명하므로, 주어진 문장이 들어가기에 가장 적절한 곳은 ⑤이다.

- efficiently ad 효율적으로
- surface ⓝ 표면
- typically ad 보통, 전형적으로
- pack ⓥ (물건 등으로) 촘촘히 채우다
- determining ⓐ 결정적인
- result in ~을 낳다, 야기하다
- transfer ⓥ 이동시키다, 전달하다
- substance ⓝ 물체
- density ⓝ 밀도

구문 풀이

12행 Solids, like wood for example, transfer the sound waves much better than air typically does / because the molecules in a solid substance are much closer and more tightly packed together than they are in air.
(Solids: 주어 / transfer: 동사 / does: =transfers / because: 이유 접속사 / the molecules: 주어 / are: 동사 / much closer: 보어1 / more tightly packed together: 보어2)

★★ 문제 해결 꿀~팁 ★★

▶ 많이 틀린 이유는?
전통적으로 오답이 많이 나오는 과학 지문을 활용한 문제이다. 주어진 문장의 This가 가리키는 바를 놓치면 ④를 오답으로 고르기 쉽다.

▶ 문제 해결 방법은?
주어진 문장의 This는 고체가 음파를 더 잘 이동시킬 수 있는 '원인'을 나타낸다. 따라서 '고체는 공기에 비해 분자가 촘촘하게 밀집되어 있다 → 고체에서 음파 이동이 쉬워진다'라는 흐름이 되도록 ⑤에 주어진 문장을 넣는 것이 적절하다.

★★★ 1등급 대비 고난도 3점 문제

12 기술 축적에 기여하는 가공품 | 정답률 39% | 정답 ②

글의 흐름으로 보아, 주어진 문장이 들어가기에 가장 적절한 곳을 고르시오. [3점]

DAY 17

[문제편 p.114]

By acting on either natural or artificial resources, / through techniques, / we alter them in various ways.
천연자원이나 인공 자원에 영향을 줌으로써, / 기술로 / 우리는 그것들을 다양한 방식으로 바꾼다.

① Thus we create *artifacts*, / which form an important aspect of technologies.
이렇게 하여 우리는 *가공품*을 만들어내는데, / 그것은 기술의 중요한 한 측면을 형성한다.

✔ A clay pot is an example of a material artifact, / which, although transformed by human activity, / is not all that far removed from its natural state.
점토 항아리는 재료 가공품의 한 사례인데, / 비록 인간 활동으로 인해 변형되었지만, / 그것의 천연 상태에서 그렇게까지 멀리 떨어진 것은 아니다.

A plastic cup, a contact lens, and a computer chip, / on the other hand, / are examples of artifacts / that are far removed from the original states / of the natural resources needed to create them.
플라스틱 컵, 콘택트렌즈, 그리고 컴퓨터 칩은 / 반면에 / 가공품의 사례이다. / 원상태에서 멀리 떨어진 / 그것을 만드는 데 필요한 천연자원의

③ Artifacts can serve as resources / in other technological processes.
가공품은 자원의 역할을 할 수 있다. / 다른 기술적 과정에서

④ This is one of the important interaction effects / within the technological system.
이것은 중요한 상호 작용 효과 중 하나이다. / 기술적 시스템 내에서의

⑤ In other words, each new technology / increases the stock of available tools and resources / that can be employed by other technologies / to produce new artifacts.
다시 말해 각각의 새로운 기술은 / 이용 가능한 도구와 자원의 축적을 늘린다. / 다른 기술에 의해 쓰일 수 있는 / 새로운 가공품을 생산하기 위해

기술로 천연자원이나 인공 자원에 영향을 줌으로써, 우리는 그것들을 다양한 방식으로 바꾼다. ① 이렇게 하여 우리는 *가공품*을 만들어내는데, 그것은 기술의 중요한 한 측면을 형성한다. ② 점토 항아리는 재료 가공품의 한 사례인데, 비록 인간 활동으로 인해 변형되었지만, 그것의 천연 상태에서 그렇게까지 멀리 떨어진 것은 아니다. 반면에 플라스틱 컵, 콘택트렌즈, 그리고 컴퓨터 칩은 그것을 만드는 데 필요한 천연자원의 원상태에서 멀리 떨어진 가공품의 사례이다. ③ 가공품은 다른 기술적 과정에서 자원의 역할을 할 수 있다. ④ 이것은 기술적 시스템 내에서의 중요한 상호 작용 효과 중 하나이다. ⑤ 다시 말해 각각의 새로운 기술은 새로운 가공품을 생산하기 위해 다른 기술에 의해 쓰일 수 있는 이용 가능한 도구와 자원의 축적을 늘린다.

Why? 왜 정답일까?

② 앞에서 가공품이 기술의 중요한 한 측면을 형성한다는 내용을 다룬 데 이어, 주어진 문장은 점토 항아리를 예로 들기 시작하고(A clay pot is an example ~), ② 뒤의 문장은 점토 항아리와 대조되는 사례를 on the other hand 이하에 제시하고 있다. 따라서 주어진 문장이 들어가기에 가장 적절한 곳은 ②이다.

- **all that** 그렇게까지
- **act on** ~에 영향을 주다
- **alter** ⓥ 바꾸다, 고치다
- **interaction effect** 상호 작용 효과
- **removed** ⓐ 떨어진, 먼
- **artificial** ⓐ 인공의
- **serve as** ~의 역할을 하다
- **employ** ⓥ 쓰다, 이용하다

구문 풀이

1행 A clay pot is an example of a material artifact, which, (although transformed by human activity), is not all that far removed from its natural state.
(which: 계속적 용법 / although: 접속사 / although transformed by human activity: 분사구문 / not all that: 그 정도로 ~하지 않다)

★★ 문제 해결 꿀~팁 ★★

▶ 많이 틀린 이유는?

가공품이 기술 축적의 기반이 된다는 추상적인 내용을 다룬 글이다. ④ 뒤의 This를 주어진 문장의 A clay pot으로 잘못 이해한 경우 ④를 답으로 골랐을 수 있다. 하지만 여기서 This는 '가공품이 다른 기술적 과정에 있어 자원으로 기능할 수 있다'는, ④ 앞의 문장 내용 전체를 받는 대명사로 보는 것이 적절하다.

▶ 문제 해결 방법은?

② 뒤의 문장에 on the other hand가 나오는데, 이는 앞의 소재와 대조할만한 소재를 뒤에서 소개할 때 쓰는 연결어이다. ② 앞의 문장에서 '플라스틱 컵, 콘택트렌즈, 컴퓨터 칩' 등과 대조될만한 가공품의 예를 언급한 바가 없으므로, ②에 주어진 문장이 들어가지 않는다면 앞뒤로 논리적인 공백이 발생하게 된다.

DAY 18 문장 삽입 03

01 ②	02 ⑤	03 ③	04 ④	05 ③
06 ④	07 ③	08 ②	09 ⑤	10 ⑤
11 ③	12 ①			

01 꼬리에 꼬리를 무는 위대한 진보

정답률 50% | 정답 ②

글의 흐름으로 보아, 주어진 문장이 들어가기에 가장 적절한 곳을 고르시오.

Ransom Olds, the father of the Oldsmobile, / could not produce his "horseless carriages" fast enough.
Oldsmobile의 창립자인 Ransom Olds는 / '말 없는 마차'를 충분히 빨리 생산할 수 없었다.

In 1901 he had an idea / to speed up the manufacturing process / — instead of building one car at a time, / he created the assembly line.
1901년에, 그는 아이디어를 내서, / 생산 과정의 속도를 높일 / 한 번에 한 대의 자동차를 만드는 대신에, / 그는 조립 라인을 고안했다.

① The acceleration in production was unheard-of / — from an output of 425 automobiles in 1901 / to an impressive 2,500 cars the following year.
생산의 가속은 전례가 없던 것이었다. / 1901년 425대의 자동차 생산량에서 / 이듬해 인상적이게도 2,500대의 자동차로

✔ While other competitors were in awe of this incredible volume, / Henry Ford dared to ask, / "Can we do even better?"
다른 경쟁사들이 이 놀라운 분량에 깊은 감명을 받는 동안, / Henry Ford는 감히 질문했다. / "우리가 훨씬 더 잘할 수 있을까?"라고

He was, in fact, able to improve upon Olds's clever idea / by introducing conveyor belts to the assembly line.
실제로 그는 Olds의 훌륭한 아이디어를 개선할 수 있었다. / 컨베이어 벨트를 조립 라인에 도입함으로써

③ As a result, / Ford's production went through the roof.
그 결과, / Ford사의 생산은 최고조에 달했다.

④ Instead of taking a day and a half to manufacture a Model T, / as in the past, / he was now able to spit them out / at a rate of one car every ninety minutes.
Model T를 제작하는 데 1.5일이 걸리는 대신에, / 과거처럼, / 그는 차를 뽑아낼 수 있게 되었다. / 90분마다 한 대씩의 속도로

⑤ The moral of the story is / that good progress is often the herald of great progress.
이 이야기의 교훈은 / 좋은 진보는 종종 위대한 진보의 선구자라는 것이다.

Oldsmobile의 창립자인 Ransom Olds는 '말 없는 마차(자동차의 초창기 호칭)'를 충분히 빨리 생산할 수 없었다. 1901년에, 그는 생산 과정의 속도를 높일 아이디어를 내서, 한 번에 한 대의 자동차를 만드는 대신에, 조립 라인을 고안했다. ① 생산의 가속은 전례가 없던 것으로, 1901년 425대의 자동차 생산량에서 이듬해 인상적이게도 2,500대의 자동차가 생산되었다. ② 다른 경쟁사들이 이 놀라운 분량에 깊은 감명을 받는 동안, Henry Ford는 감히 "우리가 훨씬 더 잘할 수 있을까?"라고 질문했다. 실제로 그는 컨베이어 벨트를 조립 라인에 도입함으로써 Olds의 훌륭한 아이디어를 개선할 수 있었다. ③ 그 결과, Ford사의 생산은 최고조에 달했다. ④ 과거처럼, Model T를 제작하는 데 1.5일이 걸리는 대신에, 그는 90분마다 한 대씩의 속도로 차를 뽑아낼 수 있게 되었다. ⑤ 이 이야기의 교훈은 좋은 진보는 종종 위대한 진보의 선구자라는 것이다.

Why? 왜 정답일까?

② 앞에서 Oldsmobile의 창립자인 Ransom Olds가 조립 라인을 만들어 자동차 생산 속도를 높였다는 내용이 소개된 후, 주어진 문장은 Henry Ford가 이에 감탄하는 데 그치지 않고 '더 잘할' 방법을 모색하기 시작했다는 내용을 이어 간다. ② 뒤의 문장에서는 Henry Ford를 He로 가리키며, 실제로 Ford가 조립 라인에 컨베이어 벨트를 도입하여 시스템을 한층 더 개선했다는 내용을 제시한다. 따라서 주어진 문장이 들어가기에 가장 적절한 곳은 ②이다.

- **competitor** ⓝ 경쟁자
- **volume** ⓝ 양
- **horseless** ⓐ 말((馬))이 없는
- **manufacturing process** 제조 과정
- **acceleration** ⓝ 가속화
- **impressive** ⓐ 인상적인
- **improve** ⓥ 향상하다
- **conveyor belt** 컨베이어 벨트
- **moral** ⓝ (이야기나 경험의) 교훈, 도덕률
- **incredible** ⓐ 놀라운, 믿기지 않는
- **dare** ⓥ 감히 ~하다
- **carriage** ⓝ 마차
- **assembly** ⓝ 조립
- **unheard-of** ⓐ 전례없는
- **following** ⓐ (시간상으로) 그 다음의
- **introduce** ⓥ 도입하다
- **go through the roof** 치솟다, 급등하다
- **progress** ⓝ 진보, 진척

구문 풀이

14행 Instead of taking a day and a half to manufacture a Model T,
전치사(~ 대신에) 동명사
as (he did) in the past, he was now able to spit them out at a rate of
생략 ~할 수 있었다
one car every ninety minutes.
접속사(~듯이)

02 기계 능력의 진화
정답률 49% | 정답 ⑤

글의 흐름으로 보아, 주어진 문장이 들어가기에 가장 적절한 곳을 고르시오.

The boundary between uniquely human creativity and machine capabilities / continues to change.
인간 고유의 창의력과 기계의 능력 사이 경계가 / 계속 변화하고 있다.

① Returning to the game of chess, back in 1956, / thirteen-year-old child prodigy Bobby Fischer / made a pair of remarkably creative moves / against grandmaster Donald Byrne.
과거 1956년의 체스 게임으로 돌아가 보면, / 13세 신동 Bobby Fischer는 / 대단히 창의적인 두 수를 두었다. / 거장 Donald Byrne을 상대로

② First he sacrificed his knight, seemingly for no gain, / and then exposed his queen to capture.
먼저 그는 겉으로 보기에 아무런 이득도 없이 자신의 나이트를 희생시켰고, / 그런 다음 퀸을 노출시켜 잡히게 했다.

③ On the surface, these moves seemed insane, / but several moves later, / Fischer used these moves to win the game.
겉으로 보기에는 이러한 수들은 비상식적으로 보였지만, / 몇 수를 더 두고 나서, / Fischer는 이 수를 이용하여 그 게임에서 승리했다.

④ His creativity was praised at the time / as the mark of genius.
당시 그의 창의성은 칭송받았다. / 천재성을 나타내는 표시로

✔ Yet today / if you program that same position into an ordinary chess program, / it will immediately suggest the exact moves / that Fischer made.
하지만 오늘날 / 여러분이 보통의 체스 프로그램에 그와 똑같은 배치를 설정하면, / 그것은 즉시 바로 그 수를 제안할 것이다. / Fischer가 두었던

It's not because the computer has memorized the Fischer-Byrne game, / but rather because it searches far enough ahead / to see that these moves really do pay off.
그것은 컴퓨터가 Fischer와 Byrne의 게임을 암기했기 때문이 아니라, / 그것이 충분히 멀리 앞을 탐색하기 때문이다. / 이러한 수가 실제로 성과를 거둔다는 것을 볼 수 있을 만큼

인간 고유의 창의력과 기계의 능력 사이 경계가 계속 변화하고 있다. ① 과거 1956년의 체스 게임으로 돌아가 보면, 13세 신동 Bobby Fischer는 거장 Donald Byrne을 상대로 대단히 창의적인 두 수를 두었다. ② 먼저 그는 겉으로 보기에 아무런 이득도 없이 자신의 나이트를 희생시켰고, 그런 다음 퀸을 노출시켜 잡히게 했다. ③ 겉으로 보기에는 이러한 수들은 비상식적으로 보였지만, 몇 수를 더 두고 나서, Fischer는 이 수를 이용하여 그 게임에서 승리했다. ④ 당시 그의 창의성은 천재성을 나타내는 표시로 칭송받았다. ⑤ 하지만 오늘날 보통의 체스 프로그램에 그와 똑같은 배치를 설정하면, 그것은 즉시 Fischer가 두었던 바로 그 수를 제안할 것이다. 그것은 컴퓨터가 Fischer와 Byrne의 게임을 암기했기 때문이 아니라, 이러한 수가 실제로 성과를 거둔다는 것을 볼 수 있을 만큼 충분히 멀리 앞을 탐색하기 때문이다.

Why? 왜 정답일까?

인간의 창의력과 기계의 능력 사이 경계가 모호해지고 있다는 내용의 글로, 서두부터 체스 게임 신동의 예가 제시되고 있다. 이 신동은 겉으로 이득이 없어 보이는 수를 두었으나 결과적으로는 승리했고, 그의 창의성은 천재성의 표시로 칭송받았다는 내용이 ⑤ 앞까지 이어진다. 한편 주어진 문장은 Yet으로 흐름을 반전시키며, 오늘날 컴퓨터에게 당시의 체스판을 똑같이 재현해주면, 컴퓨터가 바로 그 신동이 두었던 수를 제안할 것이라고 설명한다. ⑤ 뒤에서는 그 이유로 그때의 게임을 외우고 있기 때문이 아니라 그 수의 유효성을 실제로 미리 탐색할 수 있기 때문이라는 내용을 제시한다. 따라서 주어진 문장이 들어가기에 가장 적절한 곳은 ⑤이다.

- **capability** ⓝ 능력
- **sacrifice** ⓥ 희생시키다
- **insane** ⓐ 비상식적인, 제정신이 아닌
- **remarkably** ⓐⓓ 대단히, 두드러지게
- **seemingly** ⓐⓓ 겉보기에
- **pay off** 성과를 거두다

구문 풀이

14행 It's not because the computer has memorized the Fischer-
「not＋A＋but rather＋B : A가 아니라 B인(A, B 자리에 because절)」
Byrne game, but rather because it searches far enough ahead to see
「형/부＋enough＋to부정사 : ~할 만큼 충분히 …한/하게」
that these moves really do pay off.
동사 강조

03 체온 유지의 중요성
정답률 49% | 정답 ③

글의 흐름으로 보아, 주어진 문장이 들어가기에 가장 적절한 곳을 고르시오.

It is vitally important / that wherever we go and whatever we do / the body temperature is maintained / at the temperature at which our enzymes work best.
아주 중요하다. / 우리가 어디를 가든 무엇을 하든, / 체온이 유지되는 것은 / 우리 몸의 효소들이 가장 잘 작용하는 온도로

① It is not the temperature at the surface of the body / which matters.
신체의 표면 온도가 아니다. / 중요한 것은

It is the temperature deep inside the body / which must be kept stable.
바로 체내 깊은 곳의 온도이다. / 안정된 상태로 유지해야 할 것은

② At only a few degrees above or below normal body temperature / our enzymes cannot function properly.
정상적인 체온보다 단 몇 도만 높거나 낮아도 / 효소들은 원활하게 기능할 수 없다.

✔ If this goes on for any length of time / the reactions in our cells cannot continue / and we die.
만약 이 상태가 일정 시간 계속되면 / 세포 내의 반응들은 지속될 수 없고 / 우리는 죽게 될 것이다.

All sorts of things can affect internal body temperature, / including heat generated in the muscles during exercise, / fevers caused by disease, / and the external temperature.
모든 것들은 내부 체온에 영향을 미칠 수 있다. / 운동 중 근육에서 발생되는 열, / 질병으로 인한 열 / 그리고 외부 온도를 포함한

④ We can control our temperature in lots of ways: / we can change our clothing, / the way we behave / and how active we are.
우리는 다양한 방법으로 체온을 조절할 수 있는데, / 우리는 옷을 바꿀 수 있다. / 우리가 행동하는 방식 / 그리고 우리가 얼마나 활동적인지

⑤ But we also have an internal control mechanism: / when we get too hot / we start to sweat.
하지만 우리는 내부 통제 체제 또한 가지고 있어서, / 우리가 너무 더울 때 / 우리는 땀을 흘리기 시작한다.

우리가 어디를 가든 무엇을 하든, 우리 몸의 효소들이 가장 잘 작용하는 온도로 체온이 유지되도록 하는 것은 아주 중요하다. 중요한 것은 신체의 표면 온도가 아니다. ① 안정된 상태로 유지해야 할 것은 바로 체내 깊은 곳의 온도이다. ② 정상적인 체온보다 조금만 높거나 낮아도 효소들은 원활하게 기능할 수 없다. ③ 만약 이 상태가 일정 시간 계속되면 세포 내의 반응들은 지속될 수 없고 우리는 죽게 될 것이다. 운동 중 근육에서 발생되는 열, 질병으로 인한 열 및 외부 온도를 포함한 모든 것들은 내부 체온에 영향을 미칠 수 있다. ④ 우리는 다양한 방법으로 체온을 조절할 수 있는데, 옷과 행동 방식, 활동량 등을 바꿀 수 있다. ⑤ 하지만 우리는 내부 통제 체제 또한 가지고 있어서, 너무 더우면 땀을 흘리기 시작한다.

Why? 왜 정답일까?

③ 앞의 문장에서 몸 내부의 온도가 정상적 체온보다 조금만 높거나 낮아도 체내 효소들이 원활하게 기능할 수 없다고 말하는데, 주어진 문장은 이렇게 체온에 약간의 변동이 있는 상태를 this라는 대명사로 나타내며 일정 시간 '이런 상태'가 지속되면 결국 죽음에까지 이를 수 있다고 설명한다. ③ 뒤부터는 체온 조절에 영향을 미칠 수 있는 요소와 방법에 대한 이야기가 이어진다. 따라서 주어진 문장이 들어가기에 가장 적절한 곳은 ③이다.

- **vitally** ⓐⓓ 아주, 지극히, 필히
- **enzyme** ⓝ 효소
- **properly** ⓐⓓ 원활하게, 적절히
- **external** ⓐ 외부적인, 외부의
- **sweat** ⓥ 땀을 흘리다
- **maintain** ⓥ 유지하다
- **stable** ⓐ 안정된, 안정적인
- **internal** ⓐ 내부의, 내부적인
- **mechanism** ⓝ 기제, 메커니즘

구문 풀이

3행 It is vitally important [that (wherever we go and whatever we
가주어 접속사(~것) 복합관계부사(어디 ~하든) 복합관계대명사(무엇 ~이든)
do) the body temperature is maintained at the temperature {at which
주어 동사 전치사＋관계대명사
our enzymes work best}]. []: 진주어
자동사(작용하다)

04 세계 최초 대학의 유적 발견
정답률 54% | 정답 ④

글의 흐름으로 보아, 주어진 문장이 들어가기에 가장 적절한 곳을 고르시오.

In 1996, as construction workers cleared a site / in downtown Athens / for the foundations of a new Museum of Modern Art, / they found traces of a large structure / sitting on the bedrock.
1996년 건설 노동자들이 한 장소를 치웠을 때, / 아테네 시내의 / 새로운 현대 미술관의 토대를 위해 / 그들은 커다란 구조물의 흔적들을 발견했다. / 그 암반 위에 있는

[문제편 p.116]

① A building had occupied this same spot / some two-and-a-half thousand years earlier, / when it was part of a wooded sanctuary / outside the original city walls, / on the banks of the River Ilissos.
한 건물이 같은 장소를 차지했었고, / 약 2,500년 전에 / 그때 그것은 숲이 우거진 신전의 일부였다. / 본래의 도시 성벽들 밖에 있는, / Ilissos 강둑에 위치한

② The excavation uncovered the remains / of a gymnasium, a wrestling arena, changing rooms and baths.
발굴 작업에서는 유적을 찾아냈다. / 체육관, 레슬링 경기장, 탈의실 그리고 욕조의

③ This had been a place for athletics and exercise, / where the young men of Athens / had trained to become soldiers and citizens.
그곳은 운동 경기와 운동을 위한 장소였고, / 거기서 아테네의 젊은이들이 / 군인과 시민이 되기 위해 훈련했었다.

✔ But it was more than just a centre for physical improvement.
하지만 그곳은 신체적 향상을 위한 중심지 그 이상이었다.

The archaeologists soon realised / that they had found one of the most significant sites / in all of western European intellectual culture, / a site referred to continually by history's greatest philosophers: / the Lyceum of Aristotle.
고고학자들은 곧 깨달았다. / 자신들이 가장 중요한 장소 중 한 곳을 발견했음을 / 모든 서부 유럽의 지식 문화에서 / 즉 역사상 가장 위대한 철학자들에 의해 계속 언급되는 장소인 / 아리스토텔레스의 Lyceum

⑤ It was the world's first university.
그것은 바로 세계의 첫 번째 대학이었다.

1996년 건설 노동자들이 새로운 현대 미술관의 토대를 위해 아테네 시내의 한 장소를 치웠을 때, 그들은 그 암반 위에 있는 커다란 구조물의 흔적들을 발견했다. ① 약 2,500년 전에 한 건물이 같은 장소를 차지했었고, 그때 그것은 Ilissos 강둑에 위치한 본래의 도시 성벽들 밖에 있는, 숲이 우거진 신전의 일부였다. ② 발굴 작업에서는 체육관, 레슬링 경기장, 탈의실 그리고 욕조의 유적을 찾아냈다. ③ 그곳은 운동 경기와 운동을 위한 장소였고, 거기서 아테네의 젊은이들이 군인과 시민이 되기 위해 훈련했었다. ④ 하지만 그곳은 신체적 향상을 위한 중심지 그 이상이었다. 고고학자들은 자신들이 모든 서부 유럽의 지식 문화에서 가장 중요한 장소 중 한 곳, 즉 역사상 가장 위대한 철학자들에 의해 계속 언급되는 장소인 아리스토텔레스의 Lyceum(아리스토텔레스가 철학을 가르치던 학교)을 발견했음을 곧 깨달았다. ⑤ 그것은 바로 세계의 첫 번째 대학이었다.

Why? 왜 정답일까?

주어진 문장은 But으로 시작하는 것으로 보아 내용이 반전되는 곳에 들어가야 하는데, ④ 앞의 두 문장에서 건설 노동자들이 우연히 발견한 유적에 고대 아테네 사람들이 신체를 단련하던 장소가 있었음을 언급한 한편, ④ 뒤의 문장에서는 해당 유적이 세계 최초의 대학이 있었던 장소라는 내용을 제시하고 있다. 따라서 주어진 문장이 들어가기에 가장 적절한 곳은 ④이다.

- improvement ⓝ 향상, 개선
- bedrock ⓝ 암반, 기반
- sanctuary ⓝ 성소, 성역
- uncover ⓥ (숨겨진 것을) 찾아내다
- archaeologist ⓝ 고고학자
- continually ad 계속적으로, 지속적으로
- trace ⓝ 흔적
- occupy ⓥ 차지하다, 점유하다
- excavation ⓝ 발굴, 발굴지
- changing room 탈의실
- refer to ~을 언급하다

구문 풀이

12행 This had been a place for athletics and exercise, where the young men of Athens had trained to become soldiers and citizens.
(had been: 과거완료 / a place: 선행사 / where: 계속적 용법)

05 진공청소기의 명칭상 오류

정답률 47% | 정답 ③

글의 흐름으로 보아, 주어진 문장이 들어가기에 가장 적절한 곳을 고르시오. [3점]

Hubert Cecil Booth is often credited / with inventing the first powered mobile vacuum cleaner.
Herbert Cecil Booth는 공로를 자주 인정받는다. / 최초의 이동식 전동 진공청소기를 발명한 것으로

① In fact, / he only claimed to be the first / to coin the term "vacuum cleaner" / for devices of this nature, / which may explain / why he is so credited.
사실 / 그는 단지 최초의 사람이라고 주장했었고, / '진공청소기'라는 용어를 만든 / 이런 속성을 가진 장치들에 대해 / 이 점이 설명해 줄 수도 있다. / 그가 그렇게 공로를 인정받는 이유를

② As we all know, / the term "vacuum" is an inappropriate name, / because there exists no vacuum / in a vacuum cleaner.
우리 모두가 알고 있듯이, / '진공'이라는 용어는 부적절한 이름인데, / 왜냐하면 진공이 없기 때문이다. / 진공청소기에는

✔ Rather, / it is the air / moving through a small hole into a closed container, / as a result of air being blown / out of the container / by a fan on the inside.
오히려, / 그것은 공기이다. / 작은 구멍을 통해 폐쇄된 용기 안으로 유입되는 / 공기가 배출되는 결과로, / (폐쇄된) 용기에서 밖으로 / 내부에 있는 송풍기를 통해서

But / I suppose / a "rapid air movement in a closed container / to create suction" cleaner / would not sound as scientific or be as handy a name.
그러나 / 나는 생각한다. / 폐쇄된 용기 안에서의 빠른 공기의 흐름'이라는 말이 / '흡입 청소기를 만들기 위한, / 과학적이거나 편리한 이름으로 들리지 않을 것으로

④ Anyway, / we are stuck with it historically, / and it is hard to find any references to "vacuum" / prior to Booth.
어쨌든 / 우리는 역사적으로 그것을 어쩔 수 없이 사용하고 있으며, / '진공'에 대한 어떠한 언급도 찾기가 어렵다. / Booth 이전에

⑤ Interestingly, / Booth himself did not use the term "vacuum" / when he filed a provisional specification / describing in general terms his intended invention.
흥미롭게도 / Booth 자신은 '진공'이라는 용어를 사용하지 않았다. / 임시 제품 설명서를 제출할 때 / 그의 의도된 발명품을 일반적인 용어로 설명하는

Herbert Cecil Booth는 최초의 이동식 전동 진공청소기를 발명한 것으로 공로를 자주 인정받는다. ① 사실 그는 단지 자신이 이런 속성을 가진 장치들에 대해 '진공청소기'라는 용어를 만든 최초의 사람이라고 주장했었고, 이 점이 그가 그렇게 공로를 인정받는 이유를 설명해 줄 수도 있다. ② 우리 모두가 알고 있듯이, '진공'이라는 용어는 부적절한 이름인데, 왜냐하면 진공청소기에는 진공이 없기 때문이다. ③ 오히려, 그것은 내부에 있는 송풍기를 통해서 공기가 (폐쇄된) 용기에서 밖으로 배출되는 결과로 작은 구멍을 통해 폐쇄된 용기 안으로 유입되는 공기이다. 그러나 나는 '흡입을 만들기 위한, 폐쇄된 용기 안에서의 빠른 공기의 흐름' 청소기라는 말이 과학적이거나 편리한 이름으로 들리지 않을 것으로 생각한다. ④ 어쨌든 우리는 역사적으로 그것을 어쩔 수 없이 사용하고 있으며, Booth 이전에 '진공'에 대한 어떠한 언급도 찾기가 어렵다. ⑤ 흥미롭게도 Booth 자신은 그의 의도된 발명품을 일반적인 용어로 설명하는 임시 제품 설명서를 제출할 때 '진공'이라는 용어를 사용하지 않았다.

Why? 왜 정답일까?

진공청소기를 발명한 사람과 그 이름의 오류를 설명한 글이다. ③ 앞에서 진공청소기의 '진공'은 잘못된 표현임을 설명한 데 이어, Rather로 시작하는 주어진 문장은 '진공'이라고 표현되는 상태가 사실은 내부의 송풍기를 통한 공기의 빠른 흐름임을 언급하고 있다. ③ 뒤의 두 문장에서는 그러나 이러한 실질적 상태를 반영한 이름은 편의성이 떨어질 것이어서 사람들은 진공청소기라는 용어를 계속해서 사용하고 있음을 언급한다. 따라서 주어진 문장이 들어가기에 가장 적절한 곳은 ③이다.

- credited with ~로 공로를 인정받는
- vacuum ⓝ 진공
- nature ⓝ 속성
- exist ⓥ 있다, 존재하다
- container ⓝ 용기, 그릇
- suction ⓝ 흡입, 빨아들이기
- reference ⓝ 언급
- invent ⓥ 발명하다
- coin ⓥ 말을 만들다
- inappropriate ⓐ 부적절한
- closed ⓐ 폐쇄된
- rapid ⓐ 빠른
- handy ⓐ 편리한
- intend ⓥ 의도하다

구문 풀이

5행 In fact, he only claimed to be the first to coin the term "vacuum cleaner" for devices of this nature, which may explain why he is so credited.
(claimed: 동사 / to be the first: 목적어 / to coin: 형용사적 용법 / which: 계속적 용법(앞의 절이 선행사))

06 온도와 색의 연관성

정답률 48% | 정답 ④

글의 흐름으로 보아, 주어진 문장이 들어가기에 가장 적절한 곳을 고르시오. [3점]

One way of measuring temperature occurs / if an object is hot enough to visibly glow, / such as a metal poker / that has been left in a fire.
온도를 측정하는 한 가지 방법은 생긴다. / 물체가 눈에 띄게 빛이 날 정도로 뜨거울 때 / 금속 부지깽이처럼 / 불 속에 놓아둔

① The color of a glowing object / is related to its temperature: / as the temperature rises, / the object is first red and then orange, / and finally it gets white, the "hottest" color.
빛나는 물체의 색은 / 온도와 관련 있는데, / 온도가 상승함에 따라 / 물체는 먼저 빨간색, 이후 주황색으로 변하고, / 마지막으로 '가장 뜨거운' 색인 흰색이 된다.

② The relation / between temperature and the color of a glowing object / is useful to astronomers.
관련성은 / 온도와 빛나는 물체의 색 사이의 / 천문학자들에게 유용하다.

③ The color of stars is related to their temperature, / and since people cannot as yet travel the great distances to the stars / and measure their temperature in a more precise way, / astronomers rely on their color.
별의 색은 별의 온도와 관련이 있고, / 사람들이 아직 별까지의 먼 거리를 이동할 수 없기 때문에 / 그리고 더 정확한 방법으로 별의 온도를 측정할 수 없기에, / 천문학자들은 별의 색에 의존한다.

✔This temperature is of the surface of the star, / the part of the star / which is emitting the light that can be seen.
이 온도는 별 표면의 온도이다. / 별의 부분인, / 보일 수 있는 빛을 방출하는
The interior of the star / is at a much higher temperature, / though it is concealed.
별의 내부는 / 온도가 훨씬 더 높다. / 비록 그것이 숨겨져 있지만
⑤ But / the information obtained from the color of the star / is still useful.
하지만 / 별의 색깔에서 얻은 정보는 / 여전히 유용하다.

온도를 측정하는 한 가지 방법은 불 속에 놓아둔 금속 부지깽이처럼 물체가 눈에 띄게 빛이 날 정도로 뜨거울 때 생긴다. ① 빛나는 물체의 색은 온도와 관련 있는데, 온도가 상승함에 따라 물체는 먼저 빨간색, 이후 주황색으로 변하고, 마지막으로 '가장 뜨거운' 색인 흰색이 된다. ② 온도와 빛나는 물체의 색 사이의 관련성은 천문학자들에게 유용하다. ③ 별의 색은 별의 온도와 관련이 있고, 사람들이 아직 별까지 먼 거리를 이동하고 더 정확한 방법으로 별의 온도를 측정할 수 없기에, 천문학자들은 별의 색에 의존한다. ④ 이 온도는 보일 수 있는 빛을 방출하는 별의 부분인 별 표면의 온도이다. 별의 내부는 비록 숨겨져 있지만, 온도가 훨씬 더 높다. ⑤ 하지만 별의 색깔에서 얻은 정보는 여전히 유용하다.

Why? 왜 정답일까?

④ 앞에서 별의 색은 별의 온도와 관련된다고 하는데, 주어진 문장은 '이 온도'가 별 표면의 온도임을 보충 설명하고, ④ 뒤에서는 표면이 아닌 내부의 온도가 훨씬 더 높음을 자연스럽게 부연한다. 따라서 주어진 문장이 들어가기에 가장 적절한 곳은 ④이다.

- surface ⓝ 표면
- measure ⓥ 측정하다
- glow ⓥ 빛나다
- astronomer ⓝ 천문학자
- rely on ~에 의존하다
- emit ⓥ (빛이나 열을) 뿜다
- visibly ad 눈에 보이게
- poker ⓝ 부지깽이
- precise ⓐ 정확한
- interior ⓝ 내부 ⓐ 내부의

구문 풀이

4행 One way of measuring temperature occurs if an object is hot enough to visibly glow, such as a metal poker [that has been left in a fire].
(주어: One way of measuring temperature / 동사(단수): occurs / 「형/부+enough+to부정사 : ~할 만큼 충분히 …한/하게」 / 선행사: a metal poker / 주격 관·대: that)

07 순응과 구별되는 적응의 특성

정답률 63% | 정답 ③

글의 흐름으로 보아, 주어진 문장이 들어가기에 가장 적절한 곳을 고르시오. [3점]

Adaptation involves changes in a population, / with characteristics / that are passed from one generation to the next.
적응은 개체군의 변화를 수반한다. / 특성과 함께 / 한 세대로부터 다음 세대로 전해지는
This is different from acclimation / — an individual organism's changes / in response to an altered environment.
이것은 순응과는 다르다. / 개별 유기체의 변화인 / 변화된 환경에 반응한
① For example, / if you spend the summer outside, / you may acclimate to the sunlight: / your skin will increase its concentration of dark pigments / that protect you from the sun.
예를 들어, / 당신이 여름을 야외에서 보낸다면, / 당신은 햇빛에 순응하게 되어, / 당신의 피부는 어두운 색소의 농도를 증가시킬 것이다. / 당신을 태양으로부터 보호하는
② This is a temporary change, / and you won't pass the temporary change on / to future generations.
이것은 일시적인 변화이고, / 당신은 그 일시적인 변화를 물려주지 않을 것이다. / 미래 세대에
✔However, / the capacity to produce skin pigments / is inherited.
하지만, / 피부 색소를 생산하는 능력은 / 유전된다.
For populations living in intensely sunny environments, / individuals with a good ability to produce skin pigments / are more likely to thrive, or to survive, / than people with a poor ability to produce pigments, / and that trait becomes increasingly common in subsequent generations.
햇빛이 강렬한 환경에 사는 사람들의 경우, / 피부 색소를 생산하는 능력이 좋은 사람들이 / 더 번영하거나 생존하기 쉽고, / 색소 생산 능력이 좋지 않은 사람들보다 / 그 특징은 다음 세대에서 더욱 흔해진다.
④ If you look around, / you can find countless examples of adaptation.
당신이 주변을 둘러보면, / 당신은 적응의 수많은 사례를 찾을 수 있다.
⑤ The distinctive long neck of a giraffe, / for example, / developed / as individuals that happened to have longer necks / had an advantage / in feeding on the leaves of tall trees.
기린의 특징인 긴 목은 / 예를 들어, / 발달했다. / 우연히 더 긴 목을 갖게 된 개체들이 / 이점을 가짐에 따라 / 키 큰 나무의 잎을 먹는 데

적응은 한 세대로부터 다음 세대로 전해지는 특성과 함께 개체군의 변화를 수반한다. 이것은 변화된 환경에 반응한 개별 유기체의 변화인 순응과는 다르다. ① 예를 들어, 당신이 여름을 야외에서 보낸다면, 당신은 햇빛에 순응하게 되어, 당신의 피부는 당신을 태양으로부터 보호하는 어두운 색소의 농도를 증가시킬 것이다. ② 이것은 일시적인 변화이고, 당신은 그 일시적인 변화를 미래 세대에 물려주지 않을 것이다. ③ 하지만, 피부 색소를 생산하는 능력은 유전된다. 햇빛이 강렬한 환경에 사는 사람들의 경우, 피부 색소를 생산하는 능력이 좋은 사람들이 색소 생산 능력이 좋지 않은 사람들보다 더 번영하거나 생존하기 쉽고, 그 특징은 다음 세대에서 더욱 흔해진다. ④ 주변을 둘러보면, 당신은 적응의 수많은 사례를 찾을 수 있다. ⑤ 예를 들어, 기린의 특징인 긴 목은 우연히 더 긴 목을 갖게 된 개체들이 키 큰 나무의 잎을 먹는 데 유리해짐에 따라 발달했다.

Why? 왜 정답일까?

③ 앞에서 여름 햇빛에 반응해 생기는 일시적 변화를 순응의 예로 언급하는데, 주어진 문장은 이와는 달리 피부 색소를 생산하는 능력의 경우 유전적으로 전해질 수 있는 '적응'의 예시임을 설명한다. ③ 뒤의 문장은 주어진 문장에 이어 피부 색소를 생산해내는 능력에 관해 부연 설명한다. 따라서 주어진 문장이 들어가기에 가장 적절한 곳은 ③이다.

- inherit ⓥ 물려주다, 상속하다
- acclimation ⓝ (새 환경에 대한) 순응
- concentration ⓝ 농도
- thrive ⓥ 번성하다
- distinctive ⓐ 독특한
- adaptation ⓝ 적응
- alter ⓥ 바꾸다, 변경하다
- intensely ad 강렬하게
- trait ⓝ 특성

구문 풀이

18행 The distinctive long neck of a giraffe, for example, developed as individuals [that happened to have longer necks] had an advantage in feeding on the leaves of tall trees.
(주어: The distinctive long neck of a giraffe / 자동사: developed / 접속사(~함에 따라): as / 우연히 ~하다: happened to have)

08 다면 평가의 시행 배경

정답률 45% | 정답 ②

글의 흐름으로 보아, 주어진 문장이 들어가기에 가장 적절한 곳을 고르시오.

In most organizations, / the employee's immediate supervisor evaluates the employee's performance.
대부분의 조직에서 / 직원의 직속 상사는 그 직원의 성과를 평가한다.
① This is because / the supervisor is responsible for the employee's performance, / providing supervision, / handing out assignments, / and developing the employee.
이것은 ~이기 때문이다. / 그 관리자가 그 직원의 성과를 책임지기 / 감독을 제공하고, / 과업을 배정하며, / 그 직원을 계발하면서
✔A problem, however, is / that supervisors often work in locations / apart from their employees / and therefore are not able to observe their subordinates' performance.
하지만 문제는 / 관리자가 흔히 장소에서 일하고 / 직원과 떨어진 / 그렇기 때문에 자신의 부하 직원들의 성과를 관찰할 수 없다는 것이다.
Should supervisors rate employees on performance dimensions / they cannot observe?
관리자는 성과 영역에 대해 직원들을 평가해야 하는가? / 자신이 관찰할 수 없는
③ To eliminate this dilemma, / more and more organizations are implementing assessments / referred to as *360-degree evaluations*.
이 딜레마를 없애기 위해, / 점점 더 많은 조직이 평가를 시행하고 있다. / *다면 평가*라고 불리는
④ Employees are rated / not only by their supervisors / but by coworkers, / clients or citizens, / professionals in other agencies with whom they work, / and subordinates.
직원들은 평가를 받는다. / 자신의 관리자에 의해서만이 아니라, / 동료, / 고객이나 시민, / 함께 일하는 다른 대행사의 전문가들, / 그리고 부하 직원들에 의해서도
⑤ The reason for this approach is / that often coworkers and clients or citizens / have a greater opportunity / to observe an employee's performance / and are in a better position / to evaluate many performance dimensions.
이 방법을 시행하는 이유는 / 동료와 고객이나 시민들이 흔히 / 더 많은 기회를 가지며, / 어떤 직원의 성과를 관찰할 / 더 나은 위치에 있기 때문이다. / 많은 평가 영역을 평가할 수 있는

대부분의 조직에서 직원의 직속 상사는 그 직원의 성과를 평가한다. ① 이것은 그 관리자가 (직원에게) 감독을 제공하고, 과업을 배정하며, 그 직원을 계발하면서, 그 직원의 성과를 책임지기 때문이다. ② 하지만 문제는 관리자가 흔히 직원과 떨어진 장소에서 일하기 때문에 자신의 부하 직원들의 성과를 관찰할 수 없다는 것이다. 관리자는 자신이 관찰할 수 없는 성과 영역에 대해 직원들을 평가해야 하는가? ③ 이 딜레마를 없애기 위해, 점점 더 많은 조직이 *다면 평가*라고 불리는 평가를 시행하고 있다. ④ 직원들은 자신의 관리자 뿐만 아니라 동료, 고객이나 시민, 함께 일하는 다른 대행사의 전문가들, 그리고 부하 직

DAY 18

[문제편 p.118]

원들에 의해서도 평가를 받는다. ⑤ 이 방법을 시행하는 이유는 동료와 고객이나 시민들이 흔히 어떤 직원의 성과를 관찰할 더 많은 기회를 가지며, 많은 평가 영역을 평가할 수 있는 더 나은 위치에 있기 때문이다.

Why? 왜 정답일까?

② 앞에서 직속 상사는 직원의 성과를 책임지고 감독하는 입장에서 직원에 대한 성과 평가를 진행한다는 내용이 언급된다. 이어서 주어진 문장은 however로 흐름을 반전시키며, 관리자는 흔히 직원과 떨어져 있는 곳에서 일하기 때문에 부하 직원의 성과를 관찰하기 어렵다고 지적한다. ② 뒤의 문장은 이렇듯 관찰이 불가한 상황에서 직원들을 평가해야 하는지 의문을 제기한다. 따라서 주어진 문장이 들어가기에 가장 적절한 곳은 ②이다.

- supervisor ⓝ 상사
- evaluate ⓥ 평가하다
- assignment ⓝ 과업, 과제
- eliminate ⓥ 제거하다
- assessment ⓝ 평가
- observe ⓥ 관찰하다
- supervision ⓝ 감독
- rate ⓥ 평가하다
- implement ⓥ 시행하다

구문 풀이

1행 A problem(주어), however, is(동사) that(접속사(~것)) supervisors(주어) often work(동사1) in locations apart from their employees and therefore are not able to observe(동사2) their subordinates' performance.

★★★ 1등급 대비 고난도 2점 문제

09 아이들이 채소를 싫어하는 까닭 — 정답률 32% | 정답 ⑤

글의 흐름으로 보아, 주어진 문장이 들어가기에 가장 적절한 곳을 고르시오.

In the natural world, / if an animal consumes a plant / with enough antinutrients / to make it feel unwell, / it won't eat that plant again.
자연계에서 / 만약 어떤 동물이 어떤 식물을 섭취한다면, / 충분한 항영양소가 들어 있는 / 몸이 안 좋아질 만큼 / 그 동물은 그 식물을 다시는 먹지 않을 것이다.
Intuitively, / animals also know / to stay away from these plants.
직관적으로 / 동물은 또한 안다. / 이러한 식물을 멀리하는 법을
Years of evolution and information being passed down / created this innate intelligence.
오랜 시간의 진화와 전해 내려오는 정보는 / 이 타고난 지능을 만들어 냈다.
① This "intuition," / though, / is not just seen in animals.
이 '직관'은 / 그러나 / 동물에게서만 보이는 것은 아니다.
② Have you ever wondered / why most children hate vegetables?
여러분은 궁금해한 적이 있는가? / 왜 아이들 대부분이 채소를 싫어하는지
③ Dr. Steven Gundry justifies this / as part of our genetic programming, / our inner intelligence.
Dr. Steven Gundry는 이것을 정당화한다. / 우리의 유전적 프로그래밍, / 즉 우리의 내적 지능의 일부라고
④ Since many vegetables are full of antinutrients, / your body tries to keep you away from them / while you are still fragile and in development.
많은 야채들은 항영양소로 가득 차 있어서, / 여러분의 몸은 여러분이 그것을 멀리하게 하려고 노력한다. / 여러분이 아직 연약하고 성장기일 때
✔It does this / by making your taste buds perceive these flavors / as bad and even disgusting.
그것은 이렇게 한다. / 여러분의 미뢰(味蕾)가 이러한 맛을 인식하게 만들어 / 나쁘고 심지어 역겹다고
As you grow / and your body becomes stronger enough / to tolerate these antinutrients, / suddenly they no longer taste as bad as before.
여러분이 성장하고 / 여러분의 신체가 충분히 더 강해지면, / 이러한 항영양소를 견딜 만큼 / 갑자기 그것들은 더 이상 전처럼 맛이 안 좋다고 느껴지지 않는다.

자연계에서 만약 항영양소가 몸이 안 좋아질 만큼 들어 있는 식물을 어떤 동물이 섭취한다면, 그 동물은 그 식물을 다시는 먹지 않을 것이다. 직관적으로 동물은 또한 이러한 식물을 멀리할 줄 안다. 오랜 시간의 진화와 전해 내려오는 정보는 이 타고난 지능을 만들어 냈다. ① 그러나 이 '직관'은 동물에게서만 보이는 것은 아니다. ② 여러분은 왜 아이들 대부분이 채소를 싫어하는지 궁금해한 적이 있는가? ③ Dr. Steven Gundry는 이것을 우리의 유전적 프로그래밍, 즉 우리의 내적 지능의 일부라고 정당화한다. ④ 많은 야채들은 항영양소로 가득 차 있어서, 여러분이 아직 연약하고 성장기일 때 여러분의 몸은 여러분이 그것을 멀리하게 하려고 노력한다. ⑤ 그것은 여러분의 미뢰(味蕾)가 이러한 맛을 나쁘고 심지어 역겹다고 인식하게 만들어 그렇게 한다. 여러분이 성장하고 여러분의 신체가 이러한 항영양소를 견딜 만큼 충분히 더 강해지면, 갑자기 그것들은 더 이상 전처럼 맛이 안 좋다고 느껴지지 않는다.

Why? 왜 정답일까?

어린 시절에는 식물에 든 항영양소로 인해 몸이 나빠질 수 있어 직관적으로 채소를 꺼리게 된다는 내용의 글이다. ⑤ 앞에서 이 이야기가 본격적으로 언급되어서, 우리가 아직 어리고 자라는 중일 때는 우리 몸에서 채소를 멀리하게 만들려고 한다는 내용이 제시된다. 주어진 문장은 '채소를 멀리하게 하려고 한다'는 내용을 does this로 가리키며, 어떤 식으로 이런 노력이 이뤄지는지를 보충 설명한다. ⑤ 뒤로는 우리가 다 자라고 나면 상황이 달라진다는 결론이 연결된다. 따라서 주어진 문장이 들어가기에 가장 적절한 곳은 ⑤이다.

- taste bud 맛봉오리, 미뢰(味蕾)
- disgusting ⓐ 역겨운
- intuitively ad 직관적으로
- intuition ⓝ 직관
- genetic ⓐ 유전적인
- tolerate ⓥ 견디다
- flavor ⓝ 맛, 풍미
- antinutrient ⓝ 항영양소
- innate ⓐ 타고난
- justify ⓥ 정당화하다, 옳음을 보여주다
- fragile ⓐ 연약한

구문 풀이

6행 Years(주어1) of evolution and information(주어2) being passed down(수식어구) created(동사) this innate intelligence.

★★ 문제 해결 꿀~팁 ★★

▶ 많이 틀린 이유는?
가장 헷갈리는 ④ 앞의 두 문장을 보면, 아이들이 채소를 싫어하는 이유를 '우리의 내적 지능'으로 설명할 수 있다고 한다. 그리고 ④ 뒤는 채소가 우리 몸이 연약할 때는 멀리해야 하는 항영양소로 가득 차 있다고 설명한다. 즉, 앞에서 언급된 '내적 지능'을 부연 설명하기 위한 예시가 뒤에 등장하는 문맥이므로 ④ 앞뒤는 논리적 공백 없이 자연스럽다.
▶ 문제 해결 방법은?
주어진 문장의 It은 ⑤ 앞의 your body이고, does this는 keep you away from them을 가리킨다.

★★★ 1등급 대비 고난도 2점 문제

10 아이 사진을 찍을 때 주의할 점 — 정답률 43% | 정답 ⑤

글의 흐름으로 보아, 주어진 문장이 들어가기에 가장 적절한 곳을 고르시오.

The birth of a child in a family / is often the reason / why people begin to take up or rediscover photography.
가족에게 아이의 출생은 / 종종 이유이다. / 사람들이 사진을 취미로 하거나 재발견하기 시작하는
① In many ways, / photographing a child is little different / from photographing any other person.
많은 면에서 / 아이의 사진을 찍는 것은 거의 다르지 않다. / 누구든 다른 사람의 사진을 찍는 것과
② What makes it different, however, / is the relative height / between a young child and an adult.
그러나 이를 달라지게 하는 것은 / 상대적 신장이다. / 어른과 어린 아이 사이의
③ Using the camera at your own head height / works well for photographing adults, / but for children / the camera will be tilted downward.
카메라를 당신의 머리 높이에서 사용하는 것은 / 어른의 사진을 찍을 때에는 효과가 좋지만, / 아이를 찍는 경우에는 / 카메라가 아래로 기울어질 것이다.
④ You are looking down on the child, / literally and metaphorically, / and the resulting picture / can make the child look smaller and less significant / than most parents would like.
당신은 아이를 내려다보고 있고, / 말 그대로 동시에 비유적으로도 / 그 결과로 나온 사진은 / 아이를 더 작고 덜 중요해 보이도록 만들 수 있다. / 대부분의 부모들이 원할 것보다
✔It is possible to obtain more natural-looking portraits / when the camera shoots / from the same level as the child's eyeline / instead of being tilted.
더 자연스러워 보이는 인물 사진을 얻을 수 있다. / 카메라가 찍을 때 / 아이의 눈높이와 같은 높이에서 / 카메라를 기울이는 대신에
For an eight year old, / this might mean sitting down when shooting; / and for a crawling baby, / the best approach may be to lie on the floor.
8살 아이의 경우에 / 이는 (어른이) 사진을 찍어줄 때 앉는 것을 뜻할 것이며, / 기어 다니는 아기의 경우에는 / 최적의 방법이 바닥에 눕는 것일 수 있다.

가족에게 아이의 출생은 종종 사람들이 사진을 취미로 하거나 재발견하기 시작하는 이유이다. ① 많은 면에서 아이의 사진을 찍는 것은 누구든 다른 사람의 사진을 찍는 것과 거의 다르지 않다. ② 그러나 이를 달라지게 하는 것은 어른과 어린 아이 사이의 상대적 신장 (차이)이다. ③ 카메라를 (어른인) 당신의 머리 높이에서 사용하는 것은 어른의 사진을 찍을 때에는 효과가 좋지만, 아이를 찍는 경우에는 카메라가 아래로 기울어질 것이다. ④ 당신은 아이를 말 그대로 동시에 비유적으로도 내려다보고 있고, 그 결과로 나온 사진은 대개 부모들의 바람보다 아이를 더 작고 덜 중요해 보이도록 만들 수 있다. ⑤ 카메라를

기울이는 대신에 아이의 눈높이와 같은 높이에서 사진을 찍을 때 더 자연스러워 보이는 인물 사진을 얻을 수 있다. 8살 아이의 경우에 이는 (어른이) 사진을 찍어줄 때 앉는 것을 뜻할 것이며, 기어 다니는 아기의 경우에는 최적의 방법이 바닥에 눕는 것일 수 있다.

Why? 왜 정답일까?

⑤ 앞에서 어른이 자기 눈높이에서 아이를 내려다보며 사진을 찍으면 피사체인 아이가 더 작고 덜 중요해 보이게 나올 수 있다고 말한 데 이어, 주어진 문장은 '기울이는 대신 아이의 눈높이에 맞춰서 찍으면' 좋은 결과를 얻을 수 있을 것이라는 해결책을 제시한다. ⑤ 뒤의 문장에서는 아이에 따라 눈높이를 맞추는 상황의 예를 든다. 따라서 주어진 문장이 들어가기에 가장 적절한 곳은 ⑤이다.

- obtain ⓥ 얻다
- take up 취미로 시작하다
- metaphorically ad 비유적으로
- significant ⓐ 중요한, 중대한
- approach ⓝ (접근) 방법
- tilt ⓥ 기울이다
- literally ad 말 그대로, 문자 그대로
- resulting ⓐ 그 결과로 인한
- crawl ⓥ 기어 다니다
- lie ⓥ 눕다, 누워 있다

구문 풀이

12행 You are looking down on the child, (literally and metaphorically), and the resulting picture can make the child look smaller and less significant than most parents would like.

(주어1: You / 동사1(현재진행): are looking / 현재분사(그 결과로 인한): resulting / 주어2: the resulting picture / 동사2: can make / 목적격 보어(원형부정사): look / look의 보어(비교급 형용사): smaller and less significant / ~보다: than)

★★ 문제 해결 꿀~팁 ★★

▶ 많이 틀린 이유는?

'카메라를 기울인다'는 말에만 주목하면 be tilted라는 동사가 겹치는 것만 보고 ④를 답으로 고르기 쉬운 문제였다. 실제로 ①, ②, ③의 오답 분포율은 낮은 반면에 ④에만 오답률이 다소 쏠린 것을 확인할 수 있는데, 형태적으로 강력한 단서가 있더라도 답을 고른 후 주어진 문장을 그 자리에 넣고 앞뒤 흐름을 훑어보는 작업까지 거쳐야 완벽한 풀이가 가능하다.

▶ 문제 해결 방법은?

글 내용이 '문제 → 해결'의 흐름으로 구성되어 있음을 파악한다. ⑤ 앞까지는 어른이 카메라를 자기 눈높이에 맞추어 들고 이를 기울여서 아이의 사진을 찍을 경우 아이가 더 작게 나와버린다는 '문제'가 있음을 주로 이야기하고, 주어진 문장은 이에 대한 '해결'을 제시하고 있다. 문제 이야기가 충분히 마무리되어야 해결이 나올 수 있다는 데 유의한다.

★★★ 1등급 대비 고난도 3점 문제

11 언어 프레이밍의 중요성 정답률 46% | 정답 ③

글의 흐름으로 보아, 주어진 문장이 들어가기에 가장 적절한 곳을 고르시오. [3점]

Framing matters in many domains.
프레이밍은 많은 영역에서 중요하다.

① When credit cards started to become popular forms of payment in the 1970s, / some retail merchants wanted to charge different prices / to their cash and credit card customers.
신용 카드가 1970년대에 인기 있는 지불 방식이 되기 시작했을 때, / 몇몇 소매상들은 다른 가격을 청구하기를 원했다. / 현금 고객과 신용 카드 고객에게

② To prevent this, / credit card companies adopted rules / that forbade their retailers from charging different prices / to cash and credit customers.
이것을 막기 위해서, / 신용 카드 회사들은 규정을 채택했다 / 소매상들이 다른 가격을 청구하는 것을 막는 / 현금 고객과 신용 카드 고객에게

✔However, when a bill was introduced in Congress to outlaw such rules, / the credit card lobby turned its attention to language.
하지만, 그러한 규정들을 금지하기 위한 법안이 의회에 제출되었을 때, / 신용 카드 압력단체는 언어로 주의를 돌렸다.

Its preference was / that if a company charged different prices / to cash and credit customers, / the credit price should be considered the "normal" (default) price / and the cash price a discount / — rather than the alternative of making the cash price the usual price / and charging a surcharge to credit card customers.
그 단체가 선호하는 것은 / 만약 회사가 다른 가격을 청구한다면, / 현금 고객과 신용 카드 고객에게 / 신용 카드 가격이 '정상'(디폴트) 가격으로 여겨져야 한다는 것이었다. / 그리고 현금 가격이 할인으로 / 현금 가격을 보통 가격으로 만들고 / 신용 카드 고객에게 추가요금을 청구하는 방안보다는

④ The credit card companies had a good intuitive understanding / of what psychologists would come to call "framing."
신용 카드 회사들은 훌륭한 직관적 이해를 하고 있었다. / 심리학자들이 '프레이밍'이라고 부르게 된 것에 대한

⑤ The idea is that choices depend, in part, / on the way in which problems are stated.
이러한 발상은 선택이 어느 정도는 달려있다는 것이다. / 문제들이 언급되는 방식에

프레이밍은 많은 영역에서 중요하다. ① 신용 카드가 1970년대에 인기 있는 지불 방식이 되기 시작했을 때, 몇몇 소매상들은 현금 고객과 신용 카드 고객에게 다른 가격을 청구하기를 원했다. ② 이것을 막기 위해서, 신용 카드 회사들은 소매상들이 현금 고객과 신용 카드 고객에게 다른 가격을 청구하는 것을 막는 규정을 채택했다. ③ 하지만, 그러한 규정들을 금지하기 위한 법안이 의회에 제출되었을 때, 신용 카드 압력단체는 언어로 주의를 돌렸다. 그 단체가 선호하는 것은 만약 회사가 다른 가격을 현금 고객과 신용 카드 고객에게 청구한다면, 현금 가격을 보통 가격으로 만들고 신용 카드 고객에게 추가요금을 청구하는 방안보다는, 신용 카드 가격이 '정상'(디폴트) 가격, 현금 가격이 할인으로 여겨져야 한다는 것이었다. ④ 신용 카드 회사들은 심리학자들이 '프레이밍'이라고 부르게 된 것에 대한 훌륭한 직관적 이해를 하고 있었다. ⑤ 이러한 발상은 선택이 어느 정도는 문제들이 언급되는 방식에 달려있다는 것이다.

Why? 왜 정답일까?

어떤 문제가 어떤 표현으로 언급되는지, 즉 문제가 '프레이밍'되는 방식이 중요하다는 내용을 다룬 글이다. ③ 앞의 두 문장에서 신용 카드가 널리 사용되면서 소매상들이 현금 지불 시의 가격과 카드 지불 시의 가격을 달리하고 싶어 하자 카드 회사에서 이를 막는 규정을 채택했다는 내용을 말하는데, 주어진 문장에서는 이때 카드 회사의 주의가 '언어'로 향했다는 점을 환기시킨다. ③ 뒤의 문장에서는 카드 회사에서 카드 지불 시의 가격을 '정상' 가격, 현금 가격을 '할인' 가격으로 명명함으로써 문제의 인식을 달리하려고 시도했다는 내용을 이어서 말한다. 따라서 주어진 문장이 들어가기에 가장 적절한 곳은 ③이다.

- bill ⓝ (국회에 제출된) 법안
- domain ⓝ 영역, 분야
- merchant ⓝ 상인, 무역상
- default ⓝ 디폴트, (기본으로) 내정된 값
- outlaw ⓥ 금지하다, 불법화하다
- retail ⓝ 소매 ⓐ 소매의
- charge A to B A를 B에 부과하다
- surcharge ⓝ 추가 요금

구문 풀이

10행 Its preference was that (if a company charged different prices to cash and credit customers), the credit price should be considered the "normal" (default) price and the cash price (should be considered) a discount — rather than the alternative of making the cash price the usual price and charging a surcharge to credit card customers.

(접속사: that / ( ): 부사절 / 주어1: the credit price / 조동사 수동태: should be considered / 주격 보어1: the "normal" (default) price / 주어2: the cash price / 생략: (should be considered) / 주격 보어2: a discount / 전치사: of / 동명사1: making / 목적어: the cash price / 목적격 보어: the usual price / 동명사2: charging)

★★ 문제 해결 꿀~팁 ★★

▶ 많이 틀린 이유는?

문제를 기술하는 언어 표현이 중요하다는 주제를 신용 카드 회사의 예로 제시하는 글로서, 주어진 문장은 예시 부분에 있다. 주어진 문장은 However로 시작하며 '언어'에 대한 관심을 환기하므로, 이미 가격의 '표현' 문제를 언급하고 있는 'Its preference was that ~'보다 앞에 나와야 한다.

▶ 문제 해결 방법은?

③ 뒤의 대명사 Its에 주목한다. ③ 앞의 문장에서 '카드 회사'는 credit card companies와 같이 복수형으로 제시되므로 ③ 뒤에서 이를 단수대명사 Its로 받을 수는 없다. 따라서 이 Its는 주어진 문장의 the card lobby를 받는다고 보아야 한다.

★★★ 1등급 대비 고난도 3점 문제

12 인간의 비언어적 의사소통 정답률 31% | 정답 ①

글의 흐름으로 보아, 주어진 문장이 들어가기에 가장 적절한 곳을 고르시오. [3점]

For hundreds of thousands of years / our hunter-gatherer ancestors could survive / only by constantly communicating with one another / through nonverbal cues.
수십만 년 동안 / 우리의 수렵-채집인 조상들은 생존할 수 있었다. / 서로 끊임없이 의사소통해야만 / 비언어적 신호들을 통해서

Developed over so much time, / before the invention of language, / that is how the human face became so expressive, / and gestures so elaborate.
오랜 시간에 걸쳐 발달되어, / 언어의 발명 이전에 / 그렇게 인간의 얼굴은 매우 표현적이고 / 몸짓은 매우 정교해지게 되었다.

✔We have a continual desire to communicate our feelings / and yet at the same time / the need to conceal them for proper social functioning.

[문제편 p.120]

우리는 우리의 감정을 전달하고자 하는 끊임없는 욕망을 지니고 있다. / 하지만 동시에 / 적절한 사회적 기능을 위해 그것들을 감추고자 하는 욕구도

With these counterforces battling inside us, / we cannot completely control what we communicate.

이 반대 세력들이 우리 내면에서 다투면서, / 우리는 우리가 전달하는 것을 완전히 통제할 수 없다.

② Our real feelings continually leak out / in the form of gestures, tones of voice, facial expressions, and posture.

우리의 진짜 감정은 끊임없이 새어 나온다. / 몸짓, 목소리의 톤, 얼굴 표정, 그리고 자세의 형태로

③ We are not trained, however, / to pay attention to people's nonverbal cues.

그러나 우리는 훈련받지 않는다. / 사람들의 비언어적 신호에 주의를 기울이도록

④ By sheer habit, we fixate on the words people say, / while also thinking about what we'll say next.

순전한 습관으로 우리는 사람들이 하는 말에 집착하며 / 동시에 또한 우리가 다음번에 말할 것을 생각한다.

⑤ What this means is / that we are using only a small percentage of the potential social skills / we all possess.

이것이 의미하는 것은 / 우리가 잠재적인 사회적 기술들 중 오직 작은 부분만을 사용하고 있다는 것이다. / 우리 모두가 소유한

수십만 년 동안 우리의 수렵-채집인 조상들은 비언어적 신호들을 통해서 서로 끊임없이 의사소통해야만 생존할 수 있었다. 언어의 발명 이전에 오랜 시간에 걸쳐 발달되어, 그렇게 인간의 얼굴은 매우 표현적이고 몸짓은 매우 정교해지게 되었다. ① 우리는 우리의 감정을 전달하고자 하는 끊임없는 욕망을 지니고 있지만 동시에 적절한 사회적 기능을 위해 그것들을 감추고자 하는 욕구를 지니고 있다. 이 반대 세력들이 우리 내면에서 다투면서, 우리는 우리가 전달하는 것을 완전히 통제할 수 없다. ② 우리의 진짜 감정은 몸짓, 목소리의 톤, 얼굴 표정, 그리고 자세의 형태로 끊임없이 새어 나온다. ③ 그러나 우리는 사람들의 비언어적 신호에 주의를 기울이도록 훈련받지 않는다. ④ 순전한 습관으로 우리는 사람들이 하는 말에 집착하며 동시에 또한 우리가 다음번에 말할 것을 생각한다. ⑤ 이것이 의미하는 것은 우리 모두가 소유한 잠재적인 사회적 기술들 중 오직 작은 부분만을 우리가 사용하고 있다는 것이다.

Why? 왜 정답일까?

인간의 비언어적 의사소통에 관해 설명한 글로, ① 뒤의 지시어에 주목한다. ① 뒤의 문장에서 **these counterforces**를 언급하는데 앞에는 '상충되는 힘'으로 나타낼 만한 것이 없다. 이때 주어진 문장은 인간이 감정을 나타내고 싶어 하지만 동시에 감정을 감추고 싶어 한다는 내용이므로, 이 '**desire to communicate** ~'와 '**need to conceal** ~'을 ① 뒤의 문장에서 **these counterforces**로 가리키고 있음을 알 수 있다. 따라서 주어진 문장이 들어가기에 가장 적절한 곳은 ①이다.

- **continual** ⓐ 끊임없는
- **constantly** ad 끊임없이, 지속적으로
- **invention** ⓝ 발명
- **elaborate** ⓐ 정교한
- **in the form of** ~의 형태로
- **possess** ⓥ 소유하다
- **functioning** ⓝ 기능
- **nonverbal** ⓐ 비언어적인
- **expressive** ⓐ 나타내는, 표현력이 있는
- **leak out** 새어 나오다
- **fixate on** ~에 집착하다, ~을 고수하다

구문 풀이

7행 **Developed over so much time, before the invention of language, that is how the human face became so expressive, and gestures (became) so elaborate.**

(Developed over so much time: 수동분사구문 / that is how: 그렇게 ~하게 되다 / the human face: 주어1 / became: 동사1 / gestures: 주어2 / (became): 동사2(중복되어 생략))

★★ 문제 해결 꿀~팁 ★★

▶ 많이 틀린 이유는?

'With these counterforces ~' 이후로 네 문장에 걸쳐 우리가 우리의 의사소통 내용을 완벽히 통제하지 못하기에 비언어적 단서의 형태로 자꾸 진정한 감정을 내비치게 되지만, 우리는 비언어적 단서에 주목하도록 훈련받지 않아서 주로 언어적 단서에 집착한다는 내용이 논리적 공백 없이 기술되어 있다. 따라서 ②, ③, ④는 모두 오답이다.

▶ 문제 해결 방법은?

① 뒤의 **these counterforces**가 가리키는 바에 주목한다. 만일 주어진 문장이 ①에 들어가지 않으면, **these counterforces**로 받을 만한 명사는 **human face**와 **gestures** 뿐인데, '얼굴과 몸짓'을 '상충하는 힘'으로 일반화하기에는 근거가 부족하다.

DAY 19 문장 삽입 04

01 ④	02 ④	03 ④	04 ⑤	05 ⑤
06 ⑤	07 ③	08 ③	09 ③	10 ④
11 ⑤	12 ④			

01 과학 실험의 조작과 통제

정답률 49% | 정답 ④

글의 흐름으로 보아, 주어진 문장이 들어가기에 가장 적절한 곳을 고르시오.

The fundamental nature of the experimental method / is manipulation and control.

실험 방법의 근본적인 본질은 / 조작과 통제이다.

Scientists manipulate a variable of interest, / and see if there's a difference.

과학자들은 관심 변인을 조작하고, / 차이가 있는지 확인한다.

At the same time, / they attempt to control / for the potential effects of all other variables.

동시에, / 그들은 통제하려고 시도한다. / 다른 모든 변인의 잠재적 영향에 대해

The importance of controlled experiments / in identifying the underlying causes of events / cannot be overstated.

통제된 실험의 중요성은 / 사건의 근본적인 원인을 식별하는 데 있어 / 아무리 강조해도 지나치지 않다.

① In the real-uncontrolled-world, / variables are often correlated.

현실의 통제되지 않은 세계에서, / 변인들은 종종 상관관계가 있다.

② For example, / people who take vitamin supplements / may have different eating and exercise habits / than people who don't take vitamins.

예를 들어, / 비타민 보충제를 섭취하는 사람들은 / 다른 식습관과 운동 습관을 지닐 수 있다. / 비타민을 섭취하지 않는 사람들과는

③ As a result, / if we want to study the health effects of vitamins, / we can't merely observe the real world, / since any of these factors (the vitamins, diet, or exercise) / may affect health.

그 결과, / 만약 우리가 비타민의 건강에 미치는 효과를 연구하고 싶다면, / 우리는 단지 현실 세계만 관찰할 수 없는데, / 왜냐하면 이러한 요소 (비타민, 식단, 운동) 중 어느 것이든 / 건강에 영향을 미칠 수 있기 때문이다.

✔ Rather, / we have to create a situation / that doesn't actually occur in the real world.

오히려, / 우리는 상황을 만들어야 한다. / 현실 세계에서 실제로 일어나지 않는

That's just what scientific experiments do.

그것이 바로 과학 실험이 하는 일이다.

⑤ They try to separate the naturally occurring relationship in the world / by manipulating one specific variable at a time, / while holding everything else constant.

그것들은 세상에서 자연적으로 발생하는 관계를 분리하려고 애쓴다. / 한 번에 하나의 특정 변인을 조작해서 / 그 밖의 다른 모든 것을 일정하게 유지하면서

실험 방법의 근본적인 본질은 조작과 통제이다. 과학자들은 관심 변인을 조작하고, 차이가 있는지 확인한다. 동시에, 다른 모든 변인의 잠재적 영향을 통제하려고 시도한다. 사건의 근본적인 원인을 식별하는 데 있어 통제된 실험의 중요성은 아무리 강조해도 지나치지 않다. ① 현실의 통제되지 않은 세계에서, 변인들은 종종 상관관계가 있다. ② 예를 들어, 비타민 보충제를 섭취하는 사람들은 비타민을 섭취하지 않는 사람들과는 다른 식습관과 운동 습관을 지닐 수 있다. ③ 그 결과, 만약 우리가 비타민의 건강에 미치는 효과를 연구하고 싶다면, 우리는 단지 현실 세계만 관찰할 수 없는데, 왜냐하면 이러한 요소(비타민, 식단, 운동) 중 어느 것이든 건강에 영향을 미칠 수 있기 때문이다. ④ 오히려, 우리는 현실 세계에서 실제로 일어나지 않는 상황을 만들어야 한다. 그것이 바로 과학 실험이 하는 일이다. ⑤ 그것들은 그 밖의 다른 모든 것을 일정하게 유지하면서, 한 번에 하나의 특정 변인을 조작해 세상에서 자연적으로 발생하는 관계를 분리하려고 애쓴다.

Why? 왜 정답일까?

과학 실험의 조작과 통제를 설명하는 글이다. ④ 앞에서 현실 세계만 관찰해서는 여러 변인의 상호작용으로 인해 연구가 잘 이뤄지지 않는다고 하고, 주어진 문장에서는 '그래서 오히려' 현실에 없는 상황을 만들어야 한다고 설명하고 있다. ④ 뒤는 바로 '그 일'이 과학 실험에서 일어나는 일이라는 내용으로 주어진 문장과 자연스럽게 연결된다. 따라서 주어진 문장이 들어가기에 가장 적절한 곳은 ④이다.

- **fundamental** ⓐ 근본적인
- **manipulation** ⓝ 조작
- **underlying** ⓐ 근본적인, 기저에 있는
- **cannot be overstated** 아무리 과장해도 지나치지 않다
- **correlate** ⓥ 상호 관련시키다
- **constant** ⓐ 일정한

구문 풀이

1행 Rather, we have to create a situation [that doesn't actually occur in the real world].
(that: 선행사 / 주격 관·대 / 동사(단수))

02 액체의 파괴력

정답률 60% | 정답 ④

글의 흐름으로 보아, 주어진 문장이 들어가기에 가장 적절한 곳을 고르시오.

Liquids are destructive.
액체는 파괴적이다.
Foams feel soft / because they are easily compressed; / if you jump on to a foam mattress, / you'll feel it give beneath you.
발포 고무는 부드럽게 느껴지는데, / 그것이 쉽게 압축되기 때문에 / 만약 여러분이 발포 고무 매트리스 위로 점프를 한다면 / 여러분은 그것이 여러분의 밑에서 휘어지는 것을 느끼게 될 것이다.
① Liquids don't do this; / instead they flow.
액체는 이렇게 하지 않고, / 대신에 액체는 흐른다.
② You see this in a river, / or when you turn on a tap, / or if you use a spoon to stir your coffee.
여러분은 강에서 이것을 보게 된다. / 혹은 여러분이 수도꼭지를 틀 때나, / 혹은 여러분이 스푼을 사용하여 자신의 커피를 젓는다면
③ When you jump off a diving board / and hit a body of water, / the water has to flow away from you.
여러분이 다이빙 도약대에서 뛰어내려 / 많은 양의 물을 치게 될 때 / 그 물은 여러분에게서 비켜나 흘러나가야만 한다.
✔ But the flowing takes time, / and if your speed of impact is too great, / the water won't be able to flow away fast enough, / and so it pushes back at you.
그러나 흘러나가는 것은 시간이 걸리며, / 만약 여러분의 충돌 속도가 너무나도 엄청나다면 / 그 물이 충분히 빠르게 흘러나가지 못할 것이며 / 따라서 그것은 여러분을 밀어낸다.
It's that force / that stings your skin / as you belly-flop into a pool, / and makes falling into water from a great height / like landing on concrete.
바로 그 힘이다. / 여러분의 피부를 쓰리게 하며, / 여러분이 배로 수면을 치며 수영장 물속으로 떨어질 때 / 굉장한 높이에서 물속으로 떨어지는 것을 만드는 것이 / 콘크리트 위에 떨어지는 것처럼
⑤ The incompressibility of water is also / why waves can have such deadly power, / and in the case of tsunamis, / why they can destroy buildings and cities, / tossing cars around easily.
물의 비압축성은 또한 / 파도가 그러한 치명적인 힘을 가질 수 있는 이유이고, / 해일의 경우 / 그것이 건물과 도시를 부수는 이유인 것이다. / 자동차를 쉽게 던져버리며

액체는 파괴적이다. 발포 고무는 쉽게 압축되기 때문에 부드럽게 느껴지는데, 만약 여러분이 발포 고무 매트리스 위로 점프를 한다면 여러분은 그것이 밑에서 휘어지는 것을 느끼게 될 것이다. ① 액체는 이렇게 하지 않고 대신에 흐른다. ② 강에서나, 여러분이 수도꼭지를 틀 때나, 혹은 여러분이 스푼을 사용하여 자신의 커피를 젓는다면 여러분은 이것을 보게 된다. ③ 여러분이 다이빙 도약대에서 뛰어내려 많은 양의 물을 치게 될 때 그 물은 여러분에게서 비켜나 흘러나가야만 한다. ④ 그러나 흘러나가는 것은 시간이 걸리며, 만약 여러분의 충돌 속도가 너무나도 엄청나다면 그 물은 충분히 빠르게 흘러나가지 못할 것이며 따라서 여러분을 밀어낸다. 여러분이 배로 수면을 치며 수영장 물속으로 떨어질 때 여러분의 피부를 쓰리게 하며, 굉장한 높이에서 물속으로 떨어지는 것을 콘크리트 위에 떨어지는 것처럼 만드는 것이 바로 그 힘이다. ⑤ 물의 비압축성은 또한 파도가 그러한 치명적인 힘을 가질 수 있는 이유이고, 해일의 경우 그것이 건물과 도시를 부수며 자동차를 쉽게 던져버릴 수 있는 이유인 것이다.

Why? 왜 정답일까?

물은 흐르는 속성 때문에 파괴적인 힘을 가질 수 있음을 설명한 글로, ④ 앞의 문장은 다이빙대에서 뛰어내리는 경우를 예로 들고 있다. 이에 이어 주어진 문장은 다이빙처럼 급격히 떨어지는 경우 물이 흘러나가기까지 시간이 걸리기 때문에 만일 물 표면에 충돌하는 속도가 엄청나다면 물이 충분히 빨리 흘러나가지 못하여 우리를 '밀어내게' 된다고 설명한다. ④ 뒤의 문장은 바로 그러한 이유로 너무 빨리 물로 뛰어들었을 때 피부에 쓰림이 발생하고 수면이 아닌 콘크리트에라도 부딪친 것 같은 강력한 충격을 경험하게 된다고 설명한다. 따라서 주어진 문장이 들어가기에 가장 적절한 곳은 ④이다.

- impact ⓝ 충격, 충돌
- push back 밀어내다
- foam ⓝ (매트리스에 주로 쓰이는) 발포 고무
- stir ⓥ 젓다
- sting ⓥ 쓰리게 하다, 쏘다, 찌르다
- height ⓝ 높이, 고도
- incompressibility ⓝ 비압축성
- in the case of ~의 경우에
- flow away 흘러가다
- destructive ⓐ 파괴적인
- tap ⓝ 수도꼭지
- a body of (양이) 많은
- belly-flop ⓥ 배로 수면을 치며 뛰어들다
- land on ~에 착륙하다
- deadly ⓐ 치명적인
- toss ⓥ 던지다

구문 풀이

11행 It's that force that stings your skin as you belly-flop into a pool, and makes falling into water from a great height like landing on concrete.
(it is ~ that … 강조구문: …한 것은 바로 ~이다 / stings: 동사1 / as: 접속사(~할 때) / makes: 동사2 / falling into water: 목적어(동명사구) / like landing on concrete: 목적격 보어(전명구))

03 국제적 온라인 오픈 액세스의 개념

정답률 56% | 정답 ④

글의 흐름으로 보아, 주어진 문장이 들어가기에 가장 적절한 곳을 고르시오.

Open international online access is understood / using the metaphor "flat earth."
국제적인 온라인 오픈 액세스는 이해된다. / '평평한 지구'라는 은유를 사용하여
It represents a world / where information moves across the globe / as easily as a hockey puck seems to slide / across an ice rink's flat surface.
그것은 세상을 나타낸다. / 정보가 전 세계로 이동하는 / 하키 퍽이 미끄러져 가는 것만큼 쉽게 / 아이스 링크의 평평한 표면을
① This framework, however, can be misleading / — especially if we extend the metaphor.
그러나 이러한 사고방식은 오해의 소지가 있을 수 있다. / 특히 우리가 그 은유를 확장해본다면
② As anyone who has crossed an ice rink can confirm, / just because the surface of the rink appears flat and open / does not necessarily mean / that surface is smooth or even.
아이스 링크를 건너 본 사람은 누구든 확인할 수 있듯이, / 단지 링크 표면이 평평하고 탁 트인 듯 보인다고 해서 / 반드시 의미하지는 않는다. / 그 표면이 매끄럽거나 고르다는 것을
③ Rather, such surfaces tend to be covered / by a wide array of dips and cracks and bumps / that create a certain degree of pull or drag or friction / on any object moving across it.
오히려, 그러한 표면은 덮여 있는 경향이 있다. / 움푹 패이고 갈라지고 튀어나온 수많은 부분들로 / 어느 정도의 인력, 저항력 또는 마찰력을 만들어 내는, / 링크를 가로질러 이동하는 물체에 (가해지는)
✔ In much the same way, / an array of technological, political, economic, cultural, and linguistic factors / can exist / and create a similar kind of pull or drag or friction.
이와 매우 유사한 방식으로, / 수많은 기술적, 정치적, 경제적, 문화적 그리고 언어적 요소들이 / 존재할 수 있고, / 유사한 종류의 인력, 저항력 또는 마찰력을 만들어 낼 수 있다.
They affect / how smoothly or directly information can move from point to point / in global cyberspace.
그 요소들은 영향을 미친다. / 정보가 지점 간에 얼마나 원활하게, 또는 곧바로 이동할 수 있는가에 / 전 세계 사이버 공간에서
⑤ Thus, while the earth might appear to be increasingly flat / from the perspective of international online communication, / it is far from frictionless.
그러므로 지구가 점차 평평하게 보일지는 모르지만 / 국제적인 온라인 의사소통이라는 관점에서 / 결코 마찰이 없지 않다.

국제적인 온라인 오픈 액세스는 '평평한 지구'라는 은유를 사용하여 이해된다. 그것은 하키 퍽이 아이스 링크의 평평한 표면을 미끄러져 가는 것만큼 쉽게 정보가 전 세계로 이동하는 세상을 나타낸다. ① 그러나 이러한 사고방식은 특히 우리가 그 은유를 확장해본다면 오해의 소지가 있을 수 있다. ② 아이스 링크를 건너 본 사람은 누구든 확인할 수 있듯이, 단지 링크 표면이 평평하고 탁 트인 듯 보인다고 해서 그 표면이 반드시 매끄럽거나 고르다는 것을 의미하지는 않는다. ③ 오히려, 그러한 표면은 링크를 가로질러 이동하는 물체에 가해지는 어느 정도의 인력, 저항력 또는 마찰력을 만들어 내는, 움푹 패이고 갈라지고 튀어나온 수많은 부분들로 덮여 있는 경향이 있다. ④ 이와 매우 유사한 방식으로, 수많은 기술적, 정치적, 경제적, 문화적 그리고 언어적 요소들이 존재할 수 있고, 유사한 종류의 인력, 저항력 또는 마찰력을 만들어 낼 수 있다. 그 요소들은 정보가 전 세계 사이버 공간에서 지점 간에 얼마나 원활하게, 또는 곧바로 이동할 수 있는가에 영향을 미친다. ⑤ 그러므로 국제적인 온라인 의사소통이라는 관점에서 지구가 점차 평평하게 보일지는 모르지만 결코 마찰이 없지 않다.

Why? 왜 정답일까?

국제적 온라인 오픈 액세스를 아이스하키 링크에 빗대어 설명한 글이다. ④ 앞에서 아이스 링크 표면은 완전히 매끈하지 않으며 어느 정도의 인력, 저항력, 마찰력을 만들어내는 요소들로 가득하다는 내용이 언급된 후, 주어진 문장은 이와 마찬가지로 온라인에 존재하는 수많은 기술적, 정치적, 경제적, 문화적, 언어적 요소들도 온갖 인력과 저항력과 마찰력을 만들어낼 수 있다고 설명한다. ④ 뒤에서는 주어진 문장에서 언급된 갖가지 요소들을 They로 가리키며 이 모든 것들이 정보의 이동에 영향을 미칠 수 있다는 내용을 덧붙인다. 따라서 주어진 문장이 들어가기에 가장 적절한 곳은 ④이다.

DAY 19

- an array of 수많은, 다수의
- drag ⓝ 저항력, 방해물
- metaphor ⓝ 비유
- misleading ⓐ 오해의 소지가 있는
- even ⓐ 고른, 평평한
- perspective ⓝ 관점
- linguistic ⓐ 언어적인
- friction ⓝ 마찰(력)
- slide across ~을 미끄러지다
- smooth ⓐ 매끄러운
- bump ⓝ 튀어나온 부분
- far from 결코 ~ 않다

구문 풀이

11행 As anyone [who has crossed an ice rink] can confirm, just because the surface of the rink appears flat and open does not necessarily mean that surface is smooth or even.
(As: 접속사(~듯이) / anyone: 주어 / can confirm: 동사 / 「just because ~ does not (necessarily) mean …: ~라고 해서 (반드시) …인 것은 아니다」)

04 모든 욕구나 동기의 밑바탕을 이루는 감정

정답률 53% | 정답 ⑤

글의 흐름으로 보아, 주어진 문장이 들어가기에 가장 적절한 곳을 고르시오.

Emotion plays an essential role in all our pursuits / — including our pursuit of happiness.
감정은 모든 추구에서 필수적인 역할을 한다. / 행복 추구를 포함한
① It is nearly impossible for us / to imagine a life without emotion.
우리로서는 거의 불가능하다. / 감정이 없는 삶을 상상하는 것은
② Think of an emotionless robot / that, other than the capacity for emotions, / has exactly the same physical and cognitive characteristics as humans.
감정 없는 로봇을 생각해 보라. / 감정에 대한 능력을 빼고 / 인간과 정확히 동일한 신체적 및 인지적 특성을 가지고 있는
③ The robot thinks and behaves in the same way / that humans do.
이 로봇은 똑같은 방식으로 생각하고 행동한다. / 인간이 하는 것과
④ It can discuss deep philosophical issues / and follow complex logic; / it can dig tunnels and build skyscrapers.
그것은 심오한 철학적 문제에 대해 논의하고 / 복잡한 논리를 따를 수 있으며, / 터널을 파고 고층 건물을 지을 수 있다.
✔Yet, although the robot is sophisticated, / it lacks all motivation to act.
하지만, 로봇은 정교하다고 할지라도 / 행동하려는 동기가 전혀 없다.
This is because / even the most basic desires are dependent on emotions / — the one thing this robot lacks.
이는 ~ 때문이다. / 가장 기본적인 욕구마저도 감정에 좌우되기 / 이 로봇에게는 없는 한 가지인

감정은 행복 추구를 포함한 모든 추구에서 필수적인 역할을 한다. ① 감정이 없는 삶을 상상하는 것은 거의 불가능하다. ② 감정에 대한 능력을 빼고 인간과 정확히 동일한 신체적 및 인지적 특성을 가지고 있는, 감정 없는 로봇을 생각해 보라. ③ 이 로봇은 인간과 똑같은 방식으로 생각하고 행동한다. ④ 심오한 철학적 문제에 대해 논의하고 복잡한 논리를 따를 수 있으며, 터널을 파고 고층 건물을 지을 수 있다. ⑤ 하지만, 로봇은 정교하다고 할지라도 (주체적으로) 행동하려는 동기가 전혀 없다. 이는 가장 기본적인 욕구마저도, 이 로봇에게는 없는 한 가지인 감정에 좌우되기 때문이다.

Why? 왜 정답일까?

⑤ 앞의 문장에서 감정이 없고 신체 및 인지 능력이 인간과 똑같은 로봇의 경우, 인간과 마찬가지로 사고하고 행동할 수 있다고 하는데, 주어진 문장은 이러한 흐름을 Yet으로 반전시키며 아무리 이 로봇이 정교하다 한들 (주체성을 갖고) 행동하려는 동기는 가질 수 없다고 이야기한다. ⑤ 뒤의 문장에서는 이 이유로서 가장 기본적인 욕구가 바로 감정에 좌우되기 때문이라는 설명을 덧붙인다. 따라서 주어진 문장이 들어가기에 가장 적절한 곳은 ⑤이다.

- sophisticated ⓐ 정교한, 세련된
- pursuit ⓝ 추구
- capacity ⓝ 능력
- characteristic ⓝ 특성
- philosophical ⓐ 철학적인
- lack ⓥ ~이 없다, ~을 결여하다
- emotionless ⓐ 감정이 없는
- cognitive ⓐ 인지적인
- behave ⓥ 행동하다
- be dependent on ~에 좌우되다.

구문 풀이

8행 The robot thinks and behaves in the same way that humans do.
(thinks and behaves: 자동사 / in the same way: ~와 같은 방식으로 / that: 관계부사 대용(선행사에 the same이 있으면 that) / do: =think and behave)

05 객관적 증거에 의한 믿음의 검증

정답률 41% | 정답 ⑤

글의 흐름으로 보아, 주어진 문장이 들어가기에 가장 적절한 곳을 고르시오. [3점]

Most beliefs — but not all — / are open to tests of verification.
전부는 아니지만 대부분의 믿음은 / 검증 시험을 받을 수 있다.
This means / that beliefs can be tested / to see if they are correct or false.
이것은 의미한다. / 믿음이 시험될 수 있다는 것을 / 그것들이 옳거나 그른지를 확인하기 위해
① Beliefs can be verified or falsified / with objective criteria external to the person.
믿음은 진실임이 입증되거나 거짓임이 입증될 수 있다. / 그 사람의 외부에 있는 객관적인 기준을 통해
② There are people / who believe the Earth is flat and not a sphere.
사람들이 있다. / 지구가 평평하고 구가 아니라고 믿는
③ Because we have objective evidence / that the Earth is in fact a sphere, / the flat Earth belief can be shown to be false.
우리는 객관적인 증거를 가지고 있기 때문에, / 지구가 실제로 구라는 / 지구가 평평하다는 믿음은 거짓임이 증명될 수 있다.
④ Also, / the belief that it will rain tomorrow / can be tested for truth / by waiting until tomorrow / and seeing whether it rains or not.
또한, / 내일 비가 올 것이라는 믿음은 / 진실인지 확인될 수 있다. / 내일까지 기다려 / 비가 오는지 안 오는지 봄으로써
✔However, / some types of beliefs cannot be tested for truth / because we cannot get external evidence in our lifetimes / (such as a belief / that the Earth will stop spinning on its axis by the year 9999 / or that there is life on a planet 100-million light-years away).
하지만, / 어떤 종류의 믿음은 진실인지 확인될 수 없다. / 우리가 일생 동안 외부 증거를 얻을 수 없기 때문에 / (믿음 같은 / 9999년이 되면 지구가 자전하는 것을 멈출 것이라는 / 혹은 1억 광년 떨어진 행성에 생명체가 있다는 것 같은)
Also, / meta-physical beliefs / (such as the existence and nature of a god) / present considerable challenges / in generating evidence / that everyone is willing to use as a truth criterion.
또한, / 형이상학적 믿음은 / (신의 존재와 본질과 같은) / 상당한 난제가 된다. / 증거를 만드는 데 있어서 / 모든 사람이 진리 기준으로 기꺼이 사용할

전부는 아니지만 대부분의 믿음은 검증 시험을 받을 수 있다. 이것은 믿음이 옳거나 그른지를 확인하기 위해 시험될 수 있다는 것을 의미한다. ① 믿음은 그 사람의 외부에 있는 객관적인 기준을 통해 진실임이 입증되거나 거짓임이 입증될 수 있다. ② 지구가 평평하고 구가 아니라고 믿는 사람들이 있다. ③ 우리는 지구가 실제로 구라는 객관적인 증거를 가지고 있기 때문에, 지구가 평평하다는 믿음은 거짓임이 증명될 수 있다. ④ 또한, 내일 비가 올 것이라는 믿음은 내일까지 기다려 비가 오는지 안 오는지 봄으로써 진실인지 확인될 수 있다. ⑤ 하지만, (9999년이 되면 지구가 자전하는 것을 멈출 것이라는 믿음이나 1억 광년 떨어진 행성에 생명체가 있다는 것 같은) 어떤 종류의 믿음은 우리가 일생 동안 외부 증거를 얻을 수 없기 때문에 진실인지 확인될 수 없다. 또한, (신의 존재와 본질과 같은) 형이상학적 믿음은 모든 사람이 진리 기준으로 기꺼이 사용할 증거를 만드는 데 있어서 상당한 난제가 된다.

Why? 왜 정답일까?

⑤ 앞에서 지구가 둥글다는 믿음과 내일 비가 올 것이라는 믿음을 예로 들어, 믿음을 외부의 객관적 기준으로 검증할 수 있는 경우를 언급하고 있다. 이와는 반대로 주어진 문장은 지구가 미래 어느 시점에는 자전을 멈출 것이라는 믿음, 또는 외계 생명체가 있다는 믿음 등은 이를 뒷받침하는 외부적 증거를 얻을 수 없기 때문에 검증이 이루어지기 어렵다는 내용을 제시하고 있다. 이어서 ⑤ 뒤의 문장은 주어진 문장과 Also로 연결되며, 신의 존재 등에 관한 형이상학적 믿음 또한 객관적 증거로 뒷받침되기 어려울 수 있다는 점을 추가로 제시한다. 따라서 주어진 문장이 들어가기에 가장 적절한 곳은 ⑤이다.

- external ⓐ 외부의, 외적인
- verify ⓥ 검증하다, 확인하다
- criterion ⓝ 기준 (*pl.* criteria)
- meta-physical ⓐ 형이상학의
- nature ⓝ 본질
- generate ⓥ 만들어 내다
- axis ⓝ 축
- objective ⓐ 객관적인
- sphere ⓝ 구
- existence ⓝ 존재, 실재
- considerable ⓐ 상당한
- willing ⓐ 기꺼이 ~하려는

구문 풀이

13행 Also, the belief {that it will rain tomorrow} can be tested for truth by waiting until tomorrow and seeing whether it rains or not.
({ }: 동격절(= the belief) / can be tested: 조동사 수동태 / by: 전치사 / waiting: 동명사1 / seeing: 동명사2 / whether: 명사절 접속사(~인지 아닌지))

06 고정 공급 일정

정답률 38% | 정답 ⑤

글의 흐름으로 보아, 주어진 문장이 들어가기에 가장 적절한 곳을 고르시오. [3점]

A supply schedule refers to the ability of a business / to change their production rates / to meet the demand of consumers.
공급 일정은 업체의 능력을 말한다. / 생산율을 바꿀 수 있는 / 소비자의 수요를 충족하기 위해

Some businesses are able to increase their production level quickly / in order to meet increased demand.
몇몇 업체는 조업도를 빠르게 늘릴 수 있다. / 증가한 수요를 맞추고자
However, / sporting clubs have a fixed, or inflexible (inelastic) production capacity.
그러나, / 스포츠 클럽은 고정된, 혹은 유연하지 못한(비탄력적인) 생산 능력을 가지고 있다.
① They have / what is known as a fixed supply schedule.
그들은 가지고 있다. / 소위 고정 공급 일정이라는 것을
② It is worth noting / that this is not the case / for sales of clothing, equipment, memberships and memorabilia.
주목할 가치가 있다. / 이것이 해당하지 않는다는 것에 / 의류, 장비, 회원권, 기념품 판매에는
③ But / clubs and teams can only play a certain number of times / during their season.
그러나 / 클럽과 팀은 / 일정 횟수만 경기할 수 있다. / 시즌 동안
④ If fans and members are unable to get into a venue, / that revenue is lost forever.
팬과 회원이 경기장에 들어갈 수 없으면, / 그 수익은 영원히 손실된다.
✔ Although sport clubs and leagues / may have a fixed supply schedule, / it is possible / to increase the number of consumers who watch.
스포츠 클럽과 리그가 ~할지라도 / 고정 공급 일정을 가지고 있을 / 가능하다. / (경기를) 보는 소비자의 수를 늘리는 것이
For example, / the supply of a sport product can be increased / by providing more seats, / changing the venue, / extending the playing season / or even through new television, radio or Internet distribution.
예를 들어, / 스포츠 제품의 공급은 증가될 수 있다. / 더 많은 좌석을 제공하거나, / 경기장을 바꾸거나, / 경기 시즌을 연장하거나, / 심지어 새로운 텔레비전, 라디오, 혹은 인터넷 배급으로

공급 일정은 소비자의 수요를 충족하기 위해 생산율을 바꿀 수 있는 업체의 능력을 말한다. 몇몇 업체는 증가한 수요를 맞추고자 조업도를 빠르게 늘릴 수 있다. 그러나, 스포츠 클럽은 고정된, 혹은 유연하지 못한(비탄력적인) 생산 능력을 가지고 있다. ① 그들은 소위 고정 공급 일정이라는 것을 가지고 있다. ② 이것이 의류, 장비, 회원권, 기념품 판매에는 해당하지 않는다는 것에 주목할 가치가 있다. ③ 그러나 클럽과 팀은 시즌 동안 일정 횟수만 경기할 수 있다. ④ 팬과 회원이 경기장에 들어갈 수 없으면, 그 수익은 영원히 손실된다. ⑤ 스포츠 클럽과 리그가 고정 공급 일정을 가지고 있을지라도, (경기를) 보는 소비자의 수를 늘리는 것이 가능하다. 예를 들어, 더 많은 좌석을 제공하거나, 경기장을 바꾸거나, 경기 시즌을 연장하거나, 심지어 새로운 텔레비전, 라디오, 혹은 인터넷 배급으로 스포츠 제품의 공급을 늘릴 수 있다.

Why? 왜 정답일까?

⑤ 앞에서는 고정 공급 일정으로 인해 수요에 빠르게 대응하기 어려운 스포츠 클럽의 상황을 설명한다. 한편 주어진 문장은 이렇게 고정 공급 일정일지라도 소비자의 수를 늘릴 수 있다는 내용으로 흐름을 반전시키고, ⑤ 뒤에서는 그 구체적인 방법을 열거한다. 따라서 주어진 문장이 들어가기에 가장 적절한 곳은 ⑤이다.

- inflexible ⓐ 유연하지 못한, 융통성 없는
- inelastic ⓐ 비탄력적인, 적응력이 없는
- note ⓥ 알아차리다
- equipment ⓝ 장비
- revenue ⓝ 수입, 수익
- extend ⓥ 연장하다
- distribution ⓝ 배급, 분배

구문 풀이

11행 It is worth noting that this is not the case for sales of clothing, equipment, memberships and memorabilia.
「be worth+동명사 : ~할 가치가 있다」

07 중요한 정보의 원천인 인적 네트워크 정답률 41% | 정답 ③

글의 흐름으로 보아, 주어진 문장이 들어가기에 가장 적절한 곳을 고르시오. [3점]

You're probably already starting to see / the tremendous value of network analysis for businesspeople.
당신은 아마도 이미 알기 시작하고 있을 것이다. / 사업가들을 위한 네트워크 분석의 엄청난 가치를
① In the business world, information is money: / a tip about anything / from a cheap supplier / to a competitor's marketing campaign / to an under-the-table merger discussion / can inform strategic decisions / that might yield millions of dollars in profits.
사업의 세계에서 정보는 돈이다: / 어떠한 것에 대한 정보는 / 값싼 공급업자에서부터 / 경쟁자의 마케팅 활동과 / 비밀리에 이루어지는 합병 토론에 이르기까지 / 전략적 결정에 대한 정보를 줄 수 있다. / 수백만 달러를 이윤으로 산출할 수 있는
② You might catch it on TV or in the newspaper, / but that's information everyone knows.
당신은 텔레비전이나 신문에서 그것을 얻을지도 모르지만, / 그것은 모든 사람이 아는 정보이다.
✔ The most profitable information / likely comes through network connections / that provide "inside" information.
가장 수익을 창출할 수 있는 정보는 / 네트워크 연결망을 통해서 나올 가능성이 있다. / "내부" 정보를 제공하는
And it isn't just information / that travels through network connections / — it's influence as well.
그리고 정보뿐만이 아니다 / 네트워크 연결망을 통해 이동하는 것은 / 영향력 또한 그렇다.
④ If you have a connection at another company, / you can possibly ask your connection / to push that company to do business with yours, / to avoid a competitor, / or to hold off on the launch of a product.
만약 당신이 다른 회사에 인맥을 가지고 있다면 / 당신은 당신의 인맥에게 요청할 수 있다. / 그 회사가 당신의 회사와 함께 사업을 하게 하거나 / 경쟁자를 피하게 하거나 / 또는 제품의 출시를 연기하게 밀어붙여달라고
⑤ So clearly, / any businessperson wants to increase their personal network.
그래서 명확하게도, / 어떤 사업가든 그들의 개인적 네트워크를 늘리기를 원한다.

당신은 아마도 사업가들을 위한 네트워크 분석의 엄청난 가치를 이미 알기 시작하고 있을 것이다. ① 사업의 세계에서 정보는 돈이다: 값싼 공급업자에서부터 경쟁자의 마케팅 활동과 비밀리에 이루어지는 합병 토론에 이르기까지 어떠한 것에 대한 정보는 수백만 달러를 이윤으로 산출할 수 있는 전략적 결정에 대한 정보를 줄 수 있다. ② 당신은 텔레비전이나 신문에서 그것을 얻을지도 모르지만, 그것은 모든 사람이 아는 정보이다. ③ 가장 수익을 창출할 수 있는 정보는 "내부" 정보를 제공하는 네트워크 연결망을 통해서 나올 가능성이 있다. 그리고 네트워크 연결망을 통해 이동하는 것은 정보뿐만이 아니다 — 영향력 또한 그렇다. ④ 만약 당신이 다른 회사에 인맥을 가지고 있다면 당신은 당신의 인맥이 그 회사가 당신의 회사와 함께 사업을 하게 하거나 경쟁자를 피하게 하거나 또는 제품의 출시를 연기하게 밀어붙여달라고 요청할 수 있다. ⑤ 그래서 명확하게도, 어떤 사업가든 그들의 개인적 네트워크를 늘리기를 원한다.

Why? 왜 정답일까?

사업에서 정보는 중요한 가치를 지니며 이 정보를 얻는 원천으로서 인적 네트워크를 활용할 수 있다는 내용의 글이다. ③ 앞에서 텔레비전이나 신문은 정보의 원천이 될 수 있지만 이를 통해 얻는 정보는 누구나 아는 정보라는 내용이 언급된 데 이어, 주어진 문장은 정말 중요한 내부 정보는 인적 연결망을 통해 얻을 수 있다는 내용을 제시하고 있다. ③ 뒤에서는 인적 연결망을 통해 정보뿐 아니라 영향력 또한 이동할 수 있다는 내용이 추가로 제시된다. 따라서 주어진 문장이 들어가기에 가장 적절한 곳은 ③이다.

- profitable ⓐ 수익성이 있는
- likely ad 아마, 어쩌면
- tremendous ⓐ 엄청난
- supplier ⓝ 공급업자
- under-the-table 비밀리의 내밀한
- inform ⓥ 알리다
- strategic ⓐ 전략적인
- yield ⓥ 내다, 생산하다
- influence ⓝ 영향력
- hold off 미루다, 시작하지 않다
- launch ⓝ 출시, 시작

구문 풀이

6행 In the business world, {information is money}: / a tip about anything from a cheap supplier to a competitor's marketing campaign to an under-the-table merger discussion can inform strategic decisions [that might yield millions of dollars in profits].
{ } : 뒤와 동격 / 주어 / 「from A+to B+to C : A에서 B, C에 이르기까지」 / 동사 / 목적어 / 주격 관계대명사

08 숫자를 통한 상대적 크기 비교 정답률 45% | 정답 ③

글의 흐름으로 보아, 주어진 문장이 들어가기에 가장 적절한 곳을 고르시오.

We sometimes solve number problems / almost without realizing it.
우리는 가끔 숫자 문제를 해결하기도 한다. / 그것을 거의 깨닫지도 못한 채
① For example, / suppose you are conducting a meeting / and you want to ensure / that everyone there has a copy of the agenda.
예를 들어, / 여러분이 회의를 진행하고 있다고 가정해 보라. / 그리고 여러분이 확실히 갖게 하고 싶어 한다고 / 그곳에 있는 모든 사람이 의제의 사본을
② You can deal with this / by labelling each copy of the handout in turn / with the initials of each of those present.
여러분은 이것을 처리할 수 있다. / 그 유인물의 각 사본에 차례대로 적음으로써 / 참석한 사람들 각각의 이름 첫 글자들을
✔ As long as you do not run out of copies / before completing this process, / you will know / that you have a sufficient number to go around.
사본이 떨어지지 않는 한 / 이 과정을 완료하기 전에, / 여러분은 알 것이다. / (사람들에게) 돌아갈 충분한 수의 사본이 있다는 것을
You have then solved this problem / without resorting to arithmetic / and without explicit counting.
그렇다면 여러분은 이 문제를 해결한 것이다. / 산수에 의존하지 않고, / 그리고 명시적인 집계 없이

④ There are numbers at work for us here all the same / and they allow precise comparison of one collection with another, / even though the members that make up the collections / could have entirely different characters, / as is the case here, / where one set is a collection of people, / while the other consists of pieces of paper.
그래도 여기에는 우리에게 영향을 미치고 있는 숫자가 있고 / 그것(숫자)이 하나의 집합과 다른 집합을 정확히 비교할 수 있게 하는데, / 그 집합을 구성하는 것들이 / 완전히 다른 특징을 가질 수 있음에도 그러하다. / 여기서의 경우처럼 / 한 세트는 사람들의 집합인 / 다른 세트는 종이로 구성된 반면

⑤ What numbers allow us to do / is to compare the relative size of one set with another.
숫자가 우리로 하여금 할 수 있게 하는 것은 / 한 세트의 상대적인 크기를 다른 세트와 비교하는 것이다.

우리는 가끔 거의 깨닫지도 못한 채 숫자 문제를 해결하기도 한다. ① 예를 들어, 여러분이 회의를 진행하고 있고 그곳에 있는 모든 사람이 의제의 사본을 확실히 갖게 하고 싶어 한다고 가정해 보라. ② 여러분은 그 유인물의 각 사본에 참석한 사람들 각각의 이름 첫 글자들을 차례대로 적음으로써 이것을 처리할 수 있다. ③ 이 과정을 완료하기 전에 사본이 떨어지지 않는 한, 여러분은 사람들에게 돌아갈 충분한 수의 사본이 있다는 것을 알 것이다. 그렇다면 여러분은 산수에 의존하지 않고, 명시적인 집계 없이 이 문제를 해결한 것이다. ④ 그래도 여기에는 우리에게 영향을 미치고 있는 숫자가 있고 그것(숫자)이 하나의 집합과 다른 집합을 정확히 비교할 수 있게 하는데, 그 집합을 구성하는 것들이 이 경우처럼 한 세트는 사람들의 집합인 반면 다른 세트는 종이로 구성되어 완전히 다른 특징을 가질 수 있음에도 그러하다. ⑤ 숫자가 우리로 하여금 할 수 있게 하는 것은 한 세트의 상대적인 크기를 다른 세트와 비교하는 것이다.

Why? 왜 정답일까?

우리는 때로 명시적으로 수를 헤아리지 않아도 대략적으로 상대적인 크기를 비교하는 것으로 숫자 문제를 해결하기도 한다는 내용을 다룬 글이다. ③ 앞에서는 우리가 회의에서 유인물을 배부하기 앞서 종이에 사람들의 이름을 써보며 모든 구성원이 유인물을 받을 수 있는지를 따져보는 경우를 예로 드는데, 주어진 문장에서는 '이 과정'이 끝나기 전에 사본이 동나지 않는다면 우리는 유인물이 충분함을 알 수 있게 된다고 말한다. **then**으로 이어지는 ③ 뒤의 문장에서는 이 경우 우리가 명시적 계산 없이도 숫자 문제를 해결한 것이라는 결론으로 나아간다. 따라서 주어진 문장이 들어가기에 가장 적절한 곳은 ③이다.

- **sufficient** ⓐ 충분한
- **handout** ⓝ 유인물
- **explicit** ⓐ 명시적인
- **precise** ⓐ 정확한, 정밀한
- **make up** ~을 구성하다
- **as is the case** ~이 그렇듯이
- **agenda** ⓝ 의제
- **resort to** ⓥ ~에 의존하다
- **all the same** 그래도, 여전히
- **comparison** ⓝ 비교
- **entirely** ad 전적으로

구문 풀이

1행 As long as you do not run out of copies before completing this process, you will know that you have a sufficient number to go around.
(As long as: 조건 접속사 / before: 전치사 / completing: 동명사 / you: 주어 / will know: 동사(미래) / that: 접속사(~것) / to go around: 형용사적 용법)

★★★ 1등급 대비 고난도 2점 문제

09 아동 문학 텍스트의 입지 — 정답률 38% | 정답 ③

글의 흐름으로 보아, 주어진 문장이 들어가기에 가장 적절한 곳을 고르시오.

Interest in ideology in children's literature / arises from a belief / that children's literary texts are culturally formative, / and of massive importance / educationally, intellectually, and socially.
아동 문학에서의 이데올로기에 대한 관심은 / 믿음에서 비롯된다. / 아동문학의 텍스트가 문화적으로 형성되고, / 매우 중요하다는 / 교육적, 지적, 사회적으로

① Perhaps more than any other texts, / they reflect society / as it wishes to be, / as it wishes to be seen, / and as it unconsciously reveals itself to be, / at least to writers.
아마 다른 어떤 텍스트보다도 / 그것들은 사회를 반영한다. / 그것이 바라는 대로, / 그것이 보이게 하고 싶은 대로, / 그리고 그것이 무의식적으로 드러나 있는 그대로를 / 적어도 작가에게는

② Clearly, / literature is not the only socialising agent / in the life of children, / even among the media.
분명히, / 문학만이 유일한 사회화 동인은 아니다. / 아이들의 삶 속에서, / 또 심지어 매체들 가운데에서도

✔ It is possible to argue, / for example, / that, today, / the influence of books is vastly overshadowed / by that of television.
주장할 수 있다. / 예를 들어, / 오늘날 / 책의 영향은 크게 가려진다고 / 텔레비전의 영향력에 의해

There is, however, / a considerable degree of interaction / between the two media.
그러나 ~이 있다. / 상당한 수준의 상호작용이 / 두 매체 사이에는

④ Many so-called children's literary classics are televised, / and the resultant new book editions strongly suggest / that viewing can encourage subsequent reading.
소위 아동문학 고전이라고 불리는 많은 책이 TV로 방영되고 있으며, / 그 결과 나온 새로운 판본의 책은 강력하게 시사한다. / TV를 시청하는 것이 추가적으로 이어지는 독서를 장려할 수 있다는 것을

⑤ Similarly, / some television series for children / are published in book form.
마찬가지로, / 아동을 위한 몇몇 텔레비전 시리즈는 / 책 형태로 출판되기도 한다.

아동 문학에서의 이데올로기에 대한 관심은 아동문학의 텍스트가 문화적으로 형성되고, 교육적, 지적, 사회적으로 매우 중요하다는 믿음에서 비롯된다. ① 적어도 작가에게는 아동 문학의 텍스트는 아마 다른 어떤 텍스트보다도 사회를 그 사회가 바라는 대로, 보이게 하고 싶은 대로, 그리고 그것이 무의식적으로 드러나 있는 그대로를 반영한다. ② 분명히, 문학만이 아이들의 삶 속에서, 또 심지어 매체들 가운데에서도 유일한 사회화 동인은 아니다. ③ 예를 들어, 오늘날 책의 영향은 텔레비전의 영향력에 의해 크게 가려진다고 주장할 수 있다. 그러나 두 매체 사이에는 상당한 수준의 상호작용이 있다. ④ 소위 아동문학 고전이라고 불리는 많은 책이 TV로 방영되고 있으며, 그 결과 나온 새로운 판본의 책은 TV를 시청하는 것이 추가적으로 이어지는 독서를 장려할 수 있다는 것을 강력하게 시사한다. ⑤ 마찬가지로, 아동을 위한 몇몇 텔레비전 시리즈는 책 형태로 출판되기도 한다.

Why? 왜 정답일까?

③ 앞의 문장에서 오늘날 아동문학은 아이들에게 영향력을 발휘하는 유일한 매체는 아니라고 언급한 뒤, 주어진 문장에서는 예컨대 텔레비전의 영향력과 비교하면 책의 영향력이 많이 가려진다고 설명한다. 이어서 ③ 뒤의 문장은 **however**로 흐름을 반전시키며 두 매체, 즉 주어진 문장에서 언급된 텔레비전과 문학 사이에 많은 상호작용이 이루어지고 있다는 내용을 제시한다. 따라서 주어진 문장이 들어가기에 가장 적절한 곳은 ③이다.

- **vastly** ad 크게
- **ideology** ⓝ 이데올로기, 이념
- **arise from** ~에서 발생하다
- **formative** ⓐ 모양을 만드는, 형성하는
- **reflect** ⓥ 반영하다
- **reveal** ⓥ 드러내다
- **agent** ⓝ 중요한 작용을 하는 사람[것], 동인
- **so-called** ⓐ 소위 말하는
- **resultant** ⓐ 그 결과로 생긴, 그에 따른
- **overshadow** ⓥ 그늘을 드리우다, 가리다.
- **literature** ⓝ 문학
- **literary** ⓐ 문학의
- **intellectually** ad 지적으로
- **unconsciously** ad 무의식적으로
- **socialise** ⓥ 사회화시키다
- **considerable** ⓐ 상당한
- **televise** ⓥ 텔레비전으로 방송하다
- **subsequent** ⓐ 뒤이은

구문 풀이

4행 Interest in ideology in children's literature arises from a belief {that children's literary texts are culturally formative, and of massive importance educationally, intellectually, and socially}.
(children's literary texts: 주어 / are: 동사 / culturally formative: 보어1 / of massive importance: 보어2(=massively important) / { }: 동격절(=a belief))

★★ 문제 해결 꿀~팁 ★★

▶ 많이 틀린 이유는?
④ 앞뒤에 논리적 공백이 있는지 확인해 보면, 먼저 ④ 앞에서 두 미디어 간의 상호작용(**a considerable degree of interaction between the two media**)을 언급한 후, ④ 뒤에서 아동 문학 고전이 텔레비전으로 방송되는 경우를 예로 들고 있다. 즉 ④ 앞뒤로 일반론과 예시가 자연스럽게 연결되므로, ④에 주어진 문장이 들어갈 만한 논리적 공백이 존재하지 않는다.
▶ 문제 해결 방법은?
정관사 힌트에 주목해야 한다.
③ 앞에서 '두 미디어'로 지칭할 만한 대상이 언급되지 않았는데, ③ 뒤에서는 '**the two media**'라는 표현을 사용하고 있다. 이로 미루어 보아, **books**와 **television**이라는 두 가지 대상을 언급하는 주어진 문장이 ③에 반드시 들어가야 함을 알 수 있다.

★★★ 1등급 대비 고난도 2점 문제

10 자본 시장의 자유화 — 정답률 37% | 정답 ④

글의 흐름으로 보아, 주어진 문장이 들어가기에 가장 적절한 곳을 고르시오.

The liberalization of capital markets, / where funds for investment can be borrowed, / has been an important contributor / to the pace of globalization.
자본 시장의 자유화는 / 투자 자금을 빌릴 수 있는 / 중요한 기여 요인이었다. / 세계화 속도에

Since the 1970s there has been / a trend towards a freer flow of capital across borders.
1970년대 이후로 있었다. / 국경을 넘나드는 더 자유로운 자본 흐름을 향한 추세가
① Current economic theory suggests / that this should aid development.
현재의 경제 이론은 시사한다. / 이것이 발전에 도움이 될 것임을
② Developing countries have limited domestic savings / with which to invest in growth, / and liberalization allows them to tap into a global pool of funds.
개발도상국은 제한된 국내 저축을 가지고 있고, / 성장에 투자하기에 / 자유화는 그들이 국제 공동 자금을 이용하도록 허용한다.
③ A global capital market / also allows investors greater scope / to manage and spread their risks.
국제 자본 시장은 / 또한 투자자들에게 더 큰 범위를 허용한다. / 자신들의 위험을 관리하고 분산시킬 수 있는
✔ However, some say / that a freer flow of capital / has raised the risk of financial instability.
하지만 어떤 사람들은 말한다. / 더 자유로운 자본의 흐름이 / 재정적 불안정성의 위험을 증가시켰다고
The East Asian crisis of the late 1990s / came in the wake of this kind of liberalization.
1990년대 후반의 동아시아 위기는 / 이러한 자유화의 결과로 발생했다.
⑤ Without a strong financial system and a sound regulatory environment, / capital market globalization / can sow the seeds of instability in economies / rather than growth.
강한 재정 시스템과 건전한 규제 환경이 없다면, / 자본 시장 세계화는 / 경제적 불안정성의 씨를 뿌릴 수 있다. / 성장보다는

투자 자금을 빌릴 수 있는 자본 시장의 자유화는 세계화 속도에 중요한 기여 요인이었다. 1970년대 이후로 국경을 넘나드는 더 자유로운 자본 흐름을 향한 추세가 있었다. ① 현재의 경제 이론은 이것이 발전에 도움이 될 것임을 시사한다. ② 개발도상국은 성장에 투자하기에 제한된 국내 저축을 가지고 있고, 자유화는 그들이 국제 공동 자금을 이용하도록 허용한다. ③ 국제 자본 시장은 또한 투자자들에게 자신들의 위험을 관리하고 분산시킬 수 있는 더 큰 범위를 허용한다. ④ 하지만 어떤 사람들은 더 자유로운 자본의 흐름이 재정적 불안정성의 위험을 증가시켰다고 말한다. 1990년대 후반의 동아시아 위기는 이러한 자유화의 결과로 발생했다. ⑤ 강한 재정 시스템과 건전한 규제 환경이 없다면, 자본 시장 세계화는 성장보다는 경제적 불안정성의 씨를 뿌릴 수 있다.

Why? 왜 정답일까?

이 글은 자본 시장의 자유화가 초래하는 결과에 관해 논하고 있으며, ④ 앞에서는 긍정적인 내용, ④ 뒤에는 부정적인 내용이 소개된다. 이때 주어진 문장에는 역접의 연결어인 However가 있으므로, 주어진 문장이 들어가기에 가장 적절한 곳은 ④이다.

- financial ⓐ 재정적인, 금융의
- liberalization ⓝ 자유화
- contributor ⓝ 기여 요인, 원인
- aid ⓥ 돕다
- tap into ~을 이용하다
- sow ⓥ (씨를) 뿌리다, 심다
- instability ⓝ 불안정성
- investment ⓝ 투자
- globalization ⓝ 세계화
- domestic ⓐ 국내의
- regulatory ⓐ 규제력을 지닌, 규제의

구문 풀이

3행 The liberalization of capital markets, [where funds for investment can be borrowed], has been an important contributor to the pace of globalization.
(The liberalization: 주어 / where: 관계부사 / can be borrowed: 조동사 수동태 / has been: 동사(단수, 현재완료) / contributor to: ~에 대한 기여 요인)

★★ 문제 해결 꿀~팁 ★★

▶ 많이 틀린 이유는?
③ 뒤의 문장은 '위험'에 관해 언급하고 있어 얼핏 자본 시장의 자유화가 초래한 부정적인 결과를 이야기하는 문장처럼 보이지만, 이와는 정반대로 자본 시장의 자유화로 인해 '위험을 관리하고 분산시키기 좋아졌다'라는 긍정적인 내용을 다루는 문장이다. 여기까지 좋은 점이 언급되어야 ④에서 주어진 문장의 However가 흐름을 반전시켜 자본 시장의 자유화가 초래한 부정적인 결과에 관해 설명해나갈 수 있다.
▶ 문제 해결 방법은?
글을 문장 단위로 꼼꼼히 독해하기보다는 '자본 시장의 자유화'라는 소재에 관해 좋은 점을 말하는지, 나쁜 점을 말하는지를 파악하는 정도로 읽어나가며 흐름을 잡도록 한다.

★★★ 1등급 대비 고난도 3점 문제

11 소리의 밝기 — 정답률 41% | 정답 ⑤

글의 흐름으로 보아, 주어진 문장이 들어가기에 가장 적절한 곳을 고르시오. [3점]

Brightness of sounds means much energy in higher frequencies, / which can be calculated from the sounds easily.
소리의 밝기는 더 높은 주파수에서의 많은 에너지를 의미하며, / 이는 소리로부터 쉽게 계산될 수 있다.
A violin has many more overtones compared to a flute / and sounds brighter.
바이올린은 플루트에 비해 더 많은 상음(上音)을 가지고 있고 / 더 밝게 들린다.
① An oboe is brighter than a classical guitar, / and a crash cymbal brighter than a double bass.
오보에가 클래식 기타보다 더 밝고, / 크래시 심벌이 더블 베이스보다 더 밝다.
② This is obvious, / and indeed people like brightness.
이것은 명백하고 / 실제로 사람들은 밝음을 좋아한다.
③ One reason is / that it makes sound subjectively louder, / which is part of the loudness war / in modern electronic music, / and in the classical music of the 19th century.
한 가지 이유는 ~이며, / 그것이 소리를 주관적으로 더 크게 들리도록 만든다는 것 / 이는 소리의 세기 전쟁의 일환이다. / 현대 전자 음악과 / 19세기 클래식 음악에서
④ All sound engineers know / that if they play back a track to a musician / that just has recorded this track / and add some higher frequencies, / the musician will immediately like the track much better.
모든 음향 기사들은 안다. / 만약 그들이 음악가에게 곡을 틀어 주고 / 방금 이 곡을 녹음한 / 약간의 더 높은 주파수를 더하면, / 그 음악가는 곧바로 그 곡을 훨씬 더 좋아하게 되리라는 것을
✔ But this is a short-lived effect, / and in the long run, / people find such sounds too bright.
하지만 이것은 일시적인 효과이고 / 장기적으로 / 사람들은 그러한 소리가 너무 밝다는 것을 알게 된다.
So it is wise / not to play back such a track with too much brightness, / as it normally takes quite some time / to convince the musician / that less brightness serves his music better in the end.
따라서 현명한데 / 그러한 곡을 너무 밝게 틀어 주지 않는 것이 / 왜냐하면 보통 시간이 꽤 걸리기 때문이다. / 그 음악가에게 납득시키는 데 / 더 적은 밝기가 결국 음악에 더 도움이 된다는 것을

소리의 밝기는 더 높은 주파수에서의 많은 에너지를 의미하며, 이는 소리로부터 쉽게 계산될 수 있다. 바이올린은 플루트에 비해 더 많은 상음(上音)을 가지고 있고 더 밝게 들린다. ① 오보에가 클래식 기타보다 더 밝고, 크래시 심벌이 더블 베이스보다 더 밝다. ② 이것은 명백하고 실제로 사람들은 밝음을 좋아한다. ③ 한 가지 이유는 그것이 소리를 주관적으로 더 크게 들리도록 만든다는 것이며, 이는 현대 전자 음악과 19세기 클래식 음악에서 소리의 세기 전쟁의 일환이다. ④ 모든 음향 기사들은 만약 방금 이 곡을 녹음한 음악가에게 곡을 틀어 주고 약간의 더 높은 주파수를 더하면, 그 음악가는 곧바로 그 곡을 훨씬 더 좋아하게 되리라는 것을 안다. ⑤ 하지만 이것은 일시적인 효과이고, 장기적으로 사람들은 그러한 소리가 너무 밝다는 것을 알게 된다. 따라서 그러한 곡을 너무 밝게 틀어 주지 않는 것이 현명한데 왜냐하면, 그 음악가에게 더 적은 밝기가 결국 음악에 더 도움이 된다는 것을 납득시키는 데 보통 시간이 꽤 걸리기 때문이다.

Why? 왜 정답일까?

소리는 밝을수록 더 크게 느껴진다는 설명 뒤로, ⑤ 앞의 문장은 만일 음악을 녹음해서 조금 더 높은 주파수를 첨가해 틀어주면 음악가가 그 소리를 더 좋아하게 될 것이라는 예를 든다. 하지만 ⑤ 뒤의 문장은 곡을 너무 밝게 틀어주지 않는 것이 현명하다는 내용이므로, 밝은 소리가 선호될 것이라는 ⑤ 앞의 내용과 상충한다. 따라서 But으로 시작하며 밝아진 소리에 대한 선호가 일시적임을 지적하는 주어진 문장이 들어가기에 가장 적절한 곳은 ⑤이다.

- short-lived ⓐ 단기적인
- overtone ⓝ 상음(上音)
- loudness ⓝ 소리의 세기
- track ⓝ (테이프로 녹음한) 곡
- record ⓥ 녹음하다
- convince ⓥ 납득시키다
- frequency ⓝ 주파수
- subjectively ad 주관적으로
- sound engineer ⓝ 음향기사
- musician ⓝ 음악가
- immediately ad 즉시, 곧바로
- serve ⓥ 도움이 되다

구문 풀이

16행 So it is wise not to play back such a track with too much brightness, as it normally takes quite some time to convince the musician that less brightness serves his music better in the end.
(it: 가주어 / not to play back ~ brightness: 진주어 / 「it takes + 시간 + to부정사 : ~이 …하는 데 ~의 시간이 걸리다」)

★★ 문제 해결 꿀~팁 ★★

▶ 많이 틀린 이유는?
③에 주어진 문장을 넣으면 '밝은 소리는 주관적으로 크게 들린다 → 그런데 이 효과는 일시적이다 → 그 이유는 소리가 크게 들리기 때문이다'라는 흐름이 얼핏 자연스러워 보인다. 하지만 ③을 답으로 고르면, ⑤ 앞뒤의 흐름 단절이 해소되지 않은 상태로 남기 때문에 전체적인 논리 전개가 부자연스럽다.

DAY 19

[문제편 p.125]

▶ 문제 해결 방법은?
⑤ 뒤의 문장에 So가 있고, So 뒤로 곡을 너무 밝게 틀어주면 안 된다는 결론이 나오므로, ⑤ 앞에는 '밝게 틀어주는 것의 한계'를 언급하는 말이 나와야 한다. 본문에서 이 한계는 ⑤ 앞 문장이 아닌, 주어진 문장에서 언급된다(find such sounds too bright).

★★★ 1등급 대비 고난도 3점 문제

12 중요한 요소와 중추적 요소의 차이 정답률 39% | 정답 ④

글의 흐름으로 보아, 주어진 문장이 들어가기에 가장 적절한 곳을 고르시오. [3점]

Some resources, decisions, or activities / are *important* / (highly valuable on average) / while others are *pivotal* / (small changes make a big difference).
어떤 자원들, 결정들 또는 활동들은 / *중요하다*. / (평균적으로 매우 가치 있는) / 다른 것들은 *중추적*인 반면 / (작은 변화가 큰 차이를 만든다)
Consider / how two components of a car / relate to a consumer's purchase decision: / tires and interior design.
생각해보자. / 어떻게 자동차의 두 구성요소가 / 소비자의 구매결정과 관련이 있는지 / 즉 타이어와 내부 디자인
Which adds more value on average?
어떤 것이 평균적으로 더 큰 가치를 부가시키는가?
The tires.
타이어이다.
① They are essential / to the car's ability to move, / and they impact both safety and performance.
타이어는 필수적이고 / 차의 운행 능력에 / 그것은 안전과 성능 모두에 영향을 준다.
② Yet tires generally do not influence purchase decisions / because safety standards guarantee / that all tires will be very safe and reliable.
하지만 타이어는 일반적으로 구매 결정에 영향을 미치지 않는데, / 그 이유는 안전기준들이 보장해주기 때문이다. / 모든 타이어가 매우 안전하고 믿을 만하다고
③ Differences in interior features / — optimal sound system, / portable technology docks, / number and location of cup holders — / likely have far more effect / on the consumer's buying decision.
내부 디자인 사양 차이가 / 최적의 음향 시스템, / 스마트기기 거치대, / 컵홀더의 개수와 위치와 같은 / 아마도 훨씬 더 큰 영향을 미친다. / 소비자의 구매 결정에
④ In terms of the overall value of an automobile, / you can't drive without tires, / but you can drive / without cup holders and a portable technology dock.
자동차의 전반적인 가치 측면에서, / 당신은 타이어 없이는 운전할 수 없지만 / 운전할 수 있다. / 컵홀더나 스마트기기 거치대가 없어도
Interior features, however, / clearly have a greater impact / on the purchase decision.
하지만 내부 디자인 사양들은 / 확실히 더 큰 영향을 미친다. / 구매 결정에
⑤ In our language, / the tires are important, / but the interior design is pivotal.
우리 표현으로 하자면, / 타이어는 중요하지만 / 내부 디자인은 중추적이다.

어떤 자원들, 결정들 또는 활동들은 *중요한*(평균적으로 매우 가치 있는) 반면 다른 것들은 *중추적*(작은 변화가 큰 차이를 만든다)이다. 자동차의 두 구성요소인 타이어와 내부 디자인이 어떻게 소비자의 구매 결정과 관련이 있는지 생각해보자. 어떤 것이 평균적으로 더 큰 가치를 부가시키는가? 타이어이다. ① 타이어는 차의 운행 능력에 필수적이고 안전과 성능 모두에 영향을 준다. ② 하지만 타이어는 일반적으로 구매 결정에 영향을 미치지 않는데, 그 이유는 안전기준들이 모든 타이어가 매우 안전하고 믿을 만하다고 보장해주기 때문이다. ③ 최적의 음향 시스템, 스마트기기 거치대, 컵홀더의 개수와 위치와 같은 내부 디자인 사양 차이가 아마도 소비자의 구매 결정에 훨씬 더 큰 영향을 미친다. ④ 자동차의 전반적인 가치 측면에서, 당신은 타이어 없이는 운전할 수 없지만 컵홀더나 스마트기기 거치대가 없어도 운전할 수 있다. 하지만 내부 디자인 사양들은 확실히 구매 결정에 더 큰 영향을 미친다. ⑤ 우리 표현으로 하자면, 타이어는 중요하지만 내부 디자인은 중추적이다.

Why? 왜 정답일까?

자동차 구매 결정에 영향을 미치는 두 가지 요소로서 타이어와 내부 디자인을 예로 들어 비교한 글이다. ④ 앞의 두 문장에서 타이어는 보통 안전기준상 안전함을 보장받기 때문에 구매 결정에 큰 영향을 미치지 않지만, 내부 디자인은 구매 결정에 큰 영향을 미친다고 설명한다. 이어서 주어진 문장은 전반적인 가치 측면으로 보자면 타이어가 훨씬 중요하다는 점을 서술한다. 여기에 however로 연결되는 ④ 뒤의 문장은 그럼에도 불구하고 내부 디자인 사양이 구매 결정에 큰 영향을 끼친다는 점을 다시 기술한다. 따라서 주어진 문장이 들어가기에 가장 적절한 곳은 ④이다.

- in terms of ~의 면에서
- dock ⓝ 거치대
- essential ⓐ 필수적인
- reliable ⓐ 믿을 만한
- optimal ⓐ 최적의
- portable ⓐ 휴대용의
- pivotal ⓐ 중추적인
- impact ⓥ 영향을 미치다 ⓝ 영향
- feature ⓝ 기능, 특징
- have (an) effect on ~에 영향을 미치다

구문 풀이

4행 Some resources, decisions, or activities are *important* (highly valuable on average) while others are *pivotal* (small changes make a big difference).
접속사(~한 반면) = other resources

★★ 문제 해결 꿀~팁 ★★

▶ 많이 틀린 이유는?
③ 앞에서 타이어는 구매 결정에 큰 영향을 끼치지 않는다고 서술한 데 이어, ③ 뒤에서는 '타이어보다 더 큰' 영향을 끼칠 수 있는 요소로 내부 디자인 사양을 언급하고 있다. 즉 ③ 앞뒤는 타이어와 내부 디자인이 소비자의 구매 결정에 미치는 영향력의 크기를 비교하며 서로 자연스럽게 연결된다.
▶ 문제 해결 방법은?
④ 앞뒤는 똑같이 '내부 디자인 사양'에 관해 언급하는데, ④ 뒤의 문장에는 however가 있다. 즉 ④ 앞에서 내부 디자인을 언급했다가, 잠시 주어진 문장을 통해 타이어에 관해 언급한 후, ④ 뒤에서 다시 내부 디자인에 관해 설명하는 흐름임을 알 수 있다.

[문제편 p.126]

DAY 20 문장 삽입 05

01 ③	02 ④	03 ③	04 ③	05 ④
06 ④	07 ①	08 ④	09 ②	10 ③
11 ①	12 ③			

01 지구의 대기 대순환

정답률 49% | 정답 ③

글의 흐름으로 보아, 주어진 문장이 들어가기에 가장 적절한 곳을 고르시오.

On any day of the year, / the tropics / and the hemisphere that is experiencing its warm season / receive much more solar radiation / than do the polar regions and the colder hemisphere.
연중 어느 날이든, / 열대 지방과 / 따뜻한 계절을 보내고 있는 반구는 / 훨씬 더 많은 태양 복사열을 받는다. / 극지방과 더 추운 반구가 받는 것보다

① Averaged over the course of the year, / the tropics and latitudes up to about 40° / receive more total heat / than they lose by radiation.
일 년 중 평균적으로, / 열대 지역과 위도 약 40도까지의 지역은 / 더 많은 전체 열을 받는다. / 복사에 의해 잃는 열보다

② Latitudes above 40° receive less total heat / than they lose by radiation.
위도 40도 이상의 지역은 더 적은 전체 열을 받는다. / 복사열에 의해 잃는 것보다

✔ This inequality produces the necessary conditions / for the operation of a huge, global-scale engine / that takes on heat in the tropics / and gives it off in the polar regions.
이러한 불균형은 필요조건을 만들어 낸다. / 거대한 전 지구 규모의 엔진 작동을 위한 / 열대 지방에서 열을 받아서 / 극지방에서 그 열을 방출하는

Its working fluid is the atmosphere, / especially the moisture it contains.
그것의 작동유는 대기인데, / 특히 그것이 품고 있는 수분이다.

④ Air is heated over the warm earth of the tropics, / expands, rises, and flows away both northward and southward at high altitudes, / cooling as it goes.
공기는 열대 지방의 따뜻한 땅 위에서 데워지고, / 확장되고, 상승해서 높은 고도에서 북쪽과 남쪽 두 방향으로 흐르게 되고, / 이동하면서 식는다.

⑤ It descends and flows toward the equator again / from more northerly and southerly latitudes.
그것은 하강하여 다시 적도를 향해 흘러간다. / 더 북쪽과 남쪽의 위도로부터

연중 어느 날이든, 열대 지방과 따뜻한 계절을 보내고 있는 반구는 극지방과 더 추운 반구가 받는 것보다 훨씬 더 많은 태양 복사열을 받는다. ① 일 년 중 평균적으로, 열대 지역과 위도 약 40도까지의 지역은 복사에 의해 잃는 열보다 더 많은 전체 열을 받는다. ② 위도 40도 이상의 지역은 복사열에 의해 잃는 것보다 더 적은 전체 열을 받는다. ③ 이러한 불균형은 열대 지방에서 열을 받아서 극지방에서 그 열을 방출하는 거대한 전 지구 규모의 엔진 작동을 위한 필요조건을 만들어 낸다. 그것의 작동유는 대기인데, 특히 그것이 품고 있는 수분이다. ④ 공기는 열대 지방의 따뜻한 땅 위에서 데워지고, 확장되고, 상승해서 높은 고도에서 북쪽과 남쪽 두 방향으로 흐르게 되고, 이동하면서 식는다. ⑤ 그것은 하강하여 더 북쪽과 남쪽의 위도에서 다시 적도를 향해 흘러간다.

Why? 왜 정답일까?

③ 앞에서 열대 지방과 위도 40도까지의 지역은 위도 40도를 넘는 지역보다 전체적으로 더 많은 열을 받는다고 하는데, 주어진 문장은 바로 이런 '불균형' 때문에 열대에서 쌓인 열이 극지방에서 방출되는 과정이 일어날 수밖에 없다고 설명한다. ③ 뒤의 문장은 이 과정에서 열을 전달해주는 매체(Its working fluid)가 바로 공기, 특히 그 안의 수분임을 부연 설명한다. 따라서 주어진 문장이 들어가기에 가장 적절한 곳은 ③이다.

- necessary condition 필요조건
- tropics ⓝ 열대
- polar ⓐ 극지방의
- radiation ⓝ (열, 에너지 등의) 복사
- equator ⓝ 적도
- take on ~을 떠맡다
- give off 방출하다, 내뿜다
- hemisphere ⓝ 반구
- working fluid 작동유(동력을 전달해주는 매체)

구문 풀이

13행 Air is heated over the warm earth of the tropics, expands, rises, and flows away both northward and southward at high altitudes, cooling as it goes.
(is heated: 동사1, expands: 동사2, rises: 동사3, flows away: 동사4, it: 대명사(= air))

02 인간과 컴퓨터의 결합

정답률 56% | 정답 ④

글의 흐름으로 보아, 주어진 문장이 들어가기에 가장 적절한 곳을 고르시오.

It is important to remember / that computers can only carry out instructions / that humans give them.
기억하는 것이 중요하다. / 컴퓨터들은 지시 사항들을 단지 수행만 할 수 있다는 것을 / 인간이 그들에게 부여한

Computers can process data accurately at far greater speeds / than people can, / yet they are limited in many respects / — most importantly, they lack common sense.
컴퓨터들은 훨씬 더 빠른 속도로 정확하게 데이터를 처리할 수 있지만, / 사람들이 할 수 있는 것보다 / 그것들은 많은 측면에서 제한되어 있는데, / 가장 중요하게도 이것들은 상식이 부족하다.

① However, / combining the strengths of these machines with human strengths / creates synergy.
그러나, / 이러한 기계들의 강점과 인간의 강점을 결합하는 것은 / 시너지를 생성한다.

② Synergy occurs / when combined resources produce output / that exceeds the sum of the outputs of the same resources / employed separately.
시너지는 일어난다. / 결합된 자원들이 산출을 생성할 때 / 바로 그 자원들의 산출의 합을 초과하는 / 각각 사용된

③ A computer works quickly and accurately; / humans work relatively slowly and make mistakes.
컴퓨터는 빠르고 정확하게 작동하지만, / 인간은 상대적으로 느리게 일하고 실수를 한다.

✔ A computer cannot make independent decisions, however, / or formulate steps for solving problems, / unless programmed to do so by humans.
그러나, 컴퓨터는 독립적인 결정을 하거나 / 문제를 해결하기 위한 단계들을 만들어낼 수 없다. / 인간에 의해서 그렇게 하도록 프로그램되지 않는 한

Even with sophisticated artificial intelligence, / which enables the computer / to learn and then implement what it learns, / the initial programming must be done by humans.
정교한 인공지능조차, / 컴퓨터가 ~할 수 있게 하는 / 학습을 하고 학습한 것을 실행하도록 / 최초의 프로그래밍은 인간에 의해 수행되어야 한다.

⑤ Thus, a human-computer combination / allows the results of human thought / to be translated into efficient processing of large amounts of data.
따라서, 인간-컴퓨터 결합은 / 인간 사고의 결과들이 ~하게 한다. / 많은 데이터의 효율적 처리로 변환되도록

컴퓨터들은 인간이 그들에게 부여한 지시 사항들을 단지 수행만 할 수 있다는 것을 기억하는 것이 중요하다. 컴퓨터들은 사람들이 할 수 있는 것보다 훨씬 더 빠른 속도로 정확하게 데이터를 처리할 수 있지만, 그것들은 많은 측면에서 제한되어 있는데, 가장 중요하게도 이것들은 상식이 부족하다. ① 그러나, 이러한 기계들의 강점과 인간의 강점을 결합하는 것은 시너지를 생성한다. ② 시너지는 결합된 자원들이 바로 그 자원들을 각각 사용한 산출의 합을 초과하는 산출을 생성할 때 일어난다. ③ 컴퓨터는 빠르고 정확하게 작동하지만, 인간은 상대적으로 느리게 일하고 실수를 한다. ④ 그러나, 컴퓨터는 인간에 의해서 그렇게 하도록 프로그램되지 않는 한, 독립적인 결정을 하거나 문제를 해결하기 위한 단계들을 만들어낼 수 없다. 컴퓨터가 학습을 하고 학습한 것을 실행할 수 있게 하는 정교한 인공지능조차, 최초의 프로그래밍은 인간에 의해 수행되어야 한다. ⑤ 따라서, 인간-컴퓨터 결합은 인간 사고의 결과들이 많은 데이터의 효율적 처리로 변환되도록 한다.

Why? 왜 정답일까?

컴퓨터는 결국 인간의 개입을 필요로 한다는 내용을 다룬 글로, ④ 앞뒤의 논리적 공백을 잘 살펴야 한다. ④ 앞에서는 인간이 느리고 실수도 하는 반면 컴퓨터는 빠르고 정확하게 작동한다고 언급한다. 한편 ④ 뒤의 문장은 제 아무리 정교한 인공지능도 초기 프로그래밍은 결국 인간에 의해 이루어져야 한다는 내용을 제시한다. 즉 ④ 앞뒤로 컴퓨터의 능력에 대한 시각이 상반되는 것으로 볼 때, 흐름을 반전시키는 however가 포함된 주어진 문장이 들어가기에 가장 적절한 곳은 ④이다.

- independent ⓐ 독립적인
- instruction ⓝ 지시
- respect ⓝ 측면, 사항
- common sense 상식
- occur ⓥ 일어나다, 발생하다
- employ ⓥ 사용하다
- relatively ad 상대적으로, 비교적
- initial ⓐ 초기의
- translate ⓥ (다른 형태로) 바꾸다, 고치다
- formulate ⓥ 만들어 내다, 공식화하다
- process ⓥ 처리하다
- lack ⓥ ~이 부족하다
- combine ⓥ 결합하다
- exceed ⓥ 초과하다
- separately ad 각각, 별개로
- sophisticated ⓐ 정교한, 세련된
- combination ⓝ 결합
- efficient ⓐ 효율적인

구문 풀이

1행 A computer cannot make independent decisions, however, or formulate steps for solving problems, unless programmed to do so by humans.
(make: 동사1, formulate: 동사2, unless: 접속사(~하지 않는다면), programmed: 분사구문)

[문제편 p.127]

03 나이와 관련된 눈의 구조적 변화

정답률 52% | 정답 ③

글의 흐름으로 보아, 주어진 문장이 들어가기에 가장 적절한 곳을 고르시오.

Two major kinds of age-related structural changes / occur in the eye.
나이와 관련된 주요한 두 종류의 구조적 변화가 / 눈에서 일어난다.

One is a decrease in the amount of light / that passes through the eye, / resulting in the need for more light / to do tasks such as reading.
한 가지는 빛의 양의 감소인데, / 눈을 통과하는 / 이것은 더 많은 빛이 필요하게 만든다. / 독서와 같은 일을 하기 위해

① As you might suspect, / this change is one reason / why older adults do not see as well in the dark, / which may account in part for their reluctance / to go places at night.
여러분이 추측할 수 있는 대로, / 이 변화는 한 가지 이유인데, / 노인들이 어둠 속에서 그만큼 잘 보지 못하는 / 이는 부분적으로 그들이 꺼리는 이유를 설명해 줄 수 있다. / 밤에 돌아다니기를

② One possible logical response / to the need for more light / would be to increase illumination levels in general.
한 가지 가능한 논리적 대응은 / 더 많은 빛의 필요성에 대한 / 전반적으로 조도를 늘리는 것이다.

✔ However, this solution does not work in all situations / because we also become increasingly sensitive to glare.
하지만 이 해결책은 모든 상황에서 효과가 있는 것은 아닌데 / 우리가 또한 점점 환한 빛에 더 민감해지기 때문이다.

In addition, / our ability to adjust to changes in illumination, / called adaptation, / declines.
게다가 / 조도의 변화에 적응하는 우리의 능력은 / 순응이라 불리는, / 쇠퇴한다.

④ Going from outside into a darkened movie theater / involves dark adaptation; / going back outside involves light adaptation.
외부에서 캄캄해진 영화관으로 들어가는 것은 / 암(暗)순응과 관련이 있고, / 외부로 다시 나가는 것은 명(明)순응과 관련이 있다.

⑤ Research indicates / that the time it takes for both types of adaptation / increases with age.
연구는 보여 준다. / 두 가지 유형 모두 순응에 걸리는 시간이 / 나이가 들면서 증가한다는 것을

나이와 관련된 주요한 두 종류의 구조적 변화가 눈에서 일어난다. 한 가지는 눈을 통과하는 빛의 양의 감소인데, 이것은 독서와 같은 일을 하기 위해 더 많은 빛이 필요하게 만든다. ① 여러분이 추측할 수 있는 대로, 이 변화는 노인들이 어둠 속에서 그만큼 잘 보지 못하는 한 가지 이유인데, 이는 부분적으로 그들이 밤에 돌아다니기를 꺼리는 이유를 설명해 줄 수 있다. ② 더 많은 빛의 필요성에 대한 한 가지 가능한 논리적 대응은 전반적으로 조도를 늘리는 것이다. ③ 하지만 이 해결책은 모든 상황에서 효과가 있는 것은 아닌데 우리가 또한 점점 환한 빛에 더 민감해지기 때문이다. 게다가 순응이라 불리는, 조도의 변화에 적응하는 우리의 능력은 쇠퇴한다. ④ 외부에서 캄캄해진 영화관으로 들어가는 것은 암(暗)순응과 관련이 있고, 외부로 다시 나가는 것은 명(明)순응과 관련이 있다. ⑤ 연구는 두 가지 유형 모두 순응에 걸리는 시간이 나이가 들면서 증가한다는 것을 보여 준다.

Why? 왜 정답일까?

③ 앞의 문장에서 노인들이 나이가 들며 눈으로 빛을 잘 받아들이지 못하게 되는 문제에 대한 해결책으로서 '조도를 높이면 된다'는 것을 제시하는데, 주어진 문장은 **However**로 흐름을 반전시키며 이 해결책이 모든 상황에서 효과가 있지는 않다(**However, this solution does not work ~**)는 점을 지적한다. ③ 뒤의 문장은 '추가로' 눈에 일어나는 구조적 변화로서 순응 능력의 쇠퇴를 언급한다. 따라서 주어진 문장이 들어가기에 가장 적절한 곳은 ③이다.

- **sensitive** ⓐ 민감한, 예민한
- **structural** ⓐ 구조적인
- **go places** 사방으로 돌아다니다
- **reluctance** ⓝ 꺼림, 마지못해 함, 싫음
- **adjust** ⓥ 적응하다, 조정하다
- **light adaptation** 명(明)순응
- **glare** ⓝ 환한 빛
- **suspect** ⓥ (~라고) 의심하다, 추측하다
- **account for** ~을 설명하다
- **logical** ⓐ 타당한
- **dark adaptation** 암(暗)순응

구문 풀이

7행 As you might suspect, this change is one reason [why older adults do not see as well in the dark], which may account in part for their reluctance to go places at night.
(why: 관계부사 / reason: 선행사 / which: 계속적 용법 / account ... for: ~을 설명하다)

04 문화가 생물학적 과정에 미치는 영향

정답률 55% | 정답 ③

글의 흐름으로 보아, 주어진 문장이 들어가기에 가장 적절한 곳을 고르시오.

A dramatic example / of how culture can influence our biological processes / was provided by anthropologist Clyde Kluckhohn, / who spent much of his career in the American Southwest / studying the Navajo culture.
한 가지 극적인 예는 / 문화가 어떻게 우리의 생물학적인 과정에 영향을 미칠 수 있는지에 관한 / 인류학자인 Clyde Kluckhohn가 제시했는데, / 그는 생애의 많은 부분을 미대륙 남서부에서 보냈다. / Navajo 문화를 연구하며

① Kluckhohn tells of a non-Navajo woman / he knew in Arizona / who took a somewhat perverse pleasure / in causing a cultural response to food.
Kluckhohn는 Navajo인이 아닌 한 여인의 이야기를 들려준다. / 그가 아는 애리조나 사람 / 다소 심술궂은 기쁨을 얻었던, / 음식에 대한 문화적 반응을 이끌어내며

② At luncheon parties / she often served sandwiches / filled with a light meat / that resembled tuna or chicken / but had a distinctive taste.
오찬 파티에서 / 그녀는 샌드위치를 자주 대접했다. / 흰살 고기로 채운 / 참치나 닭고기와 비슷하지만 / 독특한 맛이 나는

✔ Only after everyone had finished lunch / would the hostess inform her guests / that what they had just eaten / was neither tuna salad nor chicken salad / but rather rattlesnake salad.
모든 사람이 점심 식사를 마친 후에야 / 비로소 여주인은 손님들에게 알려 주곤 했다. / 그들이 방금 먹은 것이 / 참치 샐러드나 닭고기 샐러드가 아니라 / 방울뱀 고기 샐러드였다고

Invariably, / someone would vomit / upon learning what they had eaten.
어김없이, / 누군가는 먹은 것을 토하곤 했다. / 방금 무엇을 먹었는지 알게 되자마자

④ Here, then, is an excellent example / of how the biological process of digestion / was influenced by a cultural idea.
그렇다면 이는 훌륭한 예시이다. / 생물학적 소화 과정이 어떻게 / 문화적인 관념에 의해 영향을 받았는지에 대한

⑤ Not only was the process influenced, / it was reversed: / the culturally based *idea* / that rattlesnake meat is a disgusting thing to eat / triggered a violent reversal of the normal digestive process.
그 과정은 영향을 받았을 뿐만 아니라 / 완전히 뒤집히기까지 해서, / 문화에 기초한 *관념*이 / 방울뱀 고기는 먹기에 혐오스러운 음식이라는, / 정상적인 소화 과정에 극단적인 반전을 촉발했다.

문화가 어떻게 우리의 생물학적인 과정에 영향을 미칠 수 있는지에 관한 한 가지 극적인 예는 인류학자인 Clyde Kluckhohn가 제시했는데, 그는 생애의 많은 부분을 미대륙 남서부에서 Navajo 문화를 연구하며 보냈다. ① Kluckhohn은 그가 애리조나에서 알던, 음식에 대한 문화적 반응을 이끌어내는 데서 다소 심술궂은 기쁨을 얻었던, Navajo인이 아닌 한 여인에 대한 이야기를 들려준다. ② 오찬 파티에서 그녀는 참치나 닭고기와 비슷하지만 독특한 맛이 나는 흰살 고기로 채운 샌드위치를 자주 대접했다. ③ 모든 사람이 점심 식사를 마친 후에야 비로소 여주인은 손님들에게 방금 먹은 것이 참치 샐러드나 닭고기 샐러드가 아니라 방울뱀 고기 샐러드였다고 알려 주곤 했다. 어김없이, 방금 무엇을 먹었는지 알게 되자마자 누군가는 먹은 것을 토하곤 했다. ④ 그렇다면 이는 생물학적 소화 과정이 어떻게 문화적인 관념에 의해 영향을 받았는지에 대한 훌륭한 예시이다. ⑤ 그 과정은 영향을 받았을 뿐만 아니라 완전히 뒤집히기까지 해서, 방울뱀 고기는 먹기에 혐오스러운 음식이라는, 문화에 기초한 *관념*이 정상적인 소화 과정에 극단적인 반전을 촉발했다.

Why? 왜 정답일까?

샌드위치에 든 고기가 방울뱀 고기인줄 모르고 먹었을 때는 잘 먹었던 사람들이 방울뱀 고기인 것을 알고 나서 토한 예를 통해 문화적으로 형성된 관념이 생물학적인 현상에 실제적인 영향을 줄 수 있음을 설명한 글이다. ③ 앞은 예시의 첫 문장으로, 한 여주인이 오찬 파티에서 방울뱀 고기가 들었다고 말하지 않은 샌드위치를 대접했다는 이야기를 제시하고, 주어진 문장은 이에 이어서 모두가 다 먹고 난 다음에야 주인이 사실을 고백했다는 내용을 말한다. ③ 뒤에서는 무엇을 먹었는지 알고서 바로 생물학적 반응을 일으킨 손님들이 있었다는 내용을 말한다. 따라서 주어진 문장이 들어가기에 가장 적절한 곳은 ③이다.

- **hostess** ⓝ 여주인
- **dramatic** ⓐ 극적인, 드라마틱한
- **biological** ⓐ 생물학적인
- **somewhat** ad 다소
- **resemble** ⓥ ~와 비슷하다, ~와 닮다
- **invariably** ad 예외없이, 언제나
- **digestion** ⓝ 소화
- **disgusting** ⓐ 혐오스러운, 역겨운
- **reversal** ⓝ 전환, 반전, 뒤바뀜
- **rattlesnake** ⓝ 방울뱀
- **influence** ⓥ 영향을 미치다
- **anthropologist** ⓝ 인류학자
- **luncheon** ⓝ 오찬
- **distinctive** ⓐ 독특한
- **vomit** ⓥ 토하다
- **rattlesnake** ⓝ 방울뱀
- **violent** ⓐ 강한, 심한, 극단의

구문 풀이

1행 Only (after everyone had finished lunch) would the hostess inform her guests [that {what they had just eaten} was neither tuna salad nor chicken salad but rather rattlesnake salad].
「only+(부사절)+조동사+주어+동사원형 : 부정어구의 도치」 / that: 접속사(~것) / what: 관계대명사(~것) / was: 동사
「neither A nor B : A도 아니고 B도 아닌」 「not A but (rather) B : A라기보다 B인」

05 카리스마의 학습과 단련

정답률 44% | 정답 ④

글의 흐름으로 보아, 주어진 문장이 들어가기에 가장 적절한 곳을 고르시오. [3점]

Charisma is eminently learnable and teachable, / and in many ways, / it follows one of Newton's famed laws of motion:
카리스마는 분명하게 배울 수 있고 가르칠 수 있으며, / 그리고 여러 면에서 / 뉴턴의 유명한 운동 법칙 중 하나를 따른다.

For every action, / there is an equal and opposite reaction.
'모든 작용에 대하여 / 같은 크기이면서 반대 방향인 반작용이 존재한다.'는

① That is to say / that all of charisma and human interaction / is a set of signals and cues / that lead to other signals and cues, / and there is a science to deciphering / which signals and cues work / the most in your favor.
즉 / 모든 카리스마와 인간 상호 작용은 / 일련의 신호와 단서들이며, / 다른 신호와 단서들로 이어지는 / 그리고 판독하는 과학이 있다는 것을 의미한다. / 어떤 신호와 단서들이 작용하는지를 / 자신에게 가장 유리하게

② In other words, / charisma can often be simplified / as a checklist / of what to do at what time.
다시 말하면, / 카리스마는 종종 단순화될 수 있다. / 체크리스트로 / 어떤 때에 무엇을 해야 하는지의

③ However, / it will require brief forays / out of your comfort zone.
그러나 / 그것은 일시적 시도가 필요할 것이다. / 편안한 상태에서 벗어나려는

✔ Even though there may be / a logically easy set of procedures to follow, / it's still an emotional battle / to change your habits / and introduce new, uncomfortable behaviors / that you are not used to.
비록 존재할 수 있지만, / 지켜야 할 논리적으로는 수월한 일련의 절차들이 / 여전히 감정적인 분투이다. / 습관을 바꾸고 / 새롭고 불편한 행동들을 시작하는 것은 / 익숙하지 않은

I like to say / that it's just a matter of using muscles / that have long been dormant.
나는 말하는 것을 좋아한다. / 이것이 단지 근육들을 사용하는 문제라고 / 오랫동안 활동을 중단한

⑤ It will take some time / to warm them up, / but it's only through practice and action / that you will achieve your desired goal.
시간이 좀 필요하겠지만, / 그것들을 준비시키는 데 / 오직 연습과 행동을 통해서이다. / 원하는 목표를 성취하게 되는 것은

카리스마는 분명하게 배울 수 있고 가르칠 수 있으며, 그리고 여러 면에서 *모든 작용에 대하여 같은 크기의 반작용이 존재한다*는 뉴턴의 유명한 운동 법칙 중 하나를 따른다. ① 즉 모든 카리스마와 인간 상호 작용은 다른 신호와 단서들로 이어지는 일련의 신호와 단서들이며, 어떤 신호와 단서들이 자신에게 가장 유리하게 작용하는지를 판독하는 과학이 있다. ② 다시 말하면, 카리스마는 종종 어떤 때에 무엇을 해야 하는지의 체크리스트로 단순화될 수 있다. ③ 그러나 그것은 편안한 상태에서 벗어나려는 일시적 시도를 필요로 할 것이다. ④ 비록 논리적으로는 수월한 일련의 지켜야 할 절차들이 존재할 수 있지만, 습관을 바꾸고, 익숙하지 않은 새롭고 불편한 행동들을 시작하는 것은 여전히 감정적인 분투이다. 나는 이것이 단지 오랫동안 활동을 중단한 근육들을 사용하는 문제라고 말하는 것을 좋아한다. ⑤ 그것들을 준비시키는 데 시간이 좀 필요하겠지만, 원하는 목표를 성취하게 되는 것은 바로 오직 연습과 행동을 통해서이다.

Why? 왜 정답일까?

카리스마는 마치 운동으로 단련되는 근육과 같이 키워지고 학습될 수 있다는 점을 주장하는 글이다. ④ 앞의 두 문장에서 카리스마에는 일종의 과학이 있기 때문에 카리스마라는 개념은 언제 무엇을 해야할지의 체크리스트로 단순화될 수 있지만, 그렇게 하는 데에는 현재의 편안한 상태를 깨려는 도전적인 시도가 필요할 것임을 이야기한다. 여기에 이어 **Even though**로 시작하는 주어진 문장은 비록 따라야 할 절차가 단순하다고 하더라도 습관을 바꾸는 데에는 감정적인 분투가 따를 수밖에 없다는 점을 지적한다. ④ 뒤의 문장은 이것(**it**), 즉 습관을 바꾸어 카리스마를 연마하는 일이 그저 오랫동안 사용하지 않았던 근육을 다시 쓰는 문제와 비슷하다는 비유를 제시하며 연습의 중요성을 상기시킨다. 따라서 주어진 문장이 들어가기에 가장 적절한 곳은 ④이다.

- **logically** [ad] 논리적으로
- **introduce** ⓥ 도입하다, 들여오다
- **learnable** ⓐ 배울 수 있는, 학습 가능한
- **reaction** ⓝ 반작용, 반응
- **cue** ⓝ 단서
- **in one's favor** ~에 유리하게
- **comfort zone** 안전 지대
- **procedure** ⓝ 절차, 수순
- **eminently** [ad] 분명하게, 대단히
- **teachable** ⓐ 가르칠 수 있는
- **interaction** ⓝ 상호 작용
- **work** ⓥ 작동하다
- **simplify** ⓥ 단순화하다
- **desired** ⓐ 바랐던, 희망했던

구문 풀이

8행 That is to say that all of charisma and human interaction is a set of signals and cues [that lead to other signals and cues], and there is a science to deciphering {which signals and cues work the most in your favor}.
(That is to say: 즉, 다시 말해서 / all of charisma and human interaction: 주어1 / is: 동사1 / signals and cues: 선행사 / that: 주격 관계대명사 / is: 동사2 / a science: 주어2 / to: 전치사 / deciphering: 동명사 / which: 의문사(어떤))

06 위험 관리 방법

정답률 65% | 정답 ④

글의 흐름으로 보아, 주어진 문장이 들어가기에 가장 적절한 곳을 고르시오. [3점]

Risk often arises from uncertainty / about how to approach a problem or situation.
위험은 종종 불확실성으로부터 발생한다. / 문제나 상황에 접근하는 방법에 대한

① One way to avoid such risk / is to contract with a party / who is experienced and knows how to do it.
이 위험을 피할 수 있는 한 가지 방식은 / 당사자와 계약하는 것이다. / 경험이 많고 그렇게 하는 방법을 알고 있는

② For example, / to minimize the financial risk / associated with the capital cost of tooling and equipment / for production of a large, complex system, / a manufacturer might subcontract the production of the system's major components / to suppliers familiar with those components.
예를 들어, / 재정적 위험을 최소화하기 위해, / 도구 및 장비의 자본 비용과 관련된 / 크고 복잡한 시스템의 생산을 위한 / 제조업자는 공급업자들에게 시스템 주요 부품 생산의 하청을 줄지도 모른다. / 그러한 부품에 정통한

③ This relieves the manufacturer of the financial risk / associated with the tooling and equipment / to produce these components.
이것은 제조업자에게 재정적 위험을 덜어 준다. / 도구 및 장비와 관련된 / 이러한 부품을 생산하기 위한

✔ However, / transfer of one kind of risk / often means inheriting another kind.
그러나, / 한 종류의 위험의 이전은 / 종종 다른 종류를 이어받는 것을 의미한다.

For example, / subcontracting work for the components / puts the manufacturer / in the position of relying on outsiders, / which increases the risks / associated with quality control, scheduling, and the performance of the end-item system.
예를 들어, / 부품에 대한 작업을 하청 주는 것은 / 제조업자를 처하게 하고, / 외부 업자들에 의존하는 위치에 / 이것은 위험들을 증가시킨다. / 품질 관리, 일정 관리, 완제품 시스템의 성능과 관련된

⑤ But these risks often can be reduced / through careful management of the suppliers.
그러나 이러한 위험들은 종종 감소될 수 있다. / 공급업자들의 신중한 관리를 통해

위험은 종종 문제나 상황에 접근하는 방법에 대한 불확실성으로부터 발생한다. ① 이 위험을 피할 수 있는 한 가지 방식은 경험이 많고 그렇게 하는 방법을 알고 있는 당사자와 계약하는 것이다. ② 예를 들어, 크고 복잡한 시스템의 생산을 위한 도구 및 장비의 자본 비용과 관련된 재정적 위험을 최소화하기 위해, 제조업자는 시스템의 주요 부품에 정통한 공급업자들에게 그러한 부품 생산의 하청을 줄지도 모른다. ③ 이것은 제조업자에게 이러한 부품을 생산하기 위한 도구 및 장비와 관련된 재정적 위험을 덜어 준다. ④ 그러나, 한 종류의 위험의 이전은 종종 다른 종류(위험)를 이어받는 것을 의미한다. 예를 들어, 부품에 대한 작업을 하청 주는 것은 제조업자를 외부 업자들에 의존하게 만들고, 이로 인해 품질 관리, 일정 관리, 완제품 시스템의 성능과 관련된 위험들을 증가시킨다. ⑤ 그러나 이러한 위험들은 공급업자들의 신중한 관리를 통해 종종 감소될 수 있다.

Why? 왜 정답일까?

위험은 방법의 불확실성으로 발생하기 때문에 잘 아는 사람에게 일을 맡기면 위험을 줄일 수 있고, 이로 인해 제조업자들은 부품을 잘 아는 공급업자들에게 하청을 맡기게 된다는 내용이 ④ 앞까지 전개된다. 이어서 주어진 문장은 **However**로 흐름을 반전시키며, 한 위험이 감소하면 다른 위험이 높아질 수 있다는 사실을 환기시킨다. ④ 뒤의 문장은 높아지는 '다른' 위험에 대한 예로, 제조업자가 부품 생산 하청을 맡기다 보면 외부 업체 의존도가 커지게 될 것이라는 내용을 언급하고 있다. 따라서 주어진 문장이 들어가기에 가장 적절한 곳은 ④이다.

- **inherit** ⓥ 물려받다
- **uncertainty** ⓝ 불확실성
- **minimize** ⓥ 최소화하다
- **equipment** ⓝ 장비, 용품
- **component** ⓝ 부품
- **familiar with** ~에 익숙한, 정통한
- **rely on** ~에 의존하다
- **arise** ⓥ 발생하다
- **experienced** ⓐ 경험이 풍부한
- **capital cost** ⓐ 자본 비용
- **manufacturer** ⓝ 제조업체
- **supplier** ⓝ 공급업자
- **relieve** ⓥ (문제의 심각성을) 완화하다

구문 풀이

4행 One way to avoid such risk is to contract with a party [who is experienced and knows how to do it].
(One way: 주어 / to avoid: 형용사적 용법 / is: 동사(단수) / to contract: 주격 보어 / a party: 선행사 / who: 주격 관·대 / is: 동사1 / knows: 동사2)

07 필요에 맞춰 쉽게 변하는 우리의 인식

정답률 13% | 정답 ①

글의 흐름으로 보아, 주어진 문장이 들어가기에 가장 적절한 곳을 고르시오. [3점]

[문제편 p.129]

In physics, / the principle of relativity requires / that all equations describing the laws of physics / have the same form / regardless of inertial frames of reference.
물리학에서, / 상대성 이론은 요구한다. / 물리 법칙들을 설명하는 모든 방정식이 / 동일한 형태를 가져야 한다고 / 관성좌표계에 관계없이

The formulas should appear identical to any two observers / and to the same observer in a different time and space.
그 공식들은 아무 두 관찰자에게 동일하게 보여야 한다. / 그리고 다른 시공간에 있는 같은 관찰자에게

✔ Attitudes and values, however, / are subjective to begin with, / and therefore they are easily altered / to fit our ever-changing circumstances and goals.
그러나 태도나 가치관은 / 원래 주관적이고 / 그러므로 쉽게 바뀐다. / 끊임없이 변화하는 우리의 상황과 목표에 맞게

Thus, the same task can be viewed as boring one moment / and engaging the next.
그러므로 동일한 일이 한 순간에는 지루하게 보일 수 있다. / 그리고 다음 순간에는 매력적으로

② Divorce, unemployment, and cancer / can seem devastating to one person / but be perceived as an opportunity for growth by another person, / depending on whether or not the person is married, employed, and healthy.
이혼, 실직, 그리고 암이 / 한 사람에게는 엄청나게 충격적으로 보일 수 있지만 / 또 다른 사람에게는 성장의 기회로 인식될 수 있다. / 그 사람이 결혼했는지, 취직을 했는지, 그리고 건강한지에 따라

③ It is not only beliefs, attitudes, and values / that are subjective.
신념, 태도, 가치관만이 아니다. / 주관적인 것은

④ Our brains / comfortably change our perceptions of the physical world / to suit our needs.
우리의 뇌는 / 물리적 세계에 대한 우리의 인식을 수월하게 바꾼다. / 우리의 필요에 맞게

⑤ We will never see the same event and stimuli / in exactly the same way at different times.
우리는 동일한 사건과 자극을 절대 볼 수 없을 것이다. / 다른 시간에 정확히 똑같은 방식으로는

물리학에서, 상대성 이론은 물리 법칙들을 설명하는 모든 방정식이 관성좌표계에 관계없이 동일한 형태를 가져야 한다고 요구한다. 그 공식들은 아무 두 관찰자와 다른 시공간에 있는 같은 관찰자에게 동일하게 보여야 한다. ① 그러나 태도나 가치관은 원래 주관적이어서 끊임없이 변화하는 우리의 상황과 목표에 맞게 쉽게 바뀐다. 그러므로 동일한 일이 한 순간에는 지루하게 여겨질 수 있고 다음 순간에는 매력적으로 보일 수 있다. ② 이혼, 실직, 그리고 암이 한 사람에게는 엄청나게 충격적으로 보일 수 있지만 또 다른 사람에게는 그 사람이 결혼했는지, 취직을 했는지, 그리고 건강한지에 따라 성장의 기회로 인식될 수 있다. ③ 주관적인 것은 신념, 태도, 가치관만이 아니다. ④ 우리의 뇌는 우리의 필요에 맞게 물리적 세계에 대한 우리의 인식을 수월하게 바꾼다. ⑤ 우리는 동일한 사건과 자극을 다른 시간에 정확히 똑같은 방식으로는 절대 볼 수 없을 것이다.

Why? 왜 정답일까?

물리학의 공식과는 구별되는 인간 인식의 주관적 특성을 설명한 글이다. ① 앞에서 물리학의 상대성 이론에 따르면 공식들은 서로 다른 두 명의 관찰자 또는 다른 시공간에 속한 같은 관찰자에게 동일하게 보여야 한다고 설명하는데, 주어진 문장은 태도나 가치관의 경우 원래 주관적이어서 쉽게 바뀔 수 있다고 언급하며 흐름을 반전시킨다. ① 뒤의 문장은 그리하여 같은 일도 다르게 인식될 수 있다는 내용을 이어 간다. 따라서 주어진 문장이 들어가기에 가장 적절한 곳은 ①이다.

- subjective ⓐ 주관적인
- circumstance ⓝ 상황
- equation ⓝ 방정식
- formula ⓝ 공식
- engaging ⓐ 매력적인
- depending on ~에 따라
- perception ⓝ 인식
- ever-changing 끊임없이 변하는
- relativity ⓝ 상대성
- regardless of ~에 관계없이
- identical ⓐ 동일한
- unemployment ⓝ 실직
- comfortably ad 수월하게, 편하게
- stimulus ⓝ 자극

구문 풀이

9행 Divorce, unemployment, and cancer can seem(동사1) devastating(주격 보어) to one person but (can) be perceived(동사2(수동태)) as an opportunity for growth by another person, depending on(~에 따라) whether(명사절 접속사(~인지 아닌지)) or not the person is married, employed, and healthy.

08 텃새의 서식지 선택 　정답률 67% | 정답 ④

글의 흐름으로 보아, 주어진 문장이 들어가기에 가장 적절한 곳을 고르시오.

Resident-bird habitat selection / is seemingly a straightforward process / in which a young dispersing individual moves / until it finds a place / where it can compete successfully to satisfy its needs.
텃새들의 서식지 선택은 / 외견상 간단한 과정이다. / 흩어지는 어린 개체가 옮겨 다니는, / 그것이 장소를 찾을 때까지 / (생존을 위한) 필요를 충족시키기 위해 성공적으로 경쟁할 수 있는

① Initially, these needs include only food and shelter.
처음에는, 이러한 필요에 음식과 은신처만 포함된다.

② However, eventually, / the young must locate, identify, and settle in a habitat / that satisfies not only survivorship but reproductive needs as well.
그러나 궁극적으로, / 그 어린 새는 서식지를 찾고, 확인하고, 거기에 정착해야 한다. / 생존뿐만 아니라 번식을 위한 필요조건도 충족시켜 주는

③ In some cases, the habitat / that provides the best opportunity for survival / may not be the same habitat / as the one that provides for highest reproductive capacity / because of requirements specific to the reproductive period.
일부의 경우, 서식지가 / 생존을 위한 최고의 기회를 제공하는 / 동일한 곳이 아닐 수도 있다. / 최고의 번식 능력을 가능하게 해주는 서식지와 / 번식기에만 특별히 요구되는 조건들 때문에

✔ Thus, individuals of many resident species, / confronted with the fitness benefits / of control over a productive breeding site, / may be forced to balance costs / in the form of lower nonbreeding survivorship / by remaining in the specific habitat / where highest breeding success occurs.
따라서 많은 텃새 종의 개체들은 / 합목적성에서 오는 이득과 마주하면, / 다산에 유리한 번식지를 장악하는 것이 갖는 / 대가의 균형을 맞추도록 강요당할 수도 있다. / 더 낮은 비번식기 생존율의 형태로 / 특정 서식지에 머물러 있음으로써 / 가장 높은 번식 성공이 일어나는

Migrants, however, are free to choose the optimal habitat / for survival during the nonbreeding season / and for reproduction during the breeding season.
그러나 철새들은 최적의 서식지를 자유롭게 선택한다. / 번식기가 아닌 동안에는 생존을 위한 최적의 서식지를, / 번식기 동안에는 번식을 위한

⑤ Thus, habitat selection during these different periods / can be quite different for migrants / as opposed to residents, / even among closely related species.
이와 같이 서로 다른 시기 동안의 서식지 선택은, / 철새들에게 있어서 상당히 다를 수 있다. / 텃새들과는 달리 / 심지어 밀접하게 관련이 있는 종들 사이에서조차도,

텃새들의 서식지 선택은 흩어지는 어린 개체가 (생존을 위한) 필요를 충족시키기 위해 성공적으로 경쟁할 수 있는 장소를 찾을 때까지 옮겨 다니는, 외견상 간단한 과정이다. ① 처음에는, 이러한 필요에 음식과 은신처만 포함된다. ② 그러나 궁극적으로, 그 어린 새는 생존뿐만 아니라 번식을 위한 필요조건도 충족시켜 주는 서식지를 찾고, 확인하고, 거기에 정착해야 한다. ③ 일부의 경우, 번식기에만 특별히 요구되는 조건들 때문에, 생존을 위한 최고의 기회를 제공하는 서식지가 최고의 번식 능력을 가능하게 해주는 서식지와 동일한 곳이 아닐 수도 있다. ④ 따라서 많은 텃새 종의 개체들은 다산에 유리한 번식지를 장악하는 것이 갖는 합목적성에서 오는 이득과 마주하면, 가장 높은 번식 성공이 일어나는 특정 서식지에 머물러 있음으로써 더 낮은 비번식기 생존율의 형태로 대가의 균형을 맞추도록 강요당할 수도 있다. 그러나 철새들은 번식기가 아닌 동안에는 생존을 위한 최적의 서식지를, 번식기 동안에는 번식을 위한 최적의 서식지를 자유롭게 선택한다. ⑤ 이와 같이 서로 다른 시기 동안의 서식지 선택은, 심지어 밀접하게 관련이 있는 종들 사이에서조차도, 텃새들과는 달리 철새들에게 있어서 상당히 다를 수 있다.

Why? 왜 정답일까?

텃새의 서식지 선택을 철새와 대비하여 설명한 글이다. ④ 앞에서 최적의 서식지와 최적의 번식지가 서로 다를 수 있음을 언급한 데 이어, Thus로 시작하는 주어진 문장은 그리하여 텃새가 번식에 적합한 장소에 살며 비번식기 생존율을 희생한다는, 즉 평소 서식에 있어 희생을 감당한다는 결론을 제시하고 있다. ④ 뒤에서는 이러한 텃새의 선택을 철새의 경우와 대조하고 있다. 따라서 주어진 문장이 들어가기에 가장 적절한 곳은 ④이다.

- confront ⓥ 마주하다
- straightforward ⓐ 간단한, 쉬운, 솔직한
- reproductive ⓐ 번식의
- specific ⓐ 특별한
- optimal ⓐ 최적의, 최선의
- selection ⓝ 선별
- compete ⓥ 경쟁하다
- capacity ⓝ 능력
- migrant ⓝ 철새

구문 풀이

1행 Thus, individuals(주어) of many resident species, confronted with(수동분사구문(~한 채로)) the fitness benefits of control over a productive breeding site, may be forced(동사(조동사 수동태)) to balance(보어) costs in the form of lower nonbreeding survivorship by remaining(~함으로써) in the specific habitat [where(선행사) highest breeding success occurs].

★★★ 1등급 대비 고난도 2점 문제

09 움직임에 대한 착각 정답률 19% | 정답 ②

글의 흐름으로 보아, 주어진 문장이 들어가기에 가장 적절한 곳을 고르시오.

You are in a train, / standing at a station next to another train. / Suddenly you seem to start moving.
당신은 어느 기차 안에 있다. / 어떤 역에서 다른 기차 옆에 서 있는 / 갑자기 당신은 움직이기 시작하는 것 같다.
But then you realize / that you aren't actually moving at all.
하지만 그때 당신은 깨닫는다. / 당신이 사실상 전혀 움직이지 않고 있다는 것을
① It is the second train / that is moving in the opposite direction.
바로 그 두 번째 기차이다. / 반대 방향으로 움직이고 있는 것은
② The illusion of relative movement / works the other way, too.
상대적인 움직임에 대한 착각이 / 다른 방식으로도 작동한다.
You think the other train has moved, / only to discover / that it is your own train that is moving.
당신은 다른 기차가 움직였다고 생각하지만, / 결국 발견하게 된다. / 움직이고 있는 것은 바로 당신 자신의 기차라는 것을
③ It can be hard to tell the difference / between apparent movement and real movement.
차이를 구별하는 것은 어려울 수 있다. / 외견상의 움직임과 실제 움직임 사이에
④ It's easy / if your train starts with a jolt, / of course, / but not if your train moves very smoothly.
이는 쉽지만, / 당신의 기차가 덜컥하고 움직이기 시작한다면 / 물론, / 만약 당신의 기차가 매우 부드럽게 움직인다면 쉽지 않다.
⑤ When your train overtakes a slightly slower train, / you can sometimes fool yourself into thinking / your train is still / and the other train is moving slowly backwards.
당신의 기차가 약간 더 느린 기차를 따라잡을 때, / 당신은 때때로 속아서 생각할 수 있다. / 당신의 기차가 정지해 있고 / 다른 기차가 천천히 뒤쪽으로 움직이고 있다고

당신은 어떤 역에서 다른 기차 옆에 서 있는 어느 기차 안에 있다. 갑자기 당신은 움직이기 시작하는 것 같다. 하지만 그때 당신은 당신이 사실상 전혀 움직이지 않고 있다는 것을 깨닫는다. ① 반대 방향으로 움직이고 있는 것은 바로 그 두 번째 기차이다. ② 상대적인 움직임에 대한 착각이 다른 방식으로도 작동한다. 당신은 다른 기차가 움직였다고 생각하지만, 결국 움직이고 있는 것은 바로 당신 자신의 기차라는 것을 발견하게 된다. ③ 외견상의 움직임과 실제 움직임 사이에 차이를 구별하는 것은 어려울 수 있다. ④ 물론, 당신의 기차가 덜컥하고 움직이기 시작한다면 이는 쉽지만, 만약 당신의 기차가 매우 부드럽게 움직인다면 쉽지 않다. ⑤ 당신의 기차가 약간 더 느린 기차를 따라잡을 때, 당신은 때때로 속아서 당신의 기차가 정지해 있고 다른 기차가 천천히 뒤쪽으로 움직이고 있다고 생각할 수 있다.

Why? 왜 정답일까?

② 앞의 두 문장에서 우리가 타고 있는 기차가 움직이고 있다는 느낌을 받을 때 실제로 움직이는 차는 맞은편에 있는 차일 수도 있다는 내용을 제시한 데 이어, 주어진 문장은 같은 착각이 '다른 방식'으로 일어날 수도 있음을 지적한다. ② 뒤에서는 이 '다른 방식'을 구체화하는 진술로서 다른 기차가 움직였다고 여겨질 때 실제로는 우리가 타고 있는 기차가 움직인 것일 수도 있다고 설명한다. 따라서 주어진 문장이 들어가기에 가장 적절한 곳은 ②이다.

- illusion ⓝ 착각
- relative ⓐ 상대적인
- opposite ⓐ 정반대의, 맞은편의
- tell ⓥ 구별하다
- smoothly ad 부드럽게
- overtake ⓥ 앞지르다, 추월하다
- slightly ad 약간
- fool oneself into ~ 속아서 ~하다
- still ⓐ 가만히 있는, 고요한

구문 풀이

7행 You think (that) the other train has moved, only to discover that it is your own train that is moving.
생략(접속사) 「only+to부정사 : 결국 ~하다」
「it is ~ that … : 강조 구문」

★★ 문제 해결 꿀~팁 ★★

▶ 많이 틀린 이유는?
구문이 쉽고 예시 또한 친숙한 편이지만 논리적 공백을 확실히 파악하지 못한다면 오답을 고르기 쉽다. ②를 기점으로 '직접 탄 기차가 움직인다고 착각하는 경우 vs. 맞은편 기차가 움직인다고 착각하는 경우'가 대조를 이루고 있는데 사이에 역접을 나타내는 말이 없어 논리의 흐름이 깨진다. ③과 ④는 예시 이후에 일반적인 설명을 제시하는 부분으로서 앞뒤가 서로 맞물려 이어진다.

▶ 문제 해결 방법은?
지문에 앞서 주어진 문장을 먼저 읽고 논리의 흐름을 예측해보도록 한다. 주어진 문장의 illusion과 the other way로 볼 때, 앞에 일단 움직임의 '착각'을 보여주는 예가 언급된 뒤, 이 예와 반대되는 다른 경우가 뒤에서 언급될 것임을 예측할 수 있다.

★★★ 1등급 대비 고난도 2점 문제

10 일반화하려는 본능의 순기능과 역기능 정답률 38% | 정답 ③

글의 흐름으로 보아, 주어진 문장이 들어가기에 가장 적절한 곳을 고르시오.

Everyone automatically categorizes and generalizes all the time.
모든 사람들은 항상 자동적으로 분류하고 일반화한다.
Unconsciously.
무의식적으로.
It is not a question of being prejudiced or enlightened.
그것은 편견을 갖고 있다거나 계몽되어 있다는 것의 문제가 아니다.
Categories are absolutely necessary for us to function.
범주는 우리가 제 기능을 하는 데 반드시 필요하다.
① They give structure to our thoughts.
그것들은 우리의 사고에 체계를 준다.
② Imagine / if we saw every item and every scenario as truly unique / — we would not even have a language / to describe the world around us.
상상해 보라. / 만일 우리가 모든 품목과 모든 있을 법한 상황을 정말로 유일무이한 것으로 본다고 / 우리는 언어조차 갖지 못할 것이다. / 우리 주변의 세계를 설명할
③ But the necessary and useful instinct to generalize / can distort our world view.
그러나 필연적이고 유용한 일반화 본능은 / 우리의 세계관을 왜곡할 수 있다.
It can make us / mistakenly group together things, or people, or countries / that are actually very different.
그것은 우리를 만들 수 있다. / 사물들이나, 사람들, 혹은 나라들을 하나로 잘못 묶게 / 실제로는 아주 다른
④ It can make us assume / everything or everyone in one category is similar.
그것은 우리가 가정하게 만들 수 있다. / 하나의 범주 안에 있는 모든 것이나 모든 사람이 비슷하다고
⑤ And, maybe, most unfortunate of all, / it can make us jump to conclusions about a whole category / based on a few, or even just one, unusual example.
그리고 어쩌면 모든 것 중에서 가장 유감스러운 것은, / 그것이 우리로 하여금 전체 범주에 대해 성급하게 결론을 내리게 만들 수 있다는 것이다. / 몇 가지, 또는 심지어 고작 하나의 특이한 사례를 바탕으로

모든 사람들은 항상 자동적으로 분류하고 일반화한다. 무의식적으로 (그렇게 한다). 그것은 편견을 갖고 있다거나 계몽되어 있다는 것의 문제가 아니다. 범주는 우리가 제 기능을 하는 데 반드시 필요하다. ① 그것들은 우리의 사고에 체계를 준다. ② 만일 우리가 모든 품목과 모든 있을 법한 상황을 정말로 유일무이한 것으로 본다고 상상해 보라. 우리는 우리 주변의 세계를 설명할 언어조차 갖지 못할 것이다. ③ 그러나 필연적이고 유용한 일반화 본능은 우리의 세계관을 왜곡할 수 있다. 그것은 우리가 실제로는 아주 다른 사물들이나 사람들, 혹은 나라들을 하나로 잘못 묶게 만들 수 있다. ④ 그것은 우리가 하나의 범주 안에 있는 모든 것이나 모든 사람이 비슷하다고 가정하게 만들 수 있다. ⑤ 그리고 어쩌면 모든 것 중에서 가장 유감스러운 것은, 그것이 우리로 하여금 몇 가지, 또는 심지어 고작 하나의 특이한 사례를 바탕으로 전체 범주에 대해 성급하게 결론을 내리게 만들 수 있다는 것이다.

Why? 왜 정답일까?

③ 앞까지 인간은 대상을 무의식적으로 범주에 따라 분류하고 일반화하려는 경향이 있어, 이를 토대로 체계적인 사고를 해나갈 수 있다는 내용이 언급되고 있다. But으로 시작하는 주어진 문장은 이와 같은 흐름을 반전시키며 이러한 일반화 본능이 역으로 우리 세계관을 '왜곡할' 여지가 있음을 상기시키고 있다. ③ 뒤부터는 주어진 문장의 'the necessary and useful instinct'를 It으로 가리키며, 일반화 본능으로 인해 우리가 실제로 굉장히 다른 대상을 한 범주로 잘못 묶거나 한 범주 안의 개별적인 대상들을 비슷하다고 오해할 여지가 생긴다고 설명한다. 따라서 주어진 문장이 들어가기에 가장 적절한 곳은 ③이다.

- instinct ⓝ 본능
- generalize ⓥ 일반화하다
- distort ⓥ 왜곡하다
- automatically ad 자동적으로, 저절로
- categorize ⓥ (개개의 범주로) 분류하다
- unconsciously ad 무의식적으로
- prejudice ⓥ 편견을 갖게 하다
- enlighten ⓥ 계몽하다
- function ⓥ (정상적으로) 활동하다
- structure ⓝ 체계
- group together ~을 하나로 묶다
- mistakenly ad 잘못하여, 실수로
- jump to a conclusion 성급한 결론을 내리다

DAY 20

[문제편 p.131]

구문 풀이

7행 Imagine (that) if we saw every item and every scenario as truly unique — we would not even have a language to describe the world around us.
(생략 / 「if+주어+과거 동사 ~, 주어+조동사 과거형+동사원형 ~ : 가정법 과거」 / 형용사적 용법)

★★ 문제 해결 꿀~팁 ★★

▶ 많이 틀린 이유는?
④ 앞에서, 우리는 일반화 본능 때문에 실제로 서로 다른 대상을 한 가지 범주 안에 묶을지도 모르게 된다고 언급한다. 이어서 ④ 뒤의 문장에서는 '나아가' 우리가 한 범주 안의 대상이 다 비슷할 것이라고 잘못 가정할 수도 있다는 점을 언급한다. 즉 ④ 앞뒤가 흐름 단절 없이 자연스럽게 서로 연결되므로, 주어진 문장이 ④에 들어가는 것은 적합하지 않다.
▶ 문제 해결 방법은?
③ 앞뒤의 논리적 공백을 포착해야 한다. ③ 앞에서는 우리가 일반화 본능 '덕분에' 주변 세계를 설명할 수 있다는 내용인 반면, ③ 뒤에서는 일반화 본능 '때문에' 우리가 서로 다른 대상을 하나로 잘못 묶을 수도 있다는 내용이 이어진다. 즉 '일반화 본능'이라는 한 가지 소재에 대해 ③ 앞은 긍정적 시각, ③ 뒤는 부정적 시각을 비치고 있기 때문에, ③ 앞뒤로 논리적 공백이 발생하고 있다.

★★★ 1등급 대비 고난도 3점 문제

11 행동의 원인을 내적 기질에 돌리는 이유 정답률 36% | 정답 ①

글의 흐름으로 보아, 주어진 문장이 들어가기에 가장 적절한 곳을 고르시오. [3점]

You may be wondering / why people prefer to prioritize internal disposition / over external situations / when seeking causes to explain behaviour.
당신은 궁금해 할 것이다. / 사람들이 왜 내적 기질을 우선시하기를 선호하는지를 / 외적 상황보다는 / 행동을 설명하기 위한 원인을 찾을 때

One answer is simplicity.
한 가지 답은 단순함이다.

✓ Thinking of an internal cause for a person's behaviour / is easy / — the strict teacher is a stubborn person, / the devoted parents just love their kids.
한 사람의 행동에 대한 내적 원인을 생각해내는 것은 / 쉬운데, / 엄격한 선생님은 완고한 사람이며, / 헌신적 부모는 단지 아이들을 사랑한다.

In contrast, situational explanations can be complex.
반대로, 상황적 설명은 복잡할 수 있다.

② Perhaps the teacher appears stubborn / because she's seen the consequences / of not trying hard in generations of students / and wants to develop self-discipline in them.
아마 그 선생님은 완고한 것처럼 보였을 것이다. / 그녀가 결과를 보아왔고, / 여러 세대의 학생들이 노력하지 않는 것의 / 학생들에게 자기 수양 능력을 키워주고 싶어 하기 때문에

③ Perhaps the parents / who're boasting of the achievements of their children / are anxious about their failures, / and conscious of the cost of their school fees.
아마도 부모들은 / 자기 자녀들의 성취를 뽐내는 / 그들의 실패를 걱정하고 / 수업료를 의식하고 있을 것이다.

④ These situational factors require knowledge, insight, and time / to think through.
이러한 상황적 요소들은 지식, 통찰, 그리고 시간을 필요로 한다. / 곰곰이 생각해 보려면

⑤ Whereas, jumping to a dispositional attribution is far easier.
반면에, 기질적 속성으로 넘어가는 것은 훨씬 쉽다.

당신은 행동을 설명하기 위한 원인을 찾을 때 사람들이 왜 외적 상황보다는 내적 기질을 우선시하기를 선호하는지를 궁금해 할 것이다. 한 가지 답은 단순함이다. ① 한 사람의 행동에 대한 내적 원인을 생각해내는 것은 쉬운데, (예컨대) 엄격한 선생님은 완고한 사람이며, 헌신적 부모는 단지 아이들을 사랑한다. 반대로, 상황적 설명은 복잡할 수 있다. ② 아마 그 선생님은 여러 세대의 학생들이 노력하지 않는 것의 결과를 보아왔고, 학생들에게 자기 수양 능력을 키워주고 싶어 하기 때문에 완고해 보이는 것이다. ③ 아마도 자녀들의 성취를 뽐내는 부모들은 그들의 실패를 걱정하고 수업료를 의식하고 있을 것이다. ④ 이러한 상황적 요소들은 곰곰이 생각해 보려면 지식, 통찰, 그리고 시간을 필요로 한다. ⑤ 반면에, 기질적 속성으로 넘어가는 것은 훨씬 쉽다.

Why? 왜 정답일까?

사람들이 행동의 원인을 찾을 때 상황보다 내적인 기질에 주목하는 이유를 설명한 글이다. ① 앞에서는 그 답이 '단순함'에 있다고 말한 데 이어, 주어진 문장에서는 행동의 내적 원인을 찾기는 쉽다는 것을 보여주는 예를 든다. ① 뒤의 문장에서는 이와는 달리 상황적인 설명은 복잡하다고 이야기한다. 따라서 주어진 문장이 들어가기에 가장 적절한 곳은 ①이다.

- internal ⓐ 내적인, 내부의
- stubborn ⓐ 완고한, 고집스러운
- prefer ⓥ 선호하다
- disposition ⓝ 기질, 성향, 성격
- simplicity ⓝ 단순함, 간단함
- self-discipline 자기 단련, 자기 수양
- achievement ⓝ 업적
- insight ⓝ 통찰, 이해, 간파
- attribution ⓝ (사람·사물의) 속성
- strict ⓐ 엄격한
- devoted ⓐ 헌신적인, 헌신하는
- prioritize ⓥ 우선시하다
- external ⓐ 외적인, 외부의
- consequence ⓝ 결과
- boast of ~을 뽐내다, 자랑하다
- anxious ⓐ 걱정하는, 불안해하는
- whereas conj 반면에

구문 풀이

8행 Perhaps the teacher appears stubborn / because she's seen the consequences of not trying hard in generations of students and wants to develop self-discipline in them.
(동사 / 주격 보어 / ~이기 때문에 / 동사1(현재완료) / 전치사 / 동명사 부정형 / 동사2)

★★ 문제 해결 꿀~팁 ★★

▶ 많이 틀린 이유는?
이 글은 '주제 – 예시 – 주제'의 구조로 구성되어 있다. ② 앞에서 '내적 요인>상황 요인'이라는 주제가 제시된 후, Perhaps로 시작하는 두 문장은 모두 '상황 요인'에 의존한 설명의 예를 제시하고, ④ 뒤의 두 문장은 앞의 예로 보건대 역시 '내적 요인>상황 요인'이라는 결론을 일관되게 도출한다. 큰 구조를 파악하지 않고 'simplicity vs. complex'의 대비에만 주목하여 답을 ②로 고르면 나머지 부분에서 논리적 공백을 찾을 수 없다.
▶ 문제 해결 방법은?
연결사가 가장 큰 힌트를 제공하는 문제이다. '대조적으로' 외적인 설명이 복잡하다는 내용을 이어가려면, 이 앞에 대조될만한 대상이 이미 언급되어야 한다. 따라서 ①에 논리적 공백이 있음을 유추할 수 있다.

★★★ 1등급 대비 고난도 3점 문제

12 일부 아프리카 부족의 음악의 즉흥성 정답률 33% | 정답 ③

글의 흐름으로 보아, 주어진 문장이 들어가기에 가장 적절한 곳을 고르시오. [3점]

In the West, / an individual composer writes the music / long before it is performed.
서양에서 / 개인 작곡가는 음악을 작곡한다. / 음악이 연주되기 오래 전에

The patterns and melodies we hear / are pre-planned and intended.
우리가 듣는 패턴들과 멜로디들은 / 사전에 계획되고 의도된다.

① Some African tribal music, however, / results from collaboration by the players / on the spur of the moment.
그러나 일부 아프리카 부족의 음악은 / 연주자들의 협연의 결과로 생겨난다. / 즉석에서

② The patterns heard, / whether they are the silences / when all players rest on a beat / or the accented beats / when all play together, / are not planned but serendipitous.
들리는 패턴은 / 휴지(休止)이든, / 모든 연주자가 어느 한 박자에서 쉴 때의 / 강박(强拍)이든 간에 / 모든 연주가가 함께 연주할 때의 / 계획된 것이 아니라 우연히 얻은 것이다.

✓ When an overall silence appears / on beats 4 and 13, / it is not because each musician is thinking, / "On beats 4 and 13, I will rest."
전반적인 휴지가 나타날 때, / 4박자와 13박자에 / 그것은 각각의 음악가가 생각하고 있기 때문이 아니다. / "4박자와 13박자에 나는 쉴 거야."라고

Rather, / it occurs randomly / as the patterns of all the players converge / upon a simultaneous rest.
오히려, / 그것은 무작위로 일어난다. / 모든 연주자의 패턴이 한데 모아질 때 / 동시에 쉬는 것으로

④ The musicians are probably as surprised as their listeners / to hear the silences at beats 4 and 13.
그 음악가들도 아마 청중만큼 놀란다. / 4박자와 13박자에 휴지를 듣고서

⑤ Surely that surprise is one of the joys / tribal musicians experience / in making their music.
확실히 그 놀라움은 기쁨 중 하나이다. / 부족의 음악가들이 경험하는 / 음악을 연주할 때

서양에서 개인 작곡가는 음악이 연주되기 오래 전에 음악을 작곡한다. 우리가 듣는 패턴들과 멜로디들은 사전에 계획되고 의도된다. ① 그러나 일부 아프리카 부족의 음악은 연주자들의 협연의 결과로 즉석에서 생겨난다. ② 모든 연주자가 어느 한 박자에서 쉴 때의 휴지(休止)이든, 모든 연주가가 함께 연주할 때의 강박(强拍)이든 간에 들리는 패턴은 계획된 것이 아니라 우연히 얻은 것이

다. ③ 전반적인 휴지가 4박자와 13박자에 나타날 때, 그것은 각각의 음악가가 "4박자와 13박자에 나는 쉴 거야."라고 생각하고 있기 때문이 아니다. 오히려, 이것은 모든 연주자의 패턴이 동시에 쉬는 것으로 한데 모아질 때 무작위로 일어난다. ④ 그 음악가들도 아마 4박자와 13박자에 휴지를 듣고서 청중만큼 놀란다. ⑤ 확실히 그 놀라움은 부족의 음악가들이 음악을 연주할 때 경험하는 기쁨 중 하나이다.

Why? 왜 정답일까?

일부 아프리카 부족의 음악 연주에서 관찰되는 우연성과 즉흥성을 설명한 글이다. ③ 앞에서 모든 연주자가 연주 도중 함께 쉬든 혹은 함께 특정 박자를 세게 치든 모든 것은 계획에 따른 것이 아니라 우연히 이루어진다고 서술한다. 주어진 문장은 이에 대한 예로 4박과 13박에서 휴지가 일어났을 때를 언급하며 이것이 모든 연주자가 생각하고 있던 것이 아니라고 설명한다. ③ 뒤의 문장은 주어진 문장에 Rather로 연결되며 '그렇다기보다는' 각 연주자의 연주 패턴이 동시에 쉬는 것으로 우연히 한데 모일 때 전체 휴지가 무작위로 발생하는 것임을 설명한다. 따라서 주어진 문장이 들어가기에 가장 적절한 곳은 ③이다.

- composer ⓝ 작곡가
- tribal ⓐ 부족의
- on the spur of the moment 즉석에서, 순간적인 충동으로
- accent ⓥ 강조하다
- randomly ad 무작위로
- simultaneous ⓐ 동시의

구문 풀이

8행 The patterns heard, (whether they are the silences when all players rest on a beat or the accented beats when all play together), are not planned but serendipitous.

(The patterns: 주어 / heard: 과거분사 / 「whether+A+or+B : A이든 B이든」 / ( ): 부사절 / are: 동사 / 「not+A+but+B : A가 아니라 B인」)

★★ 문제 해결 꿀~팁 ★★

▶ 많이 틀린 이유는?

④ 앞에서 모두가 4박과 13박에서 멈추는 현상이 '계획되지 않고 무작위로' 일어난다고 말한 데 이어, ④ 뒤에서는 그래서 아마 음악가들도 청중만큼 '놀랄' 수도 있다고 설명하고 있다. 즉 놀람의 이유가 무작위로 일어난 휴지(休止) 때문이므로 ④ 앞뒤는 논리적으로 자연스럽게 연결된다.

▶ 문제 해결 방법은?

앞에 not A가 나오면 but B를 떠올려야 한다. 여기서도 주어진 문장에 not(it is not because ~)이 나오므로 뒤에 but B가 이어져야 하는데, ③ 뒤의 문장이 but을 대신할 수 있는 Rather(오히려, 대신에)로 시작하며 자연스럽게 이어진다.

DAY 20

MEMO

수능 내신 1등급 대비 전국연합 학력평가

20일 완성 영어독해

수능기출 베스트셀러
리 얼 오 리 지 널

빈칸 순서 삽입

완성

The Real series ipsifly provide questions in previous real test and you can practice as real college scholastic ability test.

하루 20분! 20일 완성!

영어 독해
빈칸·순서·삽입
기본

영어 독해
빈칸·순서·삽입
완성

영어 독해
빈칸·순서·삽입
실전

Believe in yourself and show us what you can do!
자신을 믿고 자신의 능력을 당당히 보여주자.

리얼 오리지널 하루 20분 20일 완성 | 영어 독해 | 빈칸·순서·삽입 [완성]
발행처 수능 모의고사 전문 출판 입시플라이 **발행일** 2024년 6월 1일 **등록번호** 제 2017-22호
홈페이지 www.ipsifly.com **대표전화** 02-433-9979 **구입문의** 02-433-9975 **팩스** 02-6305-9907
발행인 조용규 **편집책임** 양창열 김유 이혜민 임명선 김선영 **물류관리** 김소희 이혜리 **주소** 서울특별시 중랑구 용마산로 615 정민빌딩 3층
※ 페이지가 누락되었거나 파손된 교재는 구입하신 곳에서 교환해 드립니다. ※ 발간 이후 발견되는 오류는 입시플라이 홈페이지 정오표를 통해서 알려드립니다.